ITALY

The Ultimate Cookbook

Italy: The Ultimate Cookbook

13-Digit ISBN: 978-1-64643-240-0
10-Digit ISBN:1-64643-240-1

This book may be ordered by mail from the publisher. Please include $5.99 for postage and handling.
Please support your local bookseller first!

Books published by Cider Mill Press Book Publishers are available at special discounts for bulk purchases in the United States by corporations, institutions, and other organizations.
For more information, please contact the publisher.

Cider Mill Press Book Publishers
"Where good books are ready for press"
501 Nelson Place
Nashville, Tennessee 37214

cidermillpress.com

Typography: Adobe Garamond, Brandon Grotesque, Lastra, Sackers English Script
Image Credits: Pages 721, 764, and 772 courtesy of Barbara Caracciolo.
All other photos used under official license from Shutterstock.com.

Printed in Malaysia

23 24 25 26 27 COS 5 4 3 2 1

First Edition

ITALY

The Ultimate Cookbook

BARBARA CARACCIOLO

CIDER MILL PRESS

BOOK PUBLISHERS

CONTENTS

INTRODUCTION

*I*taly is "only a geographical expression," stated the Austrian Empire's foreign minister, Count Metternich, in 1847, implying that Italy was not a nation or a people, but just the name associated with a peninsula. Metternich's statement was met with strong opposition, and around that time, Northern Italians began strategizing to free themselves from the Austrian yoke. The Northerns eventually succeeded, achieving the unification of Italy under the governance of Piedmont's royalty in 1861.

Metternich did not mean to insult Italy, however—he was simply pointing out an undeniable fact. Divided into regional principalities of assorted sizes, organized in various political systems, and influenced by myriad foreign entities since the fall of the Roman Empire, Italy was, and largely still is, the sum of its regions, each one possessing a unique culture and, up until not so long ago, a different language.

Italian dialects are in fact so distinct from one another that they often qualify as entirely separate languages rather than local variations of a general pattern.

While this diversity is starting to fade, there are many local dialects that remain very much alive—the languages of food in the various regions.

It is difficult to conceive of something as general as "Italian cuisine." Regional variations are so great that it is frequently incorrect to attribute specific foods to the whole of Italy, when they are common only in some parts of the country. The most notable differences lie between Northern and Southern Italy, with Central Italy standing in between the two, not only geographically, but also culturally.

A simple example of this phenomenon is olive oil. The whole world identifies olive oil with "Italian" cuisine, but it is only a staple in Southern Italy and in specific regions of Central and Northern Italy, like Tuscany and Liguria. Other regional cuisines use different fats in cooking—traditionally lard, and occasionally butter.

While dry pasta is ubiquitous in the South and in parts of Central Italy, egg pasta is the whole show in the North. Similarly, while rice is rarely utilized in Southern and Central Italy's cuisines, it is a staple in Northern Italy's cuisine. Each region emphasizes different vegetables, and the traditional dishes in Southern Italy are largely vegetarian, while dishes in Northern and Central Italy tend to be more carnivorous.

In short, there is not one Italian cuisine, but—at least—three, one for each large section of Italy, with as many local "dialects" as there are regions and, occasionally, towns.

In putting this book together, I aimed to represent this rich diversity, showing the many similarities between the cuisines of the smaller regions, and the significant differences between those that lie far apart.

In the North, you have the Aosta Valley, Liguria, Lombardy, Piedmont, Trentino-Alto Adige, Veneto, Friuli-Venezia Giulia, and Emilia-Romagna; Central Italy consists of Tuscany, Umbria, Abruzzo, Marche, and Lazio; and in the South sit Molise, Campania, Apulia, Basilicata, Calabria, Sicily, and Sardinia.

While the cuisine of each region is deserving of a book of its own, I elected to include only

those recipes that are the most representative of each large geographical region, thinking it was better to identify what characterizes each one rather than try to exhaustively document each regional cuisine. While I hope to compose the encyclopedia that would result from the latter approach one day, I am quite happy with the present selection.

Each section is structured according to the traditional procession of the Italian meal, which is something, for once, that the whole of Italy agrees upon.

In a departure from other cultures, Italians don't generally like to mix different courses on the same plate. For instance, meat- or vegetable-based mains are never eaten with pasta, which is instead served alone. The meal is supposed to be savored slowly, one (small) dish at a time, relishing each flavor separately, rather than combining everything in a few quick bites, as this second approach can lead to mindless consumption rather than enjoyment.

A complete meal is divided into an antipasto (appetizer), a primo (a first course that is usually a cereal-based dish like pasta or risotto, or a soup), and a secondo (a meat-, fish-, or vegetable-centered main) that can be served with (on the same plate, even!) a contorno (a side dish, generally plant based) and is almost always accompanied by pane (crusty bread or rolls). A dolce (dessert) follows and concludes the meal.

Understandably, such an elaborate meal did not grace the tables of common people every day in the past, for economic reasons, and it is not the norm for modern Italians either because of time constraints or health considerations. Besides festive days, both past and present, this complete meal is stretched across a whole day, rather than being eaten during a single sitting.

Today, Italians generally start the day with something sweet, continue with a primo for lunch, perhaps indulge in an appetizer in the afternoon, and tend to have a secondo with a contorno for dinner. In this, for once, Northern, Central, and Southern Italy are quite united.

Another aspect that I see as being truly Italian is the care and attention to detail in preparing the food. Most Italian recipes do not include a myriad of ingredients and do not require special equipment or complex techniques. They

do, however, require a deep familiarity with the ingredients, and proficient technique that allows one to prepare them in a manner that makes them fully edible, digestible, and enjoyable.

Beyond this, everything is variable. And, for me, one of the amazing things about food in Italy is how diverse the history can be within the same region. Even sticking to one region, in the same meal one could eat a dish that was originally a farmer's staple, a recipe created by the classically trained chef employed at royal court, and conclude with a sweet invented by a nun who resided in a cloistered convent.

Italian cuisine is a mixture of rural and urban food, of peasant and aristocratic dishes, origins that become less and less important due to the fact that they all entered the local culinary tradition and ended up being everyone's favorites, independent of class or vocation.

Of the thousands of recipes that best represent Italian regional cuisine, I had to limit myself to only a few hundred. In choosing, I considered how easy or difficult it would be to replicate the recipes for readers living outside of Italy, who don't have access to several local

ingredients and tools that are ordinary in Italy, but not so common abroad. And, inevitably, my own preferences also played a part in what was chosen. But I hope, and believe, that my selections will make most people happy.

I grew up with the food bible *Il talismano della felicità* by Ada Boni, a comprehensive cookbook about Italian cuisine that is not sorted according to region, but does include many regional recipes, as well as more modern, "imported" ones. Published in 1929, it is still one of the most used culinary manuals in Italy, so much so that when I moved from Rome to Sweden a couple of decades ago, I packed the 4-plus-pound cooking bible in a suitcase that was already overflowing with sweaters. It is the book I still go back to every time I need to return to the fundamentals in a recipe.

I hope this collection serves the same purpose for you, helping you dig further into traditional Italian cooking, and that you have just as much fun working your way through it as I had putting it together. Buon appetito!

Barbara Caracciolo

THE REGIONS OF ITALY

There is a powerful heritage of culinary products and traditions in each Italian region, so much so that even a book of this size is nowhere close to big enough to comprehend all of them. Here's a brief guide that will help the reader deepen their understanding of this rich food culture, an overview that will both help them navigate the present book, and further explore Italy's regional cuisines on their own.

SOUTHERN ITALY

ABRUZZI

A mountainous region that includes large forested areas, Abruzzi also has a rather large coast that faces the Adriatic, a reality which gave rise to seafood dishes such as brodetto alla pescarese. Apart from the coastal influences, Abruzzi's cuisine is, like Lazio's, marked by its tradition of sheep herding, both in the use of pecorino cheese and numerous dishes featuring lamb. The most typical pasta presentation in the area is spaghetti alla chitarra, which can be made at home only if one owns a specific tool that, with metal strings and a wooden body, resembles a guitar. Other local favorites that are renowned globally are parrozzo, the traditional sweet bread, and the area's exceptional saffron.

MOLISE

This small and mostly inland region sits south of Abruzzi. Molisan cuisine is centered around cereals, primarily durum wheat, but also corn and emmer. Some of the most popular traditional pasta formats originated here, such as cavatelli and fusilli. Molise is also the second-largest Italian producer of truffles, including white truffles, and this sector is expanding constantly. Local farming is relatively small due to the limited availability of farmland, but from this small collective comes high-quality produce.

CAMPANIA

With a large coast on the Tyrrhenian Sea, Campania is also characterized by a mountainous inland. Naples is the big city of the former piece, and has contributed immensely to what is thought of as "Italian food" abroad, being the home of pizza Napoletana, mozzarella cheese, and even tomato sauce. Campania is one of the biggest Italian producers of nuts, and the leader in production of the quality tomatoes known as San Marzano. Highly prized is the mozzarella di bufala campana that is made in this region from the milk of specific breeds of buffalo. Some notable wines also come from Campania, like Greco di Tufo and Fiano di Avellino, and the lemons and oranges from Sorrento and the Amalfi Coast are considered to be among the best in the world. Campania is also a producer of quality pasta like pasta di Gragnano, which has received the treasured Indication of Geographical Protection.

CALABRIA

This region stands just below Campania, and is characterized by a large coast that extends down to the extreme end of the Italian Peninsula and back up, covering the whole tip of the "boot." Calabria is also characterized by a steep arm of the Apennine Mountain range and the mountain plateau known as La Sila, which is covered by thick forests and is known to have the purest air in Italy. From Calabria come the spicy pork spread 'nduja and soppressata salami, as well as the popular onion variety known as cipolla rossa di Tropea. Calabria has Italy's second-highest number of organic farmers after Sicily, and it is the second-biggest olive oil producer after Apulia. Notably, Calabria is the biggest Italian producer of porcini mushrooms and its largest producer of chile peppers.

BASILICATA

Also known as Lucania, this region is characterized by mountains and has only two brief openings to the sea. Characteristic products of the region are horseradish and peperone crusco, a dried sweet pepper, and quality durum wheat and emmer. The world-famous pane di Matera also comes from this region, and has been celebrated since Roman times. Lucanica di Picerno sausage and the beloved Aglianico del Vulture red wine, as well as the popular liqueur Amaro Lucano, are other representative products of Basilicata.

APULIA

Enclosing the back and the "heel" of the Italian Peninsula's "boot," Apulia has one large coast that faces the Adriatic, and a smaller section facing the Ionian Sea. Many are this region's contributions to Italian cuisine, such as the orecchiette pasta format and the famous specialties orecchiette alla cime di rapa, focaccia Barese, pane di Altamura, panzerotti, and pasticciotti, to mention just a few. Apulia is the leading Italian producer of olive oil, durum

wheat, almonds, and grapes, and one of its main producers of tomatoes.

and, of course, the sweets cannoli and cassata are representative of Sicilian cuisine.

SICILY

The largest island in the Mediterranean Sea, Sicily is separated from the Italian Peninsula by a small stretch of water known as the Strait of Messina. Sicilian cuisine is both maritime and from the land, as it has a lot of coastline, but also a large inland. Sicilian soil has been known since antiquity for its fertility, a quality bestowed by repeated volcanic eruptions on the island. Sicily is the second-largest Italian producer of durum wheat, its third-biggest producer of wine, and one of the biggest Italian producers of tomatoes, citrus, artichokes, almonds, pistachios, and many other fruits and vegetables. Relevant also are the fishing industry, with quality tuna, bottarga, and anchovies readily available on the island, a high-quality pasta industry, and Sicilian cheeses, such as primo sale, ricotta salata, provola, and caciocavallo, to mention just a few. Among the innumerable specialties, arancini, couscous, sarde a beccafico, pasta alla Norma, pasta con le sarde,

SARDINIA

Separated from both Sicily and mainland Italy by the Tyrrhenian Sea, Sardinia's cuisine has much in common with the rest of Southern Italy, and is characterized by durum wheat, which is used to make pasta and bread, and pig and sheep farming. Sheep farming has ancient roots in Sardinia, and the island continues to have one of the highest densities of sheep in the world. As you would expect of an island, the fishing industry are a major part of the economy, and Sardinia's bottarga is highly prized. Other big culinary industries is the production of citrus, olive oil, wine, cheese (pecorino sardo is the best known of these), and, interestingly, rice. Among the many dishes that are traditional to Sardinia, roasted whole baby pig, porceddu, and many durum wheat–derived specialties are characteristic, with pastas like malloreddus, the filled culurgiones, and fregola (a pasta that is like a large-grained couscous), and the flatbread pane carasau numbering in this last group.

CENTRAL ITALY

TUSCANY

Lying just below Liguria, Tuscany has a much larger inland than its Northern neighbor, a reality which clearly influenced its cuisine. On the traditional Tuscan table, we find the famous bistecca fiorentina, which is one fruit of the storied history of cattle farming in this region, together with a myriad of vegetable and pulse–based salads and soups, like panzanella and ribollita, as well as the popular fish soup caciucco. Like Liguria, Tuscany excels with its quality olive oil, and it rivals Piedmont for the best red wines in the country, among which Brunello di Montalcino, Chianti, and Vino Nobile di Montepulciano are numbered, to mention just a few.

MARCHE

This region faces the Adriatic Sea, but it also has a large inland piece, resulting in a cuisine that has significant peasant and maritime influences. The most famous dishes from this region are olive all'ascolana and pizza di Pasqua. Marche is a producer of several quality specialties, such as olive ascolana del Piceno, lenticchia di Castelluccio, pecorino dei Monti Sibillini, and salame di Fabriano. Wine production, especially white wine, is also remarkable in the area.

UMBRIA

Unlike the neighboring Marche, Umbria has no opening to the sea. The region's hilly inland has been devoted to pig farming and meat curing for millennia, especially in the area around Norcia. Even the famous porchetta, which is commonly, and mistakenly, attributed to Rome, is originally from Umbria. The region is also notable in a culinary sense for the tartufo nero di Norcia, a black truffle that rivals Piedmont's tartufo bianco for the best in Italy, and the famous and ancient torta al testo.

LAZIO

Though it has a large area facing the Tyrrhenian Sea, Lazio's cuisine is characterized by produce from the inland portion. Renowned is the region's sheep's milk pecorino Romano cheese, as sheep herding has been traditional in Lazio since ancient times. From the countryside comes some good white wine, two of the best rustic loaves in the country, pane di Genzano and pane di Lariano, as well as top-notch guanciale, one of the main ingredients in the famous spaghetti all'amatriciana. Regarding Rome, it is renowned for the use of innards in innumerable traditional dishes, the love of fried food like fiori fritti and baccalà fritto, and pizza bianca Romana, a flatbread that is rumored to have originated during the Roman Empire.

TRENTINO-ALTO ADIGE

The Bolzano province of Trentino-Alto Adige is also known as South Tyrol. Geographically and culturally, this area belongs to the larger Tyrolean region that is part of Austria, and it used to be ruled by that country, a history which is evident in traditional regional dishes such as strudel, canederli, and schüttelbrot. Many are the characteristic products of this region, among which we find speck, a smoked ham that is popular all over Italy, the apples of the Val di Non, and wines such as Spumante Trento and Teroldego Rotaliano. Also, the unique speck di trota, a delectable smoked trout, and several varieties of polenta are representative of Trentino-Alto Adige.

FRIULI-VENEZIA GIULIA

This region is more affected by Slavic rather than Austrian influences, as shown by the festive sweet breads putizza, gubana, and presnitz, which are very closely related to Slovakian makovník, Slovenian potica, Romanian cozonac, and Polish makowiec. Among the many excellent local products are San Daniele ham, Montasio cheese, many wines, among which the world-renowned Prosecco is included, and apples.

VENETO

A relatively large region with various local cuisines, Veneto is an area where polenta is popular and rice even more so, as it was the only cereal that was easy to cultivate in this watery section. Among the most popular local dishes we find two desserts, Treviso's tiramisù—a dish whose paternity is contested by Tuscany and Friuli-Venezia Giulia—and Verona's pandoro. Veneto is the biggest wine producer in Italy, with Prosecco (together with Friuli-Venezia Giulia), Amarone della Valpolicella, and Soave among the varietals. The region is also remarkable for its excellent produce, with asparago bianco di Bassano and radicchio rosso di Treviso standing as the two strongest examples.

EMILIA-ROMAGNA

This region has a hyphenated name because it consists of two main areas, Emilia (Piacenza, Parma, Reggio Emilia, Modena, Ferrara, and Bologna) and Romagna (Cesena, Faenza, Forlì, Imola, Ravenna, and Rimini). Romagna is famous for its delicious cappelletti in brodo and its iconic piadina, while Emilia is the home of tortellini, ragù alla Bolognese, Parmigiano Reggiano, Prosciutto di Parma, and mortadella di Bologna.

THE AOSTA VALLEY

This Alpine section borders France and is largely influenced by that country's cuisine. Such is the case with popular dishes like fonduta and monte bianco, although it is possible that this latter, a chestnut dessert known in France as "mont blanc," may be originally from the Aosta Valley. The best-known product of this region is probably fontina cheese, which characterizes popular local dishes such as the abovementioned fonduta and gnocchi alla bava.

LOMBARDY

A large region that was divided into a few principalities in the past, Lombardy has large local variations in its culinary heritage. Like Veneto, Lombardy is also a big producer of rice—risotto alla Milanese originated here—and is devoted to cattle farming and milk production. World-renowned cheeses like gorgonzola, taleggio, and bel paese come from this region, and Lombardy is also one of the regions that produces Grana Padano. Milan, Lombardy's main city, is home of the popular sweet bread panettone Milanese.

PIEDMONT

This section's most notable feature is probably Langhe, a hilly area that is home to some of the most prized Italian products, such as white truffles, the wines Barolo, Barbaresco, and Barbera, and the famous Piedmont hazelnuts—Nutella has always been produced in Piedmont, and is still managed by the same family, the Ferrero clan from Alba. Also, Piedmont's cuisine is partly influenced by France, like the Aosta Valley, but also by Central Europe, as the local Savoy monarchy used to have tight relationships with several countries there. Notable among the many typical dishes that influenced Italian cuisine is risotto, which was developed at the court of the Savoia in the nineteenth century.

LIGURIA

This is northwestern Italy's opening to the Mediterranean, though separated from the rest of Northern Italy by a steep arm of the Apennines. Liguria is, by all means, a Mediterranean land, not only because it faces the sea, but for the effect that this proximity has had on its traditional cuisine. Famous primarily for its pesto alla Genovese and focaccia, Liguria is a big producer of herbs and flowers, as it seems that every plant that grows in this sun-kissed region is of the highest quality. Notable products of this region are olives of the Taggiasca variety and Ligurian olive oil, particularly the one produced around Imperia.

INGREDIENTS, TECHNIQUES & TOOLS

BASIC INGREDIENTS

TOMATOES

What matters most in nailing traditional Italian recipes is not introducing ingredients and aromas that were not present in the original recipe. For instance, when cooking something that includes tomato sauce, it is fundamental not to use ready-made, store-bought sauces, as they always feature added elements and aromas that may compromise the overall flavor profile of the dish. For this reason, throughout the book, whole and peeled canned tomatoes that have been crushed have been listed as an ingredient instead of tomato puree, as the latter often tastes like something more than just tomatoes, especially if produced outside of Italy. If you do manage to find a brand of tomato puree that is entirely undoctored, then feel free to make your life easier and use that instead of crushed whole peeled tomatoes. On the other hand, if you feel like going the extra mile, you can always use fresh tomatoes, blanching and then peeling them, instead of the canned ones. When electing to use crushed tomatoes, it is important to either crush them by hand or, if using a blender or food processor, to run the tomatoes through it for a very short time. This way the seeds contained in the tomatoes will not break, which may compromise the preparation's flavor. However, the best way to make your own tomato puree is to pass either fresh or canned tomatoes through an old-fashioned food mill. This way, peels, seeds, harder, less digestible, and tasty parts of the tomatoes are sifted out. And, of course, whole peeled tomatoes should be used with their juice; they would otherwise make a very poor tomato sauce.

OLIVE OIL, LARD & BUTTER

Olive oil is the preferred cooking fat in those Italian regions that traditionally cultivated olive trees, namely the South, part of Central Italy, and Liguria in the North. For the rest of Italy, lard was the overwhelming cooking fat of choice, as it was cheap, readily available, and, as we now know, ideal for cooking. Lard in fact does not release trans-fatty acids and other harmful chemicals when heated, as most vegetable oils—other than olive oil—do. We have also discovered that lard is rich in oleic acid, the same beneficial fatty acid contained in olive oil. It was therefore not a bad idea, in traditional cuisine, to use lard when olive oil was not available. Even in regions with a strong olive oil tradition, lard was often the fat of choice for baking before butter and vegetable oils took over recently.

In this book, I've relayed traditional recipes as faithfully as possible to what was handed down through the generations, keeping lard as

the fat of choice when it made sense to. Feel free to substitute lard with butter or olive oil, according to what is available to you and in consideration of your dietary choices and/or restrictions. There is absolutely no reason not to try out a recipe just because it contains lard—using butter or olive oil will produce quite similar, although not identical, results. Just skip the lard, not the recipe!

FLOUR

The most used flour in Italian home cooking is a superfine wheat flour which goes under the label farina "00." Although the label "00" does not say anything about the flour's strength, it is generally equated to a medium-strength white flour like all-purpose flour. When a recipe from this book calls for all-purpose flour, know that you can always replace it with farina "00," if you can get hold of it. The second-most common flour is semola rimacinata di grano duro, which in English translates to superfine durum wheat flour or superfine semolina. Semola rimacinata

is not only very finely ground but also sifted and then remilled, so it is not easy to get the right fineness in durum wheat milled outside of Italy. The best option, in cases where semola rimacinata is called for, is to get an Italian flour.

VEGETABLES

Many vegetables used in traditional Italian cuisine are difficult or impossible to find outside of Italy. I have suggested substitutions when possible, but readers can probably find even better substitutes, in light of their greater familiarity with what is available locally.

HERBS

The most common herbs in Italian cooking are rosemary, sage, basil, parsley, bay leaf, oregano, and marjoram, which are all widely available around the world. A few recommendations—do not use herb mixes, and always strive to get fresh herbs, with the exception of dried oregano and bay leaves, which are generally used in Italy.

MEAT

It is not easy to translate the cuts of meat and types of offal used in regional Italian cuisine, as many are not commonly used abroad, and can be hard to find even across different Italian regions. I have tried to minimize the need for hard-to-find cuts and offal, while not compromising on easy-to-find ingredients like salsiccia (Italian sausage), pancetta, and guanciale. When a recipe calls for salami, even if each regional recipe would traditionally feature the one produced locally, it is "good enough" to make due with any Italian salami, as non-Italian salami tends to have a very different flavor profile that could alter the recipe substantially.

CHEESE

As with vegetables, many varieties of cheese used in traditional Italian cooking are hard to find outside of Italy. In creating these recipes, I could, however, nearly always find an acceptable replacement in the form of a different Italian cheese that is readily available worldwide. The recommendation when preparing these recipes at home is to, at minimum, stick to widely available varieties of cheese like Parmesan, pecorino, and fontina, and not just use whatever is in one's fridge, as the latter will almost certainly negatively affect the resulting dish.

SALT

This is generally referring to fine sea salt in the book. It is up to you to use iodized or noniodized salt, as the differences in outcome will be minimal. Though not traditional, I do not specify using coarse salt to season pasta water, as the same result can be achieved with the proper amount of fine salt. In general, coarse salt is mentioned only in recipes in which it provides an important textural element.

SUGAR

Sugar is to be understood as granulated sugar, unless otherwise specified.

ESSENTIAL TECHNIQUES

Regional Italian cooking is at the same time simple and challenging. It is simple as it involves only a few rules. It is challenging as those few rules cannot be violated. Although a recipe may seem destined to turn out bland to you, much of the final flavor depends on how well you handle the preparation and cooking. Flavor in Italian cooking stems from the transformation of a few raw ingredients, rather than the addition of more ingredients, which may feel instinctual to some.

COOKING PASTA

A common mistake when boiling pasta is to use a pot that can hold just enough water to cover the pasta. While this can work when boiling potatoes or vegetables, it is not ideal for cooking pasta. Pasta needs plenty of water so that it can cook evenly without sticking together. And there is no need to add oil to the pasta water: if there is plenty of water, and if the pasta is added after the water reaches a full boil, the pasta will not stick together. It is also crucial to add salt when the water starts boiling and before adding the pasta. It is better to add a good amount of salt to the pasta water than to excessively season the sauce. This way you will end up consuming less salt, as most of it will remain in the water.

It is optimal to stir the pasta a couple of times during cooking and to taste it to make sure that the amount of salt added was enough, and that the pasta is cooked as desired. Depending on how you plan to finish the pasta dish, the pasta should be drained when it is more or less al dente, as in many cases the cooking will continue when it is added to the sauce. For many, but not all recipes, it is good to reserve 1 or 2 cups of pasta water, which is full of luscious starch and will help thicken the sauce.

COOKING DRIED LEGUMES & PULSES

The drawback of using dried rather than canned legumes and pulses is having to soak and cook them for long periods—however, the result will be certainly tastier, and is also healthier.

Different types of legumes need different soaking and cooking times, but it all starts the same way: soak the legumes in 3 times their volume in cold water. During the soaking period, change the water 1 to 2 times.

Soaking times by variety: beans, 12 to 24 hours; chickpeas, 12 to 48 hours; lentils and split peas, 2 hours.

After soaking the legumes or pulses, drain them and put them in a pot, ideally made of earthenware, and add twice their volume in cold water. In Italy, bay leaves and a sprig of rosemary are often added to the water, with 1 to 2 peeled garlic cloves. Bring to a simmer, partially cover the pot, and cook over low heat until whatever you are cooking is tender, which will be for a varying length of time: for beans, 1½ hours; chickpeas, about 2 hours; lentils and split peas, about 40 minutes. One more thing, wait to season the legumes and pulses with salt until you are halfway through cooking them.

HANDLING GARLIC

In traditional Italian cooking, garlic is never pressed. Most of the time, a garlic clove is simply peeled and added to the pan whole or halved in the initial stages of cooking, as happens with pasta sauces, and removed midway through. In other recipes, the garlic can be minced, and sometimes sliced thin, in which instances it will not be removed, but become part of the final dish.

MAKING A SOFFRITTO

A soffritto is a mix of chopped vegetables, generally carrots, celery, and onions, that serves as the base for a variety of traditional Italian recipes. What is crucial for a proper soffritto is finely chopping the vegetables and gently frying them over low heat until they have softened without also browning. The concept is that the soffritto should eventually dissolve in whatever is being prepared, adding flavor but not affecting the texture of the dish.

HANDLING FRESH HERBS

Herbs, more than spices, are key in traditional regional Italian cooking. Other than oregano and bay leaves, herbs should be fresh, as their dried counterparts do not create the classic flavor profiles you want. Ideally, you could keep a small herb garden in your kitchen window, which is easy, aromatic, and also rewarding. Another important consideration when using fresh herbs in Italian recipes is that the leaves are what you want to use. Besides a few recipes, generally meat based, in which an entire sprig is used, the stems of herbs are not included and should be discarded. If there's any question about what is being asked regarding an herb, assume that the leaves should be separated from the stems before being added to your dish.

GRATING CHEESE

While outside of Italy Parmesan and pecorino are grated in a variety of ways, in Italy there is near-universal agreement over the way these hard cheeses should be treated for using on pasta. To maximize the umami element they add to a dish and create the proper texture, these cheeses should not be finely shredded, but instead run over a grater with tiny, star-shaped teeth and turned into a powdery drift of thin strands that can be effectively incorporated in the pasta sauce without losing the grainy consistency of the cheeses.

MASTERING THE STOVE

Contrary to what is generally thought, a large part of Italian culinary tradition is urban in origin, not rural. Even when they did not inhabit large cities, people generally preferred to live in small towns, and in tiny dwellings rather than in large country houses. The clear impact on the cooking style is that most Italian food is not supposed to be baked but rather cooked on a stove. Since Roman times until recently, ovens were communal and not a part of the home, with the exception of farmers, who tended to have them.

The drawback of this tradition is that Italian food is generally not just thrown in the oven and left to its own devices, but instead needs constant attention. Mastering the stove implies a continual monitoring and adjustment of the temperature of the heat source according to the state of the dish being prepared. Increasing the heat when the liquid needs to thicken or the meat needs to brown, lowering the heat to slow cook ingredients that need it, covering the pan with a lid to prevent liquids from evaporating quickly, and, of course, stirring the dish as it works to completion. It is not by accident that in Italy a good home cook used to be referred to as la regina dei fornelli, "the queen of the stove." Although the term is outdated, it still holds some beneficial truth: good traditional Italian food requires complete rule over the stove, which requires many lids, nonna's wooden spoon, and an infinite amount of patience.

DEEP-FRYING

In general, the ideal temperature for deep-frying is 350°F. This temperature is high enough that the food will cook quickly, with the outside creating a crispy "shell" that will not allow the frying oil to penetrate the food. Above this temperature, the oil starts smoking, and that means that harmful compounds are being developed, which of course we want to avoid. On the other hand, below this ideal temperature, the food will not develop a "shell" soon enough and the oil will make its way into the food, resulting in unpleasantly soggy, oily, and heavy preparations.

To make sure the oil is at the proper temperature, it is best to have an instant-read thermometer at hand, or simply to do like our grandmothers did: throw a piece of the food in the oil and see if it behaves in the desired manner. To maintain the temperature, it is ideal to use a Dutch oven or a tall and narrow saucepan, and to work in small batches to avoid crowding the pot or pan. Frying too many items at a time will inevitably lower the temperature of the oil too much. Finally, make sure to have paper towels at hand to drain the food upon after it is removed from the hot oil. The best oil for frying traditional Italian food is olive oil, but there are also modern vegetable oils that are modified for frying and can be used as a cheaper alternative to olive oil.

SERVING A FULL MEAL

A full Italian meal starts with an appetizer, the antipasto, proceeds with a pasta or soup first course, the primo, and continues with a meat-, fish-, or vegetable-based second course, the secondo, which is generally served with one or more sides, the contorno or contorni, and finishes with something sweet, the dolce, which can simply be a cookie to be dipped in a glass of sweet wine, or a piece of fruit. While one may not always have the chance (or desire) to serve a full meal with this many courses, the basic structure is generally followed. For instance, except for the secondo, which is typically served with a side, the other courses are always served alone. It makes little sense to an Italian to eat an antipasto with a primo, a primo with a secondo, or a primo with a contorno. Eating salad as well as big pieces of fish or meat with pasta seems as odd as eating meat alongside cake. This means that the courses, except for secondi with contorni, should be served not only on different plates but also at different times, so that every single flavor can be enjoyed, and the pleasurable act of eating is prolonged.

ACCOMPANYING A MEAL

The main accompaniment for all Italian courses is bread. Rice is never used as a side, always as a main. Potatoes are a popular side, but only with specific dishes. Vegetables are one of the preferred sides to a second course, but they should not accompany a pasta dish—although they can be part of it, of course. Bread is the only food that is always allowed on the Italian table at every course. In old times, it was also dipped in wine and served as a dessert. This is why any food other than bread used to be called "companatico," from cum pane, which means "whatever is eaten with bread."

TOOLS

To cook proper Italian food, you will not need more than what is generally present in a well-equipped kitchen, and most recipes in this book have been selected accordingly. Some of the items listed below are just useful additions that can help you further succeed in your attempts with traditional Italian cooking.

Skillets: As much Italian food involves gently frying ingredients and some involve deep-frying, a few different skillets are needed. Since traditional Italian cooking always includes cooking with fat, it is unnecessary to use nonstick pans, some of which may not be ideal health-wise, and instead use stainless steel, cast iron, and so on. Skillets with high sides, also known as sauté pans, are fundamental for many Italian recipes that require slowly pan-roasting food or braising it, as these pans enable frequent stirring and prevent liquid (and food) from being spilled. This type of skillet also allows for even heat distribution thanks to its large surface area, so that the food can properly cook without boiling, as it would in a Dutch oven, stockpot, or saucepan, a quality that gives liquids and sauces the possibility of thickening.

Dutch oven, stockpot, and saucepans: You will certainly need a Dutch oven or a large saucepan to make pasta sauce and cook short-format pasta, and a stockpot to make soups and stocks. A tall but not too large pot is good for cooking longer-format pasta. Italian home cooks recommend copper pots for polenta, stocks, fish stews, and risotto, as they conduct heat better and make these finicky preparations easier to handle. Also, many Italian home cooks swear by their terracotta pots, believing that the way food cooks in them has a strong effect on the flavor and consistency of a dish. Among the many preparations for which terracotta is recommended as the best cooking vessel are legumes, meat sauces, and couscous, to mention just a few.

Baking dish with high edges: No lasagna or baked pasta dish is possible without a good baking dish with high edges, as it allows for proper layering and prevents the preparation from spilling over onto the floor of your oven.

Multigrater or fine cheese grater: It is essential to have the right grater for each cheese. A multigrater, also known as a box grater, allows you to both shred and finely grate cheese, as well as grate the zest of citrus. But it can be a bit bulky and tough to handle. A fine cheese grater that does not shred but effectively reduces your Parmesan or pecorino into a powdery drift of thin strands is the ideal tool for these. Remember to look at the grater, both on the individual implement and the multigrater, before using it for Parmesan or pecorino, as it must have tiny, star-shaped teeth. Because of this, a microplane is not recommended for grating

cheese, though it can be handy for zesting citrus and grating nutmeg, cinnamon sticks, and other spices.

Food mill: An old-fashioned food mill is a great tool to have if you are set upon mastering Italian cooking. It allows you to separate skins and seeds from fruit and vegetables, something that a food processor cannot do, and it is seen as essential in producing many traditional recipes. It can also allow you to make a top-notch tomato puree from scratch, with peels and seeds easily removed.

Potato ricer: This is another useful tool to have, coming in handy not only for mashing potatoes but also to make certain pastas. It is recommended that you get a ricer with interchangeable inserts to create fine or coarse textures when needed.

Blender or food processor, mortar and pestle: A blender or food processor is very useful for producing pestos and similar sauces, to crush whole peeled canned tomatoes, and to pulverize nuts. Alternatively, a large mortar and pestle is another option for all of these tasks.

Slotted spoon: It has infinite uses, and in Italian cuisine, it should almost be considered indispensable.

Wooden spoons: They are what "nonnas" use, and I won't dare risk questioning it.

Pasta fork: This implement is useful to grab pasta to taste it during cooking and it can also be used to drain pasta, instead of a colander (at least when cooking smaller amounts of pasta). It is also helpful if you want to toss a long-format pasta in a sauce before serving it.

Sharpened knives: As in traditional Italian cuisine vegetables are essential, a sharp kitchen knife will make your work easier and more precise. Meats also often need to be trimmed and/or chopped, tasks that are difficult with a dull knife.

Stainless-steel colander: Essential in Italian cooking, not only to drain pasta but also to drain mozzarella, ricotta, vegetables, and so on.

Fine-mesh strainer: Always good to strain stocks and broths with, as well as sift flour and dry ingredients.

Kneading board: It is very useful to own a kneading board that is used only for dough, and which can be removed from the area quickly, when necessary, rather than having to carefully prepare your table, make it dusty, and clean it again. Trust me, this is a time-saver!

Rolling pin: Of course, this is an essential tool if one wants to master many of the baking recipes and the handmade pastas.

Pasta maker: There is no pasta dough that cannot be rolled out just with a rolling pin, but of course a pasta maker is a great help when making handmade pasta, and will also come in handy for some other traditional Italian preparations.

Scale: For baking and handmade pasta recipes, a kitchen scale is a massive help. In Italy, food is weighed instead of measured using volume; therefore, owing a scale will enable you to access a nearly infinite number of Italian recipes without having to "translate" measurements. Most electronic kitchen scales come in both American and European units of measurement, and as such are a great help in navigating recipes written using each.

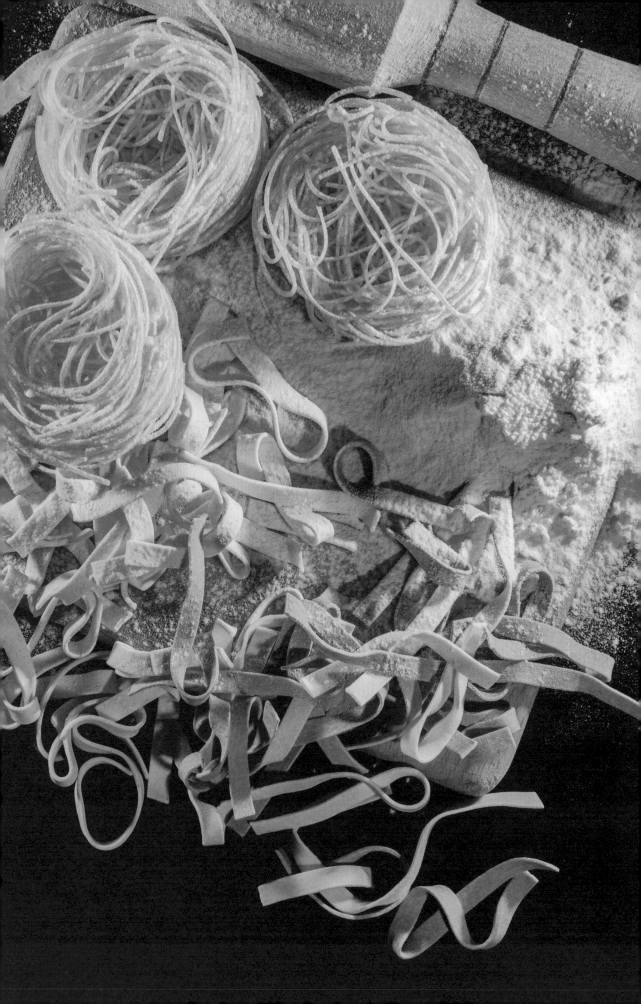

PASTA FATTA A MANO

Fresh handmade pasta was already being crafted in Italy at the time of the Ancient Romans. That pasta, known in Latin as laganum, and as lagane today, was made from a simple dough of flour and water, rolled out, and cut into strips, similar to the fettuccine and pappardelle that are popular today.

But pasta only became prominent in Italy during the Middle Ages, when Sicilians learned how to effectively dry the pasta made from their pliable durum wheat. The pasta that underwent this drying process had a very long shelf life and thus could serve as a staple during lengthy sailing trips, famines, and even sieges. From there technology progressed fast, leading to the creation of the first dried pasta production facilities around the turn of the second millennium.

The creativity of humble makers of pasta at home also progressed during this time. Although common people did not have resources to pur-chase the advanced instruments needed make dry pasta, fresh pasta remained accessible to everyone who could get hold of some flour, or even a sack of wheat grains to mill at home. From water and durum wheat flour, Southern Italian home pasta makers were capable of creating nearly infinite pasta formats, shaping them with the simple tools that were at hand, like a knitting needle or the bristle of a broom.

In the cold and wet region of Northern Italy, durum wheat could not grow and so pasta all'uovo, egg pasta, was created. This form of pasta also took on nearly infinite shapes, thanks to generations of Northern home pasta makers who devoted their skilled hands to transform this dough.

Here we guide you through some of the most common handmade pasta formats, which will help you to carry out a number of recipes in this book.

SCIALATIELLI

YIELD: 1½ LBS. / **ACTIVE TIME:** 30 MINUTES / **TOTAL TIME:** 1 HOUR

Originating on the Amalfi Coast, scialatielli is now popular throughout the Campania region. It is perfect when dressed with juicy sauces such as the Ragù di Polpo on page 201, and quite easy to make.

1. Place the flour, milk, egg, basil, and pecorino in a large bowl and work the mixture until it starts to come together as a dough.

2. Add the olive oil and work the dough until it has been incorporated.

3. Transfer the dough to a flour-dusted work surface and knead it energetically until it is a smooth and homogeneous dough, about 10 minutes.

4. Cover the dough with plastic wrap and let it rest at room temperature for 30 minutes.

5. Divide the dough into 2 pieces. Cover 1 piece with plastic wrap and place the other piece on a flour-dusted work surface.

6. Roll the dough out into a rectangle that is about ⅓ inch thick. Sprinkle flour over the dough and, working from the long sides, roll up the dough from the edges so that they meet in the center.

7. Cut the dough into ⅖-inch-thick rings, unroll them, and dust them with flour. Let them dry until they are ready to be boiled.

8. Repeat Steps 6 and 7 with the other piece of dough.

9. To cook the scialatielli, bring water to a boil in a large saucepan. Add salt, let the water return to a boil, and add the scialatelli. Cook until they are al dente, about 5 minutes.

INGREDIENTS:

- 15.8 OZ. FINELY GROUND DURUM WHEAT FLOUR (SEMOLA RIMACINATA), PLUS MORE AS NEEDED

- 7 OZ. WHOLE MILK

- 1 LARGE EGG, LIGHTLY BEATEN

- HANDFUL OF FRESH BASIL, FINELY CHOPPED

- 1 OZ. PECORINO CHEESE, GRATED

- ⅓ OZ. EXTRA-VIRGIN OLIVE OIL

FUSILLI AL FERRO

YIELD: 1½ LBS. / **ACTIVE TIME:** 1 HOUR / **TOTAL TIME:** 1 HOUR AND 30 MINUTES

In the South of Italy, fresh pasta is generally made from the simplest of doughs, based only on durum wheat flour and water. Fusilli al ferro are relatively easy to make and involve shaping a tiny string of pasta dough around a long stick and into a spiral. Traditionally, that implement would be made of iron, but at home, you can just use a long wooden skewer to shape the fusilli.

1. Place all of the ingredients in a large bowl and work the mixture until it starts to come together as a dough.

2. Transfer the dough to a flour-dusted work surface and knead it energetically until it is a smooth and homogeneous dough, about 10 minutes.

3. Cover the dough with plastic wrap and let it rest at room temperature for 30 minutes.

4. Tear the dough into small pieces and form them into logs that are about ⅓ inch thick. Cut the logs into 3-inch-long pieces.

5. Coat a long, thin metal rod or a wooden skewer with flour. Working with 1 piece of pasta at a time, wrap it around the implement to form it into a spiral. Gently remove the fusilli from the implement, taking care not to undo the spiral. Transfer the fusilli to a flour-dusted baking sheet and let them dry.

6. To cook the fusilli, bring water to a boil in a large saucepan. Add salt, let the water return to a boil, and add the fusilli. Let them float to the surface and cook for another 3 minutes.

INGREDIENTS:

15.8 OZ. FINELY GROUND DURUM WHEAT FLOUR (SEMOLA RIMACINATA), PLUS MORE AS NEEDED

7.9 OZ. WATER, AT ROOM TEMPERATURE

PINCH OF FINE SEA SALT

CAVATELLI

YIELD: 1½ LBS. / **ACTIVE TIME:** 1 HOUR / **TOTAL TIME:** 1 HOUR AND 30 MINUTES

A very ancient pasta format from the Molise region, cavatelli has become extremely popular throughout the South.

1. Place all of the ingredients in a large bowl and work the mixture until it starts to come together as a dough.

2. Transfer the dough to a flour-dusted work surface and knead it energetically until it is a smooth and homogeneous dough, about 10 minutes.

3. Cover the dough with plastic wrap and let it rest at room temperature for 30 minutes.

4. Tear the dough into small pieces and form them into logs that are about ¼ inch thick. Cut the logs into 1-inch-long pieces.

5. Press down on one side of the cavatelli with the tips of your index and middle fingers, making a movement that first pushes it forward and then comes back, rolling the pasta so that it forms a hollow in the middle. Transfer the cavatelli to a flour-dusted baking sheet and let them dry.

6. To cook the cavatelli, bring water to a boil in a large saucepan. Add salt, let the water return to a boil, and add the cavatelli. Cook until they are al dente, about 8 minutes.

INGREDIENTS:

- 15.8 OZ. FINELY GROUND DURUM WHEAT FLOUR (SEMOLA RIMACINATA), PLUS MORE AS NEEDED

- 7.9 OZ. WATER, AT ROOM TEMPERATURE

- PINCH OF FINE SEA SALT

MACCHERONI AL FERRETTO

YIELD: 1½ LBS. / **ACTIVE TIME:** 1 HOUR / **TOTAL TIME:** 1 HOUR AND 30 MINUTES

Similar to fusilli but less tightly coiled, maccheroni is one of the easiest pasta formats to make at home. It is beloved throughout the South, particularly in Calabria, where it is called either fileja or mparrettati.

1. Place all of the ingredients in a large bowl and work the mixture until it starts to come together as a dough.

2. Transfer the dough to a flour-dusted work surface and knead it energetically until it is a smooth and homogeneous dough, about 10 minutes.

3. Cover the dough with plastic wrap and let it rest at room temperature for 30 minutes.

4. Tear the dough into small pieces and form them into logs that are about ⅓ inch thick. Cut the logs into 2-inch-long pieces.

5. Coat a long, thin metal rod or a wooden skewer with flour. Working with one piece of pasta at a time, press the implement into the center of the log, creating a hollow. Roll the implement back and forth until the pasta closes around it. Gently remove the maccheroni from the implement, taking care not to unfold it. Transfer the maccheroni to a flour-dusted baking sheet and let them dry.

6. To cook the maccheroni, bring water to a boil in a large saucepan. Add salt, let the water return to a boil, and add the maccheroni. Let them float to the surface and cook for another 5 minutes.

INGREDIENTS:

15.8 OZ. FINELY GROUND DURUM WHEAT FLOUR (SEMOLA RIMACINATA), PLUS MORE AS NEEDED

7.9 OZ. WATER, AT ROOM TEMPERATURE

PINCH OF FINE SEA SALT

LAGANE

YIELD: 1 LB. / **ACTIVE TIME:** 1 HOUR / **TOTAL TIME:** 5 HOURS

Lagane is possibly the oldest pasta format, as it was known to the Romans and is still made in parts of the South.

1. Place all of the ingredients in a large bowl and work the mixture until it starts to come together as a dough.

2. Transfer the dough to a flour-dusted work surface and knead it energetically until it is a smooth and homogeneous dough, about 10 minutes.

3. Cover the dough with plastic wrap and let it rest at room temperature for 30 minutes.

4. Divide the dough into 2 pieces. Cover 1 piece with plastic wrap and place the other piece on a flour-dusted work surface.

5. Roll the dough out into a ⅛-inch-thick sheet. Roll the dough up around the rolling pin, gently slide it off, and cut it into 1-inch-thick strips. Unroll the strips and place them on a flour-dusted baking sheet. Repeat with the remaining piece of dough.

6. Dust the lagane with flour, cover with kitchen towels, and let them rest for 2 to 3 hours before cooking.

7. To cook the lagane, bring water to a boil in a large saucepan. Add salt, let the water return to a boil, and add the lagane. Cook until they are al dente, about 5 minutes.

INGREDIENTS:

- 5.3 OZ. FINELY GROUND DURUM WHEAT FLOUR (SEMOLA RIMACINATA), PLUS MORE AS NEEDED

- 5.3 OZ. ALL-PURPOSE FLOUR

- 5.3 OZ. WATER, AT ROOM TEMPERATURE

  PINCH OF FINE SEA SALT

ORECCHIETTE

YIELD: 1½ LBS. / **ACTIVE TIME:** 1 HOUR / **TOTAL TIME:** 1 HOUR AND 30 MINUTES

Orecchiette are one of the leading gastronomic symbols of Apulia, and although they are easily found packaged, they really have a different taste if made fresh. Relatively easy to make, they owe their name to the way they are shaped, as they resemble "little ears," or orecchie.

1. Place all of the ingredients in a large bowl and work the mixture until it starts to come together as a dough.

2. Transfer the dough to a flour-dusted work surface and knead it energetically until it is a smooth and homogeneous dough, about 10 minutes.

3. Cover the dough with plastic wrap and let it rest at room temperature for 30 minutes.

4. Divide the dough into 3 pieces. Cover 2 pieces with plastic wrap and place the other on a flour-dusted work surface.

5. Shape the dough into a ⅖-inch-thick log and cut it into ⅖-inch-long pieces.

6. Using a knife with a smooth blade, shape the pieces into orecchiette by running the knife over their tops to drag them toward you. Use your thumb to turn the orecchiette over. Transfer them to flour-dusted baking sheets.

7. Repeat Steps 5 and 6 with the remaining pieces of dough.

8. To cook the orecchiette, bring water to a boil in a large saucepan. Add salt, let the water return to a full boil, and add the orecchiette. Cook until they are al dente, about 5 minutes.

INGREDIENTS:

- 15.8 OZ. FINELY GROUND DURUM WHEAT FLOUR (SEMOLA RIMACINATA), PLUS MORE AS NEEDED
- 7.9 OZ. WATER, AT ROOM TEMPERATURE
- 2 PINCHES OF FINE SEA SALT

SAGNE NCANNULATE

YIELD: 1½ LBS. / **ACTIVE TIME:** 1 HOUR / **TOTAL TIME:** 3 HOURS AND 30 MINUTES

Typical of the Salento region, this long pasta format is extremely easy to make and quite beautiful to look at.

1. Place all of the ingredients in a large bowl and work the mixture until it starts to come together as a dough.

2. Transfer the dough to a flour-dusted work surface and knead it energetically until it is a smooth and homogeneous dough, about 10 minutes.

3. Cover the dough with plastic wrap and let it rest at room temperature for 15 minutes.

4. Place the dough on a flour-dusted work surface and roll into a ¹⁄₁₀-inch-thick sheet.

5. Cut the dough in half with a pasta wheel, and then cut it into 10-inch-long strips that are about ½ inch wide.

6. Dust the sagne with flour, pull the ends in opposite directions to twist them, and then bring the ends together so that the pasta has a horseshoe shape.

7. Place the sagne on a flour-dusted baking sheet and let them dry for 2 to 3 hours.

8. To cook the sagne, bring water to a boil in a large saucepan. Add salt, let the water return to a boil, and add the sagne. Cook until they are al dente, 7 to 8 minutes.

INGREDIENTS:

15.8 OZ. FINELY GROUND DURUM WHEAT FLOUR (SEMOLA RIMACINATA), PLUS MORE AS NEEDED

7.9 OZ. WATER, AT ROOM TEMPERATURE

2 PINCHES OF FINE SEA SALT

BUSIATE

YIELD: 1½ LBS. / **ACTIVE TIME:** 1 HOUR / **TOTAL TIME:** 1 HOUR AND 30 MINUTES

This popular Sicilian pasta is very similar to fusilli, only longer. Busiate owe their name to the buso, the stem of the ampelodesmos plant, that were originally used to shape them.

1. Place all of the ingredients in a large bowl and work the mixture until it starts to come together as a dough.

2. Transfer the dough to a flour-dusted work surface and knead it energetically until it is a smooth and homogeneous dough, about 10 minutes.

3. Cover the dough with plastic wrap and let it rest at room temperature for 30 minutes.

4. Place the dough on a flour-dusted work surface, tear small pieces from it, and shape them into ¼-inch-thick logs. Cut the logs into 6-inch-long strands.

5. Coat a long, thin metal rod or a wooden skewer with flour. Working with one piece of pasta at a time, wrap it around the implement to form it into a long spiral. Gently remove the busiate from the implement, taking care not to undo the spiral. Transfer it to a flour-dusted baking sheet and let it dry.

6. To cook the busiate, bring water to a boil in a large saucepan. Add salt, let the water return to a boil, and add the busiate. Cook until they are al dente, 7 to 8 minutes.

INGREDIENTS:

15.8 OZ. FINELY GROUND DURUM WHEAT FLOUR (SEMOLA RIMACINATA), PLUS MORE AS NEEDED

7.9 OZ. WATER, AT ROOM TEMPERATURE

PINCH OF FINE SEA SALT

COUSCOUS

YIELD: 10 SERVINGS / **ACTIVE TIME:** 1 HOUR AND 30 MINUTES / **TOTAL TIME:** 24 HOURS

The most common way to eat couscous today is to buy a ready-made package from the store, but in Western Sicily it is customary to make it by hand, using a technique called incocciatura that is performed in a specific ceramic plate known as a mafaradda. The couscous is then steamed in a specific couscoussiera pot. While these tools help, they are not necessary, and here is a simple recipe that will allow you to make couscous at home, from scratch.

1. Place a handful of the flour in a large, shallow bowl. Add salt to some water and add a few drops to the flour.

2. Make circular movements with your fingertips so that the flour absorbs all of the water. Continue to incorporate a few drops of water at a time until the flour starts to aggregate and form large clumps that are not moist. Transfer the aggregated couscous to a kitchen towel.

3. Repeat Steps 1 and 2 until all of the flour has been used up.

4. Let the couscous rest for anywhere from 2 hours to overnight.

5. Place the couscous in a large bowl and season it with olive oil and pepper. Toss to combine, making sure the grains of couscous remain separate.

6. If you do not have a couscoussiera, line a steaming basket with parchment paper and add the couscous.

7. Bring a few inches of water to a boil in a saucepan and add the bay leaves. Place the steaming basket over the boiling water and steam the couscous until it is tender, about 2 hours, stirring occasionally and adding more water as necessary.

INGREDIENTS:

2   LBS. COARSE DURUM WHEAT FLOUR

SALT AND PEPPER, TO TASTE

WATER, AS NEEDED

EXTRA-VIRGIN OLIVE OIL, AS NEEDED

2   BAY LEAVES

FREGOLA

YIELD: 5 SERVINGS / **ACTIVE TIME:** 1 HOUR / **TOTAL TIME:** 1 HOUR AND 30 MINUTES

Like couscous, fregola, or fregula, is also made from durum wheat but it is cooked differently. While couscous is steamed, fregola, a Sardinian specialty, is generally cooked like risotto, with liquid gradually added and absorbed. Handmade fregola generally requires a deep terracotta dish called a scivedda—in its absence, use a large bowl, possibly in ceramic.

1. Line a baking sheet with parchment paper. Place the saffron and water in a bowl and let it steep for 30 minutes.

2. Place 2 tablespoons of flour and a tablespoon of saffron water in a terracotta dish or shallow, ceramic bowl. Rub the moistened flour continuously against the bottom of the dish until it comes together in ⅙-inch balls. Transfer the fregola to the baking sheet.

3. Repeat Steps 1 and 2 until all of the flour has been used up.

4. To cook the fregola, preheat the oven to 390°F. Place it in the oven and bake until it is lightly browned, about 20 minutes.

INGREDIENTS:

¾ TEASPOON SAFFRON

9½ OZ. LUKEWARM WATER (90°F)

15.8 OZ. COARSE DURUM WHEAT FLOUR

MALLOREDDUS

YIELD: 1½ LBS. / **ACTIVE TIME:** 1 HOUR / **TOTAL TIME:** 3 HOURS

Malloreddus, known outside of Sardinia as gnocchetti sardi, have different names in local dialects, depending on the specific area of origin. The term malloreddus is typical of an area known as Campidano, while elsewhere they are called chiusoni, macarrones de punzu, or ciciones.

1. Place all of the ingredients in a large bowl and work the mixture until it starts to come together as a dough.

2. Transfer the dough to a flour-dusted work surface and knead it energetically until it is a smooth and homogeneous dough, about 10 minutes.

3. Cover the dough with plastic wrap and let it rest at room temperature for 15 minutes.

4. Divide the dough into 3 pieces. Cover 2 pieces with plastic wrap and place the other on a flour-dusted work surface.

5. Shape the dough into a ⅖-inch-thick log and cut it into ⅖-inch-long pieces.

6. Roll the pieces over a gnocchi board or a fork while gently pressing down on them to shape the malloreddus. Place them on a flour-dusted baking sheet, cover with a kitchen towel, and let them rest for 1 hour.

7. Repeat Steps 5 and 6 with the remaining pieces of dough.

8. To cook the malloreddus, bring water to a boil in a large saucepan. Add salt, let the water return to a boil, and add the malloreddus. Let them rise to the surface and cook for 1 more minute.

INGREDIENTS:

- 15.8 OZ. FINELY GROUND DURUM WHEAT FLOUR (SEMOLA RIMACINATA), PLUS MORE AS NEEDED

- 7.9 OZ. LUKEWARM WATER (90°F)

- PINCH OF FINE SEA SALT

CULURGIONES

YIELD: 40 CULURGIONES / **ACTIVE TIME:** 2 HOURS / **TOTAL TIME:** 24 HOURS

Culurgiones are a Sardinian filled pasta that are sealed in a manner that leads to them resembling an ear of wheat. Depending on their area of production, fillings can vary, but here is a recipe for the most popular type of culurgiones, typical of the Ogliastra region.

1. The day before you are going to prepare the culurgiones, prepare the filling. Place the olive oil and garlic in an airtight container and let the mixture steep for 6 hours.

2. Bring water to a boil in a large saucepan. Add salt and the potatoes and cook until they are tender. Drain the potatoes, place them in a bowl, and mash until they are smooth. Add the mint and pecorino and stir to incorporate. Strain the olive oil into the filling and stir to incorporate. Chill the filling in the refrigerator overnight.

3. Remove the filling from the refrigerator and let it rest at room temperature.

4. To begin preparations for the dough, place all of the ingredients in a large bowl and work the mixture until it starts to come together as a dough.

5. Transfer the dough to a flour-dusted work surface and knead it energetically until it is a smooth and homogeneous dough, about 10 minutes.

6. Cover the dough with plastic wrap and let it rest at room temperature for 30 minutes.

7. Place the dough on a flour-dusted work surface and roll it into a ⅒-inch-thick sheet (you can also use a pasta maker to do this). Cut the dough into 5-inch rounds.

8. Form tablespoons of the filling into patties and place them in the center of the rounds. Fold the dough over the filling to form half-moons.

9. To seal the culurgiones and give them the correct shape, it's best to watch a video, of which there are many online. You want to fold in one end of each one, and then fold one side over the other, making pleats as you do to seal in the filling.

10. To cook the culurgiones, bring water to a boil in a large saucepan. Add salt, let the water return to a boil, and add the culurgiones. Cook for about 6 minutes.

INGREDIENTS:

FOR THE FILLING

2	TABLESPOONS EXTRA-VIRGIN OLIVE OIL
2	GARLIC CLOVES, PEELED
	SALT, TO TASTE
1½	LBS. POTATOES, PEELED
20	FRESH MINT LEAVES
1½	CUPS GRATED PECORINO CHEESE

FOR THE DOUGH

8.8	OZ. FINELY GROUND DURUM WHEAT FLOUR (SEMOLA RIMACINATA), PLUS MORE AS NEEDED
4½	OZ. ALL-PURPOSE FLOUR
5.8	OZ. LUKEWARM WATER (90°F)
1	TABLESPOON EXTRA-VIRGIN OLIVE OIL
¼	TEASPOON FINE SEA SALT

STRANGOZZI

YIELD: 1 LB. / **ACTIVE TIME:** 30 MINUTES / **TOTAL TIME:** 1 HOUR

Typical of Umbria, strangozzi, or stringozzi, look like thick strands of spaghetti and are very easy to make.

1. Place all of the ingredients in a large bowl and work the mixture until it starts to come together as a dough.

2. Transfer the dough to a flour-dusted work surface and knead it energetically until it is a smooth and homogeneous dough, about 10 minutes.

3. Cover the dough with plastic wrap and let it rest at room temperature for 30 minutes.

4. Place the dough on a flour-dusted work surface and roll it into a ⅟₁₀-inch-thick sheet (you can also use a pasta maker to do this).

5. Roll the dough up around the rolling pin, gently slide it off, and cut it into ⅟₁₀-inch-thick strips. Unroll the strips and place them on a flour-dusted baking sheet.

6. To cook the strangozzi, bring water to a boil in a large saucepan. Add salt, let the water return to a boil, and add the strangozzi. Cook until they are al dente, 3 to 5 minutes.

INGREDIENTS:

- 5.3 OZ. FINELY GROUND DURUM WHEAT FLOUR (SEMOLA RIMACINATA), PLUS MORE AS NEEDED
- 5.3 OZ. ALL-PURPOSE FLOUR
- 5.3 OZ. WATER, AT ROOM TEMPERATURE
- PINCH OF FINE SEA SALT

SPAGHETTI ALLA CHITARRA

YIELD: 4 SERVINGS / **ACTIVE TIME:** 40 MINUTES / **TOTAL TIME:** 2 HOURS AND 30 MINUTES

Now one of the most popular pasta formats in Central Italy, spaghetti alla chitarra originated in the Abruzzi region. It is impossible to make them without a chitarra, a specific wooden and metal tool that is used to cut the pasta.

1. Pile the flour on a clean work surface. Make a well in the center, crack the eggs into the well, and beat the eggs with a fork until scrambled.

2. Incorporate the flour, a little at a time, until the dough starts to come together.

3. Check the dough to see if the consistency is right. Depending on a number of factors (size of the eggs, strength of the flour, and ambient humidity), you may need to incorporate 1 or 2 tablespoons of water or more flour.

4. Work the dough until it is elastic and smooth, about 10 minutes.

5. Cover the dough with plastic wrap and let it rest for 30 minutes before rolling.

6. Place the dough on a flour-dusted work surface and divide it into 6 pieces.

7. Roll out each piece of dough into a 1/5-inch-thick sheet that will fit your chitarra.

8. Let the dough dry, uncovered, for 30 minutes.

9. Turn the dough over and let the other side dry, uncovered for 30 minutes.

10. Place a sheet of pasta on the chitarra and pass the rolling pin over the sheet to cut it. Dust the strands with flour, form them into nests, and let them dry.

11. To cook spaghetti alla chitarra, bring water to a boil in a large saucepan. Add salt, let the water return to a full boil, and add the pasta. Cook until it is al dente, about 5 minutes.

INGREDIENTS:

- 14 OZ. SUPER FINE DURUM WHEAT FLOUR (SEMOLA RIMACINATA DI GRANO DURO), PLUS MORE AS NEEDED
- 4 EGGS
- 2 PINCHES OF FINE SEA SALT

TONNARELLI

YIELD: 1 LB. / **ACTIVE TIME:** 30 MINUTES / **TOTAL TIME:** 1 HOUR

Similar to Abruzzi's popular spaghetti alla chitarra, tonnarelli is a spaghettilike pasta from Lazio made from a dough containing eggs rather than water, a construction that is rare in Central Italy.

1. Place all of the ingredients in a large bowl and work the mixture until it starts to come together as a dough.

2. Transfer the dough to a flour-dusted work surface and knead it energetically until it is a smooth and homogeneous dough, about 10 minutes.

3. Cover the dough with plastic wrap and let it rest at room temperature for 30 minutes.

4. Place the dough on a flour-dusted work surface and roll it into a 1/10-inch-thick sheet (you can also use a pasta maker to do this).

5. Roll the dough up around the rolling pin, gently slide it off, and cut it into 1/10-inch-thick strips. Unroll the strips and place them on a flour-dusted baking sheet.

6. To cook the tonnarelli, bring water to a boil in a large saucepan. Add salt, let the water return to a boil, and add the tonnarelli. Cook until they are al dente, 3 to 5 minutes.

INGREDIENTS:

5.3   OZ. FINELY GROUND DURUM WHEAT FLOUR (SEMOLA RIMACINATA), PLUS MORE AS NEEDED

5.3   OZ. ALL-PURPOSE FLOUR

3   EGGS

2   PINCHES OF FINE SEA SALT

GNOCCHI DI PATATE

YIELD: 8 SERVINGS / **ACTIVE TIME:** 1 HOUR / **TOTAL TIME:** 2 HOURS

Now popular all over Italy and around the world, potato gnocchi originated in Northern Italy.

1. Place the potatoes in a large saucepan and cover them with cold water. Bring to a boil and cook until a knife inserted into the potatoes passes easily to their centers. Drain the potatoes.

2. Sift the flour onto a work surface, place the potatoes over it, and mash the potatoes.

3. Place the egg in a small bowl and season it with salt. Beat until scrambled and add it to the potato mixture. Work the mixture with your hands until it comes together as a soft, smooth dough. Be careful not to incorporate too much flour into the dough, otherwise the gnocchi will harden too much during cooking.

4. Cut the dough into pieces and form them into long, ⅗-inch-thick logs. Cut them into 1-inch-long pieces.

5. Dust a fork or a gnocchi board with flour and roll the pieces of dough over it, gently pressing down to shape the gnocchi.

6. Place the gnocchi on a flour-dusted baking sheet.

7. To cook the gnocchi, bring water to a boil in a large saucepan. Add salt, let the water return to a boil, and add the gnocchi. Cook until they rise to the surface.

INGREDIENTS:

- 2.2   LBS. STARCHY POTATOES, PEELED
- 10.6   OZ. ALL-PURPOSE FLOUR, PLUS MORE AS NEEDED
- 1   MEDIUM EGG

PICI

YIELD: 1 LB. / **ACTIVE TIME:** 30 MINUTES / **TOTAL TIME:** 4 HOURS

Traditional in Tuscany, pici is a long-format pasta that needs a bit more work than other hand-made pastas, but is well worth the effort.

1. Place the all-purpose flour, water, and salt in a large bowl and work the mixture until it starts to come together as a dough. Add the olive oil and work the dough to incorporate it.

2. Transfer the dough to a work surface dusted with all-purpose flour and knead it energetically until it is a smooth and homogeneous dough, about 10 minutes.

3. Cover the dough with plastic wrap and let it rest at room temperature for 30 minutes.

4. Place the dough on a work surface dusted with all-purpose flour and roll it into a ⅖-inch-thick sheet.

5. Roll the dough up around the rolling pin, gently slide it off, and cut it into ⅖-inch-thick strips.

6. Working with a few strands at a time, hold each end and pull in opposite directions to elongate the pici, taking care not to break them.

7. Dust the pici with semolina, place them on a baking sheet, and let them dry for 3 hours.

8. To cook the pici, bring water to a boil in a large saucepan. Add salt, let the water return to a boil, and add the pici. Cook until they are al dente, 6 to 8 minutes.

INGREDIENTS:

15.8 OZ. ALL-PURPOSE FLOUR, PLUS MORE AS NEEDED

9½ OZ. LUKEWARM WATER (90°F)

PINCH OF FINE SEA SALT, PLUS MORE AS NEEDED

2 TABLESPOONS EXTRA-VIRGIN OLIVE OIL

SEMOLINA FLOUR, AS NEEDED

CASONSEI

YIELD: 4 SERVINGS / ACTIVE TIME: 1 HOUR / TOTAL TIME: 2 HOURS

Typical of Brescia and Bergamo (Lombardy), casonsei are filled egg pasta with an interesting shape, like something you'd see at a sweet shop.

1. Place the butter in a large skillet and melt it over medium heat. Add the pear and cook, stirring, until it is browned, about 6 minutes. Remove the pan from heat and let the pear cool.

2. Place the salami in a food processor and blitz until it is a paste.

3. Place the salami in a large bowl and add all of the remaining ingredients, except for the pasta dough. Stir to combine, add the pears, and stir to incorporate. Set the filling aside.

4. Divide the dough into 2 pieces and cover 1 piece with plastic wrap.

5. Run the other piece of dough through a pasta maker until it is $\frac{1}{25}$ inch thick.

6. Cut the dough into 2-inch rounds and cover them with a kitchen towel.

7. Knead the scraps into a ball and let it rest for 15 minutes before running it through the pasta maker until it is $\frac{1}{25}$ inch thick and cutting it into 2-inch rounds.

8. Repeat Steps 5, 6, and 7 with the other piece of dough.

9. Form tablespoons of the filling into balls and place one in the center of each round. Moisten the edge of the dough with water, fold the dough over the filling, and press down on the edge to seal the casonsei.

10. Place the casonsei seam side down and press your thumb in the center, making a slight depression and forming them into crescents.

11. To cook the casonsei, bring water to a boil in a large saucepan. Add salt, let the water return to a boil, and add the casonsei. Cook them for 6 minutes.

INGREDIENTS:

- 1 TABLESPOON UNSALTED BUTTER
- 1 PEAR, PEELED, CORED, AND DICED
- 4½ OZ. SALAMI
- 3½ OZ. GROUND BEEF
- 1 TABLESPOON FINELY CHOPPED FRESH PARSLEY
- ½ GARLIC CLOVE, MINCED
- ZEST OF ½ LEMON
- 1 OZ. SULTANAS, SOAKED IN WARM WATER, DRAINED, SQUEEZED DRY, AND MINCED
- 1 SMALL EGG
- 2 AMARETTI (SEE PAGE 741), CRUMBLED FINE
- 1 (SCANT) CUP BREAD CRUMBS
- 1 (SCANT) CUP GRATED GRANA PADANO CHEESE
- SALT AND PEPPER, TO TASTE
- 2 PINCHES OF CINNAMON
- 2 PINCHES OF FRESHLY GRATED NUTMEG
- PASTA ALL'UOVO (SEE PAGE 73)

GNOCCHI DI GRANO SARACENO

YIELD: 4 SERVINGS / **ACTIVE TIME:** 40 MINUTES / **TOTAL TIME:** 1 HOUR

Typical of Valle d'Aosta, these buckwheat gnocchi may be the original form of Italian gnocchi.

1. Place the flours in a mixing bowl and stir to combine. Add the egg yolk and salt and work the mixture to incorporate them. Gradually add the water and work the mixture until it comes together as a dough.

2. Place the dough on a flour-dusted work surface and knead it until it is smooth and not sticky, incorporating more water or flour as necessary.

3. Form the dough into a loaf, cover it with plastic wrap, and chill it in the refrigerator for 1 hour.

4. Cut the dough into pieces and form them into long, ⅗-inch-thick logs. Cut them into 1-inch-long pieces.

5. Dust a fork or a gnocchi board with flour and roll the pieces of dough over it, gently pressing down to shape the gnocchi.

6. Place the gnocchi on a flour-dusted baking sheet.

7. To cook the gnocchi, bring water to a boil in a large saucepan. Add salt, let the water return to a boil, and add the gnocchi. Cook until they rise to the surface.

INGREDIENTS:

11.6 OZ. ALL-PURPOSE FLOUR, PLUS MORE AS NEEDED

8.8 OZ. BUCKWHEAT FLOUR

1 EGG YOLK

PINCH OF FINE SEA SALT

9½ OZ. WATER, PLUS MORE AS NEEDED

PASTA ALL'UOVO

YIELD: 4 SERVINGS / **ACTIVE TIME:** 30 MINUTES / **TOTAL TIME:** 1 HOUR

Typical of the North, particularly the Pianura Padana area and Emilia-Romagna, egg pasta has become a staple of Italian cuisine.

1. Pile the flour on a clean work surface. Make a well in the center, crack the eggs into the well, and beat the eggs with a fork until scrambled.

2. Incorporate the flour, a little at a time, until the dough starts to come together.

3. Check the dough to see if the consistency is right. Depending on a number of factors (size of the eggs, strength of the flour, and ambient humidity), you may need to incorporate 1 or 2 tablespoons of water or more flour.

4. Work the dough until it is elastic and smooth, about 10 minutes.

5. Cover the dough with plastic wrap and let it rest for 30 minutes before rolling it out and cutting it into the desired format.

INGREDIENTS:

14 OZ. "00" PASTA FLOUR OR ALL-PURPOSE FLOUR

4 MEDIUM EGGS

WATER, AS NEEDED

TAGLIATELLE

YIELD: 1 LB. / **ACTIVE TIME:** 30 MINUTES / **TOTAL TIME:** 1 HOUR

Typical of Emilia-Romagna, tagliatelle is the easiest pasta to make from pasta all'uovo, and the traditional format used in the famed Ragù alla Bolognese (see page 704).

1. Dust a work surface with semolina and place the pasta dough on it. Roll it out into a 1/13-inch-thick sheet (you can also use a pasta maker to do this).

2. Dust a rolling pin with all-purpose flour. Roll the dough up around the rolling pin, gently slide it off, and flatten it slightly. Cut the dough into 1/3-inch-thick strips.

3. Unroll the tagliatelle and place them on a baking sheet dusted with semolina flour.

4. If you do not intend to cook the tagliatelle right away, form them into nests and let them dry completely before storing them in a cool, dry place until ready to cook.

5. To cook the tagliatelle, bring water to a boil in a large saucepan. Add salt, let the water return to a boil, and add the tagliatelle. Cook until they are al dente, about 4 minutes.

INGREDIENTS:

SEMOLINA FLOUR,
AS NEEDED

PASTA ALL'UOVO
(SEE PAGE 73)

ALL-PURPOSE FLOUR,
AS NEEDED

PASTA ALL'UOVO VERDE

YIELD: 4 SERVINGS / **ACTIVE TIME:** 30 MINUTES / **TOTAL TIME:** 1 HOUR

In Emilia-Romagna it is common to make a variation of egg pasta that is enriched with green leafy vegetables like nettles, though nowadays it is mostly made with spinach. This is the pasta dough one should use for an authentic Lasagne alla Bolognese (see page 705).

1. Place the spinach in a large skillet, add a little bit of water, and cover the pan. Steam the spinach over low heat until it has wilted, about 5 minutes. Remove the pan from heat and let the spinach cool completely.

2. Squeeze the spinach to remove any excess water and chop it fine or blitz it in a food processor until it is pureed. Set the spinach aside.

3. Pile the flour on a clean work surface. Make a well in the center, crack the eggs into the well, and beat the eggs with a fork until scrambled.

4. Incorporate the flour, a little at a time, until the dough starts to come together. Add the spinach and salt and work the mixture to incorporate them.

5. Check the dough to see if the consistency is right. Depending on a number of factors (size of the eggs, amount of water remaining in the spinach, strength of the flour, and ambient humidity), you may need to incorporate more flour.

6. Work the dough until it is elastic and smooth, about 10 minutes.

7. Cover the dough with plastic wrap and let it rest for 30 minutes before rolling it out and cutting it into the desired format.

INGREDIENTS:

- 5½ OZ. FRESH SPINACH, RINSED WELL
- 14 OZ. "00" PASTA FLOUR OR ALL-PURPOSE FLOUR
- 3 MEDIUM EGGS

  PINCH OF FINE SEA SALT, PLUS MORE TO TASTE

SOUTH

ANTIPASTI & CONTORNI

SCAGLIUÒZZI

YIELD: 4 SERVINGS / ACTIVE TIME: 40 MINUTES / TOTAL TIME: 2 HOURS

These fried polenta triangles are generally sold in casual restaurants throughout Southern Italy, and are popular everywhere from Naples to Tuscany.

1. Line a loaf pan with parchment paper. Place the polenta, water, and salt in a saucepan and cook over medium heat, stirring frequently, until the polenta is thick and creamy, 10 to 15 minutes.

2. Transfer the polenta to the loaf pan and let it cool completely.

3. Turn the polenta out onto a cutting board and cut it into ½-inch-thick slices. Cut each slice in half diagonally, forming 2 triangles.

4. Add olive oil to a narrow, deep, and heavy-bottomed saucepan until it is about 2 inches deep and warm it to 350°F. Gently slip the polenta triangles into the hot oil and fry until they are a light golden brown, turning as necessary.

5. Remove the fried polenta from the hot oil, transfer them to a paper towel–lined plate to drain, and season them with salt. Serve once the fried polenta has drained and cooled slightly.

INGREDIENTS:

9   OZ. INSTANT POLENTA

4   CUPS WATER

1   TEASPOON KOSHER SALT, PLUS MORE FOR TOPPING

    EXTRA-VIRGIN OLIVE OIL, AS NEEDED

PANELLE

YIELD: 8 SERVINGS / **ACTIVE TIME:** 40 MINUTES / **TOTAL TIME:** 1 HOUR AND 30 MINUTES

Panelle are chickpea-flour fritters often used to stuff traditional Sicilian bread like Mafalde (see page 387). On their own, they are particularly popular in Palermo as part of the street food tradition.

1. Place the chickpea flour in a saucepan and gradually add the water, whisking to prevent lumps from forming. Stir in the salt, season the mixture with pepper, and cook over low heat, stirring continually, until the mixture starts to pull away from the side of the pan, 30 to 40 minutes.

2. Stir in the parsley and remove the pan from heat.

3. Coat a baking dish with olive oil, spoon the mixture into it, and level the surface with a rubber spatula. You want the mixture to be about ½ inch thick. Let the mixture cool completely.

4. Cut the mixture into squares. Add olive oil to a narrow, deep, heavy-bottomed saucepan with high edges until it is about 2 inches deep and warm it to 350°F. Gently slip the squares into the hot oil and fry until they are crispy and brown, turning as necessary.

5. Remove the panelle from the hot oil and transfer them to a paper towel–lined plate to drain. Serve once the panelle have drained and cooled slightly.

INGREDIENTS:

5½ (SCANT) CUPS CHICKPEA FLOUR

6 CUPS WATER

1½ TEASPOONS KOSHER SALT

BLACK PEPPER, TO TASTE

2 TABLESPOONS CHOPPED FRESH PARSLEY

EXTRA-VIRGIN OLIVE OIL, AS NEEDED

RUSTICO NAPOLETANO

YIELD: 15 TO 20 RUSTICI / **ACTIVE TIME:** 30 MINUTES / **TOTAL TIME:** 1 HOUR AND 15 MINUTES

This is a very special appetizer, with a sweet crust encasing a savory filling. Originally this delicious mini pie was part of the formal banquettes at the Neapolitan royal court, as documented by the early cookbook *Il Cuoco Galante*, which was written by Vincenzo Corrado at the end of the eighteenth century.

1. Preheat the oven to 350°F and coat 2 muffin tins with nonstick cooking spray. Place the ricotta in a mixing bowl, add the eggs, and season the mixture with salt and pepper. Whisk to combine, add the mozzarella, provola, salami, and Parmesan, and stir until well combined.

2. Beat the frolla with a rolling pin to soften it and roll it out until it is about ¼ inch thick. Using a pastry cutter or mason jar, cut the dough into rounds that are large enough to cover the wells of the muffin tins.

3. Place the rounds in the muffin tins and fill them with a generous spoonful of the cheese mixture.

4. Roll the remaining dough into a slightly thinner sheet and cut it into rounds that are large enough to use as lids for the rustici. Place them over the filling, fold the bottom layers over them, and gently press down on the seams to seal the rustici.

5. Brush the rustici with the egg yolk and place them in the oven. Cook until the rustici are golden brown, which will depend on the depth of the wells in the muffin tins. For deeper molds, bake for approximately 40 minutes. For shallower molds, bake for approximately 25 minutes. Also, do not worry if the lids of the rustici come off, as they will be reattached as the rustici cool.

6. Remove the rustici from the oven and let them cool for 5 minutes. Place a large heatproof tray over each of the muffin tins and invert the muffin tins, making sure the rustici do not come out of the tins quite yet. Let the rustici cool until they are slightly warm before removing them from the tins and enjoying.

INGREDIENTS:

- 2 CUPS RICOTTA CHEESE
- 5 EGGS
- SALT AND PEPPER, TO TASTE
- 10½ OZ. BUFFALO MOZZARELLA CHEESE, CUBED AND DRAINED IN THE REFRIGERATOR FOR 2 HOURS
- 10½ OZ. SMOKED PROVOLA CHEESE, CUBED
- 6 OZ. ITALIAN SALAMI, CHOPPED
- 1 CUP PLUS 1 TABLESPOON GRATED PARMESAN CHEESE
- PASTA FROLLA AL LARDO (SEE PAGE 817), AT ROOM TEMPERATURE
- 1 EGG YOLK, BEATEN

CROCCHÈ

YIELD: 20 CROCCHÈ / **ACTIVE TIME:** 40 MINUTES / **TOTAL TIME:** 24 HOURS

Also known as panzerotti, crocchè are a very popular appetizer in Naples, enjoyed with some local wine. Even if, nowadays, they have become a popular street food, these lovely potato croquettes most likely originated in the Neapolitan royal court.

1. Bring salted water to a boil in a large saucepan. Add the potatoes and boil until they are tender, 15 to 20 minutes. Drain the potatoes and place them in a bowl.

2. Mash the potatoes until they are smooth. Add the egg yolks, Parmesan, and parsley to the potatoes, season the mixture with salt and pepper, and knead the mixture until it feels smooth and well combined.

3. Line two baking sheets with parchment paper. To shape the crocchè, take a dollop of the potato mixture, place it in the palm of your hand, and flatten it. Place a piece of mozzarella in the center, form the mixture over the cheese, and then shape it into a 2-inch-long cylinder. Repeat until all of the potato mixture has been used.

4. Place the egg whites in a bowl, add a pinch of salt, and beat the egg whites slightly. Place the bread crumbs in a separate bowl and then dredge the croquettes in the egg whites and then in the bread crumbs until they are coated. Place the crocchè on the baking sheets, cover them with kitchen towels, and let them chill in the refrigerator overnight.

5. Remove the crocchè from the refrigerator and let them warm up at room temperature for 20 minutes.

6. Add olive oil to a narrow, deep, heavy-bottomed saucepan with high edges until it is about 2 inches deep and warm it to 350°F. Working in batches of 2 or 3, slip the crocchè into the hot oil and fry until they are golden brown, turning as necessary.

7. Remove the crocchè from the hot oil and transfer them to a paper towel–lined plate to drain. Serve once all of the crocchè have drained and cooled slightly.

INGREDIENTS:

SALT AND PEPPER, TO TASTE

2.2 LBS. POTATOES, PEELED AND CHOPPED

4 EGGS, SEPARATED

½ CUP GRATED PARMESAN CHEESE

2 HANDFULS OF FRESH PARSLEY, FINELY CHOPPED

1⅓ CUPS MOZZARELLA CHEESE, CUT INTO STRIPS AND DRAINED IN THE REFRIGERATOR FOR 1 HOUR

2 CUPS BREAD CRUMBS

EXTRA-VIRGIN OLIVE OIL, AS NEEDED

MOZZARELLA IN CARROZZA

YIELD: 6 SERVINGS / **ACTIVE TIME:** 20 MINUTES / **TOTAL TIME:** 2 HOURS AND 40 MINUTES

Popular both in Campania and Lazio, mozzarella in carrozza was probably born in the countryside of the former, since it was originally made with bufala mozzarella. In the past, distribution was not optimal and so mozzarella was often delivered past its prime, though still edible. Locals learned to turn this misfortune into a fried sandwich that is now enjoyed as an appetizer.

1. Cut the mozzarella into ½-inch-thick slices and place them in a colander. Set the colander in a bowl and let the mozzarella drain in the refrigerator for 2 hours.

2. Top 4 of the slices of bread with the mozzarella, making sure it is distributed evenly. Cover the cheese with the remaining slices of bread.

3. Place the eggs in a bowl, season them with salt and pepper, and beat them lightly. Place the bread crumbs in a separate bowl and then dredge the sandwiches in the eggs and then in the bread crumbs until they are coated. Set the breaded sandwiches aside.

4. Add olive oil to a narrow, deep, heavy-bottomed saucepan with high edges until it is about 2 inches deep and warm it to 350°F. Working with one sandwich at a time, slip it into the hot oil and fry until golden brown, turning as necessary.

5. Remove the sandwich from the hot oil, transfer it to a paper towel–lined plate to drain, and season it with salt. Serve once all of the sandwiches have drained and cooled slightly.

INGREDIENTS:

- 1   LB. FRESH MOZZARELLA CHEESE (BUFALA IS PREFERRED)
- 8   SLICES OF SANDWICH BREAD, CRUSTS REMOVED
- 3   EGGS
-   SALT AND PEPPER, TO TASTE
- 2   CUPS BREAD CRUMBS
-   EXTRA-VIRGIN OLIVE OIL, AS NEEDED

CALAMARI FRITTI

YIELD: 4 SERVINGS / **ACTIVE TIME:** 30 MINUTES / **TOTAL TIME:** 50 MINUTES

Popular in Southern and Central Italy, fried squid is not strictly Italian exclusive, as it is also common throughout the Mediterranean. The Italian iteration, calamari fritti, tends to have a very light breading, made only with flour, resulting in a lighter version than what's found elsewhere.

1. Cut the squid into 1-inch-wide rings.

2. Place the flour in a shallow bowl, add the squid, and toss them until completely coated. Place the squid in a fine-mesh sieve and gently shake to remove any excess flour.

3. Add olive oil to a narrow, deep, heavy-bottomed saucepan with high edges until it is about 2 inches deep and warm it to 350°F. Working in batches to avoid crowding the pot, slip the squid into the hot oil and fry until they are cooked through and golden brown, turning as necessary.

4. Remove the calamari from the hot oil, transfer them to a paper towel–lined plate to drain, and season them with salt. Serve with lemon wedges once all of the calamari have drained and cooled slightly.

INGREDIENTS:

2.2   LBS. SQUID, CLEANED (SEE PAGE 277)

3   CUPS ALL-PURPOSE FLOUR

EXTRA-VIRGIN OLIVE OIL, AS NEEDED

SALT, TO TASTE

LEMON WEDGES, FOR SERVING

COZZE FRITTE

YIELD: 4 SERVINGS / **ACTIVE TIME:** 20 MINUTES / **TOTAL TIME:** 40 MINUTES

These stuffed and fried mussels are a delicious appetizer from Apulia that will surprise your guests. They are often made from raw mussels, but this practice is risky if you are unsure about the freshness of your mussels. In this recipe, the mussels are instead quickly cooked before the stuffing, so that you will be able to see which mussels were fresh and which were not, as mussels that are past their prime do not open during cooking.

1. Place the olive oil in a large skillet and warm it over medium-high heat. Add the mussels and cook until the majority of them start opening, 3 to 4 minutes. Remove the mussels from the pan and place them in a bowl, upside down so that they drain. Discard any mussels that did not open.

2. Strain the liquid from the mussels into a bowl, add the bread, and let it soak until it softens.

3. Squeeze the bread and place it in a bowl. Add the eggs, bread crumbs, pecorino, parsley, and garlic, season the mixture with salt and pepper, and stir until the mixture is well combined. Add more bread crumbs if the consistency of the mixture is too soft.

4. Form the mixture into ovals that are roughly the size of the mussels.

5. Remove the piece of shell not containing the mussel from each of the mussels. Top the mussels with the bread mixture.

6. Add olive oil to a narrow, deep, heavy-bottomed saucepan with high edges until it is about 2 inches deep and warm it to 350°F. Working in batches to avoid crowding the pot, gently slip the mussels into the hot oil and fry until they are cooked through and golden brown, turning as necessary.

7. Remove the mussels from the hot oil and transfer them to a paper towel–lined plate to drain. Serve once all of the mussels have drained and cooled slightly.

INGREDIENTS:

2	TABLESPOONS EXTRA-VIRGIN OLIVE OIL, PLUS MORE AS NEEDED
2	LBS. MUSSELS, RINSED AND DEBEARDED
½	LB. DAY-OLD BREAD
2	EGGS
2	TABLESPOONS BREAD CRUMBS, PLUS MORE AS NEEDED
⅔	CUP GRATED PECORINO CHEESE
1	TABLESPOON CHOPPED FRESH PARSLEY
1	GARLIC CLOVE, MINCED
	SALT AND PEPPER, TO TASTE

ARANCINI

YIELD: 10 ARANCINI / **ACTIVE TIME:** 1 HOUR / **TOTAL TIME:** 1 HOUR AND 30 MINUTES

There are nearly infinite recipes for arancini and a wide assortment of fillings. Here is a classic version, featuring saffron risotto stuffed with a meat ragù and peas. It is best to use leftover ragù in this preparation, as it will have the time to dry out a bit.

1. Place the ragù and peas in a medium saucepan, cover the pan, and cook over low heat until the peas are tender. Remove the pan from heat and let the mixture cool.

2. Place the water, saffron, bouillon cube, salt, and butter in a medium saucepan and bring to a boil. Stir in the rice and wait for the water to start boiling again. Reduce the heat to low and cook, stirring frequently, until the rice has absorbed all of the water and is al dente, 15 to 20 minutes. Pour the rice immediately into a large baking dish so that it will cool quickly.

3. Take a handful of rice, place it in the palm of your hand, and flatten it. The portion of rice should weigh about 4½ oz. Place about 1 oz. of the ragù mixture in the center of the rice and form the rice into a cone or ball around it. Repeat with the remaining rice and ragout mixture.

4. Place the eggs in a bowl, season them with salt, and beat them lightly. Place the flour and bread crumbs in separate bowls and then dredge the arancini in the flour, eggs, and then in the bread crumbs until they are coated. Set the breaded arancini aside.

5. Add olive oil to a narrow, deep, and heavy-bottomed saucepan with high edges until it is about 2 inches deep and warm it to 350°F. Working with 2 to 3 arancini at a time, slip them into the hot oil and fry until golden brown, turning as necessary.

6. Remove the arancini from the hot oil and transfer them to a paper towel–lined plate to drain. Serve once all of the arancini have drained and cooled slightly.

INGREDIENTS:

	RAGÙ NAPOLETANO (SEE PAGE 125)
⅔	CUP PEAS
5⅓	CUPS WATER
1½	TEASPOONS SAFFRON THREADS
1	CHICKEN BOUILLON CUBE
1⅔	TEASPOONS KOSHER SALT, PLUS MORE TO TASTE
4	TABLESPOONS UNSALTED BUTTER
2½	CUPS RISOTTO RICE (CARNAROLI, VIALONE, ROMA, OR ORIGINARIO PREFERRED)
2	EGGS
2	CUPS ALL-PURPOSE FLOUR
2	CUPS BREAD CRUMBS
	EXTRA-VIRGIN OLIVE OIL, AS NEEDED

ARANCINI
SICILIANI
CON
PROSCIUTTO
E MOZZARELLA

ARANCINI
SICILIANI
CON
RAGÙ E PISELLI

ARANCINO:
THE KING OF SICILIAN STREET FOOD

King or queen? According to people from Palermo and western Sicily, the best-known Sicilian street food is not declined as arancino (plural arancini), which would make it male, but instead arancina (plural arancine), which is the form for female words in Italian. With the female suffix comes a different shape, which is round in Palermo.

On the other hand, in Catania and the whole of Eastern Sicily, arancini have a male suffix and are formed into a conical shape.

This seemingly unending battle between Palermo and Catania has been brought to an end by historical sources showing that indeed the original name of the delicious risotto ball is arancino, and not arancina.

Now that we know what to call them, we can turn to where they came from. There are plenty of origin stories swirling around arancini. The most dramatic one portrays them as being born while Sicilian people were fleeing from the cities to the mountains to escape invading Arab troops. This story holds that since people needed something portable and nutritious, the arancino, which is a full meal because it includes rice, meat, and legumes, was born. Other sources claim that arancini were born at some royal court, the brilliant invention of a skilled chef. And some think they were created by home cooks, with the intention of using up leftovers.

Whatever their true origin, arancini were surely born during or after Arab rule, so some time around or after the eleventh century. In fact, they include two ingredients brought to Sicily by the invaders—saffron and rice. Rice is not that common in Southern Italian cuisine, but there are some classics, like arancini, that have become central to local traditions. Foodies everywhere are grateful, delighting in the crunchy exterior that gives way to creamy rice and a rich center.

CIPOLLINA CATANESE

YIELD: 8 CIPOLLINE / **ACTIVE TIME:** 30 MINUTES / **TOTAL TIME:** 1 HOUR

Typical of Catania in Sicily, cipollina (little onion) is a puff pastry filled with caramelized onions, tomato sauce, ham, and cheese. It is often eaten for breakfast, but can also be enjoyed as a snack at any time of the day.

1. Preheat the oven to 370°F and line a baking sheet with parchment paper. Place the olive oil in a large skillet and warm it over low heat. Add the onions and cook, stirring occasionally, until they have softened and slightly caramelized, 10 to 15 minutes.

2. Stir in the tomatoes, season the mixture with salt and pepper, and remove the pan from heat.

3. Cut each sheet of puff pastry into 4 squares.

4. Place a slice of ham on each square and top it with the tomato sauce and cheese. Bring the 4 corners of the squares to the center and press down on the seams to seal them. Brush the cipolline with the egg and place them on the baking sheet.

5. Place the cipolline in the oven and bake until they are golden brown, about 15 minutes.

6. Remove the cipolline from the oven and let them cool slightly before serving.

INGREDIENTS:

¼ CUP EXTRA-VIRGIN OLIVE OIL

2 LARGE WHITE OR RED ONIONS, SLICED VERY THIN

1 CUP CRUSHED TOMATOES

SALT AND PEPPER, TO TASTE

2 SHEETS OF FROZEN PUFF PASTRY, THAWED

8 THIN SLICES OF HAM

3 OZ. PROVOLA CHEESE OR MOZZARELLA CHEESE, CUT INTO STRIPS AND DRAINED IN THE REFRIGERATOR FOR 2 HOURS

1 EGG, BEATEN

PANZEROTTI

YIELD: 6 TO 8 PANZEROTTI / **ACTIVE TIME:** 1 HOUR / **TOTAL TIME:** 3 HOURS

There are dozens of savory pockets in Southern Italy, the most popular ones are the calzone and panzerotti, the latter of which is characteristic of Apulian cuisine. The most common filling is mozzarella and tomato sauce, but other fillings like ground beef and peas or caciocavallo cheese and mortadella, are also popular.

1. To begin preparations for the dough, place the yeast, sugar, and water in a large bowl, gently stir to combine, and let the mixture sit until it starts to foam, about 10 minutes.

2. Add the milk and the flours and work the mixture until it just comes together as a dough.

3. Add the olive oil and salt and knead the dough until it is smooth and elastic.

4. Shape the dough into a round, place it in a clean bowl, and cover it with plastic wrap. Let the dough rest at room temperature until it has almost doubled in size, about 1½ hours.

5. Place the dough on a flour-dusted work surface and divide it into 6 pieces. Shape the pieces into rounds, cover them with a kitchen towel, and let them rest for 45 minutes.

6. Roll each round into a 16-inch disk and set them aside.

7. To begin preparations for the filling, place the tomatoes and olive oil in a bowl, season the mixture with oregano, salt, and pepper, and stir to combine.

8. Place 2 tablespoons of the tomato mixture, 2 tablespoons mozzarella, and 1 teaspoon pecorino in the center of each round and then fold the round over itself. Press down on the edges to seal the rounds, first with your fingers and then with a fork.

9. Add olive oil to a large skillet until it is about 1 inch deep and warm it to 350°F. Working with 1 panzerotto at a time, add them to the hot oil and fry until they are golden brown, turning as necessary, making sure to spoon hot oil over the tops of the panzerotti as they cook to prevent them from exploding.

10. Remove the panzerotti from the hot oil and transfer them to a paper towel–lined plate to drain. Serve once all of the panzerotti have drained and cooled slightly.

INGREDIENTS:

FOR THE DOUGH

- 1½ PACKETS OF ACTIVE DRY YEAST
- 1 TEASPOON SUGAR
- 7 OZ. LUKEWARM WATER (90°F)
- 3½ OZ. WHOLE MILK
- 7.4 OZ. FINELY GROUND SEMOLINA FLOUR (SEMOLA RIMACINATA)
- 10.2 OZ. BREAD OR "00" FLOUR, PLUS MORE AS NEEDED
- 2 TABLESPOONS EXTRA-VIRGIN OLIVE OIL
- 2 TEASPOONS FINE SEA SALT

FOR THE FILLING

- 1 (HEAPING) CUP WHOLE PEELED TOMATOES, CRUSHED
- 1 TABLESPOON EXTRA-VIRGIN OLIVE OIL
- DRIED OREGANO, TO TASTE
- SALT AND PEPPER, TO TASTE
- 4½ OZ. MOZZARELLA OR SCAMORZA CHEESE, CUBED
- 2 TABLESPOONS GRATED PECORINO CHEESE
- EXTRA-VIRGIN OLIVE OIL, AS NEEDED

INSALATA DI RINFORZO

YIELD: 6 SERVINGS / **ACTIVE TIME:** 15 MINUTES / **TOTAL TIME:** 30 MINUTES

This rich salad from Naples is typically served on Christmas Eve and New Year's Eve, and was meant to make sure people could still eat their fill on those days, when animal meat was prohibited.

1. Bring salted water to a boil in a large saucepan. Add the cauliflower and cook until it is al dente, about 10 minutes. Drain the cauliflower and let it cool completely.

2. Arrange the cooled cauliflower in a serving dish and top with the anchovies, capers, olives, pickles, and papacelle.

3. Place the olive oil, vinegar, and a pinch of salt in a bowl and whisk until the mixture has emulsified. Pour the dressing over the salad and enjoy.

INGREDIENTS:

SALT, TO TASTE

1 HEAD OF CAULIFLOWER, CUT INTO FLORETS

8 ANCHOVIES IN OLIVE OIL, DRAINED

½ CUP CAPERS IN SALT, SOAKED, DRAINED, AND SQUEEZED

¾ CUP GREEN OLIVES, PITTED

½ CUP MIXED PICKLES, DRAINED

3½ OZ. PAPACCELLE (STUFFED PEPPERS IN OIL), HALVED

5 TABLESPOONS EXTRA-VIRGIN OLIVE OIL

3 TABLESPOONS RED WINE VINEGAR

CIALLEDDA

YIELD: 4 SERVINGS / ACTIVE TIME: 20 MINUTES / TOTAL TIME: 1 HOUR AND 20 MINUTES

Also called acquasale, cialledda is a cold bread salad that is popular in Apulia. It calls for friselle, but if you do not have any at home, use any type of stale bread. The salad needs to rest before serving, so it is advisable to leave yourself plenty of time when preparing.

1. Place the onion and vinegar in a bowl, season the mixture with salt, and let it sit for 1 hour.

2. Place the bread in a bowl, gently squeeze the tomatoes over it, and then add the tomatoes. Add the remaining ingredients, season the mixture with salt, and toss to combine.

3. Cover the bowl with plastic wrap and let the salad rest for 1 hour.

4. Drain the onion and rinse it. Add it to the salad, gently toss to incorporate, and enjoy.

INGREDIENTS:

1   SMALL RED ONION, SLICED THIN

2   TABLESPOONS WHITE BALSAMIC VINEGAR

   SALT, TO TASTE

1   LB. STALE BREAD, CHOPPED

4   TOMATOES, CUT INTO WEDGES

1   CUCUMBER, FINELY DICED

1   CELERY STALK, SLICED THIN

   HANDFUL OF FRESH BASIL, CHOPPED

2   TABLESPOONS CAPERS, DRAINED

¼   CUP EXTRA-VIRGIN OLIVE OIL

   DRIED OREGANO, TO TASTE

INSALATA DI ARANCE E FINOCCHIO

YIELD: 4 SERVINGS / **ACTIVE TIME:** 15 MINUTES / **TOTAL TIME:** 30 MINUTES

An extremely simple salad from Sicily that combines oranges and fennel to provide a colorful dish with explosive flavor.

1. Peel the oranges and, using a sharp knife, remove the white pith. Slice the oranges thin and set them aside.

2. Arrange the onion and fennel on a serving platter and top with the oranges and olives.

3. Drizzle the olive oil over the salad and season it with salt and pepper.

4. Let the salad marinate for about 15 minutes before serving.

INGREDIENTS:

6	ORANGES
1	SMALL ONION, SLICED THIN
1	SMALL BULB OF FENNEL, TRIMMED AND SLICED THIN
½	CUP PITTED BLACK OLIVES
¼	CUP EXTRA-VIRGIN OLIVE OIL
	SALT AND PEPPER, TO TASTE

PEPERONATA ALLA SALENTINA

YIELD: 4 SERVINGS / **ACTIVE TIME:** 20 MINUTES / **TOTAL TIME:** 1 HOUR

A delicious pepper and olive–centered side or appetizer that is popular across all of Southern Italy.

1. Place the olive oil in a large skillet and warm it over medium-low heat. Add the onion and cook, stirring occasionally, until it has softened, about 6 minutes.

2. Add the garlic and chile and cook for 1 minute.

3. Add the bell peppers and olives, raise the heat to medium, and cook, stirring frequently, until the peppers start to brown, about 8 minutes.

4. Add the tomatoes, season the mixture with oregano and salt, and reduce the heat to low. Cover the pan and cook until the peppers are soft and nicely browned, stirring occasionally and adding water if the dish starts to look too dry, about 20 minutes. Serve immediately.

INGREDIENTS:

- 6 TABLESPOONS EXTRA-VIRGIN OLIVE OIL
- 1 LARGE ONION, FINELY DICED
- 1 GARLIC CLOVE, MINCED
- 1 HOT CHILE PEPPER, STEM AND SEEDS REMOVED, MINCED
- 4 LARGE BELL PEPPERS, STEMS AND SEEDS REMOVED, CHOPPED INTO LARGE PIECES
- ¼ CUP PITTED OLIVES
- 3 TOMATOES, DESEEDED AND CHOPPED
- DRIED OREGANO, TO TASTE
- SALT, TO TASTE

INSALATA DI PATATE E FAGIOLINI

YIELD: 4 SERVINGS / **ACTIVE TIME:** 15 MINUTES / **TOTAL TIME:** 40 MINUTES

A cold green bean-and-potato salad that is a very typical summer side dish throughout the whole of Southern Italy.

1. Bring salted water to a boil in a large saucepan. Add the potatoes and boil until they are tender, about 30 minutes. Remove the potatoes from the boiling water and let them cool.

2. Add the green beans and boil until they are tender, about 5 minutes. Drain the green beans and let them cool.

3. When the potatoes and green beans are cool enough to handle, peel the potatoes, chop them, and place them in a bowl. Chop the green beans and add them to the bowl.

4. Add the tomatoes, basil, oregano, and olive oil to the bowl, toss to combine, and either serve the salad immediately or store it in the refrigerator and serve chilled.

INGREDIENTS:

SALT, TO TASTE

4 LARGE POTATOES, SCRUBBED

1½ LBS. GREEN BEANS

1½ CUPS CHERRY TOMATOES, HALVED

FRESH BASIL, CHOPPED, TO TASTE

FRESH OREGANO, CHOPPED, TO TASTE

¼ CUP EXTRA-VIRGIN OLIVE OIL

INSALATA CAPRESE

YIELD: 4 SERVINGS / **ACTIVE TIME:** 15 MINUTES / **TOTAL TIME:** 15 MINUTES

This is possibly the most famous Italian salad and likely also the simplest. Its success lies in the freshness and quality of the ingredients, and the precision of the execution, as it is very easy to turn this lovely dish into a wet mess. Just pay attention, follow the steps, and use a sharp knife.

1. Season the tomatoes with salt and let them rest.

2. Pat the mozzarella dry with paper towels. Arrange the mozzarella, tomatoes, and basil on a platter, alternating between them.

3. Drizzle the olive oil over the salad, season it with oregano and pepper, and enjoy.

INGREDIENTS:

5   TOMATOES, CUT INTO ½-INCH-THICK SLICES

     SALT AND PEPPER, TO TASTE

2   BALLS OF FRESH MOZZARELLA CHEESE, CUT INTO ½-INCH-THICK SLICES

     HANDFUL OF FRESH BASIL LEAVES

2   TABLESPOONS EXTRA-VIRGIN OLIVE OIL

     DRIED OREGANO, TO TASTE

PATATE AL FORNO ALLA SICILIANA

YIELD: 4 SERVINGS / **ACTIVE TIME:** 25 MINUTES / **TOTAL TIME:** 1 HOUR AND 15 MINUTES

A perfect side for most meat- and fish-centered secondi. There are many variations, but this is a traditional-leaning version.

1. Preheat the oven to 390°F and line a baking dish with parchment paper. Rinse the potatoes and pat them dry. Place them in a large bowl with the olive oil, season them with salt and pepper, and toss to coat.

2. Add the remaining ingredients and toss to combine.

3. Place the mixture in the baking dish, place it in the oven, and roast until the potatoes are crispy, golden brown, and tender, about 50 minutes.

4. Remove the dish from the oven, remove the rosemary and bay leaves, and discard them. Stir the mixture so that the cooking juices are incorporated and serve immediately.

INGREDIENTS:

2.2	LBS. POTATOES, PEELED AND CHOPPED
¼	CUP EXTRA-VIRGIN OLIVE OIL
	SALT AND PEPPER, TO TASTE
1	RED ONION, SLICED
1⅓	CUPS CHERRY TOMATOES, HALVED
½	CUP PITTED BLACK OLIVES
	HANDFUL OF FRESH SAGE, CHOPPED
1	SPRIG OF FRESH ROSEMARY
3	BAY LEAVES

RAPE 'NFUCATE

YIELD: 6 SERVINGS / **ACTIVE TIME:** 20 MINUTES / **TOTAL TIME:** 1 HOUR AND 20 MINUTES

A lovely leafy greens side from Apulia that can complement any type of main. In Apulian dialect, rape 'nfucate means "drowned turnip greens," which refers to the technique—it is important that the turnips cook (drown) in the cooking liquid until very tender, which is why you keep the pan covered.

1. Place the olive oil in a large skillet and warm it over medium-low heat. Add the garlic and chile and cook for 2 minutes.

2. Add the turnip greens and water, season with salt, and cover the pan. Cook for 20 minutes.

3. Taste and adjust the seasoning as necessary. Add the wine, cover the pan again, and cook until the turnip greens are very tender, about 30 minutes. Serve immediately.

INGREDIENTS:

6   TABLESPOONS EXTRA-VIRGIN OLIVE OIL

2   GARLIC CLOVES, MINCED

1   CHILE PEPPER, STEM AND SEEDS REMOVED, MINCED

4½ LBS. TURNIP GREENS, RINSED WELL AND FIBROUS STEMS REMOVED

½   CUP WATER

    COARSE SEA SALT, TO TASTE

½   CUP DRY WHITE WINE

CAPONATA

YIELD: 4 SERVINGS / **ACTIVE TIME:** 30 MINUTES / **TOTAL TIME:** 4 HOURS

The quintessential Sicilian vegetarian dish, caponata is perfect as both a side and a starter. When selecting eggplants, those that are long and thin will serve you best.

1. Place the eggplants in a large colander and cover them with coarse salt. Place a saucepan filled with water on top of the eggplants and let them sit for 1 hour.

2. Rinse the eggplants and let them drain. Pat them dry and chop them into cubes.

3. Place half of the olive oil in a large skillet and warm it over medium-high heat. Add the eggplants and cook until they are golden brown, about 8 minutes, turning them as necessary. Transfer the eggplants to a paper towel–lined plate to drain.

4. Place the peppers in the skillet and cook, stirring occasionally, until they are starting to char, about 12 minutes. Transfer them to the paper towel–lined plate.

5. Place the remaining olive oil in a large saucepan and warm it over low heat. Add the celery and onions and cook, stirring occasionally, until they have softened, about 6 minutes.

6. Add the pine nuts, olives, and capers, raise the heat to medium, and cook, stirring occasionally, for 5 minutes.

7. Turn off the heat, stir in the tomatoes, eggplants, and peppers, and season the mixture with fine salt.

8. Combine the sugar and vinegar and add the mixture to the pan.

9. Set the heat to medium and cook until the vinegar mixture has evaporated, about 5 minutes.

10. Add the basil leaves, transfer the caponata to a serving dish, and let it cool.

11. Store the caponata in the refrigerator for a few hours before serving.

INGREDIENTS:

2.2	LBS. EGGPLANTS, SLICED
	SALT (COARSE AND FINE), TO TASTE
10	TABLESPOONS EXTRA-VIRGIN OLIVE OIL
2	RED BELL PEPPERS, STEMS AND SEEDS REMOVED, DICED
3	CELERY STALKS, SLICED
2	SMALL RED ONIONS, SLICED THIN
3½	TABLESPOONS PINE NUTS
¾	CUP PITTED GREEN OLIVES
½	CUP CAPERS IN SALT, SOAKED AND DRAINED
6	CHERRY TOMATOES, HALVED
¼	CUP SUGAR
½	CUP WHITE WINE VINEGAR
	HANDFUL OF FRESH BASIL, CHOPPED

ZUCCHINE ALLA SCAPECE

YIELD: 6 SERVINGS / **ACTIVE TIME:** 40 MINUTES / **TOTAL TIME:** 4 HOURS

A sweet-and-sour fried zucchini side that works also as an appetizer, zucchine alla scapece is a centuries-old recipe that derives its name from the Spanish term escabeche, which applies to marinating food in vinegar.

1. Season the zucchini with salt and let them sit until they look slightly shriveled. Or do as an Italian grandmother would, skip the salt, and let the zucchini dry in the sun for a couple of hours.

2. Place the olive oil in a deep skillet and warm it over medium-high heat. Working in small batches, gently slip the zucchini into the hot oil and fry until they are golden brown, turning as necessary. Transfer the fried zucchini to a paper towel–lined plate to drain and, if you chose to dry them in the sun, season them with salt.

3. Place the vinegar and mint in a bowl and stir to combine.

4. Arrange the zucchini in a layer in a serving dish and top with some of the garlic and some of the dressing. Repeat until all of the zucchini, garlic, and dressing have been used and let the dish rest for a few hours before serving.

INGREDIENTS:

- 2.2 LBS. ZUCCHINI, TRIMMED AND CUT INTO ¼-INCH-THICK SLICES
- SALT, TO TASTE
- 4 CUPS EXTRA-VIRGIN OLIVE OIL
- 1 CUP WHITE WINE VINEGAR
- HANDFUL OF FRESH MINT, CHOPPED
- 4 GARLIC CLOVES, MINCED

PRIMI

SPAGHETTI ALLA PUTTANESCA

YIELD: 4 SERVINGS / **ACTIVE TIME:** 10 MINUTES / **TOTAL TIME:** 25 MINUTES

The sauce for this pasta dish is simple yet delicious, featuring ingredients easily available on the Neapolitan coast and islands, like fresh tomatoes, capers, black Gaeta olives, and, occasionally, anchovies. The base of this dish is centuries old and tracks back to a version of it without tomatoes, called aulive e cchiapparielle ("olives and capers"). The more recent and colorful version with tomatoes is called spaghetti alla puttanesca ("spaghetti of the prostitutes") for reasons that aren't entirely clear, although there are many stories circulating around the inspiration for the name.

1. Bring water to a boil in a large saucepan. Add the tomatoes and boil them for 2 minutes. Drain the tomatoes and let them cool. When they are cool enough to handle, peel the tomatoes, remove the seeds, and chop the remaining flesh. Set the tomatoes aside.

2. Place the olive oil in a large skillet and warm it over medium-low heat. Add the garlic and cook for 2 minutes. Add the anchovies and red pepper flakes and cook for 1 minute.

3. Stir in the olives and capers and cook, stirring frequently, for 3 minutes.

4. Add the tomatoes and half of the parsley and cook, stirring occasionally, until the tomatoes start to break down, about 20 minutes.

5. Bring water to a boil in a large saucepan. Add salt, let the water return to a full boil, and add the pasta. Cook until the pasta is very al dente. Reserve ¼ cup of pasta water and drain the spaghetti.

6. Add the spaghetti and pasta water to the skillet, raise the heat to medium-high, and toss to combine. Cook until the pasta is al dente.

7. Stir in the remaining parsley and serve.

INGREDIENTS:

- 1.1 LBS. TOMATOES
- ¼ CUP EXTRA-VIRGIN OLIVE OIL
- 1 GARLIC CLOVE, CHOPPED
- 8 ANCHOVIES PACKED IN SALT, CAREFULLY RINSED AND CHOPPED
- RED PEPPER FLAKES, TO TASTE
- 1 HEAPING CUP PITTED GAETA OLIVES (OR OTHER BLACK OLIVES), CHOPPED
- 1 TABLESPOON CAPERS PACKED IN SALT, SOAKED, DRAINED, SQUEEZED DRY, AND CHOPPED
- 2 TABLESPOONS CHOPPED FRESH ITALIAN PARSLEY
- SALT, TO TASTE
- 14 OZ. SPAGHETTI

SPAGHETTI ALLA NERANO

YIELD: 4 SERVINGS / **ACTIVE TIME:** 15 MINUTES / **TOTAL TIME:** 30 MINUTES

The beautiful Nerano Bay, which lies south of the Gulf of Naples, is home to this popular pasta sauce, which is credited to Maria Grazia, a professional local cook. When selecting zucchini, opt for the smaller ones, as they have the best flavor.

1. Place ½ cup of olive oil in a large, deep skillet and warm it to 350°F. Add the zucchini to the hot oil and fry until they are starting to brown, turning as necessary. Transfer the fried zucchini to a paper towel–lined plate to drain and season it with salt.

2. Bring water to a boil in a large saucepan. Add salt, let the water return to a full boil, and add the pasta. Cook until the pasta is very al dente. Reserve 1½ cups pasta water and drain the spaghetti.

3. Place the remaining olive oil in a large skillet and warm it over medium heat. Add the garlic, cook for 2 minutes, and then remove it from the pan.

4. Add the pasta to the garlic oil and toss to combine.

5. Add some of the pasta water and the cheeses and toss until well combined and the pasta is al dente.

6. Add the fried zucchini, half of the basil, and more pasta water if it is needed and gently toss to combine.

7. Stir in the remaining basil, season the dish with black pepper, and enjoy.

INGREDIENTS:

½ CUP PLUS 3 TABLESPOONS EXTRA-VIRGIN OLIVE OIL

1½ LBS. ZUCCHINI, SLICED THIN

SALT AND PEPPER, TO TASTE

14 OZ. SPAGHETTI

2 GARLIC CLOVES

7 OZ. PROVOLONE CHEESE (PROVOLONE DEL MONACO RECOMMENDED), GRATED

2 OZ. PARMIGIANO REGGIANO CHEESE, GRATED

20 FRESH BASIL LEAVES

SPAGHETTI ALLO SCOGLIO

YIELD: 4 SERVINGS / **ACTIVE TIME:** 1 HOUR / **TOTAL TIME:** 2 HOURS

Naples has brought us the currently popular version of this dish, but it is quite certain that it was first developed in Sicily. Allo scoglio means "the sea rock way," a reference to the Sicilian tradition to harvest small sea rocks and boil them to extract the briny flavor for a humble but tasty broth, which was originally served with bread, and later on with pasta.

1. Place half of the olive oil in a large skillet and warm it over medium heat. Add 1 garlic clove and cook, stirring occasionally, for 2 minutes.

2. Add the clams and mussels, raise the heat to medium-high, and cover the pan with a lid. Cook until the majority of the clams and mussels have opened, about 5 minutes.

3. Discard any clams and/or mussels that did not open. Remove the remaining clams and mussels from the pan, remove the meat from most of the shells, and set it aside. Leave the meat in some of the mussels and clams and reserve them for garnish. Strain any liquid in the pan and set it aside.

4. Add the remaining olive oil to the pan and warm it over medium heat. Add the remaining garlic clove and cook, stirring occasionally, for 2 minutes. Add the squid, season it lightly with salt, and cook for 2 minutes.

5. Add the wine and cook until it has evaporated. Remove the garlic clove, discard it, and add the tomatoes. Cook for 5 minutes.

6. Add the shrimp and cook until they turn pink, 2 to 3 minutes. Peel the shrimp, pressing down on their heads to release the juices. Reserve these juices.

7. Add the shrimp, their juices, mussels, and clams to the sauce, season it with salt, and remove the pan from heat.

8. Bring water to a boil in a large saucepan. Add salt, let the water return to a full boil, and add the pasta. Cook until the pasta is very al dente. Drain the spaghetti and add it to the skillet.

9. Cook the pasta and sauce over medium-high heat, tossing to combine and gradually adding the reserved liquid from cooking the mussels and clams.

10. When the pasta is al dente, garnish the dish with the parsley and reserved mussels and clams and enjoy.

INGREDIENTS:

¼ CUP EXTRA-VIRGIN OLIVE OIL

2 GARLIC CLOVES

2 LBS. CLAMS, RINSED WELL

2 LBS. MUSSELS, RINSED WELL AND DEBEARDED

10 OZ. SQUID, CLEANED (SEE PAGE 277) AND CUT INTO RINGS

SALT, TO TASTE

1 CUP DRY WHITE WINE

1 CUP CHERRY TOMATOES, HALVED

10 OZ. SHRIMP, DEVEINED

1 LB. SPAGHETTI

FRESH PARSLEY, CHOPPED, FOR GARNISH

PASTA ALLO SCARPARIELLO

YIELD: 4 SERVINGS / ACTIVE TIME: 10 MINUTES / TOTAL TIME: 20 MINUTES

Pasta allo scarpariello is the classic Neapolitan pasta with tomato sauce, which can be exceptional if done right. The dish is named after the humble shoemakers who inhabited the impoverished Spagnoli quarter of Naples, as they used to take the humble ingredients of this meal for payment. If you don't want to use spaghetti, ziti spezzati and penne are good options.

1. Bring water to a boil in a large saucepan.

2. Place the olive oil in a large skillet and warm it over medium-low heat. Add the garlic and cook for 2 minutes. Add the chile and cook for 1 minute.

3. Add the tomatoes, raise the heat to medium, and cook, stirring occasionally, until the tomatoes start to collapse, about 10 minutes.

4. Add salt to the boiling water, let the water return to a full boil, and add the pasta. Cook until the pasta is very al dente. Reserve 2 cups of pasta water and drain the spaghetti.

5. Add the basil and some of the pasta water to the skillet, season the sauce with salt, and remove the garlic clove.

6. Add the pasta and more pasta water (if desired) and toss until combined and the pasta is al dente.

7. Turn off the heat, add the cheeses, and toss to combine. Serve immediately.

INGREDIENTS:

¼ CUP EXTRA-VIRGIN OLIVE OIL

1 GARLIC CLOVE

½ MILD CHILE PEPPER, STEM AND SEEDS REMOVED, MINCED

1 LB. CHERRY TOMATOES (DATTERINI RECOMMENDED), HALVED

SALT, TO TASTE

14 OZ. SPAGHETTI

LARGE HANDFUL OF FRESH BASIL

6 TABLESPOONS GRATED PECORINO ROMANO CHEESE

6 TABLESPOONS GRATED PARMIGIANO REGGIANO CHEESE

SPAGHETTI D'O PUVERIELLO

YIELD: 4 SERVINGS / **ACTIVE TIME:** 10 MINUTES / **TOTAL TIME:** 15 MINUTES

Born during the trying times of World War II, this pasta dish features eggs like the Roman classic spaghetti alla carbonara, but forgoes the guanciale to become, literally, "poor man's spaghetti."

1. Place the lard in a large skillet and melt it over medium heat. Add the eggs and fry until the whites are set and the yolks are runny, turning them just once and taking care not to overcook them. Transfer the eggs to a plate and set them aside.

2. Bring water to a boil in a large saucepan. Add salt to the boiling water, let the water return to a full boil, and add the pasta. Cook until the pasta is very al dente. Reserve ½ cup pasta water and drain the spaghetti.

3. Add the pasta to the skillet and toss to combine.

4. Add the pasta water and toss to combine.

5. When the pasta is al dente, add the pecorino and eggs, season the dish generously with pepper, toss until combined and the pasta is al dente, and enjoy.

INGREDIENTS:

3½	OZ. LARD
4	EGGS
	SALT AND PEPPER, TO TASTE
14	OZ. SPAGHETTI
¼	CUP GRATED PECORINO ROMANO CHEESE

MINESTRA MARITATA

YIELD: 6 SERVINGS / **ACTIVE TIME:** 1 HOUR / **TOTAL TIME:** 5 HOURS

This meat-and-vegetable soup from Campania is a must on big occasions like Christmas and Easter, but it is also enjoyed on cold days, particularly a winter Sunday. The word maritata means "married," and it refers to the fact that vegetables and meat are cooked separately and then brought together toward the end of cooking.

1. To begin preparations for the broth, place all of the ingredients, except for salt, in a stockpot and cover with cold water. Bring to a boil, reduce the heat to low, and gently simmer the broth until the flavor has developed to your liking, 3 to 4 hours, frequently skimming off any foam that rises to the surface.

2. Season the broth with salt, strain it, and reserve the solids. Chill the broth in the refrigerator until the layer of fat has solidified. Remove the layer of fat, discard it, and strain the broth through a fine-mesh sieve. Place the broth in a large saucepan and set it aside.

3. Remove the meat from the chicken and ribs and dice it. Dice the stew beef and sausages and set all of the meat aside.

4. To begin preparations for the vegetables, bring water to a boil in a large saucepan and prepare an ice bath. Add salt to the boiling water and then add the vegetables one at a time. Boil the vegetables for 2 minutes, remove them from the boiling water, and plunge them into the ice bath.

5. Chop the blanched vegetables and add them to the broth along with the meat. Add the lard (if desired) and simmer until the flavor has developed to your liking, 30 to 40 minutes.

6. Season the dish with salt and drizzle some olive oil over the top. Garnish with Parmesan, serve with crusty bread, and enjoy.

INGREDIENTS:

FOR THE BROTH

- 2 CELERY STALKS, EACH CUT INTO 2 TO 3 PIECES
- 2 CARROTS, PEELED AND HALVED
- 1 ONION, HALVED

    HANDFUL OF SPRIGS OF FRESH PARSLEY, SPRIGS OF FRESH THYME, AND BAY LEAVES, TIED TOGETHER WITH KITCHEN TWINE
- ½ WHOLE CHICKEN
- 1 LB. PORK RIBS
- 1 LB. STEW BEEF
- 3 ITALIAN SAUSAGES

    SALT, TO TASTE

FOR THE VEGETABLES

SALT, TO TASTE

- 1 LB. ESCAROLE OR LETTUCE, TRIMMED AND RINSED WELL
- 1 LB. CABBAGE, CHOPPED
- 1 LB. CHARD OR CHICORY, TRIMMED AND RINSED WELL
- 1 LB. COLLARD GREENS, TRIMMED AND RINSED WELL
- ½ CUP LARD, WHIPPED (OPTIONAL)

    EXTRA-VIRGIN OLIVE OIL, FOR TOPPING

    PARMESAN CHEESE, GRATED, FOR GARNISH

    CRUSTY BREAD, FOR SERVING

PASTA E PATATE

YIELD: 4 SERVINGS / **ACTIVE TIME:** 15 MINUTES / **TOTAL TIME:** 1 HOUR

A Neapolitan comfort food that resides somewhere between a pasta dish and a soup, pasta e patate is perfect for a cold day. Cooking it should not be rushed, as this pasta needs to be simmered on low heat until the preferred consistency is achieved.

1. Place the lard and olive oil in a medium saucepan and warm the mixture over low heat. Add the onion, carrot, celery, and tomatoes and cook, stirring occasionally, until they have softened, about 6 minutes.

2. Add the potatoes and cook, stirring occasionally, for 6 minutes.

3. Add the broth, raise the heat to medium, and bring to a boil. Reduce the heat to low, cover the pan, and cook until the potatoes are tender, about 40 minutes, gently stirring occasionally.

4. Add the Parmesan rinds, water, and pasta, raise the heat to medium, and cook until the pasta is al dente. If there is too much liquid, raise the heat to reduce it to the desired amount.

5. Remove the Parmesan rinds, discard them, season the dish with salt, and remove the pan from heat.

6. Stir in the provola (if desired) and enjoy.

INGREDIENTS:

2   OZ. LARD, DICED

2   TABLESPOONS EXTRA-VIRGIN OLIVE OIL

½   MEDIUM WHITE ONION, FINELY DICED

1   LARGE CARROT, PEELED AND FINELY DICED

1   CELERY STALK, FINELY DICED

1   CUP CHERRY TOMATOES, DICED

1⅓   LBS. POTATOES, PEELED AND DICED

2   CUPS BRODO VEGETALE (SEE PAGE 806)

2   PARMESAN RINDS, EXTERIORS REMOVED

1½   CUPS WATER

6   OZ. SHORT PASTA (TUBETTI OR RUOTE)

  SALT, TO TASTE

5   OZ. PROVOLA CHEESE, CUBED (OPTIONAL)

PASTA E PISELLI

YIELD: 4 SERVINGS / **ACTIVE TIME:** 10 MINUTES / **TOTAL TIME:** 25 MINUTES

The originality of this pasta recipe from Naples is that, after making a rather quick sauce with peas (and optionally pancetta), the sauce is diluted with water and the pasta is cooked directly in it. This results in a natural creaminess that makes for an easy, light, and balanced meal without compromising on taste.

1. Place the olive oil in a large skillet and warm it over medium heat. Add the onion and cook, stirring occasionally, until it has softened, about 5 minutes.

2. Add the pancetta (if desired), reduce the heat to medium-low, and cook until the fat starts to render, about 5 minutes.

3. Add the peas, raise the heat to medium, and cook, stirring occasionally, until they are tender, 3 to 5 minutes.

4. Add the water and bring to a boil. Add salt, let the water return to a full boil, and add the pasta. Cook until the pasta is al dente and has absorbed the water.

5. Season the dish with Parmesan and pepper and enjoy.

INGREDIENTS:

2	TABLESPOONS EXTRA-VIRGIN OLIVE OIL
1	ONION, FINELY DICED
6	OZ. PANCETTA, DICED (OPTIONAL)
2	CUPS PEAS
2	CUPS WATER
	SALT AND PEPPER, TO TASTE
9	OZ. PASTA (MACARONI OR BROKEN SPAGHETTI RECOMMENDED)
	PARMESAN OR PECORINO CHEESE, GRATED, TO TASTE

CALAMARATA

YIELD: 4 SERVINGS / **ACTIVE TIME:** 15 MINUTES / **TOTAL TIME:** 40 MINUTES

This Neapolitan pasta dish plays on the resemblance between mezzi paccheri pasta and squid rings. Nowadays, in fact, it is possible to find a pasta called calamari or calamarata which owes its existence to this very dish.

1. Place the olive oil in a large skillet and warm it over medium heat. Add the garlic and chile and cook, stirring occasionally, for 2 minutes.

2. Remove the garlic from the pan and discard it. Add the squid and cook for 2 minutes.

3. Add the wine and cook until it has evaporated. Add the tomatoes and cook, stirring occasionally, for 5 minutes.

4. Reduce the heat to low, cover the pan, and cook until the tomatoes have collapsed, about 20 minutes.

5. Bring water to a boil in a large saucepan. Add salt, let the water return to a full boil, and add the pasta. Cook until the pasta is very al dente.

6. Drain the pasta and add it to the skillet. Season the dish with salt, raise the heat to medium-high, and toss to combine. Cook until the pasta is al dente.

7. Garnish the dish with parsley and enjoy.

INGREDIENTS:

- ¼ CUP EXTRA-VIRGIN OLIVE OIL
- 1 GARLIC CLOVE
- 1 RED CHILE PEPPER, STEM AND SEEDS REMOVED, MINCED
- 10 OZ. SQUID, CLEANED (SEE PAGE 277) AND CUT INTO RINGS
- ½ CUP DRY WHITE WINE
- 2½ CUPS CHERRY TOMATOES, HALVED
- SALT, TO TASTE
- 14 OZ. CALAMARI OR MEZZI PACCHERI PASTA
- FRESH PARSLEY, CHOPPED, FOR GARNISH

PASTA FAGIOLI E COZZE

YIELD: 4 SERVINGS / **ACTIVE TIME:** 20 MINUTES / **TOTAL TIME:** 24 HOURS

Pasta with beans is popular throughout Italy, including Campania and Naples, where we find an interesting variation that includes mussels.

1. Bring water to a boil in a large saucepan. Add salt and the beans and cook until they are tender, about 45 minutes. Drain the beans, reserving the cooking liquid. Strain the cooking liquid and set it and the beans aside.

2. Place half of the olive oil in a large skillet and warm it over medium heat. Add half of the garlic and chile and cook, stirring occasionally, for 2 minutes.

3. Add the mussels, raise the heat to medium-high, and cover the pan with a lid. Cook until the majority of the mussels have opened, about 5 minutes. Discard any mussels that did not open. Remove the remaining mussels from the pan, remove the meat from most of the shells, and set it aside. Leave the meat in some of the mussels and reserve them for garnish. Strain any liquid in the pan and set it aside.

4. Add the remaining olive oil to the pan and warm it over medium heat. Add the remaining garlic clove and chile and cook, stirring occasionally, for 2 minutes. Add the tomatoes and cook, stirring occasionally, for 5 minutes.

5. Add the beans, half of their cooking liquid, and half of the liquid reserved from cooking the mussels. Add the pasta, cover the pan, and cook until the pasta has absorbed most of the liquid, stirring occasionally.

6. Add the remaining cooking liquid from the mussels and some more of the cooking liquid from the beans. Cook until the pasta is al dente and the sauce is creamy.

7. Add the meat from the mussels, remove the pan from heat, and season the dish with salt and pepper.

8. Garnish the dish with parsley and the reserved mussels and enjoy.

INGREDIENTS:

SALT AND PEPPER, TO TASTE

¾ LB. DRIED CANNELLINI BEANS, SOAKED OVERNIGHT AND DRAINED

¼ CUP EXTRA-VIRGIN OLIVE OIL

2 GARLIC CLOVES

½ RED CHILE PEPPER, STEM AND SEEDS REMOVED, MINCED

2 LBS. MUSSELS, RINSED WELL AND DEBEARDED

8 CHERRY TOMATOES

12 OZ. MIXED SHORT-FORM PASTA

FRESH PARSLEY, CHOPPED, FOR GARNISH

PASTA AL RAGÙ NAPOLETANO

YIELD: 6 SERVINGS / **ACTIVE TIME:** 1 HOUR / **TOTAL TIME:** 7 TO 8 HOURS

Meat sauce, or ragù in Italian, is a very serious business in Naples. Like the sauce for pasta alla Genovese, the tomato-based ragù Napoletano needs several hours of slow cooking in order to become dignified enough for its role as the star of Sunday. Although simplified versions with shorter cooking times are often used today, a real ragù Napoletano needs to cook for a very long time, to the point that it attains a deep maroon color.

1. Place the olive oil in a large saucepan and warm it over medium heat. Add the onions, beef, and pork ribs and cook until the onions have caramelized and the meat is browned all over, about 1½ hours. You will need to stay close to the pan, turning the meat as needed and increasing or decreasing the heat accordingly.

2. Add the wine and cook until it has nearly evaporated. Remove the meat from the pan and set it aside.

3. Reduce the heat to low, add the tomato paste, and cook, stirring occasionally, for 2 minutes.

4. Add the tomatoes, season with salt, partially cover the pan, and cook, stirring every 15 minutes, for 3 hours.

5. Return the meat to the pan and cook the sauce until it changes from bright red to a deep maroon and the flavor develops to your liking, 3 to 4 hours.

6. Bring water to a boil in a large saucepan. Add salt, let the water return to a full boil, and add the pasta. Cook until the pasta is al dente.

7. Drain the pasta, place it in a serving dish, and add some of the sauce and the smaller pieces of meat along with half of the pecorino and the basil. Toss to combine and top with the remaining pecorino.

8. Serve the larger pieces of meat and remaining sauce following the pasta.

INGREDIENTS:

1	CUP EXTRA-VIRGIN OLIVE OIL
2	YELLOW ONIONS, FINELY DICED
3	(1 LB.) PIECES OF STEW BEEF
6	PORK RIBS
1	CUP RED WINE
1	TABLESPOON TOMATO PASTE
4	LBS. WHOLE PEELED TOMATOES, LIGHTLY CRUSHED
	SALT, TO TASTE
1½	LBS. ZITI OR RIGATONI
2	OZ. PECORINO OR PARMESAN CHEESE, GRATED
	HANDFUL OF FRESH BASIL

GNOCCHI ALLA SORRENTINA

YIELD: 4 SERVINGS / **ACTIVE TIME:** 10 MINUTES / **TOTAL TIME:** 20 MINUTES

This recipe from Campania utilizes the simple components of Neapolitan pizza on potatoes gnocchi. The beauty of it is in how quick it can be made if you have gnocchi and leftover pasta sauce on hand.

1. Bring water to a boil in a large saucepan. Add the gnocchi and cook until they are floating on the surface.

2. Drain the gnocchi, place them in a large bowl with the tomato sauce, and gently stir to combine.

3. Transfer half of the gnocchi to a deep baking dish with high edges and cover them with half of the mozzarella and Parmesan. Repeat with the remaining gnocchi, mozzarella, and Parmesan.

4. Set the oven's broiler to high. Place the baking dish in the oven and broil until the mozzarella has melted, 5 to 8 minutes.

5. Remove the gnocchi from the oven and serve immediately.

INGREDIENTS:

2   LBS. GNOCCHI DI PATATE (SEE PAGE 65)

1½   LBS. SUGO AL BASILICO (SEE PAGE 806)

12   OZ. FRESH MOZZARELLA CHEESE, DRAINED AND TORN

⅔   CUP GRATED PARMESAN CHEESE

SCIALATIELLI ALL'AMALFITANA

YIELD: 4 SERVINGS / **ACTIVE TIME:** 40 MINUTES / **TOTAL TIME:** 1 HOUR AND 15 MINUTES

Popular on the beautiful Amalfi Coast, this seafood dish is made special by the Scialatelli, a local pasta type that luxuriates in this type of sauce.

1. Place the olive oil in a large skillet and warm it over medium-high heat. Add the garlic and cook for 1 minute.

2. Add the tomatoes and basil and cook, stirring occasionally, for 10 minutes.

3. Add the seafood, season the dish with salt, and cook until the majority of the clams and mussels have opened, about 5 minutes.

4. Remove the mussels and clams from the pan and set them aside. Discard any mussels and/or clams that did not open.

5. Add the wine, cook until it has evaporated, and remove the pan from heat.

6. Bring water to a boil in a large saucepan. Add salt, let the water return to a full boil, and add the pasta. Cook until the pasta is al dente.

7. While the pasta water is coming to a boil, remove the meat from two-thirds of the mussels and clams and reserve the remaining one-third for garnish.

8. Drain the pasta and add it to the sauce along with the mussels and clams. Cook over medium-high heat until everything is warmed through, tossing to combine.

9. Garnish the dish with parsley and the reserved mussels and clams and enjoy.

INGREDIENTS:

¼ CUP EXTRA-VIRGIN OLIVE OIL

1 GARLIC CLOVE, MINCED

5 MEDIUM TOMATOES, CHOPPED

HANDFUL OF FRESH BASIL

1 LB. MUSSELS, RINSED WELL AND DEBEARDED

½ LB. CLAMS, RINSED WELL

½ LB. SQUID, CLEANED (SEE PAGE 277) AND CHOPPED

½ LB. SHRIMP, SHELLS REMOVED, DEVEINED

SALT, TO TASTE

½ CUP DRY WHITE WINE

1 LB. SCIALATIELLI (SEE PAGE 36)

FRESH PARSLEY, CHOPPED, FOR GARNISH

PASTA ALLA GENOVESE

YIELD: 4 SERVINGS / ACTIVE TIME: 40 MINUTES / TOTAL TIME: 5 HOURS

Here a rather simple version of pasta alla Genovese, one of the most loved Neapolitan pasta dishes, but, curiously, one that is pretty much unknown outside of Naples. Although the sauce, like any proper Neapolitan ragù, takes hours to cook, the preparation is otherwise incredibly easy.

1. Leave one piece of beef as is and cut the rest of it into chunks.

2. Place some of the olive oil in a large saucepan and warm it over medium-high heat. Working in batches to avoid crowding the pan, add the beef and sear until it is browned all over, turning it as necessary.

3. Place all of the beef in the pan and cover it with the onions. Reduce the heat to low, cover the pan, and cook, stirring occasionally, until the onions start to soften.

4. Uncover the pan and cook until the meat is tender but not yet falling apart, 2 to 3 hours.

5. Season the mixture with salt, remove the biggest piece of beef from the pan, and set it aside. Cover the pan and continue cooking the sauce until the onions have almost dissolved and the sauce becomes juicy, 1 to 2 hours.

6. Bring water to a boil in a large saucepan. Add salt, let the water return to a full boil, and add the pasta. Cook until the pasta is al dente.

7. Drain the pasta, place it in a serving dish, and add some of the sauce and half of the pecorino. Toss to combine and top with the remaining pecorino.

8. Pour the remaining sauce over the large piece of beef and serve it following the pasta dish.

INGREDIENTS:

- 2½ LBS. BEEF FOR BRAISING (BEST TO USE A MIX OF DIFFERENT CUTS)
- ⅔ CUP EXTRA-VIRGIN OLIVE OIL
- 5 LBS. YELLOW OR WHITE ONIONS, SLICED THIN

  SALT, TO TASTE
- 14 OZ. ZITI SPEZZATI OR RIGATONI
- 2 OZ. PECORINO CHEESE, GRATED

PASTA ALLA GENOVESE:
A SUNDAY TRADITION

One of the most popular family meals in Naples, la Genovese is pasta served with an onion-heavy beef ragù that is cooked for a seemingly interminable amount of time. Neapolitans swear this is the ultimate comfort food, evoking dear memories of their nonne waking up early on a Sunday to cook the velvety sauce for the family's lunch.

The origins of this dish are, as usual, mysterious. It may have originated by the docks of Naples, in cheap restaurants with cooks from Genoa, or, and this sounds most likely, it was inspired by the city of Geneva, Switzerland, where a long-cooked meat stew known as carbonade is traditional. Whatever the origin, this pasta sauce has been strictly Neapolitan for a very long time, as indicated by the fact that it does not include tomatoes, which became popular in Naples only in the second half of the 1800s.

Many versions include soffritto, herbs like parsley or bay leaves, and even pancetta. This latter addition is a no-go for many hardcore Neapolitans, who feel the most authentic version contains only two main ingredients: beef and onions. This pasta sauce is traditionally centered on cheap cuts of meat that become toothsome only through slow cooking, and it substitutes remaining ragout ingredients with possibly the cheapest ingredient of all, onions, which are available even during the most austere times. Long cooking them will extract more than enough flavor, and produce a dish that displays the intelligence and simplicity that always characterize Neapolitan cuisine.

PASTA AL FORNO NAPOLETANA

YIELD: 6 SERVINGS / **ACTIVE TIME:** 40 MINUTES / **TOTAL TIME:** 1 HOUR AND 30 MINUTES

Oven-baked pasta is common to the entirety of Southern Italy, but every region has its own treasured version, and every household has its own take on that. Neapolitan pasta al forno is a great way to make use of leftover meat ragù, and it is characterized by the addition of meatballs, mozzarella, and provola and ricotta cheese. Some also like to add salami and sliced hard-boiled eggs. It's delicious almost any way you approach it, but keep in mind that the pasta should be baked until it is a bit charred on top.

1. To begin preparations for the meatballs, place all of the ingredients, except for the olive oil, in a mixing bowl and work the mixture until it is well combined. Form the mixture into small, walnut-sized meatballs.

2. Add olive oil to a large, deep skillet until it is about 1 inch deep and warm it over medium heat. Add the meatballs and cook until they are browned all over, turning them as necessary. Place the meatballs on paper towel–lined plates and let them drain.

3. Preheat the oven to 360°F. To begin preparations for the pasta, bring water to a boil in a large saucepan. Add salt, let the water return to a full boil, and add the pasta. Cook until the pasta is al dente. Drain the pasta and set it aside.

4. Place the ricotta and 1 cup of the ragù in a large mixing bowl and stir to combine. Add the mixture to the pasta along with 2 more cups of ragù and stir to combine.

5. Spread some ragù over the bottom of a 13 x 9–inch baking dish. Arrange half of the pasta, half of the provola, half of the meatballs, half of the eggs and salami (if desired), half of the mozzarella, and half of the pecorino in separate layers. Repeat the layering process with the remaining ingredients.

6. Place the dish in the oven and bake until the top is crispy, about 30 minutes.

7. Remove the dish from the oven and let it rest for 10 to 15 minutes before serving.

INGREDIENTS:

FOR THE MEATBALLS

- ½ LB. GROUND PORK
- ½ LB. GROUND BEEF
- 4 EGGS
- ½ LB. FRESH BREAD CRUMBS
- 1 CUP GRATED PECORINO OR PARMESAN CHEESE
- SALT AND PEPPER, TO TASTE
- EXTRA-VIRGIN OLIVE OIL, AS NEEDED

FOR THE PASTA

- SALT, TO TASTE
- 1 LB. ZITI, MEZZE MANICHE, OR RIGATONI
- 1 LB. RICOTTA CHEESE
- 6 CUPS RAGÙ NAPOLETANO (SEE PAGE 125)
- 9 OZ. PROVOLA CHEESE, CUBED
- 3 HARD-BOILED EGGS, SLICED (OPTIONAL)
- 4 OZ. ITALIAN SALAMI, CHOPPED (OPTIONAL)
- 1 LB. FRESH MOZZARELLA CHEESE, DRAINED AND TORN
- 1⅓ CUPS GRATED PECORINO OR PARMESAN CHEESE

THE FIRST PASTA: LASAGNA

For most people, lasagna is associated with Bologna and the practice of making egg-based pasta at home, which is so popular in Northern and Central Italy.

Lasagna, however, is not originally from Bologna. Instead, it tracks back to Southern Italy and the Greco-Roman world.

The word lasagna may derive from the Latin word laganum, used in ancient times to describe a sheet of flat dough, which was generally baked. In Greece, there still is an oval-shaped flatbread called laganos that was originally unleavened. An even more likely root for lasagna is found in the Latin word lasănum, which was the name of a three-layered casserole that was cooked slowly over the cinders in the hearth. The most influential Italian dictionary prefers this root rather than the laganum, which implies that lasagna was boiled instead of baked, making it the first pasta known in history.

This original lasagna was most likely not made from an egg-based pasta dough, but rather a simple dough of flour and water which was then boiled and layered with cheese and other ingredients like pulses and/or meat.

The addition of tomato sauce to lasagna is obviously recent, as tomatoes became popular in Naples only in the nineteenth century and from there propagated to the rest of Italy. So, even if the first recipe for lasagna containing tomato sauce was published in 1881, in the book *Principe dei cuochi o la vera cucina napolitana* by Francesco Palma, lasagna was present in Naples long before tomato sauce became part of it.

In the *Liber de coquina* from the fourteenth century, when Carlo I d'Angio' was crowned the first king of Naples, it is described as a dish made of boiled dough sheets seasoned, layer by layer, with cheese and spices. A few centuries later, a recipe for lasagna containing mozzarella cheese was published in *La lucerna de corteggiani* (1634) by Giovanni Battista Crisci, which states: "nun's stewed lasagne with mozzarella and cheese (cacio)," which specifies that after the cheese layering, the boiled lasagna should be baked in the oven. Not to forget that Francesco II, the Bourbon king of Naples in the mid-1800s, was playfully branded "the lasagna king" because of his immoderate passion for this dish.

In case you were wondering, the most popular cookbook from north-central Italy, *La Scienza in cucina*, published in 1891 by Pellegrino Artusi, does not include a recipe for lasagna.

LASAGNE ALLA NAPOLETANA

YIELD: 6 SERVINGS / **ACTIVE TIME:** 1 HOUR / **TOTAL TIME:** 2 HOURS

In Naples, lasagna sheets are not made from fresh, egg-based pasta but dried sheets of pasta made from durum wheat. The best type of pasta for an authentic Neapolitan-style lasagna is lasagna riccia, durum wheat's lasagna with the characteristic curly edges. The filling includes ricotta instead of béchamel, which is not as popular in the South of Italy as it is to the north, and it needs to include meatballs, like in any "respectable" Neapolitan layered pasta.

1. To begin preparations for the meatballs, place all of the ingredients, except for the olive oil, in a mixing bowl and work the mixture until it is well combined. Form the mixture into small, walnut-sized meatballs.

2. Add olive oil to a large, deep skillet until it is about 1 inch deep and warm it over medium heat. Add the meatballs and cook until they are browned all over, turning them as necessary. Place the meatballs on paper towel–lined plates and let them drain.

3. Preheat the oven to 360°F. To begin preparations for the lasagna, bring water to a boil in a large saucepan. Add salt, let the water return to a full boil, and add a few of the lasagna sheets at a time to avoid overcrowding the pot. Cook until the lasagna sheets are al dente. Drain the lasagna sheets and set them on kitchen towels to dry.

4. Place the ricotta and 1 cup of the ragù in a large mixing bowl and stir to combine.

5. Spread some ragù over the bottom of a 13 x 9–inch baking dish. Arrange one-third of the lasagna sheets, one-third of the ricotta mixture, one-third of the provola, one-third of the meatballs, one-third of the eggs (if desired), and half of the pecorino in separate layers. Repeat the layering process two more times with the remaining ingredients.

6. Top the lasagna with additional ragù and pecorino, place it in the oven, and bake for 50 minutes.

7. Remove the lasagna from the oven and let it rest for 10 to 15 minutes before serving.

INGREDIENTS:

FOR THE MEATBALLS

5½	OZ. GROUND BEEF
5½	OZ. GROUND PORK
2	EGGS
4	OZ. FRESH BREAD CRUMBS
2	OZ. PECORINO OR PARMESAN CHEESE, GRATED
	SALT AND PEPPER, TO TASTE
	EXTRA-VIRGIN OLIVE OIL, AS NEEDED

FOR THE LASAGNA

	SALT, TO TASTE
1½	LBS. LASAGNA SHEETS
1	LB. RICOTTA CHEESE
4	CUPS RAGÙ NAPOLETANO (SEE PAGE 125), PLUS MORE FOR TOPPING
14	OZ. PROVOLA CHEESE, CUBED
3	HARD-BOILED EGGS, SLICED (OPTIONAL)
3	OZ. PECORINO OR PARMESAN CHEESE, GRATED, PLUS MORE FOR TOPPING

PARMIGIANA DI MELANZANE ALLA NAPOLETANA

YIELD: 4 SERVINGS / **ACTIVE TIME:** 1 HOUR / **TOTAL TIME:** 2 HOURS AND 30 MINUTES

Eggplant parmigiana may seem easy to some, but it is in fact very easy to make incorrectly. The key to its success is in the correct preparation of the eggplants, leaving no room for shortcuts. The Neapolitan version of eggplant parmigiana is possibly the best known, as it includes both mozzarella and Parmesan cheese and requires the eggplants to be lightly breaded in flour and egg.

1. Slice the eggplants thin lengthwise; if you have a mandoline available, use it on a rather thick setting. Layer the sliced eggplants in a colander, seasoning each layer with coarse salt. Fill a large saucepan with water and place it on top of the eggplants. Let the eggplants drain for 1 hour.

2. Rinse the eggplants and squeeze them to remove as much water as possible. Place the eggplants on kitchen towels and let them dry.

3. Preheat the oven to 375°F. Add olive oil to a narrow, deep, heavy-bottomed saucepan with high edges until it is about 2 inches deep and warm it to 350°F.

4. Place the eggs in a bowl, season them lightly with fine salt, and whisk until scrambled. Place flour in a shallow bowl and dredge the eggplants in the flour and then the egg until they are completely coated.

5. Gently slip the eggplants into the hot oil and fry until they are golden brown, working in batches to avoid crowding the pot. Transfer the fried eggplants to a paper towel–lined plate to drain.

6. Cover the bottom of a 13 x 9–inch baking dish with some of the tomato sauce. Arrange the eggplants, mozzarella, basil, Parmesan, and tomato sauce in individual layers in the dish, continuing the layering process until everything has been used up.

7. Top the dish with additional Parmesan, place it in the oven, and bake until the cheese and sauce start to bubble, about 25 minutes.

8. Remove the parmigiana from the oven and let it rest for at least 30 minutes before slicing and serving.

INGREDIENTS:

4   **LARGE EGGPLANTS**

    SALT (FINE AND COARSE), TO TASTE

    EXTRA-VIRGIN OLIVE OIL, AS NEEDED

4   **EGGS**

    ALL-PURPOSE FLOUR, AS NEEDED

3½   **CUPS SUGO AL BASILICO (SEE PAGE 806)**

9   **OZ. FRESH MOZZARELLA CHEESE, DRAINED AND SLICED**

2   **HANDFULS OF FRESH BASIL**

1⅓   **CUPS GRATED PARMESAN CHEESE, PLUS MORE FOR TOPPING**

ZUPPA DI LENTICCHIE E CASTAGNE

YIELD: 4 SERVINGS / **ACTIVE TIME:** 1 HOUR / **TOTAL TIME:** 3 HOURS

This lovely, earthy soup from Molise is inspired by Capracotta's excellent lentils, which the locals call miccole. They are tiny, dark lentils cultivated on rocky mountainsides, and their best characteristic is their ability to keep their shape even after cooking. The pairing with chestnuts is heavenly and typical of mountain areas, where chestnuts are plentiful. The typical recipe uses dry chestnuts (which will require half the amount), but here we use fresh chestnuts, as they are easier to find, even if they require some extra work.

1. Place the chestnuts in a bowl, cover them with cold water, and let them soak for 2 to 3 minutes.

2. Bring water to a boil in a large saucepan. Make a long, shallow incision on the back of each chestnut and add them to the boiling water along with salt. Cook the chestnuts for 4 minutes and drain them.

3. Warm a large skillet over medium-high heat. Add the chestnuts and cook until they start to pop open. Remove the chestnuts from the pan and peel them.

4. Bring water to a boil in a large saucepan. Add the chestnuts and cook until they are tender, 35 to 40 minutes. Drain the chestnuts and set them aside.

5. Place the lentils, garlic, parsley, and bay leaves in a saucepan, cover the lentils with cold water, and bring to a boil. Cook for 15 minutes, season the lentils with salt, and continue cooking them until they are tender, another 15 minutes or so.

6. Remove the garlic, parsley, and bay leaves and discard them. Add the chestnuts and olive oil and cook until the chestnuts are warmed through.

7. Place a slice of bread in each of the serving bowls and ladle the soup over the top. Garnish with pecorino and additional olive oil and enjoy.

INGREDIENTS:

2   CUPS FRESH CHESTNUTS

    SALT, TO TASTE

1⅓ CUPS DARK ITALIAN LENTILS, PICKED OVER

2   GARLIC CLOVES

12 SPRIGS OF FRESH PARSLEY

2   BAY LEAVES

1   TABLESPOON EXTRA-VIRGIN OLIVE OIL, PLUS MORE FOR GARNISH

4   SLICES OF CRUSTY BREAD, TOASTED

    PECORINO CHEESE, GRATED, FOR GARNISH

VIRTÙ TERAMANE

YIELD: 4 SERVINGS / ACTIVE TIME: 1 HOUR AND 30 MINUTES / TOTAL TIME: 24 HOURS

This is an incredibly rich vegetable-and-legume soup from Teramo in Abruzzo, which is linked to the ancient celebrations of the Calendimaggio on the 1st of May. It is a welcome to spring, when the Abruzzo housewives cleaned out all of the dried legumes and various bits of broken pasta that had gathered over the winter. These "virtuous" women then combined these winter remnants with the first fruits of the spring.

1. Bring water to a boil in a large saucepan. Add salt and the spinach, zucchini, endive, carrot, and celery and cook for 5 minutes. Drain the vegetables and let them cool. When they are cool enough to handle, squeeze them to remove as much water as possible and set them aside.

2. Place the chickpeas, lentils, beans, and split peas in separate saucepans, cover them with water, and cook until they just start to soften—the cook times will differ for each legume. Drain the legumes and set them aside.

3. Place the lard in a large saucepan and warm it over medium heat. Add the onion, garlic, and pancetta and cook, stirring frequently, until the pancetta's fat starts to render.

4. Remove the garlic from the pan and discard it. Add the parsley and tomatoes and cook, stirring occasionally, until the tomatoes start to collapse, about 15 minutes.

5. Add the broth and cooked vegetables to the pan and cook for 10 minutes.

6. Add the pasta and legumes and cook until they are tender, about 30 minutes.

7. Ladle the soup into warmed bowls, garnish each portion with pecorino, and enjoy.

INGREDIENTS:

	SALT, TO TASTE
3	CUPS FRESH SPINACH
1	SMALL ZUCCHINI, CHOPPED
1	HEAD OF ENDIVE, CHOPPED
1	CARROT, PEELED AND CHOPPED
1	CELERY STALK, CHOPPED
¾	CUP DRIED CHICKPEAS, SOAKED OVERNIGHT AND DRAINED
¾	CUP LENTILS
1	(SCANT) CUP DRIED FAVA BEANS, SOAKED OVERNIGHT AND DRAINED
⅔	CUP DRIED SPLIT PEAS
2	OZ. LARD, CHOPPED
1	ONION, FINELY DICED
1	GARLIC CLOVE
5	OZ. PANCETTA, CUBED
1	TEASPOON CHOPPED FRESH PARSLEY
2	TOMATOES, CHOPPED
8	CUPS BRODO DI POLLO OR DI CARNE (SEE PAGE 805)
½	LB. SHORT-FORMAT PASTA (MIX OF DRIED SEMOLINA PASTA AND HOMEMADE EGG PASTA RECOMMENDED)
	PECORINO CHEESE, GRATED, FOR GARNISH

PASTA ALLA MUGNAIA

YIELD: 4 SERVINGS / **ACTIVE TIME**: 40 MINUTES / **TOTAL TIME**: 2 HOURS

Pasta alla mugnaia is a traditional primo in Abruzzi, in the area of Elice (Pescara) in particular. There, the pasta is handmade, without eggs, to obtain a tagliatelle with a rustic consistency.

1. Place the olive oil in a large skillet and warm it over medium heat. Add the green bell pepper, onion, and carrot and cook, stirring occasionally, until they have softened, about 5 minutes.

2. Season the beef with salt, add it to the pan, and sear it until it is browned all over, turning it as necessary.

3. Add the red bell pepper and eggplant and cook until they are browned.

4. Reduce the heat to low, add the tomatoes and water, and season the sauce with salt. Cover the pan and cook the sauce until the meat is tender, about 1 hour. Remove the sauce from heat and set it aside.

5. Bring water to a boil in a large saucepan. Add salt, let the water return to a full boil, and add the pasta. Cook until the pasta is al dente. Drain the pasta and place it in a serving dish.

6. Add the sauce to the pasta and toss to combine. Garnish the dish with pecorino and enjoy.

INGREDIENTS:

¼ CUP EXTRA-VIRGIN OLIVE OIL

1 GREEN BELL PEPPER, STEM AND SEEDS REMOVED, FINELY DICED

1 ONION, SLICED THIN

½ CARROT, PEELED AND DICED

½ LB. PIECE OF BONE-IN BEEF OR PORK

SALT, TO TASTE

1 RED BELL PEPPER, STEM AND SEEDS REMOVED, FINELY DICED

1 EGGPLANT, CUBED

1 LB. WHOLE PEELED TOMATOES, PUREED

1 CUP WATER

1 LB. TAGLIATELLE OR FETTUCCINE

PECORINO CHEESE, GRATED, FOR GARNISH

TIMBALLO ABRUZZESE

YIELD: 8 SERVINGS / **ACTIVE TIME:** 1 HOUR AND 30 MINUTES / **TOTAL TIME:** 3 HOURS AND 30 MINUTES

Timballo Abruzzese is very similar to a lasagna, but instead of using pasta, it uses the Abruzzi version of a crepe, scrippelle. It is traditional to serve it as a main dish during Christmas and/ or New Year's, but it is often also served on other special occasions, like the Sunday family lunch.

1. To begin preparations for the filling, place the butter and olive oil in a large skillet and warm the mixture over medium heat. Add the celery, carrot, and onion and cook, stirring occasionally, until the onion has softened, about 5 minutes.

2. Add the beef, veal, and pork and cook until they have browned, breaking the meats up with a wooden spoon as they cook.

3. Deglaze the pan with the wine, scraping up any browned bits from the bottom. Cook until the wine has evaporated, stir in the Parmesan, and set the filling aside.

4. To begin preparations for the sauce, place the olive oil in a large skillet and warm it over medium heat. Add the celery, carrot, and onion and cook, stirring occasionally, until the onion has softened, about 5 minutes.

5. Add the pork and sear until it is browned all over, turning it as needed.

6. Add the tomatoes, season the sauce with salt, and cook for about 1½ hours, letting the sauce thicken.

7. Preheat the oven to 320°F. Place the egg and milk in a bowl and whisk to combine. Set the mixture aside.

8. Coat a 13 x 9–inch baking pan with butter and line it with some of the Scrippelle. Cover them with a little sauce, some of the filling, and some of the mozzarella, and drizzle 1 tablespoon of the egg mixture over everything. If desired, dot the mixture with some pieces of butter. Repeat the layering process with the Scrippelle, sauce, filling, mozzarella, egg mixture, and butter (if desired).

9. Top the dish with 2 or 3 Scripelle and a few pats of butter. Place the timballo in the oven and bake for about 2 hours, taking care to not let the top burn. If the top is browning too quickly, cover the timballo with aluminum foil.

10. Remove the timballo from the oven and let it rest for 10 minutes. Invert the timballo onto a cutting board, slice it, and serve.

INGREDIENTS:

FOR THE FILLING

1	TABLESPOON UNSALTED BUTTER
2	TABLESPOONS EXTRA-VIRGIN OLIVE OIL
½	CELERY STALK, FINELY DICED
½	CARROT, PEELED AND FINELY DICED
½	WHITE ONION, FINELY DICED
1	LB. GROUND BEEF
1	LB. GROUND VEAL
1	LB. GROUND PORK
1	CUP WHITE WINE
4	OZ. PARMESAN CHEESE, GRATED

FOR THE SAUCE

3	TABLESPOONS EXTRA-VIRGIN OLIVE OIL
½	CELERY STALK, FINELY DICED
½	CARROT, PEELED AND FINELY DICED
½	WHITE ONION, PEELED AND FINELY DICED
½	LB. BONE-IN PORK
4	CUPS CRUSHED TOMATOES
	SALT, TO TASTE
1	EGG
½	CUP MILK
	UNSALTED BUTTER, AS NEEDED
2	BATCHES OF SCRIPPELLE (SEE PAGE 145), NOT DRESSED
1.2	LBS. MOZZARELLA CHEESE, DRAINED AND CUBED

SCRIPPELLE 'MBUSSE

YIELD: 12 SCRIPPELLE / **ACTIVE TIME:** 30 MINUTES / **TOTAL TIME:** 50 MINUTES

Scrippelle are crepes made with water and eggs instead of milk and eggs, and generally filled with cheese. In the popular 'mbusse, they are served, either whole or sliced, after being moistened with chicken broth. This is a specialty widespread throughout the whole Abruzzi region, but it is native to the province of Teramo, and it is a must on the Christmas table, where it is used as starter.

1. Place the eggs and flour in a bowl and whisk until the mixture is smooth. Add the water and whisk until it is incorporated.

2. Coat a large skillet with lard and warm it over medium heat.

3. Add one-twelfth of the batter to the pan and tilt it so that it is evenly distributed. Cook the scrippelle until it is browned on both sides, about 1 minute per side. Remove the scrippelle from the pan and place it on a plate. Repeat with the remaining batter, adding more lard if the the pan starts to look dry.

4. Top the scrippelle with plenty of pecorino and a little cinnamon, roll them up tightly, and place them in a deep serving dish.

5. Place the broth in a saucepan and warm it.

6. Pour the warmed broth over the scrippelle, sprinkle more pecorino over them, and enjoy.

INGREDIENTS:

4	EGGS
5	TABLESPOONS ALL-PURPOSE FLOUR
⅓	CUP WATER
	LARD, AS NEEDED
	PECORINO CHEESE, GRATED, TO TASTE
	CINNAMON, TO TASTE
4	CUPS BRODO DI POLLO (SEE PAGE 805)

BRODETTO ALL'ABRUZZESE

YIELD: 6 SERVINGS / **ACTIVE TIME:** 1 HOUR / **TOTAL TIME:** 3 HOURS

The brodetto all'Abruzzese has its roots in the ways of Abruzzi's fishermen who, at the end of the working day, needed to make good use of the leftover seafood that was less attractive to the market due to appearance and/or size. No less than six varieties of seafood are used in this dish, usually cooked whole. The variations of this recipe are numerous along the entire Adriatic coast, even within the same region.

1. Place the clams in a large bowl, cover them with cold water, and stir in 4 handfuls of salt. Let them soak for 2 hours to remove the sand.

2. Drain the clams, place them in a pot, and add the mussels. Cover the pot and cook them over high heat until the majority of the clams and mussels have opened, about 5 minutes. Transfer them to a plate and set them aside. Strain the cooking liquid and set it aside. Discard any clams and mussels that did not open.

3. Place the olive oil in a large saucepan and warm it over medium heat. Add the garlic and cook, stirring occasionally, for 2 minutes. Add the vinegar and cook until it has evaporated.

4. Add the tomatoes and chile, season the sauce with salt, and cook for about 20 minutes.

5. Add the squid and monkfish and cook for 10 minutes.

6. Add the turbot and cod, top with the sole, langoustines, and shrimp, cover the pan, and reduce the heat to medium-low. Cook for 10 minutes, gently shaking the pan occasionally.

7. Turn off the heat, taste the sauce, and adjust the seasoning as necessary.

8. Top the dish with the mussels, clams, reserved liquid, parsley, and basil, serve with toasted bread, and enjoy.

INGREDIENTS:

- 5 OZ. CLAMS
- SALT, TO TASTE
- 5 OZ. MUSSELS, RINSED WELL AND DEBEARDED
- 2 TABLESPOONS EXTRA-VIRGIN OLIVE OIL
- 2 GARLIC CLOVES
- 1 CUP WHITE WINE VINEGAR
- 4 CUPS WHOLE PEELED TOMATOES, CRUSHED
- 1 CHILE PEPPER, STEM AND SEEDS REMOVED, MINCED
- 11 OZ. SQUID, CLEANED AND SLICED INTO RINGS
- 1½ LBS. MONKFISH FILLETS, CUT INTO 2 TO 3 PIECES
- 1½ LBS. TURBOT FILLETS, CUT INTO 2 TO 3 PIECES
- 1 LB. COD FILLETS, CUT INTO 2 TO 3 PIECES
- 5 OZ. SOLE FILLETS, CUT INTO 2 TO 3 PIECES
- 4 LANGOUSTINES
- 4 MANTIS SHRIMP OR OTHER LARGE SHRIMP, LEGS AND ANTENNAE REMOVED, DEVEINED
- 1 BUNCH OF FRESH PARSLEY, CHOPPED
- 1 BUNCH OF FRESH BASIL, CHOPPED
- CRUSTY BREAD, TOASTED, FOR SERVING

PAPPARDELLE ALL'AQUILANA

YIELD: 4 SERVINGS / ACTIVE TIME: 20 MINUTES / TOTAL TIME: 50 MINUTES

Pappardelle all'aquilana is a sultry first course traditionally served on special occasions, as it features the most precious ingredients in L'Aquila gastronomy: locally produced saffron and porcini mushrooms from Monti della Laga. If you'd rather use fresh mushrooms here, use 2⅓ cups.

1. Place the porcini mushrooms in a bowl, cover them with warm water, and let them soak for 30 minutes.

2. Drain the mushrooms, reserve the soaking liquid, and squeeze the mushrooms to remove as much moisture as possible. Chop the mushrooms and set them aside. Strain the soaking liquid and set it aside.

3. Bring water to a boil in a medium saucepan. Add salt and the peas and cook for 2 minutes. Drain the peas and set them aside.

4. Place the olive oil in a large skillet and warm it over medium heat. Add the onion, cotto, and guanciale and cook, stirring occasionally, until the onion has softened, about 5 minutes.

5. Add the sausage and cook, stirring occasionally, until it has browned, about 8 minutes.

6. Add the peas, mushrooms, and some of the reserved soaking liquid. Season the dish with salt, reduce the heat to low, and cook for 15 minutes.

7. Bring water to a boil in a large saucepan. Add salt, let the water return to a full boil, and add the pasta. Cook until the pasta is very al dente. Reserve ½ cup of pasta water, drain the pasta, and set it aside.

8. Place the saffron in the pasta water and let it steep for 10 minutes.

9. Add the pasta, saffron, and some of the saffron water to the skillet and toss until well combined. You want the sauce to be thick instead of soupy, and for the pasta to be al dente.

10. Stir in the pecorino and serve.

INGREDIENTS:

- 1⅓ CUPS DRIED PORCINI MUSHROOMS
- SALT, TO TASTE
- ¾ CUP PEAS
- 2 TABLESPOONS EXTRA-VIRGIN OLIVE OIL
- ½ ONION
- ⅔ CUP DICED ITALIAN COTTO OR PARMA HAM
- 1 SLICE OF GUANCIALE, HARD SKIN REMOVED, DICED
- 1 ITALIAN SAUSAGE, CASING REMOVED, CRUMBLED
- 1 LB. PAPPARDELLE
- 1½ TEASPOONS SAFFRON THREADS
- ½ CUP GRATED PECORINO CHEESE

SAFFRON, ABRUZZI'S GOLD

In the Middle Ages, the only saffron accessible to Italians was cultivated in Spain and Tunisia, but it was too expensive to make a real impact on Italian cuisine. Things changed in the thirteenth century, when a monk named Santucci decided to import the plant and start cultivating it in the Navelli plains of Abruzzi. Here saffron found a very favorable habitat, to the point it quickly proved superior in quality to the one cultivated in other countries. The profitable cultivation of saffron quickly spread to the surrounding areas, and the families who founded the city of L'Aquila soon began trading with the cities of Milan and Venice as well as with foreign cities, such as Frankfurt, Marseille, Vienna, and Nuremberg. This enormously helped L'Aquila's economy, which had previously been based on sheep farming and wool production.

The city of L'Aquila has found itself in difficulty many times, especially under Spanish rule, but thanks to saffron the city was able to pay the heavy taxes imposed by Spain. With the arrival of the Bourbons as rulers, a new confidence was given to farmers, and by 1830 saffron production reached 45 quintals (1 quintal is equivalent to 100 kilograms).

In the twentieth century, cultivation started to recede, first due to the World Wars and then to abuses by traders who did not want to grant a fair payment to the farmers. But thanks to Silvio Sarra of Civitaretenga, the cultivation of saffron has recently been restored, perhaps not to its ancient splendor, but enough to provide important production for a spice that is sought after by gourmands all over the world.

BUCATINI CON ASPARAGI E SALSICCIA

YIELD: 4 SERVINGS / **ACTIVE TIME:** 30 MINUTES / **TOTAL TIME:** 50 MINUTES

In many Italian regions, early spring means asparagus, which grows wild throughout the country. Families make it into a ritual to go pick the green treasures, which at home become the center of many culinary preparations. Here is a version of a typical Molisan pasta with asparagus and sausage, which can of course be made with regular cultivated asparagus (the tiniest ones are the best), but shines with wild asparagus.

1. Bring water to a boil in a medium saucepan. Separate the stems from the tips of the asparagus and add salt and the asparagus stems to the boiling water. Cook until the asparagus stems are tender, about 4 minutes, drain, and set them aside.

2. Place 2 tablespoons of olive oil in a large skillet and warm it over medium heat. Add the onion and cook, stirring occasionally, until it has softened, about 5 minutes.

3. Add the sausage and cook, stirring occasionally, until it has browned, about 8 minutes.

4. Add the wine, reduce the heat to low, and cook for 15 minutes.

5. Place the remaining olive oil in a large skillet and warm it over medium heat. Add the asparagus tips and cook, stirring frequently, until they are tender, 3 to 4 minutes. Season the asparagus tips with salt and pepper, remove the pan from heat, and set the asparagus tips aside.

6. Bring water to a boil in a large saucepan. Chop the asparagus stems, add them to the sauce, and cook for 10 minutes.

7. Add salt, let the water return to a full boil, and add the pasta. Cook until the pasta is al dente. Drain the pasta, add it to the sauce, and toss to combine.

8. Top the dish with the asparagus tips and pecorino and enjoy.

INGREDIENTS:

10	OZ. FRESH ASPARAGUS, TRIMMED
	SALT AND PEPPER, TO TASTE
¼	CUP EXTRA-VIRGIN OLIVE OIL
1	ONION, FINELY DICED
11	OZ. ITALIAN SAUSAGE, CASINGS REMOVED, CRUMBLED
1	CUP WHITE WINE
1	LB. BUCATINI
⅔	CUP GRATED PECORINO CHEESE

RISO E VERZA

YIELD: 4 SERVINGS / **ACTIVE TIME:** 30 MINUTES / **TOTAL TIME:** 1 HOUR

Rice is not very common in Southern Italian cuisine, but some rice dishes have become quintessential, nonetheless. Riso e verza is an earthy cabbage-and-rice soup typical of Molise, managing to be both light and comforting.

1. Place the olive oil in a large skillet and warm it over medium heat. Add the onion, carrot, and celery and cook, stirring occasionally, until the onion has softened, about 5 minutes.

2. Add the cabbage, reduce the heat to medium-low, and cover the pan. Cook the cabbage until it is tender, 10 to 15 minutes.

3. Add the rice, season the dish with salt, and add a few ladles of hot water. Cook, stirring frequently and adding hot water as necessary, until the rice is al dente, 15 to 20 minutes.

4. Remove the pan from heat and let it rest for a few minutes.

5. Stir in the pecorino and serve.

INGREDIENTS:

2 TABLESPOONS EXTRA-VIRGIN OLIVE OIL

1 SMALL ONION, FINELY DICED

½ CARROT, PEELED AND FINELY DICED

½ CELERY STALK, FINELY DICED

1 SMALL HEAD OF SAVOY CABBAGE, SLICED VERY THIN

1 CUP VIALONE NANO RICE, RINSED WELL

   SALT, TO TASTE

   HOT WATER, AS NEEDED

⅔ CUP GRATED PECORINO CHEESE

CICELIEVITATI

YIELD: 4 SERVINGS / ACTIVE TIME: 1 HOUR / TOTAL TIME: 3 HOURS

In Poggio, Molise, homemakers used to make pasta from leftover bread dough. This recipe is an example, and requires no pasta-making expertise. Cicelievitati marries well with most sauces, such as a simple tomato-and-basil one or, even better, a meat ragù.

1. Place the flour, yeast, and eggs in the work bowl of a stand mixer fitted with the dough hook and work the mixture until combined. Add the salt, work the mixture until it has been incorporated, and then add the water, 1 tablespoon at a time. Work the mixture until it comes together as a dry dough.

2. Cover the work bowl with plastic wrap and let the dough rise until it has doubled in size, about 1½ hours.

3. Dust a work surface with semolina flour, place the dough on it, and tear off a small piece of it. Roll the small piece of dough into a 3-inch-long stick that is about the thickness of a ballpoint pen. Repeat with the remaining dough.

4. Bring water to a boil in a large saucepan. Add salt, let the water return to a full boil, and add the pasta. Cook until the pasta has the consistency of properly cooked gnocchi, light and slightly chewy.

5. Drain the pasta and place it in a serving dish. Top with the sauce and pecorino and serve.

INGREDIENTS:

17.6 OZ. ALL-PURPOSE FLOUR

1 PACKET OF ACTIVE DRY YEAST

2 EGGS

2 PINCHES OF FINE SEA SALT, PLUS MORE TO TASTE

1 CUP WATER

SEMOLINA FLOUR, AS NEEDED

2 CUPS SUGO AL BASILICO (SEE PAGE 806) OR RAGÙ NAPOLETANO (SEE PAGE 125)

2 OZ. PECORINO CHEESE, GRATED

CAVATELLI ALLA VENTRICINA

YIELD: 4 SERVINGS / ACTIVE TIME: 10 MINUTES / TOTAL TIME: 50 MINUTES

Ventricina is a salami from the area of Molise that borders Abruzzi. It is a poor man's salami, formally prepared only with the fattiest scraps of the pig, such as pork belly. Nowadays the recipe has been improved to utilize more valuable meat cuts, but the combination of sweet and chile peppers that give ventricina its characteristic red color and unique flavor remain. Ventricina sauce can be used with many different pasta formats, but it is most common to serve it with cavatelli, which is also typical of Molise.

1. Place the olive oil in a large skillet and warm it over medium heat. Add the onion and garlic and cook, stirring frequently, until the onion has softened, about 5 minutes.

2. Add the tomatoes, reduce the heat to low, and cook for 20 minutes.

3. Remove the garlic, season the sauce with salt, and stir in the ventricina. Cook for 20 minutes, stirring occasionally.

4. Bring water to a boil in a large saucepan. Add salt, let the water return to a full boil, and add the pasta. Cook until the pasta is al dente.

5. Drain the pasta and place it in a serving dish.

6. Stir the basil into the sauce. Top the pasta with the sauce and pecorino and serve.

INGREDIENTS:

3   TABLESPOONS EXTRA-VIRGIN OLIVE OIL

½   ONION, FINELY DICED

2   GARLIC CLOVES, HALVED

1   LB. WHOLE PEELED TOMATOES, CRUSHED

     SALT, TO TASTE

⅔   CUP CHOPPED VENTRICINA

1   LB. CAVATELLI (SEE PAGE 40)

     HANDFUL OF FRESH BASIL, TORN

2   OZ. PECORINO CHEESE, GRATED

CAVATELLI AL SUGO VEDOVO

YIELD: 4 SERVINGS / **ACTIVE TIME:** 40 MINUTES / **TOTAL TIME:** 40 MINUTES

Another poor man's pasta sauce from Molise, sugo vedovo means "widower sauce" and is so called because it is missing meat. Instead it contains lard, which was far more readily available and a much cheaper source of animal fat and protein in the past.

1. Place the lard in a large skillet and warm it over medium heat. Add the garlic and parsley and cook, stirring frequently, for 2 minutes.

2. Add the tomatoes and cook, stirring occasionally, until the tomatoes collapse, about 20 minutes.

3. Bring water to a boil in a large saucepan. Add salt, let the water return to a full boil, and add the pasta. Cook until the pasta is al dente.

4. Drain the pasta and place it in a serving dish.

5. Stir the basil into the sauce. Top the pasta with the sauce and pecorino, season it with salt and pepper, and serve.

INGREDIENTS:

6	OZ. LARD, FINELY DICED
1	GARLIC CLOVE, HALVED
6	SPRIGS OF FRESH PARSLEY
2	LBS. TOMATOES, CHOPPED
	SALT AND PEPPER, TO TASTE
1	LB. CAVATELLI (SEE PAGE 40)
	HANDFUL OF FRESH BASIL
⅔	CUP GRATED PECORINO CHEESE

FUSILLI ALLA MOLISANA

YIELD: 4 SERVINGS / ACTIVE TIME: 30 MINUTES / TOTAL TIME: 3 HOURS

This sultry lamb, pork, and veal–enriched sauce from Molise is traditionally used to dress handmade fusilli.

1. Place the olive oil in a large saucepan and warm it over medium heat. Add the onion, carrot, and celery and cook, stirring occasionally, until the onion has softened, about 5 minutes.

2. Add the lamb, veal, and sausages and cook over medium-high heat until they are browned, 8 to 10 minutes.

3. Deglaze the pan with the white wine, scraping up any browned bits from the bottom. Cook until the wine has evaporated.

4. Add the tomatoes, season the sauce with salt, and reduce the heat to low. Cook until the meat starts falling apart, 2 to 3 hours.

5. Bring water to a boil in a large saucepan. Add salt, let the water return to a full boil, and add the pasta. Cook until the pasta is al dente, about 3 minutes after they rise to the surface.

6. Drain the pasta and stir it into the sauce. Garnish the dish with pecorino and serve.

INGREDIENTS:

¼ CUP EXTRA-VIRGIN OLIVE OIL

1 ONION, FINELY DICED

1 CARROT, PEELED AND FINELY DICED

1 CELERY STALK, FINELY DICED

½ LB. LAMB, CHOPPED

½ LB. VEAL, CHOPPED

2 ITALIAN SAUSAGES, CASINGS REMOVED, CRUMBLED

½ CUP WHITE WINE

2 LBS. WHOLE PEELED TOMATOES, CRUSHED

SALT, TO TASTE

1 LB. FUSILLI AL FERRO (SEE PAGE 39)

PECORINO CHEESE, GRATED, FOR GARNISH

LICURDIA, ZUPPA DI CIPOLLE ALLA CALABRESE

YIELD: 6 SERVINGS / **ACTIVE TIME:** 30 MINUTES / **TOTAL TIME:** 3 HOURS

Licurdia, Calabrian onion soup, is a truly humble dish which has its roots in the pastoral culinary tradition—so much so that it is also called "the shepherds' breakfast." The original version, before potatoes were introduced, used flour as a thickener. This approach is still followed by some, so feel free to substitute potatoes with some generous sprinkles of flour. Licurdia is characteristic, compared to other traditional onion soups, for using red onions, originally the sweet ones from Tropea.

1. Place the olive oil in a large skillet and warm it over low heat. Add the onions, season them with salt, and cover the pan. Cook, stirring occasionally, until the onions are very tender, about 30 minutes, taking care not to let them brown.

2. Add the potatoes and water, partially cover the pan, and cook until the broth is very creamy, about 2 hours.

3. Place a slice of the bread in each serving bowl and top with the caciocavallo, soup, and red pepper flakes. Garnish each portion with pecorino and serve.

INGREDIENTS:

¼ CUP EXTRA-VIRGIN OLIVE OIL

2 LBS. RED ONIONS, SLICED THIN

   SALT, TO TASTE

1 LB. POTATOES, PEELED AND GRATED

4 CUPS WATER

6 SLICES OF CRUSTY BREAD, TOASTED

6 OZ. CACIOCAVALLO CHEESE, CUBED

   RED PEPPER FLAKES, TO TASTE

   PECORINO CHEESE, GRATED, FOR GARNISH

PASTA AL PESTO CALABRESE

YIELD: 4 SERVINGS / **ACTIVE TIME:** 20 MINUTES / **TOTAL TIME:** 1 HOUR

Although this pasta sauce contains typical Calabrian ingredients, its origins are recent and linked to the improved distribution of food around the globe.

1. Place the olive oil in a large skillet and warm it over medium-low heat. Add the onion and cook, stirring occasionally, until it has softened, about 6 minutes.

2. Add the peppers, cover the pan, and cook, stirring occasionally, until they are tender, about 20 minutes.

3. Add the tomatoes and season the sauce with red pepper flakes and salt. Cover the pan and cook the sauce, stirring occasionally, for 20 minutes.

4. Stir in the ricotta and caciocavallo and use an immersion blender to puree the sauce until it is smooth.

5. Bring water to a boil in a large saucepan. Add salt, let the water return to a full boil, and add the pasta. Cook until the pasta is al dente.

6. Reserve 1 cup pasta water, drain the pasta, and stir it into the sauce.

7. Toss to combine, adding pasta water as needed to get the right consistency. Serve immediately.

INGREDIENTS:

- ¼ CUP EXTRA-VIRGIN OLIVE OIL
- 1 RED ONION, FINELY DICED
- 2 RED BELL PEPPERS, STEMS AND SEEDS REMOVED, SLICED THIN
- 5 OZ. WHOLE PEELED TOMATOES, CRUSHED

  RED PEPPER FLAKES, TO TASTE

  SALT, TO TASTE
- ½ CUP RICOTTA CHEESE
- ⅔ CUP GRATED CACIOCAVALLO OR PECORINO CHEESE
- 1 LB. FUSILLI OR PENNE

FUSILLI ALLA SILANA

YIELD: 6 SERVINGS / **ACTIVE TIME:** 10 MINUTES / **TOTAL TIME:** 50 MINUTES

A pasta sauce that uses some of the delicious and earthy specialties from La Sila, the mountainous Calabrian plateau known to have the purest air in Europe. It uses the famous soppressata calabra salami, Silan caciocavallo (but it is OK to substitute it), and Calabrian chile pepper to build a pasta dish with a bite.

1. Place the olive oil in a large, deep skillet and warm it over medium heat. Add the onion, guanciale, soppressata, and chile and cook, stirring occasionally, until the guanciale's fat starts to render and the onion has softened, about 5 minutes.

2. Remove the pan from heat, add the Cognac, and place the pan over medium-low heat. Cook until the Cognac has evaporated.

3. Add the tomatoes and cook for 30 minutes, stirring occasionally.

4. Bring water to a boil in a large saucepan. Add salt, let the water return to a full boil, and add the pasta. Cook until the pasta is al dente.

5. Drain the pasta and stir it into the sauce.

6. Add the caciocavallo and parsley, cover the pan, and cook until the caciocavallo has melted.

7. Top the dish with the pecorino, season it with salt and pepper, and serve.

INGREDIENTS:

¼ CUP EXTRA-VIRGIN OLIVE OIL

1 SMALL ONION, FINELY DICED

2 OZ. GUANCIALE, HARD SKIN REMOVED, CUT INTO STRIPS

5 OZ. SOPPRESSATA, SLICED

1 CHILE PEPPER, STEM AND SEEDS REMOVED, CHOPPED

1 OZ. COGNAC OR WHISKEY

1 LB. WHOLE PEELED TOMATOES, CRUSHED

SALT AND PEPPER, TO TASTE

1 LB. DRIED FUSILLI

7 OZ. CACIOCAVALLO CHEESE, CUBED

HANDFUL OF FRESH PARSLEY, CHOPPED

⅔ CUP GRATED PECORINO CHEESE

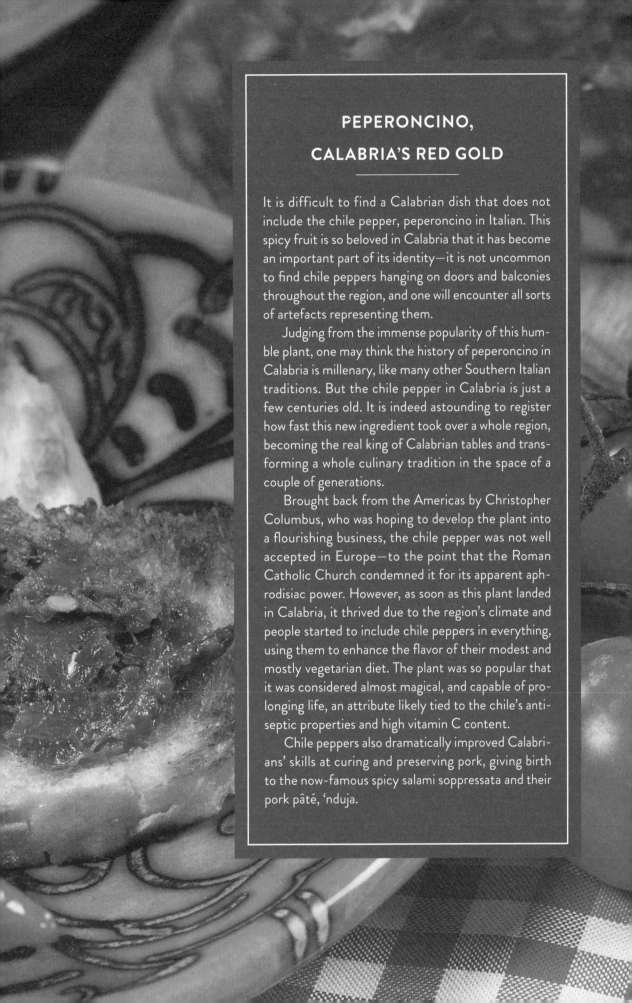

PEPERONCINO,
CALABRIA'S RED GOLD

It is difficult to find a Calabrian dish that does not include the chile pepper, peperoncino in Italian. This spicy fruit is so beloved in Calabria that it has become an important part of its identity—it is not uncommon to find chile peppers hanging on doors and balconies throughout the region, and one will encounter all sorts of artefacts representing them.

Judging from the immense popularity of this humble plant, one may think the history of peperoncino in Calabria is millenary, like many other Southern Italian traditions. But the chile pepper in Calabria is just a few centuries old. It is indeed astounding to register how fast this new ingredient took over a whole region, becoming the real king of Calabrian tables and transforming a whole culinary tradition in the space of a couple of generations.

Brought back from the Americas by Christopher Columbus, who was hoping to develop the plant into a flourishing business, the chile pepper was not well accepted in Europe—to the point that the Roman Catholic Church condemned it for its apparent aphrodisiac power. However, as soon as this plant landed in Calabria, it thrived due to the region's climate and people started to include chile peppers in everything, using them to enhance the flavor of their modest and mostly vegetarian diet. The plant was so popular that it was considered almost magical, and capable of prolonging life, an attribute likely tied to the chile's antiseptic properties and high vitamin C content.

Chile peppers also dramatically improved Calabrians' skills at curing and preserving pork, giving birth to the now-famous spicy salami soppressata and their pork pâté, 'nduja.

MACCHERONI AL FERRETTO CON 'NDUJA, SOPPRESSATA E CECI

YIELD: 4 SERVINGS / **ACTIVE TIME:** 20 MINUTES / **TOTAL TIME:** 24 HOURS

This pasta sauce makes a lovely use of the best-known Calabrian specialties—soppressata and 'nduja. The sauce is typically served with handmade maccheroni al ferretto, but it also goes well with more readily available pasta formats, such as fusilli.

1. Drain the chickpeas, place them in a large saucepan, and cover them with cold water. Add the rosemary and garlic, bring to a boil, and cook until the chickpeas are tender, about 45 minutes. Drain the chickpeas, reserve the cooking liquid, and set both aside.

2. Place the olive oil in a large, deep skillet and warm it over medium heat. Add the onion and soppressata and cook, stirring occasionally, until the onion has softened, about 5 minutes.

3. Add the tomatoes, reduce the heat to medium-low, and cook for 20 minutes, stirring occasionally.

4. Stir in the 'nduja and cook for 20 minutes.

5. Place half of the chickpeas in a blender and puree until smooth. Add the puree and remaining chickpeas to the sauce, season it with salt, and stir to combine.

6. Bring water to a boil in a large saucepan. Add salt, let the water return to a full boil, and add the pasta. Cook until the pasta is al dente.

7. Drain the pasta and stir it into the sauce along with some of the reserved cooking liquid. Toss to combine, top the dish with the pecorino, and enjoy.

INGREDIENTS:

½	LB. DRIED CHICKPEAS, SOAKED OVERNIGHT
1	SPRIG OF FRESH ROSEMARY
1	GARLIC CLOVE
2	TABLESPOONS EXTRA-VIRGIN OLIVE OIL
1	RED ONION, FINELY DICED
4	OZ. SOPPRESSATA, FINELY DICED
1	LB. WHOLE PEELED TOMATOES, CRUSHED
2	TABLESPOONS 'NDUJA
	SALT, TO TASTE
1	LB. MACCHERONI AL FERRETTO (SEE PAGE 43)
⅔	CUP GRATED PECORINO CHEESE

MACCHERONI AL FERRETTO
CON SUGO DI SALSICCIA

YIELD: 4 SERVINGS / **ACTIVE TIME:** 15 MINUTES / **TOTAL TIME:** 1 HOUR AND 30 MINUTES

Another simple and earthy Calabrian sauce that pairs wonderfully with homemade maccheroni al ferretto. Feel free to accompany this luscious sausage ragù with other pasta formats, such as strozzapreti.

1. Place the olive oil in a large skillet and warm it over medium-low heat. Add the onion and cook, stirring occasionally, until it has softened, about 6 minutes.

2. Add the sausages and cook, stirring occasionally, until they are browned, 8 to 10 minutes.

3. Add the tomatoes and chile, season the sauce with salt, and reduce the heat to low. Cover the pan and cook the sauce until the flavor has developed to your liking, about 1 hour.

4. Bring water to a boil in a large saucepan. Add salt, let the water return to a full boil, and add the pasta. Cook until the pasta is al dente.

5. Drain the pasta and stir it into the sauce along with the basil. Toss to combine, top the dish with the smoked ricotta, and serve.

INGREDIENTS:

¼ CUP EXTRA-VIRGIN OLIVE OIL

1 RED ONION, FINELY DICED

4 ITALIAN SAUSAGES WITH FENNEL, CASINGS REMOVED, CRUMBLED

1 LB. WHOLE PEELED TOMATOES, CRUSHED

1 MILD CHILE PEPPER, STEM AND SEEDS REMOVED, CHOPPED

SALT, TO TASTE

1 LB. MACCHERONI AL FERRETTO (SEE PAGE 43)

HANDFUL OF FRESH BASIL

⅔ CUP SMOKED AGED RICOTTA CHEESE, GRATED

MACCHERONI AL FERRETTO
CON 'NDUJA E RICOTTA

YIELD: 4 SERVINGS / **ACTIVE TIME:** 10 MINUTES / **TOTAL TIME:** 20 MINUTES

This simple Calabrian sauce is outrageously good and extremely easy to make. It uses a large amount of 'nduja in place of tomato sauce, and the spiciness is toned down by the addition of ricotta cheese, which also adds creaminess.

1. Bring water to a boil in a large saucepan. Place the olive oil in a large, deep skillet and warm it over medium heat. Add the onion and shallot and cook, stirring occasionally, until they have softened, about 5 minutes.

2. Add the 'nduja and cook, stirring frequently, for 5 minutes.

3. Place the ricotta and Parmesan in a bowl and stir to combine.

4. Add salt, let the water return to a full boil, and add the pasta. Cook until the pasta is al dente. Add ½ cup of pasta water to the ricotta mixture and stir to incorporate.

5. Drain the pasta and stir it into the sauce along with the ricotta mixture. Toss quickly to combine and serve.

INGREDIENTS:

¼	CUP EXTRA-VIRGIN OLIVE OIL
1	RED ONION, FINELY DICED
1	SHALLOT, FINELY DICED
7	OZ. 'NDUJA, CHOPPED
11	OZ. RICOTTA CHEESE
3	OZ. PARMESAN CHEESE, GRATED
	SALT, TO TASTE
1	LB. MACCHERONI AL FERRETTO (SEE PAGE 43)

THE CALABRIAN OBSESSION
WITH SPICY PORK

Up until relatively recent times, Calabrian cuisine was mostly vegetarian, and the use of meat was limited to pork. This is because it was inexpensive to raise a pig in one's yard, feeding it whatever food scraps happened to be available. The pig was then slaughtered and its meats were used to make sausages, lard, and guanciale, products that could last over several months of careful rationing.

Apparently, it was not always easy to cure the meat in Calabria's weather, which led at times to poor preservation of the pork. This changed drastically when Calabrians successfully learned to grow and use chile pepper during the eighteenth century. They quickly incorporated this new ingredient into their meat processing, to spectacular results.

'Nduja is a spreadable sausage characteristic of the Mount Poro area, on the Tyrrhenian coast of Calabria. It is made from the least valuable parts of the pig and a considerable amount of Calabrian hot pepper, and then smoked. Thanks to the elevated Vitamin C content of the chile pepper, 'nduja does not need preservatives. It is used as a bread spread, alone or with cheese, as well as in pasta sauces and on pizza.

Another famed sausage from Calabria is Salsiccia di Calabrese D.O.P. This sausage is made from the pig's shoulder, bottom rib, and lard. This sausage has two subtypes—piccante (spicy) and dolce (sweet)—determined by what kind of pepper is incorporated.

Finally, you have the best known of the bunch—soppressata. Technically a salami, soppressata is made with the noblest parts of the pig: the leg and the shoulder. It is commonly believed that its preparation was born from the need to find an alternative use of these highly prized parts, as the winters in some Calabrian towns are too short to properly cure a ham, which is the typical destination for the leg and shoulder. Soppressata only needs to be aged for two months, making it much easier to handle. This salami is made with very little fat added (about 15 percent), making it one of the leanest Italian salami. Both sweet and spicy chile peppers are added as well, and these chiles should come from the same area where 'nduja is produced, Mount Poro. This cultivar of chile pepper—in addition to having a balanced quantity of capsaicin which keeps it from being exasperatingly spicy—has a pulp that dries quickly and uniformly, avoiding excess humidity that would compromise the success of the salami. Once stuffed, the soppressata are pricked to make small holes in the casing, placed in perforated containers, stacked one on top of the other, and then pressed by a weight placed on top. In this way, the liquids contained in the meat will be expelled, allowing for a faster and safer curing. Afterward, the soppressata are hung and lightly smoked with aromatic woods and/or citrus peels.

LAGANE E CECI

YIELD: 4 SERVINGS / **ACTIVE TIME:** 15 MINUTES / **TOTAL TIME:** 24 HOURS

Popular across the whole South of Italy but particularly dear to Calabrian people, lagane e ceci is possibly the oldest pasta dish. This simple meal was already established enough to be celebrated by the Latin poet Horace some 2,000 years ago: "inde domum me ad porris et ciceri refero laganique catinum," which translates as "and so I come back home, to my plate of chickpeas, leeks and lagane." The original recipe did not include tomatoes, of course, but for the last couple of centuries they have been welcome. If you don't want to make lagane, pappardelle and fettuccine are good substitutes.

1. Drain the chickpeas, place them in a large saucepan, and cover them with cold water. Add the rosemary and 1 garlic clove, bring to a boil, and cook until the chickpeas are tender, about 45 minutes. Drain the chickpeas, reserve the cooking liquid, and set both aside.

2. Place the olive oil in a large skillet and warm it over medium heat. Add the remaining garlic and cook, stirring frequently, for 2 minutes.

3. Add the tomatoes and bay leaves and cook, stirring occasionally, until the tomatoes have collapsed, about 20 minutes.

4. Remove the garlic and discard it. Season the sauce with red pepper flakes and salt and stir in the chickpeas. Reduce the heat to low and cook the sauce for 20 minutes.

5. Bring water to a boil in a large saucepan. Add salt, let the water return to a full boil, and add the pasta. Cook until the pasta is al dente.

6. Reserve 1 cup pasta water, drain the pasta, and stir it into the sauce.

7. Toss to combine, adding pasta water as needed to get the right consistency. Serve immediately.

INGREDIENTS:

14 OZ. DRIED CHICKPEAS, SOAKED OVERNIGHT

1   SPRIG OF FRESH ROSEMARY

3   GARLIC CLOVES, HALVED

2   TABLESPOONS EXTRA-VIRGIN OLIVE OIL

11 OZ. WHOLE PEELED TOMATOES, LIGHTLY CRUSHED

2   BAY LEAVES

RED PEPPER FLAKES, TO TASTE

SALT, TO TASTE

1   LB. LAGANE (SEE PAGE 44) OR DRY PAPPARDELLE OR FETTUCCINE (BEST IF WITHOUT EGGS)

PASTA CON MOLLICA E PEPE ROSSO

YIELD: 4 SERVINGS / ACTIVE TIME: 15 MINUTES / TOTAL TIME: 25 MINUTES

Another delicious and easy to make Calabrian classic. This dish is perfect when one is in a rush and has next to nothing in the pantry.

1. Place three-quarters of the olive oil in a large skillet and warm it over medium heat. Add the garlic and cook, stirring frequently, for 2 minutes.

2. Stir in a generous amount of cayenne pepper, remove the pan from heat, and set it aside.

3. Place the remaining olive oil in a large skillet and warm it over medium heat. Add the bread crumbs and cook, stirring, until they are browned.

4. Bring water to a boil in a large saucepan. Add salt, let the water return to a full boil, and add the pasta. Cook until the pasta is al dente.

5. Drain the pasta and place it in a serving dish. Add the infused oil and bread crumbs, quickly toss to combine, and serve.

INGREDIENTS:

¼ CUP EXTRA-VIRGIN OLIVE OIL

3 GARLIC CLOVES, HALVED

CAYENNE PEPPER, TO TASTE

7 OZ. STALE BREAD, CRUSTS REMOVED, CRUMBLED

SALT, TO TASTE

1 LB. SPAGHETTI

PASTA CON 'NDUJA E ZUCCA GIALLA

YIELD: 4 SERVINGS / **ACTIVE TIME:** 30 MINUTES / **TOTAL TIME:** 50 MINUTES

Another delicious way to savor Calabrian 'nduja is with creamy butternut squash, which is called zucca in Italian. Zucca means both pumpkin and butternut squash, but most of the time it should be translated as the latter, as pumpkin is only popular in a few regions in Northern Italy.

1. Place the olive oil in a large, deep skillet and warm it over medium-low heat. Add the garlic and onion and cook, stirring frequently, for 5 minutes.

2. Add the butternut squash, cover the pan, and cook until the squash is tender, about 20 minutes.

3. Remove the garlic and discard it. Add the 'nduja and mash it and the squash with a wooden spoon. Season with salt and pepper.

4. Bring water to a boil in a large saucepan. Add salt, let the water return to a full boil, and add the pasta. Cook until the pasta is al dente.

5. Drain the pasta, add it to the sauce, and toss to combine. Garnish the dish with pecorino and serve.

INGREDIENTS:

3 TABLESPOONS EXTRA-VIRGIN OLIVE OIL

1 GARLIC CLOVE, HALVED

1 ONION, FINELY DICED

2 LBS. BUTTERNUT SQUASH, PEELED AND CUBED

2 TABLESPOONS 'NDUJA

SALT AND PEPPER, TO TASTE

1 LB. MACCHERONI AL FERRETTO (SEE PAGE 43)

PECORINO CHEESE, GRATED, FOR GARNISH

PASTA ALLA IONICA

YIELD: 4 SERVINGS / **ACTIVE TIME:** 30 MINUTES / **TOTAL TIME:** 50 MINUTES

This pasta dish is typical of both Apulia and the eastern coast of Calabria, since alla Ionica means "the Ionian way," and both regions face that side of the Mediterranean Sea. Instead of the Maccheroni al Ferretto, consider using bucatini or long fusilli.

1. Bring water to a boil in a large saucepan and prepare an ice bath. Add the tomatoes and peppers, boil for 1 minute, and drain. Plunge them into the ice bath, drain them, and remove the skins.

2. Remove the stem and seeds from the peppers and discard them. Place the tomatoes and peppers in a food processor, puree until smooth, and set the mixture aside.

3. Place the olive oil in a large, deep skillet and warm it over medium-low heat. Add the garlic and cook, stirring frequently, for 2 minutes.

4. Add the guanciale and cook, stirring frequently, until its fat has rendered.

5. Add the tomato-and-pepper puree and cook for 20 minutes, stirring occasionally.

6. Remove the garlic and discard it. Add the basil, season the sauce with salt, and continue cooking it over low heat.

7. Bring water to a boil in a large saucepan. Add salt, let the water return to a full boil, and add the pasta. Cook until the pasta is al dente.

8. Drain the pasta, add it to the sauce, and toss to combine. Stir in the pecorino and serve.

INGREDIENTS:

4	TOMATOES
2	MEDIUM BELL PEPPERS
2	TABLESPOONS EXTRA-VIRGIN OLIVE OIL
2	GARLIC CLOVES, HALVED
12	OZ. GUANCIALE, HARD SKIN REMOVED, CUT INTO STRIPS
2	HANDFULS OF FRESH BASIL
	SALT, TO TASTE
1	LB. MACCHERONI AL FERRETTO (SEE PAGE 43)
1	CUP GRATED PECORINO CHEESE

POLPETTE DI RICOTTA IN BRODO

YIELD: 4 SERVINGS / **ACTIVE TIME:** 40 MINUTES / **TOTAL TIME:** 1 HOUR

A light but protein-rich soup that is very easy to prepare. Characteristic of Calabria but also of Basilicata, it is the perfect comfort food for a cold day. To make this soup more substantial, serve it with toasted sourdough bread or large croutons.

1. Place all of the ingredients, except for the broth, in a mixing bowl and stir until well combined. Place the mixture in the refrigerator and chill for 30 minutes.

2. Place the broth in a medium saucepan and bring it to a boil.

3. Form the mixture into 1 oz. balls and slip them into the broth. Cook the ricotta balls for 10 minutes.

4. Ladle the soup into warmed bowls and enjoy.

INGREDIENTS:

1½ CUPS RICOTTA CHEESE (MADE FROM SHEEP'S MILK PREFERRED), DRAINED

¼ CUP GRATED PARMESAN CHEESE

⅔ CUP BREAD CRUMBS

2 HANDFULS OF FRESH PARSLEY, FINELY CHOPPED

1 EGG

SALT AND PEPPER, TO TASTE

6 CUPS BRODO VEGETALE (SEE PAGE 806)

PASTA CHJINA

YIELD: 6 SERVINGS / **ACTIVE TIME:** 1 HOUR / **TOTAL TIME:** 1 HOUR AND 30 MINUTES

Pasta chjina is traditionally eaten during festive family gatherings in Calabria—the Ferragosto festival on August 15 in particular, which is a big celebration in Calabria. Generally prepared a day ahead, it can be eaten cold or warm and thus is an easy dish to take along to family outings or to the homes of one's friends.

1. Place the bread and milk in a bowl and let the bread soak for 15 minutes.

2. Drain the bread, squeeze it to remove as much liquid as possible, and place it in a large mixing bowl. Add the beef, egg, egg yolk, and ¼ cup of pecorino, season the mixture with salt, and work the mixture until it is well combined. Form the mixture into 1 oz. balls.

3. Place the bread crumbs in a shallow bowl and dredge the meatballs in them until the meatballs are evenly coated.

4. Add olive oil to a large, deep skillet until it is about 1 inch deep and warm it over medium heat. Add the meatballs and cook them until they are browned all over, turning them as necessary. Transfer the cooked meatballs to a paper towel–lined plate to drain.

5. Place the olive oil in a large skillet and warm it over medium-low heat. Add the onion and cook, stirring frequently, until it has softened, about 6 minutes.

6. Add the tomatoes and basil, partially cover the pan, and cook, stirring occasionally, for 20 minutes. Season the sauce with salt and set it aside.

7. Preheat the oven to 390°F. Bring water to a boil in a large saucepan. Add salt, let the water return to a full boil, and add the pasta. Cook until the pasta is very al dente.

8. Drain the pasta, place it in a large bowl, and add the meatballs, eggs, soppressata, caciocavallo, two-thirds of the sauce, and two-thirds of the remaining pecorino. Gently stir to combine.

9. Transfer the mixture to a 13 x 9–inch baking pan and top it with the remaining sauce and pecorino. Place the pan in the oven and bake the chjina until the filling is bubbly, 15 to 20 minutes.

10. Remove the chjina from the oven and let it rest for 15 minutes before slicing and serving.

INGREDIENTS:

- 3½ OZ. DAY-OLD BREAD, CHOPPED
- 2 TABLESPOONS MILK
- 12 OZ. GROUND BEEF
- 1 EGG
- 1 EGG YOLK
- 1½ CUPS GRATED PECORINO OR PARMESAN CHEESE
- SALT, TO TASTE
- 1 CUP BREAD CRUMBS
- 2 TABLESPOONS EXTRA-VIRGIN OLIVE OIL, PLUS MORE AS NEEDED
- ½ RED ONION, FINELY DICED
- 2 LBS. WHOLE PEELED TOMATOES, LIGHTLY CRUSHED
- FRESH BASIL, TORN, TO TASTE
- 1 LB. RIGATONI
- 3 HARD-BOILED EGGS, CUT INTO WEDGES
- 6 OZ. SOPPRESSATA, CHOPPED
- 6 OZ. CACIOCAVALLO CHEESE, CUBED

PARMIGIANA DI MELANZANE ALLA CALABRESE

YIELD: 4 SERVINGS / ACTIVE TIME: 1 HOUR / TOTAL TIME: 3 HOURS

Eggplant parmesan is common to the whole South of Italy, but the most renowned versions are from Naples, Sicily, and Calabria. As is often the case, in addition to the regional variations, every family has its own recipe. This one is my rendition of the parmigiana di melanzane that my Calabrian grandmother used to make. It's a decadent and delicious flavor bomb, and one I deeply miss having delivered directly from my nonna's hands.

1. Slice the eggplants thin lengthwise; if you have a mandoline available, use it on a rather thick setting. Layer the sliced eggplants in a colander, seasoning each layer with coarse salt. Fill a large saucepan with water and place it on top of the eggplants. Let the eggplants drain for 1 hour.

2. Rinse the eggplants and squeeze them to remove as much water as possible. Place the eggplants on kitchen towels and let them dry.

3. Preheat the oven to 375°F. Add olive oil to a narrow, deep, heavy-bottomed saucepan with high edges until it is about 2 inches deep and warm it to 350°F.

4. Place the eggs in a bowl, season them lightly with fine salt, and whisk until scrambled. Place flour in a shallow bowl and dredge the eggplants in the flour and then in the egg until they are completely coated.

5. Gently slip the eggplants into the hot oil and fry until they are golden brown, working in batches to avoid crowding the pot. Transfer the fried eggplants to a paper towel–lined plate to drain.

6. Cover the bottom of a 13 x 9–inch baking dish with some of the tomato sauce. Arrange the eggplants, sauce, basil, hard-boiled eggs, provola, Parmesan, pecorino, and salami in individual layers in the dish, continuing the layering process until everything has been used up.

7. Top the dish with tomato sauce, provola, and pecorino, place it in the oven, and bake until the top starts to brown, about 30 minutes.

8. Remove the parmigiana from the oven and let it rest for at least 1 hour before slicing and serving.

INGREDIENTS:

4	LARGE EGGPLANTS
	SALT (COARSE AND FINE), TO TASTE
	EXTRA-VIRGIN OLIVE OIL, AS NEEDED
4	EGGS
	ALL-PURPOSE FLOUR, AS NEEDED
3½	CUPS SUGO AL BASILICO (SEE PAGE 806), PLUS MORE FOR TOPPING
2	HANDFULS OF FRESH BASIL
6	HARD-BOILED EGGS, CUT INTO THICK SLICES
9	OZ. FRESH PROVOLA CHEESE, SLICED, PLUS MORE FOR TOPPING
1⅓	CUPS GRATED PARMESAN CHEESE
1½	CUPS GRATED PECORINO CHEESE, PLUS MORE FOR TOPPING
7	OZ. SPICY SALAMI (IDEALLY FROM CALABRIA), SLICED

'NDRUPPECHE: PASTA AL RAGÙ ALLA POTENTINA

YIELD: 4 SERVINGS / **ACTIVE TIME:** 30 MINUTES / **TOTAL TIME:** 1 HOUR AND 30 MINUTES

The term 'ndruppeche means to step over something, and here it refers to the feeling of stepping over pieces of meat and salami while eating this typical Lucanian pasta dish. The original version includes slow-cooked pieces of meat and a local salami made with pork scraps, but modern versions, such as the one below, rely on more readily available ingredients.

1. Place the olive oil in a large, deep skillet and warm it over medium heat. Add the garlic and cook, stirring frequently, for 2 minutes.

2. Add the beef and salami and cook, stirring occasionally, until the meat is browned, about 8 minutes.

3. Add the wine and cook until it has evaporated.

4. Add the tomatoes and bay leaves, reduce the heat to low, partially cover the pan, and cook for 1 hour.

5. Bring water to a boil in a large saucepan. Add salt, let the water return to a full boil, and add the pasta. Cook until the pasta is al dente.

6. Remove the bay leaves from the sauce and discard them. Drain the pasta, stir it into the sauce, and toss to combine. Garnish the dish with horseradish and serve.

INGREDIENTS:

3	TABLESPOONS EXTRA-VIRGIN OLIVE OIL
1	GARLIC CLOVE, HALVED
5	OZ. GROUND BEEF
⅔	CUP CUBED THICK ITALIAN SALAMI
½	CUP DRY WHITE WINE
1	LB. WHOLE PEELED TOMATOES, LIGHTLY CRUSHED
2	BAY LEAVES
	SALT, TO TASTE
1	LB. MACCHERONI AL FERRETTO (SEE PAGE 43) OR STROZZAPRETI
	FRESH HORSERADISH, GRATED, FOR GARNISH

ZUPPA DI ASPARAGI E UOVA

YIELD: 4 SERVINGS / **ACTIVE TIME:** 30 MINUTES / **TOTAL TIME:** 45 MINUTES

In spring and early summer, it is very easy to gather delicious wild asparagus while walking through the forests of Basilicata, and this soup is a typical local way to enjoy the bounty.

1. Place the water in a large saucepan and bring it to a boil. Separate the asparagus into stems and tips. Chop the stems and set the tips aside.

2. Add salt and the asparagus stems to the water and boil for 5 minutes.

3. Add the tips to the boiling water and boil until they are just tender.

4. Place the eggs, egg whites, and pecorino in a bowl and whisk to combine.

5. Stir the mixture into the broth and serve immediately.

INGREDIENTS:

8	CUPS WATER
1	LB. ASPARAGUS, TRIMMED
	SALT, TO TASTE
2	EGGS
2	EGG WHITES
¼	CUP GRATED PECORINO OR PARMESAN CHEESE
¼	CUP EXTRA-VIRGIN OLIVE OIL

HORSERADISH: THE POOR MAN'S TRUFFLE

Horseradish, rafano in Italian, is probably native to Central Europe and was possibly brought to Southern Italy in the Middle Ages by the Normans.

Horseradish thrives in cool and water-rich places, like the Lucanian Apennines, where it grows wild and is therefore widely available and cheap, so much so that in Potenza it is called the "truffle of the poor."

In Basilicata, this root is mostly grated on pasta and soups, but also appears in fish and meat courses. Being a seasonal plant, it was used fresh from January to March, and preserved in olive oil during the rest of the year. Nowadays, it is available fresh year-round.

Probably the most traditional Lucanian dish with horseradish is rafanata, which is served at the Catholic carnival celebrations that take place in the middle of the harvest.

ORECCHIETTE ALLA MATERANA

YIELD: 4 SERVINGS / **ACTIVE TIME:** 30 MINUTES / **TOTAL TIME:** 1 HOUR AND 40 MINUTES

In Matera, the main city in the Basilicata region, it is traditional to serve orecchiette baked with this luscious lamb-based tomato sauce.

1. Place the olive oil in a large, deep skillet and warm it over medium heat. Add the lamb and cook, stirring occasionally, until it is browned, about 8 minutes.

2. Add the wine and cook until it has evaporated.

3. Add the tomatoes, reduce the heat to low, partially cover the pan, and cook for 1 hour.

4. Bring water to a boil in a large saucepan. Add salt, let the water return to a full boil, and add the pasta. Cook until the pasta is very al dente.

5. Drain the pasta, place it in a large mixing bowl, and add the sauce. Stir to combine.

6. Preheat the oven to 360°F. Place one-third of the pasta in a layer on the bottom of a 13 x 9–inch baking pan and top it with a layer of the mozzarella and pecorino. Repeat the layering process two more times.

7. Place the dish in the oven and bake until the cheese is bubbling, 20 to 25 minutes.

8. Remove the materana from the oven and let it rest for 10 minutes before serving.

INGREDIENTS:

- 3 TABLESPOONS EXTRA-VIRGIN OLIVE OIL
- 12 OZ. LEAN LAMB, CUT INTO VERY SMALL PIECES
- ½ CUP DRY WHITE WINE
- 1½ LBS. WHOLE PEELED TOMATOES, LIGHTLY CRUSHED
  SALT, TO TASTE
- 1 LB. ORECCHIETTE (SEE PAGE 47)
- 1⅔ CUPS DICED MOZZARELLA CHEESE
- 1⅔ CUPS GRATED PECORINO CHEESE

STRASCINATI ALLA MENTA

YIELD: 4 SERVINGS / **ACTIVE TIME**: 10 MINUTES / **TOTAL TIME**: 25 MINUTES

A very simple and fresh way to serve the Lucanian strascinati pasta, which is typically home-made and very similar to orecchiette, which, you might have guessed, makes an excellent substitute. The traditional recipe, which is presented here, features a local dried sweet pepper called peperone crusco, but a tiny piece of dried hot chile pepper can be substituted for those who reside far away from Basilicata.

1. Place the lard and pepper in a large skillet and warm the mixture over medium-low heat for 5 minutes.

2. Bring water to a boil in a large saucepan. Add salt, let the water return to a full boil, and add the pasta. Cook until the pasta is al dente.

3. Drain the pasta, add it to the skillet along with the mint, and toss to coat.

4. Garnish the dish with horseradish and enjoy.

INGREDIENTS:

3½   OZ. LARD, CHOPPED

1   DRIED CRUSCO PEPPER, STEM AND SEEDS REMOVED, CHOPPED

      SALT, TO TASTE

1   LB. STRASCINATI

3   TABLESPOONS CHOPPED FRESH MINT

      FRESH HORSERADISH, GRATED, FOR GARNISH

TIMBALLO DI RISO ALLA LUCANA

YIELD: 4 SERVINGS / **ACTIVE TIME:** 40 MINUTES / **TOTAL TIME:** 1 HOUR AND 30 MINUTES

Rice never really became a staple food in Southern Italy, but there are a few classic dishes based around the grain, such as this casserole from Basilicata. Due to its rich filling, timballo di riso alla lucana is perfect for a large group.

1. To begin preparations for the meatballs, place the bread and water in a bowl and let the bread soak for 15 minutes.

2. Drain the bread, squeeze it to remove as much liquid as possible, and place it in a large mixing bowl. Add the veal, egg, garlic, parsley, and pecorino, season the mixture with salt, and work the mixture until it is well combined. Form the mixture into 1 oz. balls.

3. Place the olive oil in a large, deep skillet and warm it over medium heat. Add the meatballs and cook them until they are browned all over, turning them as necessary. Transfer the cooked meatballs to a paper towel–lined plate to drain.

4. To begin preparations for the timballo, place the olive oil in a large skillet and warm it over medium heat. Add the chicken liver and sausage and cook until they are browned all over, about 8 minutes, stirring occasionally.

5. Preheat the oven to 390°F. Bring water to a boil in a large saucepan. Add salt, let the water return to a full boil, and add the rice. Cook until the rice is tender, about 15 minutes.

6. Coat a 13 x 9–inch baking pan with butter and bread crumbs. Drain the rice and spread half of it over the bottom of the baking dish. Cover the rice with the meatballs, sausage, chicken liver, eggs, provolone, and pecorino and season with pepper. Cover with the remaining rice and sprinkle pecorino generously over the top.

7. Place the timballo in the oven and bake for 20 minutes.

8. Remove the timballo from the oven and let it rest for 10 minutes before serving.

INGREDIENTS:

FOR THE MEATBALLS

2½ OZ. DAY-OLD BREAD, CHOPPED

2 TABLESPOONS WATER

6 OZ. GROUND VEAL

1 EGG

½ GARLIC CLOVE, MINCED

1 TABLESPOON FINELY CHOPPED FRESH PARSLEY

2 TABLESPOONS GRATED PECORINO CHEESE

SALT, TO TASTE

2 TABLESPOONS EXTRA-VIRGIN OLIVE OIL

FOR THE TIMBALLO

3 TABLESPOONS EXTRA-VIRGIN OLIVE OIL

3½ OZ. CHICKEN LIVER, CUBED

6 OZ. ITALIAN SAUSAGE, CASINGS REMOVED, CRUMBLED

SALT AND PEPPER, TO TASTE

1 LB. ARBORIO RICE

BUTTER, AS NEEDED

BREAD CRUMBS, AS NEEDED

2 HARD-BOILED EGGS, DICED

6 OZ. PROVOLONE CHEESE, SLICED THIN

¼ CUP GRATED PECORINO CHEESE, PLUS MORE FOR TOPPING

PASTA AL RAGÙ CON RAFANO E MOLLICA

YIELD: 4 SERVINGS / **ACTIVE TIME:** 30 MINUTES / **TOTAL TIME:** 1 HOUR AND 40 MINUTES

A very traditional Lucanian pasta sauce that features an earthy pork ragù, horseradish, and toasted bread crumbs.

1. Place 2 tablespoons of olive oil in a large, deep skillet and warm it over medium heat. Add the sausage and pork and cook, stirring occasionally, until they are browned, about 8 minutes.

2. Add the tomatoes, reduce the heat to low, partially cover the pan, and cook for 1 hour.

3. Place the remaining olive oil in a small skillet and warm it over medium heat. Add the bread crumbs and cook, stirring occasionally, until they have browned. Remove the pan from heat and set it aside.

4. Bring water to a boil in a large saucepan. Add salt, let the water return to a full boil, and add the pasta. Cook until the pasta is al dente.

5. Drain the pasta, place it in a large serving dish, and add the sauce and bread crumbs. Toss to combine, garnish with horseradish and pecorino, and enjoy.

INGREDIENTS:

3	TABLESPOONS EXTRA-VIRGIN OLIVE OIL
1	ITALIAN SAUSAGE, CASING REMOVED, CRUMBLED
6	OZ. LEAN PORK, CUBED
1	LB. WHOLE PEELED TOMATOES, LIGHTLY CRUSHED
¼	CUP BREAD CRUMBS
	SALT, TO TASTE
1	LB. FUSILLI AL FERRO (SEE PAGE 39)
	FRESH HORSERADISH, GRATED, FOR GARNISH
	PECORINO CHEESE, GRATED, FOR GARNISH

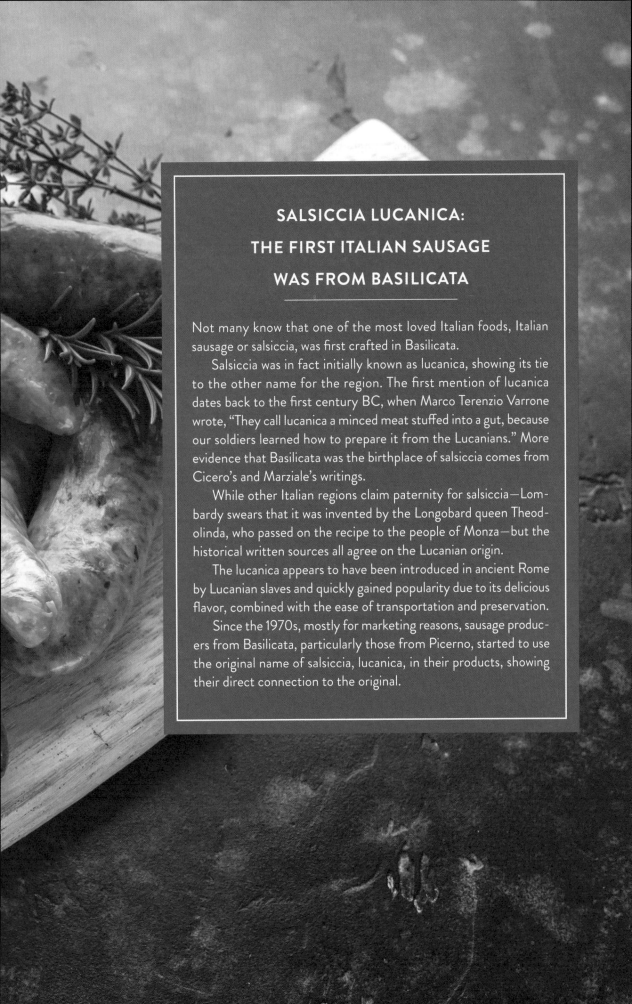

SALSICCIA LUCANICA:
THE FIRST ITALIAN SAUSAGE
WAS FROM BASILICATA

Not many know that one of the most loved Italian foods, Italian sausage or salsiccia, was first crafted in Basilicata.

Salsiccia was in fact initially known as lucanica, showing its tie to the other name for the region. The first mention of lucanica dates back to the first century BC, when Marco Terenzio Varrone wrote, "They call lucanica a minced meat stuffed into a gut, because our soldiers learned how to prepare it from the Lucanians." More evidence that Basilicata was the birthplace of salsiccia comes from Cicero's and Marziale's writings.

While other Italian regions claim paternity for salsiccia—Lombardy swears that it was invented by the Longobard queen Theodolinda, who passed on the recipe to the people of Monza—but the historical written sources all agree on the Lucanian origin.

The lucanica appears to have been introduced in ancient Rome by Lucanian slaves and quickly gained popularity due to its delicious flavor, combined with the ease of transportation and preservation.

Since the 1970s, mostly for marketing reasons, sausage producers from Basilicata, particularly those from Picerno, started to use the original name of salsiccia, lucanica, in their products, showing their direct connection to the original.

SPAGHETTI ALL'ASSASSINA

YIELD: 4 SERVINGS / **ACTIVE TIME:** 30 MINUTES / **TOTAL TIME:** 50 MINUTES

Spaghetti all'assassina, "killer's spaghetti," does not have a centuries-long history like many Apulian recipes, but was instead created in 1967 by chef Enzo Francavilla. This pasta dish became so popular worldwide that nowadays there is an association dedicated to it: the Accademia degli spaghetti all'assassina.

1. Place the olive oil in a large, deep skillet and warm it over medium heat. Add the garlic and chiles and cook, stirring frequently, for 2 minutes.

2. Remove the garlic and discard it. Add the tomatoes, season them with salt, and cook for 10 minutes.

3. Bring water to a boil in a large saucepan. Add salt, let the water return to a full boil, and add the pasta. Cook for half of the typical cooking time, 4 to 5 minutes.

4. Using a pasta fork, remove the spaghetti from the boiling water and place it in the tomato sauce.

5. Raise the heat to medium-high and stir in the tomato paste and more olive oil.

6. Stir in the spaghetti, making sure not to break the strands, and cook until it sticks to the pan and is slightly charred.

7. Turn the spaghetti over and cook until it is slightly charred all over. Serve immediately.

INGREDIENTS:

¼	CUP EXTRA-VIRGIN OLIVE OIL, PLUS MORE TO TASTE
3	GARLIC CLOVES
	HOT CHILE PEPPERS, STEMS AND SEEDS REMOVED, MINCED, TO TASTE
19½	OZ. WHOLE PEELED TOMATOES, CHOPPED
	SALT, TO TASTE
1	LB. SPAGHETTI
2	TABLESPOONS TOMATO PASTE

TIELLA BARESE

YIELD: 4 SERVINGS / ACTIVE TIME: 50 MINUTES / TOTAL TIME: 2 HOURS

Tiella refers to the earthenware pot used to cook this rice-and-potato casserole.

1. Place 3 tablespoons of olive oil in a deep pot and warm it over medium heat. Add the mussels, cover the pot, and cook until the majority of the mussels have opened, about 5 minutes. Discard any mussels that did not open. Strain the remaining mussels, reserving the liquid. Strain the liquid and set it aside.

2. Split the mussels in half, reserving the halves containing the mussels. Set them aside.

3. Coat a Dutch oven with 2 tablespoons of olive oil and cover the bottom of the pot with the onions. Arrange half of the potatoes, half of the tomatoes, the garlic, and half of the parsley in layers on top, and season the dish with salt and pepper.

4. Add the mussels, making sure the insides of their shells are facing upwards.

5. Cover the mussels with the rice, making sure that it fills both the mussels and the empty spaces in the dish. Season the dish with salt and pepper and drizzle the remaining olive oil and the reserved liquid over the dish.

6. Arrange the remaining potatoes and tomatoes on top in layers. Top with the remaining parsley, season the dish with salt and pepper, and sprinkle the pecorino and bread crumbs over the top.

7. Pour water into the pot until the rice is covered, making sure the liquid does not reach the top layer.

8. Preheat the oven to 360°F. Cover the pot and bring it to a boil over medium heat.

9. Place the pot in the oven and bake for 40 minutes.

10. Uncover the pot and bake for another 20 minutes so that the top becomes crunchy.

11. Remove the tiella Barese from the oven and serve.

INGREDIENTS:

7	TABLESPOONS EXTRA-VIRGIN OLIVE OIL
2.2	LBS. MUSSELS, RINSED WELL AND DEBEARDED
3	ONIONS, SLICED THIN
6	POTATOES, PEELED AND SLICED THIN
1	LB. CHERRY TOMATOES, QUARTERED
1	GARLIC CLOVE, MINCED
6	TABLESPOONS FINELY CHOPPED FRESH PARSLEY
	SALT AND PEPPER, TO TASTE
12	OZ. ARBORIO RICE
3½	OZ. GRATED PECORINO CHEESE
3	TABLESPOONS BREAD CRUMBS

SPAGHETTI ALLA SAN GIUANNIN

YIELD: 4 SERVINGS / **ACTIVE TIME:** 30 MINUTES / **TOTAL TIME:** 1 HOUR AND 40 MINUTES

This is an Apulian pasta dish with tomatoes, anchovies, and capers. Initially created for the Saint John's (San Giovanni) celebrations on June 24, nowadays it is eaten all year round.

1. Place the olive oil in a large, deep skillet and warm it over medium heat. Add the garlic, chile, and anchovies and cook, stirring frequently, for 2 minutes.

2. Add the tomatoes, remove the garlic, and discard the garlic. Season the tomatoes with salt and cook for 10 minutes.

3. Add the capers and a bit of water to the pan, reduce the heat to low, and let the sauce simmer gently.

4. Bring water to a boil in a large saucepan. Add salt, let the water return to a full boil, and add the pasta. Cook until the pasta is al dente.

5. Drain the pasta, add it to the sauce, and cook for 2 to 3 minutes, tossing to combine.

6. Garnish the dish with basil and pecorino and serve.

INGREDIENTS:

¼ CUP EXTRA-VIRGIN OLIVE OIL

1 GARLIC CLOVE, HALVED

1 HOT CHILE PEPPER, STEM AND SEEDS REMOVED, MINCED

6 ANCHOVIES IN OLIVE OIL, DRAINED AND CHOPPED

19½ OZ. CHERRY TOMATOES, HALVED

SALT, TO TASTE

2 TABLESPOONS CAPERS IN BRINE, DRAINED AND RINSED

1 LB. SPAGHETTI

FRESH BASIL, TORN, FOR GARNISH

PECORINO CHEESE, GRATED, FOR GARNISH

PASTA AL RAGÙ DI POLPO

YIELD: 4 SERVINGS / **ACTIVE TIME:** 50 MINUTES / **TOTAL TIME:** 1 HOUR AND 20 MINUTES

Here's a lovely seafood-enriched pasta sauce from Apulia that is simple to make, but it does require fresh octopus, which may not always be easy to find. Once you do find it, get your fishmonger to clean the octopus for you. Otherwise, carefully clean it at home, following one of the many available online tutorials. The ideal pasta for this sauce is fresh scialatielli, but dried linguine also works well.

1. Rinse the octopus thoroughly under cold water and let it drain.

2. Cut the octopus into large pieces, leaving 4 tentacles whole.

3. Place the olive oil in a large, deep skillet and warm it over medium heat. Add the garlic, onion, and chile and cook, stirring frequently, for 5 minutes.

4. Add the octopus and cook, stirring frequently, until it is browned.

5. Add the white wine, raise the heat to medium-high, and cook until the wine has evaporated.

6. Remove the garlic and discard it. Add the tomatoes and bay leaf, reduce the heat to low, and season the sauce with salt. Cook until the sauce has thickened and the octopus is tender, 30 to 35 minutes.

7. Bring water to a boil in a large saucepan. Add salt, let the water return to a full boil, and add the pasta. Cook until the pasta is al dente.

8. Drain the pasta, add it to the sauce, and toss to combine.

9. To serve, top each portion with a long octopus tentacle and parsley.

INGREDIENTS:

2	LBS. FRESH OCTOPUS
¼	CUP EXTRA-VIRGIN OLIVE OIL
1	GARLIC CLOVE
½	YELLOW ONION, FINELY DICED
⅓	HOT CHILE PEPPER, MINCED
½	CUP DRY WHITE WINE
2	LBS. WHOLE PEELED TOMATOES, LIGHTLY CRUSHED
1	BAY LEAF
	SALT, TO TASTE
1	LB. SCIALATIELLI (SEE PAGE 36)
	FRESH PARSLEY, CHOPPED, FOR GARNISH

ORECCHIETTE CON CIME DI RAPA

YIELD: 4 SERVINGS / **ACTIVE TIME:** 40 MINUTES / **TOTAL TIME:** 1 HOUR

Interestingly, the most famous Apulian pasta dish is almost entirely plant based, with just a hint of anchovy. Orecchiette alle cime di rapa is in fact centered around the most loved vegetable of the South (especially in Campania and Apulia), turnip greens. This vegetable has an intense and complex flavor, in which bitter, nutty, sweet, and umami are wonderfully blended.

1. Bring salted water to a boil in a large saucepan. Add the turnip greens and cook until just tender, about 5 minutes. Drain the turnip greens and set them aside.

2. Place the olive oil in a large, deep skillet and warm it over medium heat. Add the garlic, chile, and anchovies and cook, stirring frequently, for 2 minutes. Remove the pan from heat and set it aside.

3. Lightly coat a small skillet with olive oil and warm it over medium heat. Add the bread crumbs and cook, stirring occasionally, until they are browned, about 5 minutes.

4. Bring water to a boil in a large saucepan. Add salt, let the water return to a full boil, and add the pasta. Cook until the pasta is al dente.

5. Add the turnip greens to the garlic mixture and cook over medium heat for 2 to 3 minutes, tossing to combine.

6. Drain the pasta, add it to the sauce, and toss to combine.

7. Top the dish with the toasted bread crumbs and serve.

INGREDIENTS:

SALT, TO TASTE

2.2 LBS. TURNIP GREENS, RINSED WELL, WOODY STEMS REMOVED

¼ CUP EXTRA-VIRGIN OLIVE OIL, PLUS MORE AS NEEDED

2 GARLIC CLOVES, HALVED

1 HOT CHILE PEPPER, STEM AND SEEDS REMOVED, CHOPPED

8 ANCHOVIES IN OLIVE OIL, DRAINED AND CHOPPED

¼ CUP BREAD CRUMBS

1 LB. ORECCHIETTE (SEE PAGE 47)

PASTA ALLA NORMA

YIELD: 4 SERVINGS / **ACTIVE TIME:** 50 MINUTES / **TOTAL TIME:** 2 HOURS

Possibly the most popular Sicilian pasta dish, pasta alla Norma builds on Sicily's love for eggplants, which has given us many amazing culinary creations, such as this and eggplant parmigiana. The name is possibly a tribute to the opera *La Norma*, which was widely celebrated in Sicily since the composer, Bellini, was Sicilian.

1. Place the eggplants in a colander and season them with the coarse salt. Fill a large saucepan with water and place it on top of the eggplants. Let the eggplants drain for 1 hour.

2. Rinse the eggplants and squeeze them to remove as much water as possible. Place the eggplants on kitchen towels and let them dry.

3. Bring water to a boil in a large saucepan. Add the tomatoes and cook for 1 minute. Remove the tomatoes, peel them, and remove the seeds. Chop the remaining flesh and set them aside.

4. Place 2 tablespoons of olive oil in a medium saucepan and warm it over medium heat. Add the garlic and cook, stirring frequently, for 2 minutes.

5. Remove the garlic and discard it. Add the tomatoes, season with salt and pepper, and cook until the sauce starts to thicken, 20 to 30 minutes.

6. Place the remaining olive oil in a large skillet and warm it over medium-high heat. Add the eggplants and cook, stirring occasionally, until they are golden brown, 5 to 7 minutes. Transfer the eggplants to a paper towel–lined plate to drain.

7. Add the eggplants to the sauce and cook for a few minutes, stirring occasionally.

8. Bring water to a boil in a large saucepan. Add salt, let the water return to a full boil, and add the pasta. Cook until the pasta is very al dente.

9. Drain the pasta, add it to the sauce, and cook for 2 to 3 minutes, tossing to combine.

10. Garnish the dish with the ricotta salata and basil and serve.

INGREDIENTS:

2   LARGE EGGPLANTS, CUT INTO CHUNKS

¼   CUP COARSE SALT

2   LBS. TOMATOES

6   TABLESPOONS EXTRA-VIRGIN OLIVE OIL

1   GARLIC CLOVE, HALVED

     SALT AND PEPPER, TO TASTE

1   LB. RIGATONI

¼   CUP COARSELY GRATED RICOTTA SALATA CHEESE, FOR GARNISH

     HANDFUL OF FRESH BASIL, TORN, FOR GARNISH

SCURDIJATA

YIELD: 4 SERVINGS / **ACTIVE TIME:** 20 MINUTES / **TOTAL TIME:** 30 MINUTES

In old times, farmers from the Salento region of Apulia started their day with this plant-based, nutritious stew, made out of leftover vegetables and legumes, before heading to the fields. It is entirely fine to cook the vegetables just to make this dish, but it is best to make them one day ahead, as it will enhance the flavor of the final preparation.

1. Place the olive oil and bread in a large skillet and cook over medium heat, stirring occasionally, until it is golden brown. Remove the bread with a slotted spoon and place it on a paper towel–lined plate to drain.

2. Add the garlic and chile to the pan and cook, stirring frequently, for 2 minutes.

3. Remove the garlic and chile and discard them. Add the chickpeas and vegetables, season with salt and pepper, and cook, stirring vigorously and mashing the chickpeas slightly, for 10 minutes.

4. Stir in the fried bread and serve warm or cold.

INGREDIENTS:

6   TABLESPOONS EXTRA-VIRGIN OLIVE OIL

1   LB. STALE BREAD, CHOPPED

2   GARLIC CLOVES

½   HOT CHILE PEPPER, MINCED

1½   LBS. COOKED CHICKPEAS OR PEAS

2   LBS. COOKED LEAFY VEGETABLES (CHICORY, BEET GREENS, TURNIP GREENS, OR BROCCOLI RABE RECOMMENDED)

SALT AND PEPPER, TO TASTE

PASTA CON I POMODORI SECCHI

YIELD: 4 SERVINGS / ACTIVE TIME: 20 MINUTES / TOTAL TIME: 40 MINUTES

A simple yet delicious pasta dish from sunny Sicily, which is famous for its sun-dried tomatoes.

1. Place ¼ cup of olive oil in a large, deep skillet and warm it over medium heat. Add the garlic and cook, stirring frequently, for 2 minutes.

2. Remove the garlic and discard it. Add the tomatoes and cook for 5 minutes.

3. Place the remaining olive oil in a small skillet and warm it over medium heat. Add the bread crumbs and cook, stirring occasionally, until they are browned, about 5 minutes.

4. Bring water to a boil in a large saucepan. Add salt, let the water return to a full boil, and add the pasta. Cook until the pasta is very al dente.

5. Drain the pasta, add it to the sauce along with the parsley, and cook for 2 to 3 minutes, tossing to combine.

6. Garnish the dish with the bread crumbs and pecorino and serve.

INGREDIENTS:

6 TABLESPOONS EXTRA-VIRGIN OLIVE OIL

1 GARLIC CLOVE, HALVED

12 SUN-DRIED TOMATOES IN OLIVE OIL, DRAINED AND CHOPPED

3 TABLESPOONS BREAD CRUMBS

   SALT, TO TASTE

1 LB. SPAGHETTI

3 TABLESPOONS CHOPPED FRESH PARSLEY

   PECORINO CHEESE, GRATED, FOR GARNISH

PASTA CON LE SARDE

YIELD: 4 SERVINGS / **ACTIVE TIME:** 50 MINUTES / **TOTAL TIME:** 2 HOURS

Another Sicilian masterpiece, pasta con le sarde has attached to it a very detailed legend, dating back to the Middle Ages. The story goes that in the ninth century, the commander Eufemio da Messina tried to overthrow the Holy Roman Empire, but failed and was exiled. Eufemio found shelter in Africa and, moved by a spirit of revenge, led the Arabic fleets to conquer Sicily. When the fleet landed in Mazara del Vallo, Eufemio's cook had to use available ingredients to feed the troops—Sicilian sardines, wild fennel, and saffron, a flavorful trio that became this dish. Canned sardines can be used if they are unflavored, and as an alternative to wild fennel, use the fronds and tops of store-bought fennel.

1. Clean the sardines: scrub them, remove the heads, entrails, and spines, and open them completely. Rinse the sardines under running water and pat them dry with paper towels.

2. Bring water to a boil in a large saucepan. Add salt and the fennel and cook until the fennel is tender, about 10 minutes. Remove the fennel from the boiling water with a strainer or slotted spoon and set it aside. When the fennel has cooled slightly, chop it. Keep the water at a gentle boil.

3. Place the saffron in ½ cup water and let it steep.

4. Place the olive oil in a large skillet and warm it over medium heat. Add the onion and anchovies and cook, stirring occasionally, until the onion has softened and the anchovies have dissolved, about 5 minutes.

5. Add the saffron, saffron water, sardines, and fennel. Drain the raisins, squeeze them to remove any excess liquid, and add them to the pan. Cook until the sardines are cooked through and the sauce has thickened, about 10 minutes.

6. While the sauce is cooking, place the bread crumbs in a skillet and toast them over medium heat until they are browned, shaking the pan occasionally.

7. Add the pasta to the boiling water and cook until it is al dente.

8. Drain the pasta and add it to the sauce along with the bread crumbs, pine nuts, and almonds. Toss to combine, season with salt and pepper, remove the pan from heat, and let the dish sit for a few minutes before serving.

INGREDIENTS:

1	LB. FRESH SARDINES
	SALT AND PEPPER, TO TASTE
7	OZ. WILD FENNEL, RINSED WELL
	PINCH OF SAFFRON THREADS
¼	CUP EXTRA-VIRGIN OLIVE OIL
1	LARGE WHITE ONION, FINELY DICED
5	ANCHOVIES IN OLIVE OIL, DRAINED, RINSED, AND CHOPPED
3	TABLESPOONS RAISINS, SOAKED IN WARM WATER
3	TABLESPOONS BREAD CRUMBS
1	LB. BUCATINI
3	TABLESPOONS PINE NUTS
3	TABLESPOONS BLANCHED ALMONDS, FINELY CHOPPED

PASTA E LATTUGA

YIELD: 4 SERVINGS / **ACTIVE TIME:** 10 MINUTES / **TOTAL TIME:** 25 MINUTES

The simplest and most humble pasta dish one could imagine, this is a vegetable soup still popular in the Sicilian countryside. It requires only fresh romaine lettuce, short-cut pasta, and good olive oil.

1. Bring the water to a boil in a large saucepan. Add salt—less than you would for a typical pasta dish.

2. Add the pasta and lettuce and cook until the pasta is al dente.

3. Ladle the soup into warmed bowls, top each portion with some of the olive oil, and enjoy.

INGREDIENTS:

8	CUPS WATER
	SALT, TO TASTE
½	LB. MACARONI OR OTHER SHORT-FORM PASTA
1	HEAD OF ROMAINE LETTUCE, WASHED AND CHOPPED
2	TABLESPOONS EXTRA-VIRGIN OLIVE OIL, FOR GARNISH

PASTA CHI VRUOCCOLI ARRIMINATI

YIELD: 4 SERVINGS / **ACTIVE TIME:** 50 MINUTES / **TOTAL TIME:** 2 HOURS

Typical of the main city of Sicily, Palermo, pasta chi vruoccoli arriminati means "pasta with frequently stirred broccoli"—in Sicily, they call cauliflower "broccoli," since they have a green variety. Stirring repeatedly creates the creamy richness you want in a pasta dish.

1. Bring water to a boil in a large saucepan. Add salt and the cauliflower and cook until the cauliflower is tender, about 10 minutes. Remove the cauliflower from the boiling water with a strainer or slotted spoon and set it aside. Keep the water at a gentle boil.

2. Place 1 tablespoon of olive oil in a small skillet and warm it over medium heat. Add the bread crumbs, season them with salt, and cook, stirring occasionally, until they have browned, about 4 minutes. Remove the pan from heat and set it aside.

3. Place the remaining olive oil in a large skillet and warm it over medium heat. Add the onions and anchovies and cook, stirring occasionally, until the onions have softened and the anchovies have dissolved, about 5 minutes.

4. Place the saffron in a cup, add a bit of the boiling water, and let the saffron steep.

5. Drain the raisins, squeeze them to remove any excess liquid, and add them to the skillet along with the pine nuts. Cook for 5 minutes.

6. Add the cauliflower, season with salt and pepper, and cook for 2 minutes. Add the saffron and saffron water and cook, stirring frequently, until the sauce becomes creamy.

7. Add the pasta to the boiling water and cook until it is al dente.

8. Drain the pasta and add it to the sauce along with the bread crumbs. Toss to combine and serve.

INGREDIENTS:

- SALT AND PEPPER, TO TASTE
- 1 HEAD OF CAULIFLOWER, CUT INTO FLORETS
- 5 TABLESPOONS EXTRA-VIRGIN OLIVE OIL
- 1 (SCANT) CUP BREAD CRUMBS
- 2 SMALL ONIONS, FINELY DICED
- 4 ANCHOVIES IN OLIVE OIL, DRAINED AND CHOPPED
- 2 PINCHES OF SAFFRON THREADS
- ⅓ CUP RAISINS, SOAKED IN WARM WATER
- ⅓ CUP PINE NUTS
- 1 LB. BUCATINI

PASTA C'ANCIOVA E MUDDICA ATTURRATA

YIELD: 4 SERVINGS / **ACTIVE TIME:** 20 MINUTES / **TOTAL TIME:** 45 MINUTES

This dish, which is also called Milanisa, was probably developed by Sicilian immigrants in Northern Italy, as it features mostly canned products, which were easy for the immigrants to carry back after visiting their families in the summer.

1. Place 1 tablespoon of olive oil in a small skillet and warm it over medium heat. Add the bread crumbs, season them with salt, and cook, stirring occasionally, until they have browned, about 4 minutes. Remove the pan from heat and set it aside.

2. Place the remaining olive oil in a large skillet and warm it over medium heat. Add the onion, garlic, and anchovies and cook, stirring occasionally, until the onion has softened and the anchovies have dissolved, about 5 minutes.

3. Drain the raisins, squeeze them to remove any excess liquid, and add them to the skillet along with the pine nuts. Cook for 5 minutes.

4. Combine the tomato paste and water and stir the mixture into the pan. Raise the heat to medium-high and cook until the sauce has thickened, 5 to 10 minutes.

5. Bring water to a boil in a large saucepan. Add salt, let the water return to a full boil, and add the pasta. Cook until the pasta is al dente.

6. Drain the pasta and add it to the sauce along with the bread crumbs. Toss to combine, season with salt and pepper, and serve.

INGREDIENTS:

5	TABLESPOONS EXTRA-VIRGIN OLIVE OIL
1	(SCANT) CUP BREAD CRUMBS
	SALT AND PEPPER, TO TASTE
½	ONION, FINELY DICED
2	GARLIC CLOVES
8	ANCHOVIES IN OLIVE OIL, DRAINED AND CHOPPED
⅓	CUP RAISINS, SOAKED IN WARM WATER
⅓	CUP PINE NUTS
1	(SCANT) CUP TOMATO PASTE
1	CUP WARM WATER
1	LB. LINGUINE

PASTA 'NCASCIATA

YIELD: 4 SERVINGS / **ACTIVE TIME:** 1 HOUR / **TOTAL TIME:** 2 HOURS AND 30 MINUTES

A rich pasta casserole typical of the city of Messina, but also common in other parts of Sicily, this dish was previously a well-kept secret but has become popular outside of Sicily, thanks to the series of books written by Andrea Camilleri in which he described his Inspector Montalbano as a big fan of the dish.

1. Place 2 tablespoons of olive oil in a large, deep skillet and warm it over medium-low heat. Add the onion and cook, stirring occasionally, until it has softened, about 6 minutes.

2. Add the beef and pork, raise the heat to medium-high, and cook, breaking the meat up with a wooden spoon, until it is browned, about 8 minutes.

3. Add the wine and cook until it has evaporated.

4. Add the tomatoes and basil, season with salt and pepper, and reduce the heat to medium-low. Partially cover the pan and cook the sauce for about 40 minutes.

5. Place the eggplants in a colander and season them with salt. Fill a large saucepan with water and place it on top of the eggplants. Let the eggplants drain for 30 minutes.

6. Rinse the eggplants and squeeze them to remove as much water as possible. Place the eggplants on kitchen towels and let them dry.

7. Place the remaining olive oil in a large skillet and warm it over medium-high heat. Add the eggplants and cook, stirring occasionally, until they are golden brown, 5 to 7 minutes. Transfer the eggplants to a paper towel–lined plate to drain.

8. Bring water to a boil in a large saucepan. Add salt, let the water return to a full boil, and add the pasta. Cook until the pasta is very al dente.

9. Drain the pasta and place it in a bowl. Add half of the sauce to the bowl and toss to combine.

10. Preheat the oven to 360°F. Coat a 13 x 9–inch baking pan with olive oil and place one-half of the pasta on the bottom. Top the pasta with a layer consisting of half of the eggplant, one-third of the caciocavallo, a few tablespoons of sauce, and one-third of the pecorino. Repeat this layering process and then top with a layer of the remaining caciocavallo and pecorino. Place the 'ncasciata in the oven and bake until the cheese is melted and bubbling, about 20 minutes. Remove the 'ncasciata from the oven and let it rest for 10 minutes before serving.

INGREDIENTS:

- 1 CUP EXTRA-VIRGIN OLIVE OIL, PLUS MORE AS NEEDED
- 1 WHITE ONION, FINELY DICED
- 6½ OZ. GROUND BEEF
- 6½ OZ. GROUND PORK
- ½ CUP DRY WHITE WINE
- 1½ LBS. WHOLE PEELED TOMATOES, LIGHTLY CRUSHED
- 2 HANDFULS OF FRESH BASIL LEAVES
-   SALT AND PEPPER, TO TASTE
- 2 LARGE EGGPLANTS, CUT INTO ½-INCH-THICK SLICES
- 1 LB. SHORT-FORM PASTA
- 9 OZ. CACIOCAVALLO CHEESE, CUBED
- 1 CUP GRATED PECORINO CHEESE

COUSCOUS ALLA TRAPANESE

YIELD: 4 SERVINGS / **ACTIVE TIME:** 1 HOUR / **TOTAL TIME:** 1 HOUR AND 30 MINUTES

Possibly the most beloved main in the city of Trapani, this is a real feast. I remember ordering it in advance at a local restaurant, and it came topped with so much fresh fish that I could eat barely eat a fifth of it—and I am a good eater. In the best places, couscous is made from coarse durum wheat flour, rolled masterfully on a wooden bench, and then steamed in a specific earthenware pot with holes in the bottom. Here comes an easier—but no less scrumptious—version.

1. Place half of the olive oil in a large, deep skillet and warm it over medium-low heat. Add the onion, garlic, almonds, and parsley and cook, stirring occasionally, until the onion has softened, about 6 minutes.

2. Add the tomato paste and cook, stirring continually, for 3 minutes.

3. Add the whiting, cover it with water, and season with salt. Raise the heat to medium and cook the fish for 30 minutes.

4. Strain the broth into a bowl and set it aside. Use the solids for another preparation if desired.

5. Cook the couscous according to the package instructions. You want the grains to be separated, and not at all sticky. If they are clumping together, add some olive oil.

6. Place the couscous in a serving bowl, add the broth, and let the mixture sit for 15 minutes.

7. Place the remaining olive oil in a large skillet and warm it over medium heat. Add the langoustines and cook until they are cooked through, about 3 minutes, turning them as necessary. Remove the langoustines from the pan and set them aside.

8. Add the clams, cover the pan, and cook until the majority of them have opened, about 5 minutes. Discard any clams that did not open. Remove the clams from the pan and set them aside.

9. Place the gurnard in the pan and cook until it is just cooked through, 6 to 8 minutes, turning it over just once.

10. Top the couscous with the langoustines, clams, and gurnard and enjoy.

INGREDIENTS:

½ CUP EXTRA-VIRGIN OLIVE OIL, PLUS MORE AS NEEDED

1 WHITE ONION, FINELY DICED

2 GARLIC CLOVES, MINCED

¾ CUP ALMONDS, FINELY CHOPPED

1 BUNCH OF FRESH PARSLEY, CHOPPED

2 TABLESPOONS TOMATO PASTE

2 LBS. WHITING FILLETS, CUT INTO LARGE PIECES

SALT, TO TASTE

10 OZ. COUSCOUS

7 OZ. LANGOUSTINES

7 OZ. CLAMS, RINSED WELL

11 OZ. GURNARD FILLETS

SPAGHETTI ALL'ARAGOSTA

YIELD: 4 SERVINGS / **ACTIVE TIME:** 30 MINUTES / **TOTAL TIME:** 1 HOUR

A representative dish of the northwest coast of Sardinia, specifically the city of Alghero.

1. Bring water to a boil in a large pot. Add salt and then the lobsters, making sure they are head down, which will minimize their pain. Cover the pot, reduce the heat to low, and cook the lobsters for 15 minutes.

2. Drain the lobsters and let them cool. When they are cool enough to handle, extract the meat from the lobsters, chop it, and set it aside.

3. Place the olive oil in a large, deep skillet and warm it over medium heat. Add the onion and garlic and cook, stirring frequently, until the onion has softened, about 5 minutes.

4. Remove the garlic and discard it. Add the tomatoes, season with salt, and cook, stirring occasionally, for 20 minutes.

5. Bring water to a boil in a large saucepan. Add salt, let the water return to a full boil, and add the pasta. Cook until the pasta is very al dente.

6. Add the lobster to the sauce. Drain the pasta, add it to the sauce, and raise the heat to medium-high. Cook for 2 to 3 minutes, tossing to combine.

7. Garnish the dish with parsley and enjoy.

INGREDIENTS:

	SALT, TO TASTE
2	MEDIUM LOBSTERS
¼	CUP EXTRA-VIRGIN OLIVE OIL
1	WHITE ONION, FINELY DICED
1	GARLIC CLOVE
1	LB. WHOLE PEELED TOMATOES, LIGHTLY CRUSHED
1	LB. SPAGHETTI
	FRESH PARSLEY, CHOPPED, FOR GARNISH

BUSIATE AL PESTO ALLA TRAPANESE

YIELD: 4 SERVINGS / **ACTIVE TIME:** 30 MINUTES / **TOTAL TIME:** 45 MINUTES

If you happen to go to Trapani, you will most certainly be tempted to buy a jar of pesto alla Trapanese. While what's in that little jar will be gone way too soon, with this easy recipe you can make it at home as often as you wish.

1. Bring water to a boil in a large saucepan. Cut a cross on the bottom of the tomatoes and add them to the boiling water. Cook for 2 minutes, remove the tomatoes with a slotted spoon, and peel them. Set the tomatoes aside. Keep the water at a boil.

2. Place the almonds, basil, and garlic in a blender and pulse until finely ground. Add the olive oil and puree until the mixture is a paste.

3. Add the tomatoes and 2 tablespoons of pecorino, season the mixture with salt, pepper, and red pepper flakes, and puree until the mixture is smooth and creamy, adding more olive oil if needed to get the desired texture.

4. Add salt, let the water return to a full boil, and add the pasta. Cook until the pasta is al dente.

5. Add a few tablespoons of pasta water to the sauce and stir to combine. Drain the pasta, place it in a bowl, and add the sauce. Toss to combine.

6. Top with the remaining pecorino and serve.

INGREDIENTS:

½   LB. TOMATOES

⅓   CUP BLANCHED ALMONDS

2½   CUPS FRESH BASIL

1   GARLIC CLOVE

2   TABLESPOONS EXTRA-VIRGIN OLIVE OIL, PLUS MORE AS NEEDED

5   TABLESPOONS GRATED PECORINO CHEESE

  SALT AND PEPPER, TO TASTE

  RED PEPPER FLAKES, TO TASTE

1   LB. BUSIATE (SEE PAGE 51)

ANELLETTI AL FORNO

YIELD: 4 SERVINGS / **ACTIVE TIME:** 1 HOUR / **TOTAL TIME:** 2 HOURS AND 30 MINUTES

Possibly the most popular Sicilian pasta bake, this dish is most closely associated with the capital, Palermo. Anelletti al forno is very similar to pasta 'ncasciata, but with an even richer filling.

1. Place 2 tablespoons of olive oil in a large, deep skillet and warm it over medium-low heat. Add the onion and cook, stirring occasionally, until it has softened, about 6 minutes.

2. Add the pork and beef, raise the heat to medium-high, and cook, breaking the meat up with a wooden spoon, until it is browned, about 8 minutes.

3. Add the wine and cook until it has evaporated.

4. Add the tomatoes and peas, season with salt and pepper, and reduce the heat to medium-low. Partially cover the pan and cook the sauce for about 40 minutes.

5. Place the eggplant in a colander and season it with salt. Fill a large saucepan with water and place it on top of the eggplant. Let the eggplant drain for 30 minutes.

6. Rinse the eggplant and squeeze it to remove as much water as possible. Place the eggplant on a kitchen towel and let it dry.

7. Place the remaining olive oil in a large skillet and warm it over medium-high heat. Add the eggplant and cook, stirring occasionally, until it is golden brown, 5 to 7 minutes. Transfer the eggplant to a paper towel–lined plate to drain.

8. Bring water to a boil in a large saucepan. Add salt, let the water return to a full boil, and add the pasta. Cook until the pasta is very al dente.

9. Drain the pasta and place it in a bowl. Add half of the sauce to the bowl and toss to combine. Preheat the oven to 360°F. Coat a 13 x 9–inch baking pan with olive oil and place half of the pasta on the bottom. Top the pasta with a layer consisting of half of the eggplant, one-third of the caciocavallo, one-third of the eggs, a few tablespoons of the sauce, and one-third of the tomino. Repeat this layering process and then top with a layer of the remaining caciocavallo and tomino.

10. Place the anelletti al forno in the oven and bake until the cheese is melted and bubbling, about 35 minutes.

11. Remove the anelletti al forno from the oven and let it rest for 10 minutes before serving.

INGREDIENTS:

1	CUP EXTRA-VIRGIN OLIVE OIL, PLUS MORE AS NEEDED
1	RED ONION, FINELY DICED
9	OZ. GROUND PORK
1	OZ. GROUND BEEF
1	CUP RED WINE
9	OZ. WHOLE PEELED TOMATOES, LIGHTLY CRUSHED
9	OZ. PEAS
	SALT AND PEPPER, TO TASTE
1	LARGE EGGPLANT, CUBED
1	LB. ANELLETTI OR OTHER SHORT-FORMAT PASTA
3½	OZ. CACIOCAVALLO CHEESE, CUBED
3	HARD-BOILED EGGS, SLICED
7	OZ. TOMINO OR PECORINO CHEESE, GRATED
2	TABLESPOONS BREAD CRUMBS

COUSCOUS: A BRIDGE BETWEEN SICILY AND AFRICA

If you happen to travel to the western end of Sicily, especially the city of Trapani, you will see couscous being served at a number restaurants. This can be puzzling to one visiting Sicily for the first time, as couscous is not widely known as an Italian specialty, but rather a North African one.

The first text that mentions couscous dates back to the thirteenth century, and was written by Ibn Razīn al-Tujībī, a Tunisian gastronomic poet. The true origin of couscous is, however, believed to have come much earlier, sometime around the seventh century among the Maghreb people inhabiting Northwest Africa.

Since couscous was known to the Arabs, and Sicily was under Arabic control until 1200, it is natural to think that couscous was brought to Sicily around that time. But it is currently believed that couscous was introduced to Sicilian cuisine much later, not making its appearance until the end of the eighteenth century.

The most likely reason for this occurrence tracks couscous back to Trapani's coral fishermen. Apparently, the fishermen found a very productive coral reef on the coast of Tunisia, and their frequent trips between Sicily and Tunisia enabled some of them to get acquainted with Tunisian cuisine, including couscous, which soon became a Trapani favorite. The fishermen's origin hypothesis is consistent with the fact that the only couscous dish that became truly Sicilian is the one with fish, known as couscous alla Trapanese.

PARMIGIANA DI MELANZANE ALLA PALERMITANA

YIELD: 4 SERVINGS / **ACTIVE TIME:** 1 HOUR / **TOTAL TIME:** 3 HOURS AND 30 MINUTES

Even if the name "parmigiana" evokes Northern Italy and the city of Parma, eggplant parmesan is most definitely a Sicilian dish—eggplants are indeed Sicily's favorite vegetable, and omnipresent in its cuisine. Being a summer dish, this version of parmigiana is generally eaten cold.

1. Slice the eggplants thin lengthwise; if you have a mandoline available, use it on a rather thick setting. Layer the sliced eggplants in a colander, seasoning each layer with coarse salt. Fill a large saucepan with water and place it on top of the eggplants. Let the eggplants drain for 1 hour.

2. Rinse the eggplants and squeeze them to remove as much water as possible. Place the eggplants on kitchen towels and let them dry.

3. Add olive oil to a narrow, deep, heavy-bottomed saucepan with high edges until it is about 2 inches deep and warm it to 350°F.

4. Gently slip the eggplants into the hot oil and fry until they are golden brown, working in batches to avoid crowding the pot. Place the fried eggplants on a paper towel–lined plate to drain.

5. Cover the bottom of a 13 x 9–inch baking pan with some of the tomato sauce. Arrange some of the eggplants, sauce, basil, and pecorino in individual layers in the dish, continuing the layering process until everything has been used up.

6. Place the parmigiana in the refrigerator and chill it for 2 to 3 hours before serving.

INGREDIENTS:

4   **LARGE EGGPLANTS**

    COARSE SALT, TO TASTE

    EXTRA-VIRGIN OLIVE OIL, AS NEEDED

3½   **CUPS SUGO AL BASILICO (SEE PAGE 806)**

2   **HANDFULS OF FRESH BASIL**

1⅓   **CUPS GRATED PECORINO OR CACIOCAVALLO CHEESE**

EGGPLANT PARMIGIANA:
A SICILIAN HERITAGE

Regional "ownership" is a matter of debate for many Italian dishes, and eggplant parmigiana, or parmigiana di melanzane, is no exception. The name evokes the Northern city of Parma and its world-famous cheese, Parmigiano Reggiano, which is an ingredient in several popular versions of this dish. However, it is likely that this name is leading us astray from the real origins of the dish, which, like lasagna, seem to be Southern.

The first parmigiana was in fact most certainly from Sicily, where eggplant was first introduced by the Arabs in the fifteenth century. Research points to the dish's name being derived, instead of from Parmesan cheese, from the way the dish is assembled. The slices being arranged side by side and then on top of one another is reminiscent of an ancient object from Palermo's construction tradition, the parmiciana—a type of window shutter.

Naples also has a version of the recipe that deserves a special mention. Neapolitan parmigiana includes mozzarella cheese and Parmesan, which may be how the latter became so powerfully associated with the dish.

It is also in Naples that parmigiana first met tomato sauce, which spread to Sicily and the rest of the South before then spreading to the North, after Italy was unified under the kingdom of Piedmont in 1861.

PARMIGIANA DI MELANZANE ALLA CATANESE

YIELD: 4 SERVINGS / **ACTIVE TIME:** 1 HOUR / **TOTAL TIME:** 2 HOURS AND 30 MINUTES

In the area of Catania, on the eastern coast of Sicily, eggplant parmesan is much more substantial than the one favored in Palermo. While Palermo's simple parmigiana is not baked, Catania's version is, and it also uses hard-boiled eggs and ham or mortadella.

1. Slice the eggplants thin lengthwise; if you have a mandoline available, use it on a rather thick setting. Layer the sliced eggplants in a colander, seasoning each layer with coarse salt. Fill a large saucepan with water and place it on top of the eggplants. Let the eggplants drain for 1 hour.

2. Rinse the eggplants and squeeze them to remove as much water as possible. Place the eggplants on kitchen towels and let them dry.

3. Preheat the oven to 375°F. Add olive oil to a narrow, deep, heavy-bottomed saucepan with high edges until it is about 2 inches deep and warm it to 350°F.

4. Gently slip the eggplants into the hot oil and fry until they are golden brown, working in batches to avoid crowding the pot. Place the fried eggplants on a paper towel–lined plate to drain.

5. Cover the bottom of a 13 x 9–inch baking pan with some of the tomato sauce. Arrange some of the eggplants, sauce, basil, eggs, mozzarella, ham, and pecorino in individual layers in the dish, continuing the layering process until everything has been used up.

6. Place the parmigiana in the oven and bake until the cheese is melted and bubbling, 25 to 30 minutes.

7. Remove the parmigiana from the oven and let it rest for 30 minutes before serving.

INGREDIENTS:

4	LARGE EGGPLANTS
	COARSE SALT, TO TASTE
	EXTRA-VIRGIN OLIVE OIL, AS NEEDED
3½	CUPS SUGO AL BASILICO (SEE PAGE 806)
2	HANDFULS OF FRESH BASIL
3	HARD-BOILED EGGS, SLICED
8.8	OZ. FRESH MOZZARELLA CHEESE, DRAINED AND SLICED
7	OZ. HAM OR MORTADELLA, SLICED
1⅓	CUPS GRATED PECORINO OR CACIOCAVALLO CHEESE

SPAGHETTI ALLA BOTTARGA

YIELD: 4 SERVINGS / ACTIVE TIME: 10 MINUTES / TOTAL TIME: 30 MINUTES

A quick and delicious Sardinian pasta dish that can be put together with just a few everyday items. Admittedly, not everyone will have bottarga in the fridge, but once you try this dish, you're sure to change that.

1. Bring water to a boil in a large saucepan. Add salt, let the water return to a full boil, and add the pasta. Cook until the pasta is very al dente.

2. Place the olive oil in a large skillet and warm it over medium heat. Add the garlic and cook, stirring frequently, for 2 minutes.

3. Add two-thirds of the bottarga and parsley, and a few tablespoons of the pasta water to the pan. Cook, gently stirring, for 2 minutes.

4. Reserve 1 cup of pasta water, drain the pasta, add it to the pan, and raise the heat to medium-high. Cook for 2 to 3 minutes, tossing to combine and adding pasta water as necessary to get the desired texture.

5. Top with the remaining bottarga and parsley, season with salt and pepper, and serve.

INGREDIENTS:

SALT AND PEPPER, TO TASTE

1 LB. SPAGHETTI

¼ CUP EXTRA-VIRGIN OLIVE OIL

2 GARLIC CLOVES

3½ OZ. MULLET BOTTARGA, GRATED

¼ CUP CHOPPED FRESH PARSLEY

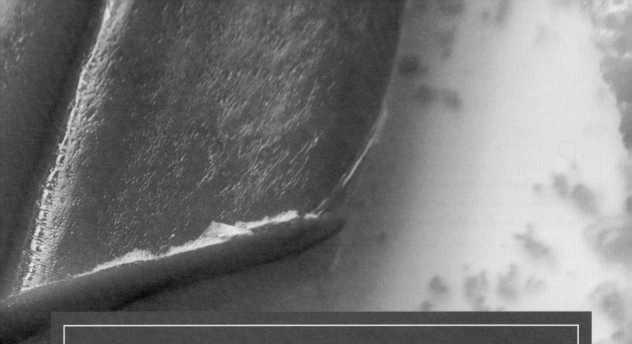

BOTTARGA:
THE SARDINIAN CAVIAR

Bottarga is salted, pressed, and dried fish roe, that is then grated and used in a number of food preparations, mostly pasta dishes.

It can be made from different types of fish roes, including tuna and mullet, and needs four to five months of drying to be ready.

Bottarga is also produced in Sicily, Calabria, Campania, and Tuscany, but the Sardinian one is possibly the most renowned and appreciated, both locally and worldwide.

Sardinian bottarga is produced mainly from mullet. The Sardinian word for bottarga is butàriga, which derives from the Arabic butarikh. The Arabs were in fact the ones who spread this item all over the Mediterranean region, but it is possible that bottarga was brought to Sardinia by the Phoenicians, who founded the Sardinian cities of Tharros and Othoca in the eighth century BC.

In ancient times, bottarga was a precious commodity, easily available only to the very fishermen who were processing it. Nowadays, it is considered to be the Sardinian gold, a luxury food to be sold in gourmet grocery stores or exported to the highest bidder.

PASTA CON NOCI E PANGRATTATO

YIELD: 4 SERVINGS / **ACTIVE TIME:** 15 MINUTES / **TOTAL TIME:** 35 MINUTES

Pasta with walnuts and bread crumbs is an extremely simple Sardinian dish that is loaded with history. A vegan pasta ante litteram, it was made for those occasions where, according to Catholic tradition, one was not supposed to eat meat. The pasta used in this dish is traditionally malloreddus, which is also called gnocchetti sardi. Malloreddus can be found dried, but can also be made at home without too much effort.

1. Place the olive oil in a large skillet and warm it over medium-low heat. Add the garlic and cook for 2 minutes.

2. Add the walnuts and parsley and cook, stirring frequently, for 2 minutes. Remove the pan from heat and set it aside.

3. Place the bread crumbs in a small skillet and toast over low heat until they are browned, shaking the pan occasionally. Remove the pan from heat and set it aside.

4. Bring water to a boil in a large saucepan. Add salt, let the water return to a full boil, and add the pasta. Cook until the pasta is al dente.

5. Reserve 1 cup of pasta water, drain the pasta, and add it to the pan containing the walnut mixture. Stir in the bread crumbs, place the pan over medium-high heat, and cook for 2 to 3 minutes, tossing to combine and adding pasta water as needed to get the desired texture. Season with salt and pepper and serve immediately.

INGREDIENTS:

¼	CUP EXTRA-VIRGIN OLIVE OIL
1	GARLIC CLOVE, MINCED
5½	OZ. WALNUTS, GROUND
2	TABLESPOONS CHOPPED FRESH PARSLEY
1	CUP BREAD CRUMBS
	SALT AND PEPPER, TO TASTE
1	LB. MALLOREDDUS (SEE PAGE 56)

FREGOLA CON I CARCIOFI

YIELD: 4 SERVINGS / **ACTIVE TIME:** 40 MINUTES / **TOTAL TIME:** 1 HOUR

This fregola dish reminds me of a good artichoke risotto, only with the smoky, nutty flavor of fregola.

1. Place the artichoke hearts and lemon juice in a bowl and cover with water.

2. Place the olive oil in a large, deep skillet and warm it over medium-low heat. Add the garlic and parsley and cook for 2 minutes.

3. Drain the artichoke hearts, add them to the pan, and cook for 3 minutes.

4. Add half of the broth and cook, stirring occasionally, for about 15 minutes.

5. Add the Fregola and cook for 20 minutes, gradually incorporating the remaining broth and letting the Fregola absorb each addition, as you would with risotto.

6. Season the dish with salt and pepper, stir in the pecorino, and serve.

INGREDIENTS:

6	FRESH ARTICHOKE HEARTS, SLICED
	JUICE OF ½ LEMON
¼	CUP EXTRA-VIRGIN OLIVE OIL
2	GARLIC CLOVES, MINCED
2	TABLESPOONS CHOPPED FRESH PARSLEY
3	CUPS BRODO VEGETALE (SEE PAGE 806), WARM
12	OZ. FREGOLA (SEE PAGE 55)
	SALT AND PEPPER, TO TASTE
½	CUP GRATED PECORINO CHEESE

FREGOLA CON SALSICCIA

YIELD: 4 SERVINGS / ACTIVE TIME: 30 MINUTES / TOTAL TIME: 50 MINUTES

A delicious Sardinian dish that requires only a few ingredients—one of which is very special, the pasta known as fregola. This pasta is similar to couscous but has much larger grains and a nutty flavor. There are small-grained and large-grained versions of fregola, and this recipe requires the larger-grained one.

1. Place the olive oil in a large skillet and warm it over medium-low heat. Add the onion and cook until it has softened, about 5 minutes.

2. Add the sausage and cook, stirring frequently, until it has browned, about 8 minutes.

3. Add the Fregola to the pan and lightly toast it. Add the broth and cook, stirring frequently, until the broth has evaporated and the dish is moist but not soupy, about 20 minutes.

4. Stir in the saffron, season the dish with salt, and cook for 1 minute. Add the grated cheese and fold to incorporate it.

5. Garnish the dish with parsley and serve.

INGREDIENTS:

¼   CUP EXTRA-VIRGIN OLIVE OIL

1   ONION, FINELY DICED

5   OZ. ITALIAN SAUSAGE, CASING REMOVED, CRUMBLED

12   OZ. FREGOLA (SEE PAGE 55)

3   CUPS BRODO VEGETALE (SEE PAGE 806), WARM

    PINCH OF SAFFRON THREADS

    SALT, TO TASTE

½   CUP GRATED SARDINIAN CHEESE

    FRESH PARSLEY, CHOPPED, FOR GARNISH

FREGOLA CON LE VONGOLE

YIELD: 4 SERVINGS / **ACTIVE TIME:** 30 MINUTES / **TOTAL TIME:** 50 MINUTES

Another traditional way to eat fregola is with clams. The traditional recipe used wedge clams, but as these are hard to find even in Sardinia nowadays, regular clams are becoming the new standard.

1. Place the clams in a large bowl, cover them with cold water, and stir in 4 handfuls of salt. Let them soak for 2 hours to remove the sand.

2. Drain the clams, rinse them, and set them aside.

3. Place 2 tablespoons of olive oil in a large, deep skillet and warm it over medium-low heat. Add the garlic and cook for 2 minutes.

4. Add the clams, cover the pan with a lid, and cook until the majority of the clams have opened, about 5 minutes. Discard any clams that did not open. Drain the clams and reserve the liquid they release. Strain the liquid and set it and the clams aside.

5. Place the remaining olive oil in the pan and warm it over medium heat. Add the Fregola and cook, stirring continually, for 2 minutes.

6. Add the tomatoes and the reserved liquid and cook for 20 minutes.

7. Remove half of the clams from their shells. Add these and the clams in their shells to the pan, season with salt and pepper, and stir to combine.

8. Garnish the dish with parsley and serve.

INGREDIENTS:

2   LBS. CLAMS

     SALT AND PEPPER, TO TASTE

¼   CUP EXTRA-VIRGIN OLIVE OIL

1   GARLIC CLOVE

12   OZ. FREGOLA (SEE PAGE 55)

1   LB. WHOLE CANNED PEELED TOMATOES, CRUSHED

     FRESH PARSLEY, FINELY CHOPPED, FOR GARNISH

ZUPPA GALLURESE

YIELD: 4 SERVINGS / **ACTIVE TIME:** 20 MINUTES / **TOTAL TIME:** 1 HOUR

Zuppa gallurese, which is also called suppa cuata, is a first course typical of the towns along the beautiful northern coast of Sardinia that overlooks Corsica. The dish makes fantastic use of day-old bread, and pane carasau is the very best option. If you don't have any on hand, any sourdough bread will suffice.

1. Place the broth in a saucepan and warm it over medium heat.

2. Place the pecorino, parsley, herbs, cinnamon, and nutmeg in a bowl and stir to combine.

3. Preheat the oven to 350°F. Layer some of the bread on the bottom of a 13 x 9–inch baking pan. Top with some of the caciocavallo and the pecorino mixture and prick the cheese with a fork. Continue the layering process until all of these ingredients have been used up.

4. Pour the broth over the dish, place it in the oven, and bake until the gallurese is golden brown, about 30 minutes.

5. Remove the gallurese from the oven and let it rest for 20 minutes before serving.

INGREDIENTS:

6	CUPS BRODO DI CARNE (SEE PAGE 805)
7	OZ. PECORINO CHEESE, GRATED
3	TABLESPOONS CHOPPED FRESH PARSLEY
1	TEASPOON CHOPPED MIXED HERBS
¼	TEASPOON CINNAMON
¼	TEASPOON FRESHLY GRATED NUTMEG
2.2	LBS. DAY-OLD BREAD, SLICED THIN
1	LB. CACIOCAVALLO CHEESE, SLICED THIN

GNOCCHETTI ALLA CAMPIDANESE

YIELD: 4 SERVINGS / ACTIVE TIME: 20 MINUTES / TOTAL TIME: 50 MINUTES

Gnocchetti is not made with potatoes, as you may expect from the name, but instead with durum wheat that is formed into concave shapes to better hold onto whichever sauce accompanies it.

1. Place the olive oil in a large skillet and warm it over medium-low heat. Add the onion and cook until it has softened, about 5 minutes.

2. Add the sausage and cook, stirring frequently, until it has browned, about 8 minutes.

3. Add the tomatoes, season with salt, and partially cover the pan. Cook for 30 minutes, stirring occasionally.

4. Place the pecorino and water in a bowl and whisk until the mixture is smooth and creamy.

5. Bring water to a boil in a large saucepan. Add salt, let the water return to a full boil, and add the pasta. Cook until the pasta is al dente.

6. Drain the pasta and add it to the sauce along with the pecorino cream. Raise the heat to medium-high and cook for 2 to 3 minutes, tossing to combine. Serve immediately.

INGREDIENTS:

- ¼ CUP EXTRA-VIRGIN OLIVE OIL
- 1 ONION, FINELY DICED
- 11 OZ. ITALIAN SAUSAGE, CASINGS REMOVED, CRUMBLED
- 1⅓ CUPS WHOLE PEELED TOMATOES, LIGHTLY CRUSHED
- SALT, TO TASTE
- 7 OZ. PECORINO CHEESE, GRATED
- ¼ CUP WATER
- 1 LB. MALLOREDDUS (SEE PAGE 56)

ZUPPA DI CASTAGNE SARDA

YIELD: 4 SERVINGS / **ACTIVE TIME:** 1 HOUR / **TOTAL TIME:** 3 HOURS

Chestnut soup is characteristic of the most mountainous Italian regions, and Sardinia is no exception. This lovely soup was traditionally a poor-man main, since chestnuts grew wild and were thus free for anyone to pick, and the pork would be scraps left after processing the pig. Some versions forgo the pasta, although its inclusion makes for an even better comfort food.

1. Preheat the oven to 160°F. Peel the chestnuts, place them on a baking sheet, and roast them for 20 minutes. Remove the chestnuts from the oven, remove the nuts, and set them aside.

2. Place the lard in a large saucepan and warm it over medium heat. Add the onion and cook, stirring occasionally, until it has softened, about 5 minutes.

3. Add the chestnuts and water, season with salt, and partially cover the pan. Bring the soup to a simmer, reduce the heat to low, and cook for 1½ hours.

4. Add the pasta and cook until it is al dente, adding more water if needed.

5. Ladle the soup into warmed bowls and enjoy.

INGREDIENTS:

1	LB. CHESTNUTS
6	OZ. LARD, CHOPPED
1	ONION, FINELY DICED
6	CUPS WATER, PLUS MORE AS NEEDED
	SALT, TO TASTE
12	OZ. SHORT-FORMAT PASTA

CULURGIONES AL POMODORO

YIELD: 4 SERVINGS / **ACTIVE TIME:** 10 MINUTES / **TOTAL TIME:** 20 MINUTES

Culurgiones are the Sardinian ravioli, though, curiously, they are shaped in a way that reminds one more of East Asian dumplings than northeastern Italian ravioli. Fillings vary by region, the most common being mint and potatoes.

1. Place the tomato sauce in a medium saucepan and warm it over medium heat.

2. Bring water to a boil in a large saucepan. Add salt, let the water return to a full boil, and add the Culurgiones. Cook until they are al dente.

3. Drain the Culurgiones and add them to the sauce. Toss to combine, garnish with the pecorino, and serve.

INGREDIENTS:

2   CUPS SUGO AL BASILICO (SEE PAGE 806)

    SALT, TO TASTE

1   LB. CULURGIONES (SEE PAGE 59)

½   CUP GRATED PECORINO CHEESE, FOR GARNISH

SECONDI

RAFANATA

YIELD: 4 SERVINGS / **ACTIVE TIME:** 10 MINUTES / **TOTAL TIME:** 45 MINUTES

This frittata is probably the result of Spain's influence over Southern Italy, as it looks exactly like the famed Spanish tortilla. Like that tortilla, it includes potatoes, but it becomes Lucanian—aka from Basilicata—via the addition of horseradish.

1. Bring salted water to a boil in a large saucepan. Add the potatoes and boil until they are tender, 15 to 20 minutes. Drain the potatoes and place them in a bowl.

2. Mash the potatoes until they are smooth and let them cool completely.

3. Place the eggs in a bowl, season them with salt and pepper, and stir to combine.

4. Add the mashed potatoes, pecorino, and horseradish and stir until the mixture is combined.

5. Place the olive oil in a large skillet and warm it over medium-high heat. Add the potato-and-egg mixture and spread it into an even layer. Cook until you see the bottom and edge of the frittata detach from the pan.

6. Using a large plate, invert the pan and flip the frittata over. Cook until the frittata is browned on the other side and cooked through, 5 to 8 minutes. Serve immediately.

INGREDIENTS:

	SALT AND PEPPER, TO TASTE
11	OZ. POTATOES, PEELED AND CHOPPED
5	EGGS
3½	OZ. PECORINO CHEESE, GRATED
3½	OZ. FRESH HORSERADISH, GRATED
3	TABLESPOONS EXTRA-VIRGIN OLIVE OIL

FRITTATA DI ZUCCHINE

YIELD: 4 SERVINGS / **ACTIVE TIME:** 20 MINUTES / **TOTAL TIME:** 30 MINUTES

Though typical of the whole Southern region, where zucchini is widely cultivated, this frittata is particularly loved in Naples and its surrounding region, Campania. The recipe usually includes a generous amount of onion and grated cheese, so keep that in mind.

1. Place half of the olive oil in a skillet and warm it over medium heat. Add the onions and cook, stirring occasionally, until they are translucent, about 3 minutes.

2. Add the zucchini and cook, stirring occasionally, until it is tender, about 10 minutes. Remove the pan from heat and let the mixture cool.

3. Place the eggs in a bowl, season them with salt and pepper, and whisk until scrambled. Add the pecorino, bread crumbs, and parsley and whisk to combine.

4. Add the cooled vegetable mixture and fold to incorporate.

5. Place the remaining olive oil in a large skillet and warm it over medium-low heat. Add the egg mixture, cover the pan, and cook until the bottom is set, 5 to 8 minutes.

6. Gently lift the frittata on one side and check to see if it is golden brown. When it is, use a large plate to invert the pan and flip the frittata over. Cook until the frittata is browned on the other side, 3 to 4 minutes. Serve immediately.

INGREDIENTS:

- 6 TABLESPOONS EXTRA-VIRGIN OLIVE OIL
- 2 LARGE ONIONS, SLICED THIN
- 1⅓ LBS. ZUCCHINI, TRIMMED AND CHOPPED
- 5 EGGS
-   SALT AND PEPPER, TO TASTE
- 3½ OZ. PECORINO OR PARMESAN CHEESE, GRATED
- 3 TABLESPOONS BREAD CRUMBS
- 1 TABLESPOON CHOPPED FRESH PARSLEY

UOVA E PEPERONI FRITTI ALLA COSENTINA

YIELD: 4 SERVINGS / **ACTIVE TIME:** 15 MINUTES / **TOTAL TIME:** 30 MINUTES

I f you are looking for a different way to enjoy your eggs for breakfast, this colorful, pepper and cheese–enriched dish from Cosenza (Calabria) just may be it.

1. Place the olive oil in a large skillet and warm it over medium-low heat. Add the garlic, anchovies, and red pepper flakes and cook for 2 minutes.

2. Add the cherry tomatoes and cook, stirring occasionally, until they have softened.

3. Add the bell peppers, season the dish with salt, and raise the heat to medium. Cover the pan and cook for about 30 minutes, stirring occasionally and adding water if the dish starts to look dry.

4. Add the eggs and scramble them until they are almost set.

5. Sprinkle the pecorino over the eggs and cook until it has melted. Season the dish with oregano and salt and serve immediately with slices of sourdough bread.

INGREDIENTS:

¼ CUP EXTRA-VIRGIN OLIVE OIL

2 GARLIC CLOVES

5 ANCHOVIES IN OLIVE OIL, DRAINED AND CHOPPED

RED PEPPER FLAKES OR 'NDUJA, TO TASTE

8 CHERRY TOMATOES, HALVED

1 RED BELL PEPPER, STEM AND SEEDS REMOVED, SLICED

1 YELLOW BELL PEPPER, STEM AND SEEDS REMOVED, SLICED

SALT, TO TASTE

8 EGGS, BEATEN

⅔ CUP GRATED PECORINO CHEESE

DRIED OREGANO, TO TASTE

4 SLICES OF SOURDOUGH BREAD, TOASTED OR GRILLED, FOR SERVING

PITTA DI PATATE

YIELD: 6 SERVINGS / **ACTIVE TIME:** 40 MINUTES / **TOTAL TIME:** 1 HOUR AND 30 MINUTES

The vegetarian equivalent of gattò di patate is pitta di patate, a dish popular in the Salento region.

1. Place half of the olive oil in a large skillet and warm it over medium-low heat. Add the onions and cook, stirring occasionally, until they have softened, about 6 minutes.

2. Add the tomatoes and cook, stirring occasionally, until the mixture has thickened.

3. Stir in the olives, capers, and mint, season the mixture with salt and oregano, and cook for about 2 minutes. Remove the pan from heat and let the mixture cool.

4. Bring salted water to a boil in a large pot. Add the potatoes and boil until they are tender, about 40 minutes.

5. Preheat the oven to 390°F. Drain the potatoes and run them under cold water. Peel the potatoes, mash them, and season them with salt and pepper.

6. Add the remaining olive oil, the eggs, pecorino, and milk and stir to combine.

7. Coat a deep baking dish with butter. Sprinkle half of the bread crumbs over the bottom and then spread half of the potato mixture on top. Top with the tomato mixture, spread the remaining potato mixture over the top, and sprinkle the remaining bread crumbs over it.

8. Place the baking dish in the oven and bake for 35 minutes.

9. Set the oven's broiler to high and place the baking dish directly below it. Broil until the top is golden brown.

10. Turn off the broiler and let the dish cool in the oven, which will allow it to become firmer when you serve it.

INGREDIENTS:

- ¼ CUP EXTRA-VIRGIN OLIVE OIL
- 3 LARGE YELLOW OR RED ONIONS, SLICED THIN
- 1 LB. WHOLE PEELED TOMATOES, CRUSHED
- ½ CUP PITTED BLACK OLIVES, CHOPPED
- 1 TABLESPOON CAPERS IN BRINE, RINSED AND DRAINED
- 4 FRESH MINT LEAVES, FINELY CHOPPED
- SALT AND PEPPER, TO TASTE
- DRIED OREGANO, TO TASTE
- 2½ LBS. POTATOES
- 2 EGGS
- 1 CUP GRATED PECORINO CHEESE
- 3½ TABLESPOONS WHOLE MILK
- BUTTER, AS NEEDED
- ¼ CUP BREAD CRUMBS

AFFUNNIATELLA MOLISANA

YIELD: 4 SERVINGS / ACTIVE TIME: 10 MINUTES / TOTAL TIME: 30 MINUTES

A traditional vegetarian dish from Molise, the original recipe calls for Italian friggitelli peppers, but regular bell peppers make for a reasonable substitute.

1. Place the olive oil in a large skillet and warm it over medium heat. Add the onion and cook, stirring occasionally, until it has softened, about 5 minutes.

2. Add the sweet peppers and cook, stirring occasionally, until they have softened, about 5 minutes.

3. Add the chile, parsley, and tomatoes, season with salt, and reduce the heat to low. Cook until the sauce has thickened, 15 to 20 minutes.

4. Add the eggs and scramble until they are almost set.

5. Sprinkle the pecorino over the eggs and cook until it has melted. Serve immediately.

INGREDIENTS:

¼   CUP EXTRA-VIRGIN OLIVE OIL

1   ONION, FINELY DICED

13   OZ. SWEET ITALIAN PEPPERS, STEMS AND SEEDS REMOVED, CUT INTO STRIPS

½   CHILE PEPPER, STEM AND SEEDS REMOVED, MINCED

1   TABLESPOON CHOPPED FRESH PARSLEY

3   TOMATOES, CHOPPED

     SALT, TO TASTE

4   EGGS, LIGHTLY BEATEN

⅔   CUP GRATED PECORINO CHEESE

SCAROLA MBUTTUNAT

YIELD: 4 SERVINGS / **ACTIVE TIME:** 30 MINUTES / **TOTAL TIME:** 1 HOUR

There are several dishes that stuff meat into leafy vegetable pockets in European cuisine, but not so many with a vegetarian filling. These meatless escarole pockets from Campania are scrumptious, highly nutritious, and easy to make vegan, should you want to. If you can find Gaeta black olives, use them here.

1. Preheat the oven to 480°F. Bring salted water to a boil in a large saucepan. Remove the core and outer leaves from the heads of escarole and rinse them under cold water. Tie the heads of escarole tightly with kitchen twine, place them in the boiling water, and boil for 2 minutes. Drain the escarole and let it cool.

2. Place the olive oil in a large skillet and warm it over medium heat. Add the garlic and red pepper flakes and cook for 1 minute. Add the anchovies, olives, capers, raisins, pine nuts, walnuts, and parsley, season with salt, and cook for 5 minutes.

3. Add the pecorino and bread crumbs and cook for 2 minutes.

4. Gently open the heads of escarole and fill them with the olive mixture. Tie the stuffed escarole closed with kitchen twine and place it in a baking dish.

5. Drizzle olive oil over the stuffed escarole and sprinkle bread crumbs on top. Place the stuffed escarole in the oven and roast until it is golden brown, about 20 minutes.

6. Remove the stuffed escarole from the oven and let it cool slightly before serving.

INGREDIENTS:

	SALT, TO TASTE
4	SMALL HEADS OF ESCAROLE
5	TABLESPOONS EXTRA-VIRGIN OLIVE OIL, PLUS MORE FOR TOPPING
1	GARLIC CLOVE, MINCED
	RED PEPPER FLAKES, TO TASTE
5	ANCHOVIES IN OLIVE OIL, DRAINED AND CHOPPED
½	CUP PITTED BLACK OLIVES, CHOPPED
½	CUP PITTED GREEN OLIVES, CHOPPED
2	TABLESPOONS CAPERS, RINSED IF PACKED IN SALT OR DRAINED IF PACKED IN BRINE
½	CUP RAISINS, SOAKED IN WARM WATER FOR 10 MINUTES, DRAINED, AND SQUEEZED
3	TABLESPOONS PINE NUTS
2	TABLESPOONS CHOPPED WALNUTS
2	TABLESPOONS CHOPPED FRESH PARSLEY
2	OZ. PECORINO CHEESE, SHAVED
½	CUP BREAD CRUMBS, PLUS MORE FOR TOPPING

THE LEAF EATERS:
SOUTHERN ITALIANS'
PASSION FOR VEGETABLES

A popular Italian saying is "di necessità virtù," which translates to "virtue arises out of necessity." This saying captures the country's ability to make the most of what's available, a talent that is almost always in evidence in recipes from Southern Italy.

Centuries ago, meat was not readily available to common people in Southern Italy. Animals, both domesticated and wild, were too expensive for all but the largest landowners. The only exceptions were the odd pig or hen, both of which were fed with table scraps.

As meat was a luxury reserved for the rich, and even wheat was too expensive to consume in large amounts, the only food group common people could source abundantly was vegetables. The rich soil of Southern Italy, combined with the mild weather, proved ideal for the cultivation of a variety of edible plants, meaning that even poor families could make the most of what little land they had.

As a result, Neapolitans—a term applied to residents of Naples that was eventually extended to refer to all Southern Italians—were derogatively labeled i mangiatori di foglia, "the leaf eaters," by Luigi Pulci at Lorenzo il Magnifico's court in Florence. But, surrounded by all that delicious produce, the people of the south reveled in the bounty, with even the children learning to love the abundance they'd been provided.

Today, nutritionists, scientists, and environmental activists are continually lecturing us to eat more vegetables. And while it's a struggle for most, Southern Italians have no issues, happily consuming the foods they've always known and loved, from cime di rapa (turnip greens) and scarola (a type of escarole) to tenerumi (leaves and shoots of a Sicilian squash).

PIZZA DI SCAROLA

YIELD: 6 SERVINGS / ACTIVE TIME: 40 MINUTES / TOTAL TIME: 4 HOURS

Pizza di scarola, typical of Campania and Naples, is made with a rather dry yeasted dough and is technically more of a savory pie than a focaccia. This is great as a buffet offering at a party, and, if escarole is not available, can easily be made with other leafy greens.

1. To begin preparations for the dough, place the yeast, water, and sugar in a large bowl, gently stir to combine, and let the mixture sit until it starts to foam, about 10 minutes.

2. Add the flour and work the mixture until it just comes together as a dough.

3. Add the olive oil and salt and knead the dough until it is smooth and elastic.

4. Shape the dough into a round, place it in a clean bowl, and cover it with plastic wrap. Let the dough rest at room temperature until it has almost doubled in size, about 3 hours.

5. To begin preparations for the filling, place the olive oil in a large skillet and warm it over medium-low heat. Add the garlic and anchovies, season with red pepper flakes, and cook for 2 minutes.

6. Add the escarole, cover the pan with a lid, and cook until the escarole has wilted, about 15 minutes.

7. Add the olives and capers, lightly season the mixture with salt, and cook for 5 more minutes. Remove the pan from heat and let the filling cool.

8. Preheat the oven to 430°F. Place the dough on a flour-dusted work surface and divide it into 2 pieces, one larger than the other. Roll out the larger piece into a ¼-inch-thick, 10-inch round.

9. Coat a 9-inch pie plate with olive oil and place the 10-inch round over it. Place the filling on top of the dough, roll out the remaining piece of dough, and place it on top of the filling. Fold the bottom crust down over the top crust and press down on the seam to seal. Brush the top crust with olive oil and place the scarola in the oven.

10. Bake until the scarola is golden brown, about 30 minutes. Remove it from the oven and enjoy warm or at room temperature.

INGREDIENTS:

FOR THE DOUGH

1	SACHET OF ACTIVE DRY YEAST
15.8	OZ. LUKEWARM WATER (90°F)
1	TABLESPOON SUGAR
28.2	OZ. ALL-PURPOSE FLOUR, PLUS MORE AS NEEDED
2	TABLESPOONS EXTRA-VIRGIN OLIVE OIL
⅔	OZ. FINE SEA SALT

FOR THE FILLING

5	TABLESPOONS EXTRA-VIRGIN OLIVE OIL, PLUS MORE AS NEEDED
1	GARLIC CLOVE, MINCED
3	ANCHOVIES IN OLIVE OIL, DRAINED AND CHOPPED
	RED PEPPER FLAKES, TO TASTE
1	LARGE HEAD OF ESCAROLE, RINSED WELL AND CHOPPED
½	CUP PITTED BLACK OLIVES
2	TABLESPOONS CAPERS, RINSED IF PACKED IN SALT OR DRAINED IF PACKED IN BRINE
	SALT, TO TASTE

GATTÒ DI PATATE

YIELD: 6 SERVINGS / **ACTIVE TIME:** 40 MINUTES / **TOTAL TIME:** 1 HOUR AND 30 MINUTES

Served mostly on special occasions, gattò di patate is a Neapolitanization of the French potato gateau, a dish encountered by chefs who studied abroad before going to work in the kitchens of the region's nobles. To make the perfect gattò, use old, but not sprouted, potatoes, as their reduced water content is an advantage.

1. Preheat the oven to 390°F. Bring salted water to a boil in a large pot. Add the potatoes and boil until they are tender, about 40 minutes.

2. Drain the potatoes and run them under cold water. Peel the potatoes, mash them, and season them with salt and pepper.

3. Add the olive oil, eggs, Parmesan, and milk and stir to combine.

4. Coat a deep baking dish with butter. Sprinkle half of the bread crumbs over the bottom and then spread half of the potato mixture on top.

5. Top with the provola, salami, and ham, spread the remaining potato mixture over the top, and sprinkle the remaining bread crumbs over it.

6. Place the baking dish in the oven and bake for 35 minutes.

7. Set the oven's broiler to high and place the baking dish directly below it. Broil until the top is golden brown.

8. Turn off the broiler and let the gattò cool in the oven, which will allow it to become firmer when you serve it.

INGREDIENTS:

- SALT AND PEPPER, TO TASTE
- 2½ LBS. POTATOES
- 2 TABLESPOONS EXTRA-VIRGIN OLIVE OIL
- 2 EGGS
- ⅓ CUP GRATED PARMESAN CHEESE
- 3½ TABLESPOONS WHOLE MILK
- BUTTER, AS NEEDED
- ¼ CUP BREAD CRUMBS
- 7 OZ. SMOKED PROVOLA OR SMOKED SCAMORZA CHEESE, DICED
- 3½ OZ. SALAMI, CHOPPED
- 3½ OZ. HAM, DICED

THE MONZÙ,
THE CHEFS OF THE SOUTHERN ELITE

Until recently, common people in Europe were mostly confined to the locations where they were born. Mobility, encouraged through arranged marriages, political maneuvering, education, or leisurely travel, was a sign of nobility.

As a result, the cuisine featured in the mansions of the nobles was not exclusively based on local traditions, but strongly influenced by the trends circulating among the elites throughout Europe. These trends were passed on mostly through the import of cooks with experience in foreign courts, who could then train local chefs, creating an interesting fusion.

In the sixteenth century, cooks rose to increasing fame and relevance in courts throughout Southern Italy, and they became even more influential with the advent of the monzù. This term was coined during the times of Maria Carolina of Austria (Marie Antoinette's sister), who married and coreigned with King Ferdinand I over Naples and Sicily in the 1700s. The word derives from the French monsieur, which was the title given to the head of the royal kitchen in Maria Carolina's kingdom. The queen was extremely active in promoting Naples as a cultural center, and she also brought some of her sister Marie Antoinette's cooks to Naples. These cooks introduced many French terms and dishes into Neapolitan cuisine, as well as standardizing the role of the court's head cook. Monzù in Naples and monsù in Sicily, these terms remained in use until the middle of the twentieth century, when they were replaced by "chef."

The monzù, who were for the most part Italians, were highly regarded and enjoyed independence and generous salaries. They could either keep their own name and become famous with it, or take the name of the noble family they worked for and enjoy the beneficial social associations that came along with it.

Eventually, some of the amazing dishes developed by these skilled cooks became so popular that they were incorporated in the local cooking tradition, a reality that has formed the identities of Southern Italian cuisine, which is a perfect blend of peasant and noble influence.

FRIARIELLI E SALSICCIA

YIELD: 4 SERVINGS / **ACTIVE TIME:** 30 MINUTES / **TOTAL TIME:** 1 HOUR

Turnip greens and sausages are a match made in heaven. This pairing is also the topping of one of the most traditional Neapolitan pizzas, pizza alla carrettiera, and it makes a lovely, simple secondo on its own.

1. Bring salted water to a boil in a large saucepan. Add the turnip greens and cook until just tender, about 5 minutes. Drain the turnip greens and set them aside.

2. Place 5 tablespoons of olive oil in a large skillet and warm it over medium-low heat. Add the garlic and chile and cook for 2 minutes. Remove the pan from heat and season the mixture with salt.

3. Place the remaining olive oil in a large skillet and warm it over medium heat. Poke holes in the sausages, place them in the pan, and cook until they are browned all over and nearly cooked through, about 10 minutes.

4. Stir in the garlic mixture and turnip greens and cook until the sausages are completely cooked through, 3 to 4 minutes. Serve immediately.

INGREDIENTS:

	SALT, TO TASTE
2.2	LBS. TURNIP GREENS, RINSED WELL, WOODY STEMS REMOVED
6	TABLESPOONS EXTRA-VIRGIN OLIVE OIL
4	GARLIC CLOVES, HALVED
1	CHILE PEPPER, STEM AND SEEDS REMOVED, CHOPPED
8	ITALIAN SAUSAGES

PALLOTTE CACE E OVE

YIELD: 20 PALLOTTE / **ACTIVE TIME:** 30 MINUTES / **TOTAL TIME:** 1 HOUR

Pallotte cace e ove, literally balls with cheese and eggs, are traditional to the Abruzzi region. Born out of the need to reuse stale bread and find a substitute for meat, which was not always available, they are often served in a pepper-and-tomato sauce, accompanied by bread.

1. Place all of the cheeses in a large bowl and stir to combine. Incorporate the eggs 1 at a time and then add the bread crumbs. Gently stir until the mixture holds together enough to keep its shape during the cooking process. If necessary, incorporate more bread crumbs.

2. Add olive oil to a narrow, deep, heavy-bottomed saucepan with high edges until it is about 2 inches deep and warm it to 350°F. Form the cheese mixture into ovals (each should weigh approximately 2 oz.) and gently slip them into the hot oil. Fry the pallotte until they are crispy and golden brown, turning as necessary.

3. Remove the pallotte from the hot oil and transfer them to a paper towel–lined plate to drain.

4. Place the sauce in a large skillet and warm it over low heat. Add the pallotte and cook them for 10 minutes. Serve immediately with crusty bread.

INGREDIENTS:

2 CUPS GRATED GRANA PADANO CHEESE

2 CUPS GRATED PARMESAN CHEESE

1 CUP GRATED PECORINO CHEESE

1 CUP DRAINED RICOTTA CHEESE

5 EGGS

1 CUP FRESH BREAD CRUMBS, PLUS MORE AS NEEDED

EXTRA-VIRGIN OLIVE OIL, AS NEEDED

SUGO AI PEPERONI (SEE PAGE 807)

CRUSTY BREAD, FOR SERVING

POLPETTE DI MELANZANE

YIELD: 4 SERVINGS / **ACTIVE TIME:** 30 MINUTES / **TOTAL TIME:** 1 HOUR

Popular in Calabria and Sicily, these delicious eggplant balls are a great alternative to meat-based ones and are also extremely easy to make. These are also great to eat cold, over a salad.

1. Bring salted water to a boil in a large saucepan. Add the eggplants and cook until they soften slightly, about 5 minutes. Drain the eggplants and let them cool.

2. Squeeze the eggplants to remove any excess water and place them in a large bowl. Add the stale bread, eggs, parsley, garlic, bread crumbs, and pecorino, season the mixture with salt and pepper, and stir to combine.

3. Add olive oil to a narrow, deep, heavy-bottomed saucepan with high edges until it is about 2 inches deep and warm it to 350°F. Form the eggplant mixture into ovals (each should weigh approximately 2 oz.) and gently slip them into the hot oil. Fry the polpettes until they are crispy and golden brown, turning as necessary.

4. Remove the polpettes from the hot oil and transfer them to a paper towel–lined plate to drain. Serve once all of the polpettes have drained and cooled slightly.

INGREDIENTS:

	SALT AND PEPPER, TO TASTE
4	LARGE EGGPLANTS, TRIMMED AND CUT INTO STRIPS
2	SLICES OF STALE BREAD, BRIEFLY SOAKED IN WATER AND SQUEEZED DRY
2	EGGS
2	TABLESPOONS FINELY CHOPPED FRESH PARSLEY
1	GARLIC CLOVE, MINCED
1	TABLESPOON BREAD CRUMBS
½	CUP GRATED PECORINO CHEESE
	EXTRA-VIRGIN OLIVE OIL, AS NEEDED

FALSOMAGRO

YIELD: 6 SERVINGS / **ACTIVE TIME:** 40 MINUTES / **TOTAL TIME:** 2 HOURS

A classic of Sicilian festive days, this stuffed roast is relatively easy to make and very tasty. The only challenge may be finding a large and thin slice of beef, easier to achieve if you have access to a real butcher rather than the supermarket meat section. Also called farsumagru or bruciuluni, this is not a peasant dish but was instead created at the Spanish court of Palermo in the fifteenth century.

1. Beat the slice of beef with a meat tenderizer to ensure that it is uniformly thick.

2. Place the ground beef, pecorino, and bread crumbs in a large bowl and stir to combine. Season the mixture with salt and pepper and then spread it over the slice of beef, leaving a ½ inch border around the edge.

3. Layer the guanciale, caciocavallo, and mortadella on top and then place the hard-boiled eggs in the center.

4. Roll up the slice of beef, starting from a short side, and tie it with kitchen twine.

5. Place ¼ cup of olive oil in a large skillet and warm it over medium heat. Add the slice of beef and sear it until it is browned all over, turning it as necessary. Remove the pan from heat and set it aside.

6. Place the remaining olive oil in a Dutch oven and warm it over medium heat. Add the carrot, celery, and onion and cook, stirring occasionally, until the vegetables have softened, about 5 minutes.

7. Add the seared beef to the pot and cook for about 5 minutes.

8. Add the red wine and cook until it has almost evaporated, scraping up any browned bits from the bottom of the pot.

9. Stir in the tomatoes and tomato paste, season the dish with salt and pepper, and reduce the heat to low. Cover the pan and cook, stirring occasionally, until the beef is tender, about 1 hour.

10. Cut the twine off of the beef and let it rest for 5 minutes before slicing and serving.

INGREDIENTS:

1½ LBS. LEAN BEEF, IN 1 LARGE AND THIN SLICE

5 OZ. GROUND BEEF

2 TABLESPOONS GRATED PECORINO CHEESE

¼ CUP BREAD CRUMBS

SALT AND PEPPER, TO TASTE

1 OZ. GUANCIALE, CUT INTO STRIPS

2 OZ. CACIOCAVALLO CHEESE, CUT INTO STRIPS

2 OZ. MORTADELLA, CUT INTO STRIPS

3 HARD-BOILED EGGS, CHOPPED

½ CUP EXTRA-VIRGIN OLIVE OIL

1 CARROT, PEELED AND FINELY CHOPPED

1 CELERY STALK, FINELY DICED

1 ONION, FINELY DICED

¼ CUP RED WINE

1½ LBS. WHOLE PEELED TOMATOES, CRUSHED

1 TABLESPOON TOMATO PASTE

POLPETTE AL SUGO

YIELD: 6 SERVINGS / **ACTIVE TIME:** 30 MINUTES / **TOTAL TIME:** 1 HOUR

Polpette al sugo, also called polpette in umido, are a classic secondo throughout Italy, and are particularly popular in Southern Italy. While in North America these are generally served with spaghetti, in Italy big meatballs in tomato sauce are instead served as a dish of their own, accompanied by bread to mop up any sauce that is left over.

1. Place all of the ingredients, except for the sauce and bread, in a large bowl and work the mixture until well combined. Form the mixture into balls (each should weigh approximately 2 oz.) and set them aside.

2. Place the sauce in a large, deep skillet and warm it over low heat.

3. Add the meatballs, cover the pan, and cook for 10 minutes.

4. Shake the pan a few times to coat the meatballs in the sauce, cover the pan again, and cook for another 5 minutes.

5. Gently turn the meatballs over, raise the heat to medium, and cook until the meatballs are cooked through, 10 to 15 minutes. Serve immediately with crusty bread.

INGREDIENTS:

- ¾ LB. GROUND BEEF
- ¾ LB. GROUND PORK
- 4 EGGS
- 4 LARGE SLICES OF DAY-OLD BREAD, SOAKED IN WATER AND SQUEEZED DRY
- 1½ CUPS GRATED PECORINO OR PARMESAN CHEESE
- 1 GARLIC CLOVE, MINCED
- 2 TABLESPOONS FINELY CHOPPED FRESH PARSLEY
- SALT AND PEPPER, TO TASTE
- SUGO AL BASILICO (SEE PAGE 806)
- CRUSTY BREAD, FOR SERVING

BRACIOLE NAPOLETANE

YIELD: 6 SERVINGS / **ACTIVE TIME:** 20 MINUTES / **TOTAL TIME:** 40 MINUTES

This dish carries quite a confusing name: braciole in fact means meat chops in Italian, but in Neapolitan it refers to a lean cut of beef filled with a stuffing. This type of preparation is known as involtino in the center and north of the country, leading to still more confusion. What makes this form of involtino special is that braciole has a vegetarian filling, as opposed to the popular filling in the north, which is ham.

1. Beat the slices of beef with a meat tenderizer to ensure that they are uniformly thick. Season them with salt and pepper and set them aside.

2. Place the minced garlic, raisins, pine nuts, and parsley in a bowl and stir to combine. Evenly distribute the mixture and the pecorino over the slices of beef.

3. Starting from a short side, roll up the slices of beef and then secure them with skewers or large toothpicks.

4. Place the olive oil in a large skillet and warm it over medium heat. Add the remaining garlic and cook for 1 minute.

5. Add the slices of stuffed beef and sear until they are browned all over, turning them as necessary.

6. Remove the garlic from the pan and add the red wine. Cook until it has nearly evaporated, about 5 minutes.

7. Add the sauce, stir to combine, and cover the pan. Reduce the heat to low and cook until the slices of stuffed beef are just cooked through, 10 to 15 minutes. Serve immediately.

INGREDIENTS:

8   THIN SLICES OF LEAN BEEF (EACH ABOUT 5 OZ.)

    SALT AND PEPPER, TO TASTE

4   GARLIC CLOVES, 2 MINCED; 2 HALVED

6   TABLESPOONS RAISINS, CHOPPED

¼   CUP PINE NUTS, CHOPPED

3   TABLESPOONS CHOPPED FRESH PARSLEY

1   CUP GRATED PECORINO CHEESE

3   TABLESPOONS EXTRA-VIRGIN OLIVE OIL

1   CUP RED WINE

    SUGO AL BASILICO (SEE PAGE 806)

POLLO ALLA PIZZAIOLA

YIELD: 4 SERVINGS / **ACTIVE TIME:** 20 MINUTES / **TOTAL TIME:** 1 HOUR

What meat cannot be improved by tomato sauce? Apparently none, according to Italians, as cooking meat in umido ("in tomato sauce") is one of their favorite things to do. A quick scientific fact: it has been proven that cooking meat in a liquid, rather than roasting it, has some health benefits, a further reason to love this yummy chicken stew.

1. Trim the fattiest parts from the chicken, season it with salt and pepper, and set it aside.

2. Place the olive oil in a large skillet and warm it over low heat. Add the garlic and cook until it starts to brown, about 2 minutes.

3. Add the chicken, skin side down, raise the heat to medium-high, and sear until it is browned all over, turning it as necessary.

4. Add the wine and cook until it has nearly evaporated.

5. Add the tomatoes, reduce the heat to low, and cover the pan. Cook until the chicken is tender, about 30 minutes.

6. Add the olives and capers, season the dish with salt and pepper, and cook, uncovered, until the sauce has thickened, about 10 minutes.

7. Add the mozzarella, season the dish with oregano, and cover the pan. Cook until the mozzarella has melted, about 5 minutes, and serve immediately.

INGREDIENTS:

4	LARGE BONE-IN, SKIN-ON CHICKEN THIGHS
	SALT AND PEPPER, TO TASTE
¼	CUP EXTRA-VIRGIN OLIVE OIL
2	GARLIC CLOVES, MINCED
⅔	CUP WHITE WINE
1½	LBS. WHOLE PEELED TOMATOES, CRUSHED
½	CUP PITTED BLACK OLIVES, SLICED
2	TABLESPOONS CAPERS, RINSED IF PACKED IN SALT OR DRAINED IF PACKED IN BRINE
6	OZ. FRESH MOZZARELLA CHEESE, DRAINED AND SLICED
	DRIED OREGANO, TO TASTE

IL CIF E CIAF

YIELD: 5 SERVINGS / **ACTIVE TIME:** 20 MINUTES / **TOTAL TIME:** 1 HOUR AND 40 MINUTES

A traditional pork-based dish from Abruzzi that uses those parts of the pig that are not suitable to become cured pork. Dried sweet peppers, which are not easy to find outside of Southern Italy, can be swapped out for a smaller amount of dried chile peppers.

1. Place the olive oil in a large cast-iron skillet and warm it over medium-high heat. Add the rosemary and bay leaves and cook for 1 minute.

2. Add the pork to the pan and sear until it is browned all over, turning it as necessary.

3. Deglaze the pan with the wine, scraping up any browned bits from the bottom. Cook until the wine has evaporated, cover the pan, and reduce the heat to low. Cook, stirring occasionally, for 30 minutes.

4. Remove the bay leaves and discard them. Season the dish with salt and pepper and check to see if the pork is sticking to the pan. If it is, add 1 cup water, cover the pan, and cook for another 30 minutes.

5. Preheat the oven to 390°F.

6. Add the garlic and peppers, transfer the pan to the oven, and braise the pork until it is very tender, about 20 minutes.

7. Remove the pan from the oven and serve with toasted bread.

INGREDIENTS:

½ CUP EXTRA-VIRGIN OLIVE OIL

1 SPRIG OF FRESH ROSEMARY

3 BAY LEAVES

2½ LBS. ASSORTED CUTS OF PORK (BACON, RIBS, LEAN CUTS, ETC.)

1 CUP DRY WHITE WINE

SALT AND PEPPER, TO TASTE

10 GARLIC CLOVES, PEELED

5 DRIED SWEET PEPPERS, STEMS AND SEEDS REMOVED, TORN

CRUSTY BREAD, TOASTED, FOR SERVING

POLLO ALLO ZAFFERANO

YIELD: 4 SERVINGS / **ACTIVE TIME:** 20 MINUTES / **TOTAL TIME:** 1 HOUR

Abruzzi is known for the high-quality saffron that grows there, which has produced a number of wonderful saffron-based dishes.

1. Trim the fattiest parts from the chicken, season it with salt, and set it aside.

2. Place the butter and olive oil in a large skillet and warm the mixture over medium-high heat. Add the chicken, skin side down, and sear until it is browned on both sides, turning it as necessary.

3. Deglaze the pan with the wine and Cognac, scraping up any browned bits from the bottom of the pan. Cook until the liquid has nearly evaporated.

4. Add two-thirds of the broth, reduce the heat to medium-low, and cover the pan. Cook for 20 minutes.

5. Uncover the pan, raise the heat to medium-high, and cook for 5 to 10 minutes. Remove the chicken from the pan, transfer it to a plate, and cover loosely with aluminum foil to keep it warm.

6. Add the remaining broth, cream, saffron, parsley, and flour, season the mixture with salt, and cook, stirring continually, until the flavor of the sauce has developed to your liking.

7. Ladle the sauce over the chicken and enjoy.

INGREDIENTS:

- 4   LB. WHOLE CHICKEN, BROKEN DOWN
-     SALT, TO TASTE
- 4   TABLESPOONS UNSALTED BUTTER
- 3   TABLESPOONS EXTRA-VIRGIN OLIVE OIL
- ½   CUP WHITE WINE
- ¼   CUP COGNAC OR BRANDY
- 1   CUP BRODO DI CARNE (SEE PAGE 805)
- 1   CUP LIGHT CREAM
- 1   TABLESPOON SAFFRON THREADS
- 2   TABLESPOONS CHOPPED FRESH PARSLEY
- 3   TABLESPOONS ALL-PURPOSE FLOUR

ARROSTICINI

YIELD: 4 SERVINGS / **ACTIVE TIME:** 20 MINUTES / **TOTAL TIME:** 30 MINUTES

A simple way to enjoy lamb is to chop it into small pieces and make skewers out of them. This recipe is traditional to the Abruzzi region, but has become popular throughout the rest of Italy.

1. Thread the lamb onto skewers and season it with salt and pepper.

2. Place the olive oil in a large cast-iron skillet and warm it over high heat.

3. Add the skewers to the pan and cook until they are seared all over and just medium-rare (the interior temperature should be 125°F), turning them as necessary.

4. Remove the skewers from the pan and let them rest for 2 minutes before serving.

INGREDIENTS:

2   LBS. BONELESS LEG OF LAMB, TRIMMED AND CUT INTO ½-INCH CUBES

SALT AND PEPPER, TO TASTE

1   TABLESPOON EXTRA-VIRGIN OLIVE OIL

PAMPANELLA MOLISANA

YIELD: 4 SERVINGS / ACTIVE TIME: 15 MINUTES / TOTAL TIME: 2 HOURS AND 20 MINUTES

Pampanella is the center of a local fair that takes place every year in San Martino during August.

1. Preheat the oven to 350°F. Place the chili powder, paprika, and garlic in a bowl, season the mixture with salt, and stir to combine.

2. Cut the pork every ½ inch, taking care not to cut all the way through so that the tenderloin remains together. Rub the seasoning blend over every part of the pork, place it in a roasting pan, and cover it with aluminum foil.

3. Place the pan in the oven and roast the pork for 2 hours.

4. Remove the pork from the oven, drizzle the vinegar over it, and return the pork to the oven, uncovered. Roast until it is nicely browned, about 10 minutes.

5. Remove the pork from the oven and let it rest for a few minutes before serving.

INGREDIENTS:

2 TABLESPOONS CHILI POWDER

2 TABLESPOONS SWEET PAPRIKA

4 GARLIC CLOVES, MINCED

SALT, TO TASTE

2 LBS. PORK TENDERLOIN

2 TABLESPOONS WHITE WINE VINEGAR

MAIALE CON I PEPERONI

YIELD: 4 SERVINGS / **ACTIVE TIME:** 20 MINUTES / **TOTAL TIME:** 1 HOUR

A typical meat-based main course in Basilicata, this dish has a sweet-and-sour flavor thanks to the peppers cooked in vinegar.

1. Place the vinegar in a medium saucepan and bring to a boil. Add the peppers and cook for 5 minutes. Drain the peppers and set them aside.

2. Place the olive oil in a large skillet and warm it over low heat. Add the garlic and cook for about 2 minutes.

3. Raise the heat to medium, add the pork chops, bay leaves, and cloves, and sear the pork chops until they are browned on both sides, turning them as necessary.

4. Add the peppers and 1 cup water, season the dish with salt and pepper, and cook until the pork chops are cooked through (the interior is 145°F). Serve immediately.

INGREDIENTS:

- 2 CUPS WHITE VINEGAR
- 5 BELL PEPPERS, STEMS AND SEEDS REMOVED, CUT INTO STRIPS
- 2 TABLESPOONS EXTRA-VIRGIN OLIVE OIL
- 2 GARLIC CLOVES
- 8 PORK CHOPS
- 4 BAY LEAVES
- 2 WHOLE CLOVES

SALT AND PEPPER, TO TASTE

AGNELLO CACIO E OVA

YIELD: 4 SERVINGS / **ACTIVE TIME:** 20 MINUTES / **TOTAL TIME:** 1 HOUR AND 20 MINUTES

A classic Easter dish in Abruzzi, agnello cacio e ova (lamb with eggs and cheese) includes the two main symbols of this holiday, eggs and lamb.

1. Place the olive oil in a large skillet and warm it over medium heat. Add the onion and juniper berries and cook, stirring occasionally, until the onion has softened, about 5 minutes.

2. Season the lamb with salt and pepper and add it to the pan along with the rosemary, thyme, and bay leaf. Sear until the lamb is browned, turning it as necessary.

3. Add the wine, scraping up any browned bits from the bottom of the pan. Cook until the wine has nearly evaporated and then add enough water to cover the lamb. Cover the pan and braise the lamb until it is tender, about 40 minutes.

4. Uncover the pan and let the sauce reduce. Remove the rosemary, thyme, and bay leaf and discard the herbs. Reduce the heat to low.

5. Place the eggs in a bowl, whisk until scrambled, and then whisk in the pecorino. Add the egg mixture to the lamb and cook until it has set, 3 to 4 minutes. Serve immediately.

INGREDIENTS:

¼	CUP EXTRA-VIRGIN OLIVE OIL
1	YELLOW ONION, SLICED THIN
5	JUNIPER BERRIES
2.2	LBS. BONELESS LEG OF LAMB, TRIMMED AND CUT INTO 1-INCH CUBES
	SALT AND PEPPER, TO TASTE
1	SPRIG OF FRESH ROSEMARY
1	SPRIG OF FRESH THYME
1	BAY LEAF
½	CUP WHITE WINE
7	EGGS
2	CUPS GRATED PECORINO CHEESE

PEPERONI RIPIENI DI TONNO

YIELD: 8 SERVINGS / **ACTIVE TIME:** 20 MINUTES / **TOTAL TIME:** 1 HOUR AND 20 MINUTES

This recipe is a version of my mother's rendition of tuna-stuffed bell peppers, a Sicilian staple. It was one of my childhood favorites and what I always ask my daughter to cook on my birthday. For me, it is the contrast between the sweet peppers and salty filling that makes this dish special.

1. Preheat the oven to 350°F. Place all of the ingredients, except for the peppers, in a bowl and stir until well combined.

2. Cut off the top of the peppers and set the tops aside. Remove the seeds and ribs from the peppers, taking care not to break the peppers.

3. Stuff the peppers with the filling and place the pepper tops back on top. Place the peppers in a baking dish, on their sides so that they sit end to end, lightly season them with salt, and drizzle olive oil over them.

4. Place the peppers in the oven and bake until they start to look slightly charred, about 1 hour, turning them over halfway through.

5. Remove the peppers from the oven and let them cool completely.

6. Chill the peppers in the refrigerator for 1 hour before serving.

INGREDIENTS:

- 1.3 LBS. STALE BREAD, SOAKED IN WATER AND SQUEEZED DRY
- 1 LB. TUNA IN OLIVE OIL, DRAINED
- 14 ANCHOVIES IN OLIVE OIL, DRAINED AND CHOPPED
- ⅔ CUP PITTED GREEK OLIVES, CHOPPED
- 3 TABLESPOONS CAPERS IN SALT, SOAKED, DRAINED, AND SQUEEZED
- 2 GARLIC CLOVES, MINCED
- 3 TABLESPOONS FINELY CHOPPED FRESH PARSLEY
- ½ CUP EXTRA-VIRGIN OLIVE OIL, PLUS MORE TO TASTE
- SALT AND PEPPER, TO TASTE
- 8 RED OR YELLOW BELL PEPPERS

AGNELLO A CUTTURIEDDE

YIELD: 5 SERVINGS / **ACTIVE TIME:** 30 MINUTES / **TOTAL TIME:** 5 HOURS

A recipe common to parts of both Basilicata and Apulia, agnello a cutturiedde is a lamb stew that is typically made for Christmas and other convivial occasions. For those wondering, lampascioni are bulbs of wild hyacinth, and they carry an inimitable bittersweet flavor.

1. Place the lamb, vinegar, and bay leaves in a bowl, add water until the lamb is covered, and let it marinate for 2 hours.

2. Place the olive oil in a Dutch oven and warm it over medium heat. Add the onion, celery, and carrot and cook, stirring occasionally, until they have softened, about 5 minutes.

3. Add the tomatoes and cook, stirring occasionally, for about 5 minutes.

4. Add the potatoes, lampascioni, greens, and enough water to cover the vegetables, season with salt and pepper, and bring to a boil.

5. Drain the lamb and add it to the pot along with the bay leaves. Add water until the lamb is covered and bring to a simmer.

6. Reduce the heat to low, cover the pot, and cook until the lamb is tender, about 2 hours.

7. Remove the lid, remove the lamb from the pot, and raise the heat to high. Cook until the liquid has reduced.

8. To serve, ladle the sauce and vegetables over the lamb, top with the pecorino, and enjoy.

INGREDIENTS:

- 2½ LBS. BONELESS LEG OF LAMB OR MUTTON, TRIMMED AND CUT INTO ½-INCH CUBES
- 1 CUP RED WINE VINEGAR
- 4 BAY LEAVES
- 6 TABLESPOONS EXTRA-VIRGIN OLIVE OIL
- 1 YELLOW ONION, FINELY DICED
- 1 CELERY STALK, FINELY DICED
- 1 CARROT, PEELED AND FINELY DICED
- 1 LB. TOMATOES, CHOPPED
- 1 LB. POTATOES, PEELED AND DICED
- 3½ OZ. LAMPASCIONI OR BABY ONIONS, CLEANED AND LEFT WHOLE
- 7 OZ. CHICORY OR COLLARD GREENS, RINSED WELL
- SALT AND PEPPER, TO TASTE
- 1 CUP GRATED PECORINO CHEESE, FOR GARNISH

AGNELLO ALLA GALLURESE

YIELD: 5 SERVINGS / **ACTIVE TIME:** 20 MINUTES / **TOTAL TIME:** 1 HOUR AND 20 MINUTES

Sardinia is known for its whole pig roast porcheddu, which is not possible to make in a kitchen oven, but also has other delicious and earthy meat dishes, like this easy lamb recipe from the Gallura region.

1. Place the butter in a large skillet and melt it over medium heat. Season the lamb with salt and pepper and add it to the pan with the garlic and juniper berries. Sear the lamb until it is browned all over, turning it as necessary.

2. Add the rosemary, thyme, bay leaves, and potatoes, season the dish with salt and pepper, and cook, stirring occasionally, for 5 minutes.

3. Add water until the lamb is covered and bring to a simmer. Reduce the heat to medium-low, cover the pan, and cook for 30 minutes.

4. Remove the rosemary, thyme, and bay leaves and discard them. Add the olives and cook until the lamb and potatoes are tender, about 20 minutes, stirring occasionally. Serve immediately.

INGREDIENTS:

- 7 TABLESPOONS UNSALTED BUTTER
- 3 LBS. BONELESS LEG OF LAMB, TRIMMED AND CUT INTO 2-INCH CUBES
- SALT AND PEPPER, TO TASTE
- 2 GARLIC CLOVES
- 2 JUNIPER BERRIES
- 2 SPRIGS OF FRESH ROSEMARY
- 2 SPRIGS OF FRESH THYME
- 4 BAY LEAVES
- 6 POTATOES, PEELED AND CUBED
- ½ CUP PITTED GREEN OLIVES

CALAMARI RIPIENI

YIELD: 4 SERVINGS / **ACTIVE TIME:** 30 MINUTES / **TOTAL TIME:** 1 HOUR

S quid is extremely versatile and a quite inexpensive seafood that is worth learning to incorporate into your cooking more often. Here is a Sicilian version of a stuffed squid recipe that will help you do just that.

1. Preheat the oven to 390°F. Place 2 tablespoons of olive oil in a large skillet and warm it over medium-low heat. Dice the squid tentacles, pat them dry, and add them to the pan. Cook, stirring frequently, until they are cooked through, about 2 minutes. Remove the tentacles from the pan and place them in a bowl.

2. Add 2 tablespoons of olive oil, the olives, capers, anchovies, garlic, parsley, and bread crumbs to the bowl, season the mixture with salt and pepper, and stir to combine.

3. Place the mixture on the strips of squid, roll them up, and secure them with toothpicks.

4. Coat a baking dish with some of the remaining olive oil. Place the squid in the dish, season with salt, top with additional parsley and bread crumbs, and drizzle the remaining olive oil over the top.

5. Place the squid in the oven and bake until they just start to brown, 15 to 20 minutes. Take care not to overcook the squid, as they will harden.

6. Remove the squid from the oven and serve immediately.

INGREDIENTS:

½   CUP EXTRA-VIRGIN OLIVE OIL

8   SQUID, CLEANED (SEE PAGE 277)

⅔   CUP PITTED BLACK OLIVES, MINCED

1   TABLESPOON CAPERS IN BRINE, DRAINED AND RINSED

10   ANCHOVIES IN OLIVE OIL, DRAINED AND CHOPPED

3   GARLIC CLOVES, FINELY MINCED

2   TABLESPOONS FINELY CHOPPED FRESH PARSLEY, PLUS MORE FOR TOPPING

⅔   CUP BREAD CRUMBS, PLUS MORE FOR TOPPING

     SALT AND PEPPER, TO TASTE

SEPPIE CON I PISELLI

YIELD: 4 SERVINGS / **ACTIVE TIME:** 30 MINUTES / **TOTAL TIME:** 1 HOUR AND 10 MINUTES

A classic seafood-and-legumes dish from Southern Italy, seppie con i piselli ("squid with peas") is most popular in Sicily, but it is also treasured in other regions, like Abruzzi.

1. To clean the squid, find the bone and make a transversal cut to eliminate it. Remove the internal organs of the squid and the ink sac (if present). Separate the head from the body and remove the innards of the head. Remove the tentacles and the beak that is positioned in the center of the tentacles. Make a small incision on the back and remove the skin. Remove the eyes, rinse the squid, and cut the body into wide strips. Set the strips and tentacles aside.

2. Place the olive oil in a large skillet and warm it over low heat. Add the onion and cook, stirring occasionally, until it has softened, about 6 minutes.

3. Add half of the broth and the squid, season with salt and pepper, and raise the heat to medium. Cook until the liquid has evaporated.

4. Add the wine and cook until it has evaporated.

5. Add the peas, tomatoes, and remaining broth, cover the pan, and reduce the heat to low. Cook for 15 minutes.

6. Stir in the parsley and serve.

INGREDIENTS:

2.2 LBS. SQUID, CLEANED

¼ CUP EXTRA-VIRGIN OLIVE OIL

1 WHITE ONION, FINELY DICED

1 CUP BRODO VEGETALE (SEE PAGE 806)

SALT AND PEPPER, TO TASTE

¼ CUP WHITE WINE

1 LB. PEAS

1 LB. WHOLE PEELED TOMATOES, CRUSHED

2 TABLESPOONS CHOPPED FRESH PARSLEY

COZZE ALLO ZAFFERANO

YIELD: 4 SERVINGS / **ACTIVE TIME:** 20 MINUTES / **TOTAL TIME:** 40 MINUTES

You won't be surprised to learn that this unique, saffron-spiked seafood dish is from the Abruzzi region, which is renowned for its top-notch saffron.

1. Place 2 tablespoons of olive oil in a Dutch oven and warm it over medium heat. Add the onion and bay leaf and cook, stirring occasionally, until the onion has softened, about 5 minutes.

2. Add the mussels, cover the pot, and cook until the majority of the mussels have opened, 5 to 7 minutes. Discard any mussels that did not open. Strain the mussels through a fine-mesh sieve, reserving any liquid.

3. Place the reserved liquid in a large saucepan and bring it to a boil. Add the saffron and remaining olive oil and whisk until the mixture has emulsified. If desired, add the cornstarch to thicken the emulsion.

4. Season the emulsion with salt, drizzle it over the mussels, garnish with parsley, and enjoy.

INGREDIENTS:

7	TABLESPOONS EXTRA-VIRGIN OLIVE OIL
½	ONION, CHOPPED
1	BAY LEAF
4½	LBS. MUSSELS, RINSED WELL AND DEBEARDED
1	TABLESPOON SAFFRON THREADS
1	TEASPOON CORNSTARCH (OPTIONAL)
	SALT, TO TASTE
	FRESH PARSLEY, FINELY CHOPPED, FOR GARNISH

INVOLTINI DI PESCE SPADA

YIELD: 4 SERVINGS / **ACTIVE TIME:** 30 MINUTES / **TOTAL TIME:** 1 HOUR

Many people love the flavor of swordfish, but are at a loss when it comes time to do anything other than grill it. This traditional Sicilian recipe is a delicious alternative.

1. Preheat the oven to 390°F. Place 2 tablespoons of olive oil in a large skillet and warm it over medium-high heat. Add two-thirds of the bread crumbs and cook, stirring occasionally, until they are golden brown, 5 to 7 minutes.

2. Transfer the toasted bread crumbs to a bowl, add the garlic, raisins, pine nuts, pecorino, parsley, lemon juice, and 3 tablespoons of olive oil, and stir to combine. Season the mixture with salt and pepper.

3. Top the slices of swordfish with the bread crumb mixture, roll them up, and thread the rolls, bay leaves, and lemon slices onto skewers, portioning three rolls to each skewer and alternating between the rolls, bay leaves, and lemon slices.

4. Place the skewers in a baking dish, drizzle the remaining olive oil over them, and sprinkle the remaining bread crumbs on top.

5. Place the baking dish in the oven and bake until the swordfish is just golden brown, about 20 minutes.

6. Remove the swordfish from the oven and serve it alongside the Salmoriglio Sauce.

SALMORIGLIO SAUCE

1. Place all of the ingredients in a small bowl and stir until well combined. Use immediately or store in the refrigerator.

INGREDIENTS:

7	TABLESPOONS EXTRA-VIRGIN OLIVE OIL
1	CUP BREAD CRUMBS
1	GARLIC CLOVE, MINCED
2	TABLESPOONS RAISINS
2	TABLESPOONS PINE NUTS
3	TABLESPOONS GRATED PECORINO CHEESE
2	TABLESPOONS CHOPPED FRESH PARSLEY
	JUICE OF ½ LEMON
	SALT AND PEPPER, TO TASTE
12	LONG, THIN SLICES OF SWORDFISH
8	BAY LEAVES
1	LEMON, CUT INTO 8 SLICES
	SALMORIGLIO SAUCE (SEE RECIPE), FOR SERVING

SALMORIGLIO SAUCE

½	CUP EXTRA-VIRGIN OLIVE OIL
½	CUP HOT WATER
1	TABLESPOON CHOPPED FRESH PARSLEY
1	GARLIC CLOVE, MINCED
	JUICE OF ½ LEMON
	DRIED OREGANO, TO TASTE
	SALT AND PEPPER, TO TASTE

SARDE A BECCAFICU

YIELD: 4 SERVINGS / **ACTIVE TIME:** 20 MINUTES / **TOTAL TIME:** 1 HOUR

One of the most renowned Sicilian specialties, sarde a beccaficu is the poor man's version of a delicacy from the 1800s, as only the nobility had access to game. Everyone had access to the humble sardine, however, and this dish is a result—one that is even tastier than the recipe that inspired it.

1. Preheat the oven to 350°F and coat a baking dish with olive oil. Place 2 tablespoons of olive oil in a large skillet and warm it over medium-high heat. Add the bread crumbs and cook, stirring occasionally, until they are golden brown, 5 to 7 minutes.

2. Set 2 tablespoons of the toasted bread crumbs aside and place the rest in a bowl. Add the orange juice, raisins, pine nuts, anchovies, parsley, garlic, sugar, and 2 tablespoons of olive oil and stir to combine. Season the mixture with salt and pepper.

3. Top the sardines with the bread crumb mixture, roll them up from head to tail, and arrange them in the baking dish, packing them together tightly so that they do not open.

4. Put the bay leaves and orange slices between the sardines, drizzle the remaining olive oil over them, and sprinkle the reserved bread crumbs on top.

5. Place the baking dish in the oven and bake until the sardines are cooked through and starting to brown, about 10 to 15 minutes.

6. Remove the sardines from the oven and enjoy.

INGREDIENTS:

7	TABLESPOONS EXTRA-VIRGIN OLIVE OIL, PLUS MORE AS NEEDED
1	CUP BREAD CRUMBS
	JUICE OF ½ ORANGE
½	CUP RAISINS
⅓	CUP PINE NUTS
7	ANCHOVIES IN OLIVE OIL, DRAINED AND CHOPPED
2	TABLESPOONS CHOPPED FRESH PARSLEY
1	GARLIC CLOVE, MINCED
1	TABLESPOON SUGAR
	SALT AND PEPPER, TO TASTE
2.2	LBS. FRESH SARDINES, CLEANED, DEBONED, AND RINSED
4	BAY LEAVES
½	ORANGE, SLICED

PESCESTOCCO:
HISTORY AND LEGEND

In Messina, the Sicilian city closest to the Italian peninsula, there is a saying: *sciroccu, malanova e piscistoccu e Messina non mancanu mai*, which literally translates into "scirocco wind, bad news, and dried cod are never missing in Messina." Dried cod (pescestocco in local dialect), though no longer easy to find in many places, is in fact very common in Sicilian cuisine, particularly in Messina and surrounding areas. This is tied to Messina's long history as an international harbor, which made it easy for vessels coming from Northern Europe that were stocked with dried cod to land in this town.

Inexpensive, nourishing, and gifted with an extremely long shelf life, dried cod, which is also known as stockfish, became a staple in Sicilian cuisine, and was particularly important during Lent and on Fridays, when, according to Catholic customs, no meat was allowed on the table.

Particularly dear to the inhabitants of Messina is the collective memory of a specific restaurant owner, Epifanio Fiumara, who operated a popular osteria. It was at the end of the nineteenth century that Fiumara began to offer a stockfish stew commonly known as stoccafisso alla messinese. His stew aimed to be delicious, substantial, and affordable enough that even the poorest of his customers could eat it. Fiumara was known to price offerings according to the depth of his clients' pockets, a trait that made him beloved. The memory of Fiumara and his osteria has stood the test of time, so much that the street where the restaurant was located is still informally called Piazza Don Fano, after the osteria's name.

STOCCAFISSO ALLA MESSINESE

YIELD: 4 SERVINGS / **ACTIVE TIME:** 30 MINUTES / **TOTAL TIME:** 2 HOURS

Though it is not terribly easy to find nowadays, dried cod, or stockfish, is still very popular in Sicily, and this famed recipe is a big reason why.

1. Place flour in a shallow bowl and dredge the stockfish in it until the stockfish is completely coated.

2. Place 2 tablespoons of olive oil in a large skillet and warm it over medium heat. Working in batches to avoid crowding the pan, add the stockfish and fry until it is golden brown, about 5 minutes, turning it as necessary. Transfer the fried stockfish to a paper towel–lined plate and let it drain.

3. Place the remaining olive oil in a large saucepan and warm it over medium heat. Add the onion and cook, stirring occasionally, until it has softened, about 5 minutes.

4. Add the tomatoes, olives, capers, and celery, reduce the heat to low, and cover the pan. Cook for 15 minutes.

5. Add the stockfish and enough water so that the mixture is covered. Cover the pan and cook for 30 minutes.

6. Add the potatoes and more water if there doesn't seem to be enough liquid. Season the dish with salt and red pepper flakes, cover the pan, and cook until the potatoes are tender, 30 to 40 minutes.

7. Serve with crusty bread and enjoy.

INGREDIENTS:

	ALL-PURPOSE FLOUR, AS NEEDED
2	LBS. STOCKFISH (DRIED COD), SOAKED, CLEANED, AND CHOPPED
6	TABLESPOONS EXTRA-VIRGIN OLIVE OIL
1	ONION, SLICED THIN
1	LB. WHOLE PEELED TOMATOES, CRUSHED BY HAND
⅔	CUP PITTED OLIVES
6	TABLESPOONS CAPERS IN SALT, SOAKED, DRAINED, AND SQUEEZED DRY
1	CELERY STALK WITH ITS LEAVES, SLICED THIN
2	LBS. POTATOES, PEELED AND CHOPPED
	SALT, TO TASTE
	RED PEPPER FLAKES, TO TASTE
	CRUSTY BREAD, FOR SERVING

DOLCI & PANE

ROCCOCÒ

YIELD: 20 COOKIES / **ACTIVE TIME:** 1 HOUR / **TOTAL TIME:** 1 HOUR AND 30 MINUTES

In the past, Christmas was the one time when common people were allowed to splurge on ingredients, and these cookies are a splendid representation of what can come of such freedom. Roccocò are now baked all year round by bakeries but are traditionally baked at home on December 8, a practice dating back to the 1300s. There are likely as many recipes for roccocò as there are households in Naples—here's one that produces a crunchy, but not stone-hard, cookie.

1. Preheat the oven to 350°F. Place the almonds on a baking sheet, place them in the oven, and toast them for 5 minutes. Remove the almonds from the oven and let them cool completely. Leave the oven on.

2. Place the flour, cocoa powder, Pisto, baker's ammonia, sugar, citrus zests, candied orange peels, and salt in the work bowl of a stand mixer fitted with the dough hook.

3. Place the orange juice and water in a measuring cup and warm the mixture to 105°F. With the mixer running on low, gradually add the mixture to the flour mixture until it has all been incorporated and the mixture comes together as a dough.

4. Add the almonds and work the dough until they are incorporated. The dough should be dense and not sticky.

5. Work the dough on low until it is smooth, about 5 minutes. Divide the dough into 3 pieces, place them on a flour-dusted work surface, and roll each piece into a log. Tear the logs into pieces that are approximately 3 oz. and roll them into thin logs.

6. Line two baking sheets with parchment paper. Form each log into a ring and place them on the baking sheets.

7. Place the egg and egg yolk in a bowl and whisk until combined. Brush the rings, inside and out, with the mixture.

8. Place the baking sheets in the oven and bake the roccocò until they are golden brown and hard, about 25 minutes.

9. Remove the roccocò from the oven and let them cool on the baking sheets for a few minutes before transferring them to wire racks to cool completely.

PISTO

1. Place all of the ingredients in a bowl and stir to combine.

INGREDIENTS:

17.6 OZ. UNPEELED ALMONDS

17.6 OZ. ALL-PURPOSE FLOUR, PLUS MORE AS NEEDED

1 TEASPOON UNSWEETENED COCOA POWDER

1½ TEASPOONS PISTO (SEE RECIPE)

1 TEASPOON BAKER'S AMMONIA

17.6 OZ. SUGAR

ZEST OF 1 ORANGE

ZEST OF 1 CLEMENTINE

ZEST OF ½ LEMON

⅓ CUP CANDIED ORANGE PEELS, MINCED

PINCH OF FINE SEA SALT

3½ TABLESPOONS FRESH ORANGE JUICE

½ CUP WATER

1 EGG

1 EGG YOLK

PISTO

1 TEASPOON CINNAMON

½ TEASPOON CORIANDER

½ TEASPOON BLACK PEPPER

½ TEASPOON FRESHLY GRATED NUTMEG

¼ TEASPOON GROUND CLOVES

PINCH OF GROUND STAR ANISE

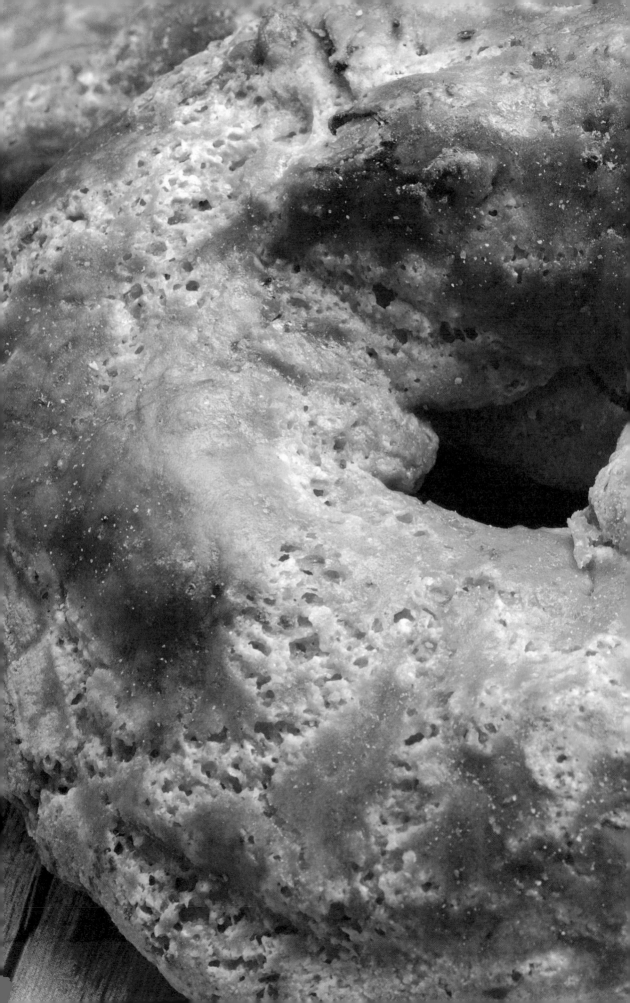

ROCCOCÒ:
THE CRUNCHY STONES WITH
A FASCINATING HISTORY

Delicious Christmas cookies that can be enjoyed all year round, roccocò owe their name to the French word rocaille, which means "rocky." These cookies are in fact quite hard in their original version, as they are supposed to be dipped in a beverage, traditionally sweet wine.

The origin of this food specialty is, for once, not obscure. Instead, it's quite certain, and fairly fascinating.

Sources agree that roccocò were created in the second decade of the thirteenth century by the skilled hands of the nuns of the Real Convento della Maddalena, in the Maddalena district of Naples. It was not uncommon for delicious food to come out of convents, but this specific convent was particularly blessed culinarily—the Maddalena nuns were also behind the famous pasta reale, which is what marzipan is called in Naples. The term "reale" is in fact a tribute to the nuns from the Real Convento della Maddalena, who were the first to make this pastry base popular.

Roccocò are traditionally baked at home on December 8 for the Festa dell'Immacolata Concezione and then eaten all the way through the Christmas festivities. They can have a variable consistency, but Neapolitans swear that the authentic roccocò needs to be hard on the outside and soft inside.

Like susamielli and mostaccioli, roccocò are flavored with a spice mix called pisto that includes coriander, star anise, cinnamon, black pepper, cloves, and nutmeg. In Naples, pisto can be found in stores, but it is otherwise easy to make at home.

ROCCOCÒ MORBIDI

YIELD: 20 COOKIES / **ACTIVE TIME:** 1 HOUR / **TOTAL TIME:** 1 HOUR AND 30 MINUTES

The classic roccocò cookies are hard on the outside and soft inside, and are at their best if dipped in sweet wine. Since this use has gradually become less popular, a softer version of roccocò has been developed. It is very similar to the original recipe but includes honey and more baker's ammonia.

1. Preheat the oven to 350°F. Place the almonds on a baking sheet, place them in the oven, and toast them for 5 minutes. Remove the almonds from the oven and let them cool completely. Leave the oven on.

2. Place the flour, cocoa powder, Pisto, baker's ammonia, sugar, zests, honey, candied orange peels, and salt in the work bowl of a stand mixer fitted with the dough hook.

3. Place the orange juice and water in a measuring cup and warm the mixture to 105°F. With the mixer running on low, gradually add the mixture to the flour mixture until it has all been incorporated and the mixture comes together as a dough.

4. Add the almonds and work the dough until they are incorporated. The dough should be dense and not sticky.

5. Work the dough on low until it is smooth, about 5 minutes. Divide the dough into 3 pieces, place them on a flour-dusted work surface, and roll each piece into a log. Tear the logs into pieces that are approximately 3 oz. and roll them into thin logs.

6. Line two baking sheets with parchment paper. Form each log into a ring and place them on the baking sheets.

7. Place the egg and egg yolk in a bowl and whisk until combined. Brush the rings, inside and out, with the mixture.

8. Place the baking sheets in the oven and bake the roccocò until they are golden brown and hard, about 25 minutes.

9. Remove the roccocò from the oven and let them cool on the baking sheets for a few minutes before transferring them to wire racks to cool completely.

INGREDIENTS:

17.6 OZ. UNPEELED ALMONDS

17.6 OZ. ALL-PURPOSE FLOUR, PLUS MORE AS NEEDED

1 TEASPOON UNSWEETENED COCOA POWDER

1½ TEASPOONS PISTO (SEE PAGE 287)

2 TEASPOONS BAKER'S AMMONIA

17.6 OZ. SUGAR

ZEST OF 1 ORANGE

ZEST OF 1 CLEMENTINE

ZEST OF ½ LEMON

1 TABLESPOON PLUS 1 TEASPOON HONEY

⅓ CUP CANDIED ORANGE PEELS, MINCED

PINCH OF FINE SEA SALT

3½ TABLESPOONS FRESH ORANGE JUICE

½ CUP WATER

1 EGG

1 EGG YOLK

MOSTACCIOLI

YIELD: 15 COOKIES / **ACTIVE TIME:** 40 MINUTES / **TOTAL TIME:** 1 HOUR

Although there are countless regional variations of mostaccioli, the most popular one is from Naples. Their name refers to the original version of them, which included mosto, the must derived from the initial processing in wine making. Neapolitan mostaccioli have lost their must but are scrumptious nonetheless, and surely easier to make.

1. Preheat the oven to 350°F and line two baking sheets with parchment paper. Place the flours, honey, sugar, baker's ammonia, Pisto, cocoa powder, orange zest, and orange juice in the work bowl of a stand mixer fitted with the paddle attachment. With the mixer running, gradually add the hot water and work the mixture until it comes together as a soft, smooth dough. Depending on the all-purpose flour you end up using, you may not need to use all of the water; you also may need to add more water if the dough is too stiff.

2. Place the dough on a flour-dusted work surface and roll it out until it is about ½ inch thick. Cut the dough into diamonds and place them on the baking sheets.

3. Place the cookies in the oven and bake until they are golden brown, 10 to 15 minutes. Remove the cookies from the oven and let them cool.

4. While the cookies are cooling, bring a few inches of water to a simmer in a medium saucepan. Place the chocolate in a heatproof bowl, place it over the simmering water, and stir until the chocolate has melted.

5. Using kitchen tongs, dip the cookies into the melted chocolate and place them on wire racks. Let the chocolate set before serving.

INGREDIENTS:

17.6   OZ. ALL-PURPOSE FLOUR, PLUS MORE AS NEEDED

5.3   OZ. ALMOND FLOUR

5.3   OZ. HONEY

5.3   OZ. SUGAR

1½   TEASPOONS BAKER'S AMMONIA

2   TEASPOONS PISTO (SEE PAGE 287)

1.2   OZ. UNSWEETENED COCOA POWDER

ZEST AND JUICE OF 1 ORANGE

3½   OZ. HOT WATER (140°F), PLUS MORE AS NEEDED

7   OZ. BITTERSWEET CHOCOLATE, CHOPPED

CELLI PIENI

YIELD: 40 COOKIES / **ACTIVE TIME:** 40 MINUTES / **TOTAL TIME:** 1 HOUR AND 30 MINUTES

Celli pieni, also called celli ripieni or cill pijn, are delicious grape jam and toasted almond–filled cookies from Ortona in Abruzzi. They look like giant fortune cookies and make fantastic presents around the holidays.

1. Place the cookies and almonds in a bowl and stir to combine. Add the jam, lemon zest, cocoa powder, and cinnamon and stir to incorporate. Let the mixture rest for 30 minutes.

2. Place the wine and sugar in a saucepan and warm the mixture over medium heat, stirring to dissolve the sugar.

3. Place the wine syrup in a heatproof bowl, add the olive oil and flour, and work the mixture with your hands until it comes together as a smooth dough. Cover the dough and let it rest for 30 minutes.

4. Preheat the oven to 350°F and line two baking sheets with parchment paper. Place the dough on a flour-dusted work surface and roll it out into a very thin sheet. It is also possible to use a pasta maker to get the dough thin enough.

5. Distribute teaspoons of the jam mixture on the dough, leaving 1 inch between each dollop. Use a glass or ring cutter to cut out rounds of dough with the jam mixture in the center. Fold the rounds over the filling, shape them into crescents, and pinch the seams to seal the cookies. Bring the two points of the crescents together to form the shape of a fortune cookie or tortellino. Dust the cookies with sugar and place them on the baking sheets.

6. Place the cookies in the oven and bake until they are a light golden brown, about 15 minutes.

7. Remove the cookies from the oven and let them cool on the baking sheets for a few minutes before transferring them to wire racks to cool completely.

INGREDIENTS:

- ¾ CUP CRUSHED BISCUITS OR OTHER DRY COOKIES
- ⅔ CUP BLANCHED AND TOASTED ALMONDS, FINELY CHOPPED
- 1⅓ CUPS GRAPE JAM
- ZEST OF 1 LEMON
- 2 TEASPOONS UNSWEETENED COCOA POWDER
- ½ TEASPOON CINNAMON
- ⅔ CUP DRY WHITE WINE
- 2 TABLESPOONS SUGAR, PLUS MORE FOR TOPPING
- ⅔ CUP EXTRA-VIRGIN OLIVE OIL
- 17.6 OZ. ALL-PURPOSE FLOUR, PLUS MORE AS NEEDED

SUSAMIELLI

YIELD: 12 COOKIES / **ACTIVE TIME:** 40 MINUTES / **TOTAL TIME:** 1 HOUR

Susamielli are part of the wide range of Neapolitan Christmas sweets. They have a characteristic "S" shape and are prepared with ground almonds, flour, sugar, honey, and pisto, a spice mix found also in other Neapolitan Christmas cookies. This is one of three traditional versions, susamielli nobili, which, as you might have guessed, was reserved for the nobility.

1. Preheat the oven to 350°F and line a baking sheet with parchment paper. Place the almonds and sugar in a food processor and blitz until the almonds are finely ground.

2. Place the almond mixture, flour, baker's ammonia, Pisto, and honey in the work bowl of a stand mixer fitted with the paddle attachment and beat until the mixture comes together as a smooth dough.

3. Divide the dough into 2 pieces and form them into logs. Tear each log into 2-oz. pieces, roll these pieces into thin logs, and shape them into an S.

4. Place the cookies on the baking sheet, brush them with the egg white, and press almonds into the tops.

5. Place the cookies in the oven and bake until they are golden brown, about 15 minutes.

6. Remove the cookies from the oven and let them cool on the baking sheet for a few minutes before transferring them to wire racks to cool completely.

INGREDIENTS:

¾ CUP BLANCHED ALMONDS, PLUS MORE FOR TOPPING

3½ OZ. SUGAR

8.8 OZ. ALL-PURPOSE FLOUR

½ TEASPOON BAKER'S AMMONIA

2 TEASPOONS PISTO (SEE PAGE 287)

¾ CUP HONEY

1 EGG WHITE, BEATEN

BISCOTTI ALL'AMARENA

YIELD: 10 COOKIES / **ACTIVE TIME:** 1 HOUR / **TOTAL TIME:** 1 HOUR AND 30 MINUTES

These sour cherry–filled cookies were born out of a desire to repurpose the leftovers of other desserts. A favorite of the Neapolitans, they are perfect enjoyed with espresso.

1. To begin preparations for the frolla, place all of the ingredients in a mixing bowl and quickly work the mixture with your hands until it just comes together as a dough. Place the dough on a flour-dusted surface and shape it into a compact ball. Cover the dough with plastic wrap and chill it in the refrigerator for 30 minutes.

2. To prepare the filling, place all of the ingredients in a bowl and stir until well combined.

3. Place the dough on a flour-dusted work surface and roll it into a rectangle.

4. Line a baking sheet with parchment paper. Shape the filling into a log that is the same length as the dough. Place the filling in the center of the dough and roll the long sides of the dough over the filling, making sure the sides meet at the center. Pinch the seam closed, turn the dough over, and place it on the baking sheet. Chill the dough in the refrigerator for 15 minutes.

5. To prepare the glaze, place the confectioners' sugar and egg whites in a small bowl and beat until the mixture is a thick glaze. Set the glaze aside.

6. Preheat the oven to 350°F. Take the dough out of the refrigerator and trim away the 2 ends that have little filling inside. Spread the glaze evenly over the dough.

7. Using a toothpick, cut two long strips in the glaze. Place cherry jam in a piping bag fitted with a fine tip and pipe the jam into the strips.

8. Cut the dough into 1½-inch-thick slices, place them in the oven, and bake until they are golden brown, about 20 minutes.

9. Remove the cookies from the oven and let them cool on the baking sheet for a few minutes before transferring them to a wire rack to cool completely.

INGREDIENTS:

FOR THE FROLLA

10.6 OZ. ALL-PURPOSE FLOUR, PLUS MORE AS NEEDED

4.2 OZ. SUGAR

4.2 OZ. UNSALTED BUTTER, SOFTENED AND CHOPPED INTO PIECES

1 EGG

1 EGG YOLK

1 TEASPOON BAKING POWDER

1 TEASPOON PURE VANILLA EXTRACT

FOR THE FILLING

12 OZ. LEFTOVER SPONGE CAKE, CRUMBLED

5½ TABLESPOONS UNSWEETENED COCOA POWDER

1 CUP PLUS 2 TABLESPOONS SOUR CHERRIES OR BLACK CHERRY JAM

2 TABLESPOONS ALCHERMES OR ANOTHER SWEET LIQUEUR

FOR THE GLAZE

1 CUP PLUS 2 TABLESPOONS CONFECTIONERS' SUGAR

2 TABLESPOONS EGG WHITES

BLACK CHERRY JAM, AS NEEDED

PEPATELLI MOLISANI

YIELD: 40 COOKIES / **ACTIVE TIME:** 30 MINUTES / **TOTAL TIME:** 1 HOUR

Typical of Molise and Abruzzi, pepatelli are traditionally made during the Christmas season. They look like the Tuscan cantucci, but have a very different taste due to the use of whole wheat flour and the addition of black pepper and orange zest.

1. Line a 13 x 9–inch baking dish with parchment paper. Sift the flour into a large bowl, add the baking soda, and stir to combine. Set the mixture aside.

2. Place the honey in a medium saucepan and warm it over medium heat. Stir in the almonds, orange zest, and pepper, add the flour mixture, and stir vigorously until the mixture comes together as a dough.

3. Pour the dough into the baking dish and level it until it is about 1 inch thick. Let the dough cool completely.

4. Preheat the oven to 340°F. Line two baking sheets with parchment paper. Cut the dough into 2 x ½–inch strips and place them on the baking sheets.

5. Place the cookies in the oven and bake until they are a light golden brown, about 15 minutes. Turn off the oven and leave the cookies in the cooling oven for 5 minutes.

6. Remove the cookies from the oven and let them cool on the baking sheets for a few minutes before transferring them to wire racks to cool completely.

INGREDIENTS:

17.6 OZ. WHOLE WHEAT FLOUR

1 TEASPOON BAKING SODA

17.6 OZ. HONEY

3 CUPS BLANCHED AND TOASTED ALMONDS

ZEST OF 1 ORANGE

1 TABLESPOON BLACK PEPPER

TARALLI DI AVIGLIANO

YIELD: 4 LARGE TARALLI / **ACTIVE TIME:** 1 HOUR / **TOTAL TIME:** 2 HOURS

Also called lu mstazzuol, these large sweets from Avigliano in Basilicata were traditionally given away to guests at wedding banquets, but are now enjoyed year-round.

1. To begin preparations for the dough, place the eggs and salt in a bowl and whisk to combine.

2. Place the remaining ingredients in a large bowl and stir to combine. Work the mixture until it comes together as a shaggy dough.

3. Transfer the dough to a flour-dusted working surface and knead it until it is soft and smooth. If the dough feels too dry, incorporate another egg.

4. Tear the dough into 4 pieces and form them into logs that are about 8 inches long and 1 inch thick (each one should weigh just under 1 lb.). Join the ends together to form large rings and pinch the seams.

5. Bring water to a boil in a large pot. Add the taralli a few at a time and cook until they rise to the surface. Remove, score the taralli at their equators, and place them on a paper towel–lined plate to dry.

6. Preheat the oven to 350°F and line a baking sheet with parchment paper.

7. Place the taralli on the baking sheet, place them in the oven, and bake until they are golden brown, about 20 minutes.

8. Remove the taralli from the oven and let them cool completely.

9. To prepare the glaze, place the water and sugar in a saucepan and bring it to a boil, stirring to dissolve the sugar.

10. Remove the pan from heat and place it on a heat-resistant surface. Work the syrup quickly and energetically with a spatula until it becomes a white paste. Transfer the paste to a heatproof bowl.

11. Bring a few inches of water to a boil in a saucepan. Place the paste over the simmering water and let it melt slowly. Add the anise, stir to incorporate, and then add the taralli, turning them to ensure they are coated evenly.

12. Remove the taralli from the glaze and place them on wire racks. Enjoy once the glaze has hardened.

INGREDIENTS:

FOR THE DOUGH

5	EGGS, PLUS MORE AS NEEDED
	PINCH OF SALT
17.6	OZ. ALL-PURPOSE FLOUR, PLUS MORE AS NEEDED
½	CUP SUGAR
1	TEASPOON BAKING POWDER
3½	OZ. LARD
½	CUP ANISE LIQUEUR

FOR THE GLAZE

½	CUP WATER
17.6	OZ. SUGAR
4	DROPS OF ANISE EXTRACT

TARALLI DOLCI PUGLIESI

YIELD: 60 COOKIES / **ACTIVE TIME:** 40 MINUTES / **TOTAL TIME:** 1 HOUR AND 15 MINUTES

Not as famous as the savory version on page 380, sweet Apulian taralli are delicious treats that make good use of some of the best products of their native land: wine and olive oil.

1. Preheat the oven to 340°F and line two baking sheets with parchment paper. Sift the flour into a mixing bowl, add the baking soda and sugar, and stir to combine. Add the olive oil and wine and work the mixture until it comes together as a shaggy dough.

2. Transfer the dough to a flour-dusted working surface and knead it until it is soft and smooth.

3. Tear the dough into walnut-sized pieces and roll them into 4-inch-long logs. Join the ends together to form rings and gently press down on the seams.

4. Fill a small bowl with sugar and dip the taralli in it until evenly coated.

5. Place the taralli on the baking sheets, place them in the oven, and bake until they are golden brown, about 25 minutes.

6. Remove the taralli from the oven and let them cool on the baking sheets for a few minutes before transferring them to wire racks to cool completely.

INGREDIENTS:

17.6 OZ. ALL-PURPOSE FLOUR, PLUS MORE AS NEEDED

2 TEASPOONS BAKING SODA

4.6 OZ. SUGAR, PLUS MORE FOR COATING

5.3 OZ. EXTRA-VIRGIN OLIVE OIL

¾ CUP SWEET WHITE WINE

CIAMBELLE STROZZOSE

YIELD: 6 CIAMBELLE / **ACTIVE TIME:** 40 MINUTES / **TOTAL TIME:** 24 HOURS

Ciambelle strozzose are big taralli that tend to appear upon Easter tables in the Marche region, though they are also made in parts of Abruzzi. They are traditionally leavened with sourdough or yeast and have the aroma of anise, given to them by Mistrà, a local anise liqueur. In the absence of Mistrà, one can use another liqueur and add some anise extract, or a few anise seeds.

1. Place the flour, yeast, eggs, all but 2 tablespoons of the olive oil, and the liqueur in the work bowl of a stand mixer fitted with the dough hook and stir to combine. Add the sugar and salt and beat the mixture until it comes together as a smooth, elastic dough.

2. Cover the dough and let it rest for 2 to 3 hours in a naturally warm place.

3. Place the dough on a flour-dusted work surface, divide it into 6 pieces, and roll each piece into a round.

4. Make a hole in the center of each round and slowly enlarge it to create doughnuts with rather large holes in their centers. Cover the ciambelle and let them rest for 1 hour.

5. Bring water to a boil in a large pot. Add salt and the remaining olive oil, stir to incorporate, and add the ciambelle, 1 at a time. Boil the ciambelle for 3 to 5 minutes on each side, transfer them to a kitchen towel, and let them dry. Make a cut all the way around the ciambelle at their equators. Cover the ciambelle with a kitchen towel and let them rest overnight.

6. Preheat the oven to 445°F (if you have an oven with a convection mode, use it here) and line two baking sheets with parchment paper.

7. Place the ciambelle on the baking sheets, place them in the oven, and bake until they are hardened, about 15 minutes, taking care not to let them get too hard.

8. Remove the ciambelle from the oven and let them cool on the baking sheets for a few minutes before transferring them to wire racks to cool completely.

INGREDIENTS:

2.2	LBS. ALL-PURPOSE FLOUR, PLUS MORE AS NEEDED
1	PACKET OF INSTANT YEAST
10	EGGS
½	CUP PLUS 3 TABLESPOONS EXTRA-VIRGIN OLIVE OIL
½	CUP MISTRÀ (ANISE LIQUEUR)
4¾	OZ. SUGAR
	PINCH OF SALT, PLUS MORE TO TASTE

PASTE DI MANDORLA SICILIANE

YIELD: 20 COOKIES / **ACTIVE TIME:** 20 MINUTES / **TOTAL TIME:** 40 MINUTES

Possibly the most popular Sicilian cookie, paste di mandorla is ubiquitous in Sicily, and popular through the entirety of Southern Italy. If you prefer to shape them by hand, just remove the water from the recipe and make sure to let the dough rest in the fridge overnight before shaping it into balls.

1. Place the egg whites in the work bowl of a stand mixer fitted with the whisk attachment and whip them until they are very firm.

2. Place the flour and sugar in a bowl and stir to combine. Add the water and almond extract and stir until the mixture comes together.

3. Add the egg whites and fold until the mixture is soft enough to be squeezed out of a piping bag. If the mixture feels too hard, incorporate a splash of water.

4. Place the dough in a piping bag and chill it in the refrigerator for 1 hour.

5. Preheat the oven to 330°F and line a baking sheet with parchment paper. Pipe small dollops of the dough onto the baking sheet.

6. Press either almonds or candied cherries into the centers of the cookies. Place them in the oven and bake until they are golden brown, about 15 minutes.

7. Remove the cookies from the oven and let them cool on the baking sheet for a few minutes before transferring them to wire racks to cool completely.

INGREDIENTS:

2   EGG WHITES

7   OZ. ALMOND FLOUR

4.9   OZ. CONFECTIONERS' SUGAR

3   TABLESPOONS WATER OR LIQUEUR, PLUS MORE AS NEEDED

3   DROPS OF BITTER ALMOND EXTRACT

  ALMONDS, FOR TOPPING (OPTIONAL)

  CANDIED CHERRIES, HALVED, FOR TOPPING (OPTIONAL)

BUCCELLATI

YIELD: 20 COOKIES / **ACTIVE TIME:** 40 MINUTES / **TOTAL TIME:** 3 HOURS

This Sicilian cookie leans upon the very best that summer on that island produces: figs and almonds. Up until a few decades ago, the dough was made at home and then taken to the local bakeries to be baked. Now everyone, including you, can produce them in their own homes.

1. To begin preparations for the dough, place the flours in a large mixing bowl, add the lard, and use a pastry cutter to work the mixture until it is like wet sand.

2. Add the sugar, baker's ammonia, vanilla, and milk and work the mixture until it just comes together as a dough.

3. Transfer the dough to a flour-dusted work surface and quickly knead the dough until it is smooth and dense. Cover the dough with plastic wrap and chill it in the refrigerator for 1 hour.

4. To prepare the filling, place all of the ingredients in a mixing bowl and stir to combine.

5. Preheat the oven to 350°F and line a baking sheet with parchment paper. Place the dough on a flour-dusted work surface and roll it out into a ½-inch-thick rectangle. Spread the filling over the dough and then roll the dough up tightly, starting from a long side.

6. Cut the dough into 1-inch-thick slices, place them on the baking sheet, and gently press down on them to flatten them slightly.

7. Sprinkle sugar sprinkles over the cookies, place them in the oven, and bake until they are golden brown, about 25 minutes.

8. Remove the cookies from the oven and let them cool on the baking sheet for a few minutes before transferring them to wire racks to cool completely.

INGREDIENTS:

FOR THE DOUGH

9.7	OZ. ALL-PURPOSE FLOUR, PLUS MORE AS NEEDED
7.9	OZ. FINELY GROUND DURUM WHEAT FLOUR (SEMOLA RIMACINATA), PLUS MORE AS NEEDED
5	OZ. LARD
5.3	OZ. SUGAR
2	TEASPOONS BAKER'S AMMONIA
1	TEASPOON PURE VANILLA EXTRACT
1	CUP LUKEWARM WHOLE MILK (90°F)

FOR THE FILLING

3	CUPS DRIED FIGS, CHOPPED
⅓	CUP ALMONDS, FINELY CHOPPED
⅓	CUP HONEY OR FIG JAM
1¾	OZ. DARK CHOCOLATE, GRATED
1	CUP CANDIED ORANGE PEELS
	COLORED SUGAR SPRINKLES, FOR TOPPING

REGINELLE

YIELD: 40 COOKIES / **ACTIVE TIME:** 30 MINUTES / **TOTAL TIME:** 2 HOURS

The reginelle, literally the queen's cookies, are characteristic of Palermo. They are coated in sesame seeds, just like traditional Sicilian bread, and are great with an aperitivo and, surprisingly, tea.

1. Place the flour, sugar, and saffron in a mixing bowl and stir to combine.

2. Place the baker's ammonia and milk in a bowl and stir until the baker's ammonia has dissolved. Add the milk mixture, lard, eggs, lemon zest, and salt to the mixing bowl and work the mixture until it just comes together.

3. Place the dough on a flour-dusted work surface and knead it until it is smooth. Form the dough into a ball, cover it with plastic wrap, and chill it in the refrigerator for 30 minutes.

4. Preheat the oven to 390°F and line two baking sheets with parchment paper. Place the dough on a flour-dusted work surface, divide it into 8 pieces, and roll each piece into a 1-inch-thick cylinder. Cut the cylinders into 2-inch-long pieces.

5. Place the sesame seeds in a bowl, spray the pieces of dough with water, and roll them in the sesame seeds until they are completely coated.

6. Place the cookies on the baking sheets, place them in the oven, and bake them until they are golden brown, 10 to 15 minutes.

7. Reduce the oven's temperature to 300°F and bake the cookies for another 15 minutes.

8. Remove the cookies from the oven and let them cool on the baking sheets for a few minutes before transferring them to wire racks to cool completely.

INGREDIENTS:

- 17.6 OZ. ALL-PURPOSE FLOUR, PLUS MORE AS NEEDED
- 5.3 OZ. SUGAR
- ¼ TEASPOON SAFFRON THREADS
- 1 TEASPOON BAKER'S AMMONIA
- 1½ TABLESPOONS WHOLE MILK
- 5 OZ. LARD OR UNSALTED BUTTER
- 2 EGGS
- ZEST OF 1 LEMON
- PINCH OF SALT
- 1 CUP SESAME SEEDS

PASTICCIOTTI LECCESI

YIELD: 15 PASTICCIOTTI / **ACTIVE TIME:** 1 HOUR / **TOTAL TIME:** 2 HOURS

Pasticciotti are oval miniature pies characteristic of Salento, which lies in the extreme south of Apulia. Depending on the location, pasticciotti can have different fillings. In Lecce, they are filled with custard, while in other areas the filling can be fruit jam, ricotta-and-lemon cream, ricotta and cherries, or ricotta and chocolate. As it is not easy to get hold of the oval pasticciotti tins that are traditional, feel free to use a regular muffin pan.

1. Coat the wells of a muffin pan with butter, dust them with flour, and knock out any excess.

2. Preheat the oven to 350°F. Place the frolla on a flour-dusted work surface and beat it with a rolling pin to soften it. Roll out the frolla into a ¼-inch-thick rectangle and use a glass or ring cutter to cut out rounds that are large enough to cover the bottom and sides of the wells in the muffin pan. Place the rounds in the wells and trim away any excess dough. Roll the excess dough out into a thin sheet that will cover the muffin pan.

3. Fill each pastry with a generous spoonful of the custard.

4. Cut rounds slightly larger than the wells from the sheet of dough. Place them over the pasticciotti and press down on the edges to seal so that the tops hold tight in the oven.

5. Prick the tops of the pasticciotti with a toothpick. Place the egg yolk and water in a small bowl, beat to combine, and brush the pasticciotti with the egg wash.

6. Place the pasticciotti in the oven. Baking times will depend on the depth of the wells in the muffin pan. For deeper wells, bake for about 30 minutes. For shallower wells, bake for about 20 minutes. Also, do not worry if the tops detach, they will be reattached later.

7. Remove the pasticciotti from the oven and let them cool for 5 minutes. Cover the pan with a similarly sized tray, invert the pan, and let it rest on the counter for 1 hour.

8. Turn the pan back over, remove the pasticciotti from the pan, dust them generously with confectioners' sugar, and enjoy.

INGREDIENTS:

BUTTER, AS NEEDED

ALL-PURPOSE FLOUR, AS NEEDED

PASTA FROLLA AL LARDO (SEE PAGE 817)

1½ CUPS CREMA PASTICCERA NAPOLETANA (SEE PAGE 820)

1 EGG YOLK

½ TEASPOON WATER

CONFECTIONERS' SUGAR, FOR TOPPING

PISTOCCHEDDUS DE CAPPA

YIELD: 40 COOKIES / **ACTIVE TIME:** 1 HOUR / **TOTAL TIME:** 2 HOURS

This is a very elegant Sardinian cookie that was traditionally baked for important formal events such as weddings, baptisms, confirmations, and holidays. Pistoccheddus can take numerous shapes, some of which are very elaborate. Here we offer a simple version that is no less delicious.

1. Preheat the oven to 350°F and line two baking sheets with parchment paper. To begin preparations for the dough, sift the flours into a mixing bowl, add the baking powder, and stir to combine.

2. Place the baker's ammonia and milk in a separate bowl, stir to dissolve the baker's ammonia, and set the mixture aside.

3. Place the egg yolks and sugar in a separate mixing bowl and whisk until the mixture is pale yellow. Stir in the vanilla, lemon zest, and lard, add the flour mixture, and work the mixture until it comes together.

4. Place the mixture on a flour-dusted work surface, add the milk mixture, and work the mixture until it is a smooth dough. Tear the dough into pieces that are the size of a large walnut and roll each piece into a cylinder. Shape the cylinders into ovals, circles, hearts, or S-shaped cookies.

5. Place the cookies on the baking sheets, place them in the oven, and bake until they are a light golden brown, about 20 minutes.

6. To prepare the glaze, place the egg whites and confectioners' sugar in a heatproof bowl and whisk to combine. Bring a few inches of water to a boil in a medium saucepan and place the bowl over it. Whisk until the sugar has dissolved.

7. Remove the cookies from the oven, turn them over, and brush their bottoms with the glaze.

8. Reduce the oven's temperature to 250°F. Place the cookies back in the oven and bake for 10 minutes, making sure the glaze does not brown.

9. Remove the cookies from the oven, turn them over, and brush their tops with the glaze. Sprinkle the sugar sprinkles over the cookies, place them back in the oven, and bake for 10 minutes.

10. Remove the cookies from the oven and let them cool on the baking sheets for a few minutes before transferring them to wire racks to cool completely.

INGREDIENTS:

FOR THE DOUGH

8.8 OZ. ALL-PURPOSE FLOUR, PLUS MORE AS NEEDED

8.8 OZ. FINELY GROUND DURUM WHEAT FLOUR (SEMOLA RIMACINATA)

1 TEASPOON BAKING POWDER

1 TEASPOON BAKER'S AMMONIA

½ CUP WHOLE MILK

4 EGG YOLKS

3½ OZ. SUGAR

1 TEASPOON PURE VANILLA EXTRACT

ZEST OF 1 LEMON

2 OZ. LARD, SOFTENED

FOR THE GLAZE

4 EGG WHITES

2 CUPS CONFECTIONERS' SUGAR

COLORED SUGAR SPRINKLES, FOR TOPPING (SILVER ARE THE MOST TYPICAL)

CROSTATA DI RICOTTA

YIELD: 1 PIE / **ACTIVE TIME:** 1 HOUR / **TOTAL TIME:** 2 HOURS

In Italy, this pie is enjoyed for breakfast, merenda (coffee break), or after a meal, typically dinner. It is popular both in its most traditional version with raisins or with the more modern version with chocolate chips. If using raisins, make sure they are thoroughly dried, or else the consistency of the cream will be off.

1. Place the ricotta, vanilla, eggs, lemon zest, orange zest, sugar, and cinnamon in a mixing bowl and stir until the mixture is thick and creamy.

2. Place the ricotta mixture in a saucepan and bring it to a simmer over low heat. Let the mixture simmer for 3 minutes and remove the pan from heat. Let the mixture cool until it is lukewarm.

3. Add the raisins to the mixture and stir to combine.

4. Preheat the oven to 340°F. Place the frolla on a flour-dusted work surface, remove a 3½ oz. piece of dough, and set it aside. Beat the remaining dough with a rolling pin to soften it and roll it out into a ⅛-inch-thick disk.

5. Coat a 9-inch pie plate with butter, dust it with flour, and knock out any excess. Place the dough in the pie plate, prick it with a fork, and trim away any excess dough.

6. Roll out the 3½-oz. piece of dough into a ⅛-inch-thick disk and cut it into 7 strips.

7. Pour the filling into the dough and arrange the strips of dough in a lattice pattern over the filling.

8. Place the crostata in the oven and bake until the crust is golden brown, about 1 hour.

9. Remove the crostata from the oven, let it cool completely, and dust with confectioners' sugar before serving.

INGREDIENTS:

2.2 LBS. RICOTTA CHEESE, DRAINED

1 TEASPOON PURE VANILLA EXTRACT

4 EGGS

ZEST OF 1 LEMON

ZEST OF 1 ORANGE

1½ CUPS SUGAR

½ TEASPOON CINNAMON

½ CUP RAISINS, SOAKED IN WARM WATER, DRAINED, AND SQUEEZED DRY

PASTA FROLLA (SEE PAGE 816)

ALL-PURPOSE FLOUR, AS NEEDED

UNSALTED BUTTER, AS NEEDED

CONFECTIONERS' SUGAR, FOR TOPPING

PASTIERA NAPOLETANA

YIELD: 1 PIE / **ACTIVE TIME:** 1 HOUR / **TOTAL TIME:** 24 HOURS

Pastiera is undoubtedly the best known and most beloved pie in Southern Italy. The origins of this pie stretch back to ancient history, as the wheat berries in the dough are obviously symbols of fertility and rebirth, two elements that were the focus of pagan celebrations of spring.

1. Place the wheat berries, milk, sugar, and butter in a saucepan and bring the mixture to a boil over low heat, stirring continually. Cook until the mixture thickens, about 15 minutes.

2. Remove the pan from heat and let the mixture cool.

3. Add the ricotta, eggs, egg yolks, orange blossom water, vanilla seeds, candied citrus peels, and candied orange peels and stir to combine.

4. Preheat the oven to 340°F. Place the frolla on a flour-dusted work surface, remove a 3½-oz. piece of dough, and set it aside. Beat the remaining dough with a rolling pin to soften it and roll it out into a ⅛-inch-thick disk.

5. Coat a 9-inch pie plate with butter, dust it with flour, and knock out any excess. Place the dough in the pie plate, prick it with a fork, and trim away any excess dough.

6. Roll out the 3½-oz. piece of dough into a ⅛-inch-thick disk and cut it into 7 strips.

7. Pour the filling into the dough and arrange the strips of dough in a lattice pattern over the filling.

8. Place the pastiera in the oven and bake until the crust is golden brown, about 1 hour.

9. Remove the pastiera from the oven and let it cool completely. Cover it with plastic wrap and chill it in the refrigerator overnight.

10. Dust the pastiera with confectioners' sugar and serve.

INGREDIENTS:

8.8   OZ. COOKED WHEAT BERRIES

⅔   CUP WHOLE MILK

1½   CUPS SUGAR

1½   TABLESPOONS UNSALTED BUTTER, PLUS MORE AS NEEDED

1½   CUPS RICOTTA CHEESE, DRAINED (RICOTTA MADE FROM SHEEP'S MILK PREFERRED)

2   EGGS

2   EGG YOLKS

1½   (HEAPING) TABLESPOONS ORANGE BLOSSOM WATER

SEEDS OF 1 VANILLA BEAN

¼   CUP CANDIED CITRUS PEELS, FINELY DICED

¼   CUP CANDIED ORANGE PEELS, FINELY DICED

PASTA FROLLA (SEE PAGE 816)

ALL-PURPOSE FLOUR, AS NEEDED

CONFECTIONERS' SUGAR, FOR TOPPING

PIZZA DI CREMA E AMARENE

YIELD: 1 PIE / **ACTIVE TIME:** 30 MINUTES / **TOTAL TIME:** 3 HOURS AND 15 MINUTES

No, not that kind of pizza. Instead, this is a cherry-and-custard confection from Sorrento that was typically made for Saint Antonino's celebrations on February 14, but is now popular year-round.

1. Preheat the oven to 350°F. Place the frolla on a flour-dusted work surface, remove a 3½-oz. piece of dough, and set it aside. Beat the remaining dough with a rolling pin to soften it and roll it out into a ⅛-inch-thick disk.

2. Coat a 9-inch pie plate with butter, dust it with flour, and knock out any excess. Place the dough in the pie plate, prick it with a fork, and trim away any excess dough.

3. Roll out the 3½-oz. piece of dough into a ⅛-inch-thick disk and cut it into 7 strips.

4. Distribute half of the cherries in the crust, cover them with the Crema Pasticcera Napoletana, and then top the custard with the remaining cherries.

5. Arrange the strips of dough in a lattice pattern over the cherries.

6. Place the pie in the oven and bake until the crust is golden brown, about 45 minutes.

7. Remove the pie from the oven and let it cool for a few hours.

8. Dust the pie with confectioners' sugar and serve.

INGREDIENTS:

PASTA FROLLA (SEE PAGE 816)

ALL-PURPOSE FLOUR, AS NEEDED

UNSALTED BUTTER, AS NEEDED

7 OZ. CHERRIES IN SYRUP, DRAINED

CREMA PASTICCERA NAPOLETANA (SEE PAGE 820)

CONFECTIONERS' SUGAR, FOR TOPPING

MIGLIACCIO

YIELD: 1 CAKE / *ACTIVE TIME:* 1 HOUR / *TOTAL TIME:* 2 HOURS AND 30 MINUTES

This cake was originally made from two ingredients that used to be readily available to local farmers: millet and pig's blood. As durum wheat became more common, it replaced the millet, and, around the eighteenth century, pig's blood was replaced by milk, thank heavens.

1. Preheat the oven to 350°F. Place the milk, salt, butter, orange peel, and lemon peel in a saucepan and bring the mixture to a boil.

2. Remove the orange peel and lemon peel and discard them. Add the semolina and stir continually until the mixture thickens.

3. Remove the pan from heat, cover it with plastic wrap, and let the mixture cool.

4. Place the eggs, sugar, vanilla, limoncello, orange blossom water, cinnamon, orange zest, and lemon zest in a bowl and whisk to combine. Incorporate the ricotta a little bit at a time. When all of the ricotta has been incorporated, add the semolina mixture gradually and whisk until incorporated.

5. Coat a round 12-inch cake pan with low edges with butter. Pour the mixture into the pan, place it in the oven, and bake for 1½ hours.

6. Remove the migliaccio from the oven and let it cool completely. Dust it with confectioners' sugar before serving.

INGREDIENTS:

4	CUPS WHOLE MILK
¼	TEASPOON FINE SEA SALT
4	TABLESPOONS UNSALTED BUTTER, PLUS MORE AS NEEDED
½	ORANGE PEEL, PITH REMOVED
½	LEMON PEEL, PITH REMOVED
1½	CUPS COARSE SEMOLINA FLOUR
6	EGGS
1¾	CUPS SUGAR
2	TEASPOONS PURE VANILLA EXTRACT
2	TABLESPOONS LIMONCELLO
2	TEASPOONS ORANGE BLOSSOM WATER
¼	TEASPOON CINNAMON
	ZEST OF ½ ORANGE
	ZEST OF ½ LEMON
2	CUPS RICOTTA CHEESE, DRAINED
	CONFECTIONERS' SUGAR, FOR TOPPING

SFOGLIATELLE DI FROLLA

YIELD: 12 SFOGLIATELLE / **ACTIVE TIME:** 1 HOUR / **TOTAL TIME:** 3 HOURS

Sfogliatelle are delectable pastries with a filling of ricotta cheese and cream of semolina, enclosed in a shell made of either crunchy puff pastry or a simple short-crust, known as frolla in Italian. Born in the Convent of Santa Rosa on the beautiful Amalfi Coast at the turn of the seventeenth century, sfogliatelle were brought to Naples by a pastry baker named Pasquale Pintauro about a century later.

1. Place the milk, salt, half of the butter, and the lemon peel in a medium saucepan and bring the mixture to a boil.

2. Remove the lemon peel and discard it. Add the semolina and stir continually until the mixture thickens.

3. Remove the pan from heat, cover it with plastic wrap, and let the mixture cool.

4. Place the egg, confectioners' sugar, vanilla, orange blossom water, cinnamon, and candied citrus peels in another bowl and whisk to combine. Incorporate the ricotta a little bit at a time. When all of the ricotta has been incorporated, add the semolina mixture gradually and whisk until incorporated.

5. Cover the mixture with plastic wrap and chill it in the refrigerator for 1 hour.

6. Line two baking sheets with parchment paper. Place the frolla on a flour-dusted work surface and beat it with a rolling pin to soften it. Divide the frolla into 12 pieces and roll out each piece into ¼-inch-thick oval.

7. Place 1 tablespoon of the ricotta cream on the bottom half of each oval, making sure to maintain a small border around the edge, and fold the other half of the dough over the filling.

8. Press down on the edges of the sfogliatelle to seal them and trim away any excess dough.

9. Place the sfogliatelle on the baking sheets and chill them in the refrigerator for 1 hour.

10. Preheat the oven to 390°F (if your oven has convection mode, set it to that).

11. Brush the sfogliatelle with the egg yolk, place them in the oven, and bake until they are golden brown, about 15 minutes.

12. Remove the sfogliatelle from the oven and let them cool slightly before serving.

INGREDIENTS:

- 1⅔ CUPS WHOLE MILK
- PINCH OF SALT
- ½ CUP UNSALTED BUTTER
- 1 LEMON PEEL, PITH REMOVED
- ¾ CUP COARSE SEMOLINA FLOUR
- 1 EGG
- 2 (SCANT) CUPS CONFECTIONERS' SUGAR
- 1 TEASPOON PURE VANILLA EXTRACT
- 1 TEASPOON ORANGE BLOSSOM WATER
- PINCH OF CINNAMON
- ½ CUP CANDIED CITRUS PEELS, FINELY CHOPPED
- 1 CUP RICOTTA CHEESE
- PASTA FROLLA NAPOLETANA (SEE PAGE 817)
- ALL-PURPOSE FLOUR, AS NEEDED
- 1 EGG YOLK, BEATEN

BOCCONOTTI ABRUZZESI

YIELD: 15 BOCCONOTTI / **ACTIVE TIME:** 1 HOUR / **TOTAL TIME:** 4 HOURS

These chocolate and almond cream–filled pastries are usually baked in special copper or aluminum molds, but they can also be baked in regular muffin pans.

1. Place the water in a saucepan and warm it until it is lukewarm. Add the chocolate and sugar and bring to a boil. Remove the pan from heat and let the mixture cool until it is lukewarm.

2. Stir in 3 of the egg yolks, place the mixture over medium heat, and let it come to a gentle simmer.

3. Stir in the almonds and gently simmer the mixture until it thickens. Stir in the cinnamon, remove the pan from heat, and cover the custard with plastic wrap, placing it directly on the surface to prevent a skin from forming. Chill the custard in the refrigerator for 1 hour.

4. Coat the wells of a muffin pan with butter, dust them with flour, and knock out any excess.

5. Preheat the oven to 350°F. Place the frolla on a flour-dusted work surface and beat it with a rolling pin to soften it. Roll out the frolla into a ¼-inch-thick rectangle and use a glass or ring cutter to cut out rounds that are large enough to cover the bottom and sides of the wells in the muffin pan. Place the rounds in the wells and trim away any excess dough. Roll the excess dough out into a thin sheet that will cover the muffin pan.

6. Fill each pastry with a spoonful of the custard, keeping in mind that it will expand in the oven. Lay the thin sheet of dough over the muffin pan and trim away the dough that is not directly over the bocconotti, leaving just a little bit over the edge of each well. You can also cut out properly sized rounds from the sheet of dough instead of placing the sheet over the tins all at once. Press down on the edges to seal so that the tops hold tight in the oven. Prick the tops of the bocconotti with a toothpick. Beat the remaining egg yolk and brush the bocconotti with it.

7. Place the bocconotti in the oven. Baking times will depend on the depth of the wells in the muffin pan. For deeper wells, bake for about 30 minutes. For shallower wells, bake for about 20 minutes. Also, do not worry if the tops detach; they will be reattached later.

8. Remove the bocconotti from the oven and let them cool for 5 minutes. Cover the pan with a similarly sized tray, invert the pan, and let it rest on the counter for 1 hour.

9. Turn the pan back over, remove the bocconotti from the pan, dust them generously with confectioners' sugar, and enjoy.

INGREDIENTS:

- 1½ CUPS WATER
- 5 OZ. BITTERSWEET CHOCOLATE
- ½ CUP PLUS 2 TABLESPOONS SUGAR
- 4 EGG YOLKS
- ⅔ CUP BLANCHED AND TOASTED ALMONDS, FINELY CHOPPED
- LARGE PINCH OF CINNAMON
- UNSALTED BUTTER, AS NEEDED
- ALL-PURPOSE FLOUR, AS NEEDED
- PASTA FROLLA (SEE PAGE 816)
- CONFECTIONERS' SUGAR, FOR TOPPING

BOCCONOTTI CALABRESI

YIELD: 15 BOCCONOTTI / **ACTIVE TIME:** 1 HOUR / **TOTAL TIME:** 2 HOURS

Calabrian bocconotti are quite special, being filled not with chocolate like the Abruzzi ones, or with custard. Instead, a black grape marmalade does the honors. In the absence of such a marmalade, you can substitute whatever marmalade or jam you prefer.

1. Coat the wells of a muffin pan with butter, dust them with flour, and knock out any excess.

2. Preheat the oven to 350°F. Place the frolla on a flour-dusted work surface and beat it with a rolling pin to soften it. Roll out the frolla into a ¼-inch-thick rectangle and use a glass or ring cutter to cut out rounds that are large enough to cover the bottom and sides of the wells in the muffin pan. Place the rounds in the wells and trim away any excess dough. Roll the excess dough out into a thin sheet that will cover the muffin pan.

3. Fill each pastry with a heaping spoonful of the marmalade.

4. Cut rounds slightly larger than the wells from the sheet of dough. Place them over the bocconotti and press down on the edges to seal so that the tops hold tight in the oven.

5. Prick the tops of the bocconotti with a toothpick. Beat the egg yolk and brush the bocconotti with it.

6. Place the bocconotti in the oven. Baking times will depend on the depth of the wells in the muffin pan. For deeper wells, bake for about 30 minutes. For shallower wells, bake for about 20 minutes. Also, do not worry if the tops detach, they will be reattached later.

7. Remove the bocconotti from the oven and let them cool for 5 minutes. Cover the pan with a similarly sized tray, invert the pan, and let it rest on the counter for 1 hour.

8. Turn the pan back over, remove the bocconotti from the pan, dust them generously with confectioners' sugar, and enjoy.

INGREDIENTS:

UNSALTED BUTTER, AS NEEDED

ALL-PURPOSE FLOUR, AS NEEDED

PASTA FROLLA (SEE PAGE 816)

1½ CUPS BLACK GRAPE MARMALADE (MOSTARDA D'UVA)

1 EGG YOLK

CONFECTIONERS' SUGAR, FOR TOPPING

BOCCONOTTI & PASTICCIOTTI:
THE SOUTHERN OBSESSION WITH MINI PIES

Southern Italy has a real passion for sweets of all kinds, and for miniature pies in particular. The best known of these is the Abruzzi confection known as bocconotti, which are round and have a thin crust enveloping a cream made of egg yolks, almonds, and, unsurprisingly, chocolate—one of Abruzzi's favorite ingredients. Before the nineteenth century, when chocolate was still not readily available in Europe, these pastries were most likely filled with cooked mosto cotto—a jammy by-product of the wine harvest.

Part of bocconotti's appeal is that the metal tins they were cooked in could be placed directly on the hearth, and did not require something as technologically evolved as an oven.

In Molise, bocconotti are filled with custard and cherries, while in Basilicata, bocconotti are generally filled with cherries only.

In Apulia and Campania, the miniature pie is known as pasticciotti. Apulia and Campania's pasticciotti have a characteristic oval shape and use a thicker shortcrust shell compared with classic bocconotti. Pasticciotti, however, are not known throughout all of Apulia, only in the Salento region, Lecce in particular. Here they are filled with custard and have become a real institution. In Naples, pasticciotti are filled exactly like Molisan bocconotti, with custard and cherries.

BOCCONOTTI MOLISANI

YIELD: 15 BOCCONOTTI / **ACTIVE TIME:** 1 HOUR / **TOTAL TIME:** 2 HOURS

Here we have what is perhaps the most luscious bocconotti filling, cherries and custard.

1. Coat the wells of a muffin pan with butter, dust them with flour, and knock out any excess.

2. Preheat the oven to 350°F. Place the frolla on a flour-dusted work surface and beat it with a rolling pin to soften it. Roll out the frolla into a ¼-inch-thick rectangle and use a glass or ring cutter to cut out rounds that are large enough to cover the bottom and sides of the wells in the muffin pan. Place the rounds in the wells and trim away any excess dough. Roll the excess dough out into a thin sheet that will cover the muffin pan.

3. Fill each pastry with a few cherries and a generous spoonful of the custard.

4. Cut rounds slightly larger than the wells from the sheet of dough. Place them over the bocconotti and press down on the edges to seal so that the tops hold tight in the oven.

5. Prick the tops of the bocconotti with a toothpick. Place the egg yolk and water in a small bowl, beat to combine, and brush the bocconotti with the egg wash.

6. Place the bocconotti in the oven. Baking times will depend on the depth of the wells in the muffin pan. For deeper wells, bake for about 30 minutes. For shallower wells, bake for about 20 minutes. Also, do not worry if the tops detach, they will be reattached later.

7. Remove the bocconotti from the oven and let them cool for 5 minutes. Cover the pan with a similarly sized tray, invert the pan, and let it rest on the counter for 1 hour.

8. Turn the pan back over, remove the bocconotti from the pan, dust them generously with confectioners' sugar, and enjoy.

INGREDIENTS:

	UNSALTED BUTTER, AS NEEDED
	ALL-PURPOSE FLOUR, AS NEEDED
2	BATCHES OF PASTA FROLLA (SEE PAGE 816)
½	LB. CHERRIES IN SYRUP, DRAINED AND PATTED DRY
1½	CUPS CREMA PASTICCIERA NAPOLETANA (SEE PAGE 817)
1	EGG YOLK
½	TEASPOON WATER
	CONFECTIONERS' SUGAR, FOR TOPPING

CASSATELLE DI PARTINICO

YIELD: 20 CASSATELLE / **ACTIVE TIME:** 1 HOUR / **TOTAL TIME:** 24 HOURS

Characteristic of Partinico and Lascari, these cassatelle have a delectable and very unique filling composed of chickpeas, butternut squash, honey, and chocolate.

1. Place the chickpeas in a bowl, cover them with water, and stir in the baking soda. Let the chickpeas soak overnight.

2. Drain the chickpeas and place them in a large saucepan. Cover them with water, add a few pinches of salt, and bring to a boil. Cook the chickpeas until they are tender, drain them, and let them cool.

3. Add the butternut squash, honey, and chocolate chips to the chickpeas and stir to combine.

4. Preheat the oven to 350°F and line two baking sheets with parchment paper. Place the frolla on a flour-dusted work surface and roll it out until it is a ⅛-inch-thick rectangle. Use a glass or ring cutter to cut 4-inch rounds out of the dough.

5. Place a teaspoon of the filling in the center of each round and fold the rounds into half-moons. Press down on the edge to seal the dumplings and trim away any excess dough using a pasta wheel.

6. Add olive oil to a large, deep skillet until it is about 1 inch deep and warm it to 350°F. Add the cassatelle and fry until they are crispy and golden brown, 4 to 6 minutes, turning them as necessary.

7. Transfer the fried cassatelle to a paper towel–lined plate to drain. Place sugar and cinnamon in a shallow bowl and stir to combine. Sprinkle the mixture over the cassatelle and enjoy.

INGREDIENTS:

3	CUPS DRIED CHICKPEAS
1	TEASPOON BAKING SODA
	SALT, TO TASTE
3½	OZ. ROASTED BUTTERNUT SQUASH, DICED
¼	CUP HONEY
½	CUP BITTERSWEET CHOCOLATE CHIPS
	PASTA FROLLA DI SEMOLA (SEE PAGE 818), SUBSTITUTE LARD FOR BUTTER
	ALL-PURPOSE FLOUR, AS NEEDED
	EXTRA-VIRGIN OLIVE OIL, AS NEEDED
	SUGAR, FOR TOPPING
	CINNAMON, FOR TOPPING

CASSATELLE SICILIANE

YIELD: 20 CASSATELLE / **ACTIVE TIME:** 1 HOUR / **TOTAL TIME:** 1 HOUR AND 30 MINUTES

Typical of Carnival celebrations, cassatelle—cassateddi, cappiduzzu, or raviola in local dialects—are fried miniature pies typically filled with ricotta cheese. They likely originated in the small town of Calatafimi Segesta and subsequently spread throughout western Sicily, creating plenty of interesting (and delicious) variations along the way.

1. Place all of the ingredients, except for the frolla, flour, and olive oil, in a large bowl and stir until well combined.

2. Place the frolla on a flour-dusted work surface and roll it out into a ¼-inch-thick rectangle. Use a glass or ring cutter to cut 4-inch rounds out of the dough.

3. Place a teaspoon of the ricotta mixture in the center of each round and fold the rounds into half-moons. Press down on the edge to seal the dumplings and trim away any excess dough using a pasta wheel.

4. Add olive oil to a large, deep skillet until it is about 1 inch deep and warm it to 350°F. Add the cassatelle and fry until they are crispy and golden brown, 4 to 6 minutes, turning them as necessary.

5. Transfer the fried cassatelle to a paper towel–lined plate to drain. Dust them with confectioners' sugar and enjoy.

INGREDIENTS:

1   LB. RICOTTA CHEESE, DRAINED IN THE REFRIGERATOR FOR A FEW HOURS

1   (SCANT) CUP CONFECTIONERS' SUGAR, PLUS MORE FOR TOPPING

3½   OZ. BITTERSWEET CHOCOLATE CHIPS

1   EGG YOLK

½   TEASPOON CINNAMON

        ZEST OF 1 ORANGE

        PASTA FROLLA AL MARSALA (SEE PAGE 818)

        ALL-PURPOSE FLOUR, AS NEEDED

        EXTRA-VIRGIN OLIVE OIL, AS NEEDED

SEADAS SARDE

YIELD: 20 SEADAS / **ACTIVE TIME:** 1 HOUR AND 30 MINUTES / **TOTAL TIME:** 2 HOURS

Seadas, seada, sebada, seatta, sevada, every town has a name for these lovely fresh-cheese-filled "ravioli" that are similar to the Sicilian cassatelle, only round instead of half-moon shaped. Originally from Sardinia's barren inland, seadas were traditionally made on special occasions, such as Christmas or Easter, and were not sweet but savory, and served as a main course.

1. Place 3 cups of flour and the water in the work bowl of a stand mixer fitted with the dough hook and stir to combine. Add the salt and lard and work the mixture until it comes together as a smooth dough.

2. Cover the dough with plastic wrap and chill it in the refrigerator for 30 minutes.

3. Place the ricotta, lemon zest, and remaining flour in a saucepan and warm the mixture over low heat, stirring occasionally, until it is creamy and not watery. Remove the pan from heat and let the mixture cool.

4. Place the dough on a flour-dusted work surface and roll it out until it is about 1/10 inch thick. You can also use a pasta maker to get the dough to the proper thinness. Cut the dough into 5-inch rounds.

5. Place a tablespoon of the ricotta mixture in the center of each round.

6. Roll out the leftover dough until it is 1/10 inch thick and cut it into 5-inch rounds. Place them over the filling and press down on the edges to seal the seadas. Trim away any excess dough using a pasta wheel.

7. Add olive oil to a large, deep skillet until it is about 1 inch deep and warm it to 350°F. Add the seadas and fry until they are crispy and golden brown, 4 to 6 minutes, turning them as necessary.

8. Transfer the fried seadas to a paper towel–lined plate to drain. Drizzle honey over them and enjoy.

INGREDIENTS:

3½ CUPS PLUS 3 TABLESPOONS FINELY GROUND DURUM WHEAT FLOUR (SEMOLA RIMACINATA), PLUS MORE AS NEEDED

1 CUP WARM WATER (105°F), PLUS MORE AS NEEDED

PINCH OF FINE SEA SALT

¼ CUP LARD

2 CUPS RICOTTA CHEESE (MADE FROM SHEEP'S MILK PREFERRED)

ZEST OF 1 LEMON

EXTRA-VIRGIN OLIVE OIL, AS NEEDED

HONEY, FOR TOPPING

CASSATELLE DI AGIRA

YIELD: 20 CASSATELLE / **ACTIVE TIME:** 1 HOUR AND 30 MINUTES / **TOTAL TIME:** 24 HOURS

These cassatelle are the version typical of Agira, which lies deep inland in Sicily. They are special among the cassatelle family because they are not fried, but baked.

1. Place the almonds and lemon zest in a food processor and blitz until the mixture is a slightly coarse powder.

2. Place the ground almond mixture, cocoa powder, sugar, cinnamon, vanilla, and water in a medium saucepan and stir to combine. Bring the mixture to a simmer over low heat and cook until it thickens, stirring continually.

3. Remove the pan from heat, sift the chickpea flour into the pan, and stir vigorously until the mixture is smooth.

4. Transfer the filling to an airtight container and let it sit at room temperature overnight.

5. Preheat the oven to 350°F and line two baking sheets with parchment paper. Place the frolla on a flour-dusted work surface and roll it out until it is a ⅛-inch-thick rectangle. Use a glass or ring cutter to cut 4-inch rounds out of the dough.

6. Place a teaspoon of the filling in the center of each round and fold the rounds into half-moons. Press down on the edge to seal the dumplings and trim away any excess dough using a pasta wheel. Place the cassatelle on the baking sheets.

7. Place the cassatelle in the oven and bake until they are just about to start browning, 10 to 15 minutes.

8. Remove the cassatelle from the oven and let them cool completely.

9. Place confectioners' sugar and cinnamon in a shallow bowl and stir to combine. Sprinkle the mixture over the cassatelle and enjoy.

INGREDIENTS:

7	OZ. ALMONDS, TOASTED
	ZEST OF 1 LEMON
½	CUP UNSWEETENED COCOA POWDER
¾	CUP SUGAR
1	TEASPOON CINNAMON, PLUS MORE FOR TOPPING
1	TEASPOON PURE VANILLA EXTRACT
1½	(SCANT) CUPS WATER
½	(HEAPING) CUP CHICKPEA FLOUR, PLUS MORE AS NEEDED
	PASTA FROLLA AL LARDO (SEE PAGE 817)
	ALL-PURPOSE FLOUR, AS NEEDED
	CONFECTIONERS' SUGAR, FOR TOPPING

GENOVESI DI ERICE

YIELD: 20 GENOVESI / **ACTIVE TIME:** 45 MINUTES / **TOTAL TIME:** 1 HOUR

Erice, situated on a steep promontory with a breathtaking view of Trapani's coast, may be one of the prettiest and best-preserved medieval Sicilian villages. Among the many specialties native to this very special town is the genovesi, a delectable custard-filled pastry that lies somewhere between bocconotti and cassatelle. The most famous ones are made by Maria Grammatico's pastry shop, which is a stop not to miss if visiting Erice.

---

1. Preheat the oven to 375°F and line two baking sheets with parchment paper. Place the frolla on a flour-dusted work surface and beat it with a rolling pin to soften it. Roll out the frolla into a ¼-inch-thick rectangle. Use a glass or ring cutter to cut 4-inch rounds out of the dough.

2. Place a teaspoon of the custard in the center of each round. Roll the remaining dough into a ¼-inch-thick rectangle. Use a glass or ring cutter to cut 4-inch rounds out of the dough. Place the rounds over the filling and press down on the edges to seal the genovesi. Trim away any excess dough using a pasta wheel.

3. Place the genovesi on the baking sheets, place them in the oven, and bake until they are just about to brown, 10 to 15 minutes.

4. Remove the genovesi from the oven and let them cool.

5. Dust the genovesi generously with confectioners' sugar and enjoy.

INGREDIENTS:

PASTA FROLLA DI SEMOLA (SEE PAGE 818)

ALL-PURPOSE FLOUR, AS NEEDED

CREMA PASTICCERA SICILIANA (SEE PAGE 820)

CONFECTIONERS' SUGAR, FOR TOPPING

CASSATA SICILIANA

YIELD: 1 CAKE / **ACTIVE TIME:** 1 HOUR / **TOTAL TIME:** 5 HOURS

A sumptuous and very sweet combination of sponge cake, ricotta cream, marzipan, and candied fruit, modern cassata is a development of a medieval Sicilian Easter cake that was popular during Moorish rule.

1. To prepare the ricotta cream, place the ricotta in a bowl, add the sugar and vanilla sugar, and stir to combine. Add the chocolate chips and fold until they are evenly distributed. Chill the ricotta cream in the refrigerator.

2. To begin preparations for the marzipan, place the sugar, water, and food coloring in a saucepan and bring to a boil, stirring to dissolve the sugar. Turn off the heat, add the almond flour, and stir until the mixture is dense, smooth, and soft, and starts to pull away from the side of the pan.

3. Spray a pastry board or cutting board with water, pour the marzipan onto it, and let it cool.

4. Knead the marzipan for a few minutes until it feels smoother. Roll it out into a ¼-inch-thick rectangle and cut the marzipan into 7 or 8 trapezoids that are approximately one-third as high as the edge of the pan on which the cassata will be arranged.

5. To prepare the bagna, place all of the ingredients in a bowl and whisk until combined.

6. Cut the Pan di Spagna, horizontally, into 3 equally thick pieces. Place the top piece in a round cake pan, cut side up.

7. Cut out trapezoids from the middle piece of cake and line the side of the pan with them and the pieces of marzipan, alternating between them.

8. Pour the bagna over the pieces of the cake and then spread the ricotta cream inside the cake. Place the remaining piece of cake on top, cut side down, and place the cassata in the refrigerator for 2 to 3 hours.

9. To prepare the icing, place the confectioners' sugar in a bowl and incorporate the water 1 tablespoon at a time until the icing has the desired consistency. Set the mixture aside.

10. Remove the cake from the refrigerator, place a large plate over the pan, and invert the cake. Spread the icing over the top and sides of the cake, top it with candied fruit, and enjoy.

INGREDIENTS:

FOR THE RICOTTA CREAM

2.3 LBS. RICOTTA CHEESE (MADE FROM SHEEP'S MILK PREFERRED), DRAINED FOR A FEW HOURS IN THE REFRIGERATOR

2 CUPS SUGAR

1 TABLESPOON VANILLA SUGAR OR 1 TEASPOON PURE VANILLA EXTRACT

1¾ CUPS BITTERSWEET CHOCOLATE CHIPS

FOR THE MARZIPAN (PASTA REALE)

1 CUP SUGAR

3½ TABLESPOONS WATER

2–3 DROPS OF BRIGHT GREEN FOOD COLORING

2 CUPS ALMOND FLOUR

FOR THE BAGNA

⅓ CUP MARSALA, LUXARDO MARASCHINO LIQUEUR, OR SWEET LIQUEUR

⅔ CUP WATER

¼ CUP SUGAR

2.3 LBS. PAN DI SPAGNA (SEE PAGE 819)

FOR THE ICING

2 (SCANT) CUPS CONFECTIONERS' SUGAR

¼ CUP WATER

CANDIED FRUIT, FOR TOPPING

CASADINAS

YIELD: 15 CASADINAS / **ACTIVE TIME:** 1 HOUR / **TOTAL TIME:** 2 HOURS

These pies are called casadinas in north and central Sardinia, and pardulas in the south of the island. Consisting of a semolina-based crust and a sweet cheese filling, they are a must around Easter time.

1. Place the flour, lard, water, and salt in a mixing bowl and work the mixture until it comes together as a smooth dough.

2. Cover the dough with plastic wrap and let it rest for 30 minutes.

3. Place the remaining ingredients in a mixing bowl and stir until well combined.

4. Preheat the oven to 350°F and line two baking sheets with parchment paper.

5. Place the dough on a flour-dusted work surface and roll it out until it is about ⅛ inch thick. Cut the dough into 4-inch rounds and place them on the baking sheets.

6. Place a tablespoon of the ricotta mixture in the center of each round.

7. To shape the casadinas, pinch the edge of the rounds around the filling, forming a sort of small basket that encases it. Generally, the perimeter of the pastry has 7 or 8 corners.

8. Place the casadinas in the oven and bake until the filling is golden brown and puffy, about 30 minutes.

9. Remove the casadinas from the oven and let them cool slightly before enjoying.

INGREDIENTS:

10.6 OZ. FINELY GROUND DURUM WHEAT FLOUR (SEMOLA RIMACINATA), PLUS MORE AS NEEDED

2.8 OZ. LARD

5.6 OZ. LUKEWARM WATER (90°F)

PINCH OF FINE SEA SALT

2 CUPS RICOTTA CHEESE (BEST IF FROM SHEEP'S MILK)

1 (SCANT) CUP CONFECTIONERS' SUGAR

2 TABLESPOONS ALL-PURPOSE FLOUR

1 EGG

PINCH OF SAFFRON THREADS

ZEST OF 1 ORANGE

ZEST OF 1 LEMON

SISE DELLE MONACHE

YIELD: 10 PASTRIES / *ACTIVE TIME:* 40 MINUTES / **TOTAL TIME:** 1 HOUR

The name translates to "nuns' breasts," probably because these pastries have three peaks, and in the past nuns used to put fabric between their breasts to hide their shape.

1. Preheat the oven to 360°F and line a baking sheet with parchment paper. Place the egg whites in the work bowl of a stand mixer fitted with the whisk attachment and whip until they hold medium peaks. Add half of the sugar and whip until the meringue holds stiff peaks.

2. Place the egg yolks and remaining sugar in a separate bowl and beat until the mixture is pale and well combined. Add the flour and cornstarch and whisk to combine.

3. Add the meringue and fold to incorporate it. Place the batter in a piping bag.

4. In groups of three, pipe small cones of the batter onto the baking sheet. Place the pan in the oven and bake until the sise delle monache are lightly golden brown, 15 to 20 minutes.

5. Turn off the oven and let the sise delle monache rest in the cooling oven for 5 minutes.

6. Remove the sise delle monache from the oven and let them cool completely.

7. Cut off the tips of the sise delle monache with a sharp knife, fill them with the custard, and put the tips back on. Dust the sise delle monache with confectioners' sugar and enjoy.

INGREDIENTS:

- 4 EGGS, SEPARATED
- ½ CUP SUGAR
- 3½ OZ. ALL-PURPOSE OR CAKE FLOUR
- 7 TABLESPOONS CORNSTARCH
- ½ BATCH OF CREMA PASTICCERA NAPOLETANA (SEE PAGE 820)
- CONFECTIONERS' SUGAR, FOR TOPPING

CASSATA ABRUZZESE

YIELD: 1 CAKE / **ACTIVE TIME:** 1 HOUR / **TOTAL TIME:** 1 HOUR AND 30 MINUTES

A traditional layered cake from Sulmona, a town that is also famous for its candied almond confetti—a product that frequently is used to decorate this cake. The base is pan di spagna soaked in a liqueur known as centerbe, which is made by macerating herbs in alcohol. Should centerbe not be available, use your favorite liqueur in its place.

1. Place the milk and liqueur in a bowl, stir to combine, and set it aside.

2. Place the butter and sugar in the work bowl of a stand mixer fitted with the paddle attachment and cream it on medium speed until pale and fluffy. With the mixer running, incorporate the egg yolks one at a time.

3. Divide the mixture into three equal portions.

4. Add the hazelnuts to the first portion, the torrone and chocolate to the second portion, and the cocoa powder to the third portion. Stir until the additions have been incorporated.

5. Place a spoonful of each frosting in a separate bowl and stir to combine.

6. Cut the Pan di Spagna, horizontally into 4 equally thick pieces.

7. Place a piece of cake on a plate, moisten it with the liqueur mixture, and spread the cocoa powder frosting over the cake.

8. Place another piece of cake on top, moisten it with the liqueur mixture, and spread the hazelnut frosting over the cake.

9. Place another piece of cake on top, moisten it with the liqueur mixture, and spread the torrone frosting over the cake.

10. Top with the final piece of cake, moisten it with the liqueur mixture, and spread the mixture of all three frostings over the top.

11. Top the cake with confetti and/or cherries (if desired) and enjoy.

INGREDIENTS:

- ½ CUP WHOLE MILK
- 1 OZ. CENTERBE
- 7 OZ. UNSALTED BUTTER
- 7 OZ. SUGAR
- 6 EGG YOLKS (FROM VERY FRESH EGGS)
- ½ CUP HAZELNUTS, BLANCHED, TOASTED, AND FINELY CHOPPED
- 2 OZ. TORRONE, FINELY DICED
- ⅓ CUP MILK CHOCOLATE, FINELY CHOPPED
- ¼ CUP UNSWEETENED COCOA POWDER
- 1 LB. PAN DI SPAGNA (SEE PAGE 819)
- CONFETTI (CANDIED ALMONDS), FOR TOPPING (OPTIONAL)
- CHERRIES IN SYRUP, DRAINED, FOR TOPPING (OPTIONAL)

CASSATINE SICILIANE

YIELD: 15 CASSATINE / **ACTIVE TIME:** 1 HOUR / **TOTAL TIME:** 5 HOURS

The traditional cassata Siciliana can also be made as individual miniature cakes known as cassatine.

1. To prepare the ricotta cream, place the ricotta in a bowl, add the sugar and vanilla sugar, and stir to combine. Add the chocolate chips and fold until they are evenly distributed. Chill the ricotta cream in the refrigerator.

2. To begin preparations for the marzipan, place the sugar, water, and food coloring in a saucepan and bring to a boil, stirring to dissolve the sugar. Turn off the heat, add the almond flour, and stir until the mixture is dense, smooth, and soft, and starts to pull away from the side of the pan.

3. Spray a pastry board or cutting board with water, pour the marzipan onto it, and let it cool.

4. Knead the marzipan for a few minutes until it feels smoother. Roll it out into a ¼-inch-thick rectangle and cut the marzipan into rounds that are the size of the bottom of the wells in a cupcake pan. Place the rounds in the wells of the cupcake pan.

5. Cut the Pan di Spagna, horizontally, into 3 equally thick pieces. Cut rounds large enough to cover the marzipan out of the pieces of cake.

6. Place pieces of cake on top of the marzipan and spread some of the ricotta cream over the top, almost filling the wells of the cupcake pan. Place the remaining pieces of cake on top of each portion of ricotta cream. Place the cassatine in the refrigerator for 2 to 3 hours.

7. To prepare the icing, place the confectioners' sugar in a bowl and incorporate the water a little at a time until the icing has the desired consistency. Set the mixture aside.

8. Remove the cassatine Siciliane from the refrigerator, place a large tray over the pan, and invert the cakes. Spread the icing over the top and sides of the cakes, top them with candied fruit, and enjoy.

INGREDIENTS:

PAN DI SPAGNA (SEE PAGE 819)

FOR THE RICOTTA CREAM

1.1 LBS. RICOTTA CHEESE (MADE FROM SHEEP'S MILK PREFERRED), DRAINED FOR A FEW HOURS IN THE REFRIGERATOR

1 CUP SUGAR

2 TEASPOONS VANILLA SUGAR OR ½ TEASPOON PURE VANILLA EXTRACT

1 CUP BITTERSWEET CHOCOLATE CHIPS

FOR THE MARZIPAN (PASTA REALE)

½ CUP SUGAR

1½ TABLESPOONS WATER

2 DROPS OF BRIGHT GREEN FOOD COLORING

1 CUP ALMOND FLOUR

FOR THE ICING

1 (SCANT) CUP CONFECTIONERS' SUGAR

2 TABLESPOONS WATER

CANDIED FRUIT, FOR TOPPING

CANNOLI SICILIANI

YIELD: 30 CANNOLI / **ACTIVE TIME:** 1 HOUR / **TOTAL TIME:** 4 HOURS

Sicilian cannoli, the crunchy fried shells filled with ricotta cream, are possibly the best- known Sicilian specialty worldwide. And, as is often the case with Southern Italian food, their origins are very ancient, likely dating back to the Romans. There are numerous recipes for the shells, and while tradition insists upon lard, feel free to substitute it with your shortening of choice.

1. To begin preparations for the shells, place the flour, sugar, salt, cocoa powder, and cinnamon in a mixing bowl and stir to combine.

2. Add the lard, wine, vinegar, and egg and work the mixture until it just comes together as a shaggy dough.

3. Place the dough on a flour-dusted work surface and knead it until it is smooth and elastic, about 10 minutes.

4. Cover the dough in plastic wrap and chill it in the refrigerator for 3 hours.

5. To prepare the ricotta cream, place all of the ingredients in a mixing bowl and stir until well combined. Store it in the refrigerator.

6. Place the dough on a flour-dusted work surface and roll it out into a ⅛-inch-thick sheet.

7. Cut the dough into 4-inch rounds and form them into shells around cannoli molds, brushing the edges with the beaten egg white and pressing down to seal them.

8. Add olive oil to a narrow, deep, heavy-bottomed saucepan with high edges until it is about 2 inches deep and warm it to 340°F. Working in batches to avoid crowding the pot, add the cannoli shells and fry until they are golden brown, 3 to 4 minutes. Transfer the fried cannoli shells to a paper towel–lined plate to drain and cool.

9. When the cannoli shells are cold, place the ricotta cream in a piping bag and fill the shells with them. Garnish the two ends with chocolate chips, candied cherries, candied orange peels, or pistachios, dust the cannoli with confectioners' sugar, and enjoy.

INGREDIENTS:

FOR THE SHELLS

17.6 OZ. ALL-PURPOSE FLOUR, PLUS MORE AS NEEDED

1.4 OZ. SUGAR

PINCH OF FINE SEA SALT

1 TEASPOON UNSWEETENED COCOA POWDER

1 TEASPOON CINNAMON

1.4 OZ. LARD

1.4 OZ. MARSALA OR WHITE WINE

1.4 OZ. VINEGAR

1 EGG

1 EGG WHITE, BEATEN

EXTRA-VIRGIN OLIVE OIL, AS NEEDED

FOR THE RICOTTA CREAM

3 CUPS RICOTTA CHEESE (MADE FROM SHEEP'S MILK PREFERRED), DRAINED FOR A FEW HOURS IN THE REFRIGERATOR

1½ CUPS CONFECTIONERS' SUGAR

½ CUP SMALL BITTERSWEET CHOCOLATE CHIPS (OPTIONAL)

BITTERSWEET CHOCOLATE CHIPS, CANDIED CHERRIES, CHOPPED PISTACHIOS, CANDIED ORANGE PEELS, AND/OR CONFECTIONERS' SUGAR, FOR GARNISH

PARROZZO

YIELD: 1 CAKE / **ACTIVE TIME:** 30 MINUTES / **TOTAL TIME:** 2 HOURS

A beautiful and delectable cake from Abruzzi that features semolina and almond flour, a combination that confers a very distinctive texture and taste to parrozzo, which was created relatively recently, at the beginning of the twentieth century by a pastry chef named Luigi D'Amico.

1. Preheat the oven to 320°F. To begin preparations for the cake, place the egg yolks and sugar in a bowl and whisk until the mixture is pale yellow. Add the remaining ingredients, except for the egg whites, and stir until the mixture comes together as a smooth batter.

2. Place the egg whites in the work bowl of a stand mixer fitted with the whisk attachment and whip until they hold soft peaks. Add the egg whites to the batter and fold to incorporate them.

3. Coat a 6 x 3–inch hemisphere pan with butter and pour the batter into it.

4. Place the cake in the oven and bake until a toothpick inserted into the center of it comes out clean, about 20 minutes.

5. Remove the cake from the oven, let it cool for 10 minutes, and then remove it from the pan. Place the cake on a wire rack and let it cool completely.

6. To prepare the ganache, bring a few inches of water to a simmer in a medium saucepan. Place the chocolate and butter in a heatproof bowl, place it over the simmering water, and stir until the mixture is melted and smooth.

7. Place a piece of waxed paper beneath the cake on the wire rack and pour the ganache over the cake.

8. Collect the ganache from the waxed paper and spread it over the cake.

9. Let the ganache set before slicing and serving the cake.

INGREDIENTS:

FOR THE CAKE

4	LARGE EGGS, SEPARATED
3½	OZ. SUGAR
	ZEST OF 1 LEMON
2.8	OZ. UNSALTED BUTTER, MELTED, PLUS MORE AS NEEDED
1	OZ. AMARETTO DI SARONNO
4.2	OZ. SEMOLINA FLOUR
3½	OZ. BLANCHED ALMONDS, VERY FINELY GROUND

FOR THE CHOCOLATE GANACHE

7	OZ. BITTERSWEET CHOCOLATE, CHOPPED
1½	TABLESPOONS UNSALTED BUTTER

ZIPPULA SARDE

YIELD: 12 TO 14 ZIPPOLE / **ACTIVE TIME:** 40 MINUTES / **TOTAL TIME:** 2 HOURS

Typical of Carnival season in Sardinia, and of Oristano in particular, zippula are one of the many forms Italian doughnuts take, made unique by their spiral shape and by being made with durum flour.

1. Place the yeast and water in a mixing bowl, gently stir, and let the mixture proof until it is foamy, about 10 minutes.

2. Add the remaining ingredients, except for the olive oil and sugar, and work the mixture until it comes together as a smooth batter that is soft enough to be extruded from a piping bag.

3. Cover the bowl with plastic wrap and let the batter rest at room temperature until bubbles start forming on the surface, about 1 hour.

4. Add extra-virgin olive oil to a narrow, deep, heavy-bottomed saucepan with high edges until it is 2 inches deep and warm it to 340°F. Pipe a few spirals of batter at a time into the hot oil and fry until they are just golden brown, turning as necessary.

5. Place the fried zippula on a paper towel–lined plate to drain.

6. Place the sugar in a bowl, add the zippula, toss until they are completely coated, and enjoy.

INGREDIENTS:

1	PACKET OF ACTIVE DRY YEAST
½	CUP LUKEWARM WATER (90°F)
17.6	OZ. SEMOLINA FLOUR
½	CUP LUKEWARM WHOLE MILK
1	EGG
	ZEST AND JUICE OF 1 ORANGE
¼	CUP BRANDY OR ANISE LIQUEUR
1½	TEASPOONS FINE SEA SALT
	EXTRA-VIRGIN OLIVE OIL, AS NEEDED
3	CUPS SUGAR

IRIS

YIELD: 12 IRIS / **ACTIVE TIME:** 50 MINUTES / **TOTAL TIME:** 6 HOURS

Iris are decadent sweet pastries filled with ricotta cream, breaded, and deep-fried, producing a real explosion of flavor. The name is a tribute to an opera of the same name which premiered in Palermo in 1901. The popular pastry chef Antonio Lo Verso designed this pastry for that event, and it became so popular that he later changed the name of his pastry shop to Iris—it remains a hip meeting spot for breakfast in Palermo.

1. To begin preparations for the dough, warm the milk to 90°F, place it in a bowl, and add the yeast. Gently stir and let the mixture proof until it starts to foam, about 10 minutes.

2. Place the mixture in the work bowl of a stand mixer fitted with the dough hook, add the flours and egg, and work the mixture on low speed until it is combined.

3. Add the sugar and work the mixture until it comes together as a smooth and elastic dough.

4. Add the butter, raise the mixer's speed to medium, and knead until the dough is very elastic.

5. Cover the bowl with plastic wrap, place it in a warm spot, and let the dough rise until it doubles in size, about 4 hours.

6. To prepare the filling, place all of the ingredients in a mixing bowl and stir to combine.

7. Line a baking sheet with parchment paper. Place the dough on a flour-dusted work surface, divide it into 12 pieces, and shape them into rounds. Place the rounds on the baking sheet, cover them with a kitchen towel, and let them rise for 1 hour.

8. Working with one round at a time, place it on a flour-dusted work surface, flatten it, and place 1 tablespoon of filling in the center. Form the dough around the filling, seal it, and flip it over. Work the dough in a circular motion until it is a seamless round.

9. Place the eggs in a bowl and beat until scrambled. Place the bread crumbs in a shallow bowl. Dredge the iris in the eggs and then in the bread crumbs until it is completely coated.

10. Repeat Steps 8 and 9 with the remaining rounds and filling.

11. Add olive oil to a narrow, deep, heavy-bottomed saucepan with high edges until it is about 2 inches deep and warm it to 350°F. Add 2 iris to the hot oil at a time and fry until they are golden brown, turning them over halfway through. Transfer the fried iris to a paper towel–lined plate to drain and serve once all of the iris have been cooked.

INGREDIENTS:

FOR THE DOUGH

9.8 OZ. WHOLE MILK

⅓ PACKET OF ACTIVE DRY YEAST

14.1 OZ. BREAD FLOUR

5.3 OZ. ALL-PURPOSE FLOUR, PLUS MORE AS NEEDED

1 MEDIUM EGG

2 TABLESPOONS SUGAR

2 OZ. UNSALTED BUTTER

FOR THE FILLING

1½ CUPS RICOTTA CHEESE (MADE FROM SHEEP'S MILK PREFERRED), DRAINED IN THE REFRIGERATOR FOR A FEW HOURS

1¼ CUPS CONFECTIONERS' SUGAR

2 OZ. BITTERSWEET CHOCOLATE CHIPS, FROZEN FOR 30 MINUTES BEFORE USING (OPTIONAL)

2 EGGS

1½ CUPS BREAD CRUMBS

EXTRA-VIRGIN OLIVE OIL, AS NEEDED

TORTA SAVOIA

YIELD: 1 CAKE / **ACTIVE TIME:** 1 HOUR / **TOTAL TIME:** 5 HOURS

An elegant, yet simple, layered cake with a luscious chocolate-hazelnut filling. The cake was probably created in the second half of the 1800s by the Benedictine nuns of Catania, to honor the Piedmont kings, the Savoia, who had just annexed Sicily to their kingdom. According to others, torta Savoia was created by a pastry chef from Palermo during a visit to Savoia. The base is a type of pan di spagna called pasta biscotto, but the classic pan di spagna works just as well. Similarly, purists would only use homemade hazelnut butter for the filling, but modern versions also utilize Nutella.

1. Cut the larger Pan di Spagna, horizontally, into three equally thick rounds. Cut the smaller one, horizontally, into three equally thick rounds. Set them aside.

2. To begin preparations for the chocolate and hazelnut cream, place the hazelnuts and sugar in a food processor and blitz until the mixture is a smooth paste.

3. Bring a few inches of water to a simmer in a medium saucepan. Place the chocolate in a heatproof bowl, place it over the simmering water, and stir until it is melted and smooth. Add the Nutella, stir to incorporate, and then incorporate the hazelnut paste. Remove the bowl from heat.

4. Spread the chocolate and hazelnut cream over the pieces of cake, stacking the frosted pieces on top of one another and pressing down gently on them to make sure they stay together.

5. Chill the cake in the refrigerator or freezer for 2 to 3 hours.

6. Bring a few inches of water to a simmer in a medium saucepan. To prepare the glaze, place the chocolate in a heatproof bowl, place it over the simmering water, and stir until it is melted and smooth. Add the coconut oil and stir until the mixture is very smooth and shiny. Remove the bowl from heat.

7. Reserve a few tablespoons of the glaze and pour the rest over the cake. Use a rubber spatula to smooth out any smudges on the bottom of the cake.

8. Using two spatulas, transfer the cake onto a clean serving plate. Place it back in the freezer or refrigerator and chill until the icing has set.

9. Place the reserved glaze in a piping bag fitted with a fine tip and pipe the word "Savoia" on the top of the cake. Decorate the cake with any remaining glaze and enjoy.

INGREDIENTS:

1½ BATCHES OF PAN DI SPAGNA (SEE PAGE 819), FULL BATCH PREPARED IN 1 PAN, ½ BATCH PREPARED IN ANOTHER PAN, AT ROOM TEMPERATURE

FOR THE CHOCOLATE & HAZELNUT CREAM

2 (HEAPING) CUPS BLANCHED HAZELNUTS

¼ CUP SUGAR

10 OZ. MILK CHOCOLATE, CHOPPED

1 CUP NUTELLA

FOR THE GLAZE

15 OZ. BITTERSWEET CHOCOLATE, CHOPPED

¼ CUP COCONUT OIL

TORTA FEDORA

YIELD: 1 CAKE / **ACTIVE TIME:** 30 MINUTES / **TOTAL TIME:** 3 HOURS

Possibly the oldest Sicilian cake that is still around, torta fedora is pan di spagna soaked with orange-flavored syrup, filled with ricotta cream, and covered with almonds and pistachios. It is truly delicious and extremely easy to make.

1. To prepare the ricotta cream, place all of the ingredients in a bowl and stir until well combined. Chill the ricotta cream in the refrigerator.

2. To prepare the bagna, place the water, sugar, and orange zest in a small saucepan and bring to a boil, stirring to dissolve the sugar. Remove the pan from heat and let the syrup cool. When the syrup has cooled, stir in the liqueur.

3. Cut the Pan di Spagna, horizontally, into two equally thick pieces and moisten them both with the bagna.

4. Spread two-thirds of the ricotta cream over the bottom piece of cake. Place the other piece of cake on top and coat the entire cake with the remaining ricotta cream.

5. Top the sides of the cake with the almonds and the top with the pistachios. Place the cake in the refrigerator and chill it for at least 1 hour before serving.

INGREDIENTS:

FOR THE RICOTTA CREAM

4 CUPS RICOTTA CHEESE (MADE FROM SHEEP'S MILK PREFERRED), DRAINED FOR A FEW HOURS IN THE REFRIGERATOR

1¼ CUPS CONFECTIONERS' SUGAR

½ CUP BITTERSWEET CHOCOLATE CHIPS

FOR THE BAGNA

¾ CUP WATER

½ CUP SUGAR

ZEST OF 1 ORANGE

2 TABLESPOONS ORANGE LIQUEUR

PAN DI SPAGNA (SEE PAGE 819)

1 CUP SLIVERED ALMONDS, TOASTED, FOR TOPPING

1 CUP UNSALTED PISTACHIOS, FINELY CHOPPED, FOR TOPPING

TORTA CAPRESE

YIELD: 1 CAKE / ACTIVE TIME: 30 MINUTES / TOTAL TIME: 3 HOURS

There are plenty of evocative stories swirling around the origins of this peculiar chocolate cake from Capri. It is probably a cake born around the court of Naples during the first half of the eighteenth century, possibly made by a baker from Capri, as caprese means "from Capri." Other stories include a Mafia visit to Capri in 1920 or a yearning Austrian queen. Regarding the latter, legend holds that Maria Carolina D'Asburgo was nostalgic for her native sacher torte but was not quite precise in telling its ingredients to the court's baker, and so torta caprese was born. Whatever the origins, this cake is delicious and easy to make, with the added bonus that it can be enjoyed also by gluten-sensitive guests and family members, since it uses almond flour.

1. Preheat the oven to 360°F. Place the butter and sugar in the work bowl of a stand mixer fitted with the paddle attachment and cream the mixture on medium speed until it is pale and fluffy.

2. Add the egg yolks, orange zest, and liqueur and beat until incorporated.

3. Bring a few inches of water to a simmer in a medium saucepan. Place the chocolate in a heatproof bowl, place it over the simmering water, and stir until it is melted and smooth. Remove the bowl from heat, add the almond flour to the melted chocolate, and stir to combine.

4. Add the butter mixture to the melted chocolate mixture and stir until well combined.

5. Clean out the work bowl of the stand mixer and fit the mixer with the whisk attachment. Place the egg whites in the work bowl and whip until they hold stiff peaks.

6. Add the whipped egg whites to the batter and fold to incorporate.

7. Coat a round 9-inch cake pan with butter, dust it with cocoa powder, and knock out any excess. Pour the batter into the pan, place it in the oven, and bake until a toothpick inserted into the center comes out clean, about 40 minutes.

8. Remove the cake from the oven and let it cool.

9. Dust the cake with cocoa powder and confectioners' sugar and enjoy.

INGREDIENTS:

- 7 OZ. UNSALTED BUTTER, PLUS MORE AS NEEDED
- 7 OZ. SUGAR
- 6 EGGS, SEPARATED
- ZEST OF 1 ORANGE
- 2 TABLESPOONS ORANGE LIQUEUR
- 9 OZ. BITTERSWEET CHOCOLATE
- 8.8 OZ. ALMOND FLOUR
- UNSWEETENED COCOA POWDER, AS NEEDED
- CONFECTIONERS' SUGAR, FOR TOPPING

NAPOLI AND SICILY:
CENTERS OF ROYALTY AND LUXURY SWEETS

The 1861 unification of Italy had been dreamed about by Southern Italians for centuries and pursued with bloody battles for decades. It did not, however, bring the results most had hoped for, at least not for the South. This led to the biggest wave of emigration Italy had ever known, as Italians fled in the hope that they would find abroad, most often in America, the improved standard of living the revolution failed to provide.

Nowadays, not many are aware that prior to Italy's unification, Naples and Sicily were themselves centers of flourishing kingdoms. Although there was never a Southern kingdom independent of foreign sovereignty—the administration was always made up of nobles representing Spanish or French royalty—these proxy monarchs were in fact Southern Italians by birth or culture, different from the northern Savoia monarchy that unified the country.

Ferdinando I Re Delle Due Sicilie, who ruled over most of the South, represented one bright example of the Italianization of southern kings. Born in Naples, Ferdinando I could only speak Neapolitan, and was famous for having refused to learn any of the other languages commonly spoken at his court, including Italian, Spanish, and French, as well as German, the mother tongue of his wife, Maria Carolina D'Asburgo. He hated etiquette and loved to hang out with the poor of Naples, the lazzaroni, with whom he had a special bond that earned him the nickname "King Lazzarone."

Having local monarchs meant that also the court was composed of locals, which meant that all of the delicious creations made by the court's kitchen staff slowly filtered out into the community and became assimilated into traditional Southern Italian cuisine. This is the reason why both Naples and the main Sicilian cities, Palermo and Catania, are meccas of delicious sweets. Indeed, also the first Italian cookbooks are emanations of this opulence, as they were developed by the early gourmands and chefs orbiting around Neapolitan royalty. The most influential of these tomes are the *Liber de Coquina*, written at the court of Carlo II D'Angió at the end of the thirteenth century, and *Lo Scalco alla moderna* by Antonio Latini, written at the end of the seventeenth century. This latter book is where we find the first written recipes for sorbet and ice cream (sorbetto al latte).

A special mention goes also to the intertwined worlds of aristocracy and clergy, as many Southern delicacies were developed by nuns, who often belonged to aristocratic families. Most convents in Naples were shut down after the unity of Italy, a happening that caused a loss of some crucial techniques. Still, many of their creations had already become part of the local culinary fabric, like sfogliatelle, to name just one.

Similarly, many amazing Sicilian sweets also originated from royal courts, aristocracy's mansions, and convents. Several of the spared convents in Sicily deliver top-notch pastries to this very day, while the sweets once developed for the aristocracy are now accessible to everyone thanks to the local bakeries that keep manufacturing these delicacies, and the cooks who learned to reproduce them at home.

SORBETTO AL LIMONE

YIELD: 4 CUPS / **ACTIVE TIME:** 30 MINUTES / **TOTAL TIME:** 9 HOURS

This lemon sorbet is as delicious as it is simple to make, and it does not require any special appliances. It is interesting to note that sorbet was first developed in Sicily under the Moorish domination, about 1,000 years ago, using ice extracted from Mount Etna. The technique to make sorbet was then largely forgotten and only rediscovered in the sixteenth century, when it evolved into ice cream, and then quickly spread to the rest of Europe.

1. Place the water, sugar, and lemon peels in a saucepan and bring it to a boil, stirring to dissolve the sugar. Remove the pan from heat and let the syrup cool.

2. Remove the lemon peels, discard them, and stir in the lemon juice.

3. Pour the lemon syrup into a container and freeze it for 5 to 6 hours.

4. Remove the syrup from the freezer and let it thaw at room temperature for at least 25 minutes. Scoop the sorbet into a blender and briefly mix until it is creamy.

INGREDIENTS:

17.6 OZ. WATER

8.8 OZ. SUGAR

2 LEMON PEELS, PITH REMOVED

6.3 OZ. FRESH LEMON JUICE

BABÀ

YIELD: 1 CAKE / **ACTIVE TIME:** 40 MINUTES / **TOTAL TIME:** 8 HOURS

One of the most renowned Neapolitan desserts, babà is a cake with a spongy texture smothered in a rumcentric syrup. As the dough is somewhat challenging, it is best to prepare with a stand mixer.

1. To prepare the lievitino, place all of the ingredients in a bowl and stir to combine. Cover the bowl with plastic wrap and let the lievitino rest for 1 hour.

2. To begin preparations for the dough, place the lievitino and flour in the work bowl of a stand mixer fitted with the dough hook and work the mixture at low speed until combined.

3. Incorporate the eggs one at a time. Add the sugar and salt and work the mixture until they have been incorporated.

4. Work the mixture until it is a smooth and elastic dough. Gradually add the butter and knead the dough until it has been incorporated.

5. Raise the speed to medium and knead the dough until it is soft, very elastic, and not sticky.

6. Cover the bowl with plastic wrap and let the dough rest in a naturally warm spot (86°F is ideal). Let the dough rise until it has tripled in size, about 4 hours.

7. Dust a pastry board or cutting board with flour, place the dough on it, and shape it into a round. Make a hole in the center of the round.

8. Coat a 10-inch Bundt pan with butter, place the dough in it, and place it in a naturally warm spot. Let the dough rise until it has almost reached the edge of the pan.

9. Preheat the oven to 350°F.

10. Place the cake in the oven and bake until a toothpick inserted into the center comes out clean, about 30 minutes. Remove the cake from the oven and let it cool completely.

11. To prepare the bagna, place the sugar, water, and lemon peel in a saucepan and bring to a boil, stirring to dissolve the sugar. Remove the pan from heat and stir in the rum. Pour one-quarter of the bagna over the cake and let it soak for 20 minutes. Repeat two more times.

12. Invert the cake onto a serving platter, pour the remaining bagna over the cake, and serve.

INGREDIENTS:

FOR THE LIEVITINO (STARTER)

1	PACKET OF INSTANT YEAST
3	TABLESPOONS LUKEWARM WATER (90°F)
1	TEASPOON SUGAR
2	TABLESPOONS BREAD FLOUR

FOR THE DOUGH

10.6 OZ.	STRONG BREAD FLOUR (SUCH AS MANITOBA FLOUR), PLUS MORE AS NEEDED
5	MEDIUM EGGS
2	TABLESPOONS SUGAR
	PINCH OF FINE SEA SALT
3½ OZ.	UNSALTED BUTTER, PLUS MORE AS NEEDED

FOR THE BAGNA

2	CUPS SUGAR
3⅓	CUPS WATER
1	LEMON PEEL, PITH REMOVED
2	CUPS RUM

BABÀ:
A ROYAL DESSERT

For most, the babà is a Neapolitan pastry through and through, with a select few knowing its true origins.

In the first half of the eighteenth century, King Stanislaw Leszczyński was exiled from Poland and settled in the Alsace region of France. During his stay, King Stanislaw developed many hobbies, one of which was gastronomy. He took inspiration from a local sponge cake called kugelhopf, which is not truly French but rather Austro-Hungarian, and improved it. Sources report that the exiled king found kugelhopf to be too dry and so he developed it into the babà. The dough was devised to be extremely spongy to absorb as much rum-spiked syrup as possible, creating the luscious dessert we all know and love today.

The king also gave the babà its name, but the reasons why he chose it are not entirely known. There are two leading hypotheses: the first traces the origins of the name back to the Polish word for old lady, baba, highlighting the resemblance of the cake's shape and an elderly woman made heavier by age. The other possible origin of the name is linked to the famed Ali Baba of *One Thousand and One Nights*, a book that was translated just around the time Leszczy≈Ñski invented his cake, and indeed was the king's favorite book.

The king's recipe was then refined by the famous pastry chef Nicolas Stohrer and became so popular in France that it soon reached the Bourbon court of Naples. In time, the babà slipped out of the royal kitchens and entered the bakeries frequented by the common people, becoming a luxury available to many (if not to all).

In Neapolitan bakeries, the cake took on different shapes, in particular the mushroom-shaped one, and became declined into endless variations: topped with custard, whipped cream, berries, cherries, candied fruit, nuts, and so on. The "mignon," a miniature version of the babà, is now also very popular.

BRIOCHE COL TUPPO

YIELD: 8 BRIOCHE / **ACTIVE TIME:** 1 HOUR / **TOTAL TIME:** 16 HOURS

Italians have the habit of eating "dessert" for breakfast, something that often surprises people born outside of Italy. In Sicily, the quintessential breakfast is this brioche and granita. The brioche col tuppo was, like Neapolitan babà, imported from France, most likely by an aristocratic Sicilian family in the 1700s.

1. To begin preparations for the lievitino, place the milk and vanilla seeds in a saucepan and warm until it is just about to come to a simmer. Remove the pan from heat and let the mixture cool until it is lukewarm (about 90°F).

2. Add the yeast, gently stir, and let the mixture proof until it starts to foam, about 10 minutes.

3. Add the flour and clementine zest, stir to combine, and transfer the lievitino to an airtight container. Chill it in the refrigerator for 10 to 12 hours.

4. To begin preparations for the dough, warm ½ cup of the milk to 90°F, place it in a bowl, and add the yeast and honey. Gently stir and let the mixture proof until it starts to foam, about 10 minutes.

5. Place the mixture in the work bowl of a stand mixer fitted with the dough hook, add the flours and lievitino, and work the mixture on low speed until it is combined.

6. Add 2 of the eggs and work the mixture until they have been incorporated. Add the sugar and salt and work the mixture until it comes together as a smooth and elastic dough.

7. Add the lard, raise the mixer's speed to medium, and knead until the dough is very elastic.

8. Cover the bowl with plastic wrap, place it in a warm spot, and let the dough rise until it doubles in size, about 2½ hours.

9. Line a baking sheet with parchment paper. Place the dough on a flour-dusted work surface and divide it into 5 pieces. Divide 4 of the pieces in half, and then divide the remaining large piece into 8 small pieces. Shape the pieces of dough into rounds.

10. Make a hole in the top of each of the larger rounds and gently widen the openings. Place a smaller round in each of the openings. Place the brioche on the baking sheet.

INGREDIENTS:

FOR THE LIEVITINO (STARTER)

½ CUP WHOLE MILK

SEEDS OF ½ VANILLA BEAN

¼ PACKET OF ACTIVE DRY YEAST

1 CUP BREAD FLOUR

ZEST OF 2 CLEMENTINES

FOR THE DOUGH

½ CUP PLUS 2 TEASPOONS WHOLE MILK

¼ PACKET OF ACTIVE DRY YEAST

2 TEASPOONS HONEY

5.6 OZ. STRONG BREAD FLOUR (SUCH AS MANITOBA FLOUR)

4½ OZ. ALL-PURPOSE FLOUR, PLUS MORE AS NEEDED

3 LARGE EGGS

2.8 OZ. SUGAR

1 TEASPOON FINE SEA SALT

3.8 OZ. LARD OR UNSALTED BUTTER

11. Place the remaining milk and egg in a bowl and whisk to combine. Brush the brioche with some of the egg wash and let them rise until they have doubled in size, about 1½ hours. Place the remaining egg wash in the refrigerator.

12. Preheat the oven to 375°F.

13. Brush the brioche again with the egg wash and place them in the oven. Bake the brioche until they are golden brown, about 20 minutes.

14. Remove the brioche from the oven and let them cool slightly before serving.

GRAFFE

YIELD: 20 GRAFFE / **ACTIVE TIME:** 1 HOUR / **TOTAL TIME:** 4 HOURS

Graffe are typical doughnuts from Naples, where they are part of the Carnival celebrations in February. Compared to regular doughnuts, they are notable both in their shape and in their consistency, as they contain potatoes.

1. Place the potatoes in a large saucepan, cover them with water, and bring to a boil. Cook until the potatoes are fork-tender, about 20 minutes.

2. Drain the potatoes, peel them while they are still hot, and mash them. Let the potatoes cool.

3. Warm the milk to 90°F, place it in a bowl, and add the yeast. Gently stir and let the mixture proof until it starts to foam, about 10 minutes.

4. Place the mixture in the work bowl of a stand mixer fitted with the dough hook, add the flour, egg, egg yolks, mashed potatoes, vanilla, sugar, salt, liqueur, lemon zest, and orange zest, and work the mixture on low speed until it is combined.

5. As the water content of potatoes can vary, check the dough. If it is too dry, incorporate a little more milk; if it is too wet, incorporate a little more flour.

6. Add the butter and work the mixture until it comes together as a smooth dough.

7. Raise the mixer's speed to medium and knead the dough until it is very elastic.

8. Form the dough into a ball and place it in a clean mixing bowl. Cover the bowl with plastic wrap, place it in a warm spot, and let the dough rise until it doubles in size, about 1½ hours.

9. Line two baking sheets with parchment paper. Place the dough on a flour-dusted work surface and divide it into 2 pieces. Divide each piece into 10 pieces and roll each piece out into a 4-inch-long and ¾-inch-thick log. Form the logs into doughnuts and pinch the seams to seal them.

10. Place the graffe on the baking sheets, cover them with kitchen towels, and let them rise for 1 hour.

INGREDIENTS:

17.6	OZ. YELLOW-FLESHED POTATOES, CHOPPED
½	CUP WHOLE MILK, PLUS MORE AS NEEDED
1	PACKET OF ACTIVE DRY YEAST
17.6	OZ. BREAD FLOUR, PLUS MORE AS NEEDED
1	EGG
3	EGG YOLKS
2	TEASPOONS PURE VANILLA EXTRACT
3	TABLESPOONS SUGAR, PLUS MORE FOR COATING
	PINCH OF FINE SEA SALT
2	TABLESPOONS ANISE LIQUEUR
	ZEST OF ½ LEMON
	ZEST OF ½ ORANGE
3½	OZ. UNSALTED BUTTER, SOFTENED
	EXTRA-VIRGIN OLIVE OIL, AS NEEDED

11. Add olive oil to a narrow, deep, heavy-bottomed saucepan with high edges until it is about 2 inches deep and warm it to 340°F. Add 2 graffe to the hot oil at a time and fry until they are golden brown, turning them over halfway through.

12. Transfer the fried graffe to a paper towel–lined plate to drain.

13. Place sugar in a shallow dish, dredge the graffe in it until coated, and enjoy.

SFINCE DI SAN GIUSEPPE

YIELD: 20 SFINCE / **ACTIVE TIME:** 1 HOUR / **TOTAL TIME:** 2 HOURS

A delicious fried eclair from Sicily, sfince is particularly popular on the western part of the island. Typically made on Saint Joseph's Day, they were created by the nuns at the Saint Francis's Stigmata convent in Palermo.

1. To prepare the ricotta cream, place all of the ingredients in a mixing bowl, stir to combine, and store the ricotta cream in the refrigerator.

2. To begin preparations for the batter, place the butter, water, and salt in a saucepan and bring to a simmer over medium-low heat. Remove the pan from heat, add the flour, and stir quickly until it has been incorporated.

3. Place the saucepan over low heat and cook for a few minutes, stirring continually. Remove the pan from heat and let the batter cool until it is just warm.

4. Incorporate the eggs into the batter one at a time.

5. Add olive oil to a narrow, deep, heavy-bottomed saucepan with high edges until it is 2 inches deep and warm it to 340°F. Add 2 or 3 dollops of the batter to the hot oil and fry until golden brown, turning them as necessary.

6. Place the fried sfince on a paper towel–lined plate. To serve, top them with the ricotta cream, candied orange peels, candied cherries, pistachios, and confectioners' sugar.

INGREDIENTS:

FOR THE RICOTTA CREAM

- 2.2 LBS. RICOTTA CHEESE, DRAINED IN THE REFRIGERATOR FOR A FEW HOURS
- 3¼ CUPS CONFECTIONERS' SUGAR, PLUS MORE FOR TOPPING
- 1 (SCANT) CUP BITTERSWEET CHOCOLATE CHIPS

FOR THE BATTER

- 3½ OZ. LARD OR UNSALTED BUTTER
- 8.8 OZ. WATER
- ⅔ TEASPOON FINE SEA SALT
- 5.3 OZ. ALL-PURPOSE FLOUR
- 4 MEDIUM EGGS

  EXTRA-VIRGIN OLIVE OIL, AS NEEDED

  CANDIED ORANGE PEELS, FOR TOPPING

  CANDIED CHERRIES, FOR TOPPING

  UNSALTED PISTACHIOS, CHOPPED, FOR TOPPING

  CONFECTIONERS' SUGAR, FOR TOPPING

ZEPPOLE DI SAN GIUSEPPE

YIELD: 9 ZEPPOLE / **ACTIVE TIME:** 1 HOUR / **TOTAL TIME:** 1 HOUR AND 30 MINUTES

A fried Neapolitan eclair similar to the Sicilian sfince, zeppole are traditional for Saint Joseph's Day, just like their Sicilian counterpart.

1. Place the butter, water, salt, and sugar in a saucepan and bring to a simmer over medium-low heat. Remove the pan from heat, add the flour, and stir quickly until it has been incorporated.

2. Place the saucepan over low heat and cook for a few minutes, stirring continually. Remove the pan from heat and let the batter cool until it is just warm.

3. Incorporate the eggs into the batter 2 at a time, using either a whisk or the paddle attachment on a stand mixer.

4. Place the batter in a piping bag fitted with a star tip and pipe 4-inch rings of the batter onto a large piece of parchment paper, making sure to leave space between each ring.

5. Add olive oil to a narrow, deep, heavy-bottomed saucepan with high edges until it is 2 inches deep and warm it to 340°F. Cut the parchment paper into squares around each zeppola and gently slip the zeppola and parchment paper into the hot oil, frying one at a time. Fry the zeppole until they are golden brown, turn them over, and remove the parchment paper. Fry for another 1 to 2 minutes.

6. Place the fried zeppole on a paper towel–lined plate. To serve, top each one with some custard, a cherry, and confectioners' sugar.

INGREDIENTS:

6	OZ. UNSALTED BUTTER
2	CUPS WATER
1	TEASPOON FINE SEA SALT
2	TEASPOONS SUGAR
10.6	OZ. BREAD FLOUR
10	MEDIUM EGGS
	EXTRA-VIRGIN OLIVE OIL, AS NEEDED
	CREMA PASTICCERA NAPOLETANA (SEE PAGE 820)
9	CHERRIES IN SYRUP, DRAINED
	CONFECTIONERS' SUGAR, FOR TOPPING

STRUFFOLI NAPOLETANI

YIELD: 60 STRUFFOLI / **ACTIVE TIME:** 40 MINUTES / **TOTAL TIME:** 2 HOURS

Ubiquitous in Neapolitan Christmas and New Year's spreads, struffoli are bites of fried unleavened dough smothered in honey.

1. Place the flour, sugar, and salt in a mixing bowl and stir to combine. Add the eggs and work the mixture until they have been incorporated.

2. Add the butter, orange zest, lemon zest, and rum and work the mixture until it comes together as a smooth dough. Cover the dough with plastic wrap and chill it in the refrigerator for 1 hour.

3. Place the dough on a flour-dusted work surface, flatten it slightly, and cut it into ½-inch-thick strips. Roll the strips into long, thin logs, cut each log into ½-inch-long pieces, and shape the pieces into rounds.

4. Add olive oil to a narrow, deep, heavy-bottomed saucepan with high edges until it is 2 inches deep and warm it to 340°F. Add a handful of struffoli at a time and fry until they are just golden, about 1 minute. Remove the fried struffoli with a slotted spoon and place them on a paper towel–lined plate to drain.

5. Place the honey and confectioners' sugar in a saucepan and warm the mixture over low heat until the honey has liquefied.

6. Add all of the struffoli to the pan and gently stir until they are all coated.

7. Pile the struffoli on a serving dish or arrange them in a circle. Top with sugar sprinkles and candied fruit and enjoy.

INGREDIENTS:

14.1 OZ. ALL-PURPOSE FLOUR, PLUS MORE AS NEEDED

1.4 OZ. SUGAR

1 TEASPOON FINE SEA SALT

3 EGGS

2.8 OZ. UNSALTED BUTTER

ZEST OF 1 ORANGE

ZEST OF 1 LEMON

1½ TABLESPOONS RUM OR ANISE LIQUEUR

EXTRA-VIRGIN OLIVE OIL, AS NEEDED

1 (SCANT) CUP HONEY

¼ CUP CONFECTIONERS' SUGAR

COLORED SUGAR SPRINKLES, FOR TOPPING

CANDIED FRUIT, FOR TOPPING

CASATIELLO

YIELD: 1 LOAF / **ACTIVE TIME:** 1 HOUR / **TOTAL TIME:** 6 HOURS

Casatiello is a traditional Easter bread from Naples. Seasoned with lard and pepper, this lovely savory bread is shaped like a large doughnut and topped by whole eggs, symbolizing both life and resurrection. The term casatiello derives from cheese in Neapolitan dialect, referring to the bread's abundant cheese filling, which is made even richer by the addition of various cured meats.

1. To begin preparations for the dough, place the yeast and water in a mixing bowl, gently stir, and let the mixture proof until it is foamy, about 10 minutes.

2. Add the flour and work the mixture until it comes together as a smooth dough.

3. Place the dough on a flour-dusted work surface, add the salt and pepper, and then gradually incorporate the lard. Knead the dough until it is smooth and elastic. Shape the dough into a ball, place it in a clean mixing bowl, and cover it with plastic wrap. Place the dough in a naturally warm place and let it rise for 2 hours.

4. To prepare the filling, place all of the ingredients in a mixing bowl and stir to combine.

5. Remove a handful of dough, cover it with plastic wrap, and set it aside. Place the remaining dough on a flour-dusted work surface and roll it out into a ½-inch-thick rectangle.

6. Distribute the filling evenly over the dough and gently fold the dough over itself, lengthwise. Gently pinch the seam to seal it.

7. Coat a 10-inch Bundt pan with lard, place the dough in the pan, seam side down, and pinch the ends of the dough together to join them together.

8. Cover the dough with a kitchen towel, place it in a naturally warm spot, and let it rise for 2 hours.

9. Preheat the oven to 390°F.

10. Arrange the eggs on the top of the casatiello, spaced regularly, and secure them using cross strips made from the reserved dough. Brush the dough with melted lard and place it in the oven.

11. Bake for 10 minutes, reduce the oven's temperature to 340°F, and bake until a toothpick inserted into the center of the bread comes out clean, about 35 minutes.

12. Remove the bread from the oven and let it cool completely before serving.

INGREDIENTS:

FOR THE DOUGH

1	PACKET OF ACTIVE DRY YEAST
14.1	OZ. WARM WATER (105°F)
24.7	OZ. BREAD FLOUR, PLUS MORE AS NEEDED
2	TEASPOONS FINE SEA SALT
1	TABLESPOON BLACK PEPPER
5	OZ. LARD, SOFTENED, PLUS MORE AS NEEDED

FOR THE FILLING

5	OZ. PROVOLONE CHEESE, CUBED
3½	OZ. CACIOCAVALLO CHEESE, CUBED
6	OZ. SALAMI, CHOPPED
2	OZ. PANCETTA, CUBED
¼	CUP GRATED PECORINO CHEESE
1	TEASPOON BLACK PEPPER
5	EGGS, LEFT WHOLE, FOR TOPPING

TORTANO

YIELD: 1 LOAF / ACTIVE TIME: 1 HOUR / TOTAL TIME: 6 HOURS

Tortano is very similar to casatiello, but with one big difference: the eggs are in the filling instead of being used on top as a decorative piece. This quality makes tortano both richer in taste and easier to assemble.

1. To begin preparations for the dough, place the yeast and water in a mixing bowl, gently stir, and let the mixture proof until it is foamy, about 10 minutes.

2. Add the flour and work the mixture until it comes together as a smooth dough.

3. Place the dough on a flour-dusted work surface, add the salt and pepper, and then gradually incorporate the lard. Knead the dough until it is smooth and elastic. Shape the dough into a ball, place it in a clean mixing bowl, and cover it with plastic wrap. Place the dough in a naturally warm place and let it rise for 2 hours.

4. To prepare the filling, place all of the ingredients in a mixing bowl and stir to combine.

5. Place the dough on a flour-dusted work surface and roll it out into a ½-inch-thick rectangle.

6. Distribute the filling evenly over the dough and gently fold the dough over itself, lengthwise. Gently pinch the seam to seal it.

7. Coat a 10-inch Bundt pan with lard, place the dough in the pan, seam side down, and pinch the ends of the dough together to join them together.

8. Cover the dough with a kitchen towel, place it in a naturally warm spot, and let it rise for 2 hours.

9. Preheat the oven to 390°F.

10. Brush the dough with melted lard and place it in the oven.

11. Bake for 10 minutes, reduce the oven's temperature to 340°F, and bake until a toothpick inserted into the center of the bread comes out clean, about 35 minutes.

12. Remove the bread from the oven and let it cool completely before serving.

INGREDIENTS:

FOR THE DOUGH

1	PACKET OF ACTIVE DRY YEAST
14.1	OZ. WARM WATER (105°F)
24.7	OZ. BREAD FLOUR, PLUS MORE AS NEEDED
2	TEASPOONS FINE SEA SALT
1	TABLESPOON BLACK PEPPER
5	OZ. LARD, SOFTENED, PLUS MORE AS NEEDED

FOR THE FILLING

5	OZ. PROVOLONE CHEESE, CUBED
3½	OZ. CACIOCAVALLO CHEESE, CUBED
6	OZ. SALAMI, CHOPPED
2	OZ. PANCETTA, CUBED
4	HARD-BOILED EGGS, CHOPPED
¼	CUP GRATED PECORINO CHEESE
1	TEASPOON BLACK PEPPER

PANE AQUILANO

YIELD: 1 LOAF / **ACTIVE TIME:** 1 HOUR / **TOTAL TIME:** 15 HOURS

Not many are aware of this fact, even in Italy, but bread from the Abruzzi region is outstanding. This traditional sourdough loaf is a clear example of the mastery residing in that baking tradition.

1. Place the bread flour, whole wheat flour, and two-thirds of the water in the work bowl of a stand mixer fitted with the dough hook and work the mixture on low speed. Gradually add the starter and work the mixture until it comes together as a shaggy dough.

2. Add the potato and continue to work the dough until it is smooth.

3. Gradually add the salt and remaining water and work the dough until they have been incorporated. Shape the dough into a ball, place it in a clean bowl, and cover it with plastic wrap. Let the dough rise at room temperature for 1 hour, fold it, and let it rise for another hour. Fold the dough again and let it rise for 6 hours.

4. Place the dough on a bread flour–dusted work surface and fold it over itself. Cover the dough with a kitchen towel and let it rest for 30 minutes.

5. Spread the dough with your hands into a rectangle. Fold a long side toward the center of the dough and then fold the other long side over it.

6. Place the dough, seam side down, on a semolina-dusted kitchen towel that is large enough to also cover the top of the dough. Let it rest for 1 hour.

7. Preheat the oven to 390°F and place a baking stone in the oven as it warms.

8. Place the dough on a semolina-dusted oven peel and slide it onto the baking stone. Bake until the crust is dark brown, about 50 minutes.

9. Remove the bread from the oven and let it cool, upright, for at least 4 hours before serving.

INGREDIENTS:

- 11.6 OZ. BREAD FLOUR, PLUS MORE AS NEEDED
- 3½ OZ. FINELY GROUND WHOLE WHEAT FLOUR
- 10.9 OZ. WATER
- 3½ OZ. STIFF SOURDOUGH STARTER (SEE PAGE 823)
- 1 SMALL POTATO, BOILED, PEELED, AND PRESSED THROUGH A POTATO RICER
- 2 TEASPOONS FINE SEA SALT
- SEMOLINA FLOUR, AS NEEDED

PARROZZO MOLISANO

YIELD: 1 LOAF / ACTIVE TIME: 1 HOUR / TOTAL TIME: 10 HOURS

In Molise, a region traditionally poor of resources, corn from the Americas became a staple. This local bread called parrozzo (from pane rozzo, "coarse bread") is an example of using both corn and potatoes to replace a portion of the wheat flour in a bread, and the result is a loaf with a very interesting consistency and flavor.

1. Place the bread flour, whole wheat flour, and two-thirds of the water in the work bowl of a stand mixer fitted with the dough hook and work the mixture on low speed. Gradually add the starter and work the mixture until it comes together as a shaggy dough.

2. Add the Polenta and potatoes and continue to work the dough until it is smooth.

3. Gradually add the salt and remaining water and work the dough until they have been incorporated. Shape the dough into a ball, place it in a clean bowl, and cover it with plastic wrap. Let the dough rise at room temperature for 30 minutes, fold it, and let it rise for another 30 minutes. Fold the dough again and let it rise for another hour.

4. Place the dough on a bread flour–dusted work surface and fold it over itself. Cover the dough with a kitchen towel and let it rest for 30 minutes.

5. Spread the dough with your hands into a rectangle. Fold a long side toward the center of the dough and then fold the other long side over it.

6. Place the dough, seam side down, on a semolina-dusted kitchen towel that is large enough to also cover the top of the dough. Let it rest for 4 hours.

7. Preheat the oven to the maximum possible temperature and place a baking stone in the oven as it warms.

8. Place the dough on a semolina-dusted oven peel and slide it onto the baking stone. Bake for 15 minutes and reduce the oven's temperature to 390°F. Bake until the crust is dark brown, about 30 minutes.

9. Remove the bread from the oven and let it cool for 2 hours before serving.

INGREDIENTS:

5.3 OZ. BREAD FLOUR, PLUS MORE AS NEEDED

3½ OZ. WHOLE WHEAT FLOUR

11.6 OZ. WATER

5.3 OZ. STIFF SOURDOUGH STARTER (SEE PAGE 823)

5.3 OZ. POLENTA (SEE PAGE 668), COOLED

5.3 OZ. MASHED POTATOES, COOLED

1½ TEASPOONS SALT

SEMOLINA FLOUR, AS NEEDED

SEMPRE FRESCHI

YIELD: 9 ROLLS / **ACTIVE TIME:** 1 HOUR / **TOTAL TIME:** 3 HOURS AND 30 MINUTES

Meaning "always fresh," these rolls are readily available in Sicilian bakeries, and particularly popular in Palermo.

1. Place the yeast, honey, and water in the work bowl of a stand mixer fitted with the dough hook, gently stir, and let the mixture proof until it is foamy, about 10 minutes.

2. Add the flours and work the mixture until it just comes together as a dough.

3. Add the sugar, olive oil, and salt and work the dough until it is smooth and elastic. Form the dough into a ball, place it in a clean bowl, and cover the bowl with plastic wrap. Let the dough rest for 40 minutes.

4. Line two baking sheets with parchment paper. Place the dough on a flour-dusted work surface and divide it into 9 pieces. Roll each piece into a ¼-inch-thick rectangle. Roll the rectangles up, starting from a short side.

5. Place the rolls on the baking sheets, seam side down, and let them rise for 1½ hours, brushing them with water a few times so they don't get dry.

6. Preheat the oven to 430°F and set it on convection mode if it is available.

7. Place the rolls in the oven and bake until they are golden brown, 12 to 15 minutes.

8. Remove the rolls from the baking sheets, wrap them in linen towels, and let them cool. Wrapping them up as they cool makes for a very soft crumb that is very much worth it.

INGREDIENTS:

1	PACKET OF ACTIVE DRY YEAST
1	TEASPOON HONEY
15.8	OZ. WARM WATER (105°F)
14.1	OZ. FINELY GROUND DURUM WHEAT FLOUR (SEMOLA RIMACINATA)
14.1	OZ. ALL-PURPOSE FLOUR, PLUS MORE AS NEEDED
2	TEASPOONS SUGAR
2	TABLESPOONS EXTRA-VIRGIN OLIVE OIL
3½	TEASPOONS FINE SEA SALT

PITTA CALABRESE

YIELD: 3 LOAVES / **ACTIVE TIME:** 1 HOUR / **TOTAL TIME:** 14 HOURS

A Calabrian sandwich bread, pitta Calabrese has most certainly Greek origins, as the name clearly suggests. Generally ring shaped and quite flat, pitta is great filled with meat, and in Catanzaro it forms the foundation of two popular sandwiches: u'suffritt, with pork and offal, and u'morzeddhu, with entrails and tripe.

1. If using active dry yeast, warm the water to 105°F, place it in the work bowl of a stand mixer fitted with the dough hook, and add the yeast and honey. Gently stir and let the mixture proof until it is foamy, about 10 minutes.

2. Add the flours and work the mixture on low speed until combined. If using a starter, add it gradually and work the mixture until it comes together as a dough.

3. Raise the speed and work the dough until it is smooth and elastic.

4. Add the salt and work the dough for another 10 minutes.

5. Coat a clean bowl with olive oil, place the dough in it, and cover the bowl with plastic wrap. Place the dough in a naturally warm spot and let it rise for 3 hours.

6. Transfer the dough to a flour-dusted work surface, divide it into 3 pieces, and shape them into rounds. Cover the dough with a kitchen towel and let it rise for another 3 hours.

7. Preheat the oven to 410°F and place a baking stone in the oven as it warms.

8. Roll out each round into a disk and make a hole in the center with a glass or ring cutter. Use a peel to slide the dough onto the baking stone and bake for 15 minutes.

9. Reduce the temperature to 355°F and cook the bread until it is golden brown, about 15 minutes.

10. Remove the bread from the oven and let it cool for 2 hours before serving.

INGREDIENTS:

- 1   PACKET OF ACTIVE DRY YEAST OR 6.3 OZ. STIFF SOURDOUGH STARTER (SEE PAGE 823)
- 16.9 OZ. WATER
- 2   TEASPOONS HONEY (OPTIONAL)
- 12.3 OZ. BREAD FLOUR
- 12.3 OZ. STONE-GROUND ALL-PURPOSE FLOUR, PLUS MORE AS NEEDED
- 1   TEASPOON FINE SEA SALT

   EXTRA-VIRGIN OLIVE OIL, AS NEEDED

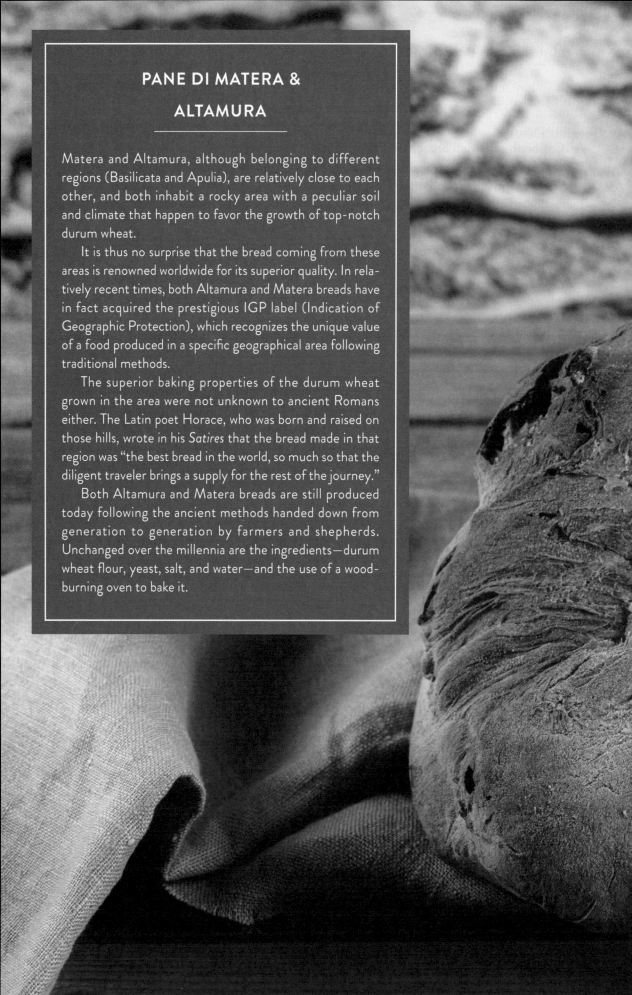

PANE DI MATERA & ALTAMURA

Matera and Altamura, although belonging to different regions (Basilicata and Apulia), are relatively close to each other, and both inhabit a rocky area with a peculiar soil and climate that happen to favor the growth of top-notch durum wheat.

It is thus no surprise that the bread coming from these areas is renowned worldwide for its superior quality. In relatively recent times, both Altamura and Matera breads have in fact acquired the prestigious IGP label (Indication of Geographic Protection), which recognizes the unique value of a food produced in a specific geographical area following traditional methods.

The superior baking properties of the durum wheat grown in the area were not unknown to ancient Romans either. The Latin poet Horace, who was born and raised on those hills, wrote in his *Satires* that the bread made in that region was "the best bread in the world, so much so that the diligent traveler brings a supply for the rest of the journey."

Both Altamura and Matera breads are still produced today following the ancient methods handed down from generation to generation by farmers and shepherds. Unchanged over the millennia are the ingredients—durum wheat flour, yeast, salt, and water—and the use of a wood-burning oven to bake it.

PANE DI MATERA

YIELD: 2 LOAVES / **ACTIVE TIME:** 2 HOURS / **TOTAL TIME:** 24 HOURS

The real pane di Matera can only be made around Matera, with local ingredients and using a very specific method involving fresh wild yeast derived from fermented fruit. It is possible to get close in your home, however, and this recipe helps you do just that.

1. Place the flour and 21.1 oz. of water in the work bowl of a stand mixer fitted with the dough hook and work the mixture until it just comes together and there are no lumps. Cover the bowl and let the dough rest for 1 hour.

2. Add the starter and the remaining water and work the dough until it is smooth and elastic. Add the salt and work the dough until it has been incorporated.

3. Transfer the dough to a large bowl, cover it with plastic wrap, and let it rest for 30 minutes.

4. Stretch and fold the dough over itself a few times. Cover the dough, let it rest for 30 minutes, and stretch and fold the dough over itself a few times. Rest for another 30 minutes, repeat the stretches and folds, and place the dough back in the bowl. Cover the bowl and store the dough in the refrigerator overnight.

5. Remove the dough from the refrigerator and let it rest at room temperature for 3 hours.

6. Place the dough on a flour-dusted work surface and divide it into 2 pieces.

7. Preheat the oven to 480°F and place a baking stone in the oven as it warms.

8. Slightly flatten each piece of the dough and shape them into ovals. Fold the edges of both sides of the ovals underneath the dough, roll the edges up tightly, and form the pieces of dough into logs. Bend the log into half-moons and score 3 perpendicular cuts on the curved sides of the half-moons, where the 2 halves meet. Squeeze a bit of the loaves from the side opposite to the cuts so that they open.

9. Place a small cast-iron skillet of water on the bottom of the oven. Use a peel to slide the loaves onto the baking stone and bake for 10 minutes.

10. Reduce the oven's temperature to 390°F and bake for 30 minutes.

11. Reduce the oven's temperature to 350°F, remove the saucepan, and leave the oven door open a crack. Bake for another 15 minutes.

12. Remove the bread from the oven and let it cool for 2 hours before serving.

INGREDIENTS:

- 2.2 LBS. FINELY GROUND DURUM WHEAT FLOUR (SEMOLA RIMACINATA), PLUS MORE AS NEEDED
- 24.3 OZ. WATER
- 6.3 OZ. STIFF SOURDOUGH STARTER (SEE PAGE 823), FED TWICE WITH FINELY GROUND DURUM WHEAT FLOUR
- 1 (HEAPING) TABLESPOON FINE SEA SALT

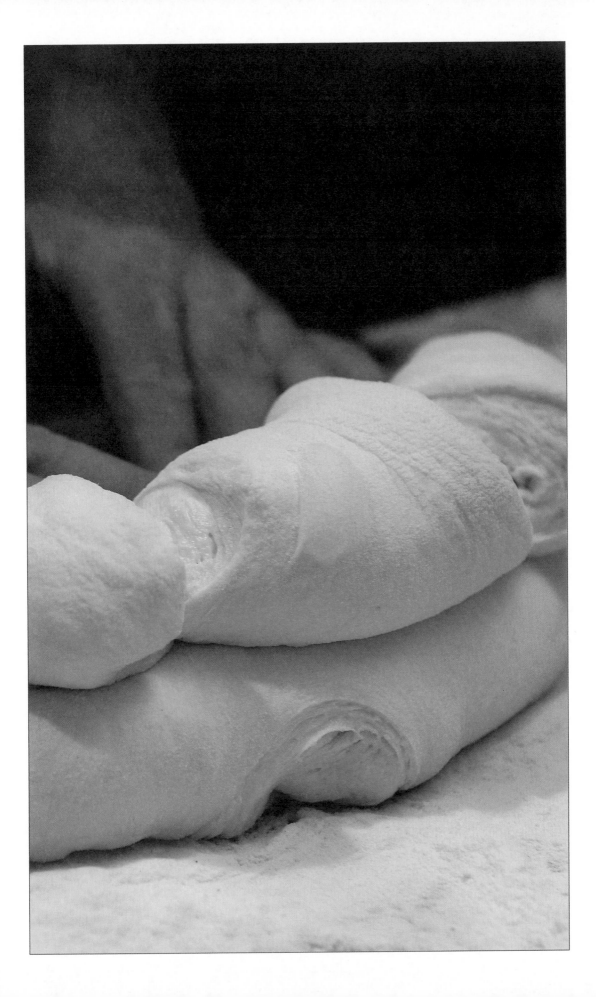

PANE DI ALTAMURA

YIELD: 2 LOAVES / **ACTIVE TIME:** 2 HOURS / **TOTAL TIME:** 24 HOURS

Like pane di Matera, Altamura's famed bread can only be made there. Here's a recipe for those who can't wait to try it, but can't get to Italy anytime soon.

1. Place the flours and 21.1 oz. of water in the work bowl of a stand mixer fitted with the dough hook and work the mixture until it just comes together and there are no lumps. Cover the bowl and let the dough rest for 1 hour.

2. Add the starter and remaining water and work the dough until it is smooth and elastic. Add the salt and work the dough until it has been incorporated.

3. Transfer the dough to a large bowl, cover it with plastic wrap, and let it rest for 30 minutes.

4. Stretch and fold the dough over itself a few times. Cover the dough, let it rest for 30 minutes, and stretch and fold the dough over itself a few times. Rest for another 30 minutes, repeat the stretches and folds, and place the dough back in the bowl. Cover the bowl and store the dough in the refrigerator overnight.

5. Remove the dough from the refrigerator and let it rest at room temperature for 30 minutes.

6. Place the dough on a flour-dusted work surface, divide it into 2 pieces, and shape them into rounds. Cover the rounds with a kitchen towel and let them rest for 2½ hours.

7. Preheat the oven to 480°F and place a baking stone in the oven as it warms.

8. Using a lame or sharp knife, make 2 cuts in the shape of a cross on the top of each round.

9. Place a small cast-iron skillet of water on the bottom of the oven. Use a peel to slide the loaves onto the baking stone and bake for 10 minutes.

10. Reduce the oven's temperature to 390°F and bake for 30 minutes.

11. Reduce the oven's temperature to 350°F, remove the saucepan, and leave the oven door open a crack. Bake for another 15 minutes.

12. Remove the bread from the oven and let it cool for 2 hours before serving.

INGREDIENTS:

28.2 OZ. FINELY GROUND DURUM WHEAT FLOUR (SEMOLA RIMACINATA), PLUS MORE AS NEEDED

7.7 OZ. BREAD FLOUR

24.3 OZ. WATER

6.3 OZ. STIFF SOURDOUGH STARTER (SEE PAGE 823), FED TWICE WITH FINELY GROUND DURUM WHEAT FLOUR

1 (HEAPING) TABLESPOON FINE SEA SALT

TARALLI

YIELD: 80 TARALLI / **ACTIVE TIME:** 2 HOURS / **TOTAL TIME:** 6 HOURS

There are nearly infinite ways to make taralli: big, small, with herbs, with spices, with cheese, etc. The typical recipe being used in Apulia, though, is simple and similar to the one below.

1. Place all of the ingredients in a mixing bowl and work the mixture until it just comes together as a dough.

2. Place the dough on a flour-dusted work surface and knead it quickly until the dough is smooth. Form the dough into a ball, cover it with plastic wrap, and let it rest at room temperature for 30 minutes.

3. Quickly knead the dough to make sure there are no lumps.

4. Tear small pieces that are approximately the size of a cherry from the dough. Roll each piece into a log and shape the logs into 5-inch circles. Pinch the ends of the circles to join them together.

5. Bring a large saucepan of lightly salted water to a boil. Add 10 taralli at a time to the boiling water and boil until they rise to the surface. Remove the taralli with a strainer, place them on a kitchen towel, and let them dry for 3 to 4 hours.

6. Preheat the oven to 390°F and line two baking sheets with parchment paper.

7. Place the taralli on the baking sheets, place them in the oven, and bake until they are golden brown, about 1 hour.

8. Remove the taralli from the oven and let them cool for 1 hour before serving.

INGREDIENTS:

- 2.2 LBS. ALL-PURPOSE FLOUR, PLUS MORE AS NEEDED
- 12.3 OZ. DRY WHITE WINE
- 10.6 OZ. EXTRA-VIRGIN OLIVE OIL
- ⅔ OZ. FINE SEA SALT, PLUS MORE TO TASTE

TARALLI AND FRISELLE:
BETWEEN HISTORY AND LEGEND

The quintessential Apulian baked good, taralli, are said to date back to the fifteenth century, when Southern Italy was facing a harsh famine. Apulians swear that the credit for having kneaded the very first taralli goes to a mother with limited resources who needed to feed her children. Using the only food items she had at hand, flour, olive oil, salt, and white wine, she made a dough, and the rest is . . . history? . . . legend? Whatever the true origin is, we know a few things: for innumerable generations Apulian housewives carried large pans full of taralli dough to the town's communal ovens, that taralli have become an accompaniment to every Apulian meal, and that taralli stand as the very symbol of Southern conviviality.

Friselle are another bread that is omnipresent on Apulian tables. From a baked loaf cut in the middle and rebaked is derived a rusk, typically topped with the emblems of the Italian South: tomatoes, olive oil, and oregano. It is believed that something close to friselle was being enjoyed on Phoenician ships some 3,000 years ago, as this type of bread is very portable and has a long shelf life. As you might imagine for a bread with such a long history, friselle also have their own legend, which says that they were brought to Apulia by none other than Aeneas, the mythical son of Anchises and Aphrodite, during his escape from the city of Troy.

FRISELLE

YIELD: 6 FRISELLE / **ACTIVE TIME:** 1 HOUR / **TOTAL TIME:** 5 HOURS

These crunchy bread "wheels" from Apulia are relatively easy to make at home and can last a few weeks if stored properly. Eaten as the base for an open-faced sandwich, they are best if slightly wet with water before proceeding to add the typical topping of olive oil, tomatoes, oregano, and anchovies.

1. Place the yeast and water in the work bowl of a stand mixer fitted with the dough hook, gently stir, and let the mixture proof until it is foamy, about 10 minutes.

2. Add the remaining ingredients and work the mixture until it comes together as a smooth, elastic dough. Form the dough into a ball, cover the work bowl with plastic wrap, and let it rest for 2 hours.

3. Line two baking sheets with parchment paper. Place the dough on a flour-dusted work surface, divide it into 6 pieces, and shape them into 14-inch-long logs.

4. Shape the logs into circles and pinch the ends of the circles to join them together. Place them on the baking sheets, cover them with kitchen towels, and let them rest for 1 hour.

5. Preheat the oven to 430°F.

6. Place the friselle in the oven and bake them for 20 minutes.

7. Remove the friselle from the oven and let them cool.

8. Cut them in half at their equators and place them back on the baking sheets, cut side up.

9. Reduce the oven's temperature to 340°F. Place the friselle back in the oven and bake them until they are golden brown, about 1 hour.

10. Remove the friselle from the oven and let them cool before serving.

INGREDIENTS:

- 3½ TEASPOONS ACTIVE DRY YEAST
- 9 OZ. WARM WATER (105°F)
- 17.6 OZ. BREAD FLOUR
- 17.6 OZ. FINELY GROUND DURUM WHEAT FLOUR (SEMOLA RIMACINATA), PLUS MORE AS NEEDED
- 2 TEASPOONS FINE SEA SALT

CUDDURA C'A CIUCIULENA

YIELD: 1 LOAF / **ACTIVE TIME:** 1 HOUR / **TOTAL TIME:** 6 HOURS

This traditional Calabrian bread is characteristic of the province of Reggio, where it is enjoyed during holidays and seen as an omen of good fortune and prosperity.

1. Line a baking sheet with parchment paper. Place the yeast, sugar, and water in the work bowl of a stand mixer fitted with the dough hook, gently stir, and let the mixture proof until it is foamy, about 10 minutes.

2. Add the flour and olive oil and work the mixture until it comes together as a smooth and elastic dough, incorporating the salt toward the end.

3. Place the dough on a flour-dusted work surface and divide it into 2 pieces, keeping one piece half the size of the other. Roll the pieces into logs that are the same length.

4. Place the larger piece of dough on the baking sheet and form it into a circle. Form the smaller piece of dough into a circle and place it on top of the larger piece of dough. Cover the dough with a kitchen towel, place it in a naturally warm spot, and let it rise for 3 hours.

5. Preheat the oven to 350°F and set it to convection mode if it is available. Moisten the dough with a bit of water and sprinkle the sesame seeds over it. Using scissors, make incisions that resemble ears of wheat all over the top circle.

6. Place a small cast-iron skillet filled with water on the bottom of the oven. Place the bread in the oven and bake until it is golden brown, about 30 minutes.

7. Remove the bread from the oven and let it cool for 2 hours before serving.

INGREDIENTS:

1   **PACKET OF ACTIVE DRY YEAST**

1   **TEASPOON SUGAR**

10.6   **OZ. WARM WATER (105°F), PLUS MORE AS NEEDED**

21.1   **OZ. FINELY GROUND DURUM WHEAT FLOUR (SEMOLA RIMACINATA), PLUS MORE AS NEEDED**

3½   **OZ. EXTRA-VIRGIN OLIVE OIL**

2   **TEASPOONS FINE SEA SALT**

⅓   **CUP SESAME SEEDS**

MAFALDE

YIELD: 10 ROLLS / **ACTIVE TIME:** 1 HOUR / **TOTAL TIME:** 3 HOURS AND 30 MINUTES

Mafalde are the quintessential Sicilian bread. Made with semola and shaped to resemble either the rod of Asclepius (the symbol of medicine) or an S, they are often filled with the chickpea fritters known as Panelle (see page 82).

1. Place the yeast, honey, and water in the work bowl of a stand mixer fitted with the dough hook, gently stir, and let the mixture proof until it is foamy, about 10 minutes.

2. Add the flours and work the mixture until it just comes together as a dough.

3. Add the olive oil and salt and work the dough until it is smooth and elastic. Form the dough into a ball, place it in a clean bowl, and cover the bowl with plastic wrap. Let the dough rest for 15 minutes.

4. Line two baking sheets with parchment paper. Place the dough on a flour-dusted work surface and divide it into 10 pieces. Roll each piece into a 6-inch-long log. Brush the tops of the logs with water, dip the tops in sesame seeds until coated, and place the logs on the baking sheets. Cover with kitchen towels and let the mafalde rise for 1½ hours.

5. Preheat the oven to 410°F.

6. Place the mafalde in the oven and bake for 20 minutes. Reduce the oven's temperature to 350°F and bake until they are golden brown, about 10 minutes.

7. Remove the mafalde from the baking sheets and let them cool before serving.

INGREDIENTS:

1½   PACKETS OF ACTIVE DRY YEAST

1   TEASPOON HONEY

24.7   OZ. WARM WATER (105°F)

28.2   OZ. FINELY GROUND DURUM WHEAT FLOUR (SEMOLA RIMACINATA)

7   OZ. ALL-PURPOSE FLOUR, PLUS MORE AS NEEDED

2.8   OZ. EXTRA-VIRGIN OLIVE OIL

⅔   OZ. FINE SEA SALT

    SESAME SEEDS, FOR TOPPING

PANE CARASAU

YIELD: 20 CARASAU / **ACTIVE TIME:** 1 HOUR / **TOTAL TIME:** 3 HOURS

Pane carasau is one of the most famous Sardinian specialties and can be used in innumerable ways. A very ancient bread, it is also known as carta musica ("music paper") in Italy for the noise it makes when chewed, while the name carasau derives from the method of baking the bread twice to make it crispy, a practice known as carasatura.

1. Place the yeast, sugar, and water in the work bowl of a stand mixer fitted with the dough hook, gently stir, and let the mixture proof until it is foamy, about 10 minutes.

2. Add the flour and work the mixture until it just comes together as a dough.

3. Add the salt and work the dough until it is smooth and elastic. Form the dough into a ball, place it in a clean bowl, and cover the bowl with plastic wrap. Let the dough rest for 1 hour.

4. Preheat the oven to the maximum temperature and place a baking stone in it as it warms. Place the dough on a flour-dusted work surface, divide it into 10 pieces, and shape them into rounds. Cover the rounds with kitchen towels and let them rest for 30 minutes.

5. Flatten the rounds into a ¹⁄₁₀-inch-thick disks, cover them with kitchen towels, and let them rest for another 30 minutes.

6. Using a peel, slide 1 round at a time onto the baking stone and bake until it puffs up, 3 to 5 minutes.

7. Remove the bread from the oven and let it cool slightly.

8. When all of the carasau have been baked, cut them in half at their equators and gently press down to flatten them.

9. Slide a few carasau at a time onto the baking stone and bake until they are crispy, about 30 seconds. Remove them from the oven and let the carasau cool before serving.

INGREDIENTS:

- ¾   PACKET OF ACTIVE DRY YEAST
- 1   TEASPOON SUGAR
- 9.3   OZ. WARM WATER (105°F)
- 17.6   OZ. FINELY GROUND DURUM WHEAT FLOUR (SEMOLA RIMACINATA), PLUS MORE AS NEEDED
- 1   TEASPOON FINE SEA SALT

SARDINIA: THE ITALIAN BLUE ZONE

The concept of a Blue Zone was introduced in the early 2000s by the French scholar Michel Poulain to indicate areas in the world where people lived unusually long and healthy lives. Together with Gianni Pes, who had been studying the extraordinary longevity of Sardinian people for 20 years, Poulain mapped five "Blue Zones" in the world and journeyed to discover what factors were responsible for this increased longevity. Unsurprisingly, the answer was food.

Sardinian centenaries are mostly concentrated in the Ogliastra and Barbagia regions, which are home to some of the most renowned Sardinian specialties, like culurgiones (see page 59) and pane carasau (see page 388), both of which are wheat based. It is interesting to note that the traditional Sardinian diet is primarily based on wheat, although the wheat that is eaten by Sardinians is not the same that is available in North America—or even Northern Italy. As they are in much of Southern Italy, traditional Sardinian bread and pasta are in fact based on locally grown durum wheat, which is possibly healthier than other types of wheat, as it contains more dietary fiber and as such may be more digestible. Other staples of the Sardinian diet are legumes, garden vegetables, fruits, and pecorino cheese made from the milk of grass-fed sheep, which is known to be higher in omega-3 fatty acids than cow's milk.

In short, preparing Sardinian and Southern Italian recipes doesn't just make us happier, it may help us live a longer life. At least, this is what the Blue Zone research says!

PANE COCCOI

YIELD: 2 LOAVES / **ACTIVE TIME:** 1 HOUR / **TOTAL TIME:** 7 HOURS

This is an ancient Sardinian bread which was traditionally prepared for special occasions like weddings and Easter but is now an everyday item. Coccoi is generally made with a piece of dough saved from a previous bake called su framentu, which we replace with Stiff Sourdough Starter here.

1. Place the water and salt in the work bowl of a stand mixer fitted with the dough hook and stir to combine.

2. Add the flour and work the mixture until it just comes together as a dough. Add the starter and work the dough until it is smooth and elastic. Form the dough into a ball, place it in a clean bowl, and cover the bowl with plastic wrap. Let the dough rest for 1 hour.

3. Place the dough on a flour-dusted work surface, divide it into 2 pieces, and shape them into logs.

4. Flatten the logs, dust them with flour, and use your hands to create a depression in the center of each log. The depressions should run the entire length of the logs.

5. Fold each log over itself, like a long pocket, and make incisions along the edges.

6. You can shape the log into a crown or just curve it a bit, making the cuts open up slightly.

7. Place the loaves on parchment-lined baking sheets, cover them with kitchen towels, and let them rise until they have doubled in size, about 1½ hours.

8. Preheat the oven to 450°F. If the cuts became less visible during the rise, redo them.

9. Place the loaves in the oven and bake until they are golden brown, about 35 minutes.

10. Remove the loaves from the oven and let them cool for 2 hours before serving.

INGREDIENTS:

- 1 CUP WATER

- 2 TEASPOONS FINE SEA SALT

- 17.6 OZ. FINELY GROUND DURUM WHEAT FLOUR (SEMOLA RIMACINATA), PLUS MORE AS NEEDED

- 3½ OZ. STIFF SOURDOUGH STARTER (SEE PAGE 823), FED 8 TO 12 HOURS EARLIER WITH FINELY GROUND DURUM WHEAT FLOUR

THE HISTORY OF PIZZA

The first written record of the word "pizza" dates back to 997 AD in a document from Gaeta, an island near Naples. Later on, the term was found in records from other Italian cities. The word pizza, however, meant different things depending on the place, and this ambiguity is still present in contemporary Italian language. In some regions, for instance, pizza refers to a round, leavened cake. The type of pizza that became a global phenomenon, however, is a very specific incarnation of Italian pizza. What we commonly refer to when we speak of pizza outside of Italy is mostly Neapolitan pizza.

The history of Neapolitan pizza starts before the eighteenth century, in Naples. At that time, it was common to use flattened rounds of dough to test the oven's temperature before baking bread. The discarded baked dough became a plate for the poor, because it was quick to bake and, therefore, less valuable. It was sold in the streets, topped with a white sauce. The white sauce topping was later replaced with pancetta, lard, cheese, tomatoes, or fish, as described in 1843 by the writer Alexandre Dumas, visiting Naples. As Dumas recounted, pizza was the food of the lazzaroni, the people who inhabited the streets of Naples, doing small jobs or not working at all. Pizza was the food eaten in the streets during the winter, and the topping depended on what was most abundant at every moment. If fishing had been good, then plenty of fish-topped pizza was sold, if there was a lot of leftover lard from butchers' shops, then there was plenty of pizza with lard, and so on.

It is quite certain that by the early 1820s there were already pizzerias in Naples, since we know that Naples's king, Ferdinand I of Bourbon (who died in 1825), visited one of them. The story holds that Ferdinand, always very close to his people and to the lazzaroni in particular, wanted to taste some freshly baked pizza, and so he violated court etiquette and visited a pizzeria in a poor district of Naples—and we are sure he did not regret it.

In a few decades, pizza became popular also among the middle and privileged classes, and after Piedmont's kingdom took over Italy, a special pizza was dedicated to the new visiting queen, Margherita di Savoia. That version of pizza had a simple topping of tomato sauce, mozzarella cheese, and basil, to honor the three colors of the national flag set down by the Savoia. From there pizza spread to the whole of Italy, and it traveled with the early Italian migratory wave to North America, where it soon became an extremely popular food. From there, Neapolitan pizza spread to every corner of the world.

FORMING A PIZZA ROUND

There are several ways to create a tight "skin" around a ball of dough, so that it will better retain gases from fermentation even when pressed to form a pizza disk.

One way is to pull all of the sides of a piece of dough toward the bottom of the dough, pinching them together.

Alternatively, the piece of dough can be slightly flattened and folded in on itself from different angles a few times until it looks like a ball.

Either way, the final step is to roll the resulting ball over an unfloured counter, cupping your hand over the ball and moving it in a circular motion, counterclockwise.

NEAPOLITAN PIZZA DOUGH

YIELD: 4 BALLS OF DOUGH / **ACTIVE TIME:** 30 MINUTES / **TOTAL TIME:** 8 TO 12 HOURS

The dough that eventually took over the culinary world.

1. If using active dry yeast, warm 3½ tablespoons of the water until it is about 105°F. Add the yeast and water to a bowl and gently stir. Let the mixture sit until it is foamy, 5 to 10 minutes.

2. In a large bowl, combine the bread flour, yeast, and water. Work the mixture until it just comes together as a dough. Transfer it to a flour-dusted work surface and knead the dough until it is compact, smooth, and elastic.

3. Add the salt and knead until the dough is developed and elastic, meaning it pulls back energetically when pulled. Transfer the dough to an airtight container, cover it, and let it rest for 2 to 3 hours at room temperature. For a classic Neapolitan dough, room temperature should be 77°F. If your kitchen is colder, let the dough rest longer before shaping it into rounds.

4. Dust a baking dish with high edges with semolina. Divide the dough into 4 pieces and shape them into very tight rounds, as it is important to create tension in the outer layer of dough. Place the rounds in the baking dish, leaving enough space between rounds that they won't touch when fully risen. Cover with a kitchen towel and let them rest for 6 to 8 hours, depending on the temperature in the room, before using them to make pizza.

INGREDIENTS:

15   OZ. WATER

⅙   TEASPOON PLUS 1 PINCH
      ACTIVE DRY YEAST OR ⅙
      TEASPOON INSTANT YEAST

25   OZ. BREAD FLOUR, PLUS
      MORE AS NEEDED

1   TABLESPOON TABLE SALT

      SEMOLINA FLOUR, AS
      NEEDED

MARGHERITA

YIELD: 1 PIZZA / ACTIVE TIME: 15 MINUTES / TOTAL TIME: 45 MINUTES

For most, both in Italy and abroad, this is the true original Neapolitan pizza: gooey mozzarella and a tomato sauce base.

1. Preheat the oven to the maximum temperature and place a baking stone or steel on the bottom of the oven as it warms. Dust a work surface with semolina flour, place the dough on the surface, and gently stretch it into a disk. Cover the dough with the sauce and top with the mozzarella and basil leaves.

2. Season the pizza with salt and drizzle olive oil over the top.

3. Dust a peel or flat baking sheet with semolina flour and use it to transfer the pizza to the heated baking implement in the oven. Bake for 8 to 10 minutes, until the crust is golden brown and starting to char. Remove and let it cool slightly before slicing and serving.

PIZZA SAUCE

1. Place the tomatoes and their juices in a bowl, add the olive oil, and stir until it has been thoroughly incorporated.

2. Season the sauce with salt and oregano and stir to incorporate. If using within 2 hours, leave the sauce at room temperature. If storing in the refrigerator, where the sauce will keep for up to 3 days, return to room temperature before using.

INGREDIENTS:

	SEMOLINA FLOUR, AS NEEDED
1	BALL OF PIZZA DOUGH
⅓	CUP PIZZA SAUCE (SEE RECIPE)
4	OZ. FRESH MOZZARELLA CHEESE, DRAINED AND CUT INTO SHORT STRIPS
	FRESH BASIL LEAVES, TO TASTE
	SALT, TO TASTE
	EXTRA-VIRGIN OLIVE OIL, TO TASTE

PIZZA SAUCE

1	LB. PEELED, WHOLE SAN MARZANO TOMATOES, WITH THEIR LIQUID, CRUSHED
1½	TABLESPOONS EXTRA-VIRGIN OLIVE OIL
	SALT, TO TASTE
	DRIED OREGANO, TO TASTE

ROMANA

YIELD: 1 PIZZA / **ACTIVE TIME:** 15 MINUTES / **TOTAL TIME:** 45 MINUTES

There are two different versions of this pizza: with or without mozzarella. It also has two names: it is Romana to the Neapolitans, who created the topping, and Napoli for everyone else. What never changes in this pizza is the presence of tomato sauce, anchovies, capers, and oregano.

1. Preheat the oven to the maximum temperature and place a baking stone or steel on the bottom of the oven as it warms. Dust a work surface with semolina flour, place the dough on the surface, and gently stretch it into a disk. Cover the dough with the sauce and top with the mozzarella, anchovies, and capers.

2. Season the pizza with salt and oregano and drizzle olive oil over the top.

3. Dust a peel or flat baking sheet with semolina flour and use it to transfer the pizza to the heated baking implement in the oven. Bake for about 8 to 10 minutes, until the crust is golden brown and starting to char. Remove and let it cool slightly before slicing and serving.

INGREDIENTS:

SEMOLINA FLOUR, AS NEEDED

1 BALL OF PIZZA DOUGH

⅓ CUP PIZZA SAUCE (SEE PAGE 398)

2½ OZ. FRESH MOZZARELLA CHEESE, DRAINED AND CUT INTO SHORT STRIPS

4–5 ANCHOVIES IN OLIVE OIL, DRAINED AND CHOPPED

1 TABLESPOON CAPERS, DRAINED AND RINSED

SALT, TO TASTE

DRIED OREGANO, TO TASTE

EXTRA-VIRGIN OLIVE OIL, TO TASTE

CAPRICCIOSA

YIELD: 1 PIZZA / **ACTIVE TIME:** 15 MINUTES / **TOTAL TIME:** 30 MINUTES

Capricciosa means "capricious" in Italian, and in Neapolitan pizza jargon this means a topping that, as it cannot make a simple decision, simply overdoes it.

1. Place a baking stone or steel on the middle rack of the oven and preheat the oven to the maximum temperature. Dust a work surface with semolina flour, place the dough on it, and gently stretch it into a disk.

2. Cover the dough with the sauce and top with the artichokes and mushrooms. Season the pizza with salt and drizzle olive oil over the top.

3. Using a peel or flat baking sheet, transfer the pizza to the heated baking implement in the oven. Bake for about 5 minutes, until the crust starts to brown. Remove the pizza, distribute the mozzarella, prosciutto, and olives over the top, and return the pizza to the oven. Bake for 8 to 10 minutes, until the crust is golden brown and starting to char. Remove the pizza from the oven and let it cool slightly before topping with basil, slicing, and serving.

INGREDIENTS:

SEMOLINA FLOUR, AS NEEDED

1 BALL OF PIZZA DOUGH

⅓ CUP PIZZA SAUCE (SEE PAGE 398)

2 ARTICHOKE HEARTS IN OLIVE OIL, CUT INTO WEDGES

¼ CUP MUSHROOMS, SLICED

SALT, TO TASTE

EXTRA-VIRGIN OLIVE OIL, TO TASTE

3 OZ. FRESH MOZZARELLA CHEESE, DRAINED AND CUT INTO SHORT STRIPS

2 SLICES OF PROSCIUTTO, TORN

SMALL HANDFUL OF PITTED BLACK OLIVES

FRESH BASIL LEAVES, FOR TOPPING

BOSCAIOLA

YIELD: 1 PIZZA / **ACTIVE TIME:** 25 MINUTES / **TOTAL TIME:** 40 MINUTES

Boscaiola means "from the woods" in Italian, referring to mushrooms and game. Here, the game component is just humble sausage, but the pizza retains its earthy and substantial promise.

1. Place a baking stone or steel on the middle rack of the oven and preheat the oven to the maximum temperature. Coat the bottom of a skillet with olive oil and warm over medium-high heat. When the oil starts to shimmer, add the sausage and cook, stirring occasionally, until it starts to brown, about 6 minutes. Remove from heat and set aside.

2. Dust a work surface with semolina flour, place the dough on it, and gently stretch it into a disk.

3. Cover the dough with the sauce and top with the mushrooms and sausage. Season the pizza with salt and drizzle olive oil over the top.

4. Using a peel or a flat baking sheet, transfer the pizza to the heated baking implement in the oven. Bake for about 5 minutes, until the crust starts to brown. Remove the pizza, distribute the mozzarella over the top, and return the pizza to the oven. Bake for 8 to 10 minutes, until the crust is golden brown and starting to char. Remove and let it cool slightly before slicing and serving.

INGREDIENTS:

	EXTRA-VIRGIN OLIVE OIL, TO TASTE
½	LINK OF ITALIAN SAUSAGE, CHOPPED
	SEMOLINA FLOUR, AS NEEDED
1	BALL OF PIZZA DOUGH
⅓	CUP PIZZA SAUCE (SEE PAGE 398)
⅓	CUP MUSHROOMS, SLICED
	SALT, TO TASTE
3	OZ. FRESH MOZZARELLA CHEESE, DRAINED AND CUT INTO SHORT STRIPS

CARRETTIERA

YIELD: 1 PIZZA / **ACTIVE TIME:** 25 MINUTES / **TOTAL TIME:** 1 HOUR

The name refers to a sandwich filling popular with the Neapolitan carrettieri, who spent the day pushing around goods in a wooden trolley. Substantial and extremely tasty, this is a must, assuming one can get hold of broccoli rabe.

1. Coat the bottom of a skillet with olive oil and warm it over medium-high heat. When the oil starts to shimmer, add the garlic and broccoli rabe and cook, stirring frequently, until the broccoli rabe has softened, about 8 minutes. Season with salt and pepper, add the sausage, and cook until the sausage is browned, about 8 minutes. Remove from heat and let it cool.

2. Dust a work surface with semolina flour, place the dough on the surface, and gently stretch it into a disk. Spread the sautéed broccoli rabe and sausage over the pizza and top with the mozzarella. Drizzle olive oil over the pizza.

3. Dust a peel or flat baking sheet with semolina flour and use it to transfer the pizza to the heated baking implement in the oven. Bake for 8 to 10 minutes, until the crust is golden brown and starting to char. Remove and let it cool slightly before slicing and serving.

INGREDIENTS:

	EXTRA-VIRGIN OLIVE OIL, AS NEEDED
½	GARLIC CLOVE, MINCED
5	OZ. BROCCOLI RABE, TRIMMED
	SALT AND PEPPER, TO TASTE
1	LINK OF ITALIAN SAUSAGE, CHOPPED
	SEMOLINA FLOUR, AS NEEDED
1	BALL OF PIZZA DOUGH
3	OZ. FRESH MOZZARELLA CHEESE, DRAINED AND CUT INTO SHORT STRIPS

DIAVOLA

YIELD: 1 PIZZA / ACTIVE TIME: 15 MINUTES / TOTAL TIME: 50 MINUTES

A "devilish" pie that becomes more and more tempting as the spice level rises.

1. Preheat the oven to the maximum temperature and place a baking stone or steel on the bottom of the oven as it warms. Combine the olive oil and red pepper flakes in a small bowl and set the mixture aside.

2. Dust a work surface with semolina flour, place the dough on the surface, and gently stretch it into a disk. Cover the dough with the sauce and top with the cheese and salami. Drizzle the spicy olive oil over the top and season with salt and oregano.

3. Dust a peel or flat baking sheet with semolina flour and use it to transfer the pizza to the heated baking implement in the oven. Bake for 8 to 10 minutes, until the crust is golden brown and starting to char. Remove and let it cool slightly before slicing and serving.

INGREDIENTS:

2	TABLESPOONS EXTRA-VIRGIN OLIVE OIL, PLUS MORE TO TASTE
	RED PEPPER FLAKES, TO TASTE
	SEMOLINA FLOUR, AS NEEDED
1	BALL OF PIZZA DOUGH
⅓	CUP PIZZA SAUCE (SEE PAGE 398)
2½	OZ. CACIOCAVALLO OR PROVOLA CHEESE, CUBED
5	SLICES OF SPICY SALAMI
	SALT, TO TASTE
	DRIED OREGANO, TO TASTE

QUATTRO STAGIONI

YIELD: 1 PIZZA / **ACTIVE TIME:** 15 MINUTES / **TOTAL TIME:** 30 MINUTES

Meaning "four seasons" in Italian, the name here refers to the topping being divided into four sections, each one featuring a different ingredient. The toppings here are the same used in pizza capricciosa, the difference being that here they are kept separate.

1. Place a baking stone or steel on the middle rack of the oven and preheat the oven to the maximum temperature. Dust a work surface with semolina flour, place the dough on it, and gently stretch it into a disk.

2. Cover the dough with the sauce and mozzarella. Place each of the artichokes, prosciutto, mushrooms, and olives on their own section of the pizza. Season the pizza with salt and drizzle olive oil over the top.

3. Using a peel or flat baking sheet, transfer the pizza to the heated baking implement in the oven. Bake for 8 to 10 minutes, until the crust is golden brown and starting to char. Remove the pizza from the oven and let it cool slightly before slicing and serving.

NOTE: If your oven is not very hot, it is recommended that you wait to add the olives and prosciutto a few minutes before the pizza is fully baked, so as not to dry out the prosciutto or burn the olives.

INGREDIENTS:

	SEMOLINA FLOUR, AS NEEDED
1	BALL OF PIZZA DOUGH
⅓	CUP PIZZA SAUCE (SEE PAGE 398)
3	OZ. FRESH MOZZARELLA CHEESE, DRAINED AND CUT INTO SHORT STRIPS
2	ARTICHOKE HEARTS IN OLIVE OIL, CUT INTO WEDGES
2	SLICES OF PROSCIUTTO, TORN
¼	CUP MUSHROOMS, SLICED
	HANDFUL OF PITTED BLACK OLIVES
	SALT, TO TASTE
	EXTRA-VIRGIN OLIVE OIL, TO TASTE

QUATTRO FORMAGGI

YIELD: 1 PIZZA / **ACTIVE TIME:** 15 MINUTES / **TOTAL TIME:** 45 MINUTES

As you might expect, this pizza is exceptionally gooey, and nothing short of miraculous for cheese lovers.

1. Preheat the oven to the maximum temperature and place a baking stone or steel in the oven as it warms. Dust a work surface with semolina flour, place the dough on the surface, and gently stretch it into a disk. Distribute the cheeses over the dough.

2. Season the pizza with salt and pepper and drizzle olive oil over the top.

3. Dust a peel or a flat baking sheet with semolina flour and use it to transfer the pizza to the heated baking implement in the oven. Bake for 8 to 10 minutes, until the crust is golden brown and starting to char. Remove and let it cool slightly before slicing and serving.

INGREDIENTS:

SEMOLINA FLOUR, AS NEEDED

1   BALL OF PIZZA DOUGH

2   OZ. FRESH MOZZARELLA CHEESE, DRAINED AND CUT INTO SHORT STRIPS

2   OZ. FONTINA OR PROVOLONE CHEESE, GRATED

2   OZ. GORGONZOLA CHEESE, CRUMBLED

2   OZ. PECORINO OR PARMESAN CHEESE, GRATED

SALT AND PEPPER, TO TASTE

EXTRA-VIRGIN OLIVE OIL, TO TASTE

PESCATORA

YIELD: 1 PIZZA / **ACTIVE TIME:** 25 MINUTES / **TOTAL TIME:** 1 HOUR

This variation on the margherita pizza was inspired by the classic caprese salad. A perfect pie for a hot summer night.

1. Preheat the oven to the maximum temperature and place a baking stone or steel on the bottom of the oven as it warms. Coat the bottom of a skillet with olive oil and warm it over medium-high heat. When the oil starts to shimmer, add all of the seafood and the garlic. Season with salt and red pepper flakes and cook until most of the mussels have opened and the rest of the seafood is just cooked through, about 4 minutes. Remove from heat, discard any mussels that did not open, and remove the meat from those that have opened.

2. Dust a work surface with semolina flour, place the dough on the surface, and gently stretch it into a round. Cover the dough with the sauce and season with oregano and pepper.

3. Dust a peel or a flat baking sheet with semolina flour and use it to transfer the pizza to the heated baking implement in the oven. Bake for about 5 minutes, until the crust starts to brown. Remove the pizza, distribute the seafood over it, drizzle olive oil on top, and return the pizza to the oven. Bake for about 5 minutes, until the crust is golden brown and starting to char. Remove and let it cool slightly before garnishing with the parsley, slicing, and serving.

INGREDIENTS:

- EXTRA-VIRGIN OLIVE OIL, AS NEEDED
- 5 LARGE SHRIMP, SHELLED AND DEVEINED
- HANDFUL OF SQUID RINGS
- 6 MUSSELS, DEBEARDED AND RINSED WELL
- HANDFUL OF BABY OCTOPUS
- ½ GARLIC CLOVE, MINCED
- SALT AND PEPPER, TO TASTE
- RED PEPPER FLAKES, TO TASTE
- SEMOLINA FLOUR, AS NEEDED
- 1 BALL OF PIZZA DOUGH
- ½ CUP PIZZA SAUCE (SEE PAGE 398)
- DRIED OREGANO, TO TASTE
- FRESH PARSLEY, FOR GARNISH

Pescatora, see page 411

MARI E MONTI

YIELD: 1 PIZZA / **ACTIVE TIME:** 35 MINUTES / **TOTAL TIME:** 55 MINUTES

Translated as "sea and mountains," this pizza does indeed combine frutti di mare with the mushrooms that grow in the mountain forests.

1. Place a baking stone or steel on the middle rack of the oven and preheat the oven to the maximum temperature. Place the mushrooms in a bowl, season with salt and pepper, and generously drizzle olive oil over them. Stir to combine and let the mixture sit for 10 minutes. Drain and set aside.

2. Coat the bottom of a skillet with olive oil and warm over medium-high heat. Add the shrimp, mussels, and garlic, season with salt and red pepper flakes, and cook, stirring occasionally, until the shrimp are cooked through and the majority of the mussels have opened, about 5 minutes. Remove the pan from heat, discard any mussels that did not open, and remove the meat from those that did open.

3. Dust a work surface with semolina flour, place the dough on it, and gently stretch it into a disk. Cover the dough with the mozzarella and mushrooms, season with salt, and drizzle olive oil over the pizza.

4. Using a peel or a flat baking sheet, transfer the pizza to the heated baking implement in the oven. Bake for 5 to 8 minutes, until the crust starts to brown. Remove the pizza, distribute the seafood over the top, and return the pizza to the oven. Bake for about 5 minutes, until the crust is golden brown and starting to char. Remove the pizza from the oven and let it cool slightly before garnishing with the parsley, slicing, and serving.

INGREDIENTS:

⅓	CUP MUSHROOMS, CHOPPED
	SALT AND PEPPER, TO TASTE
	EXTRA-VIRGIN OLIVE OIL, AS NEEDED
5	LARGE SHRIMP, SHELLS REMOVED, DEVEINED
	SMALL HANDFUL OF MUSSELS, RINSED WELL AND DEBEARDED
½	GARLIC CLOVE, MINCED
	RED PEPPER FLAKES, TO TASTE
	SEMOLINA FLOUR, AS NEEDED
1	BALL OF PIZZA DOUGH
3	OZ. FRESH MOZZARELLA CHEESE, DRAINED AND CUT INTO SHORT STRIPS
	FRESH PARSLEY, CHOPPED, FOR GARNISH

CAPRESE

YIELD: 1 PIZZA / **ACTIVE TIME:** 15 MINUTES / **TOTAL TIME:** 45 MINUTES

This variation on the Margherita pizza was inspired by the classic caprese salad. A perfect pie for a hot summer night.

1. Preheat the oven to the maximum temperature and place a baking stone or steel on the bottom of the oven as it warms. Dust a work surface with semolina flour, place the dough on the surface, and gently stretch it into a disk. Cover the dough with the sauce and top with the mozzarella and tomato.

2. Season the pizza with salt, pepper, and oregano and drizzle olive oil over the top.

3. Dust a peel or a flat baking sheet with semolina flour and use it to transfer the pizza to the heated baking implement in the oven. Bake for 8 to 10 minutes, until the crust is golden brown and starting to char. Remove and let it cool slightly before garnishing with the basil, slicing, and serving.

INGREDIENTS:

SEMOLINA FLOUR, AS NEEDED

1   BALL OF PIZZA DOUGH

⅓   CUP PIZZA SAUCE (SEE PAGE 398)

4½ OZ. FRESH MOZZARELLA CHEESE, DRAINED AND SLICED

1   TOMATO, SLICED

SALT AND PEPPER, TO TASTE

DRIED OREGANO, TO TASTE

EXTRA-VIRGIN OLIVE OIL, TO TASTE

FRESH BASIL LEAVES, FOR GARNISH

ORTOLANA

YIELD: 1 PIZZA / **ACTIVE TIME:** 30 MINUTES / **TOTAL TIME:** 1 HOUR AND 15 MINUTES

As you may expect of a pizza that trumpets being "from the garden," the topping features no cheese—just tomato sauce and a selection of vegetables.

1. Preheat the oven to the maximum temperature and place a baking stone or steel on the bottom of the oven as it warms. Place the mushrooms in a bowl, season with salt and pepper, and generously drizzle olive oil over them. Stir to combine and let the mixture sit for 10 minutes. Drain and set aside.

2. Place the bell pepper and eggplant on an aluminum foil–lined baking sheet, season with salt and pepper, drizzle olive oil over the vegetables, and place in the oven. Roast until they are tender and browned, about 25 minutes. Remove from the oven and let it cool.

3. Dust a work surface with semolina flour, place the dough on the surface, and gently stretch it into a disk. Cover the dough with the sauce and top with the mushrooms, bell pepper, eggplant, onion, and basil leaves.

4. Season the pizza with salt and drizzle olive oil over the top.

5. Dust a peel or a flat baking sheet with semolina and use it to transfer the pizza to the heated baking implement in the oven. Bake for 8 to 10 minutes, until the crust is golden brown and starting to char. Remove and let it cool slightly before slicing and serving.

INGREDIENTS:

¼ CUP MUSHROOMS, CHOPPED

SALT AND PEPPER, TO TASTE

EXTRA-VIRGIN OLIVE OIL, TO TASTE

½ BELL PEPPER, SLICED

½ SMALL EGGPLANT, SLICED

SEMOLINA FLOUR, AS NEEDED

1 BALL OF PIZZA DOUGH

⅓ CUP PIZZA SAUCE (SEE PAGE 398)

¼ ONION, SLICED

FRESH BASIL LEAVES, TO TASTE

DRIED OREGANO, TO TASTE

MARINARA

YIELD: 1 PIZZA / **ACTIVE TIME:** 15 MINUTES / **TOTAL TIME:** 30 MINUTES

According to the European Union, there are only two authentic Neapolitan pizzas that deserve the TSG (Traditional Speciality Guaranteed) appellation: this and pizza margherita. Pizza marinara is possibly the oldest variety of Neapolitan pizza still popular today, and it is surprising in its simplicity. The key to making a good version of this pizza at home is to use top-notch ingredients, as that is the only way to do justice to this simple topping.

1. Place a baking stone or steel on the middle rack of the oven and preheat the oven to the maximum temperature. Dust a work surface with semolina flour, place the dough on the surface, and gently stretch it into a round.

2. Cover the dough with the sauce and top with the garlic. Season the pizza with salt and dried oregano and drizzle olive oil over the top.

3. Using a peel or a flat baking sheet, transfer the pizza to the heated baking implement in the oven. Bake for 5 to 12 minutes, depending on your oven, until the crust is golden brown and starting to char. Remove and let cool slightly before slicing and serving.

INGREDIENTS:

SEMOLINA FLOUR, AS NEEDED

1 BALL OF PIZZA DOUGH

5.3 OZ. PIZZA SAUCE (SEE PAGE 398)

1 GARLIC CLOVE, SLICED THIN

SALT, TO TASTE

DRIED OREGANO, TO TASTE

EXTRA-VIRGIN OLIVE OIL, TO TASTE

FOCACCIA VELOCE

YIELD: DOUGH FOR 1 LARGE FOCACCIA / **ACTIVE TIME:** 15 MINUTES / **TOTAL TIME:** 1 HOUR AND 30 MINUTES

The simplest and quickest focaccia dough in my repertoire, providing a wonderfully soft dough in just a couple of hours.

1. Combine the yeast and water in a bowl, gently stir, and let the mixture sit for a few minutes, until it starts to foam.

2. In a large bowl, combine the flours, sugar, and yeast mixture and work the mixture until it just holds together. Transfer it to a flour-dusted work surface and knead the dough until it is compact, smooth, and elastic.

3. Add the olive oil and salt and knead until the dough is developed, elastic, and extensible, about 5 minutes. Form the dough into a ball and place it in an airtight container that has been greased with olive oil. Let it rest in a naturally warm spot (in the oven with the light on is a good option) until it has doubled in size, about 1 hour.

4. After 1 hour, the dough can be spread and flavored as desired. It will need another 30 minutes to 1 hour for the second rise before baking.

INGREDIENTS:

- 3½ TEASPOONS ACTIVE DRY YEAST
- 2 CUPS WARM WATER (105°F)
- 17.6 OZ. BREAD FLOUR
- 7 OZ. ALL-PURPOSE FLOUR, PLUS MORE AS NEEDED
- 2 TEASPOONS SUGAR
- 5 TABLESPOONS EXTRA-VIRGIN OLIVE OIL, PLUS MORE AS NEEDED
- 2½ TEASPOONS FINE SEA SALT

FOCACCIA CLASSICA

YIELD: DOUGH FOR 1 LARGE FOCACCIA / **ACTIVE TIME:** 30 MINUTES / **TOTAL TIME:** 5 HOURS

This dough will give you a soft focaccia with a nice, complex texture. It takes several hours to make, but keep in mind that most of it is rising time, during which you can attend to other activities (my favorite is napping). This dough is extremely versatile and can be used in most of the focaccia recipes in this book.

1. Combine the yeast and water in a bowl, gently stir, and let the mixture sit for a few minutes, until it starts to foam.

2. In a large bowl, combine the flours and yeast mixture. Work the mixture until it just holds together. Transfer it to a flour-dusted work surface and knead the dough until it is compact, smooth, and elastic.

3. Add the olive oil and salt and knead until the dough is developed, elastic, and extensible, about 5 minutes. Form the dough into a ball, cover it with a damp kitchen towel or greased plastic wrap, and let it rest at room temperature until it has doubled in size, 3 to 4 hours. The time for this first fermentation can be reduced if you place the dough in a naturally warm spot. In the oven with the light on is a good option if you're going to go this route.

4. Stretch and flavor the dough as desired. It will need another 1½ to 2 hours for the second rise before baking. The extra rising time can only benefit the dough, as the relatively low amount of yeast means the risk of overproofing is small.

INGREDIENTS:

¾ TEASPOON ACTIVE DRY YEAST

17 OZ. WARM WATER (105°F)

21 OZ. BREAD FLOUR

3 OZ. ALL-PURPOSE FLOUR, PLUS MORE AS NEEDED

2 TABLESPOONS EXTRA-VIRGIN OLIVE OIL, PLUS MORE AS NEEDED

2 TEASPOONS FINE SEA SALT

FOCACCIA ASCIUTTA

YIELD: DOUGH FOR 1 LARGE FOCACCIA / **ACTIVE TIME:** 30 MINUTES / **TOTAL TIME:** 24 HOURS

This dough is rather dry for a focaccia, making it perfect for recipes that need a rather thin and substantial focaccia base. You can use this dough with several of the traditional Italian focaccia recipes, including many of the focaccia from Northern and Central Italy, which are often less hydrated than those from the South.

1. Combine the yeast and water in a bowl, gently stir, and let the mixture sit for a few minutes, until it starts to foam.

2. In a large bowl, combine the flours and yeast mixture. Work the mixture until it just holds together. Transfer it to a flour-dusted work surface and knead the dough until it is compact, smooth, and elastic.

3. Add the salt and knead until the dough is developed, elastic, and extensible, about 5 minutes. Add the olive oil and knead the dough until the oil has been incorporated. Form the dough into a ball, place it in an airtight container that is at least three times bigger, cover, and refrigerate for 24 hours.

4. Remove the dough from the refrigerator and let it warm to room temperature before making focaccia.

INGREDIENTS:

1	(HEAPING) TEASPOON ACTIVE DRY YEAST
13	OZ. WARM WATER (105°F)
10.6	OZ. BREAD FLOUR
10.6	OZ. ALL-PURPOSE FLOUR, PLUS MORE AS NEEDED
2⅔	TEASPOONS FINE SEA SALT
2	TABLESPOONS EXTRA-VIRGIN OLIVE OIL

FOCACCIA MORBIDA

YIELD: DOUGH FOR 1 LARGE FOCACCIA / **ACTIVE TIME:** 30 MINUTES / **TOTAL TIME:** 24 HOURS

This dough is rather wet, but not "liquid," like the more hydrated focaccia doughs. It is perfect for a Focaccia Genovese (see page 786) and for focaccia that need to be thick without being overly pillowy.

1. Combine the yeast and water in a bowl, gently stir, and let the mixture sit for a few minutes, until it starts to foam.

2. In a large bowl, combine the flours and yeast mixture. Work the mixture until it just holds together. Transfer it to a flour-dusted work surface and knead the dough until it is compact, smooth, and elastic.

3. Add the salt and knead until the dough is developed, elastic, and extensible, about 5 minutes. Add the olive oil and knead the dough until the oil has been incorporated. Form the dough into a ball, place it in an airtight container that is at least three times bigger, cover, and refrigerate for 24 hours.

4. Remove the dough from the refrigerator and let it warm to room temperature before making focaccia.

INGREDIENTS:

1⅔ TEASPOONS ACTIVE DRY YEAST

17.3 OZ. WARM WATER (105°F)

1.1 LBS. BREAD FLOUR OR "00" FLOUR

7 OZ. ALL-PURPOSE FLOUR, PLUS MORE AS NEEDED

1 TABLESPOON FINE SEA SALT

2 TABLESPOONS EXTRA-VIRGIN OLIVE OIL

PIZZA DI GRANOTURCO

YIELD: 8 SMALL FOCACCIA / **ACTIVE TIME:** 10 MINUTES / **TOTAL TIME:** 45 MINUTES

Pizza di granoturco was traditionally made from cornmeal and cooked among the embers of a fireplace or a wood-fired stove. Serve with sautéed vegetables, such as broccoli rabe.

1. Preheat the oven to 430°F and place a baking stone or steel in the oven as it warms. In a large bowl, combine the cornmeal and salt. Using a wooden spoon, gradually incorporate the boiling water and work the mixture until the dough is just holding together. Transfer the dough to a cornmeal-dusted work surface and knead until it is smooth. Divide the dough into 8 pieces, form them into rounds, and flatten them into rather thick disks.

2. Place the disks directly on the heated baking implement and bake for about 25 minutes, until the tops are crispy. Remove the focaccia from the oven and let them cool slightly before serving.

INGREDIENTS:

- 17.6 OZ. CORNMEAL, PLUS MORE AS NEEDED
- 1 TEASPOON FINE SEA SALT
- 31¾ OZ. BOILING WATER

PIZZ'ONTA

YIELD: 12 SMALL FOCACCIA / **ACTIVE TIME:** 30 MINUTES / **TOTAL TIME:** 3 HOURS

In Abruzzi, it is very common to eat a fried crunchy focaccia called pizz'onta, or "greasy pizza." This focaccia is very easy to make at home, and it is out-of-this-world scrumptious, perfect beside cheese and cold cuts or grilled steak tips.

1. If using active dry yeast, warm 3½ tablespoons of the water until it is about 105°F. Add the water and yeast to a bowl and gently stir. Let the mixture sit until it is foamy, 5 to 10 minutes. Instant yeast does not need to be proofed.

2. In a large bowl, combine the flour, water, yeast, and sugar. Work the mixture until it just holds together. If kneading by hand, transfer the dough to a flour-dusted work surface. Work it until it is compact, smooth, and elastic.

3. Add the salt and olive oil and work the dough until it is developed, elastic, and extensible, about 5 minutes. Form the dough into a ball and place it in an airtight container that has been coated with olive oil. Let the dough rest at room temperature until it has doubled in size, about 2 hours.

4. Divide the dough into 12 pieces and form them into rounds, taking care not to overwork the dough. Cover the dough with a linen towel and let it rest for 30 minutes.

5. Add olive oil to a narrow, deep, heavy-bottomed saucepan with high edges until it is approximately 2 inches deep and warm it to 350°F. Flatten the rounds and, working in batches, fry them until they are golden brown on both sides, about 4 minutes. Transfer the fried focaccia to a paper towel–lined plate to drain and season them with salt before serving.

INGREDIENTS:

1¼ TEASPOONS ACTIVE DRY YEAST OR 1 TEASPOON INSTANT YEAST

8½ OZ. WATER

14 OZ. BREAD FLOUR, PLUS MORE AS NEEDED

2 TEASPOONS SUGAR

1 TEASPOON TABLE SALT, PLUS MORE TO TASTE

2 TABLESPOONS EXTRA-VIRGIN OLIVE OIL, PLUS MORE AS NEEDED

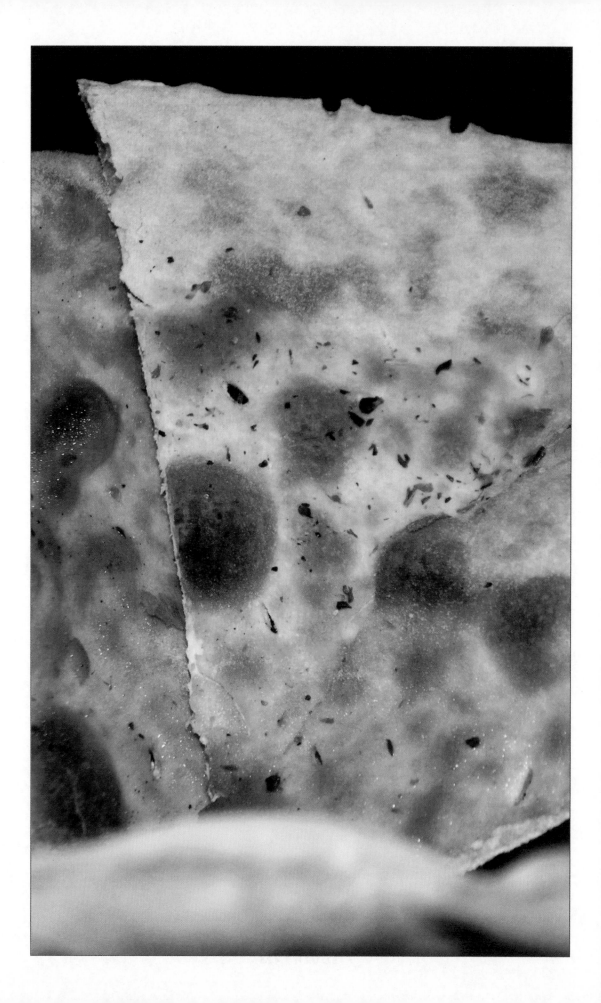

PIZZA ASSETTATA

YIELD: 1 LARGE FOCACCIA / **ACTIVE TIME:** 25 MINUTES / **TOTAL TIME:** 1 HOUR AND 15 MINUTES

This unleavened focaccia is made with a mix of semolina and bread flour and flavored with fennel seeds and red pepper flakes. As it is unleavened, it is among the quickest and easiest focaccia to make.

1. In a large bowl, combine the flours and fine sea salt. Gradually incorporate the water and work the mixture with your hands until it just holds together. Add the olive oil, fennel seeds, and red pepper flakes and work the dough until they have been incorporated.

2. If kneading by hand, transfer the dough to a flour-dusted work surface. Work it until it is smooth, compact, and elastic, about 10 minutes. Form the dough into a ball, cover it in plastic wrap, and let it rest at room temperature for 30 minutes.

3. Preheat the oven to 430°F.

4. Grease an 18 × 13–inch baking pan with olive oil, roll the dough out into a rectangle that will fit within the pan, and place the dough in the pan. Drizzle olive oil over the dough and sprinkle coarse salt on top.

5. Place the focaccia in the oven and bake for 20 to 25 minutes, until it is a light golden brown. Remove the focaccia from the oven and let it cool slightly before serving.

INGREDIENTS:

- 12.3 OZ. BREAD FLOUR, PLUS MORE AS NEEDED
- 12.3 OZ. FINELY GROUND DURUM WHEAT FLOUR (SEMOLA RIMACINATA)
- 2 TEASPOONS FINE SEA SALT
- 16.6 OZ. WARM WATER (110°F)
- 1¾ OZ. EXTRA-VIRGIN OLIVE OIL, PLUS MORE AS NEEDED
- 1 TABLESPOON FENNEL SEEDS
- 1 TEASPOON RED PEPPER FLAKES
- COARSE SEA SALT, FOR TOPPING

PANUOZZO

YIELD: 6 SMALL FOCACCIA / **ACTIVE TIME**: 20 MINUTES / **TOTAL TIME**: 3 HOURS AND 30 MINUTES

A focaccia traditionally made with pizza dough, what is truly special about Panuozzo is that it is baked twice: first to cook the bread, and then to incorporate the fillings. The most typical fillings are thin slices of pancetta or bacon with mozzarella, but the options are endless for this scrumptious flatbread.

1. Place the dough on a flour-dusted work surface and cut it into 6 pieces. Stretch the pieces of dough into 8- to 10-inch-long ovals, place them on pieces of flour-dusted parchment paper, and cover them with kitchen towels or plastic wrap coated with olive oil. Let the dough rest in a warm spot for 2 to 3 hours.

2. Preheat the oven to 410°F and place a baking stone or steel in the oven as it warms.

3. Using a peel or flat baking sheet, slide the focaccia onto the heated baking implement and bake for 15 to 20 minutes, until the crust is set. Remove the focaccia and let them cool before cutting a slit along the equator of each focaccia.

4. Fill each focaccia with an equal amount of the pancetta, mozzarella, tomatoes, and lettuce. Sprinkle red pepper flakes and salt over the filling and drizzle olive oil over it.

5. Return the focaccia to the oven and bake for about 10 minutes, until the pancetta looks cooked and the mozzarella has melted. Remove the focaccia from the oven and let them cool briefly before serving.

INGREDIENTS:

FOCACCIA MORBIDA (SEE PAGE 423)

ALL-PURPOSE FLOUR, AS NEEDED

EXTRA-VIRGIN OLIVE OIL, TO TASTE

12.7 OZ. PANCETTA OR BACON, SLICED THIN

26.4 OZ. FRESH MOZZARELLA CHEESE, DRAINED AND SLICED

2 TOMATOES, SLICED

12 LETTUCE LEAVES

RED PEPPER FLAKES, TO TASTE

SALT, TO TASTE

PARIGINA

YIELD: 1 LARGE FOCACCIA / **ACTIVE TIME:** 20 MINUTES / **TOTAL TIME:** 3 HOURS AND 30 MINUTES

If you are walking the streets of Naples during the day, you will probably stumble upon this beloved street food. Decadent and delicious, parigina typically features multiple layers of toppings, such as tomato sauce, ham, cheese, puff pastry, and heavy cream.

1. Coat an 18 x 13–inch baking sheet with olive oil, place the dough on it, and stretch it toward the edges of the pan, taking care not to tear it. Cover the dough with olive oil–coated plastic wrap and let it rest at room temperature for 2 hours. As the dough rests, stretch it toward the edges of the pan every 20 minutes until it covers the entire pan.

2. Preheat the oven to 390°F. Spread the tomatoes over the dough, making sure to leave a 1-inch border of dough at the edges. Season the tomatoes with salt. Cover with a layer of ham and top this with a layer of cheese. Cover the focaccia with the puff pastry, beat the egg yolks and cream together until combined, and brush the puff pastry with the egg wash.

3. Place the focaccia in the oven and bake until golden brown, 30 to 35 minutes.

4. Remove the focaccia from the oven and let it cool slightly before cutting into squares.

INGREDIENTS:

EXTRA-VIRGIN OLIVE OIL, AS NEEDED

FOCACCIA ASCIUTTA (SEE PAGE 422)

23 OZ. CANNED WHOLE PEELED TOMATOES, DRAINED AND CRUSHED

SALT, TO TASTE

7 OZ. HAM, SLICED

14 OZ. CACIOCAVALLO CHEESE OR LOW-MOISTURE MOZZARELLA CHEESE, SLICED THIN

1 SHEET OF FROZEN PUFF PASTRY, THAWED

2 EGG YOLKS

¼ CUP HEAVY CREAM

MONTANARE

YIELD: 20 MINIATURE FOCACCIA / **ACTIVE TIME:** 45 MINUTES / **TOTAL TIME:** 2 HOURS AND 45 MINUTES

A recipe that dates back to a time when people living in cities didn't have a kitchen large enough to accommodate an oven, and so focaccia was fried rather than baked. These miniature focaccia are a real treat, particularly beloved by children. A good way to use up leftover dough.

1. Place the dough on a flour-dusted work surface, divide it into 20 pieces, and shape each piece into a ball. Coat a piece of plastic wrap with olive oil, place it over the balls of dough, and let them sit at room temperature until they have doubled in size, about 2 hours.

2. Add olive oil to a deep skillet until it is about 1 inch deep and warm it to 350°F. Flatten the balls of dough. Working in batches of three, add them to the oil and cook until they are golden brown, turning them frequently, about 5 minutes. Place the cooked focaccia on paper towel–lined plates to drain.

3. When all of the focaccia have been cooked, top with the Marinara Sauce, pecorino, basil, and, if desired, mozzarella. Drizzle olive oil over the focaccia and serve.

INGREDIENTS:

½ BATCH OF NEAPOLITAN PIZZA DOUGH (SEE PAGE 397)

ALL-PURPOSE FLOUR, AS NEEDED

EXTRA-VIRGIN OLIVE OIL, AS NEEDED

26.4 OZ. SUGO AL BASILICO (SEE PAGE 806), WARMED, FOR TOPPING

PECORINO CHEESE, GRATED, FOR TOPPING

FRESH BASIL, FOR TOPPING

MOZZARELLA CHEESE, SLICED, FOR TOPPING (OPTIONAL)

GRUPARIATA

YIELD: 1 FOCACCIA / **ACTIVE TIME:** 30 MINUTES / **TOTAL TIME:** 3 HOURS AND 30 MINUTES

Hailing from Calabria, this is a very tall and fluffy focaccia with a pleasantly red crumb that is due to the presence of tomatoes and chili powder in the dough.

1. Line a deep, round 13-inch cake pan with parchment paper and coat it with olive oil. Place the yeast and water in a bowl, gently stir, and let the mixture sit until it starts to foam, 5 to 10 minutes.

2. In a large bowl, combine the flours, peeled tomatoes, chili powder, olive oil, salt, and yeast mixture and work the mixture until the dough is thoroughly combined.

3. Incorporate the garlic and a few pinches of fresh oregano and transfer the dough into the cake pan. Cover the pan with a kitchen towel and let the dough rest at room temperature until it has doubled in size, about 2½ hours.

4. Preheat the oven to 390°F. Cover the focaccia with anchovies and the fresh tomato slices, pressing down on them so that they are embedded deep within the dough. Sprinkle rosemary and additional oregano and salt over the dough and drizzle some olive oil over the top.

5. Place the focaccia in the oven and bake for 30 to 35 minutes, until it is golden brown. Remove the focaccia from the oven and let it cool slightly before serving.

INGREDIENTS:

1.2 OZ. EXTRA-VIRGIN OLIVE OIL, PLUS MORE AS NEEDED

2½ TEASPOONS ACTIVE DRY YEAST

14 OZ. WARM WATER (105°F)

17.6 OZ. BREAD FLOUR

10.6 OZ. "00" FLOUR

1 LB. WHOLE PEELED TOMATOES, DRAINED AND CHOPPED

2 TABLESPOONS CHILI POWDER

2½ TEASPOONS FINE SEA SALT, PLUS MORE TO TASTE

2 GARLIC CLOVES, MINCED

FRESH OREGANO, FINELY CHOPPED, TO TASTE

ANCHOVIES IN OLIVE OIL, DRAINED AND TORN, TO TASTE

1 FRESH TOMATO, SLICED

FRESH ROSEMARY, TO TASTE

PIZZA SCIMA

YIELD: 1 LARGE FOCACCIA / **ACTIVE TIME:** 25 MINUTES / **TOTAL TIME:** 1 HOUR AND 15 MINUTES

Notwithstanding the name, which implies that it is "dull," this focaccia carries a distinctive flavor and crunchiness, both of which are provided by the high amount of olive oil in the dough. The "dull," then, refers to it being unleavened, as was typical in the Jewish communities that traditionally inhabited parts of Abruzzi.

1. In a large bowl, combine the flours with the baking soda and salt. Incorporate the olive oil, wine, and water gradually and work the mixture until it just holds together. Transfer the dough to a flour-dusted work surface and knead until it is compact, smooth, and elastic. Form the dough into a ball, cover it with plastic wrap, and let it rest at room temperature for 30 minutes.

2. Preheat the oven to 430°F and place a baking stone or steel in the oven as it warms.

3. Using a rolling pin, roll the dough out until it is approximately ¾ inch thick. Place the dough on a piece of parchment paper and make deep cuts in it in a crosshatch pattern, taking care not to cut all the way through. Using a peel or a flat baking sheet, transfer the dough onto the heated baking implement and bake for 20 to 30 minutes, until it is golden brown. Remove the focaccia from the oven and let it cool slightly before serving.

INGREDIENTS:

17.6 OZ. BREAD FLOUR

7 OZ. ALL-PURPOSE FLOUR, PLUS MORE AS NEEDED

¼ TEASPOON BAKING SODA

2 TEASPOONS FINE SEA SALT

2.8 OZ. EXTRA-VIRGIN OLIVE OIL

2.8 OZ. WHITE WINE

6.3 OZ. WATER

LESTOPITTA

YIELD: 8 SMALL FOCACCIA / **ACTIVE TIME:** 45 MINUTES / **TOTAL TIME:** 2 HOURS AND 45 MINUTES

This fried focaccia is crunchy when hot, but becomes soft as it cools. It is usually wrapped around a savory filling when eaten soft.

1. Combine the flour, water, and olive oil in a mixing bowl and work the mixture until it is smooth and elastic. Cover the bowl with plastic wrap and let the dough rest at room temperature for 1 hour.

2. Divide the dough into 8 pieces and form them into balls. Coat a piece of plastic wrap with olive oil, place it over the balls of dough, and let them sit at room temperature until they have doubled in size, about 1 hour.

3. Add olive oil to a deep skillet until it is about 1 inch deep and warm it to 350°F. Flatten the balls of dough. Working in batches of three, add them to the hot oil and cook until golden brown, turning them frequently. Place the cooked focaccia on paper towel–lined plates to drain. Serve them warm or wait until they have cooled and fill with anything you desire.

INGREDIENTS:

- 14 OZ. FINELY GROUND DURUM WHEAT FLOUR (SEMOLA RIMACINATA)

- 7 OZ. WATER

- 2 TABLESPOONS EXTRA-VIRGIN OLIVE OIL, PLUS MORE AS NEEDED

FOCACCIA BARESE

YIELD: 2 SMALL FOCACCIA / **ACTIVE TIME:** 30 MINUTES / **TOTAL TIME:** 4 HOURS

B ari is the birthplace of one of the most prototypical Italian focaccia, the Barese. This is the most popular version—round and topped with fresh tomatoes and olives—but many variations can be found.

1. If using active dry yeast, warm 3½ tablespoons of the water until it is about 105°F. Add the water and the yeast to a bowl and gently stir. Let the mixture sit until it is foamy, 5 to 10 minutes. Instant yeast does not need to be proofed.

2. In a large bowl, combine the flours, potato, yeast, and water. Work the mixture until it comes together as a dough. If kneading by hand, transfer the dough to a flour-dusted work surface. Work it until it is compact, smooth, and elastic.

3. Add the salt and work the dough until it is developed, elastic, and extensible, about 5 minutes. Form the dough into a ball and place it in an airtight container that has been coated with olive oil. Let the dough rest at room temperature until it has doubled in size, about 2 hours.

4. Generously coat two 10-inch cast-iron skillets or round cake pans with olive oil. Place the dough on a flour-dusted work surface and divide it in two. Place the pieces of dough in the pans and spread them to the edge of each one, making sure not to press down too hard and deflate the focaccia. Let the dough rest in a warm spot for 1 hour.

5. Preheat the oven to its maximum temperature and position a rack in the middle. Top the focaccia with the tomatoes, olives, and oregano, season with salt, and drizzle olive oil over everything. Place the pans directly on the bottom of the oven and bake for 10 minutes.

6. Transfer the pans to the middle rack and bake until the edges look brown and crunchy, 5 to 7 more minutes.

7. Remove the focaccia from the oven and let them cool slightly before serving.

INGREDIENTS:

- 2   TEASPOONS ACTIVE DRY YEAST OR 1⅗ TEASPOONS INSTANT YEAST
- 14   OZ. WATER
- 14   OZ. BREAD FLOUR, PLUS MORE AS NEEDED
- 7   OZ. FINE SEMOLINA FLOUR
- 1   POTATO, BOILED, PEELED, AND MASHED
- 2½   TEASPOONS TABLE SALT, PLUS MORE TO TASTE
-    EXTRA-VIRGIN OLIVE OIL, AS NEEDED
- 2   VERY RIPE TOMATOES, CHOPPED
-    GREEN OLIVES, PITTED AND CHOPPED, TO TASTE
-    FRESH OREGANO, CHOPPED, TO TASTE

FOCACCIA DI ALTAMURA

YIELD: 2 SMALL FOCACCIA / **ACTIVE TIME:** 30 MINUTES / **TOTAL TIME:** 4 HOURS

I n Altamura, focaccia is made from 100 percent durum wheat flour and features a topping of onions and fresh tomatoes.

1. Place the water and yeast in a bowl, gently stir, and let the mixture sit until it starts to foam, 5 to 10 minutes.

2. In a large bowl, combine the flour and yeast mixture and work the mixture until it just holds together. If kneading by hand, transfer the dough to a flour-dusted work surface. Work it until it is compact, smooth, and elastic.

3. Add the salt and work the dough until it is developed, elastic, and extensible, about 5 minutes. Form the dough into a ball and place it in an airtight container that has been coated with olive oil. Let the dough rest at room temperature until it has doubled in size, about 2 hours.

4. Generously coat two 10-inch cast-iron skillets or round cake pans with olive oil. Place the dough on a flour-dusted work surface and divide it in two. Place a piece of dough in each pan and spread it to the edge, making sure not to press down too hard and deflate it. Let the dough rest at room temperature for 1 hour.

5. Preheat the oven to its maximum temperature and position a rack in the center of the oven. Top the focaccia with the onion, press the tomatoes into the dough, season with salt and oregano, and drizzle olive oil over the top. Place the pans directly on the bottom of the oven and bake for 10 minutes.

6. Transfer the pans to the center rack and bake until the edges look brown and crunchy, 5 to 7 more minutes. Remove the focaccia from the oven and let them cool slightly before serving.

INGREDIENTS:

14   OZ. WARM WATER (105°F)

2   TEASPOONS ACTIVE DRY YEAST

21.1 OZ. FINELY GROUND DURUM WHEAT FLOUR (SEMOLA RIMACINATA), PLUS MORE AS NEEDED

2½   TEASPOONS FINE SEA SALT, PLUS MORE TO TASTE

    EXTRA-VIRGIN OLIVE OIL, AS NEEDED

1   LARGE ONION, SLICED

2   VERY RIPE TOMATOES, SLICED

    FRESH OREGANO, FINELY CHOPPED, TO TASTE

PUDDICA SALENTINA

YIELD: 2 SMALL FOCACCIA / **ACTIVE TIME:** 30 MINUTES / **TOTAL TIME:** 4 HOURS

In Salento, particularly in the city of Brindisi, Apulian focaccia is made without durum flour and with capers in place of olives as a topping.

1. If using active dry yeast, warm 3½ tablespoons of the water until it is about 105°F. Add the water and the yeast to a bowl and gently stir. Let the mixture sit until it is foamy, 5 to 10 minutes. Instant yeast does not need to be proofed.

2. In a large bowl, combine the flours, yeast, and water and work the mixture until it comes together as a dough. If kneading by hand, transfer the dough to a flour-dusted work surface. Work it until it is compact, smooth, and elastic.

3. Add the salt and work the dough until it is developed, elastic, and extensible, about 5 minutes. Form the dough into a ball and place it in an airtight container that has been coated with olive oil. Let the dough rest at room temperature until it has doubled in size, about 2 hours.

4. Generously coat two 10-inch cast-iron skillets or round cake pans with olive oil. Place the dough on a flour-dusted work surface and divide it in two. Place a piece of dough in each of the pans and spread them to the edges, making sure not to press down too hard and deflate the dough. Let the dough rest at room temperature for 1 hour.

5. Preheat the oven to its maximum temperature and position a rack in the middle. Top the focaccia with the capers, press the tomatoes into the dough, season with salt and oregano, and drizzle olive oil over the top. Place the pans directly on the bottom of the oven and bake for 10 minutes.

6. Transfer the pans to the middle rack and bake until the edges look brown and crunchy, 5 to 7 more minutes.

7. Remove the focaccia from the oven and let them cool slightly before serving.

INGREDIENTS:

- 2 TEASPOONS ACTIVE DRY YEAST OR 1⅗ TEASPOONS INSTANT YEAST
- 14 OZ. WATER
- 14 OZ. BREAD FLOUR
- 7 OZ. ALL-PURPOSE FLOUR, PLUS MORE AS NEEDED
- 2½ TEASPOONS TABLE SALT, PLUS MORE TO TASTE

  EXTRA-VIRGIN OLIVE OIL, AS NEEDED

  CAPERS, DRAINED AND RINSED, TO TASTE
- 2 VERY RIPE TOMATOES, CHOPPED

  FRESH OREGANO, CHOPPED, TO TASTE

PAPOSCIA DEL GARGANO

YIELD: 5 MEDIUM FOCACCIA / **ACTIVE TIME:** 30 MINUTES / **TOTAL TIME:** 9 HOURS AND 30 MINUTES

From the beautiful Gargano region of Apulia, this focaccia is possibly the original version of ciabatta. Traditionally made with scraps of leftover dough and baked in wood-fired ovens, it can be made at home—with some adjustments—and it is surely worth trying, as it also makes a delicious bread for sandwiches.

1. Place the water and yeast in a bowl, gently stir, and let the mixture sit until it starts to foam, 5 to 10 minutes.

2. In a large bowl, combine the bread flour and yeast mixture and work the mixture until it just holds together. Transfer the dough to a flour-dusted work surface and knead until it is compact, smooth, and elastic.

3. Add the salt and knead until the dough is smooth, elastic, and extensible. Divide the dough into 5 pieces, shape them into balls, and place them in an airtight container that has been coated with olive oil. Let the dough rest at room temperature for at least 8 hours.

4. Preheat the oven to the maximum temperature and place a baking stone or steel in the oven as it warms.

5. Dust a peel or a flat baking sheet with semolina flour. Place 2 to 3 focaccia on it at a time and stretch them into long ovals. Use the peel to transfer the focaccia to the heated baking implement and bake for about 10 minutes, until golden brown and crispy. Remove the focaccia from the oven and let them cool slightly before serving.

INGREDIENTS:

14.8 OZ. WARM WATER (105°F)

1 (SCANT) TEASPOON ACTIVE DRY YEAST

22.9 OZ. BREAD FLOUR, PLUS MORE AS NEEDED

2½ TEASPOONS FINE SEA SALT

EXTRA-VIRGIN OLIVE OIL, AS NEEDED

SEMOLINA FLOUR, AS NEEDED

CAVICIONE

YIELD: 1 MEDIUM FOCACCIA / **ACTIVE TIME:** 45 MINUTES / **TOTAL TIME:** 5 HOURS

I n Ischitella, the typical Apulian calzone is filled with sautéed spring onions, which give it a very special flavor.

1. Place the water and yeast in a bowl, gently stir, and let the mixture sit until it starts to foam, 5 to 10 minutes.

2. In a large bowl, combine the flour and yeast mixture and work the mixture until it just holds together. Transfer the dough to a flour-dusted work surface and knead until it is compact, smooth, and elastic.

3. Add the salt and knead until the dough is smooth, elastic, and extensible. Form the dough into a ball and place it in an airtight container that has been coated with olive oil. Let the dough rest at room temperature until it has doubled in size, about 2 hours.

4. Preheat the oven to the maximum temperature and place a baking stone or steel in the oven as it warms.

5. Coat the bottom of a skillet with olive oil and warm it over medium-high heat. Add the onions and cook, stirring occasionally, until they are tender, about 10 minutes. Remove the pan from heat and let the onions cool completely.

6. Coat a 10-inch cast-iron skillet or round cake pan with olive oil. Transfer the dough to a flour-dusted work surface and divide it into 2 pieces, making sure 1 piece is slightly bigger than the other. Roll out 1 piece into a disk that is slightly larger than the pan. Place the disk in the pan and top it with the onions, olives, and anchovies.

7. Roll out the second piece of dough so that it will fit within the pan, place it over the filling, and crimp the edge to seal the focaccia. Brush the top of the focaccia with olive oil and use a fork to poke holes in it. Coat a piece of plastic wrap with olive oil, place it over the pan, and let the focaccia rest for 1 hour.

8. Preheat the oven to 430°F. Place the focaccia in the oven and bake for 20 minutes. Reduce the oven's temperature to 350°F and bake for another 20 to 25 minutes, until the focaccia is golden brown on top and on the bottom. Remove the focaccia from the oven and let it cool slightly before serving.

INGREDIENTS:

- 8.8 OZ. WARM WATER (105°F), PLUS MORE AS NEEDED
- 2 TEASPOONS ACTIVE DRY YEAST
- 17.6 OZ. ALL-PURPOSE FLOUR, PLUS MORE AS NEEDED
- 1½ TEASPOONS FINE SEA SALT, PLUS MORE TO TASTE
- EXTRA-VIRGIN OLIVE OIL, AS NEEDED
- 17.6 OZ. SPRING ONIONS, CHOPPED
- 5.3 OZ. PITTED BLACK OLIVES
- 4.2 OZ. ANCHOVIES IN OLIVE OIL, DRAINED

SCEBLASTI & PIZZO LECCESE

YIELD: 1 LARGE FOCACCIA / **ACTIVE TIME:** 45 MINUTES / **TOTAL TIME:** 3 HOURS

Deep in the Apulian inland, one can still find a focaccia that dates back to Greek times. It is rich with healthy, yummy vegetables and makes a great way to present them to your family. There are two main variations: in Zollino this focaccia is called sceblasti, a Greek word that means "without shape," because the dough is more like a batter. It includes a blend of different vegetables, and is richer than the version that we find in Lecce, which is known as Pizzo Leccese. Here is a method for both versions.

1. Place the water and yeast in a bowl, gently stir, and let the mixture sit until it starts to foam, 5 to 10 minutes.

2. In a large bowl, combine the flour and yeast mixture and work the mixture until it just holds together. Transfer the dough to a flour-dusted work surface and knead until it is compact, smooth, and elastic.

3. Add the salt and knead until the dough is smooth, elastic, and extensible. Form the dough into a ball and place it in an airtight container that has been coated with olive oil. Let the dough rest at room temperature until it has doubled in size, about 2 hours.

4. Preheat the oven to the maximum temperature and place a baking stone or steel in the oven as it warms. While the dough is rising, clean and mince all of the vegetables and combine with the sauce, olive oil, salt, oregano, and red pepper flakes (if using).

5. Flatten the dough and spread the vegetables over it, folding the dough over the vegetables and working with your hands to incorporate them into the dough. Place the dough on a peel or flat baking sheet and transfer it to the heated baking implement. Bake the focaccia until golden brown, about 20 minutes. Remove the focaccia from the oven and let it cool briefly before serving.

INGREDIENTS:

- 14.8 OZ. WARM WATER (ABOUT 105°F)
- 2 TEASPOONS ACTIVE DRY YEAST
- 21.1 OZ. ALL-PURPOSE FLOUR, PLUS MORE AS NEEDED
- 2½ TEASPOONS FINE SEA SALT, PLUS MORE TO TASTE
- 2.8 OZ. EXTRA-VIRGIN OLIVE OIL, PLUS MORE AS NEEDED
- 2 MEDIUM ONIONS, SLICED
- 7 OZ. CHERRY TOMATOES
- 1 ZUCCHINI (OMIT IF MAKING PIZZO LECCESE)
- 7 OZ. FRESH PUMPKIN (OMIT IF MAKING PIZZO LECCESE)
- 7 OZ. PITTED BLACK OLIVES
- 3½ OZ. PIZZA SAUCE (SEE PAGE 398)
- FRESH OREGANO, FINELY CHOPPED, TO TASTE
- RED PEPPER FLAKES, TO TASTE (OPTIONAL)

CALZONE PUGLIESE

YIELD: 1 MEDIUM FOCACCIA / **ACTIVE TIME:** 45 MINUTES / **TOTAL TIME:** 4 HOURS

Although the name calzone evokes the popular Neapolitan pizza pockets, in Apulia it refers to a round pie made from two layers of focaccia dough.

1. Place the water and yeast in a bowl, gently stir, and let the mixture sit until it starts to foam, 5 to 10 minutes.

2. In a large bowl, combine the flour and yeast mixture and work the mixture until it just holds together. Transfer the dough to a flour-dusted work surface and knead until it is compact, smooth, and elastic.

3. Add the salt and knead until the dough is smooth, elastic, and extensible. Form the dough into a ball and place it in an airtight container that has been coated with olive oil. Let the dough rest at room temperature until it has doubled in size, about 2 hours.

4. Coat the bottom of a skillet with olive oil and warm it over medium-high heat. Add the onions and cook, stirring occasionally, until they are translucent, about 3 minutes. Add the cherry tomatoes and cook until they start to collapse, about 10 minutes. Remove the pan from heat and let the mixture cool completely.

5. Coat a 10-inch cast-iron skillet or round cake pan with olive oil. Transfer the dough to a flour-dusted work surface and divide it into 2 pieces, making sure 1 piece is slightly bigger than the other. Roll out 1 piece into a disk that is slightly larger than the pan. Place the disk in the pan, top it with the onion-and-tomato mixture, and distribute the olives, anchovies, and capers over the mixture.

6. Roll out the second piece of dough so that it will fit within the pan, place it over the filling, and crimp the edge to seal the focaccia. Brush the top of the focaccia with olive oil and use a fork to poke holes in it. Coat a piece of plastic wrap with olive oil, place it over the pan, and let the focaccia rest for 1 hour.

7. Preheat the oven to 430°F. Place the focaccia in the oven and bake for 20 minutes. Reduce the oven's temperature to 350°F and bake for another 20 to 25 minutes, until the focaccia is golden brown on top and on the bottom. Remove the focaccia from the oven and let it cool slightly before serving.

INGREDIENTS:

- 8.8 OZ. WARM WATER (ABOUT 105°F)
- 2 TEASPOONS ACTIVE DRY YEAST
- 17.6 OZ. ALL-PURPOSE FLOUR, PLUS MORE AS NEEDED
- 1½ TEASPOONS FINE SEA SALT, PLUS MORE TO TASTE
- EXTRA-VIRGIN OLIVE OIL, AS NEEDED
- 3 ONIONS, SLICED
- 5.3 OZ. CHERRY TOMATOES
- 5.3 OZ. PITTED BLACK OLIVES
- 1 OZ. ANCHOVIES, DRAINED
- 2 TABLESPOONS CAPERS IN BRINE, DRAINED AND RINSED

VASTEDDA CON SAMBUCO

YIELD: 1 MEDIUM FOCACCIA / **ACTIVE TIME**: 30 MINUTES / **TOTAL TIME**: 4 HOURS

A focaccia enriched with eggs, flavored with elderflowers, and filled with salami and cheese. Delicious and really different.

1. Place the water and yeast in a bowl, gently stir, and let the mixture sit until it starts to foam, 5 to 10 minutes.

2. In a large bowl, combine the flour, lard, a handful of elderflowers, and yeast mixture and work the mixture until it just holds together. Transfer the dough to a flour-dusted work surface and knead until it is compact, smooth, and elastic.

3. Add the salt and eggs and knead until the dough is smooth, elastic, and extensible. Form the dough into a ball and place it in an airtight container that has been coated with olive oil. Let the dough rest at room temperature until it has doubled in size, about 2 hours.

4. Coat a 10-inch cast-iron skillet or round cake pan with olive oil. Transfer the dough to a flour-dusted work surface and divide it into 2 pieces, making sure 1 piece is slightly bigger than the other. Roll out 1 piece into a round that is slightly larger than the pan. Place the round in the pan and layer the salami and caciocavallo on top.

5. Roll out the second piece of dough so that it will fit within the pan, place it over the filling, and crimp the edge to seal the focaccia. Brush the top of the focaccia with olive oil and use a fork to poke holes in it. Coat a piece of plastic wrap with olive oil, place it over the pan, and let the focaccia rest for 1 hour.

6. Preheat the oven to 390°F. Sprinkle elderflowers over the focaccia and drizzle olive oil over the top. Place the focaccia in the oven and bake for 30 to 35 minutes, until it is golden brown and crispy. Remove the focaccia from the oven and let it cool slightly before serving.

INGREDIENTS:

12.3 OZ. WARM WATER (105°F)

2½ TEASPOONS ACTIVE DRY YEAST

21.1 OZ. ALL-PURPOSE FLOUR, PLUS MORE AS NEEDED

3½ OZ. LARD OR BUTTER

ELDERFLOWERS, FRESH OR DRIED, TO TASTE

1½ TEASPOONS FINE SEA SALT

5 EGGS

EXTRA-VIRGIN OLIVE OIL, AS NEEDED

17.6 OZ. SLICED SALAMI

17.6 OZ. CACIOCAVALLO OR TUMA CHEESE

FOCACCIA DI CARNEVALE SALENTINA

YIELD: 1 SMALL FOCACCIA / **ACTIVE TIME:** 45 MINUTES / **TOTAL TIME:** 4 HOURS

This rich and delicious Apulian calzone is typical of the region of Salento, where it is presented during the Carnival.

1. If using active dry yeast, warm 3½ tablespoons of the water until it is about 105°F. Add the water and the yeast to a bowl and gently stir. Let the mixture sit until it is foamy, 5 to 10 minutes.

2. In a large bowl, combine the flour, yeast, and water until the mixture comes together as a dough. If kneading by hand, transfer the dough to a flour-dusted work surface. Work it until it is compact, smooth, and elastic.

3. Add the salt and work the dough until it is developed, elastic, and extensible, about 5 minutes. Form the dough into a ball and place it in an airtight container that has been coated with olive oil. Let the dough rest at room temperature until it has doubled in size, about 2 hours.

4. Coat the bottom of a skillet with olive oil and warm it over medium-high heat. When the oil starts to shimmer, add the onion and sausage, season with salt and pepper, and cook, stirring frequently, until the sausage is browned and the onion is soft, about 10 minutes. Remove from heat and let it cool.

5. Grease a 10-inch cast-iron skillet or a round cake pan with olive oil. Transfer the dough to a flour-dusted work surface and divide it into 2 pieces, with one piece slightly bigger than the other. Roll out one piece into a disk that is slightly larger than the pan. Place it in the pan, top with the onion-and-sausage mixture, and distribute the tomatoes, pecorino, and mozzarella over the mixture.

6. Roll out the second piece of dough so that it will fit within the pan, place it over the filling, and crimp the edge to seal the focaccia. Brush the top of the focaccia with olive oil and use a fork to poke holes in it. Cover with olive oil–coated plastic wrap and let it rest for 1 hour.

7. Preheat the oven to 430°F. Place the focaccia in the oven and bake for 20 minutes. Lower the temperature to 350°F and bake for another 20 to 25 minutes, until it is golden brown, both on top and on the bottom. Remove and let it cool slightly before serving.

INGREDIENTS:

2   TEASPOONS ACTIVE DRY YEAST OR 1⅔ TEASPOONS INSTANT YEAST

8.8   OZ. WATER

17½   OZ. ALL-PURPOSE FLOUR, PLUS MORE AS NEEDED

1½   TEASPOONS TABLE SALT, PLUS MORE TO TASTE

EXTRA-VIRGIN OLIVE OIL, AS NEEDED

1   ONION, SLICED

14   OZ. ITALIAN SAUSAGE, CHOPPED

BLACK PEPPER, TO TASTE

3   SMALL TOMATOES, PEELED, SEEDS REMOVED, AND SLICED

2½   OZ. PECORINO CHEESE, FRESHLY GRATED

10   OZ. FRESH MOZZARELLA CHEESE, TORN

SFINCIONE PALERMITANO

YIELD: 1 LARGE FOCACCIA / **ACTIVE TIME:** 1 HOUR / **TOTAL TIME:** 4 HOURS AND 30 MINUTES

The soft and spongy consistency of this Sicilian focaccia's crumb makes this one of the greatest treats the Mediterranean region has to offer.

1. If using active dry yeast, warm 3½ tablespoons of the water until it is about 105°F. Add the water and the yeast to a bowl and gently stir. Let the mixture sit until it is foamy, 5 to 10 minutes. Instant yeast does not need to be proofed.

2. In a large bowl, combine the flours, yeast, and water until the mixture comes together as a dough. If kneading by hand, transfer the dough to a flour-dusted work surface. Work the dough until it is compact, smooth, and elastic.

3. Add the salt and work the dough until it is developed, elastic, and extensible, about 5 minutes. Form the dough into a ball, place it in a bowl, and cover the bowl with a damp linen towel. Let it rest at room temperature until it has doubled in size, about 2 hours.

4. Coat the bottom of a skillet with olive oil and warm it over medium-low heat. When the oil starts to shimmer, add the onions and cook, stirring frequently, until they are starting to brown, about 12 minutes. Add the tomatoes and three of the anchovies, cover the skillet, reduce the heat, and simmer until the flavor is to your liking, 20 to 30 minutes. Season with salt and pepper and let it cool completely.

5. Coat an 18 x 13–inch baking pan with olive oil, place the dough on the pan, and gently stretch it until it covers the entire pan. Cover the dough with plastic wrap and let it rest for 1 hour.

6. Preheat the oven to 430°F. Top the focaccia with the cubed caciocavallo and the remaining anchovies and press down on them until they are embedded in the dough. Cover with the tomato sauce, generously sprinkle oregano over the sauce, and drizzle olive oil over everything. Sprinkle the grated caciocavallo and a generous handful of bread crumbs over the focaccia.

7. Place it in the oven and bake for 20 minutes. Lower the temperature to 180°F and bake for another 15 to 20 minutes, until the focaccia is golden brown, both on the edges and on the bottom.

8. Remove the focaccia from the oven and let it cool slightly before serving.

INGREDIENTS:

2½ TEASPOONS ACTIVE DRY YEAST OR 2 TEASPOONS INSTANT YEAST

22½ OZ. WATER

19¾ OZ. BREAD FLOUR, PLUS MORE AS NEEDED

8.4 OZ. FINE SEMOLINA FLOUR

1 TABLESPOON TABLE SALT, PLUS MORE TO TASTE

EXTRA-VIRGIN OLIVE OIL, AS NEEDED

2 ONIONS, SLICED

22.9 OZ. CRUSHED TOMATOES, WITH THEIR LIQUID

11–14 ANCHOVIES IN OLIVE OIL, DRAINED AND TORN

BLACK PEPPER, TO TASTE

1 LB. CACIOCAVALLO CHEESE, TWO-THIRDS CUBED, ONE-THIRD GRATED

FRESH OREGANO, CHOPPED, TO TASTE

BREAD CRUMBS, TO TASTE

FACCIA DI VECCHIA

YIELD: 6 MEDIUM FOCACCIA / **ACTIVE TIME:** 1 HOUR / **TOTAL TIME:** 5 HOURS

The toppings here are the same as the ones used in sfincione, but the smaller focaccia are baked directly on the stone, as a Neapolitan pizza would be. Some versions omit both the cheese and the anchovies from the topping, so if that sounds more to your taste, don't hesitate to go that route.

1. Place the water and yeast in a bowl, gently stir, and let the mixture sit until it starts to foam, 5 to 10 minutes.

2. In a large bowl, combine the flours and yeast mixture and work the mixture until it just holds together. Transfer the dough to a flour-dusted work surface and knead until it is compact, smooth, and elastic.

3. Add the salt and knead until the dough is smooth, elastic, and extensible. Form the dough into a ball and place it in a bowl that has been coated with olive oil. Cover the bowl with a damp kitchen towel and let the dough rest at room temperature until it has doubled in size, about 2 hours.

4. Coat the bottom of a skillet with olive oil and warm it over medium-low heat. Add the onions and cook, stirring occasionally, until they are tender, about 10 minutes. Add the tomatoes and 3 of the anchovies, cover the skillet, reduce the heat to low, and cook until the flavor of the mixture is to your liking, 20 to 30 minutes. Remove the pan from heat, season the mixture with salt and pepper, and let it cool completely.

5. Place the dough on a flour-dusted work surface and divide it into 6 pieces. Shape the pieces into balls, coat a piece of plastic wrap with olive oil, and place it over the balls of dough. Let them rest for 1 hour.

6. Preheat the oven to its maximum temperature and place a baking stone or steel in the oven as it warms.

7. Gently flatten the balls of dough and cover them with the tomato sauce. Top with the tuma, the remaining anchovies, the caciocavallo, and a generous amount of oregano, bread crumbs, and olive oil.

8. Using a peel or a flat baking sheet, transfer the focaccia onto the heated baking implement and bake for about 30 minutes, until the edges are golden brown. Remove the focaccia from the oven and let them cool slightly before serving.

INGREDIENTS:

19.4	OZ. WARM WATER (105°F)
2½	TEASPOONS ACTIVE DRY YEAST
19¾	OZ. BREAD FLOUR, PLUS MORE AS NEEDED
8.4	OZ. FINELY GROUND DURUM WHEAT FLOUR (SEMOLA RIMACINATA)
1	TABLESPOON FINE SEA SALT, PLUS MORE TO TASTE
	EXTRA-VIRGIN OLIVE OIL, AS NEEDED
2	ONIONS, SLICED
22.9	OZ. WHOLE PEELED TOMATOES, WITH THEIR LIQUID, MASHED
11–14	ANCHOVIES IN OLIVE OIL, DRAINED AND TORN
	BLACK PEPPER, TO TASTE
10.6	OZ. TUMA CHEESE, CUBED
7	OZ. CACIOCAVALLO CHEESE, GRATED
	FRESH OREGANO, FINELY CHOPPED, TO TASTE
	BREAD CRUMBS, TO TASTE

MUSTAZZEDDU

YIELD: 1 LARGE FOCACCIA / **ACTIVE TIME:** 40 MINUTES / **TOTAL TIME:** 4 HOURS AND 30 MINUTES

Traditionally, this was the sustenance food of the Sardinian women who baked for their community; they used to make this focaccia to feed themselves during the day-long process of making large batches of bread.

1. Place the tomatoes, garlic, basil leaves, and a generous amount of olive oil in a bowl, season with salt, and stir to combine. Let the mixture sit for 2 hours, drain it in a colander, and let it drain further for 1 hour.

2. If using active dry yeast, warm 3½ tablespoons of the water until it is about 105°F. Add the water and the yeast to a bowl and gently stir. Let sit for 5 to 10 minutes.

3. In a large bowl, combine the flours, olive oil, yeast, and water until the dough holds together. Add the salt and work the dough until it is compact, smooth, and elastic. Cover the bowl with a damp kitchen towel and let it rest at room temperature until it has doubled in size, about 2 hours.

4. Place the dough on a flour-dusted work surface and roll it out until it is an approximately ¾-inch-thick disk. Place it on a parchment-lined baking sheet, cover with the kitchen towel, and let it rest for another hour.

5. Preheat the oven to 430°F and place a rack in the middle position. Place the tomato mixture on the focaccia, making sure to leave some dough at the edge. Season with salt and pepper and fold the dough over the filling. You can leave the filling exposed or cover it completely; both are traditional in Sardinia.

6. Brush the dough with olive oil, place the pan directly on the bottom of the oven, and bake for 10 minutes. Lower the temperature to 390°F, transfer the focaccia to the middle rack, and bake for 30 to 40 minutes, until golden brown on the edges and on the bottom. Remove and let cool slightly before serving.

INGREDIENTS:

28.2 OZ. CHERRY TOMATOES, CHOPPED

2 GARLIC CLOVES, CHOPPED

3–4 BASIL LEAVES

1 TABLESPOON OLIVE OIL, PLUS MORE AS NEEDED

1½ TEASPOONS TABLE SALT, PLUS MORE TO TASTE

2 TEASPOONS ACTIVE DRY YEAST OR 1⅔ TEASPOONS INSTANT YEAST

11.6 OZ. WATER

12.3 OZ. FINE SEMOLINA FLOUR (SEMOLA RIMACINATA)

5.3 OZ. BREAD FLOUR, PLUS MORE AS NEEDED

BLACK PEPPER, TO TASTE

FOCACCIA MESSINESE

YIELD: 1 LARGE FOCACCIA / **ACTIVE TIME:** 40 MINUTES / **TOTAL TIME:** 4 HOURS AND 30 MINUTES

This delicious focaccia reigns in Messina, where escarole is queen. If you're searching for some way to make salad look and taste amazing, look no further.

1. Place the water and yeast in a bowl, gently stir, and let the mixture sit until it starts to foam, 5 to 10 minutes.

2. In a large bowl, combine the flours, olive oil, and yeast mixture and work the mixture until it just holds together. Transfer the dough to a flour-dusted work surface and knead until it is compact, smooth, and elastic.

3. Add the salt and knead until the dough is smooth, elastic, and extensible. Form the dough into a ball and place it in an airtight container that has been coated with olive oil. Let the dough rest at room temperature until it has doubled in size, about 2 hours.

4. Coat an 18 × 13–inch baking pan with olive oil, place the dough on it, and brush the dough with more olive oil. Cover the pan with a kitchen towel and let the dough rest for 30 minutes.

5. Gently stretch the dough until it covers the entire pan. Let it rest for another hour.

6. Preheat the oven to 390°F. Press the anchovies and caciocavallo into the dough and top it with the escarole and tomatoes. Season with oregano, salt, and pepper and drizzle olive oil over the focaccia.

7. Place the focaccia in the oven and bake for 20 to 30 minutes, until it is golden brown and crisp on the edges and the bottom. Remove the focaccia from the oven and let it cool slightly before slicing and serving.

INGREDIENTS:

- 14.8 OZ. WARM WATER (105°F)
- 2½ TEASPOONS ACTIVE DRY YEAST
- 1 LB. BREAD FLOUR, PLUS MORE AS NEEDED
- 8.8 OZ. FINELY GROUND DURUM WHEAT FLOUR (SEMOLA RIMACINATA)
- 0.7 OZ. EXTRA-VIRGIN OLIVE OIL, PLUS MORE AS NEEDED
- 1 TABLESPOON FINE SEA SALT, PLUS MORE TO TASTE
- 12 ANCHOVIES IN OLIVE OIL, DRAINED AND TORN
- 21.1 OZ. CACIOCAVALLO CHEESE, CUBED
- 14 OZ. ESCAROLE, CHOPPED
- 3 TOMATOES, CHOPPED
- FRESH OREGANO, FINELY CHOPPED, TO TASTE
- BLACK PEPPER, TO TASTE

RIANATA

YIELD: 1 LARGE FOCACCIA / ACTIVE TIME: 40 MINUTES / TOTAL TIME: 4 HOURS AND 45 MINUTES

A simple and scrumptious focaccia loaded with tomatoes and oregano. Don't hesitate to be extravagant with the latter, as rianata means "with oregano."

1. If using active dry yeast, warm 3½ tablespoons of the water until it is about 105°F. Add the water and the yeast to a bowl and gently stir. Let the mixture sit until it starts to foam. Instant yeast does not need to be proofed.

2. In a large bowl, combine the flours, olive oil, yeast, and water until the mixture comes together as a dough. Transfer it to a flour-dusted work surface and knead the dough until it is compact, smooth, and elastic.

3. Add the salt and knead until the dough is developed, elastic, and extensible, about 5 minutes. Form the dough into a ball and place it in an airtight container that has been coated with olive oil. Let the dough rest at room temperature until it has doubled in size, about 2 hours.

4. Coat an 18 x 13–inch baking sheet with olive oil, place the dough on it, and brush the dough with more olive oil. Cover with a linen towel and let the dough rest for 30 minutes.

5. Gently stretch the dough until it covers the entire pan. Let it rest for another hour.

6. Preheat the oven to 430°F. Press the anchovies and tomatoes into the dough, sprinkle the pecorino over the focaccia, season it with salt and oregano, and drizzle olive oil over everything.

7. Place the focaccia in the oven and bake for 20 to 30 minutes, until the focaccia is golden brown and crispy on the edges and the bottom.

8. Remove the focaccia from the oven and let it cool slightly before serving.

INGREDIENTS:

- 2½ TEASPOONS ACTIVE DRY YEAST OR 2 TEASPOONS INSTANT YEAST
- 14.8 OZ. WATER
- 1 LB. BREAD FLOUR, PLUS MORE AS NEEDED
- 8.8 OZ. FINE SEMOLINA FLOUR
- 1 TABLESPOON PLUS 1 TEASPOON EXTRA-VIRGIN OLIVE OIL, PLUS MORE AS NEEDED
- 1 TABLESPOON TABLE SALT, PLUS MORE TO TASTE
- 7–8 ANCHOVIES IN OLIVE OIL, DRAINED
- 30 CHERRY TOMATOES, HALVED
- ½ LB. PECORINO CHEESE, GRATED

  FRESH OREGANO, CHOPPED, TO TASTE

SCACCIA RAGUSANA

YIELD: 3 MEDIUM FOCACCIA / **ACTIVE TIME:** 1 HOUR AND 15 MINUTES / **TOTAL TIME:** 3 HOURS AND 20 MINUTES

This layered focaccia from Ragusa and Modica is a beloved street food and comes in many variations. Popular fillings are eggplant with tomato sauce, broccoli with Italian sausage, and this one with tomato sauce, onions, and caciocavallo cheese.

1. Place the water and yeast in a bowl, gently stir, and let the mixture sit until it starts to foam, 5 to 10 minutes.

2. In a large bowl, combine the flour and yeast mixture and work the mixture until it just holds together. Transfer the dough to a flour-dusted work surface and knead until it is compact, smooth, and elastic.

3. Add the salt and knead until the dough is smooth, elastic, and extensible. Form the dough into a ball and place it in an airtight container that has been coated with olive oil. Let the dough rest at room temperature until it has doubled in size, about 2 hours.

4. Coat the bottom of a skillet with olive oil and warm it over medium-low heat. Add the onions and cook, stirring occasionally, until they are tender, about 10 minutes. Add the tomatoes, cover the skillet, reduce the heat to low, and cook until the flavor of the mixture is to your liking, 20 to 30 minutes. Remove the pan from heat, season the mixture with salt, and let it cool completely.

5. Preheat the oven to 430°F and line a baking sheet with parchment paper. Place the dough on a flour-dusted work surface, divide it into 3 pieces, and shape them into balls. Roll each ball into a thin rectangle. Cover each focaccia with some of the tomato sauce and a generous sprinkle of the caciocavallo, leaving a 1-inch border around the edges. Fold the short ends of the focaccia toward the center, lengthwise. Cover the focaccia with more tomato sauce and caciocavallo, leaving a border near the edges again. Fold the short ends of the focaccia toward the center. Cover the focaccia with more sauce and caciocavallo and fold the focaccia in half.

6. Place the focaccia on the baking sheet, brush them with olive oil, and poke holes in them with a fork. Place the focaccia in the oven and bake for 25 to 30 minutes, until they are crispy and golden brown. Remove the focaccia from the oven and let them cool slightly before serving.

INGREDIENTS:

11.8 OZ. WARM WATER (105°F)

2 TEASPOONS ACTIVE DRY YEAST

21.1 OZ. FINELY GROUND DURUM WHEAT FLOUR (SEMOLA RIMACINATA), PLUS MORE AS NEEDED

1½ TEASPOONS FINE SEA SALT, PLUS MORE TO TASTE

EXTRA-VIRGIN OLIVE OIL, AS NEEDED

21.1 OZ. ONIONS, SLICED THIN

21.1 OZ. WHOLE PEELED TOMATOES, MASHED

10.6 OZ. CACIOCAVALLO CHEESE, GRATED

FOCACCIA PORTOSCUSESE

YIELD: 4 MEDIUM FOCACCIA / **ACTIVE TIME:** 40 MINUTES / **TOTAL TIME:** 3 HOURS AND 45 MINUTES

A traditional Sardinian focaccia that looks like a Neapolitan pizza but has a special dough that contains more potato than flour. A must try!

1. Warm 3½ tablespoons of milk until it is about 105°F. Add the milk and yeast to a bowl, gently stir, and let the mixture sit until it starts to foam, 5 to 10 minutes.

2. In a large bowl, combine the flour, potatoes, and yeast mixture until a soft and not too sticky dough forms. If needed, gradually add the remaining milk; how much you need depends on how watery the potatoes are.

3. Work the salt into the dough, transfer it to a flour-dusted work surface, and work the dough until it is smooth. Place the dough in an airtight container that has been coated with olive oil and let it rest at room temperature until it has doubled in size, about 2 hours.

4. Coat the bottom of a skillet with olive oil and warm it over medium-low heat. Add the onions and cook, stirring occasionally, until they are tender, about 10 minutes. Add the tomatoes, cover the skillet, reduce the heat to low, and cook until the flavor of the mixture is to your liking, 20 to 30 minutes. Remove the pan from heat, season the mixture with salt, and let it cool completely.

5. Place the dough on a flour-dusted work surface and divide it into 4 pieces. Shape the pieces into balls, coat a piece of plastic wrap with olive oil, and place it over the dough. Let the dough rest for 1 hour.

6. Preheat the oven to 390°F and place a baking stone or steel in the oven as it warms. Gently flatten the balls of dough and cover them with the tomato sauce. Sprinkle the pecorino over the focaccia and drizzle olive oil on top. Use a peel to transfer the focaccia onto the heated cooking implement and bake for about 20 to 25 minutes, until the edges and bottom are golden brown. Remove the focaccia from the oven and let them cool slightly before serving.

INGREDIENTS:

5.3   OZ. MILK

2   TEASPOONS ACTIVE DRY YEAST

10.6   OZ. BREAD FLOUR, PLUS MORE AS NEEDED

28.2   OZ. POTATOES, BOILED, PEELED, AND MASHED

1½   TEASPOONS FINE SEA SALT, PLUS MORE TO TASTE

  EXTRA-VIRGIN OLIVE OIL, AS NEEDED

14   OZ. ONIONS, SLICED THIN

14   OZ. WHOLE PEELED TOMATOES, MASHED

7   OZ. PECORINO CHEESE, GRATED

CENTRAL

ANTIPASTI & CONTORNI

OLIVE ALL'ASCOLANA

YIELD: 60 PIECES / *ACTIVE TIME*: 30 MINUTES / **TOTAL TIME**: 50 MINUTES

One of the most popular Italian appetizers both in Italy and abroad, olive all'ascolana are a real treat—large green olives stuffed with meat, vegetables, and spices. Making them at home is time-consuming but, on the bright side olive all'ascolana are perfect to freeze after preparing. If you do, just thaw them before frying. High-quality olives are a must, and ascolana tenere are ideal.

1. Place the olive oil in a large skillet and warm it over medium-low heat. Add the onion, carrot, and garlic and cook, stirring frequently, until the onion has softened, about 6 minutes.

2. Add the meat and cook, stirring occasionally, until it has browned on all sides, over, about 5 minutes.

3. Deglaze the pan with the wine, scraping up any browned bits from the bottom. Cook until the wine has evaporated.

4. Stir in the pepper and nutmeg, season with salt, and cover the pan. Cook until the meat is cooked through, 10 to 15 minutes.

5. Remove the pan from heat and let the mixture cool.

6. Remove the garlic and discard it. Strain the mixture, add it to a blender along with 2 tablespoons of bread crumbs and the Parmesan, and puree until the mixture is a smooth paste.

7. To pit the olives, cut the flesh away from the pit and into a spiral. This will make it easy to wrap the olives around the filling.

8. Place the pitted olives in a bowl of water and add the lemon zest. When all of the olives have been pitted, form the meat into olive-shaped nuggets and wrap the olives around them. It is OK to leave some of the filling exposed, as it will help the breading adhere.

9. Place the eggs, flour, and remaining bread crumbs in separate bowls. Dredge the stuffed olives in the flour, then in the eggs, and finally in the bread crumbs until they are completely coated.

10. Add olive oil to a narrow, deep, and heavy-bottomed saucepan with high edges until it is about 2 inches deep and warm it to 350°F. Working in batches to avoid crowding the pot, gently slip the stuffed olives into the hot oil and fry until they are golden brown, turning as necessary.

11. Transfer the fried olives to a paper towel–lined plate to drain and cool before serving.

INGREDIENTS:

2	TABLESPOONS EXTRA-VIRGIN OLIVE OIL, PLUS MORE AS NEEDED
1	ONION, FINELY DICED
1	CARROT, PEELED AND FINELY DICED
3	GARLIC CLOVES
3½	OZ. BONELESS, SKINLESS CHICKEN BREAST, CHOPPED
3½	OZ. PORK, CHOPPED
3½	OZ. VEAL, CHOPPED
½	CUP DRY WHITE WINE
1	TEASPOON BLACK PEPPER
1	TEASPOON FRESHLY GRATED NUTMEG
	SALT, TO TASTE
1½	CUPS PLUS 2 TABLESPOONS BREAD CRUMBS
2	TABLESPOONS GRATED PARMESAN CHEESE
2.2	LBS. LARGE GREEN OLIVES
	ZEST OF 1 LEMON
2	EGGS, LIGHTLY BEATEN
1	CUP ALL-PURPOSE FLOUR

OLIVE ALL'ASCOLANA:
THE IRRESISTIBLE APPETIZER FROM MARCHE

Fried stuffed olives, known as olive all'ascolana, are a staple in pizzerias all over Italy, a perfect appetizer to kick off a meal. They are also popular items at cafés and bars, as their salty, crunchy character makes them a great accompaniment for alcoholic beverages. In their region of origin, Marche, olive all'ascolana are also a fixture on tables around the holidays.

Traditionally, they are made with a specific type of green olives known as ascolana tenera, then filled with meat, bread crumbs, and nutmeg, and breaded and deep-fried.

The history of these stuffed olives begins with the Romans, who gave olives to troops to sustain them during long campaigns. Olive all'ascolana as we know them, though, are a relatively recent development—in the early eighteenth century, the chef for some aristocratic family in Ascoli Piceno, looking for a smart way to utilize the excess meat in rich households' kitchens, came up with them. Soon, the meat-stuffed treats spread to the local population, and from there to the rest of Italy. In 1875, industrial production of olive all'ascolana began thanks to Mariano Mazzocchi, who saw the potential of these irresistible savory nuggets.

In recent times, to safeguard the ascolana tenera variety, a local manufacturer obtained the Oliva Ascolana del Piceno DOP recognition.

According to regulations, the olives are harvested by hand from early September to mid-October, and, in the Ascoli Piceno area, they then undergo a debittering process, are subsequently pitted and stuffed with a mixture of beef, pork, and a small percentage of chicken or turkey, and seasoned with Parmesan, nutmeg, and cloves. After resting for a few hours, they are breaded and deep-fried.

FIORI DI ZUCCA FRITTI

YIELD: 12 SERVINGS / **ACTIVE TIME:** 30 MINUTES / **TOTAL TIME:** 50 MINUTES

If you manage to find some fresh and large zucchini blossoms in the summer, this traditional Roman recipe makes the most of them. Filled with mozzarella and anchovies, dipped into a simple batter, and then fried, fiori di zucca fritti are the typical Roman starter when dining in a pizzeria or enjoying a summertime dinner with family or friends.

1. Carefully wash the zucchini blossoms and place them on a kitchen towel to dry.

2. Open each zucchini blossom, making sure not to tear it, and stuff it with a strip of mozzarella and 1 anchovy. Close the tip of the flower over itself to seal the stuffing inside.

3. Place the flour, sugar, and salt in a bowl. While whisking, gradually add the sparkling water until the mixture comes together as a smooth batter.

4. Add olive oil to a narrow, deep, and heavy-bottomed saucepan with high edges until it is about 2 inches deep and warm it to 350°F.

5. Dredge the zucchini blossoms, 1 at a time, in the batter until they are completely coated.

6. Working in batches to avoid crowding the pot, gently slip the stuffed zucchini blossoms into the hot oil and fry until they are golden brown, turning them over once.

7. Transfer the zucchini blossoms to a paper towel–lined plate to drain and cool before serving.

INGREDIENTS:

- 12 LARGE ZUCCHINI BLOSSOMS, STAMENS REMOVED
- 1 BALL OF FRESH MOZZARELLA CHEESE, CUT INTO STRIPS AND DRAINED
- 12 ANCHOVIES IN OLIVE OIL, DRAINED
- 1⅓ CUPS ALL-PURPOSE FLOUR
- 1 TEASPOON SUGAR
- 2 PINCHES OF KOSHER SALT
- 7 OZ. SPARKLING WATER, ICE COLD

  EXTRA-VIRGIN OLIVE OIL, AS NEEDED

BACCALÀ FRITTO

YIELD: 6 SERVINGS / **ACTIVE TIME**: 30 MINUTES / **TOTAL TIME**: 24 HOURS

This Roman appetizer is a tasty way to use up dried cod. Traditionally, it is part of the Roman-style mixed fry, usually served accompanied by fried zucchini blossoms (see page 465), Supplì al Telefono (see page 471), and Carciofi alla Giudia (see page 481).

1. Carefully rinse the dried cod, handling it very delicately.

2. Place the cod in a large bowl, cover it with cold water, and chill it in the refrigerator for 24 hours, changing the water every 8 hours.

3. Drain the cod and set it aside.

4. Place the flour and 2 pinches of salt in a bowl. While whisking, gradually add the sparkling water until the mixture comes together as a smooth batter.

5. Hold each cod fillet by the tail, remove the skin, and cut it into large chunks.

6. Add olive oil to a narrow, deep, and heavy-bottomed saucepan with high edges until it is about 2 inches deep and warm it to 350°F.

7. Dredge the cod in the batter until it is completely coated.

8. Working in batches to avoid crowding the pot, gently slip the cod into the hot oil and fry until they are golden brown, turning them over once.

9. Transfer the fried cod to a paper towel–lined plate to drain and cool. Season them with salt and serve.

INGREDIENTS:

1	LB. DRIED COD
2¾	CUPS ALL-PURPOSE FLOUR
	SALT, TO TASTE
1⅔	CUPS SPARKLING WATER, ICE COLD
	EXTRA-VIRGIN OLIVE OIL, AS NEEDED

BRUSCHETTA

YIELD: 4 SERVINGS / **ACTIVE TIME:** 10 MINUTES / **TOTAL TIME:** 15 MINUTES

The quintessential garlic bread, the classic version of bruschetta does not include tomatoes, which were a later addition. It appears that this type of bruschetta was already popular in ancient Rome, as the name is derived from the Latin word bruscare, which means "to toast" and "to roast over charcoal."

1. Toast both sides of the bread on the grill, or in a grill pan on the stove.

2. Remove the toasted bread from the cooking surface and rub both sides with the garlic.

3. Place the bread on a serving plate, drizzle olive oil generously over it, and season with salt. Serve immediately.

INGREDIENTS:

8 SLICES OF CRUSTY BREAD

2 GARLIC CLOVES, HALVED

EXTRA-VIRGIN OLIVE OIL, FOR GARNISH

SALT, TO TASTE

FRITTELLE DI BROCCOLO ROMANESCO

YIELD: 15 FRITTERS / **ACTIVE TIME:** 30 MINUTES / **TOTAL TIME:** 1 HOUR

These fritters are a must at Christmas Eve celebrations in Rome and the surrounding areas.

1. Rinse the broccoli and cut it into florets. Cut the florets that are especially large in half.

2. Bring water to a boil in a large saucepan. Add salt and the broccoli and cook until it is just tender. Drain the broccoli and let it cool.

3. Place the flour and 2 pinches of salt in a bowl. While whisking, gradually add the sparkling water until the mixture comes together as a smooth batter.

4. Add olive oil to a narrow, deep, and heavy-bottomed saucepan with high edges until it is about 2 inches deep and warm it to 350°F.

5. Dredge the broccoli in the batter until it is completely coated.

6. Working in batches of 2 or 3 to avoid crowding the pot, gently slip the broccoli into the hot oil and fry until it is golden brown, turning it over once.

7. Transfer the fried broccoli to a paper towel–lined plate to drain and cool before serving.

INGREDIENTS:

2   LBS. ROMANESCO BROCCOLI

      SALT, TO TASTE

2¾   CUPS ALL-PURPOSE FLOUR

1⅔   CUPS SPARKLING WATER, ICE COLD

      EXTRA-VIRGIN OLIVE OIL, AS NEEDED

SUPPLÌ AL TELEFONO

YIELD: 20 CROQUETTES / **ACTIVE TIME:** 30 MINUTES / **TOTAL TIME:** 1 HOUR

Supplì al telefono are risotto croquettes that are generally one of the pillars of Roman ros-ticceria and are also served in pizzerias as starters. Instead of tomatoes, you can also use a ragù as the base for the filling. If you do, just add enough water to reach the same consistency of canned crushed tomatoes.

1. Place the rice and water in a medium saucepan and bring to a boil.

2. Add the tomatoes and basil, reduce the heat to low, and season with salt. Cook, stirring frequently, until the rice is al dente, 15 to 20 minutes. Pour the rice immediately into a large rimmed baking sheet so that it will cool quickly, add the pecorino, and gently stir to combine.

3. When the rice is cool enough to handle, take a handful, place it in the palm of your hand, and flatten it. The portion of rice should weigh about 3½ oz. Place a strip of mozzarella in the center and form the rice into a ball around it. Repeat with the remaining rice and mozzarella.

4. Place the eggs in a bowl, season them with salt, and beat them lightly. Place the flour and bread crumbs in separate bowls and then dredge the supplì in the flour, then in the eggs, and then in the bread crumbs until they are coated. Set the breaded supplì aside.

5. Add olive oil to a narrow, deep, and heavy-bottomed saucepan with high edges until it is about 2 inches deep and warm it to 350°F. Working with batches of 2 to 3 supplì at a time, slip them into the hot oil and fry until golden brown, turning as necessary.

6. Remove the supplì from the hot oil and transfer them to a paper towel–lined plate to drain and cool slightly before serving.

INGREDIENTS:

- 2.2 **LBS. RISOTTO RICE, RINSED AND DRAINED**
- 6 **CUPS WATER**
- 6 **CUPS WHOLE PEELED TOMATOES, MASHED**
- 3 **HANDFULS OF FRESH BASIL, TORN**
- **SALT, TO TASTE**
- 7 **OZ. PECORINO CHEESE, GRATED**
- 4 **BALLS OF MOZZARELLA CHEESE, CUT INTO STRIPS AND DRAINED IN THE REFRIGERATOR FOR 1 HOUR**
- 6 **EGGS, LIGHTLY BEATEN**
- 1½ **CUPS ALL-PURPOSE FLOUR**
- 2 **CUPS BREAD CRUMBS**
- **EXTRA-VIRGIN OLIVE OIL, AS NEEDED**

POMODORI RIPIENI DI TONNO

YIELD: 4 SERVINGS / **ACTIVE TIME:** 15 MINUTES / **TOTAL TIME:** 1 HOUR AND 15 MINUTES

A modern summer starter that is as simple as it is delicious.

1. Core the tomatoes and turn them upside down in a colander to drain.

2. Place the tuna, mayonnaise, capers, and anchovies in a food processor and briefly blitz to combine. Season the mixture with salt and pepper, place it in an airtight container, and chill it in the refrigerator for 30 minutes.

3. Stuff the tomatoes with the tuna mixture and arrange them on a serving plate. Garnish the stuffed tomatoes with the olives and additional mayonnaise and enjoy.

INGREDIENTS:

8	MEDIUM TOMATOES
9	OZ. TUNA IN OLIVE OIL, DRAINED
3	TABLESPOONS MAYONNAISE, PLUS MORE FOR GARNISH
2	TEASPOONS CAPERS IN BRINE, DRAINED
2	ANCHOVIES IN OLIVE OIL, DRAINED
	SALT AND PEPPER, TO TASTE
4	PIMENTO-STUFFED OLIVES, HALVED, FOR GARNISH

CROSTINI AL PÂTÉ DI FEGATINI

YIELD: 6 SERVINGS / **ACTIVE TIME:** 30 MINUTES / **TOTAL TIME:** 1 HOUR AND 15 MINUTES

Also known as crostini toscani, these are a favorite starter, especially at barbecues. Typical of Tuscany, but also popular in Umbria and Lazio, the pâté is nowadays most often made with chicken liver, differently from the past when the livers and offal from other animals were used.

1. Rinse the liver under cold water and pat it dry with paper towels. Chop the liver, trimming away any green-hued parts.

2. Place the olive oil in a large skillet and warm it over medium heat. Add the onions and cook, stirring occasionally, until they are translucent, about 3 minutes.

3. Add the liver, rosemary, sage, and capers to the pan and cook, stirring occasionally, until the liver is browned all over, about 10 minutes.

4. Deglaze the pan with the wine, scraping up any browned bits from the bottom. Raise the heat to medium-high and cook until the wine has evaporated.

5. Season with salt and pepper and stir in the broth and lemon slices. Reduce the heat to low and cook for 50 minutes, stirring frequently and adding more broth as needed.

6. Remove the herbs and the lemon slices and discard them. Add the anchovy paste, stir until incorporated, and remove the pan from heat. Let the mixture cool.

7. Place the mixture in a food processor. With the food processor running, stream in olive oil until the pâté has the desired texture.

8. Serve the pâté with toasted bread and enjoy.

INGREDIENTS:

- **1.1 LBS. CHICKEN LIVER**
- **¼ CUP EXTRA-VIRGIN OLIVE OIL, PLUS MORE AS NEEDED**
- **2 ONIONS, SLICED THIN**
- **1 SPRIG OF FRESH ROSEMARY**
- **5 FRESH SAGE LEAVES**
- **1¾ OZ. CAPERS IN BRINE, DRAINED AND RINSED**
- **1 CUP DRY WHITE WINE**
- **SALT AND PEPPER, TO TASTE**
- **2 CUPS BRODO DI POLLO (SEE PAGE 805), PLUS MORE AS NEEDED**
- **2 LEMON SLICES**
- **½ TEASPOON ANCHOVY PASTE**
- **CRUSTY BREAD, SLICED AND TOASTED, FOR SERVING**

PANZANELLA ROMANA

YIELD: 4 SERVINGS / **ACTIVE TIME:** 10 MINUTES / **TOTAL TIME:** 10 MINUTES

In Tuscany, panzanella is a salad, but in Rome it's an open-faced sandwich. A popular way to recycle stale bread for centuries, this preparation was a beloved afternoon snack during my childhood.

1. Quickly dip the bread in a bowl of cold water and arrange it on a serving plate.

2. Coarsely chop the tomatoes, distribute them over the bread, and press down on them with a fork, making sure their juices moisten the bread.

3. Top the bread with the basil, drizzle olive oil over it, and season with salt. Serve immediately.

INGREDIENTS:

- 8 SLICES OF STALE CRUSTY BREAD
- 4 MEDIUM-LARGE, EXTRA-RIPE TOMATOES
- 2 HANDFULS OF FRESH BASIL, FOR TOPPING

  EXTRA-VIRGIN OLIVE OIL, FOR TOPPING

  SALT, TO TASTE

BRUSCHETTA AL POMODORO

YIELD: 4 SERVINGS / **ACTIVE TIME:** 10 MINUTES / **TOTAL TIME:** 15 MINUTES

This is one of the most popular appetizers at Italian restaurants, both in Italy and abroad. Originally from the Tuscan countryside but popular throughout Central Italy, this tomato-laden bruschetta is simpler than it is often presented abroad, forgoing the onions and olives that are typical inclusions.

1. Place the tomatoes and basil in a bowl, season with olive oil, salt, and pepper, and toss to combine.

2. Toast both sides of the bread on the grill, or in a grill pan on the stove.

3. Remove the toasted bread from the cooking surface and rub both sides with the garlic.

4. Place the bread on a serving plate, top it with the tomato mixture, and drizzle olive oil over the dish. Serve immediately.

INGREDIENTS:

4   MEDIUM-LARGE, EXTRA-RIPE TOMATOES, DESEEDED AND DICED

2   HANDFULS OF FRESH BASIL LEAVES, TORN

    EXTRA-VIRGIN OLIVE OIL, TO TASTE

    SALT AND PEPPER, TO TASTE

8   SLICES OF STALE CRUSTY BREAD

2   GARLIC CLOVES, HALVED

TUSCAN OLIVE OIL:
A MODERN EXCELLENCE

Tuscany is renowned for its beautiful hilly landscape, for its wine, and for its highly prized olive oil. The latter has become a regional treasure, with artisan producers contending for the title of the region's best. The product has indeed obtained the IGP title, which stands for Indication of Geographic Protection, given to excellent products that are closely linked to the territory they come from. The level of pomp and circumstance around Tuscan olive oil is like little else in the Italian food scene, with endless tasting events and competitions.

The iconic image of Tuscany is indeed that of a slice of bread smothered in olive oil, possibly with a glass of red wine, and the Tuscan hills in the background. With this is mind, one may think olive oil in Tuscany has been a thing since ancient times; however, this is not the case, as the cultivation of olives is a relatively recent development in the region.

While the South of Italy, especially Apulia, were big olive (and olive oil) producers since pre-Roman times, in Tuscany, olives started to be cultivated in specific areas during the fifteenth century, with the industry spreading throughout the region in the second half of the nineteenth century. The now-bustling industry got off to a slow start, as production was expensive—it took several years for new trees to become productive, and even then, productivity was low, as common people could not afford to grow olives, as it was much more profitable to use the land for wheat cultivation.

However, after centuries of incremental gains and devastating setbacks—including the disastrous Great Frost of 1709—some areas of Tuscany succeeded in becoming steady olive oil producers, namely, the upper Tyrrhenian belt and the central hills around the Arno River. Slowly, consumption of olive oil also increased among common people, who started to season bread and vegetables with the now-affordable liquid gold, creating early versions of the classics we all know and love today, like bruschetta al pomodoro and panzanella alla Toscana.

The final leap forward in olive cultivation happened between the second half of the nineteenth century and the first half of the twentieth century, when, thanks to modern techniques, the cultivation of olive trees became possible all through the region, with 25 million producing trees by the end of the 1960s, resulting in an average of 220,000 quintals of oil annually.

Nowadays, olive oil is a flourishing industry in Tuscany, with over 70,000 companies focusing their efforts around its production.

CROSTINI PROSCIUTTO E MOZZARELLA

YIELD: 4 SERVINGS / **ACTIVE TIME:** 10 MINUTES / **TOTAL TIME:** 1 HOUR AND 20 MINUTES

Ham and cheese the Italian way, baking crusty bread, Parma ham, and mozzarella in the oven.

1. Preheat the oven to 390°F and line a baking sheet with parchment paper. Arrange the bread on the baking sheet and cover each piece with a slice of ham.

2. Top the ham with the mozzarella, distributing it evenly among the slices.

3. Drizzle olive oil over the open-faced sandwiches and place them in the oven. Bake until the mozzarella has melted and the bread is golden brown, about 10 minutes.

4. Remove the open-faced sandwiches from the oven and enjoy.

INGREDIENTS:

8   SLICES OF STALE CRUSTY BREAD

8   SLICES OF PARMA HAM

3   BALLS OF MOZZARELLA CHEESE, SLICED AND DRAINED IN THE REFRIGERATOR FOR 1 HOUR

    EXTRA-VIRGIN OLIVE OIL, TO TASTE

CARCIOFI ALLA GIUDIA

YIELD: 4 SERVINGS / **ACTIVE TIME:** 40 MINUTES / **TOTAL TIME:** 2 HOURS

A must-have in Roman trattorias, carciofi alla giudia are deep-fried artichokes with an appealing melt-in-your-mouth quality. This way of cooking artichokes was developed within Rome's Jewish community, which began to populate Rome as early as 150 BCE.

1. To trim the artichokes, remove the outer layer of leaves, usually at least the first 3 layers. Cut the rest of the leaves short, in a way that only the pale green or yellow leaves remain.

2. Open the top of the artichokes and remove as much of the white pieces as possible.

3. Cut the stems, leaving only the edible hearts. Place the artichokes in a bowl of water and add the lemon juice.

4. Place one-third of the olive oil, the mint, parsley, garlic, and bread crumbs in a bowl, season with salt, and stir to combine.

5. Drain the artichokes and fill them with the herb mixture.

6. Place the remaining olive oil in a skillet and warm it over medium-high heat. Add the artichokes, upside down, season them with salt, and fry for about 10 minutes.

7. Carefully add water to the pan until the liquid covers half of the artichokes' heads. Cover the pan, reduce the heat, and cook until the artichokes are fork-tender, 1 to 1½ hours.

8. Season the artichokes with salt and pepper and serve immediately.

INGREDIENTS:

4	LARGE ARTICHOKES OR 6 MEDIUM ONES
	JUICE OF 1 LEMON
1	CUP EXTRA-VIRGIN OLIVE OIL
3	TABLESPOONS CHOPPED FRESH MINT
3	TABLESPOONS CHOPPED FRESH PARSLEY
2	GARLIC CLOVES, MINCED
⅓	CUP BREAD CRUMBS
	SALT AND PEPPER, TO TASTE

PANZANELLA ALLA TOSCANA

YIELD: 4 SERVINGS / **ACTIVE TIME:** 15 MINUTES / **TOTAL TIME:** 1 HOUR AND 15 MINUTES

Probably the most famous Tuscan salad, panzanella alla Toscana used to be one of the many ways to recycle stale bread in rural Central Italy, where bread could never be thrown away.

1. Place the vinegar and water in a bowl and stir to combine. Dip the bread in the mixture until it has softened.

2. Squeeze the bread and tear it into large pieces.

3. Place the bread in a bowl, season it with salt and olive oil, and add the tomatoes. Toss until the bread has turned red.

4. Add the cucumber, onion, and basil, season the salad with salt and pepper, and drizzle olive oil over the top.

5. Cover the bowl with plastic wrap and chill it in the refrigerator for at least 1 hour before serving.

INGREDIENTS:

3   TABLESPOONS WHITE WINE VINEGAR

2   CUPS WATER

1   LB. STALE CRUSTY BREAD, SLICED

    SALT AND PEPPER, TO TASTE

    EXTRA-VIRGIN OLIVE OIL, TO TASTE

2   RIPE ROMA TOMATOES, FINELY DICED

1   CUCUMBER, SLICED

1   LARGE RED OR WHITE ONION, FINELY DICED

2   HANDFULS OF FRESH BASIL LEAVES, TORN

CAVOLO NERO IN PADELLA

YIELD: 4 SERVINGS / **ACTIVE TIME:** 20 MINUTES / **TOTAL TIME:** 50 MINUTES

In Central Italy, cavolo nero, or Tuscan kale, rules. It is a beloved vegetable that has a pungent, earthy flavor but a much smoother and more palatable consistency than regular kale (cavolo riccio).

1. Bring water to a boil in a large saucepan and prepare an ice bath. Add salt and the kale to the boiling water and cook until the toughest parts of the kale have softened, about 15 minutes.

2. Drain the kale and plunge it into the ice bath. Drain it again, squeeze the kale to remove any excess water, chop it, and set it aside.

3. Place the olive oil in a large skillet and warm it over low heat. Add the garlic and chile and until the garlic is lightly browned, about 1 minute.

4. Add the kale, season with salt, and reduce the heat to low. Cook for 10 to 15 minutes, stirring occasionally.

5. Top the dish with the mozzarella and cook until the cheese has melted. Serve immediately.

INGREDIENTS:

SALT, TO TASTE

1.1 LBS. TUSCAN KALE, WOODY STEMS REMOVED

3 TABLESPOONS EXTRA-VIRGIN OLIVE OIL

1 GARLIC CLOVE, MINCED

½ MEDIUM-HOT CHILE PEPPER, MINCED

2 BALLS OF MOZZARELLA CHEESE, SLICED AND DRAINED IN THE REFRIGERATOR FOR 1 HOUR

PISELLI AL PROSCIUTTO

YIELD: 4 SERVINGS / **ACTIVE TIME:** 20 MINUTES / **TOTAL TIME:** 50 MINUTES

Perfect beside Saltimbocca alla Romana (see page 539), this dish is also delicious on its own, served with toasted slices of crusty bread.

1. Place half of the butter and the fatty pieces of ham in a skillet and warm the mixture over medium heat. Add the onion and cook, stirring occasionally, until it is translucent, about 3 minutes.

2. Add the peas and cook, stirring occasionally, until they start to brown.

3. Add the broth, season with salt and pepper, and cover the pan. Cook until the peas are tender, adding more broth if the mixture starts to look dry.

4. Add the remaining ham and butter and stir to combine. Cook for 5 minutes and serve immediately.

INGREDIENTS:

2 TABLESPOONS UNSALTED BUTTER

3½ OZ. PARMA HAM, CUT INTO STRIPS, FATTY PARTS REMOVED AND RESERVED

1 SMALL WHITE ONION, FINELY DICED

2.2 LBS. PEAS

1 CUP BRODO DI POLLO (SEE PAGE 805), PLUS MORE AS NEEDED

 SALT AND PEPPER, TO TASTE

PUNTARELLE ALLA ROMANA

YIELD: 4 SERVINGS / **ACTIVE TIME:** 20 MINUTES / **TOTAL TIME:** 20 MINUTES

Puntarelle are the sprouts of a type of chicory, and are considered a real delicacy in Rome. If you manage to get hold of some, this is the way they are traditionally prepared.

1. Using a mortar and pestle, work the garlic, anchovies, olive oil, and vinegar until combined. Set the mixture aside.

2. To trim the puntarelle, remove the outer leaves and cut them into long strips. There is a specific tool for cutting puntarelle, but you can achieve decent results with a sharp knife.

3. Place the puntarelle in a bowl, add some cold water, and toss until they curl up.

4. Drain the puntarelle, add the vinaigrette, and toss to combine. Serve immediately.

INGREDIENTS:

½ GARLIC CLOVE, MINCED

4 ANCHOVIES PACKED IN SALT, RINSED AND DRAINED

¼ CUP EXTRA-VIRGIN OLIVE OIL

1 TABLESPOON WHITE WINE VINEGAR

1 HEAD OF PUNTARELLE

FRICANDÒ DI VERDURE

YIELD: 4 SERVINGS / **ACTIVE TIME:** 20 MINUTES / **TOTAL TIME:** 1 HOUR

Typical of the Marche region, fricandò, or frecantò, is the Italian equivalent of ratatouille. This lovely stew of summer vegetables and potatoes is as easy to make as it is enjoyable to eat.

1. Place the olive oil in a large skillet and warm it over medium-low heat. Add the garlic and cook, stirring frequently, for 2 minutes.

2. Add the zucchini, potatoes, eggplant, peppers, and onions, season with salt, and stir to combine. Raise the heat to high and cook for 10 minutes.

3. Reduce the heat and cover the pan. Cook for about 20 minutes, tossing the vegetables occasionally and taking care not to break them.

4. Add the tomatoes and gently toss to incorporate them. Cover the pan and cook for another 15 minutes. Serve immediately.

INGREDIENTS:

¼ CUP EXTRA-VIRGIN OLIVE OIL

2 GARLIC CLOVES

3 ZUCCHINI, DICED

2 MEDIUM POTATOES, PEELED AND DICED

1 ROUND EGGPLANT, DICED

2 BELL PEPPERS, STEMS AND SEEDS REMOVED, DICED

2 ONIONS, CHOPPED

   SALT, TO TASTE

2 RED TOMATOES, PEELED AND CHOPPED

PRIMI

ACQUACOTTA DELLA TRANSUMANZA

YIELD: 4 SERVINGS / ACTIVE TIME: 20 MINUTES / TOTAL TIME: 1 HOUR AND 20 MINUTES

Acquacotta ("cooked water") is a shepherd's soup that is particularly appreciated in Maremma, Tuscany. This type of soup was traditionally eaten during the transumanza (when the herds are moved to different grazing areas) and was made with wild vegetables foraged from the pastures, water, eggs, and, when available, grated cheese.

1. Place the olive oil in a large saucepan and warm it over medium heat. Add the onions and cook, stirring occasionally, until they have softened, about 5 minutes.

2. Add the celery, carrots, potatoes, and leafy greens, raise the heat to medium-high, and cook, stirring occasionally, for 5 minutes.

3. Deglaze the pan with the wine, scraping up any browned bits from the bottom. Cook for 5 minutes.

4. Add enough water to cover the vegetables, season with salt and red pepper flakes, and reduce the heat to medium-low. Cover the pan with a lid and simmer the vegetables until they are tender, about 50 minutes.

5. Stir in the eggs and cook until they are set.

6. To serve, divide the bread among the serving bowls, ladle the acquacotta over each one, and garnish with the pecorino.

INGREDIENTS:

- 3 TABLESPOONS EXTRA-VIRGIN OLIVE OIL
- 8 WHITE ONIONS, FINELY DICED
- 4 CELERY STALKS, PEELED AND CHOPPED
- 2 CARROTS, PEELED AND CHOPPED
- 4 POTATOES, PEELED AND CHOPPED
- 3 CUPS LEAFY GREEN VEGETABLES, CHOPPED
- 1 CUP WHITE WINE
-   SALT, TO TASTE
-   RED PEPPER FLAKES, TO TASTE
- 4 EGGS
- 4 SLICES OF STALE OR TOASTED BREAD, FOR SERVING
- ¼ CUP GRATED PECORINO CHEESE, FOR GARNISH

STRACCIATELLA ALLA ROMANA

YIELD: 4 SERVINGS / **ACTIVE TIME:** 10 MINUTES / **TOTAL TIME:** 20 MINUTES

A simple soup that is a favorite at Easter celebrations in Rome, as it contains eggs, a symbol of rebirth, and it is light, leaving space for the lamb roast that usually serves as the entree on such occasions. Stracciatella is also frequently prepared when one is feeling under the weather, as it is nourishing and easy to make and digest.

1. Place the eggs and pecorino in a bowl and whisk until well combined.

2. Place the broth in a medium saucepan and warm it over medium heat. When it is almost boiling, pour the egg-and-cheese mixture into the broth, whisking vigorously. You want to make sure that the egg sets in thin strands, avoiding the formation of lumps.

3. Season the soup with salt, pepper, and nutmeg and cook for 2 minutes.

4. Ladle the soup into warmed bowls and enjoy.

INGREDIENTS:

4   EGGS

¼   CUP GRATED PECORINO
       CHEESE

6   CUPS BRODO DI CARNE
       (SEE PAGE 805)

       SALT AND PEPPER, TO
       TASTE

       FRESHLY GRATED NUTMEG,
       TO TASTE

PAPPA AL POMODORO

YIELD: 4 SERVINGS / **ACTIVE TIME:** 10 MINUTES / **TOTAL TIME:** 1 HOUR

Pappa al pomodoro, literally "tomato mash," is a simple tomato-and-bread soup from rural Tuscany that is very versatile, as it is enjoyable served hot or cold.

1. Place the beans in a large pot, cover them with cold water, and bring to a boil. Reduce the heat and simmer the beans until they are tender, 45 minutes to 1 hour, seasoning them with salt halfway through. Drain the beans and set them aside.

2. Rub the slices of bread with the garlic.

3. Place half of the olive oil in a large pot and arrange the slices of bread on the bottom.

4. Pour the tomatoes and broth over the bread. Add the sugar, season with salt and pepper, and gently stir. Cover the pan and cook the soup over low heat, stirring occasionally, until the bread becomes pulpy, about 50 minutes.

5. Taste the soup and adjust the seasoning as necessary. Ladle the soup into warmed bowls, drizzle the remaining olive oil over each portion, garnish with the fresh basil, and serve.

INGREDIENTS:

12   OZ. STALE CRUSTY BREAD, SLICED AND LIGHTLY TOASTED

2   GARLIC CLOVES, HALVED

¼   CUP EXTRA-VIRGIN OLIVE OIL

2   LBS. WHOLE PEELED TOMATOES, CRUSHED

4   CUPS BRODO VEGETALE (SEE PAGE 806)

1   TEASPOON SUGAR

     SALT AND PEPPER, TO TASTE

2   HANDFULS OF FRESH BASIL, TORN, FOR GARNISH

ZUPPA DI CAVOLO NERO

YIELD: 4 SERVINGS / **ACTIVE TIME:** 20 MINUTES / **TOTAL TIME:** 24 HOURS

It is interesting that in the land of the famed Fiorentina steaks, so many traditional dishes are vegan. This quintessential Tuscan soup features the earthy Tuscan kale and Tuscany's favorite bean, the cannellini.

1. Place the beans in a large pot, cover them with cold water, and bring to a boil. Reduce the heat and simmer the beans until they are tender, 45 minutes to 1 hour, seasoning them with salt halfway through. Drain the beans and set them aside.

2. Place the olive oil in a medium saucepan and warm it over medium heat. Add the onion, carrot, and celery and cook, stirring occasionally, until they have softened, about 6 minutes.

3. Stir in the kale, potatoes, and bay leaf and then add the broth and tomatoes. Season with salt, cover the pan, and cook until the potatoes and carrots are tender, 15 to 20 minutes.

4. Remove the bay leaf and discard it. Add the beans, season with salt, and simmer the soup for 10 minutes.

5. Ladle the soup into warmed bowls, serve with crusty bread, and enjoy.

INGREDIENTS:

1.1 LBS. CANNELLINI BEANS, SOAKED OVERNIGHT AND DRAINED

SALT, TO TASTE

¼ CUP EXTRA-VIRGIN OLIVE OIL

1 WHITE ONION, SLICED

1 CARROT, PEELED AND SLICED

1 CELERY STALK, SLICED

1 LB. TUSCAN KALE, TOUGH STEMS REMOVED, LEAVES HALVED

2 POTATOES, PEELED AND DICED

1 BAY LEAF

4 CUPS BRODO VEGETALE (SEE PAGE 806)

1 CUP WHOLE PEELED TOMATOES, CRUSHED

STALE CRUSTY BREAD, SLICED AND TOASTED, FOR SERVING

ZUPPA DI PORRI ALLA TOSCANA

YIELD: 4 SERVINGS / *ACTIVE TIME:* 20 MINUTES / *TOTAL TIME:* 1 HOUR

If you prefer, you can prepare this in a deep baking dish, layering the bread on the bottom, covering it with the soup, and topping with the pine nuts and cheese. Bake for 10 to 15 minutes at 350°F.

1. Place the olive oil in a medium saucepan and warm it over low heat. Add the leeks and cook, stirring occasionally, until they are tender, about 10 minutes. If the leeks start sticking to the pan, add a few tablespoons of water.

2. Add the flour and stir until it has been incorporated.

3. Add the broth, season with salt, and cook until the leeks have almost dissolved.

4. Divide the bread among the serving bowls and ladle the soup over it. Garnish each portion with the pine nuts and Parmesan and serve.

INGREDIENTS:

¼ CUP EXTRA-VIRGIN OLIVE OIL

2.2 LBS. LEEKS, WHITE PARTS ONLY, RINSED WELL AND SLICED

2 TABLESPOONS ALL-PURPOSE FLOUR

4 CUPS BRODO VEGETALE (SEE PAGE 806)

SALT, TO TASTE

8 SLICES OF STALE CRUSTY BREAD

3 TABLESPOONS PINE NUTS, FOR GARNISH

3½ OZ. PARMESAN CHEESE, GRATED, FOR GARNISH

PICI AL RAGÙ BIANCO

YIELD: 4 SERVINGS / **ACTIVE TIME:** 10 MINUTES / **TOTAL TIME:** 20 MINUTES

Pici are a handmade pasta typical of southern Tuscany and Umbria. The Ragù Bianco can also be used with other pasta formats, but it is excellent over pici.

1. Place the ragù in a large skillet and warm it over medium heat.

2. Bring water to a boil in a large saucepan. Add salt, let the water return to a full boil, and add the pasta. Cook the pasta until it is very al dente. Reserve ½ cup pasta water and drain the pasta.

3. Add the pasta to the ragù. Add pasta water until the sauce has the desired consistency and cook, tossing to combine, for 2 to 3 minutes. Serve immediately.

INGREDIENTS:

RAGÙ BIANCO (SEE PAGE 809)

SALT, TO TASTE

PICI (SEE PAGE 66)

RIBOLLITA TOSCANA

YIELD: 6 SERVINGS / **ACTIVE TIME:** 30 MINUTES / **TOTAL TIME:** 24 HOURS

Probably the most famous Tuscan soup, ribollita is one of the many ways small farmers used up every bit of their bread allowance. The key to a proper ribollita is letting the bread soak up all of the soup before it is reheated, as ribollita means "reboiled."

1. Place the beans in a large pot, cover them with cold water, and bring to a boil. Reduce the heat and simmer the beans until they are tender, 45 minutes to 1 hour, seasoning them with salt halfway through. Drain the beans and set them aside.

2. Place the olive oil in a medium saucepan and warm it over medium heat. Add the onions, carrots, celery, and rosemary and cook, stirring occasionally, until they have softened, about 6 minutes.

3. Add the leafy greens and potatoes, and then add the broth and tomatoes. Season the soup with salt and pepper, cover the pan, and cook until the potatoes and carrots are tender, 15 to 20 minutes.

4. Place half of the beans in a bowl and mash them.

5. Remove the rosemary and discard it. Add the beans, season the soup with salt and pepper, and cook for 10 minutes.

6. Arrange half of the bread in a Dutch oven and cover it with half of the soup.

7. Top with the remaining bread and ladle the remaining soup over it.

8. Cover the pot and let the ribollita rest at room temperature for 1 hour.

9. Place the pot on the stove and cook the ribollita over medium heat until it is hot, about 10 minutes.

10. Ladle the ribollita into warmed bowls, drizzle olive oil over each portion, and serve.

INGREDIENTS:

- 2 LBS. DRIED CANNELLINI BEANS, SOAKED OVERNIGHT AND DRAINED
- SALT AND PEPPER, TO TASTE
- ¼ CUP EXTRA-VIRGIN OLIVE OIL, PLUS MORE FOR GARNISH
- 2 SMALL WHITE ONIONS, SLICED
- 3 CARROTS, PEELED AND SLICED
- 2 CELERY STALKS, SLICED
- 2 SPRIGS OF FRESH ROSEMARY
- 2 LBS. MIXED LEAFY GREEN VEGETABLES (TUSCAN KALE, SAVOY CABBAGE, COLLARD GREENS), TOUGH STEMS REMOVED, CHOPPED
- 4 MEDIUM POTATOES, PEELED AND DICED
- 6 CUPS BRODO VEGETALE (SEE PAGE 806)
- 1 CUP WHOLE PEELED TOMATOES, CRUSHED
- 8 THICK SLICES OF STALE CRUSTY BREAD

IMBRECCIATA UMBRA

YIELD: 6 SERVINGS / **ACTIVE TIME:** 20 MINUTES / **TOTAL TIME:** 1 HOUR AND 30 MINUTES

An ancient Umbrian soup traditionally made to utilize leftover pulses and cereals in the pantry, imbrecciata is delicious served hot or cold.

1. Place the chickpeas and beans in a large pot, cover them with cold water, and bring to a boil. Reduce the heat and simmer the chickpeas and beans until they are tender, 1 to 1½ hours, seasoning them with salt halfway through. Drain the legumes and set them aside.

2. Place the lentils in a saucepan and cover them with water. Bring to a boil, reduce the heat so that the water simmers, and cook until the lentils are tender, 15 to 20 minutes. Drain the lentils and set them aside.

3. Place the barley in a bowl, cover it with boiling water, and cover the bowl with a kitchen towel. Let the barley sit until it has absorbed the water and become tender, 25 to 30 minutes. Set the barley aside.

4. Place the lard in a medium saucepan and warm it over medium heat. When most of the lard has melted, remove any parts that did not melt.

5. Add the olive oil and warm it. Add the onions, garlic, celery, and carrots and cook, stirring occasionally, until they are tender, about 10 minutes.

6. Add the water and tomatoes and cook until the water has reduced by half.

7. Either strain the broth to remove the vegetables or puree the broth with an immersion blender.

8. Add the chickpeas, beans, corn, lentils, and barley, season the soup with salt and pepper, and cook until everything is warmed through and the flavor has developed to your liking, 10 to 15 minutes.

9. Ladle the soup into warmed bowls, drizzle olive oil over each portion, and serve.

INGREDIENTS:

- 1 CUP DRIED CHICKPEAS, SOAKED OVERNIGHT AND DRAINED
- 1 CUP DRIED CANNELLINI OR BORLOTTI BEANS, SOAKED OVERNIGHT AND DRAINED
- 1 DRIED BROAD BEANS, SOAKED OVERNIGHT AND DRAINED
- SALT AND PEPPER, TO TASTE
- ¾ CUP LENTILS
- 1 CUP BARLEY
- 2 OZ. LARD, FINELY DICED
- 3 TABLESPOONS EXTRA-VIRGIN OLIVE OIL, PLUS MORE FOR GARNISH
- 2 SMALL ONIONS, FINELY DICED
- 2 GARLIC CLOVES, MINCED
- 2 CELERY STALKS, FINELY DICED
- 2 CARROTS, PEELED AND FINELY DICED
- 12 CUPS WATER
- 1 CUP WHOLE PEELED TOMATOES, CRUSHED
- 1 CUP CORN

BARZOFFIA CIOCIARA

YIELD: 6 SERVINGS / **ACTIVE TIME:** 30 MINUTES / **TOTAL TIME:** 1 HOUR AND 15 MINUTES

A lovely spring soup from the Appenine Mountains in Lazio, specifically Monti Lepini.

1. To trim the artichokes, cut the stems, leaving just 1 inch attached to the flower. Remove the outer leaves and trim the hearts, removing the pointy ends and the beards. Cut the artichokes into thin wedges, place them in a bowl, and cover them with cold water. Add the lemon juice and set the artichokes aside.

2. Place the olive oil in a large saucepan and warm it over medium heat. Add the onion and cook, stirring occasionally, until it is translucent, about 3 minutes.

3. Add the chard, lettuce, peas, and beans. Drain the artichokes and add them along with the water. Season the broth with salt and pepper, cover the pan, and bring the broth to a simmer.

4. Reduce the heat to low and gently simmer the soup until the artichokes, beans, and chard are tender.

5. Gently slide the eggs into the soup and poach until the whites are set, 4 to 5 minutes.

6. Remove the eggs with a slotted spoon and set them aside.

7. Divide the bread among the serving bowls and ladle the soup over it. Top each portion with a poached egg and some pecorino and serve.

INGREDIENTS:

4	ARTICHOKES
	JUICE OF 1 LEMON
¼	CUP EXTRA-VIRGIN OLIVE OIL
1	ONION, SLICED
2	LEAVES OF CHARD, CHOPPED
5	LEAVES OF ROMAINE LETTUCE, CHOPPED
2½	CUPS GREEN PEAS
2½	CUPS BROAD BEANS
6	CUPS BOILING WATER
	SALT AND PEPPER, TO TASTE
4	EGGS
8	SLICES OF STALE CRUSTY BREAD
¼	CUP GRATED PECORINO CHEESE, FOR GARNISH

PAPPARDELLE AL RAGÙ DI CINGHIALE

YIELD: 4 SERVINGS / **ACTIVE TIME:** 10 MINUTES / **TOTAL TIME:** 20 MINUTES

Wild boars are very common in Central Italy, and as such, we find several dishes based around their rich meat.

1. Place the ragù in a large skillet and warm it over medium heat.

2. Bring water to a boil in a large saucepan. Add salt, let the water return to a full boil, and add the pasta. Cook the pasta until it is al dente. Reserve ½ cup pasta water and drain the pasta.

3. Add the pasta to the ragù. Add pasta water until the sauce has the desired consistency and cook, tossing to combine, for 2 to 3 minutes. Serve immediately.

INGREDIENTS:

RAGÙ DI CINGHIALE (SEE PAGE 810)

SALT, TO TASTE

14 OZ. PAPPARDELLE

GNUDI TOSCANI

YIELD: 6 SERVINGS / **ACTIVE TIME**: 30 MINUTES / **TOTAL TIME**: 40 MINUTES

Gnudi look like big gnocchi but are made of spinach and cheese, which would traditionally fill ravioli. They are indeed "naked" ravioli, as their name suggests.

1. Bring water to a boil in a large saucepan. Add salt and the spinach and cook for 3 minutes. Drain the spinach and let it cool. When it is cool enough to handle, squeeze the spinach to remove as much water as possible.

2. Place the spinach in a bowl, add the ricotta, egg, and Parmesan, and season the mixture with salt and pepper. Stir until well combined.

3. Check to see if the mixture is dry enough to shape. If it is not, incorporate 1 teaspoon of flour at a time until the mixture has the right consistency.

4. Dust your hands with flour and shape the mixture into rounds or ovals.

5. Bring water to a boil in a large saucepan. Working with a few gnudi at a time, add them to the water. Once they rise to the surface, cook the gnudi for another minute and then gently remove them with a strainer or pasta fork.

6. Place the gnudi in a serving dish, add the tomato sauce, and gently toss to combine. Top with the basil and olive oil and serve.

INGREDIENTS:

SALT AND PEPPER, TO TASTE

8 CUPS FRESH SPINACH

1 CUP RICOTTA CHEESE, DRAINED IN THE REFRIGERATOR FOR AT LEAST 1 HOUR

1 SMALL EGG

½ CUP GRATED PARMESAN CHEESE

ALL-PURPOSE FLOUR, AS NEEDED

SUGO AL BASILICO (SEE PAGE 806), WARM

HANDFUL OF FRESH BASIL, TORN, FOR GARNISH

EXTRA-VIRGIN OLIVE OIL, FOR GARNISH

VINCISGRASSI

YIELD: 6 SERVINGS / **ACTIVE TIME:** 20 MINUTES / **TOTAL TIME:** 1 HOUR

This is a type of lasagna popular in Marche, particularly in the city of Ancona. Its name has a belligerent origin: in 1799, Ancona was under attack. When the Austrian general Alfred von Windisch-Graetz won, the city gave him this recipe as a present. From then on it was called vincisgrassi, for that was how the locals pronounced the general's name.

1. Preheat the oven to 350°F. If using dried lasagna sheets, bring water to a boil in a large saucepan. Add salt, let the water return to a full boil, and add the lasagna. Cook until it is al dente. Drain the pasta.

2. Spread some ragù over the bottom of a large baking dish. Place some lasagna on top, spread a thin layer of ragù on top, and top this with a generous sprinkle of Parmesan. Repeat until you have 10 layers.

3. Place the lasagna in the oven and bake until it is bubbling, about 30 minutes. Remove the lasagna from the oven and let it rest for 20 minutes before slicing and serving.

INGREDIENTS:

SALT, TO TASTE

10 LARGE LASAGNA SHEETS OR 40 SMALL ONES

RAGÙ RICCO (SEE PAGE 808)

1½ CUPS GRATED PARMESAN CHEESE

STRANGOZZI AL TARTUFO NERO

YIELD: 4 SERVINGS / **ACTIVE TIME:** 15 MINUTES / **TOTAL TIME:** 25 MINUTES

Strangozzi (or stringozzi) are a handmade pasta popular in Umbria, particularly in the areas including Foligno and Spoleto. They can also be found in the Marche region, and in parts of Lazio.

1. Bring water to a boil in a large saucepan. Using a kitchen brush, remove any soil from the truffles. Cut them into small, thin flakes and set them aside.

2. Place the olive oil in a large skillet and warm it over medium-low heat. Add the garlic and cook, stirring frequently, for 2 minutes.

3. Remove the pan from heat, remove the garlic, and discard it. Stir the truffles into the infused oil and set it aside.

4. Add salt, let the water return to a full boil, and add the pasta. Cook the pasta until it is al dente.

5. Drain the pasta, add it to the truffle oil, and toss to combine. Serve immediately.

INGREDIENTS:

3½ OZ. BLACK TRUFFLES

5 TABLESPOONS EXTRA-VIRGIN OLIVE OIL

2 GARLIC CLOVES, HALVED

SALT, TO TASTE

STRANGOZZI (SEE PAGE 60)

PENNE ALL'ARRABBIATA

YIELD: 4 SERVINGS / **ACTIVE TIME:** 20 MINUTES / **TOTAL TIME:** 30 MINUTES

A popular Roman pasta dish that was developed during the 1950s, arrabbiata means "angry" in Italian, referring to the spiciness of the chile-enriched sauce.

1. Place the olive oil in a large skillet and warm it over low heat. Add the garlic and chiles and cook until the garlic is lightly browned.

2. Add the tomatoes, season with salt, and raise the heat to medium, cook stirring occasionally, for 10 to 15 minutes.

3. Remove the garlic from the pan, reduce the heat to medium-low, and gently simmer the sauce.

4. Bring water to a boil in a large saucepan. Add salt, let the water return to a full boil, and add the pasta. Cook the pasta until it is al dente. Drain the pasta and place it in a bowl.

5. Add the sauce, parsley, and pecorino to the bowl and toss to combine. Serve immediately with additional pecorino.

INGREDIENTS:

¼ CUP EXTRA-VIRGIN OLIVE OIL

2 GARLIC CLOVES, HALVED

2 HOT CHILE PEPPERS, STEMS AND SEEDS REMOVED, SLICED THIN

1.1 LBS. WHOLE PEELED TOMATOES, LIGHTLY CRUSHED

SALT, TO TASTE

1 LB. PENNE RIGATE

HANDFUL OF FRESH PARSLEY, CHOPPED

1 (HEAPING) CUP GRATED PECORINO CHEESE, PLUS MORE FOR SERVING

PASTA ALLA NORCINA

YIELD: 4 SERVINGS / **ACTIVE TIME:** 20 MINUTES / **TOTAL TIME:** 35 MINUTES

This dish is also good with fettuccine in place of the penne.

1. Bring water to a boil in a large saucepan. Place the olive oil in a large skillet and warm it over medium-high heat. Add the onion and garlic and cook, stirring frequently, until the onion is translucent, about 3 minutes.

2. Add the sausage and cook, stirring occasionally, until it starts to brown.

3. Deglaze the pan with the wine and cook until it has evaporated.

4. Add salt, let the water return to a full boil, and add the pasta. Cook the pasta until it is al dente. Reserve 1 cup pasta water and drain the pasta.

5. Add the ricotta and a few tablespoons of pasta water to the skillet and stir to combine.

6. Add the Parmesan and pasta, season with salt and pepper, and cook for 2 to 3 minutes, tossing to combine.

7. Garnish the dish with truffle flakes and serve.

INGREDIENTS:

3	TABLESPOONS EXTRA-VIRGIN OLIVE OIL
½	ONION, SLICED THIN
1	GARLIC CLOVE, HALVED
11	OZ. ITALIAN SAUSAGE, CASINGS REMOVED, CRUMBLED
½	CUP WHITE WINE
	SALT AND PEPPER, TO TASTE
1	LB. PENNE
7	OZ. RICOTTA CHEESE
½	CUP GRATED PARMESAN CHEESE
	TRUFFLES, CUT INTO SMALL, THIN FLAKES, FOR GARNISH

THE ELUSIVE CARBONARA

Over the decades of making my way through traditional Italian food, I have discovered that pasta alla carbonara is, by far, the dish surrounded by the most heated debate.

It appears that everyone knows the proper way to cook this classic of Roman and Italian cuisine, which is currently one of the most popular pasta dishes in the world. With pasta water and never with cream, with egg yolks and never egg whites, with guanciale and never pancetta or bacon, with pecorino cheese and never with Parmesan. And only with spaghetti, right?

The truth is that no one knows what the truly authentic recipe for pasta carbonara is. Was it really made only with egg yolks? Was the meat of choice really guanciale? Where does carbonara come from? When was it first developed?

All we know for sure is that this way to serve pasta became popular after World War II in Rome, when it started to appear on the menus of several restaurants in the Italian capital. Around that time, the current go-to recipe was developed, which did include egg yolks, guanciale, pecorino, and spaghetti as the preferred pasta format. But what about prior to then?

Little is known around the origins of carbonara, but a few facts are certain. First, the most extensive Italian cookbook at the time, *Il talismano della felicità* by Ada Boni, which was first published in 1929, did not have a carbonara recipe in its prewar editions. Boni was Roman, thus, we know that the dish was not around in Rome before the war. We also know from its name that carbonara had something to do with the carbonari, the seasonal workers who were tasked with harvesting wood and burning it to make charcoal. Many carbonari were working in the Apennine Mountains on the border between Lazio and Abruzzi, and they were known to have a favorite meal consisting of a simple pasta with cheese and eggs, pasta cacio e uova. It is therefore not too difficult to imagine that during the war something happened, and cacio e ova turned into the carbonara we know and love today, thanks to the simple addition of cured pork.

Others think that carbonara was born in Rome after the American troops reached it, as it was a means of using the dried eggs and bacon brought by the soldiers. Possible, but then why the name carbonara? And how come this pasta was so similar to the carbonari's go-to meal?

In either of these scenarios, it is likely that the first carbonara did not use guanciale, but bacon, and made use of whole eggs instead of just egg yolks. It appears that the current fashionable version was a late development, devised by Roman professional cooks.

SPAGHETTI ALLA CARBONARA

YIELD: 4 SERVINGS / **ACTIVE TIME:** 20 MINUTES / **TOTAL TIME:** 25 MINUTES

Here follows the contemporary version of pasta carbonara, with no claim of authenticity. The trick to making this pasta restaurant perfect is speed, as it is crucial to work fast toward the end, as just a few extra minutes will spoil the creaminess of the sauce and result in a yellow glue instead of a sultry carbonara.

1. Place the guanciale in a large skillet and warm it over medium-low heat. Cook until the guanciale has rendered most of its fat and is lightly browned. Remove the guanciale from the pan and set it aside.

2. Place the egg yolks and Pecorino in a large bowl and lightly beat to combine. Season the mixture with a generous amount of pepper and set it aside.

3. Bring water to a boil in a large saucepan. Add salt, let the water return to a full boil, and add the pasta. Cook the pasta until it is al dente.

4. Drain the pasta and add it to the bowl containing the egg-and-cheese mixture along with the guanciale. Toss to combine and serve immediately.

INGREDIENTS:

6½ OZ. GUANCIALE, CUT INTO 1-INCH-LONG AND ¼-INCH-THICK STRIPS

5 EGG YOLKS

⅔ CUP GRATED PECORINO CHEESE

SALT AND PEPPER, TO TASTE

1 LB. SPAGHETTI

SPAGHETTI CON RICOTTA

YIELD: 4 SERVINGS / **ACTIVE TIME:** 10 MINUTES / **TOTAL TIME:** 20 MINUTES

Though not as famous as other Roman pasta dishes, this creamy preparation was a childhood favorite of mine, and something I still go back to when I want something easy and comforting.

1. Bring water to a boil in a large saucepan. Add salt, let the water return to a full boil, and add the pasta. Cook the pasta until it is al dente.

2. Place the ricotta and pecorino in a large bowl and add a few tablespoons of pasta water. Season with salt and pepper and whisk to combine.

3. Reserve 1 cup of pasta water, drain the pasta, and place it in the bowl.

4. Toss to combine, adding pasta water as needed to get the desired consistency. Serve immediately.

INGREDIENTS:

SALT AND PEPPER, TO TASTE

1 LB. SPAGHETTI

1.1 LBS. RICOTTA CHEESE (MADE FROM SHEEP'S MILK PREFERRED)

1½ CUPS GRATED PECORINO CHEESE

PASTA CACIO E PEPE

YIELD: 4 SERVINGS / **ACTIVE TIME:** 20 MINUTES / **TOTAL TIME:** 25 MINUTES

A dish that originated in Lazio's countryside, pasta cacio e pepe has become one of the classic dishes of Roman cuisine, served in countless restaurants and trattorias. The ingredients are few but need to be utilized masterfully to achieve the desired result.

1. Use a spice grinder or mortar and pestle to coarsely grind the peppercorns. Set them aside.

2. Bring water to a boil in a large saucepan. Add salt, let the water return to a full boil, and add the pasta. Cook the pasta until it is very al dente. Reserve 1 cup of pasta water, drain the pasta, and set it aside.

3. Place 1 tablespoon of the ground pepper in a large skillet and toast it over medium heat for 1 minute. Add a few tablespoons of pasta water and stir to incorporate.

4. Place the pecorino and a few tablespoons of pasta water in a bowl and stir to combine. Set the mixture aside.

5. Add the pasta to the skillet, raise the heat to medium-high, and cook for 2 to 3 minutes, tossing to combine.

6. Pour the pasta into the bowl with the pecorino cream and toss to combine, adding more pasta water if needed to get the desired consistency.

7. Serve with the remaining ground pepper and additional pecorino on the side.

INGREDIENTS:

2 TABLESPOONS BLACK PEPPERCORNS

SALT, TO TASTE

1 LB. TONNARELLI (SEE PAGE 64) OR SPAGHETTI

3 CUPS GRATED PECORINO CHEESE, PLUS MORE TO TASTE

PASTA ALLA GRICIA

YIELD: 4 SERVINGS / **ACTIVE TIME:** 20 MINUTES / **TOTAL TIME:** 25 MINUTES

Also called amatriciana bianca, pasta alla gricia features several of Lazio's typical ingredients: guanciale, pecorino, and black pepper. Its name derives either from the "grici," sellers of basic foods like cured meats and cheese, or a small town called Grisciano, which is close to Amatrice, the city that gave birth to the famous amatriciana. This pasta is delicious only if the main ingredients are top-notch, especially the guanciale.

1. Place the guanciale in a large skillet and warm it over medium-low heat. Cook until the guanciale has rendered most of its fat and is lightly browned. Remove the guanciale from the pan with a slotted spoon and set it aside.

2. Bring water to a boil in a large saucepan. Add salt, let the water return to a full boil, and add the pasta. Cook the pasta until it is al dente. Reserve 1 cup of pasta water, drain the pasta, and set it aside.

3. Add a few tablespoons of pasta water to the skillet and place it over medium-high heat. Add the pasta and cook for 2 to 3 minutes, tossing to combine.

4. Season with a generous amount of pepper and remove the pan from heat.

5. Add the cheese and a few tablespoons of pasta water and toss to incorporate. Add the guanciale, toss to combine, garnish with additional pecorino, and serve.

INGREDIENTS:

½   LB. GUANCIALE, CUT IN 1-INCH-LONG AND ¼-INCH-WIDE STRIPS

SALT AND PEPPER, TO TASTE

14   OZ. RIGATONI

1   (HEAPING) CUP GRATED PECORINO CHEESE, PLUS MORE FOR GARNISH

AMATRICE:
THE HOME OF AMATRICIANA

I am not typically keen on including personal anecdotes in my writng, but I will make an exception for pasta amatriciana, which has a very special place in my heart.

A couple of summers prior to moving to Sweden, I decided to ignore my poor driving skills—I tend to get lost in my own thoughts—and travel by car all the way from Rome to Amatrice to attend the annual amatriciana festival. The road to Amatrice was like something out of a fairy tale, winding up through beautiful mountains, the breathtaking scenery punctuated by charming stone and brick houses. Once I arrived at my destinaton, the town was just as beautiful, a perfectly preserved medieval settlement with friendly people and plenty of quality food stores—in short, my dream place. The festival itself was also what I'd hoped for: filled with great, honest food that finally taught me the proper way to make pasta amatriciana. I remember staying over at the Hotel Roma because the pasta tasting happened quite late in the evening, and, yes, because I am a bad driver.

The morning after the festival, I went around town to shop for local guanciale and pecorino, and I still remember the nice lady who sold me some guanciale apologizing because it was not the right season for it and the taste may not be optimal.

Back home, I made amatriciana for my whole family, following the recipe published by the municipality of Amatrice and using the ingredients I bought on my trip. I do not exaggerate when I say that it was the best amatriciana I have ever tasted, and my picky Roman family was also astounded by it, particularly by the flavor of the seemingly subpar guanciale.

I kept dreaming of going back for a longer stay to explore more of that beautiful town, and follow the locals' suggestion to come when it's the right season (between late winter and early spring) for that mind-blowing guanciale.

And then, one sad day, news came that Amatrice had been reduced to rubble by an earthquake. Tragically, this happened just before the annual festival, when many tourists as well as locals were visiting. Many died, including several guests at the Hotel Roma, who were trapped when it collapsed.

To help with my grief, I started making pasta amatriciana regularly, but I was never happy with the result. I knew it was missing Amatrice's guanciale, aged in the impossibly crisp air of the Monti della Laga. And so, I know that I must go back sometime soon and see for myself what still remains of that fairy tale place.

Though many of the historical buildings that charmed me on my one trip have been lost, Amatrice keeps going, as it does its festival, the Sagra degli Spaghetti all'Amatriciana. Even the Hotel Roma has been rebuilt, albeit in a slightly different location. All great news for the residents of that magical town—and those who, like me, can't get enough of pasta amatriciana.

AMATRICIANA

YIELD: 4 SERVINGS / **ACTIVE TIME:** 30 MINUTES / **TOTAL TIME:** 40 MINUTES

Amatriciana is without a doubt the queen of Roman pastas—carbonara is a relatively new addition to osteria menus, while amatriciana has been there for centuries. The recipe is originally from the beautiful Laga Mountains, where possibly the best guanciale in Lazio, and the world, is produced. Here is my adaptation of the original amatriciana recipe proffered by Amatrice's municipality, following the dish's one sacred rule: the amount of guanciale should always be one-quarter of the pasta's weight.

1. Bring water to a boil in a large saucepan. Add the tomatoes and boil them for 2 minutes. Drain the tomatoes and let them cool. When they are cool enough to handle, peel the tomatoes, remove the seeds, and chop the remaining flesh. Set the tomatoes aside.

2. Place the olive oil in a large cast-iron skillet and warm it over medium heat. Add the guanciale and chile and cook until the guanciale starts to render its fat. Raise the heat to medium-high and cook until the guanciale has browned.

3. Add the wine and cook until it has evaporated.

4. Remove the guanciale from the pan with a slotted spoon. Set it aside.

5. Add the tomatoes to the pan, season with salt, and reduce the heat to medium. Cook for 2 minutes.

6. Remove the chile, return the guanciale to the pan, and gently simmer the sauce.

7. Bring water to a boil in a large saucepan. Add salt, let the water return to a full boil, and add the pasta. Cook the pasta until it is al dente. Drain the pasta and place it in a bowl.

8. Add the pecorino to the bowl and toss to combine. Add the sauce, toss to combine, and serve with additional pecorino.

INGREDIENTS:

6   RIPE SAN MARZANO TOMATOES

1   TABLESPOON EXTRA-VIRGIN OLIVE OIL

4½   OZ. GUANCIALE (GUANCIALE AMATRICIANO PREFERRED), CUT INTO 1-INCH-LONG AND ¼-INCH-WIDE STRIPS

1   PIECE OF CHILE PEPPER

2   TABLESPOONS DRY WHITE WINE

     SALT, TO TASTE

18   OZ. SPAGHETTI

1   (HEAPING) CUP GRATED PECORINO CHEESE, PLUS MORE FOR SERVING

SPAGHETTI AGLIO OLIO E PEPERONCINO

YIELD: 4 SERVINGS / **ACTIVE TIME:** 10 MINUTES / **TOTAL TIME:** 20 MINUTES

In Rome, when you have almost nothing in the pantry, this is the pasta you make. Famous as a cure for hunger that descends late at night, it is a pasta dish that is as easy to make as it is to enjoy.

1. Bring water to a boil in a large saucepan.

2. Place the olive oil in a large skillet and warm it over low heat. Add the garlic and chiles and cook until the garlic is lightly browned. Then remove the garlic from the pan and set aside.

3. Add salt to the boiling water, let it return to a full boil, and add the pasta. Cook until the pasta is al dente.

4. Drain the pasta and add it to the skillet along with the parsley. Raise the heat to medium-high and cook for 2 to 3 minutes, tossing to combine. Serve immediately.

INGREDIENTS:

SALT, TO TASTE

1   LB. SPAGHETTI

6   TABLESPOONS EXTRA-
    VIRGIN OLIVE OIL

2   GARLIC CLOVES, HALVED

2   HOT CHILE PEPPERS,
    STEMS AND SEEDS
    REMOVED, MINCED

    HANDFUL OF FRESH
    PARSLEY, CHOPPED

GNOCCHI ALLA ROMANA

YIELD: 4 SERVINGS / **ACTIVE TIME:** 40 MINUTES / **TOTAL TIME:** 1 HOUR AND 20 MINUTES

The origins of this dish are obscure, but it has surely been around for a long time. According to Ada Boni, the author of the most influential Italian cookbook to date (*Il talismano della felicità*, first published in 1929), it was the standard dish that Romans served at their celebrations.

1. Place the milk in a saucepan, season it with salt, pepper, and nutmeg, and bring to a simmer.

2. Add the semolina and cook, whisking continually, until the mixture thickens.

3. Remove the pan from heat, add the butter, and stir until it has melted.

4. Add the egg yolks and pecorino, and stir until blended.

5. Coat a baking pan with olive oil and pour the mixture into it. Spread it to ½ inch thick and let the mixture cool completely.

6. Preheat the oven to 350°F. Cut the mixture into 1½-inch rounds. Coat a clean baking dish with olive oil and lay the rounds in it, making sure they overlap slightly.

7. Brush the rounds with melted butter and sprinkle additional pecorino over the top.

8. Place the gnocchi alla Romana in the oven and bake for 15 minutes.

9. Set the oven's broiler to high. Set the gnocchi alla Romana under the broiler and broil until it is golden brown.

10. Remove the gnocchi alla Romana from the oven and serve.

INGREDIENTS:

4   CUPS WHOLE MILK

SALT AND PEPPER, TO TASTE

FRESHLY GRATED NUTMEG, TO TASTE

9   OZ. SEMOLINA FLOUR

4   TABLESPOONS UNSALTED BUTTER, PLUS MORE, MELTED, FOR TOPPING

2   EGG YOLKS

3½   OZ. PECORINO CHEESE, GRATED, PLUS MORE FOR TOPPING

EXTRA-VIRGIN OLIVE OIL, AS NEEDED

SECONDI

FRITTATA PASQUALE

YIELD: 4 SERVINGS / **ACTIVE TIME:** 30 MINUTES / **TOTAL TIME:** 1 HOUR

This frittata is an Umbrian dish that is traditionally prepared for Easter breakfast. In the countryside, it will feature wild spring vegetables like asparagus, wild leafy greens like chicory, and aromatic herbs. Here is a version that can be made with foraged or store-bought ingredients.

1. Carefully rinse the leafy greens, asparagus, and herbs. Remove any woody stems, tough ends, or damaged leaves and discard. Chop the vegetables and herbs and set them aside.

2. Place half of the olive oil in a large skillet and warm it over low heat. Add the garlic and cook until it is lightly browned, about 2 minutes.

3. Add the asparagus and cook, stirring occasionally, until it has softened, about 5 minutes.

4. Add the leafy greens, herbs, and a few tablespoons of water, season with salt and pepper, and cover the pan. Cook, stirring occasionally, for 15 minutes.

5. Place the eggs, Parmesan, and milk in a large bowl and whisk to combine.

6. Remove the pan from heat and let the vegetables and herbs cool.

7. Pour the mixture into the egg mixture and stir to combine.

8. Place the remaining olive oil in a large skillet and warm it over medium heat.

9. Add the vegetable-and-egg mixture to the pan, reduce the heat to medium-low, and cover the pan.

10. Cook the frittata until the bottom is browned and sides are set. Place a plate over the frittata and invert the pan so the frittata falls on the plate. Place the frittata back in the pan and cook until it is browned on that side.

11. Remove the frittata from the pan and serve immediately.

INGREDIENTS:

5   OZ. LEAFY GREEN VEGETABLES (CHICORY, DANDELION GREENS, BEET GREENS, COLLARD GREENS)

3   OZ. ASPARAGUS

2   HANDFULS OF MIXED FRESH HERBS (ROSEMARY, PARSLEY, SAGE, MARJORAM, CHIVES, AND/OR MINT)

6   TABLESPOONS EXTRA-VIRGIN OLIVE OIL

1   GARLIC CLOVE

    SALT AND PEPPER, TO TASTE

8   EGGS

2   TABLESPOONS GRATED PARMESAN CHEESE

2   TABLESPOONS WHOLE MILK

PARMIGIANA DI GOBBI

YIELD: 4 SERVINGS / ACTIVE TIME: 40 MINUTES / TOTAL TIME: 2 HOURS

Gobbi alla parmigiana is a delicious, layered gratin made with cardoons, which are called cardi or gobbi in Italian. Cardoons are common in certain areas of Northern and Central Italy, particularly Marche and Umbria, and taste a bit like artichokes. The recipe below is vegetarian; however, there are versions that include ground beef or sausage.

1. Remove the flower buds from the cardoons and cut the stems into 3-inch-long pieces. While working with the cardoons, place the cut pieces in a bowl of water and stir in the lemon juice to prevent them from blackening.

2. Bring water to a boil in a large saucepan. Add salt and the cardoons and boil until they are tender. Cooking times will vary based on the quality of your cardoons. Drain the cardoons and let them cool. When they are cool enough to handle, squeeze them to remove any excess water.

3. Place the eggs in a bowl, add a pinch of salt, and beat until scrambled. Place the flour in a shallow bowl.

4. Add olive oil to a narrow, deep, and heavy-bottomed saucepan with high edges until it is about 2 inches deep and warm it to 350°F.

5. Dredge the cardoons in the flour and then in the beaten eggs until they are completely coated. Working in batches to avoid crowding the pot, gently slip them into the hot oil and fry until they are golden brown.

6. Remove the fried cardoons and place them on a paper towel–lined plate to drain and cool. Preheat the oven to 350°F.

7. Spread some tomato sauce over the bottom of a large baking dish. Top with half of the cardoons, sprinkle one-third of the Parmesan on top, and arrange one-third of the mozzarella on top of the Parmesan. Spread a thin layer of tomato sauce over the cheeses. Repeat this layering process and then top the dish with the remaining Parmesan and mozzarella.

8. Place the dish in the oven and bake until the top looks crunchy, about 40 minutes. Remove the parmigiana from the oven and let it rest for 15 minutes before slicing and serving.

INGREDIENTS:

- 4 LBS. CARDOONS
- JUICE OF ½ LEMON
- SALT, TO TASTE
- 3 EGGS
- 1 CUP ALL-PURPOSE FLOUR
- EXTRA-VIRGIN OLIVE OIL, AS NEEDED
- SUGO CON SOFFRITTO (SEE PAGE 807)
- 2 CUPS GRATED PARMESAN CHEESE
- 1.1 LBS. FRESH MOZZARELLA CHEESE, DRAINED FOR 1 HOUR AND CUBED

POMODORI RIPIENI DI RISO

YIELD: 4 SERVINGS / **ACTIVE TIME:** 30 MINUTES / **TOTAL TIME:** 2 HOURS AND 30 MINUTES

One of the most treasured summer dishes in Rome, pomodori ripieni di riso, or rice-stuffed tomatoes, has a mysterious origin. It was most likely brought to Rome by the Jewish immigrants who settled there.

1. Rinse the ripe tomatoes, cut off the tops, and reserve the tops. Extract the pulp and juice from the tomatoes and put them aside. Place the hollowed-out tomatoes on a plate upside down to drain.

2. Remove the white parts from the tomato pulp, place them in a food processor, and blitz until pureed. Place the puree in a bowl, add the parsley, mint, and olive oil, and stir to combine.

3. Stir in the garlic, rice, crushed tomatoes, and remaining tomato pulp and juices. Season the mixture with salt and pepper and toss to combine.

4. Cover the bowl with plastic wrap, place it in the refrigerator, and chill for 1 hour.

5. Preheat the oven to 350°F. Coat a deep baking dish with olive oil. Arrange the hollowed-out tomatoes, right side up, in the dish and fill each tomato with the rice mixture. Do not fill the tomatoes to the top, as the rice will expand during cooking.

6. Place the tops back on the tomatoes. Season them with salt and pepper and drizzle olive oil over the top.

7. Place the stuffed tomatoes in the oven and bake until the tops look slightly charred and their skins start to wrinkle.

8. Remove the stuffed tomatoes from the oven and let them cool. Serve them lukewarm or cold.

INGREDIENTS:

8   RIPE, ROUND TOMATOES (EACH ABOUT 8 OZ.)

   HANDFUL OF FRESH PARSLEY, CHOPPED

   HANDFUL OF FRESH MINT, CHOPPED

3   TABLESPOONS EXTRA-VIRGIN OLIVE OIL, PLUS MORE AS NEEDED

1   GARLIC CLOVE, MINCED

8.8   OZ. CARNAROLI OR ARBORIO RICE

5   OZ. WHOLE PEELED TOMATOES, CRUSHED

   SALT AND PEPPER, TO TASTE

FAGIOLI CON LE COTICHE

Raw pork rind can be hard to find in the United States, and you will rarely (if ever) find it in a supermarket. There is no real substitute for it in this dish—after all, the name of the dish is "beans and pork rind"! Try your best to find a good butcher who carries it. If you don't have any luck, I'd venture that substituting pork belly or some other fatty cut of pork would result in something quite tasty.

1. Place the beans in a large pot, cover them with cold water, and bring to a boil. Reduce the heat and simmer the beans until they are tender, 45 minutes to 1 hour, seasoning them with salt halfway through. Drain the beans and set them aside.

2. Bring salted water to a boil in a large saucepan. Remove the fat from the pork rind, place it in the boiling water, and boil it for 5 minutes.

3. Drain the pork rind and cut it into short and thin strips.

4. Bring unsalted water to a boil in a large saucepan. Add the pork rind and cook until it is tender, about 1 hour. Drain the pork rind and set it aside.

5. Place the ham fat in a Dutch oven and warm it over low heat until it has rendered. Add the onion and garlic and cook, stirring occasionally, until they start to brown, about 5 minutes.

6. Add the tomatoes and cook, stirring occasionally, for 15 minutes.

7. Add the beans and pork rind, season with salt and pepper, and cook for 45 minutes, adding water as necessary if the dish starts to look dry.

8. Stir in the parsley and cook for 1 minute. Serve with toasted bread and enjoy.

INGREDIENTS:

14	OZ. DRIED WHITE BEANS, SOAKED OVERNIGHT AND DRAINED
	SALT AND PEPPER, TO TASTE
6	OZ. PORK RIND
2	OZ. PARMA HAM FAT, CHOPPED
1	WHITE ONION, FINELY DICED
1	GARLIC CLOVE, MINCED
1.1	LBS. WHOLE PEELED TOMATOES, CRUSHED
	HANDFUL OF FRESH PARSLEY, CHOPPED
	SLICES OF BREAD, TOASTED, FOR SERVING

POLLO ALLA CACCIATORA

YIELD: 4 SERVINGS / **ACTIVE TIME:** 30 MINUTES / **TOTAL TIME:** 1 HOUR AND 30 MINUTES

A Tuscan recipe that is popular in the whole of Central Italy, pollo alla cacciatora means "chicken the hunter's way," referring to the preparation of meat with rosemary and garlic, which is generally used to prepare game. Abroad this dish is often served over pasta, but in Italy, that's a no-go. Instead, serve with a loaf of good bread.

1. Place the olive oil in a large, deep skillet and warm it over medium heat. Add the carrot, celery, onion, garlic, and rosemary and cook, stirring occasionally, until they have softened, about 5 minutes.

2. Add the chicken, season with salt and red pepper flakes, and sear the chicken until it is browned all over.

3. Add the wine and cook until it has evaporated.

4. Remove the garlic and rosemary and discard them. Add the tomatoes, bay leaves, and olives (if desired), season with salt and red pepper flakes, and cover the pan. Reduce the heat to low and cook until the chicken is tender, about 45 minutes, turning it occasionally.

5. Serve with crusty bread and enjoy.

INGREDIENTS:

¼   CUP EXTRA-VIRGIN OLIVE OIL

1   CARROT, PEELED AND FINELY DICED

½   CELERY STALK, FINELY CHOPPED

1   ONION, FINELY DICED

6   GARLIC CLOVES

2   SPRIGS OF FRESH ROSEMARY

3.3   LBS. CHICKEN THIGHS AND WINGS

     SALT, TO TASTE

     RED PEPPER FLAKES, TO TASTE

⅔   CUP RED WINE

14   OZ. WHOLE PEELED TOMATOES, CRUSHED

2   BAY LEAVES

1   (HEAPING) CUP PITTED BLACK OLIVES (OPTIONAL)

     CRUSTY BREAD, FOR SERVING

TRIPPA ALLA ROMANA

YIELD: 4 SERVINGS / **ACTIVE TIME:** 30 MINUTES / **TOTAL TIME:** 2 HOURS

An iconic Roman dish, trippa alla Romana is something you must try at least once, assuming you can get hold of the main ingredient, ready-to-cook tripe. To be edible, tripe undergoes a treatment known as sbiancamento ("whitening"), which removes any unpleasant residues and gives it a whiter color.

1. Bring water to a boil in a large saucepan. Cut the tripe into 2-inch-long strips, rinse them under cold water, and add them to the boiling water. Boil for about 10 minutes. Drain the tripe and set it aside.

2. Place the olive oil in a large, deep skillet and warm it over medium heat. Add the carrot, celery, onion, and garlic and cook, stirring occasionally, until they have softened, about 5 minutes.

3. Add the tripe and cook until it has browned, about 5 minutes.

4. Add the mint, cloves, and wine and cook until the wine has evaporated. Stir in half of the pecorino cheese and cook until it has melted.

5. Add the tomatoes and tomato paste, season with salt and red pepper flakes, and cook for about 30 minutes, stirring occasionally.

6. Garnish the dish with the remaining pecorino cheese and additional mint and serve with crusty bread.

INGREDIENTS:

1	LB. READY-TO-COOK TRIPE (SBIANCATA)
2	TABLESPOONS EXTRA-VIRGIN OLIVE OIL
½	CARROT, PEELED AND FINELY DICED
½	CELERY STALK, FINELY DICED
½	ONION, FINELY DICED
1	GARLIC CLOVE, MINCED
1	TEASPOON CHOPPED FRESH MINT, PLUS MORE FOR GARNISH
3	WHOLE CLOVES
½	CUP DRY WHITE WINE
1	(HEAPING) CUP GRATED PECORINO CHEESE
14	OZ. WHOLE PEELED TOMATOES, CRUSHED
1	TABLESPOON TOMATO PASTE
	SALT, TO TASTE
	RED PEPPER FLAKES, TO TASTE
	CRUSTY BREAD, FOR SERVING

SALTIMBOCCA ALLA ROMANA

YIELD: 4 SERVINGS / **ACTIVE TIME:** 20 MINUTES / **TOTAL TIME:** 40 MINUTES

This elegant Roman secondo is of uncertain origin. According to Pellegrino Artusi's *La scienza in cucina e l'arte di mangiar bene*, which was published in 1891, saltimbocca was already a popular dish in Roman restaurants. However, the use of dry-cured ham suggests a possible Northern Italian origin.

1. Beat the veal cutlets with a meat tenderizer to make them thinner.

2. Place a piece of ham over each cutlet and place a sage leaf in the middle of the ham. Secure the ham and sage with a toothpick, but do not roll the slice up.

3. Place the flour in a shallow bowl and dredge the bottom of the cutlets in it until coated.

4. Place two-thirds of the butter in a large skillet and melt it over low heat until it starts to brown.

5. Raise the heat to high and add the veal, floured side down. Season with pepper and cook until the bottoms of the cutlets are golden.

6. Add the wine and cook until it has evaporated.

7. Cover the pan with a lid and cook for 1 minute.

8. Remove the veal from the pan, place it on a plate, and tent it with aluminum foil.

9. Place the water and remaining butter in the pan and cook over medium heat, scraping up any browned bits from the bottom of the pan, until the sauce thickens.

10. Pour the sauce over the veal and serve with Carciofi alla Giudia and crusty bread.

INGREDIENTS:

8   MEDIUM VEAL CUTLETS

4   SLICES OF PARMA HAM, HALVED

8   FRESH SAGE LEAVES

½   CUP ALL-PURPOSE FLOUR

4   TABLESPOONS UNSALTED BUTTER

    BLACK PEPPER, TO TASTE

⅔   CUP DRY WHITE WINE

2   TABLESPOONS WATER

    CARCIOFI ALLA GIUDIA (SEE PAGE 481), FOR SERVING

    CRUSTY BREAD, FOR SERVING

BRACIOLA RIFATTA TOSCANA

YIELD: 4 SERVINGS / ACTIVE TIME: 20 MINUTES / TOTAL TIME: 40 MINUTES

Cooking meat in tomato sauce is very common in Italy, and the simplest way is in fettine alla pizzaiola, where thin beef steaks are cooked in a simple tomato sauce. The Tuscan version of this recipe is a bit more interesting, as the beef steaks are first breaded and fried and then cooked in umido ("in tomato sauce").

1. Place the eggs and a pinch of salt in a shallow bowl and beat until scrambled. Place the bread crumbs in a separate bowl.

2. Place the olive oil in a large skillet and warm it over medium heat.

3. Dredge the steaks in the egg and then in the bread crumbs until they are completely coated. Place them in the skillet and cook until they are browned on both sides, 3 to 5 minutes.

4. Transfer the steaks to a paper towel–lined plate to drain.

5. Place the tomato sauce in a large skillet and warm it over medium heat.

6. Place the steaks in the sauce, reduce the heat to medium-low, and cook until the steaks are cooked through, about 10 minutes.

7. Garnish with the parsley and serve.

INGREDIENTS:

3 EGGS

SALT, TO TASTE

1 CUP BREAD CRUMBS

1 CUP EXTRA-VIRGIN OLIVE OIL

8 BEEF STEAKS, SLICED THIN

SUGO AL BASILICO (SEE PAGE 806)

HANDFUL OF FRESH PARSLEY, CHOPPED, FOR GARNISH

CINGHIALE ALLA CACCIATORA

YIELD: 4 SERVINGS / **ACTIVE TIME:** 30 MINUTES / **TOTAL TIME:** 15 HOURS

Typical of Umbria but also loved in other regions in Northern and Central Italy, cinghiale alla cacciatora is an extremely tasty and rich game stew.

1. To prepare the marinade, place all of the ingredients in a large bowl and stir to combine.

2. To begin preparations for the cacciatora, add the boar to the marinade and let it marinate in the refrigerator for 12 hours.

3. Drain the boar and chop it into small pieces.

4. Place the lard in a large, deep skillet and melt it over medium heat. Add the boar, garlic, onion, celery, carrot, and bay leaves and cook, stirring occasionally, until the boar is browned all over, about 10 minutes.

5. Season with salt and red pepper flakes and add the wine. Cook until the wine has evaporated.

6. Add the tomato paste and broth, reduce the heat to low, and cover the pan. Cook for 2 hours, stirring occasionally and adding more broth as needed if the dish starts to look dry.

7. Remove the bay leaves and discard them. Cook the cacciatora for another 30 minutes and serve immediately.

INGREDIENTS:

FOR THE MARINADE

4	CUPS RED WINE
1	GARLIC CLOVE
2	SPRIGS OF FRESH ROSEMARY
1	SPRIG OF FRESH THYME
1	SPRIG OF FRESH MARJORAM
2	BAY LEAVES
5	FRESH SAGE LEAVES
5	JUNIPER BERRIES

FOR THE CACCIATORA

2.2	LBS. WILD BOAR TENDERLOIN
2	TABLESPOONS LARD
3	GARLIC CLOVES
½	ONION, SLICED THIN
½	CELERY STALK, FINELY DICED
½	CARROT, PEELED AND FINELY DICED
2	BAY LEAVES
	SALT, TO TASTE
	RED PEPPER FLAKES, TO TASTE
1	CUP DRY WHITE WINE
¼	CUP TOMATO PASTE
2	CUPS BRODO DI CARNE (SEE PAGE 805), PLUS MORE AS NEEDED

STRACOTTO ALLA FIORENTINA

YIELD: 4 SERVINGS / **ACTIVE TIME:** 30 MINUTES / **TOTAL TIME:** 4 HOURS

A rich Sunday roast from Florence, stracotto alla Fiorentina is a perfect winter dish, and often served with mashed potatoes.

1. Place the olive oil in a Dutch oven and warm it over medium heat. Add the onion, garlic, and rosemary and cook, stirring frequently, until the onion is translucent, about 3 minutes.

2. Add the pot roast and sear until it is browned all over, turning it as necessary.

3. Add the celery and carrots and cook, stirring occasionally, for 15 minutes.

4. Deglaze the pot with the wine, scraping up any browned bits from the bottom. Cover the pot and cook for 30 minutes, turning the pot roast often.

5. Add the tomatoes and 1 cup of water, season with salt and pepper, and bring to a boil.

6. Reduce the heat to low, cover the pot, and cook until the pot roast is very tender, 2 or 3 hours, turning the pot roast occasionally and adding more water as needed.

7. Remove the pot roast and let it rest for 10 minutes. Transfer the broth and vegetables to a food processor and blitz until smooth.

8. Slice the pot roast and serve with the sauce and mashed potatoes.

INGREDIENTS:

¼	CUP EXTRA-VIRGIN OLIVE OIL
1	ONION, CHOPPED
1	GARLIC CLOVE
1	SPRIG OF FRESH ROSEMARY
2.2	LBS. POT ROAST
2	CELERY STALKS, CHOPPED
3	CARROTS, PEELED AND CHOPPED
2	CUP CHIANTI
5	TOMATOES, CHOPPED
	SALT AND PEPPER, TO TASTE
	MASHED POTATOES, FOR SERVING

CONIGLIO IN POTACCHIO

YIELD: 4 SERVINGS / **ACTIVE TIME:** 20 MINUTES / **TOTAL TIME:** 1 HOUR AND 15 MINUTES

A classic of Marche cuisine, coniglio in potacchio is braised rabbit with herbs, wine, and plenty of garlic.

1. Place the rosemary, sage, garlic, chile, olive oil, and wine in a Dutch oven.

2. Place the rabbit and tomatoes on top of the aromatics, season with salt and pepper, and cover the pot. Cook over low heat for about 50 minutes, turning the rabbit and tomatoes over halfway through.

3. Uncover the pot, raise the heat to medium, and cook until the sauce has reduced. Serve immediately.

INGREDIENTS:

1	SPRIG OF FRESH ROSEMARY
6	FRESH SAGE LEAVES
8	GARLIC CLOVES, HALVED
½	FRESH CHILE PEPPER, CHOPPED
¼	CUP EXTRA-VIRGIN OLIVE OIL
⅔	CUP DRY WHITE WINE
1	RABBIT, CHOPPED INTO LARGE PIECES
8	CHERRY TOMATOES, HALVED
	SALT AND PEPPER, TO TASTE

PEPOSO ALLA FORNACINA

YIELD: 4 SERVINGS / **ACTIVE TIME:** 30 MINUTES / **TOTAL TIME:** 4 HOURS

This slow-cooked Tuscan stew was created by the fornacini, makers of earthenware from the Impruneta area. Take a cue from those artisans anytime you make this, or any, stew—cook it in an earthenware pot.

1. Place all of the ingredients, except for the beans and bread, in a Dutch oven and add water until the beef is covered. Stir to combine and bring to a simmer.

2. Cover the pot, reduce the heat to low, and cook until the beef is very tender, about 3 hours, stirring occasionally.

3. Uncover the pot, raise the heat, and cook until the sauce has reduced.

4. Season with pepper and serve with white beans and crusty bread.

INGREDIENTS:

2.2   LBS. STEW BEEF, CUT INTO BIG CHUNKS

8   GARLIC CLOVES

3   CUPS CHIANTI

1   TABLESPOON TOMATO PASTE

2   TABLESPOONS BLACK PEPPERCORNS

SALT AND GROUND BLACK PEPPER, TO TASTE

WHITE BEANS, COOKED, FOR SERVING

CRUSTY BREAD, FOR SERVING

PASTICCIATA ALLA PESARESE

YIELD: 4 SERVINGS / **ACTIVE TIME:** 40 MINUTES / **TOTAL TIME:** 3 HOURS AND 30 MINUTES

An earthy pot roast that is cooked twice, the second time in tomato sauce. Traditional to Pesaro and Fano in the Marche region, it is traditionally served at festivities such as Christmas and Easter.

1. Place the olive oil in a Dutch oven and warm it over medium heat. Add the carrot, celery, onion, garlic, and cloves and cook, stirring frequently, until the onion is translucent, about 3 minutes.

2. Add the veal and sear until it is browned all over, turning it as necessary.

3. Deglaze the pot with the wine, scraping up any browned bits from the bottom. Cover the pot and cook for 30 minutes, turning the veal often.

4. Add 1 cup of hot water, season with salt and pepper, and bring to a boil.

5. Reduce the heat to low, cover the pot, and cook until the veal is very tender, about 1 hour, adding more water as needed.

6. Remove the veal and vegetables from the pan. Cut the veal into ¼-inch-thick slices. Set the vegetables aside.

7. Add the tomatoes to the pot and return the veal to the pot. Season with salt and pepper, cover the pot, and cook over low heat until the flavor has developed to your liking, about 1 hour.

8. Serve with the vegetables and crusty bread.

INGREDIENTS:

¼ CUP EXTRA-VIRGIN OLIVE OIL

1 CARROT, PEELED AND CHOPPED

1 CELERY STALK, COARSELY CHOPPED

1 ONION, CHOPPED

2 GARLIC CLOVES

2 WHOLE CLOVES

1 LB. VEAL TOP ROUND

1 CUP RED WINE

SALT AND PEPPER, TO TASTE

1½ CUPS WHOLE PEELED TOMATOES, CRUSHED

CRUSTY BREAD, FOR SERVING

PAJATA

YIELD: 4 SERVINGS / **ACTIVE TIME:** 40 MINUTES / **TOTAL TIME:** 2 HOURS

A classic from the traditionally less-affluent quarters of Rome, Testaccio and Trastevere, pajata is the upper intestines of veal, cooked in tomato sauce. Often used as a sauce for rigatoni, it can also be served as a secondo, accompanied by bread and a vegetable-centered side dish.

1. Rinse the pajata under cold water for a few minutes and cut it into 8-inch-long pieces. Knot the ends of each piece together, forming them into rings.

2. Place the olive oil in a Dutch oven and warm it over medium heat. Add the carrot, celery, and onion and cook, stirring frequently, until the onion is translucent, about 3 minutes.

3. Add the pajata and sear until it is browned on both sides, turning it over once.

4. Add the wine and cook until it has evaporated.

5. Add the tomatoes and parsley, season with salt, pepper, and oregano, and cook for 15 minutes.

6. Add 1 cup of hot water, cover the pot, and cook for 1 hour, stirring occasionally and adding more hot water as needed.

7. Uncover the pot, raise the heat to medium, and cook until the sauce has reduced. Serve immediately.

INGREDIENTS:

2.2	LBS. VEAL PAJATA
¼	CUP EXTRA-VIRGIN OLIVE OIL
1	CARROT, PEELED AND FINELY DICED
1	CELERY STALK, FINELY DICED
1	ONION, FINELY DICED
1	CUP DRY WHITE WINE
14	OZ. WHOLE PEELED TOMATOES, CRUSHED
	HANDFUL OF FRESH PARSLEY, CHOPPED
	SALT AND PEPPER, TO TASTE
	FRESH OREGANO, CHOPPED, TO TASTE

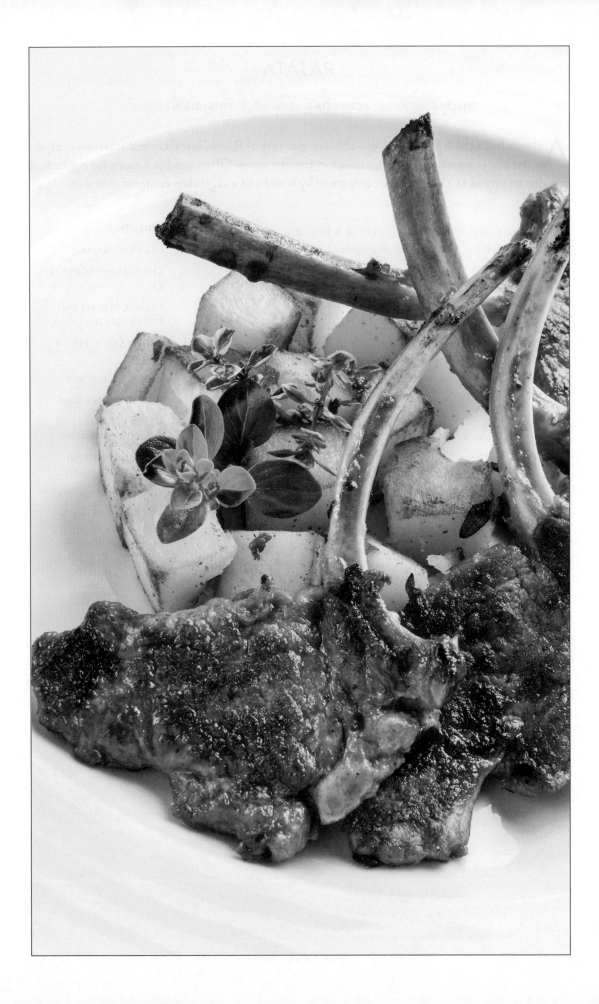

ABBACCHIO ALLA SCOTTADITO

YIELD: 4 SERVINGS / **ACTIVE TIME:** 10 MINUTES / **TOTAL TIME:** 40 MINUTES

Abbacchio alla scottadito means "burning fingers lamb," which refers to the way of cooking these lamb chops for a short time over high heat, and then eating them right off the grill, with one's hands.

1. Pat the lamb dry with paper towels and set it aside.

2. Place the olive oil, garlic, and rosemary in a bowl and stir to combine.

3. Add the lamb to the marinade and let it marinate at room temperature for 30 minutes.

4. Warm a large cast-iron skillet over high heat. Place the lamb in the skillet and cook until it is browned on both sides and medium-rare (the interior is 125°F), turning it over just once.

5. Transfer the lamb to a serving platter, tent it with aluminum foil, and let it rest for 3 minutes.

6. Season the lamb with salt and pepper and serve with Bruschetta.

INGREDIENTS:

8	LAMB CHOPS
½	CUP EXTRA-VIRGIN OLIVE OIL
2	GARLIC CLOVES
1	TEASPOON CHOPPED FRESH ROSEMARY
	SALT AND PEPPER, TO TASTE
	BRUSCHETTA (SEE PAGE 467), FOR SERVING

ABBACCHIO AL FORNO

YIELD: 4 SERVINGS / **ACTIVE TIME:** 20 MINUTES / **TOTAL TIME:** 1 HOUR AND 30 MINUTES

The most traditional Roman Easter dish, abbacchio al forno is oven-baked lamb with potatoes. Abbacchio refers to a lamb butchered very young, which is the way it is still done in the Lazio region.

1. Preheat the oven to 390°F. Pat the lamb dry with paper towels.

2. Coat a large, deep baking dish with half of the olive oil and arrange the lamb in it in a single layer.

3. Season the lamb with salt and pepper, add the rosemary, wine, and garlic, and toss to combine.

4. Place the dish in the oven and roast for 30 minutes.

5. Place the potatoes and remaining olive oil in a bowl, season with salt and pepper, and toss to combine.

6. Remove the dish from the oven, add the potatoes, and toss to combine. Place the dish back in the oven and roast until the potatoes are tender and golden brown, 40 to 50 minutes, stirring occasionally.

7. Remove the abbacchio al forno from the oven and let it cool slightly before serving.

INGREDIENTS:

2½   LBS. LAMB, CUBED

6   TABLESPOONS EXTRA-VIRGIN OLIVE OIL

SALT AND PEPPER, TO TASTE

2   SPRIGS OF FRESH ROSEMARY

⅔   CUP DRY WHITE WINE

3   GARLIC CLOVES, MINCED

2½   LBS. POTATOES, PEELED AND CHOPPED

STOCCO ALL'ANCONETANA

YIELD: 4 SERVINGS / **ACTIVE TIME:** 40 MINUTES / **TOTAL TIME:** 2 HOURS AND 40 MINUTES

If you can get hold of stockfish, this is a delicious way to cook it. Stocco all'Anconetana is a popular dish in Ancona, Marche, a historically relevant seaport on the Adriatic, where Norwegian stockfish was readily available in the past. This dish is made special by the use of Verdicchio dei Castelli di Jesi, a lovely local white wine.

1. Preheat the oven to 280°F. Coat a large, deep baking dish with olive oil and arrange the stockfish in it in a single layer.

2. Place the celery, carrots, onion, capers, anchovies, and rosemary in a bowl and stir to combine.

3. Pour half of the mixture over the stockfish, season with salt, and toss to combine.

4. Drizzle the olive oil over the mixture and top with the potatoes.

5. Top the potatoes with the other half of the vegetable mixture and then distribute the tomatoes and olives over the top.

6. Add the chile, season the stocco with salt and pepper, and add the wine. Add water until the stocco is covered and place it in the oven.

7. Bake for about 2 hours. Remove the stocco from the oven and let it rest for 2 to 3 hours before serving.

INGREDIENTS:

- 2 CUPS EXTRA-VIRGIN OLIVE OIL, PLUS MORE AS NEEDED
- 2.2 LBS. STOCKFISH, SOAKED, CLEANED, AND CHOPPED
- 2 CELERY STALKS, FINELY DICED
- 3 CARROTS, PEELED AND FINELY DICED
- 1 ONION, FINELY DICED
- 2 OZ. CAPERS IN SALT, SOAKED, RINSED, AND SQUEEZED DRY
- 5 ANCHOVIES IN SALT, RINSED, PATTED DRY, AND CHOPPED
- 2 TEASPOONS CHOPPED FRESH ROSEMARY
- 2.2 LBS. POTATOES, PEELED AND CUT INTO WEDGES
- 2.2 LBS. TOMATOES, CUT INTO WEDGES
- 1 (HEAPING) CUP PITTED BLACK OLIVES
- 1 CHILE PEPPER, STEM AND SEEDS REMOVED, MINCED
- ¾ CUP VERDICCHIO
- SALT AND PEPPER, TO TASTE

AGNELLO AL TARTUFO NERO

YIELD: 4 SERVINGS / **ACTIVE TIME:** 20 MINUTES / **TOTAL TIME:** 1 HOUR AND 30 MINUTES

A fancy lamb preparation featuring black truffles, which ideally would come from Norcia in Umbria, an area renowned for its cured meats and truffles.

1. Place half of the olive oil in a large, deep skillet and warm it over medium heat. Add 2 garlic cloves and the rosemary and cook, stirring continually, for 2 minutes.

2. Add the lamb and sear until it is browned all over, turning it as needed.

3. Add the wine and cook until it has evaporated.

4. Cover the pan, reduce the heat to low, and cook for 20 minutes.

5. Using a mortar and pestle, grind the remaining garlic, the capers, and vinegar into a paste.

6. Stir the paste into the pan, cover, and cook until the lamb is tender, about 30 minutes.

7. Uncover the pan, raise the heat to medium, and cook until the sauce has reduced.

8. Using a mortar and pestle, grind the truffles, lemon juice, and remaining olive oil until combined. Season the truffle oil with salt and pepper.

9. To serve, divide the lamb and sauce among the serving dishes and top each portion with truffle oil.

INGREDIENTS:

- ½ CUP EXTRA-VIRGIN OLIVE OIL
- 3 GARLIC CLOVES
- 2 SPRIGS OF FRESH ROSEMARY
- 3.3 LBS. LAMB, CUBED
- ⅔ CUP DRY WHITE WINE
- 2 TABLESPOONS CAPERS IN SALT, SOAKED, RINSED, AND DRAINED
- 2 TABLESPOONS WHITE VINEGAR
- 2 OZ. NORCIA BLACK TRUFFLES
- JUICE OF ¼ LEMON
- SALT AND PEPPER, TO TASTE

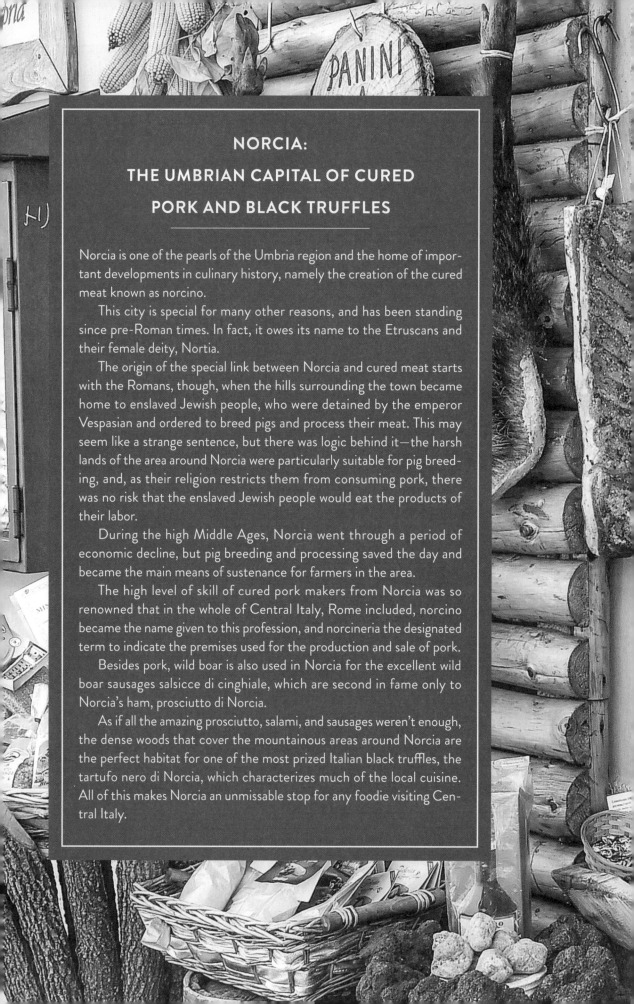

NORCIA:
THE UMBRIAN CAPITAL OF CURED PORK AND BLACK TRUFFLES

Norcia is one of the pearls of the Umbria region and the home of important developments in culinary history, namely the creation of the cured meat known as norcino.

This city is special for many other reasons, and has been standing since pre-Roman times. In fact, it owes its name to the Etruscans and their female deity, Nortia.

The origin of the special link between Norcia and cured meat starts with the Romans, though, when the hills surrounding the town became home to enslaved Jewish people, who were detained by the emperor Vespasian and ordered to breed pigs and process their meat. This may seem like a strange sentence, but there was logic behind it—the harsh lands of the area around Norcia were particularly suitable for pig breeding, and, as their religion restricts them from consuming pork, there was no risk that the enslaved Jewish people would eat the products of their labor.

During the high Middle Ages, Norcia went through a period of economic decline, but pig breeding and processing saved the day and became the main means of sustenance for farmers in the area.

The high level of skill of cured pork makers from Norcia was so renowned that in the whole of Central Italy, Rome included, norcino became the name given to this profession, and norcineria the designated term to indicate the premises used for the production and sale of pork.

Besides pork, wild boar is also used in Norcia for the excellent wild boar sausages salsicce di cinghiale, which are second in fame only to Norcia's ham, prosciutto di Norcia.

As if all the amazing prosciutto, salami, and sausages weren't enough, the dense woods that cover the mountainous areas around Norcia are the perfect habitat for one of the most prized Italian black truffles, the tartufo nero di Norcia, which characterizes much of the local cuisine. All of this makes Norcia an unmissable stop for any foodie visiting Central Italy.

TRIGLIE ALLA LIVORNESE

YIELD: 4 SERVINGS / **ACTIVE TIME:** 20 MINUTES / **TOTAL TIME:** 40 MINUTES

Red mullet has been highly prized in Italy since Roman times. This way of cooking it, with plenty of tomatoes, is typical of Livorno, Tuscany, a port city where fresh seafood is unsurprisingly abundant.

1. Rinse the fish under cold water and set it aside.

2. Place the garlic and parsley in a small bowl and stir to combine. Place the olive oil in a large, deep skillet and warm it over low heat. Add the garlic mixture and cook until the garlic is lightly browned, about 2 minutes.

3. Add the tomatoes, season with salt, and cook for 15 minutes, stirring frequently.

4. Set the fish on top of the tomatoes, drizzle olive oil over it, and season with salt and pepper.

5. Cook the fish for 5 minutes per side, shaking the pan regularly to prevent the fish from sticking. Serve immediately with crusty bread.

INGREDIENTS:

- 2.2 LBS. RED MULLET, CLEANED AND DESCALED
- 2 GARLIC CLOVES, MINCED
- HANDFUL OF FRESH PARSLEY, CHOPPED
- ¼ CUP EXTRA-VIRGIN OLIVE OIL, PLUS MORE TO TASTE
- 2.2 LBS. TOMATOES, PEELED, DESEEDED, AND CHOPPED
- SALT AND PEPPER, TO TASTE
- CRUSTY BREAD, FOR SERVING

CACIUCCO

YIELD: 4 SERVINGS / ACTIVE TIME: 40 MINUTES / TOTAL TIME: 2 HOURS

Probably the most renowned Italian seafood soup, caciucco comes from Livorno, Tuscany, a port city that historically teemed with a diverse mix of people and fruits of the sea. Originally, this was a poor man's dish, made with whatever leftover seafood was available. Then it became something special, and it is said that the traditional recipe required 16 different types of seafood: cuttlefish, octopus, dogfish, conger eel, moray eel, gurnard, redfish, tub gurnard, goby, blenny, painted comber, sea cicadas, horse mackerel, eel, red snapper, and sea bass. Here follows my adaptation of the official caciucco recipe registered at the Italian Chamber of Commerce and approved by the Italian Academy of Cuisine.

1. Place half of the olive oil in a large saucepan and warm it over low heat. Add half of the garlic, the chile, and sage and cook, stirring frequently, for 3 minutes.

2. Add the octopus and cook for about 20 minutes.

3. Add the squid and cuttlefish and cook for another 5 minutes.

4. Add the wine and tomatoes and cook over low heat for 10 minutes.

5. Place the remaining olive oil in another large saucepan and warm it over low heat. Add the onion, celery, and remaining garlic and cook, stirring occasionally for 3 minutes.

6. Add the fish soup from the other pan, stir in the tomato paste and water, and season the soup with salt. Raise the heat to medium-high and bring the soup to a boil.

7. Reduce the heat and simmer for 20 minutes.

8. Add the prawns, eel, and scorpionfish and simmer for another 10 minutes.

9. Strain the soup, return the broth to the saucepan, and cook until it thickens.

10. Remove the bones from the scorpionfish. Return all of the seafood and vegetables to the soup, cook until warmed through, and serve with Bruschetta.

INGREDIENTS:

- 1   CUP EXTRA-VIRGIN OLIVE OIL
- 2   GARLIC CLOVES, HALVED
- 1   CHILE PEPPER, STEM AND SEEDS REMOVED, CHOPPED
-    HANDFUL OF FRESH SAGE
- 1.1   LBS. OCTOPUS, CLEANED AND DICED
- 1.1   LBS. SQUID AND CUTTLEFISH, CLEANED (SEE PAGE 277) AND SLICED
- 1   CUP RED WINE
- 1.1   LBS. RIPE TOMATOES, PEELED, DESEEDED, AND CHOPPED
- 1   ONION, CHOPPED
- 1   CELERY STALK, CHOPPED
- 1   TABLESPOON TOMATO PASTE
- 2   CUPS WATER
-    SALT, TO TASTE
- 11   OZ. PRAWNS, SHELLS REMOVED, DEVEINED
- 11   OZ. MORAY EEL, CONGER, OR SWORDFISH
- 9   OZ. SCORPIONFISH, GURNARD, WEEVER, OR ANY INEXPENSIVE SMALL WHOLE FISH
-    BRUSCHETTA (SEE PAGE 467), TO TASTE, FOR SERVING

DOLCI & PANE

TOZZETTI

YIELD: 50 TOZZETTI / **ACTIVE TIME:** 30 MINUTES / **TOTAL TIME:** 1 HOUR

Tozzetti are the Umbrian version of Tuscany's famed cantucci. Truth is, this type of cookie is very common in several regions of Italy, including Sicily, where they are called pepatelli. There are infinite versions, and one of the typical Umbrian ones includes hazelnuts and candied fruits. Serve these with an Italian dessert wine like Vin Santo.

1. Preheat the oven to 350°F and line a baking sheet with parchment paper. In a large bowl, combine the flour, baker's ammonia, and salt.

2. In a separate large bowl, beat the eggs and sugar until combined. Add the citrus zests and anise seeds (if desired) and whisk to incorporate.

3. Gradually add the flour mixture, working the mixture just enough to incorporate each addition.

4. Add the hazelnuts, raisins, pine nuts, and candied fruit and knead the dough until just incorporated.

5. Divide the dough into 3 pieces and shape each one into a 1½-inch-wide log.

6. Place the logs on the parchment-lined baking sheet and place them in the oven.

7. Bake for about 20 minutes, remove the tozzetti from the oven, and cut them into ⅔-inch-thick slices. Place the tozzetti back on the baking sheets, cut side up, and return them to the oven.

8. Bake for 10 minutes, turning the tozzetti over halfway through. Remove them from the oven, transfer them to a wire rack, and let them cool completely before serving.

INGREDIENTS:

- 14 OZ. ALL-PURPOSE FLOUR
- 1½ TEASPOONS BAKER'S AMMONIA
- PINCH OF FINE SEA SALT
- 3 MEDIUM EGGS
- 7 OZ. SUGAR
- ZEST OF 1½ ORANGES
- ZEST OF 1½ LEMONS
- ½ TEASPOON ANISE SEEDS (OPTIONAL)
- 2½ OUNCES HAZELNUTS, CHOPPED
- ¼ CUP RAISINS
- 2½ TABLESPOONS PINE NUTS
- 1½ OZ. CANDIED FRUIT, DICED

CANTUCCI

YIELD: 50 CANTUCCI / **ACTIVE TIME:** 30 MINUTES / **TOTAL TIME:** 1 HOUR

Cantucci are probably the most internationally known Italian cookies. Originally made in Tuscany, they became famous in the nineteenth century, when a pastry chef from Prato refined the recipe and presented them at 1867 World's Fair in Paris.

1. Preheat the oven to 350°F and line a baking sheet with parchment paper. In a large bowl, combine the flour, baker's ammonia, and salt.

2. In a separate large bowl, beat the eggs and sugar until combined. Add the citrus zests and vanilla and whisk to incorporate.

3. Gradually add the flour mixture, working the mixture just enough to incorporate each addition.

4. Add the almonds and knead the dough just enough to incorporate them.

5. Divide the dough into 3 pieces and shape each one into a 1½-inch-wide log.

6. Place the logs on the parchment-lined baking sheet and place them in the oven.

7. Bake for about 20 minutes, remove the cantucci from the oven, and cut them into ⅔-inch-thick slices. Place the cantucci back on the baking sheets, cut side up, and return them to the oven.

8. Bake for 10 minutes, turning the cantucci over halfway through. Remove them from the oven, transfer them to a wire rack, and let them cool completely before serving.

INGREDIENTS:

14	OZ. ALL-PURPOSE FLOUR
1½	TEASPOONS BAKER'S AMMONIA
	PINCH OF FINE SEA SALT
3	MEDIUM EGGS
7	OZ. SUGAR
	ZEST OF 1½ ORANGES
	ZEST OF 1½ LEMONS
1	TEASPOON PURE VANILLA EXTRACT
1¼	CUPS ALMONDS

CIAMBELLINE AL VINO ROSSO

YIELD: 20 COOKIES / **ACTIVE TIME:** 30 MINUTES / **TOTAL TIME:** 1 HOUR AND 15 MINUTES

Typical of the hilly countryside surrounding Rome, ciambelline al vino rosso, or "red wine doughnuts," are probably very ancient. Since that time, many versions have arisen, and this recipe is a popular one.

1. Place the flour, sugar, baker's ammonia, salt, and star anise (if desired) in a mixing bowl and stir to combine.

2. Add the olive oil and wine and work the mixture quickly until it just comes together as a dough. Form the dough into a ball, cover it with plastic wrap, and let it rest for 20 minutes.

3. Preheat the oven to 350°F and line a baking sheet with parchment paper. Place some sugar on a plate.

4. Place the dough on a flour-dusted work surface and divide it into 2 oz. pieces. Roll each piece into a log, shape them into small rings, and pinch the ends together.

5. Dip each cookie in the sugar until coated all over and place them on the baking sheet.

6. Place the cookies in the oven and bake until they are just golden brown, about 20 minutes.

7. Remove the cookies from the oven, transfer them to a wire rack, and let them cool completely before serving.

INGREDIENTS:

- 14 OZ. ALL-PURPOSE FLOUR, PLUS MORE AS NEEDED
- 3½ OZ. SUGAR, PLUS MORE FOR COATING
- 1½ TEASPOONS BAKER'S AMMONIA
- PINCH OF FINE SEA SALT
- PINCH OF GROUND STAR ANISE (OPTIONAL)
- ½ CUP EXTRA-VIRGIN OLIVE OIL
- 1 (SCANT) CUP RED WINE

RICCIARELLI

YIELD: 25 COOKIES / **ACTIVE TIME:** 40 MINUTES / **TOTAL TIME:** 25 HOURS

This delicious marzipan cookie was born in the royal kitchens of Siena several centuries ago. Today, it is traditionally eaten around Christmas.

1. Place the egg whites, lemon juice, vanilla seeds, bitter almond extract, and orange zest in a mixing bowl and whisk until the mixture is foamy.

2. Add the almond flour and confectioners' sugar and whisk until the mixture comes together as a soft dough.

3. Form the dough into a ball, cover it in plastic wrap, and chill in the refrigerator for 24 hours.

4. Preheat the oven to 300°F and line a baking sheet with parchment paper. Generously dust a work surface with confectioners' sugar and place more on a plate. Place the dough on the work surface, and shape it into a 1-inch-thick cylinder. Slice it into 1 oz. pieces, roll them in the confectioners' sugar until coated all over, and form them into ovals or diamonds, flattening and lengthening them.

5. Place the ricciarelli on the baking sheet. Wet your fingers, moisten the cookies, and generously sprinkle more confectioners' sugar over the cookies.

6. Place the cookies in the oven and bake for 5 minutes. Raise the oven's temperature to 350°F and cook until the cookies start to crack, about 5 minutes.

7. Reduce the oven's temperature to 320°F and cook for another 5 minutes.

8. Remove the ricciarelli from the oven, transfer them to a wire rack, and let them cool before serving.

INGREDIENTS:

2	**EGG WHITES**
1	**TEASPOON FRESH LEMON JUICE**
	SEEDS OF 1 VANILLA POD
2	**DROPS OF BITTER ALMOND EXTRACT**
	ZEST OF 1 ORANGE
7	**OZ. ALMOND FLOUR**
7	**OZ. CONFECTIONERS' SUGAR, PLUS MORE AS NEEDED**

PINOCCATA

YIELD: 40 CANDIES / *ACTIVE TIME*: 20 MINUTES / *TOTAL TIME*: 1 HOUR

Pinoccata is an ancient pine nut candy from Central Italy that was originally made with honey. This type of candy became particularly popular in the city of Perugia during the Middle Ages, when they were wrapped and thrown to the knights who were dueling in singolar tenzone. There is also a dark version, which you can make by swapping 2 oz. of bittersweet cocoa powder in for the vanilla.

1. Preheat the oven to 350°F and line two baking dishes with parchment paper, making sure it overlaps the sides. Place the sugar and water in a saucepan and bring to a boil, stirring to dissolve the sugar.

2. Whisking continually, add the flour. Reduce the heat to low and cook the mixture for 30 minutes, stirring frequently.

3. Place the pine nuts on a baking sheet, place them in the oven, and toast for 5 minutes. Remove the pine nuts from the oven and set them aside.

4. Remove the pan from heat and stir in the pine nuts, lemon zest, and vanilla.

5. Pour the mixture into the parchment-lined baking dishes and let it cool.

6. Cut the candies into large diagonal strips, make diagonal cuts in the opposite direction, creating diamond-shaped candies, and enjoy.

INGREDIENTS:

2.2 LBS. SUGAR

1½ CUPS WATER

5 TABLESPOONS ALL-PURPOSE FLOUR

2 CUPS PINE NUTS

ZEST OF 1 LEMON

2 TEASPOONS PURE VANILLA EXTRACT

BOMBOLONI

YIELD: 25 BOMBOLONI / **ACTIVE TIME:** 1 HOUR / **TOTAL TIME:** 7 HOURS

Bomboloni are filled doughnuts that are similar to the Austrian confection krapfen. Popular throughout Central Italy, they are particularly dear to Romans, who enjoy them by the beach in the summer, morning, noon, and night. If custard is not to your liking as a filling, Nutella and apricot jam are other beloved options.

1. Warm half of the milk to 90°F. Add the yeast, gently stir, and let the mixture proof until it starts to foam, about 10 minutes.

2. Place the flours, yeast mixture, remaining milk, citrus zests, and liqueur in the work bowl of a stand mixer fitted with the dough hook and work the mixture until combined.

3. Add the sugar and work the mixture to incorporate it.

4. Incorporate the eggs 1 at a time, with the mixer running on low speed.

5. Add the lard and salt and work the mixture until it is a smooth, elastic dough.

6. Cover the bowl with plastic wrap and let the dough rise until it has nearly doubled in size, 3 to 4 hours.

7. Line two large baking dishes with parchment paper. Dust a work surface with all-purpose flour, place the dough on it, and divide it into 25 pieces. Shape them into rounds, place them in the baking dishes, and gently press down on the rounds to flatten them slightly.

8. Cover the rounds with kitchen towels and let them rise until nearly doubled in size, about 2 hours.

9. Add olive oil to a narrow, deep, and heavy-bottomed with high edges until it is 2 inches deep and warm it to 350°F. Working in batches to avoid crowding the pot, gently slip the bomboloni into the hot oil and fry until they are golden brown.

10. Transfer the fried bomboloni to a paper towel–lined plate to drain.

11. Place the custard in a piping bag fitted with a plain tip and insert it into the centers of the bomboloni's tops. Fill them with the custard and serve.

INGREDIENTS:

1¾	CUPS MILK
⅓	PACKET OF ACTIVE DRY YEAST
21.1	OZ. ALL-PURPOSE FLOUR, PLUS MORE AS NEEDED
14	OZ. STRONG BREAD FLOUR (SUCH AS MANITOBA FLOUR)
	ZEST OF 1 ORANGE
	ZEST OF 1 LEMON
¼	CUP SWEET LIQUEUR
3½	OZ. SUGAR, PLUS MORE FOR TOPPING
4	EGGS
3½	OZ. LARD
⅓	OZ. FINE SEA SALT
	EXTRA-VIRGIN OLIVE OIL, AS NEEDED
	CREMA PASTICCERA NAPOLETANA (SEE PAGE 820)

BIGNÈ DI SAN GIUSEPPE

YIELD: 10 BIGNÈ / **ACTIVE TIME:** 50 MINUTES / **TOTAL TIME:** 1 HOUR AND 15 MINUTES

Typical of Rome and its surrounding areas, bignè di San Giuseppe are fried cream puffs filled with custard, one of many fried pastries prepared for March 19, Saint Joseph's Day.

1. Place the butter, water, and salt in a saucepan and bring to a boil.

2. Remove the pan from heat, add the flour, and stir energetically until incorporated.

3. Place the saucepan over medium heat and cook until the dough starts to detach from the side of the pan, stirring continually. Reduce the heat to low and cook for 2 to 3 minutes, stirring continually.

4. Remove the pan from heat and let the dough cool for a few minutes.

5. Incorporate 1 egg at a time. Add the sugar and stir until it has been incorporated.

6. Pour the dough into a heatproof bowl, cover it with plastic wrap, and let the dough cool for 30 minutes.

7. Add olive oil to a narrow, deep, and heavy-bottomed saucepan with high edges until it is 2 inches deep and warm it to 350°F. Using two spoons, drop balls of dough into the hot oil, working in batches to avoid crowding the pot. Fry the bignè until they are golden brown.

8. Transfer the fried bignè to a paper towel–lined plate to drain.

9. Place the custard in a piping bag fitted with a plain tip and fill the bignè with it. Sprinkle confectioners' sugar over them and serve.

INGREDIENTS:

3 OZ. UNSALTED BUTTER

7 OZ. WATER

PINCH OF FINE SEA SALT

5.3 OZ. ALL-PURPOSE FLOUR

4 EGGS

2.3 OZ. SUGAR

EXTRA-VIRGIN OLIVE OIL OIL, AS NEEDED

CREMA PASTICCERA NAPOLETANA (SEE PAGE 820)

CONFECTIONERS' SUGAR, FOR TOPPING

MARITOZZI

YIELD: 12 MARITOZZI / **ACTIVE TIME**: 40 MINUTES / **TOTAL TIME**: 4 HOURS

An ancient Roman sweet bread that is commonly eaten for breakfast or between meals, accompanied by espresso.

1. Line a large baking dish with parchment paper. Dust a work surface with flour, place the dough on it, and divide it into 12 pieces. Shape them into rounds and then pull them at the ends to form ovals. Place them in the baking dish and gently press down on the rounds to flatten them slightly.

2. Cover the rounds with kitchen towels and let them rise until nearly doubled in size, about 2 hours.

3. Preheat the oven to 350°F.

4. Place the egg and 1 teaspoon of water in a bowl and whisk to combine. Brush the maritozzi with the egg wash, place them in the oven, and bake until they are golden brown, about 20 minutes.

5. While the maritozzi are in the oven, place the caster sugar and remaining water in a saucepan and bring to a boil, stirring to dissolve the caster sugar. Remove the pan from heat.

6. Remove the maritozzi from the oven and brush them with the syrup. Let the maritozzi cool completely.

7. Place the cream in the work bowl of a stand mixer fitted with the whisk attachment and whip until it holds stiff peaks.

8. Cut the maritozzi lengthwise and fill them with a generous amount of whipped cream. Level the top of the cream with a rubber spatula.

9. Sprinkle confectioners' sugar over the maritozzi and serve.

INGREDIENTS:

	ALL-PURPOSE FLOUR, AS NEEDED
½	BATCH OF BOMBOLONI DOUGH (SEE PAGE 571)
1	EGG
1	CUP PLUS 1 TEASPOON WATER
3	TABLESPOONS CASTER SUGAR
2	CUPS WHIPPING CREAM
	CONFECTIONERS' SUGAR, FOR TOPPING

BUDINO DI RISO ALLA TOSCANA

YIELD: 18 BUDINO / **ACTIVE TIME:** 40 MINUTES / **TOTAL TIME:** 2 HOURS

This is not strictly rice pudding, but actually miniature pies filled with rice pudding. It is not clear if this pastry originated in a royal's kitchen or came out of the oven of some skilled home baker—the only sure thing is how unique and delicious it is.

1. Place the milk, sugar, salt, and citrus zests in a saucepan and bring to a simmer, stirring to dissolve the sugar.

2. Add the rice, reduce the heat to low, and cook, stirring frequently, until the rice is tender, 20 to 30 minutes.

3. Remove the pan from heat and stir in the butter. Let the rice pudding cool to room temperature.

4. Stir the custard into the rice pudding and set the mixture aside.

5. Place the frolla on a flour-dusted work surface and roll it out into a ¼-inch-thick rectangle.

6. Preheat the oven to 350°F. Coat the wells of two muffin pans with butter. Please note that the recipe is for 1½ pans, so not all of the wells need to be greased.

7. Use a glass or ring cutter to cut the dough into rounds that are large enough to cover the bottom and sides of the wells in the muffin pan. Place the rounds in the wells and trim away any excess dough.

8. Fill the crusts with the rice pudding and place the budino in the oven.

9. Bake for 20 minutes, reduce the oven's temperature to 320°F, and bake until the budino are golden brown, about 15 minutes.

10. Remove the budino from the oven, transfer them to a wire rack, and let them cool completely. Dust the budino with confectioners' sugar before serving.

INGREDIENTS:

2½   **CUPS WHOLE MILK**

½   **CUP SUGAR**

   PINCH OF FINE SEA SALT

   ZEST OF 1 ORANGE

   ZEST OF ½ LEMON

1   **(SCANT) CUP RISOTTO RICE (CARNAROLI, VIALONE, ROMA, OR ORIGINARIO PREFERRED)**

1   **TABLESPOON UNSALTED BUTTER, PLUS MORE AS NEEDED**

1¾   **CUPS CREMA PASTICCERA NAPOLETANA (SEE PAGE 820)**

   PASTA FROLLA (SEE PAGE 816)

   ALL-PURPOSE FLOUR, AS NEEDED

   CONFECTIONERS' SUGAR, FOR TOPPING

TORCOLO

YIELD: 1 CAKE / **ACTIVE TIME:** 40 MINUTES / **TOTAL TIME:** 1 HOUR AND 30 MINUTES

Torcolo is the name given in Umbria to the classic, doughnut-shaped pound cake that is typically made for Easter. It is called ciambellone in other regions, like Lazio, and while it is extremely simple, it is delicious nonetheless.

1. Preheat the oven to 350°F. Place the butter, sugar, salt, vanilla seeds, and lemon zest in the work bowl of a stand mixer fitted with the whisk attachment and whip the mixture for 10 to 15 minutes, until it is foamy.

2. With the mixer running, incorporate the eggs 1 at a time. Add the milk and whisk to incorporate.

3. Place the flour and baking powder in a mixing bowl and stir to combine.

4. Add the flour mixture to the work bowl and fold to incorporate it into the batter.

5. Coat a 10-inch Bundt pan with butter, dust it with flour, and knock out any excess. Pour the batter into the pan and place it in the oven.

6. Bake until a toothpick inserted into the center of the cake comes out clean, about 40 minutes.

7. Remove the cake from the oven and let it cool in the pan.

8. Invert the cake onto a serving plate and enjoy.

INGREDIENTS:

6	OZ. UNSALTED BUTTER, SOFTENED, PLUS MORE AS NEEDED
8.8	OZ. SUGAR
	PINCH OF FINE SEA SALT
	SEEDS OF 1 VANILLA POD
	ZEST OF 1 LEMON
5	EGGS
8.8	OZ. WHOLE MILK
17.6	OZ. ALL-PURPOSE FLOUR, PLUS MORE AS NEEDED
1	TABLESPOON BAKING POWDER

CIARAMICOLA

YIELD: 1 CAKE / **ACTIVE TIME:** 40 MINUTES / **TOTAL TIME:** 1 HOUR AND 30 MINUTES

This simple pound cake comes from Perugia, and is special due to the addition of a baking liqueur called Alchermes, which is extremely popular in certain regions of Central and Southern Italy. Alchermes provides a red tint to any food it is added to, so it can be swapped out for a mild liqueur (the alcoholic content in Alchermes ranges from 20 to 30 percent) and some drops of red food coloring.

1. Preheat the oven to 350°F. To begin preparations for the cake, place the butter, sugar, vanilla seeds, and lemon zest in the work bowl of a stand mixer fitted with the whisk attachment and whip the mixture for 10 to 15 minutes, until it is foamy.

2. With the mixer running, incorporate the eggs 1 at a time. Add the milk and liqueur and whisk to incorporate.

3. Place the flour and baking powder in mixing bowl and stir to combine.

4. Add the flour mixture to the work bowl and fold to incorporate it into the batter.

5. Coat a 10-inch Bundt pan with butter, dust it with flour, and knock out any excess. Pour the batter into the pan and place it in the oven.

6. Bake until a toothpick inserted into the center of the cake comes out clean, about 40 minutes.

7. Remove the cake from the oven and let it cool in the pan.

8. While the cake is cooling, prepare the glaze. Wipe out the stand mixer's work bowl and clean the whisk. Place the egg whites in the work bowl and whip until they hold stiff peaks. With the mixer running, add the sugar in three increments. Add the vanilla seeds and whip until they are incorporated. Set the glaze aside.

9. Invert the cake onto a serving plate and cover it with the glaze. Top with the sugar sprinkles and serve.

INGREDIENTS:

FOR THE CAKE

5.3 OZ. UNSALTED BUTTER, SOFTENED, PLUS MORE AS NEEDED

7 OZ. SUGAR

SEEDS OF 1 VANILLA POD

ZEST OF 1 LEMON

3 EGGS

3½ OZ. WHOLE MILK

1 (SCANT) CUP ALCHERMES LIQUEUR

10.6 OZ. ALL-PURPOSE FLOUR, PLUS MORE AS NEEDED

2 TEASPOONS BAKING POWDER

FOR THE GLAZE

2 EGG WHITES

1 CUP SUGAR

SEEDS OF 1 VANILLA POD

COLORED SUGAR SPRINKLES, FOR TOPPING

ROCCIATA

YIELD: 1 CAKE / **ACTIVE TIME:** 40 MINUTES / **TOTAL TIME:** 1 HOUR AND 30 MINUTES

A strudel-like pastry from East Umbria, rocciata likely dates back to the Longobards' domination of Central Italy, as this is a classic Northern dessert.

1. To begin preparations for the filling, place the raisins and rum in a bowl and let the mixture steep.

2. To begin preparations for the dough, place all of the ingredients in a mixing bowl and work the mixture until it comes together as a smooth dough. Form the dough into a ball, cover it with plastic wrap, and let it rest for 30 minutes.

3. Preheat the oven to 390°F and line a baking sheet with parchment paper. Place the dough on a flour-dusted work surface and roll it out into a paper-thin sheet. Transfer the sheet of dough to a flour-dusted tablecloth.

4. Resume preparations for the filling. Sprinkle the sugar over the dough and then sprinkle the cinnamon and cocoa powder over it. Sprinkle the anise seeds (if desired) and lemon zest over the dough.

5. Distribute the apples evenly over the dough. Drain the raisins and distribute them, the walnuts, and pine nuts over the dough.

6. With the help of the tablecloth, roll up the dough into a not-too-tight log and pinch the ends to seal, taking care not to break the thin sheet.

7. Transfer the rocciata to the baking sheet and shape it into a spiral.

8. Place the rocciata in the oven and bake until it is golden brown, about 25 minutes, taking care not to burn it.

9. Remove the rocciata from the oven, drizzle alchermes over the top, sprinkle confectioners' sugar over it, and serve.

INGREDIENTS:

FOR THE FILLING

⅖	CUP RAISINS
⅖	CUP RUM
⅓	CUP SUGAR
1½	TABLESPOONS CINNAMON
2	TABLESPOONS UNSWEETENED COCOA POWDER
1	TABLESPOON ANISE SEEDS, GROUND (OPTIONAL)
	ZEST OF 1 LEMON
4	MEDIUM GOLDEN DELICIOUS APPLES, CORED AND DICED
1	(SCANT) CUP WALNUTS
⅔	CUP PINE NUTS

FOR THE DOUGH

8.8	OZ. ALL-PURPOSE FLOUR, PLUS MORE AS NEEDED
¼	CUP EXTRA-VIRGIN OLIVE OIL
½	CUP WATER
2	PINCHES OF FINE SEA SALT
	ALCHERMES LIQUEUR, FOR TOPPING
	CONFECTIONERS' SUGAR, FOR TOPPING

PANGIALLO

YIELD: 4 CAKES / **ACTIVE TIME:** 40 MINUTES / **TOTAL TIME:** 27 HOURS

Pangiallo, or "yellow bread," is a traditional Roman and Lazio Christmas cake that dates back to ancient Rome, when it was made to celebrate the winter solstice and the return of the sun.

1. Line a baking sheet with parchment paper. Place the almonds, walnuts, hazelnuts, pine nuts, and raisins in a mixing bowl and stir to combine. Add the flour and toss to combine. Set the mixture aside.

2. Place the honey in a saucepan and warm it over medium heat until it has completely liquefied.

3. Add the olive oil and stir to combine. Pour the mixture into the mixing bowl and stir until everything is combined.

4. Working with flour-dusted hands, form the mixture into 4 rounds and place them on the baking sheet. Press down on the rounds to flatten them slightly. Cover the rounds with a kitchen towel and let them rest at room temperature for 2 hours.

5. Preheat the oven to 320°F.

6. Place the pangiallo in the oven and bake for 20 minutes. Remove them from the oven and shape them into compact rounds.

7. Cover each pangiallo with plastic wrap. Let them rest for 1 day before serving.

INGREDIENTS:

- 9   OZ. BLANCHED ALMONDS
- 9   OZ. WALNUTS
- 9   OZ. BLANCHED HAZELNUTS
- 3½   OZ. PINE NUTS
- 9   OZ. RAISINS, SOAKED IN WARM WATER FOR 1 HOUR, DRAINED, AND SQUEEZED DRY
- 7.7 OZ. ALL-PURPOSE FLOUR, PLUS MORE AS NEEDED
- 17.6 OZ. HONEY
- 2   TABLESPOONS EXTRA-VIRGIN OLIVE OIL

PANPEPATO

YIELD: 4 CAKES / **ACTIVE TIME:** 40 MINUTES / **TOTAL TIME:** 27 HOURS

The Umbrian panpepato is a modern development of Roman pangiallo, as it includes chocolate and spices. There are more decadent versions that cover the cakes with a chocolate glaze, but that is entirely optional.

1. Line a baking sheet with parchment paper. Place the almonds, walnuts, hazelnuts, pine nuts, raisins, and candied fruit in a mixing bowl and stir to combine. Add the flour, pepper, cinnamon, and nutmeg and toss to combine. Set the mixture aside.

2. Place the honey and chocolate in a saucepan and warm over medium heat until the mixture has liquefied.

3. Pour the mixture into the mixing bowl and stir until everything is combined.

4. Working with flour-dusted hands, form the mixture into 4 rounds and place them on the baking sheet. Press down on the rounds to flatten them slightly. Cover the rounds with a kitchen towel and let them rest at room temperature for 2 hours.

5. Preheat the oven to 320°F.

6. Place the panpepato in the oven and bake for 20 minutes. Remove them from the oven and shape them into compact rounds.

7. Cover each panpepato with plastic wrap. Let them rest for 1 day before serving.

INGREDIENTS:

9	OZ. BLANCHED ALMONDS
9	OZ. WALNUTS
9	OZ. BLANCHED HAZELNUTS
3½	OZ. PINE NUTS
9	OZ. RAISINS, SOAKED IN WARM WATER FOR 1 HOUR, DRAINED, AND SQUEEZED DRY
3½	OZ. CANDIED FRUIT, DICED
17.6	OZ. ALL-PURPOSE FLOUR, PLUS MORE AS NEEDED
2	TABLESPOONS BLACK PEPPER
1	TABLESPOON CINNAMON
¼	TEASPOON FRESHLY GRATED NUTMEG
17.6	OZ. HONEY
3½	OZ. BITTERSWEET CHOCOLATE

ZUCCOTTO

YIELD: 1 CAKE / **ACTIVE TIME:** 1 HOUR / **TOTAL TIME:** 4 HOURS

This is a rather fancy cake that is frequently displayed in Italian pastry shops. It was apparently invented by a famous architect and artist in the de Medici court, Bernardo Buontalenti, in the 1500s, and it has since been iterated into infinite versions.

1. Line a baking sheet with parchment paper. Bring a few inches of water to a simmer in a medium saucepan. Place the chocolate in a heatproof bowl, place it over the simmering water, and stir until it is melted and smooth. Remove the bowl from heat and set one-third of it aside. Place the remaining melted chocolate in a piping bag fitted with a plain tip and pipe short strips of it over the parchment paper.

2. Remove the crust from the Pan di Spagna, cut the cake in half at the equator, and cut triangular slices from one of the halves.

3. Cover a 6 x 3–inch hemisphere pan with plastic wrap and line it with the slices of Pan di Spagna.

4. Place the liqueurs and brandy in a bowl and stir to combine. Brush the slices of cake with the mixture.

5. Place the cream in the work bowl of a stand mixer fitted with the whisk attachment and whip until it holds stiff peaks, adding the sugar and vanilla toward the end.

6. Add the chocolate strips and nuts and fold to incorporate.

7. Divide the mixture into two parts. Add the reserved melted chocolate to one portion and stir to combine.

8. Fill the cake-lined pan with the white cream, spreading it evenly with the help of a rubber spatula.

9. Fill the center of the zuccotto, all the way to the top, with the chocolate cream.

10. Cover the zuccotto with a disk of Pan di Spagna of appropriate size. Cover it with plastic wrap and refrigerate for 3 hours.

11. Place a plate over the zuccotto and invert the cake onto the plate.

12. Place the cocoa powder and confectioners' sugar in a bowl and stir to combine. Sprinkle the mixture over the zuccotto and enjoy.

INGREDIENTS:

- 7 OZ. BITTERSWEET CHOCOLATE
- 14 OZ. PAN DI SPAGNA (SEE PAGE 819)
- 2 TABLESPOONS CRÈME DE CACAO
- 3 TABLESPOONS GRAND MARNIER
- 2 TABLESPOONS BRANDY
- 4 CUPS WHIPPING CREAM
- 1 (HEAPING) CUP CONFECTIONERS' SUGAR, PLUS MORE FOR TOPPING
- 1 TEASPOON PURE VANILLA EXTRACT
- ½ CUP BLANCHED ALMONDS, TOASTED AND FINELY CHOPPED
- ½ CUP BLANCHED HAZELNUTS, TOASTED AND FINELY CHOPPED
- 3 TABLESPOONS UNSWEETENED COCOA POWDER

PAN CACIATO DI SAN MARTINO

YIELD: 9 ROLLS / **ACTIVE TIME:** 1 HOUR / **TOTAL TIME:** 4 HOURS AND 30 MINUTES

Also called pan nociato ("bread with nuts"), pan caciato ("bread with cheese") is a delicious Umbrian bread that is typically made to celebrate Saint Martin's Day, November 11.

1. Place the yeast and milk in a bowl, gently stir, and let the mixture proof until it starts to foam, about 10 minutes.

2. Place the flours, Parmesan, water, and yeast mixture in the work bowl of a stand mixer fitted with the dough hook. Work the mixture until it comes together as a dough.

3. Add the olive oil and salt and knead the dough until it is smooth and elastic.

4. Dust a work surface with all-purpose flour. Roll the dough out into a rectangle, distribute the walnuts and pecorino over it, and roll the dough up. Knead it until the walnuts and pecorino are evenly distributed. Form the dough into a ball. Coat a bowl with olive oil, place the dough in it, and cover it with plastic wrap. Let the dough rest for 1½ hours.

5. Line a baking sheet with parchment paper. Place the dough on the flour-dusted work surface and divide it into 9 pieces. Shape each piece into a round, press down to flatten them slightly, and arrange the rolls on the baking sheet.

6. Cover them with a kitchen towel and let them rest for 1½ hours.

7. Preheat the oven to 340°F.

8. Place the rolls in the oven and bake until they are just golden brown, 20 to 25 minutes.

9. Remove the rolls from the oven and let them cool slightly before serving.

INGREDIENTS:

1	PACKET OF ACTIVE DRY YEAST
½	CUP LUKEWARM WHOLE MILK (90°F)
11.6	OZ. ALL-PURPOSE FLOUR, PLUS MORE AS NEEDED
6	OZ. BREAD FLOUR
3	OZ. PARMESAN CHEESE, GRATED
½	CUP WATER
¼	CUP EXTRA-VIRGIN OLIVE OIL, PLUS MORE AS NEEDED
1	TEASPOON FINE SEA SALT
1½	CUPS WALNUTS, COARSELY CHOPPED
3	OZ. PECORINO CHEESE, DICED

TORTA DI PASQUA

YIELD: 1 TORTA / **ACTIVE TIME:** 30 MINUTES / **TOTAL TIME:** 4 HOURS AND 30 MINUTES

The most beloved Easter treat in Central Italy is not a cake but this savory bread. Torta di Pasqua has a long tradition behind it, dating to the Middle Ages, when it was supposedly created by the nuns in the Ancona monastery known as Santa Maria Maddalena di Serra de' Conti. Here is a simplified version that requires a cake pan that is substantially deeper than normal.

1. Place the yeast and milk in a bowl, gently stir, and let the mixture proof until it starts to foam, about 10 minutes.

2. Place the eggs, olive oil, Parmesan, pecorino, and yeast mixture in the work bowl of a stand mixer fitted with the dough hook. Work the mixture until it comes together as a dough.

3. Add the flour, salt, and a generous pinch of black pepper and knead the dough until it is smooth and elastic.

4. Coat a deep, round 9-inch cake pan with olive oil, place the dough in it, and distribute the Emmental over it, pushing the cubes deep into the dough. Cover the pan with plastic wrap and let the dough rise until it has reached the edge of the pan, 2 to 3 hours.

5. Preheat the oven to 350°F.

6. Place the bread in the oven and bake it until is just dark brown, about 1 hour. If the bread is darkening too much, cover it with aluminum foil toward the end of baking. Remove the bread from the oven and let it cool completely before slicing and serving.

INGREDIENTS:

1	PACKET OF ACTIVE DRY YEAST
⅓	CUP LUKEWARM WHOLE MILK (90°F)
5	EGGS
½	CUP EXTRA-VIRGIN OLIVE OIL, PLUS MORE AS NEEDED
2	CUPS GRATED PARMESAN CHEESE
½	CUP GRATED PECORINO CHEESE
17.6	OZ. BREAD FLOUR
1½	TEASPOONS FINE SEA SALT
	BLACK PEPPER, TO TASTE
3½	OZ. EMMENTAL CHEESE

PANE TOSCANO

YIELD: 1 LOAF / ACTIVE TIME: 1 HOUR / TOTAL TIME: 30 HOURS

Pane Toscano is also called pane sciapo or pane sciocco, which both refer to the peculiar absence of salt. One popular story for this unique characteristic is tied to the rivalry between Pisa and Florence, and to the Pisan block of the salt supply, which caused Florentines to learn to make bread without salt, rather than stomach the shame of surrender. Another tale holds that Florentines simply did not want to pay the tax on salt. Either way, pane Toscano has become central to Tuscan cuisine and is the absolute king of many iconic recipes, from ribollita and panzanella alla Toscana to caciucco.

1. To prepare the biga, place the yeast and water in a bowl, gently stir, and let the mixture sit until it starts to foam, about 10 minutes. Add the flour and stir until it has been incorporated. Cover the bowl and let the biga chill in the refrigerator for 1 day.

2. To begin preparations for the dough, warm one-third of the water to 90°F. Add the yeast, gently stir, and let the mixture sit until it starts to foam, about 10 minutes.

3. Place the flour, yeast mixture, and remaining water in the work bowl of a stand mixer fitted with the dough hook and work the mixture until combined.

4. Add the biga and work the mixture until it comes together as a smooth, elastic dough.

5. Form the dough into a round and place it in a large, clean bowl. Cover the bowl with plastic wrap and let the dough rise until it has almost doubled in size, about 3 hours.

6. Transfer the dough to a flour-dusted work surface and flatten it into a rectangle. Working from the short sides, fold the dough over itself like a letter and shape it into a log, or filone.

7. Place the dough on a flour-dusted kitchen towel, fold the towel over the loaf, and let it rest, seam side up, for 2 hours. Preheat the oven to 480°F and place a baking stone in the oven as it warms.

8. Invert the dough onto a flour-dusted peel and make two diagonal cuts in it with a razor. Throw a few ice cubes in the bottom of the oven. Slide the dough onto the baking stone and bake for 15 minutes.

9. Reduce the oven's temperature to 420°F and bake until a pale crust has formed, 20 to 25 minutes. Keep in mind that this bread won't take on much color because there is no salt.

10. Remove the bread from the oven, transfer it to a wire rack, and let it cool completely before slicing and serving.

INGREDIENTS:

FOR THE BIGA

⅓   TEASPOON ACTIVE DRY YEAST

⅓   CUP LUKEWARM WATER (90°F)

1   CUP BREAD FLOUR

FOR THE DOUGH

8½   OZ. WATER

½   TEASPOON ACTIVE DRY YEAST

14   OZ. BREAD FLOUR, PLUS MORE AS NEEDED

PANE DI GENZANO

YIELD: 2 LOAVES / ACTIVE TIME: 1 HOUR / TOTAL TIME: 32 HOURS

This is one of the most celebrated Italian breads, and its true recipe is a trade secret of the bakers from Genzano, a beautiful town in the hills overlooking Rome. Here's a cheat version to try at home.

1. To prepare the biga, place all of the ingredients in a bowl and stir until combined. Cover the bowl and let the biga chill in the refrigerator for 1 day.

2. To begin preparations for the dough, place the flour and four-fifths of the water in the work bowl of a stand mixer fitted with the dough hook and work the mixture until combined. Let the mixture rest for 1 hour.

3. Add the biga and work the mixture until it has been incorporated. Add the salt and remaining water and work the mixture until it comes together as a smooth, elastic dough.

4. Form the dough into a round and place it in a large, clean bowl. Cover the bowl with plastic wrap and let the dough rise until it has almost doubled in size, about 4 hours.

5. Transfer the dough to a flour-dusted work surface and divide it into 2 pieces. Flatten them into rectangles. Working from the short sides, fold the rectangles over themselves like a letter and shape them into loaves.

6. Dust two kitchen towels with wheat bran. Place the loaves on the towels, fold the towels over the them into loaves, and let them rest, seam side down, for 2 to 3 hours.

7. Preheat the oven to the maximum temperature and place a baking stone in the oven as it warms.

8. Invert the loaves onto a flour-dusted peel. Throw a few ice cubes in the bottom of the oven. Slide the loaves onto the baking stone, reduce the oven's temperature to 480°F, and bake for 15 minutes.

9. Reduce the oven's temperature to 420°F and bake until a dark crust has formed, 30 to 35 minutes.

10. Remove the loaves from the oven, transfer it to a wire rack, and let them cool completely before slicing and serving.

INGREDIENTS:

FOR THE BIGA

2.6 OZ. SOURDOUGH STARTER (SEE PAGE 822)

2.6 OZ. WATER

5.3 OZ. BREAD FLOUR

FOR THE DOUGH

31 OZ. BREAD FLOUR, PLUS MORE AS NEEDED

22.9 OZ. WATER

1 TABLESPOON FINE SEA SALT

WHEAT BRAN, AS NEEDED

PANE DI GENZANO

Genzano is a small town in the hilly countryside surrounding Rome that is famous for its bread, pane di Genzano, which was the first Italian bread to receive the IGP, the protected geographical indication. This trademark recognizes the value of products linked to a specific area and to specific ingredients and methods, meaning they cannot be made "authentically" anywhere else.

It is not clear if this bread is similar to the country bread made in late Roman times, but pane di Genzano has surely been around since at least the Middle Ages. For centuries, it has been the duty of the women living around Genzano to make the dough at home and carry it to the town's large wood-fired ovens, each of them impressing symbols on the surface of their loaves to distinguish them from those of other families.

Around the seventeenth century, the quality of pane di Genzano came to the attention of the Roman elite—including the Pope—and this fueled its commercial production in local bakeries, from where it began to be brought daily to Rome.

This habit has not changed since, and one can always find fresh Genzano bread in well-stocked Roman bakeries, and even in some supermarkets.

The official method is based on sourdough, with a pre-ferment known as biga. The loaves are generally shaped like logs, filoni, or flattened rounds, and the bread is baked in wood-fired ovens (gas ovens are allowed) at high temperatures, to achieve a thick and dark crust.

The detailed method is otherwise a secret well-kept, and any available recipes are only imitations of the real thing. Without a doubt, it is one of the products not to miss when visiting Rome and its countryside.

PANE DI LARIANO

YIELD: 2 LOAVES / **ACTIVE TIME:** 1 HOUR / **TOTAL TIME:** 32 HOURS

Pane di Lariano is similar to pane di Genzano, but made with a finely ground and partly sifted whole wheat flour known as tipo 2. The recipe below is an adaptation with regular flours and is of course not the real thing, which only the bakers from Lariano know how to make.

1. To prepare the biga, place all of the ingredients in a bowl and stir until combined. Cover the bowl and let the biga chill in the refrigerator for 1 day.

2. To begin preparations for the dough, place the flours and four-fifths of the water in the work bowl of a stand mixer fitted with the dough hook and work the mixture until combined. Let the mixture rest for 1 hour.

3. Add the biga and work the mixture until it has been incorporated. Add the salt and remaining water and work the mixture until it comes together as a smooth, elastic dough.

4. Form the dough into a round and place it in a large, clean bowl. Cover the bowl with plastic wrap and let the dough rise until it has almost doubled in size, about 4 hours.

5. Transfer the dough to a flour-dusted work surface and divide it into 2 pieces. Flatten them into rectangles. Working from the short sides, fold the rectangles over themselves like a letter and shape them into logs.

6. Dust two kitchen towels with wheat bran. Place the loaves on the towels, fold the towels over the loaves, and let them rest, seam side down, for 2 to 3 hours.

7. Preheat the oven to 480°F and place a baking stone in the oven as it warms.

8. Invert the loaves onto a flour-dusted peel. Throw a few ice cubes in the bottom of the oven. Slide the loaves onto the baking stone and bake for 15 minutes.

9. Reduce the oven's temperature to 420°F and bake until a dark crust has formed, 30 to 35 minutes.

10. Remove the loaves from the oven, transfer them to a wire rack, and let them cool completely before slicing and serving.

INGREDIENTS:

FOR THE BIGA

2.6 OZ. SOURDOUGH STARTER (SEE PAGE 822)

2.6 OZ. WATER

5.3 OZ. BREAD FLOUR

FOR THE DOUGH

23.2 OZ. BREAD FLOUR, PLUS MORE AS NEEDED

8.1 OZ. FINELY GROUND WHOLE-WHEAT FLOUR

22.9 OZ. WATER

1 TABLESPOON FINE SEA SALT

WHEAT BRAN, AS NEEDED

FOCACCETTE DI AULLA

YIELD: 16 SMALL FOCACCIA / **ACTIVE TIME:** 30 MINUTES / **TOTAL TIME:** 4 HOURS

These miniature focaccia are really fragrant due to the presence of cornmeal. Focaccette di Aulla are traditionally baked in special pans called testi, which are placed directly over an open fire. Here you find a recipe developed for the standard kitchen oven. Focaccette are delicious when cut open while still warm and filled with fresh cheese and cold cuts.

1. Combine the yeast and water in a bowl, gently stir, and let the mixture sit for a few minutes, until it starts to foam.

2. In a large bowl, combine the flour and cornmeal and then incorporate the yeast mixture. Work the mixture until it just holds together. If kneading by hand, transfer the dough to a flour-dusted work surface. Work it until it is compact, smooth, and elastic.

3. Add the salt and knead until the dough is developed, elastic, and extensible, about 5 minutes. Form the dough into a ball and place it in an airtight container that has been coated with olive oil. Let the dough rest at room temperature until it has doubled in size, about 2 hours.

4. Divide the dough into 16 pieces and shape each piece into a ball. Cover the balls with plastic wrap and let them rest for 1 hour.

5. Preheat the oven to 390°F and position a rack in the middle of the oven. Place a baking stone or steel in the oven as it warms. Flatten the balls until they are approximately ½ inch thick.

6. Using a peel or flat baking sheet, transfer the focaccia onto the heated baking implement and bake until they are golden brown, 15 to 20 minutes.

7. Remove the focaccia from the oven and let them cool slightly before serving.

INGREDIENTS:

1 ¾ TEASPOONS ACTIVE DRY YEAST

10.6 OZ. LUKEWARM WATER (90°F)

8.8 OZ. ALL-PURPOSE FLOUR, PLUS MORE AS NEEDED

8.8 OZ. FINELY GROUND CORNMEAL

1 ¾ TEASPOONS FINE SEA SALT

EXTRA-VIRGIN OLIVE OIL, AS NEEDED

SCHIACCIATA CON CIPOLLA E SALVIA

YIELD: 1 LARGE FOCACCIA / **ACTIVE TIME:** 40 MINUTES / **TOTAL TIME:** 4 HOURS AND 30 MINUTES

In Umbria, it is very typical to eat a thin focaccia flavored with golden onions and sage, a delicious combination that can provide warmth on a cold winter day.

1. Combine the yeast and water in a bowl, gently stir, and let the mixture sit for a few minutes, until it starts to foam.

2. In a large bowl, combine the flour, sugar, and yeast mixture. Work the mixture until it just holds together. If kneading by hand, transfer the dough to a flour-dusted work surface. Work it until it is compact, smooth, and elastic.

3. Add the salt and half of the sage leaves and knead until they have been incorporated and the dough appears smooth and elastic again. Coat an airtight container with olive oil, shape the dough into a ball, place it in the container, and let it rest at room temperature until it has doubled in size, about 2 hours.

4. Place the onions on a piece of parchment paper, sprinkle salt over them, and let them dry out.

5. Generously coat an 18 × 13–inch baking pan with olive oil, place the dough in the center of the pan, and gently flatten it into an oval. Brush the dough generously with olive oil, cover it with a kitchen towel, and let it rest for 30 minutes.

6. Use your hands to flatten the dough and stretch it toward the edges of the baking pan. If the dough does not want to extend to the edges of the pan right away, let it rest for 15 to 20 minutes before trying again.

7. Brush the focaccia with more olive oil and use your fingers to make indentations in the dough. Cover it with plastic wrap and let it rest for another 30 minutes. Preheat the oven to 390°F.

8. Distribute the onions and remaining sage leaves over the focaccia. Drizzle with olive oil and season with just a bit of salt, keeping in mind that the onions are salted.

9. Place the focaccia in the oven and bake for 30 to 35 minutes, until the edges are golden brown. Remove the focaccia from the oven and let it cool slightly before serving.

INGREDIENTS:

- 1¾ TEASPOONS ACTIVE DRY YEAST
- 10.6 OZ. WARM WATER (105°F)
- 17.6 OZ. ALL-PURPOSE FLOUR, PLUS MORE AS NEEDED
- 2½ TEASPOONS SUGAR
- 1 TEASPOON FINE SEA SALT, PLUS MORE TO TASTE
- 30 FRESH SAGE LEAVES, FINELY CHOPPED
- EXTRA-VIRGIN OLIVE OIL, AS NEEDED
- 4 LARGE YELLOW ONIONS, SLICED THIN

SCHIACCIA TOSCANA

YIELD: 1 LARGE FOCACCIA / **ACTIVE TIME:** 30 MINUTES / **TOTAL TIME:** 4 HOURS AND 30 MINUTES

This focaccia is rather thin and crunchy, making it the perfect bread to pair with an aperitif.

1. Combine the yeast and water in a bowl, gently stir, and let the mixture sit for a few minutes, until it starts to foam.

2. In a large bowl, combine the flour, wine, milk, sugar, and yeast mixture. Work the mixture until it just holds together. If kneading by hand, transfer the dough to a flour-dusted work surface and knead the dough until it is compact, smooth, and elastic.

3. Add the salt and work the dough until it is developed, elastic, and extensible, about 5 minutes. Coat an airtight container with olive oil, shape the dough into a ball, place it in the container, and let it rest at room temperature until it has doubled in size, about 2 hours.

4. Generously coat an 18 × 13–inch baking pan with olive oil, place the dough in the center of the pan, and gently flatten it into an oval. Brush the dough with olive oil, cover it with plastic wrap, and let it rest for 30 minutes.

5. Use your hands to flatten the dough and spread it toward the edges of the baking pan. If the dough does not want to extend to the edges of the pan right away, let it rest for 15 to 20 minutes before trying again.

6. Brush the focaccia with more olive oil and use your fingers to make indentations in the dough. Cover the focaccia with plastic wrap and let it rest for another 30 minutes.

7. Preheat the oven to 480°F.

8. Brush the dough with more olive oil and season it with salt. Place the focaccia in the oven and bake for 15 minutes, until the valleys between the bubbles are a deep golden brown. As this focaccia is supposed to be slightly crunchy, you want the bottom to be golden brown as well.

9. Remove the focaccia from the oven and let it cool slightly before serving.

INGREDIENTS:

- 1¾ TEASPOONS ACTIVE DRY YEAST
- 7 OZ. WARM WATER (105°F)
- 17.6 OZ. ALL-PURPOSE FLOUR, PLUS MORE FOR DUSTING
- 1¾ OZ. WHITE WINE
- 1¾ OZ. MILK
- 1 TABLESPOON SUGAR
- 1 TEASPOON FINE SEA SALT, PLUS MORE TO TASTE
- EXTRA-VIRGIN OLIVE OIL, AS NEEDED

SCHIACCIA ALL'UVA

YIELD: 1 LARGE FOCACCIA / **ACTIVE TIME:** 40 MINUTES / **TOTAL TIME:** 3 HOURS

Popular in Tuscany since the days of the Etruscans, this grape-enriched focaccia was linked to the rituals of the vendemmia, the local wine grape harvest, and made with the unsalted bread dough that is traditional in the region.

1. Combine the yeast and water in a bowl, gently stir, and let the mixture sit for a few minutes, until it starts to foam.

2. In a large bowl, combine the flour, honey, and yeast mixture. Work the mixture until it just holds together. If kneading by hand, transfer the dough to a flour-dusted work surface. Work it until it is compact, smooth, and elastic. Coat an airtight container with olive oil, shape the dough into a ball, place it in the container, and let it rest at room temperature until it has doubled in size, about 2 hours.

3. Preheat the oven to 360°F. Working the mixture with your hands, incorporate the sugar and olive oil. Divide the dough into 2 pieces and roll each piece into a rectangle that is approximately the size of an 18 × 13–inch baking sheet.

4. Coat the baking sheet with olive oil and place 1 piece of dough on it. Place half of the grapes on top of the dough and gently press down on them. Sprinkle caster sugar and drizzle olive oil over the grapes.

5. Cover the grapes with the second piece of dough and crimp the edges to seal. Place the remaining grapes on top of the second sheet of dough, and gently press down on them. Sprinkle caster sugar and drizzle olive oil over the grapes.

6. Place the focaccia in the oven and bake for 40 minutes, until it is golden brown. Remove the focaccia from the oven and let it cool briefly before serving.

INGREDIENTS:

1	TABLESPOON ACTIVE DRY YEAST
18.3	OZ. WATER
31¾	OZ. ALL-PURPOSE FLOUR, PLUS MORE AS NEEDED
2	TEASPOONS HONEY
2.8	OZ. EXTRA-VIRGIN OLIVE OIL, PLUS MORE AS NEEDED
4	OZ. SUGAR
2.8	LBS. PURPLE GRAPES
	CASTER SUGAR, FOR TOPPING

TORTA AL TESTO CON I CICCIOLI

YIELD: 2 SMALL FOCACCIA / **ACTIVE TIME:** 25 MINUTES / **TOTAL TIME:** 1 HOUR AND 15 MINUTES

This classic version of torta al testo includes small bites of a rustic cured pork known as ciccioli. In the absence of ciccioli, cubed pancetta or bacon will do.

1. Place the ciccioli in a large skillet and cook over medium heat until the fat has rendered and it starts to turn crispy, about 6 minutes. Transfer the ciccioli to a plate and let it cool.

2. In a large bowl, combine the flour, salt, and baking soda. Incorporate the water gradually and work the mixture until it comes together. Add the ciccioli. If kneading by hand, transfer the dough to a flour-dusted work surface. Work it until it is compact, smooth, and elastic. Divide the dough into 2 pieces and shape each piece into a ball. Cover the balls with plastic wrap and let them rest at room temperature for 30 minutes.

3. Warm a 10-inch cast-iron skillet over medium heat. Using a rolling pin, flatten each ball until it is a disk that is approximately ¼ inch thick. Use a fork to poke holes in the disks.

4. Working with 1 disk at a time, place it in the pan and cook until it is golden brown all over, about 6 minutes per side.

5. Cut the cooked focaccia into wedges. These can be enjoyed as is, or filled with cold cuts, cheese, or sautéed vegetables.

INGREDIENTS:

- **5.3** OZ. CICCIOLI, DICED
- **17.6** OZ. ALL-PURPOSE FLOUR, PLUS MORE FOR DUSTING
- **1** TEASPOON FINE SEA SALT
- **1** TEASPOON BAKING SODA
- **8.8** OZ. WATER

TORTA AL TESTO

YIELD: 2 SMALL FOCACCIA / **ACTIVE TIME:** 25 MINUTES / **TOTAL TIME:** 1 HOUR

One of the many unleavened focaccia from Central Italy that have survived the test of time. Popular in Etruscan times (approximately 2,500 years ago), torta al testo is faster to make than a regular focaccia. It is traditionally cooked in a specific pan called a testo, but still tastes delicious if cooked in a cast-iron or nonstick skillet.

1. In a large bowl, combine the flour, salt, and baking soda. Incorporate the water gradually and work the mixture until it comes together. If kneading by hand, transfer the dough to a flour-dusted work surface. Work it until it is compact, smooth, and elastic. Divide the dough into 2 pieces and shape each piece into a ball. Cover the balls with plastic wrap and let them rest at room temperature for 30 minutes.

2. Warm a 10-inch cast-iron skillet over medium heat. Using a rolling pin, flatten each ball until it is a disk that is approximately ¼ inch thick. Use a fork to poke holes in the disks.

3. Working with 1 disk at a time, place it in the pan and cook until it is golden brown all over, about 6 minutes per side.

4. Cut the cooked focaccia into wedges. These can be enjoyed as is, or filled with cold cuts, cheese, or sautéed vegetables.

INGREDIENTS:

17.6 OZ. ALL-PURPOSE FLOUR, PLUS MORE AS NEEDED

1 TEASPOON FINE SEA SALT

1 TEASPOON BAKING SODA

8.8 OZ. WATER

TORTA AL TESTO CON FARINA DI MAIS

YIELD: 2 SMALL FOCACCIA / **ACTIVE TIME:** 25 MINUTES / **TOTAL TIME:** 1 HOUR

A popular version of the Umbrian torta al testo uses cornmeal. Here's an easy recipe made for the modern home.

1. In a large bowl, combine the flour, cornmeal, salt, and baking soda. Incorporate the water gradually and work the mixture until it comes together. If kneading by hand, transfer the dough to a flour-dusted work surface. Work it until it is compact, smooth, and elastic. Divide the dough into 2 pieces and shape each piece into a ball. Cover the balls with plastic wrap and let them rest at room temperature for 30 minutes.

2. Warm a 10-inch cast-iron skillet over medium heat. Using a rolling pin, flatten each ball until it is a disk that is approximately ⅓ inch thick. Use a fork to poke holes in the disks.

3. Working with 1 disk at a time, place it in the pan and cook until it is golden brown all over, about 6 minutes per side.

4. Cut the cooked focaccia into wedges. These can be enjoyed as is, or filled with cold cuts, cheese, or sautéed vegetables.

INGREDIENTS:

- 8.8 OZ. ALL-PURPOSE FLOUR, PLUS MORE AS NEEDED
- 8.8 OZ. CORNMEAL
- 1 TEASPOON FINE SEA SALT
- 1 TEASPOON BAKING SODA
- 8.8 OZ. WATER

CHICHIRIPIENO

YIELD: 1 LARGE FOCACCIA / **ACTIVE TIME:** 45 MINUTES / **TOTAL TIME:** 3 HOURS

From the Marche region comes this scrumptious flatbread, the name of which is the local term for "filled focaccia." Originally made with leftover bread dough, this focaccia was traditionally filled with whatever was locally available. Chichiripieno stands as a perfect picnic food, with every slice standing as a meal in itself.

1. Line a baking sheet with parchment paper. Combine the yeast and water in a bowl, gently stir, and let the mixture sit for a few minutes, until it starts to foam.

2. In a large bowl, combine the flour, honey, and yeast mixture and work the mixture until it just holds together. If kneading by hand, transfer the dough to a flour-dusted work surface. Work it until it is compact, smooth, and elastic.

3. Add the salt and work the dough until it is incorporated and the dough is smooth, elastic, and extensible. Divide the dough into 2 pieces and shape each piece into a ball. Place them on the baking sheet, cover them with plastic wrap, and let them rest at room temperature until they have doubled in size, about 2 hours.

4. Preheat the oven to 390°F. Roll out both balls of dough until they are approximately the size of an 18 × 13–inch baking sheet. Generously coat the baking sheet with olive oil and place 1 piece of dough on the pan.

5. Add all of the remaining ingredients to a mixing bowl and stir to combine. Cover the dough in the pan with the mixture and place the second sheet of dough on top. Cut away any excess dough with a sharp knife and crimp the edges to seal. Brush the focaccia with olive oil, season it with salt, and use a fork to poke several holes in the surface.

6. Place the focaccia in the oven and bake for 20 to 25 minutes, until it is golden brown. Remove the focaccia from the oven and let it cool slightly before serving.

INGREDIENTS:

1	TABLESPOON ACTIVE DRY YEAST
18.3	OZ. WARM WATER (105°F)
2	LBS. ALL-PURPOSE FLOUR
2½	TEASPOONS HONEY
1½	TEASPOONS FINE SEA SALT, PLUS MORE AS NEEDED
	EXTRA-VIRGIN OLIVE OIL, AS NEEDED
1	LB. SMOKED PAPRIKA
6	OZ. ANCHOVIES IN OLIVE OIL, DRAINED
3.2	OZ. CAPERS
10	OZ. GREEN OLIVES, PITTED
10	OZ. ARTICHOKES IN OLIVE OIL, DRAINED AND CHOPPED
14	OZ. TUNA IN OLIVE OIL, DRAINED

CRESCIA SFOGLIATA

YIELD: 6 SMALL FOCACCIA / **ACTIVE TIME:** 45 MINUTES / **TOTAL TIME:** 4 HOURS

As one would expect from the stylish city of Urbino in the Marche region, this focaccia is a luxurious take on the piadina. Crescia sfogliata is rumored to have been born during the Renaissance, specifically in the kitchen of the duke of Urbino. It is wonderful on its own but is at its best if accompanied by Italian soft cheeses, like crescenza or stracchino, and vegetables or cold cuts.

1. In a large bowl, combine the flour, water, lard, eggs, salt, and pepper and work the mixture until it just comes together as a dough. If kneading by hand, transfer the dough to a flour-dusted work surface. Work it until it is compact, smooth, and elastic.

2. Form the dough into a ball, cover it with plastic wrap, and let it rest at room temperature for 30 minutes.

3. Divide the dough into 6 pieces and form them into balls. Flatten each ball into a disk, brush it with lard, and roll it up as tightly as possible. Twist the dough into spirals, transfer them to a parchment-lined baking sheet, and cover them with plastic wrap. Refrigerate for 30 minutes to 1 hour.

4. Remove the spirals from the refrigerator and flatten them into disks that are approximately ⅛ inch thick.

5. Warm a 10-inch skillet over medium heat. Working with one disk at a time, cook until dark spots appear all over, about 5 minutes per side.

6. Let the focaccia cool briefly before enjoying.

INGREDIENTS:

- 17⅔ OZ. ALL-PURPOSE FLOUR, PLUS MORE AS NEEDED
- 7 OZ. WATER
- 3½ OZ. LARD, PLUS MORE AS NEEDED
- 2 EGGS
- 1¾ TEASPOONS TABLE SALT
- 2 PINCHES OF BLACK PEPPER

CACCIANNANZE

YIELD: 1 LARGE FOCACCIA / **ACTIVE TIME:** 30 MINUTES / **TOTAL TIME:** 3 HOURS

A very simple and easy focaccia from the rural portion of the Marche region, cacciannanze is great as an appetizer but can also work as a side for dinner.

1. Place the dough on a flour-dusted work surface and form it into a loose ball, making sure not to press down too hard on the core of the mass and deflate it. Coat an 18 × 13–inch baking sheet with olive oil, place the dough in the center, and gently flatten it into an oval. Brush the dough with olive oil, cover it with plastic wrap, and let it rest at room temperature for 1 hour.

2. Place the rosemary, garlic, and a few pinches of salt in a mixing bowl and stir to combine. Use your hands to flatten the dough and stretch it toward the edges of the baking sheet. If the dough does not want to extend to the edges of the pan right away, let it rest for 15 to 20 minutes before trying again.

3. Brush the dough with olive oil, sprinkle the garlic-and-rosemary mixture over the top, and let the focaccia rest at room temperature for another 30 minutes. If desired, you can also sprinkle chunks of lard over the focaccia. Preheat the oven to 390°F.

4. Place the focaccia in the oven and bake for 15 to 20 minutes, until it is golden brown and slightly crispy on the edges. Remove the focaccia from the oven and let it cool slightly before serving.

INGREDIENTS:

FOCACCIA CLASSICA (SEE PAGE 420)

ALL-PURPOSE FLOUR, AS NEEDED

EXTRA-VIRGIN OLIVE OIL, AS NEEDED

2 TABLESPOONS FRESH ROSEMARY

3 GARLIC CLOVES, SLICED THIN

SALT, TO TASTE

LARD (OPTIONAL), AS NEEDED

PIZZA BIANCA ROMANA

YIELD: 2 SMALL FOCACCIA / **ACTIVE TIME:** 30 MINUTES / **TOTAL TIME:** 8 HOURS

I n Rome, focaccia is referred to as pizza bianca, which can be found in virtually every bakery. Compared to other regional focaccias, this is probably the most alveolated one, due to the long fermentation time, strong flour used, and relatively high water content. It is scrumptious filled with cold cuts—ideally mortadella or Parma ham—and fresh figs, but there are countless possible fillings.

1. Combine the yeast and water in a bowl, gently stir, and let the mixture sit for a few minutes, until it starts to foam.

2. In a large bowl, combine the flour, yeast mixture, malt, sugar, and olive oil and work the mixture until it just holds together. Using your hands or a stand mixer, work the dough until it is smooth and elastic, 10 to 15 minutes.

3. Add the salt and knead the dough until it is extremely elastic. Coat an airtight container with olive oil, place the dough in it, and let it rest at room temperature until it has risen and is full of bubbles, about 5 hours.

4. Preheat the oven to 480°F and place a baking stone or steel in the oven as it warms. Line two baking sheets with parchment paper. Invert the dough onto a flour-dusted work surface and divide it into 2 pieces. Place each piece of dough on a baking sheet and flatten it into an oval. Let it rest for 2 to 3 hours in a naturally warm spot, stretching the dough lengthwise every 30 minutes and being careful not to deflate excessively. After the last stretch, generously drizzle olive oil and sprinkle salt over the pieces of dough.

5. Using a peel or flat baking sheet, transfer one of the focaccia and its parchment paper onto the heated baking implement. Bake for 10 to 15 minutes, until it is golden brown. Remove the focaccia from the oven and brush it with olive oil. Repeat with the remaining focaccia.

INGREDIENTS:

- 1¼ TEASPOONS ACTIVE DRY YEAST
- 18½ OZ. WARM WATER (105°F)
- 24.7 OZ. BREAD FLOUR OR "00" PIZZA FLOUR, PLUS MORE AS NEEDED
- 2 TEASPOONS DIASTATIC MALT
- 1¾ TEASPOONS SUGAR
- 1.4 OZ. EXTRA-VIRGIN OLIVE OIL, PLUS MORE AS NEEDED
- 1 TABLESPOON FINE SEA SALT, PLUS MORE TO TASTE

FALIA DI PRIVERNO

YIELD: 2 MEDIUM FOCACCIA / **ACTIVE TIME:** 1 HOUR / **TOTAL TIME:** 5 HOURS AND 30 MINUTES

Lazio is not a big region for local variations on focaccia, because it has long been dominated by Roman pizza. But this is an exception, and it is still baked in the small town of Priverno. It is traditionally made with sourdough, but biga can also be used. If you can get hold of baby broccoli, sauté it and use it as a filling.

1. In a large bowl, combine all of the ingredients, except for the salts, and work the mixture with your hands or a stand mixer until it comes together as a dough. This will take about 20 minutes, with a few intervals of rest.

2. Add the fine sea salt and work the dough until it has been incorporated and the dough is smooth and elastic. Coat an airtight container with olive oil, place the dough in it, and let it rest for 3 to 4 hours, until it has doubled in size.

3. Preheat the oven to 450°F and place a baking stone or steel in the oven as it warms. Dust 2 pieces of parchment paper with flour. Place the dough on a flour-dusted work surface and divide it into 2 pieces. Place the pieces of dough on the pieces of parchment paper and stretch them lengthwise, being careful not to deflate the dough. They should have a rough oval shape.

4. Place the focaccia and their associated parchment paper sheets on a peel or flat baking sheet. Before loading them into the oven, generously drizzle olive oil over the focaccia, sprinkle coarse salt on top, and make three deep, lengthwise cuts in each piece. Slide the focaccia onto the heated baking implement (bake 1 at a time if your oven is small). Bake for 20 minutes, until the focaccia are golden brown.

5. Remove the focaccia from the oven, brush them with olive oil, and let them cool slightly. When they are cool enough to handle, slice the focaccia open and fill them with whatever your heart desires.

INGREDIENTS:

6.3   OZ. SOURDOUGH STARTER
       (SEE PAGE 822)

17.6   OZ. BREAD FLOUR OR "00"
       PIZZA FLOUR, PLUS MORE
       AS NEEDED

13.2   OZ. WATER

1   TEASPOON DIASTATIC
       MALT OR SUGAR

1   TABLESPOON EXTRA-
       VIRGIN OLIVE OIL, PLUS
       MORE AS NEEDED

2   TEASPOONS FINE SEA SALT

       COARSE SEA SALT, FOR
       TOPPING

CIACCINO SENESE

YIELD: 1 LARGE FOCACCIA / **ACTIVE TIME:** 30 MINUTES / **TOTAL TIME:** 4 HOURS

Typical of the town of Siena in Tuscany, ciaccino is just too good to be true. Here you can savor steamy ham and cheese baked directly inside a flaky focaccia, a must try for all lovers of ham-and-cheese sandwiches.

1. Combine the yeast and water in a bowl, gently stir, and let the mixture sit for a few minutes, until it starts to foam.

2. In a large bowl, combine the flour, yeast mixture, and sugar and work the mixture until the dough just holds together. If kneading by hand, transfer the dough to a flour-dusted work surface. Work the dough until it is compact, smooth, and elastic.

3. Add the olive oil and salt and work the dough until it is developed, elastic, and extensible, about 5 minutes. Coat an airtight container with olive oil, form the dough into a ball, and place it in the container. Let the dough rest at room temperature until it has doubled in size, about 2 hours.

4. Transfer the dough to a flour-dusted work surface and divide it into 2 pieces. Roll each piece of dough into a rectangle that is approximately 1/16 inch thick.

5. Coat an 18 × 13–inch baking pan with olive oil and place one of the rectangles on it. Distribute the slices of ham and mozzarella over the dough. Cover with the second sheet of dough and crimp the edges to seal. Let the focaccia rest at room temperature for 1 hour.

6. Preheat the oven to 390°F. Use a fork to poke holes in the top of the focaccia. Brush the focaccia with olive oil and sprinkle salt over the top.

7. Place the focaccia in the oven and bake for 20 minutes, until the top is golden brown and crispy. Remove the focaccia from the oven and let it cool slightly before serving.

INGREDIENTS:

- 2½ TEASPOONS ACTIVE DRY YEAST
- 13.2 OZ. WARM WATER (105°F)
- 26.4 OZ. ALL-PURPOSE FLOUR, PLUS MORE AS NEEDED
- 2 TEASPOONS SUGAR
- 3.7 OZ. EXTRA-VIRGIN OLIVE OIL, PLUS MORE AS NEEDED
- 2½ TEASPOONS FINE SEA SALT, PLUS MORE TO TASTE
- 11 OZ. SLICED HAM (PROSCIUTTO COTTO PREFERRED)
- 13.2 OZ. FRESH MOZZARELLA CHEESE, DRAINED AND SLICED

ANTIPASTI & CONTORNI

GNOCCO FRITTO

YIELD: 40 SERVINGS / **ACTIVE TIME:** 40 MINUTES / **TOTAL TIME:** 4 HOURS

A beloved street food from Emilia-Romagna, gnocco fritto is traditionally served as a starter alongside salami, mortadella, prosciutto, and aged cheese.

1. Warm one-quarter of the water to 90°F. Place it in a bowl, add the yeast, gently stir, and let the mixture proof until it starts to foam, about 10 minutes.

2. Add ½ cup of flour to the yeast mixture, stir to combine, cover it with plastic wrap, and let the mixture sit in a naturally warm spot for about 1 hour.

3. Place the mixture in the work bowl of a stand mixer fitted with the dough hook. Add the remaining water and flour and work the mixture until it just comes together as a dough.

4. With the mixer running, gradually add the lard and work the dough until it is smooth and elastic. Add the salt and work the dough until it is incorporated.

5. Form the dough into a ball, place it in a clean bowl, and cover it with plastic wrap. Let the dough rise in a naturally warm spot until it has doubled in size, about 2 hours.

6. Place the dough on a flour-dusted work surface. Roll it out into a ⅓-inch-thick rectangle and cut the dough into 2-inch-wide strips.

7. Cut the strips into 2-inch-long diamonds.

8. Add olive oil to a narrow, deep, heavy-bottomed saucepan with high sides until it is about 2 inches deep and warm it to 350°F. Working in batches to avoid crowding the pot, add the gnocco and fry until they are golden brown on both sides, turning them as necessary.

9. Transfer the fried gnocco to a paper towel–lined plate to drain before serving.

INGREDIENTS:

1	CUP WATER
⅔	PACKET OF ACTIVE DRY YEAST
4½	CUPS BREAD FLOUR, PLUS MORE AS NEEDED
3	OZ. LARD
2	TEASPOONS FINE SEA SALT
	EXTRA-VIRGIN OLIVE OIL, AS NEEDED

CHIZZE REGGIANE

YIELD: 15 CHIZZE / **ACTIVE TIME**: 40 MINUTES / **TOTAL TIME**: 4 HOURS

In Reggio, home of the famed Parmigiano Reggiano cheese, there is a variation of gnocco fritto called chizza that is filled with Parmesan.

1. Warm one-quarter of the water to 90°F. Place it in a bowl, add the yeast, gently stir, and let the mixture proof until it starts to foam, about 10 minutes.

2. Add ½ cup of flour to the yeast mixture, stir to combine, cover it with plastic wrap, and let the mixture sit in a naturally warm spot for about 1 hour.

3. Place the mixture in the work bowl of a stand mixer fitted with the dough hook. Add the remaining water and flour and work the mixture until it just comes together as a dough.

4. With the mixer running, gradually add the lard and work the dough until it is smooth and elastic. Add the salt and work the dough until it is incorporated.

5. Form the dough into a ball, place it in a clean bowl, and cover it with plastic wrap. Let the dough rise in a naturally warm spot until it has doubled in size, about 2 hours.

6. Place the dough on a flour-dusted work surface. Roll it out into a ⅕-inch-thick rectangle and cut the dough into 2-inch-wide strips.

7. Cut the strips into 4-inch-long rectangles. Place a few pieces of Parmesan on each rectangle, moisten the edges of the dough with water, and, working from a long side, fold the dough over itself, pressing down on the edges to seal.

8. Add olive oil to a narrow, deep, heavy-bottomed saucepan with high sides until it is about 2 inches deep and warm it to 350°F. Working in batches to avoid crowding the pot, add the chizze and fry until they are golden brown on both sides, turning them as necessary.

9. Transfer the fried chizze to a paper towel–lined plate to drain before serving.

INGREDIENTS:

1	CUP PLUS 1 TABLESPOON WATER, PLUS MORE AS NEEDED
⅔	PACKET OF ACTIVE DRY YEAST
4½	CUPS BREAD FLOUR, PLUS MORE AS NEEDED
3	OZ. LARD
2	TEASPOONS FINE SEA SALT
7	OZ. PARMESAN CHEESE, SHAVED
	EXTRA-VIRGIN OLIVE OIL, AS NEEDED

GATTAFIN

YIELD: 15 GATTAFIN / **ACTIVE TIME:** 1 HOUR / **TOTAL TIME:** 1 HOUR AND 30 MINUTES

In Levanto, a lovely town on the eastern coast of Liguria, there is a special type of fried ravioli known as gattafin. The specialty is so dear to the locals that the Associazione Sapori di Levanto trademarked it.

1. To prepare the dough, place the flour in a large bowl and make a well in the center. Add the water and olive oil to the well and work the mixture until it comes together as a smooth and elastic dough. Form the dough into a ball, cover it with plastic wrap, and chill it in the refrigerator for 30 minutes.

2. To begin preparations for the filling, place the olive oil in a large skillet and warm it over medium heat. Add the onion and leek and cook, stirring occasionally, until they have softened, about 5 minutes.

3. Add the prebuggiùn and water, cover the pan, and cook until the mixture is tender, stirring occasionally.

4. Uncover the pan and cook until the liquids have evaporated. Remove the pan from heat and let the mixture cool.

5. Squeeze the mixture to remove any excess liquid. Place it in a bowl, add the remaining ingredients, and stir to combine. Set the filling aside.

6. Place the dough on a flour-dusted work surface and roll it out into a very thin sheet that is about ⅛ inch thick. Cut 5-inch rounds out of the dough, place a spoonful of the filling in the center, and fold the dough over the filling to create a half-moon. Crimp the edges of the ravioli with a fork.

7. Add olive oil to a skillet until it is about 1 inch deep and warm it to 325°F. Working in batches to avoid crowding the pot, add the gattafin and fry until they are crispy and golden brown, 4 to 6 minutes, turning them as necessary.

8. Transfer the fried gattafin to a paper towel–lined plate to drain before serving.

PREBUGGIÙN: This is a bouquet of wild leafy green vegetables such as borage, nettle, chard, dandelion, wild fennel, wild radicchio, wild poppy leaves, horseradish leaves, wild arugula, pimpinella, and/or chicory. In the absence of these wild greens, use baby spinach, small leaves of chard, arugula, and whatever other small leafy greens you prefer.

INGREDIENTS:

FOR THE DOUGH

- 4½ CUPS ALL-PURPOSE FLOUR, PLUS MORE AS NEEDED
- 1 CUP PLUS 1 TABLESPOON WATER
- 1¾ OZ. EXTRA-VIRGIN OLIVE OIL

FOR THE FILLING

- 2 TABLESPOONS EXTRA-VIRGIN OLIVE OIL, PLUS MORE AS NEEDED
- 1 ONION, FINELY DICED
- ½ LEEK, WHITE PART ONLY, RINSED WELL AND FINELY DICED
- 1 LARGE BUNCH OF PREBUGGIÙN (SEE NOTE)
- 2 TABLESPOONS WATER
- 2 EGGS, LIGHTLY BEATEN
- 2 HANDFULS OF FRESH MARJORAM, FINELY CHOPPED
- 1 (HEAPING) CUP GRATED GRANA PADANO CHEESE
- 1 (HEAPING) CUP GRATED PECORINO CHEESE
- SALT, TO TASTE

FONDUTA ALLA VALDOSTANA

YIELD: 4 SERVINGS / **ACTIVE TIME:** 1 HOUR / **TOTAL TIME:** 4 HOURS AND 30 MINUTES

Valle d'Aosta is a small mountainous region bordering France and Switzerland, and thus shares much of these countries' cuisine. Fonduta, which you likely know as fondue, is a typical example, as it is common to the whole Alpine region. In Valle d'Aosta, the cheese used is fontina, so if you want to make a real Italian fonduta that is the cheese you should be using.

1. Remove the rind from the fontina cheese and slice the cheese thin.

2. Place the fontina and milk in a bowl, cover it with plastic wrap, and chill the mixture in the refrigerator for 4 hours.

3. Bring a few inches of water to a gentle simmer in a large saucepan. Place half of the butter in a heatproof bowl and place it over the simmering water. Stir occasionally until the butter has melted.

4. Drain the fontina and add it to the bowl.

5. When the cheese starts to melt, whisk the mixture, making sure all of the lumps dissolve and the temperature does not rise above 140°F.

6. Add the rest of the butter and whisk until it is incorporated. While whisking continually, incorporate the eggs 1 at a time. Season the fonduta with salt and white pepper.

7. Place the fonduta over a heat source to serve it, accompanied by the toasted bread.

INGREDIENTS:

- 11 OZ. FONTINA CHEESE
- ⅔ CUP WHOLE MILK
- 4 TABLESPOONS UNSALTED BUTTER
- 4 EGGS

  SALT AND WHITE PEPPER, TO TASTE
- 5 SLICES OF CRUSTY BREAD, CUBED AND TOASTED, FOR SERVING

BAGNA CÀUDA

YIELD: 4 SERVINGS / **ACTIVE TIME:** 1 HOUR / **TOTAL TIME:** 1 HOUR

Bagna càuda means "hot sauce"—in the sense of warm, not spicy—in Piedmont's local dialect and is an olive oil–based dip for vegetables, loaded with garlic and anchovies. The origins of this dish are lost in time but are probably very ancient. This recipe is an adaptation of the official one registered by the delegation of Asti of the Italian Academy of Cuisine and makes for a lovely (and extremely healthy) appetizer to be enjoyed in a cozy, convivial atmosphere. If you're looking for some vegetables to serve alongside, consider using a combination of raw and cooked veggies.

1. Place half of the olive oil in a saucepan and warm it over medium-low heat. Add the garlic and cook, stirring continually to ensure it does not brown.

2. Add the anchovies and cook, stirring to dissolve them.

3. Add the remaining olive oil, reduce the heat to low, and cook the bagna cauda for 30 minutes, making sure that it does not start to fry at any point.

4. Add the butter and stir to incorporate. Place the bagna cauda over a heat source to serve it, accompanied by vegetables.

INGREDIENTS:

2　CUPS EXTRA-VIRGIN OLIVE OIL

　CLOVES FROM 4 HEADS OF GARLIC, SLICED THIN

7　OZ. ANCHOVIES PACKED IN SALT, SOAKED AND CHOPPED

2　TABLESPOONS UNSALTED BUTTER

　VEGETABLES, FOR SERVING

GIARDINIERA PIEMONTESE

YIELD: 6 PINTS / **ACTIVE TIME:** 1 HOUR / **TOTAL TIME:** 1 MONTH

La giardiniera means "garden salad" in Italian, and this summer vegetable preserve was traditionally made at the end of the summer, in Piedmont, to extend the bounty of the warm season. It is generally served as a side dish for heavy secondi or with cold cuts as a starter.

1. Place six mason jars in a canning pot, cover them with cold water, and bring to a boil. Boil the jars for 30 minutes to sterilize them. Remove the jars from the boiling water and place them on a wire rack, upside down, to drain and cool.

2. Place the water, wine, and vinegar in a large pot and bring to a boil.

3. Add the bay leaves, peppercorns, salt, sugar, carrots, celery, and green beans and boil for 2 minutes.

4. Add the peppers, fennel, and cauliflower and boil for another 2 minutes.

5. Add the pearl onions, radishes, and cucumbers, gently stir, and boil for 2 minutes.

6. Drain the vegetables, reserving the brine.

7. Distribute the vegetables among the sterilized jars, leaving about 1 inch free on top. Pour the reserved brine into the jars until it nearly reaches their rims.

8. Seal the jars tight and place them in the canning pot. Cover them with cold water and bring to a boil. Reduce the heat and let the jars simmer for 5 to 10 minutes.

9. Remove the jars from the hot water and place them on the wire rack to cool. As they are cooling, you should hear the classic "ping and pop" sound of the lids creating a seal.

10. After 6 hours, check the lids. There should be no give in them, and they should be suctioned onto the jars. Discard any lids and food that did not seal properly.

11. Keep the giardiniera in a dark place for 1 month before serving. It should keep for up to 1 year.

INGREDIENTS:

2½	CUPS WATER
3	CUPS PLUS 3 TABLESPOONS DRY WHITE WINE
3½	CUPS WHITE WINE VINEGAR
8	BAY LEAVES
1½	TABLESPOONS BLACK PEPPERCORNS
4	TEASPOONS COARSE SEA SALT
½	CUP SUGAR
7	OZ. CARROTS, PEELED AND SLICED
9	OZ. CELERY STALKS, LIGHTLY PEELED AND CHOPPED
7	OZ. GREEN BEANS, TRIMMED AND HALVED
3½	OZ. YELLOW BELL PEPPERS, STEM AND SEEDS REMOVED, SLICED
3½	OZ. RED BELL PEPPERS, STEM AND SEEDS REMOVED, SLICED
3½	OZ. GREEN BELL PEPPERS, STEM AND SEEDS REMOVED, SLICED
7	OZ. FENNEL, TRIMMED AND CUT INTO WEDGES
11	OZ. CAULIFLOWER FLORETS
7	OZ. PEARL ONIONS
9	OZ. RADISHES, TRIMMED AND HALVED
7	OZ. CUCUMBERS, CHOPPED

CUNDIGIUN

YIELD: 4 SERVINGS / **ACTIVE TIME:** 15 MINUTES / **TOTAL TIME:** 2 HOURS

Cundigiun, also known as condiggion or condiglione, used to be a Ligurian sailor's salad that included whatever vegetables were at hand and some canned or dried fish. While the dish has evolved some, it is still accompanied by Ligurian crackers known as gallette del marinaio that were created with the intention of keeping during long periods at sea.

1. Bring water to a boil in a large saucepan. Add salt and the green beans and cook until the green beans are just tender, about 3 minutes. Drain the green beans, run them under cold water, and set them aside.

2. Place the vinegar and water in a bowl. Add the sea biscuits and toss until they have absorbed the liquid.

3. Rub the garlic over the inside of a salad bowl. Add the remaining ingredients and the sea biscuits, season with salt, and toss to combine.

4. Refrigerate the cundigiun for 1 hour before serving.

INGREDIENTS:

	SALT, TO TASTE
6	OZ. GREEN BEANS, TRIMMED AND HALVED
1	TABLESPOON WHITE WINE VINEGAR
1	TABLESPOON WATER
4	GALLETTE DEL MARINAIO (SEE PAGE 767), BROKEN
1	GARLIC CLOVE, HALVED
4	TOMATOES, SLICED
1	RED BELL PEPPER, STEM AND SEEDS REMOVED, SLICED
1	YELLOW BELL PEPPER, STEM AND SEEDS REMOVED, SLICED
6	SPRING ONIONS, SLICED
2	HANDFULS OF FRESH BASIL, CHOPPED
2	HANDFULS OF GREEN OLIVES, PITTED
2	HANDFULS OF TAGGIASCA BLACK OLIVES, PITTED
1	CAN OF TUNA IN OLIVE OIL, DRAINED
3½	OZ. PIECE OF BOTTARGA, SLICED
¼	CUP EXTRA-VIRGIN OLIVE OIL

CAVOLFIORE IN BESCIAMELLA

YIELD: 4 SERVINGS / **ACTIVE TIME:** 15 MINUTES / **TOTAL TIME:** 40 MINUTES

In Emilia-Romagna, it is common to serve this cauliflower gratin as a rich side dish.

1. Preheat the oven to 350°F. Bring water to a boil in a large saucepan. Add salt and the cauliflower to the boiling water and cook until the cauliflower is just tender, about 10 minutes. Drain the cauliflower and set it aside.

2. Coat a baking dish with butter and cover the bottom with a layer of Béchamel Sauce and a generous sprinkle of Parmesan.

3. Chop the cauliflower and place it in the baking dish in an even layer. Cover with the butter and remaining béchamel and Parmesan. Sprinkle the bread crumbs over the top.

4. Place the cavolfiore in the oven and bake until the top is golden brown, about 20 minutes.

5. Remove the cavolfiore from the oven and let it cool slightly before serving.

INGREDIENTS:

SALT, TO TASTE

1 HEAD OF CAULIFLOWER, TRIMMED AND CUT INTO 4 PIECES

4 TABLESPOONS UNSALTED BUTTER, PLUS MORE AS NEEDED

2 (HEAPING) CUPS BESCIAMELLA (SEE PAGE 810)

2 OZ. PARMESAN CHEESE, GRATED

⅔ CUP BREAD CRUMBS

RADICCHIO ROSSO FRITTO

YIELD: 4 SERVINGS / **ACTIVE TIME:** 15 MINUTES / **TOTAL TIME:** 30 MINUTES

In the area around Treviso, Veneto, the best radicchio, called radicchio rosso di Treviso tardivo, or late red radicchio, grows. These fritters are a delicious way to enjoy this special vegetable and make for a refined appetizer.

1. Prepare an ice bath. To trim the radicchio, remove the outer leaves if they are damaged. Remove the base of each radicchio without breaking the bunch. Cut them into wedges and soak them in the ice bath until their tips curl, about 10 minutes.

2. Place the flour, cornmeal, egg, and Prosecco in a bowl and whisk until the mixture comes together as a smooth batter.

3. Drain the radicchio and pat them dry with a paper towel.

4. Add olive oil to a narrow, deep, heavy-bottomed saucepan with high sides until it is 2 inches deep and warm it to 350°F. Dredge the radicchio in the batter until completely coated and, working in batches to avoid crowding the pot, gently slip them into the hot oil. Fry until they are golden brown.

5. Transfer the fritters to a paper towel–lined plate to drain. Season them with salt before serving.

INGREDIENTS:

5	HEADS OF LATE RED RADICCHIO
1	CUP ALL-PURPOSE FLOUR, PLUS MORE AS NEEDED
⅔	CUP CORNMEAL
1	EGG
1⅓	CUPS PROSECCO
	EXTRA-VIRGIN OLIVE OIL, AS NEEDED
	SALT, TO TASTE

RADICCHIO E BRUCIATINI

YIELD: 4 SERVINGS / ACTIVE TIME: 15 MINUTES / TOTAL TIME: 30 MINUTES

This lovely radicchio salad is popular on the Romagna side of Emilia-Romagna. It calls for round radicchio (or radicchio di Chioggia), which is less bitter and has softer leaves compared with radicchio di Treviso.

1. Rinse the radicchio and pat it dry.

2. Place the pancetta in a large skillet and cook it over medium heat until the fat has rendered, stirring occasionally.

3. Add the vinegar and cook, stirring occasionally, until the pancetta has browned.

4. Arrange the radicchio leaves on a serving plate, top with the pancetta, and drizzle olive oil over the dish. Season it with salt and serve immediately.

INGREDIENTS:

- 14 OZ. RADICCHIO DI CHIOGGIA
- 3½ OZ. PANCETTA OR BACON, DICED
- 2½ TABLESPOONS BALSAMIC VINEGAR
- EXTRA-VIRGIN OLIVE OIL, TO TASTE
- SALT, TO TASTE

CIPOLLE RIPIENE

YIELD: 4 SERVINGS / **ACTIVE TIME:** 30 MINUTES / **TOTAL TIME:** 1 HOUR

A traditional dish from Piedmont, which can be served as an appetizer, a rich contorno, or a secondo. The best onions for this recipe are white onions that are round and flat.

1. Preheat the oven to 430°F. Bring water to a boil in a large saucepan. Peel the onions and cut off their ends. Add them and salt to the boiling water and cook until the onions are tender, about 15 minutes.

2. Drain the onions and remove the inner petals, leaving the 3 outer layers. Finely chop the inner petals and set them aside.

3. Place the stale bread and milk in a bowl and soak for 10 minutes.

4. Drain the bread, reserving the milk. Squeeze the bread and set it aside.

5. Place the pork, veal, ham, parsley, bread, and chopped onion in a bowl and stir to combine.

6. Season the mixture with salt and add 1 of the eggs, stirring to incorporate.

7. Stuff the onions with the mixture. Coat a baking dish with butter and arrange the stuffed onions in it.

8. Place the remaining egg, the reserved milk, the Parmesan, and a couple of pinches of salt in a bowl and stir to combine. Pour the mixture over the stuffed onions and sprinkle the butter over them.

9. Place the stuffed onions in the oven and bake until the tops are golden brown and crispy, about 20 minutes.

10. Remove the stuffed onions from the oven and let them cool slightly before serving.

INGREDIENTS:

8	WHITE ONIONS
	SALT, TO TASTE
2	OZ. STALE BREAD
¼	CUP WHOLE MILK
3½	OZ. GROUND PORK
3½	OZ. GROUND VEAL
3½	OZ. HAM, DICED
2	HANDFULS OF FRESH PARSLEY, FINELY CHOPPED
2	EGGS
4	TABLESPOONS UNSALTED BUTTER, DICED, PLUS MORE AS NEEDED
¼	CUP GRATED PARMESAN CHEESE

FUNGHI TRIFOLATI

YIELD: 4 SERVINGS / *ACTIVE TIME*: 15 MINUTES / *TOTAL TIME*: 30 MINUTES

This dish is pretty much just another version of funghi al funghetto, though the latter mostly uses porcini, while this recipe will work with any fresh mushroom. Originally from Piedmont but now common throughout Italy, this preparation is best served warm, but is still good served cold the day after.

1. Brush the mushrooms to remove any residual soil and then pat them with a moist kitchen towel. Cut the mushrooms into 1-inch-thick slices and set the mushrooms aside.

2. Place the olive oil in a large skillet and warm it over medium heat. Add the garlic and cook, stirring continually, for 1 minute.

3. Remove the garlic and discard it. Add the mushrooms, reduce the heat to low, and cover the pan. Cook the mushrooms for 7 minutes, stirring occasionally.

4. Season the mushrooms with salt, add two-thirds of the parsley and the chile (if desired), cover the pan, and cook for 7 minutes.

5. Stir in the remaining parsley and serve warm or at room temperature.

INGREDIENTS:

- 14 OZ. FRESH MUSHROOMS
- ¼ CUP EXTRA-VIRGIN OLIVE OIL
- 1 GARLIC CLOVE, HALVED

    SALT, TO TASTE
- 2 HANDFULS OF FRESH PARSLEY, FINELY CHOPPED
- ½ CHILE PEPPER, MINCED (OPTIONAL)

PATATE IN TECIA

YIELD: 4 SERVINGS / ACTIVE TIME: 20 MINUTES / TOTAL TIME: 1 HOUR

A beloved side in Trieste, patate in tecia means "potatoes in a pan," as they used to be prepared strictly in heavy cast-iron skillets. Enriched by pancetta, this makes for a great accompaniment with both meat and seafood.

1. Bring water to a boil in a large saucepan. Add salt and the potatoes and cook until they are fork-tender.

2. Drain the potatoes and let them cool. When they are cool enough to handle, peel the potatoes and roughly chop them.

3. Place the butter in a large cast-iron skillet and melt it over medium heat. Add the onion and cook, stirring occasionally, until it has softened, about 5 minutes.

4. Add the pancetta and cook, stirring occasionally, until it is browned and crispy.

5. Add the potatoes, season with salt and pepper, and raise the heat to medium-high. Cook, stirring continually and adding the broth a little at a time to keep the potatoes from sticking to the pan, until the potatoes are crispy and golden brown, and have absorbed all of the liquid, 10 to 15 minutes. Serve immediately.

INGREDIENTS:

SALT AND PEPPER, TO TASTE

1½ LBS. POTATOES

5 TABLESPOONS UNSALTED BUTTER

1 ONION, FINELY DICED

4½ OZ. PANCETTA OR BACON, CUBED

1 CUP BRODO DI CARNE (SEE PAGE 805)

FUNGHI AL FUNGHETTO

YIELD: 4 SERVINGS / **ACTIVE TIME:** 15 MINUTES / **TOTAL TIME:** 30 MINUTES

In the beautiful hinterlands of Genoa there are plenty of shady and humid woods that are perfect for growing porcini. Funghi al funghetto is a traditional way of cooking these mushrooms, and this dish has also spread to other regions as a contorno or a starter.

1. Brush the mushrooms to remove any residual soil and then pat them with a moist kitchen towel. Cut the mushrooms into 1-inch-thick slices and set them aside.

2. Place the olive oil in a large skillet and warm it over medium heat. Add the garlic and parsley and cook until the garlic is golden brown.

3. Add the mushrooms and water and cook until the mushrooms start to brown, 10 to 12 minutes, stirring occasionally.

4. Season with salt and oregano and serve warm or at room temperature.

INGREDIENTS:

1   LB. PORCINI MUSHROOMS

3   TABLESPOONS EXTRA-VIRGIN OLIVE OIL

1   GARLIC CLOVE, MINCED

1   TABLESPOON FINELY CHOPPED FRESH PARSLEY

2   TABLESPOONS WATER

SALT, TO TASTE

DRIED OREGANO, TO TASTE

ASPARAGI AL PROSCIUTTO

YIELD: 6 SERVINGS / **ACTIVE TIME:** 15 MINUTES / **TOTAL TIME:** 40 MINUTES

Asparagus with Parma ham is a lovely appetizer or side dish that is extremely quick to make.

1. Preheat the oven to 350°F. Bring water to a boil in a tall, narrow pot. Add salt to the boiling water, tie the asparagus tightly with kitchen twine, and stand them in the pot with their tips facing up. Cook until the asparagus is al dente, about 5 minutes. Drain the asparagus and let it cool.

2. Wrap 2 to 3 asparagus stalks in each piece of ham—how many asparagus stalks you put in each one depends on how thick they are.

3. Coat a baking dish with high sides with butter and arrange the ham-wrapped asparagus in it.

4. Top with the butter and Parmesan and place the dish in the oven. Bake until the cheese has melted and the ham is golden brown, about 10 minutes.

5. Remove the dish from the oven and serve immediately, drizzling any pan juices over the top.

INGREDIENTS:

	SALT, TO TASTE
24-36	ASPARAGUS STALKS, TRIMMED
12	SLICES OF PARMA HAM
4	TABLESPOONS UNSALTED BUTTER, CHOPPED, PLUS MORE AS NEEDED
2	OZ. PARMESAN CHEESE, GRATED

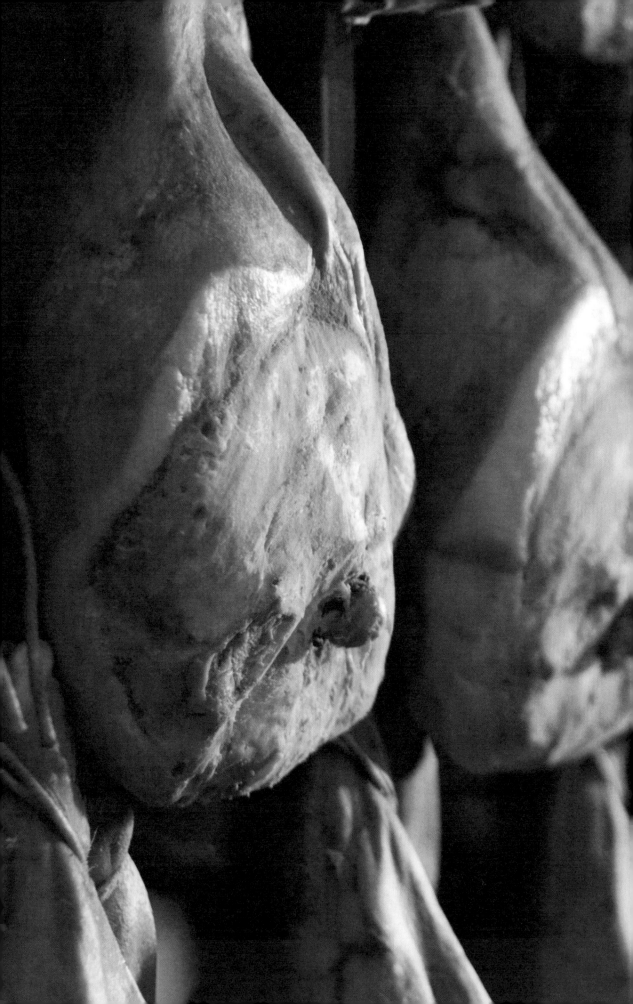

THE ANCIENT HISTORY OF PARMA HAM

The king of all Italian cured meats, prosciutto crudo, or Parma ham, has a very long history dating back to pre-Roman times.

Evidence found in the remains of an Etruscan settlement north of Parma, in Bagnolo San Vito, from the sixth century BC proves that the area around Parma has been devoted to curing ham for 2,500 years and counting, making it no surprise that their technique has become exceptional and probably impossible to exceed.

The Romans continued the Etruscan tradition of ham curing, and there are writings from Cato the Censor from the third century BCE that mention a technique for the preservation of the pork leg based on salting and drying.

In the second century, Marco Terenzio Varrone devotes a whole chapter in his *De Re Rustica* to the processing of ham, specifying that the production area is the one around Parma, which back then was called Gallia Padana.

Since then, this delicious and nutritious cured meat has continued to gain popularity, until the producers finally joined forces and created the Consorzio del Prosciutto di Parma in 1963 to protect and promote this product in Italy and the world.

But what is it that makes Parma ham so special?

First, its production area. Parma ham can be produced only in the low-lying land south of the Via Emilia between the East Enza stream and the West Stirone stream. The bulk of the production is concentrated around the town of Langhirano, which holds an annual Parma ham festival in September. Only this area is gifted with the climatic conditions for the natural curing of Parma ham.

Second, the pigs can be only from the large white Landrace and Duroc breeds (and related crossbreeds) from farms located in the center of Northern Italy. These pigs eat a specific diet of maize, barley, and Parmigiano Reggiano whey, and they cannot be younger than 9 months old.

Then there is the first processing of the meat, which includes cutting out excess fat and skin, the rifilatura, resulting in a loss of up to one-quarter of the initial weight of the leg. The next step is the salting of the meat, and after several other steps, the salt is washed away from the ham, which is then left hanging to dry in natural conditions, using fresh air from open windows.

After the drying, it is time for the sugnatura, when the ham is coated in sugna, lard mixed with salt and pepper. After 7 months of curing, the meat is seasoned and aged for a minimum of 12 months and a maximum of 3 years.

From this lengthy labor of love results a product the world has come to enjoy.

PROSCIUTTO E MELONE

YIELD: 4 SERVINGS / ACTIVE TIME: 10 MINUTES / TOTAL TIME: 10 MINUTES

Parma ham with cantaloupe is omnipresent as a starter or light lunch during the summer in Italy. The origins of this dish are quite recent, as cantaloupe was not common in Europe before the end of the nineteenth century. The recipe was first made popular by the Emilian Pellegrino Artusi, who published it in his famous cookbook, *La scienza in cucina e l'arte di mangiar bene*.

1. Split the cantaloupe in half, remove all of the seeds and the rind, and discard them. Cut the cantaloupe into 8 slices.

2. Wrap each slice of cantaloupe with 2 slices of Parma ham. You can also arrange the slices of ham over the cantaloupe, but if you do, make sure not to cover them entirely.

3. Arrange the wrapped cantaloupe on a serving platter, drizzle olive oil over the top, and either serve immediately or chill in the refrigerator.

INGREDIENTS:

1   CANTALOUPE

16   SLICES OF PARMA HAM

     EXTRA-VIRGIN OLIVE OIL,
     FOR TOPPING

CROSTINI ALLA SALSA PEVERADA

YIELD: 4 SERVINGS / **ACTIVE TIME:** 20 MINUTES / **TOTAL TIME:** 40 MINUTES

S alsa peverada is a dish traditional to Veneto, particularly the city of Padua. Its name means "peppered sauce," in reference to the generous amounts of black pepper included in the recipe. It is a sort of chunky liver pâté and as such it goes great on bread. However, its original intended use is to accompany roasted meats, enhancing the flavor and moistness.

1. Place the olive oil in a large skillet and warm it over medium heat. Add the garlic and parsley and cook until the garlic is golden brown.

2. Add the anchovies, chicken livers, salami, and lemon zest, season generously with salt and pepper, and toss to combine.

3. Add the vinegar and bring to a simmer. Reduce the heat to low and cook, stirring occasionally, for 10 minutes.

4. Spread the peverada over the toasted slices of bread and serve immediately.

INGREDIENTS:

- 3 TABLESPOONS EXTRA-VIRGIN OLIVE OIL, PLUS MORE TO TASTE
- 1 GARLIC CLOVE, MINCED
- 2 HANDFULS OF FRESH PARSLEY, FINELY CHOPPED
- 2 ANCHOVIES PACKED IN SALT, SOAKED, DRAINED, AND MINCED
- 3 CHICKEN LIVERS, FINELY DICED
- 3½ OZ. SOPRESSA VENETA, FINELY DICED
- ZEST OF ½ LEMON
- SALT AND PEPPER, TO TASTE
- ¼ CUP WHITE WINE VINEGAR
- 4 SLICES OF CRUSTY BREAD, TOASTED

CICCHETTI VENEZIANI:
THE ITALIAN TAPAS

Venetian cicchetti are bite-size appetizers served with wine, similar to the more internationally known Spanish tapas, even if they are not related to them.

The name of cicchetti derives from the Latin ciccus, small quantity, referring not only to the size of the food morsel but also to the volume of the wine that should accompany it.

In old Venice, it was common for merchants and traders to take a break under the shade of the bell tower in Piazza San Marco and eat something small, while drinking and chatting with other merchants.

Soon a myriad of tiny taverns called bacari (from Bacchus, the god of wine) flourished in Piazza San Marco and the nearby streets, selling all sorts of delicious appetizers to pair with the wine, and this tradition has never stopped.

Nowadays, the modern bacari (osterias and wine bars) sometimes do not even have seats, and guests just grab their plate with the chosen cicchetti and a takeaway glass of wine, making cicchetti a perfect food to eat on the go.

Regarding the variety of cicchetti, well, that is nearly infinite. Among the most popular we find polpette alla vedova, sarde in saor, polenta e schie, baccalà mantecato, and moscardini alla veneziana, among many others—a collection that deserves a book (or a trip) of its own.

Prosecco is the wine most often consumed with cicchetti because it is the most versatile, though it particularly shines with seafood or poultry cicchetti. Cold cuts on bread excel with a Rosé or a young red wine, and vegetarian cicchetti call for a smooth, dry white wine.

POLPETTE ALLA VEDOVA

YIELD: 20 MEATBALLS / **ACTIVE TIME:** 30 MINUTES / **TOTAL TIME:** 1 HOUR

Venetian meatballs are part of the cicchetti veneziani commonly served in local bars. Small and generally fried, they come in many flavors, are made with different meats and can also be vegetarian. Here is a recipe for a specific type, alla vedova (the widow's way), which is attributed to a cook known as Ada, who skillfully made them for over 40 years for the guests of the Venetian Trattoria Cá D'oro.

1. Bring water to a boil in a large saucepan. Add salt and the potato and cook until it is fork-tender.

2. Drain the potato and let it cool. When it is cool enough to handle, peel the potato and mash it.

3. Place the ground beef, eggs, mortadella, parsley, garlic, and mashed potato in a mixing bowl, season with salt and pepper, and stir to combine. Check the consistency of the mixture: if it seems to be too soft, incorporate bread crumbs until it is the right consistency.

4. Add olive oil to a narrow, deep, heavy-bottomed saucepan with high sides until it is about 2 inches deep and warm it to 350°F.

5. Place some bread crumbs in a shallow bowl. Form the mixture into small meatballs that are about the size of a walnut. Roll the meatballs in the bread crumbs until they are coated all over.

6. Working in batches to avoid crowding the pot, gently slip the meatballs into the hot oil and fry until they are cooked through and golden brown, turning as necessary.

7. Transfer the fried meatballs to a paper towel–lined plate to drain before serving.

INGREDIENTS:

	SALT AND PEPPER, TO TASTE
1	MEDIUM POTATO
¾	LB. GROUND BEEF
2	EGGS
3	OZ. MORTADELLA, FINELY DICED
	HANDFUL OF FRESH PARSLEY, FINELY CHOPPED
1	GARLIC CLOVE, MINCED
	BREAD CRUMBS, AS NEEDED
	EXTRA-VIRGIN OLIVE OIL, AS NEEDED

SARDE IN SAOR

YIELD: 4 SERVINGS / **ACTIVE TIME:** 25 MINUTES / **TOTAL TIME:** 50 MINUTES

Sarde in saor is one of the most beloved traditional Venetian recipes, and always present as part of the cicchetti veneziani. This way of eating sardines dates back to the fourteenth century, when Venetian sailors needed to preserve fish during long sea crossings. The contemporary recipe features raisins, making this dish palatable to all.

1. Place two-thirds of the olive oil in a large skillet and warm it over medium heat. Place the flour in a shallow bowl and dredge the sardines in it until they are coated all over.

2. Add the sardines to the pan and fry until they are golden brown and crispy on both sides, taking care not to break them. Transfer the fried sardines to a paper towel–lined plate, season with salt and black pepper, and let them drain.

3. Using a mortar and pestle, grind the coriander seeds, green peppercorns, and cloves into a fine powder.

4. Place the remaining olive oil in a small saucepan and warm it over medium heat. Add the onions and cook, stirring occasionally, until they have browned, about 10 minutes.

5. Stir in the raisins, pine nuts, and ground spices, cover the mixture with the vinegar and white wine, and bring to a simmer. Cook until the liquid has reduced and thickened, 10 to 15 minutes.

6. Top the onion stew with the fried sardines and serve.

INGREDIENTS:

6	TABLESPOONS EXTRA-VIRGIN OLIVE OIL
1	CUP ALL-PURPOSE FLOUR
1⅓	LBS. FRESH SARDINES, CLEANED AND DEBONED
	SALT AND BLACK PEPPER, TO TASTE
1	TABLESPOON CORIANDER SEEDS
1	TABLESPOON GREEN PEPPERCORNS
2	WHOLE CLOVES
2	WHITE ONIONS, SLICED THIN
2	OZ. SULTANAS, SOAKED IN WARM WATER, DRAINED, AND SQUEEZED DRY
2	OZ. PINE NUTS
1⅓	CUPS WHITE WINE VINEGAR
1	CUP DRY WHITE WINE

POLENTA E SCHIE

YIELD: 4 SERVINGS / **ACTIVE TIME:** 30 MINUTES / **TOTAL TIME:** 1 HOUR

In Venice, schie is the name given to a local type of shrimp that grows in the Venetian laguna. They are small and grey and sold alive, as they spoil very fast once they are dead. The traditional way to eat schie is on a bed of white polenta. As schie are available only in Venezia, it is best to substitute them with medium-large shrimp elsewhere, as other small shrimp may not have the same effect in this dish as schie.

1. Place the polenta and water in a medium saucepan, season with salt, and bring to a boil. Reduce the heat to low and cook, stirring frequently, until the polenta is creamy, about 8 minutes for fast-cooking polenta and 45 minutes for the slow-cooking version.

2. While the polenta is cooking, place the schie in a bowl, sprinkle the flour over them, and toss to combine.

3. Add olive oil to a narrow, deep, heavy-bottomed saucepan with high sides until it is about 2 inches deep and warm it to 350°F. Gently slip the schie into the hot oil and fry until they are cooked through and golden brown, 2 to 4 minutes.

4. Transfer the fried schie to a paper towel–lined plate to drain.

5. Stir the butter into the polenta, ladle it into warmed bowls, top each portion with some of the fried schie, and serve.

INGREDIENTS:

6	OZ. WHITE POLENTA
3	CUPS WATER
	SALT, TO TASTE
3½	OZ. SCHIE OR 8 LARGE SHRIMP, HEADS AND SHELLS REMOVED, TAILS LEFT ON, DEVEINED
2	TABLESPOONS ALL-PURPOSE FLOUR
	EXTRA-VIRGIN OLIVE OIL, AS NEEDED
1	TABLESPOON UNSALTED BUTTER

BACCALÀ MANTECATO

YIELD: 4 SERVINGS / **ACTIVE TIME:** 25 MINUTES / **TOTAL TIME:** 50 MINUTES

A thick spread made with ample parts of boiled stockfish and olive oil, baccalà mantecato is so dear to Venetians that they created a fraternity, La Confraternita del Baccalà Mantecato, devoted to the preparation.

1. Place the stockfish and water in a saucepan, season with salt, and then add the lemon and bay leaves. Bring to a boil and cook the stockfish for 20 minutes.

2. Remove the stockfish with a slotted spoon, place it in a bowl, and add the olive oil. Stir to combine, breaking the stockfish into small pieces.

3. Using a handheld mixer, whip the mixture until it is dense and creamy and there are only a few pieces of stockfish left whole, adding water as necessary to get the proper consistency.

4. Season the cream with salt and pepper, garnish with parsley, and serve alongside crusty bread.

INGREDIENTS:

11	OZ. STOCKFISH, SOAKED, DRAINED, SKIN REMOVED, DEBONED
4	CUPS WATER, PLUS MORE AS NEEDED
	SALT AND PEPPER, TO TASTE
½	LEMON
2	BAY LEAVES
1½	CUPS EXTRA-VIRGIN OLIVE OIL
	FRESH PARSLEY, CHOPPED, FOR GARNISH
	CRUSTY BREAD, TOASTED, FOR SERVING

MOSCARDINI ALLA VENEZIANA

YIELD: 4 SERVINGS / **ACTIVE TIME:** 20 MINUTES / **TOTAL TIME:** 40 MINUTES

Moscardini alla veneziana are baby octopus that are boiled, split in half, and served with a lemon vinaigrette. A simple seafood appetizer, this is also a popular cicchetto at wine bars in Venice, and is often served with boiled potatoes.

1. Place the water and vinegar in a saucepan, season with salt, and bring to a boil. Submerge the ends of the moscardini in the boiling water, holding them by the head, until the tentacles curl up. Drop the moscardini in the water and cook for 30 minutes.

2. Remove the moscardini, cut them in half and season with salt and pepper.

3. Place the lemon juice and olive oil in a bowl and whisk until it has emulsified. Drizzle the emulsion over the moscardini, sprinkle the parsley on top, and serve.

INGREDIENTS:

4	CUPS WATER
2	TABLESPOONS WHITE WINE VINEGAR
	SALT AND PEPPER, TO TASTE
12	MOSCARDINI (BABY OCTOPUS), CLEANED AND RINSED
	JUICE OF 1 LEMON
¼	CUP EXTRA-VIRGIN OLIVE OIL
1	HANDFUL OF FRESH PARSLEY, FINELY CHOPPED, FOR GARNISH

CAPESANTE ALLA VENEZIANA

YIELD: 4 SERVINGS / **ACTIVE TIME:** 15 MINUTES / **TOTAL TIME:** 20 MINUTES

A beloved Venetian seafood appetizer, scallops, or capesante in Italian, are popular throughout the whole region around the upper Adriatic Sea. A fun fact about the word capesante: it means "holy head," because in the past scallop shells were used as a vessel for blessed water during the Baptism ceremony.

1. Preheat the oven to 200°F. Using a sharp knife, remove the scallops from their shells, including the orange part, and rinse them under cold water.

2. Rinse and dry the 4 largest scallop shells. Place them in the oven to keep them warm.

3. Place half of the olive oil in a large skillet and warm it over medium heat. Add the garlic and parsley and cook, stirring continually, for 2 minutes.

4. Add the scallops and sear on both sides until they are browned and just cooked through. Season them with salt and pepper.

5. Place 3 scallops in each shell, drizzle the lemon juice and remaining olive oil over them, and serve.

INGREDIENTS:

12   LARGE SCALLOPS IN THEIR SHELLS

½   CUP EXTRA-VIRGIN OLIVE OIL

1   GARLIC CLOVE, MINCED

1   HANDFUL OF FRESH PARSLEY, FINELY CHOPPED

SALT AND PEPPER, TO TASTE

JUICE OF ½ LEMON

CAPPON MAGRO

YIELD: 6 SERVINGS / ACTIVE TIME: 1 HOUR / TOTAL TIME: 3 HOURS

One of the fanciest meatless dishes of Italian cuisine, the Ligurian cappon magro was originally nothing more than a sailor's salad on a cracker, similar to cundigiun. In later times, the cooks of Genoa's aristocrats turned cappon magro into a baroque display of vegetables and seafood, smothered with a rich green sauce, salsa verde ligure. Now made on special occasions like Christmas, it is a labor of love but certainly worth the effort.

1. Fill a large saucepan with water and bring to a simmer. Place the fish in a steaming basket, place the steaming basket over the simmering water, and steam the fish until it is cooked through, 12 to 15 minutes.

2. Remove the fish from the steaming basket, drizzle olive oil and lemon juice over it, season with salt, and set it aside.

3. Bring the water to a boil. Add the cauliflower, beet, carrots, green beans, scorzonera, and artichoke hearts one at a time and cook until they are al dente.

4. Cut the cooked vegetables into small pieces, place them in separate bowls, season with olive oil, salt, and vinegar, and toss to combine. Set the vegetables aside.

5. Place the crackers in a bowl, sprinkle water and vinegar over them, and let them soak for a few minutes. Press down on the crackers to remove excess moisture and set them aside.

6. Line a 9 x 5–inch loaf pan with plastic wrap. Layer the fish and each of the vegetables in the pan, inserting 2 layers of bottarga between the vegetable layers and topping each layer with some of the salsa verde.

7. Top the cappon magro with the crackers and press down on it to compact it slightly.

8. Chill the cappon magro in the refrigerator for 2 hours.

9. Invert the cappon magro onto a serving dish and remove the plastic wrap. Spread any remaining salsa verde over it and serve alongside the seafood.

INGREDIENTS:

2 WHITEFISH FILLETS

EXTRA-VIRGIN OLIVE OIL, TO TASTE

FRESH LEMON JUICE, TO TASTE

SALT, TO TASTE

1 SMALL HEAD OF CAULIFLOWER, TRIMMED AND CHOPPED

1 BEET, PEELED AND CHOPPED

3 CARROTS, PEELED AND CHOPPED

7 OZ. GREEN BEANS, TRIMMED

3 SCORZONERA ROOTS OR 11 OZ. CELERIAC, TRIMMED

6 ARTICHOKE HEARTS

WHITE WINE VINEGAR, TO TASTE

4 GALLETTE DEL MARINAIO (SEE PAGE 767)

3½ OZ. BOTTARGA, SLICED

2 BATCHES OF SALSA VERDE LIGURE (SEE PAGE 811)

1 LB. ASSORTED SEAFOOD, COOKED, FOR SERVING

PRIMI

ZUPPA ALLA PAVESE

YIELD: 4 SERVINGS / **ACTIVE TIME:** 10 MINUTES / **TOTAL TIME:** 20 MINUTES

An earthy and extremely simple soup from Pavia, Lombardia. One tip, if possible, serve this in earthenware bowls.

1. Place the broth in a medium saucepan and bring to a boil.

2. Place the butter in a large skillet and melt it over low heat. Add the bread and cook until it is browned on both sides, 4 to 6 minutes.

3. Divide the bread among the serving bowls and sprinkle half of the Parmesan over the top. Season with salt and pepper and crack an egg over the top, taking care not to break the yolk.

4. Ladle a cup of the warm broth into each bowl, making sure not to let it hit the egg yolk.

5. Sprinkle the remaining Parmesan over each portion and serve immediately.

INGREDIENTS:

4	CUPS BRODO DI CARNE (SEE PAGE 805)
4	TABLESPOONS UNSALTED BUTTER
8	SLICES OF STALE CRUSTY BREAD
⅔	CUP GRATED PARMESAN CHEESE
	SALT AND PEPPER, TO TASTE
4	EGGS

SEUPA À LA VAPELENENTSE

YIELD: 4 SERVINGS / **ACTIVE TIME:** 10 MINUTES / **TOTAL TIME:** 10 MINUTES

One of the most popular soups from Valle d'Aosta, Seupa à la Vapelenentse features fontina and cabbage. Every July, the town of Valpelline holds the La sagra della Zuppa, a festival where one can taste the real thing while taking in the beautiful scenery.

1. Preheat the oven to 390°F. Place the broth in a medium saucepan and bring to a boil. Add the cabbage and cook until the cabbage is tender. Remove the pan from heat and set it aside.

2. Coat a baking dish with high edges with butter and cover the bottom with one-third of the bread, making sure not to leave any empty spaces.

3. Cover the bread with one-third of the fontina. Repeat until you have 3 layers of bread and cheese.

4. Pour the broth over the dish, pricking the layers of bread and cheese with a fork several times to make sure the stock is evenly distributed.

5. Place the butter in a saucepan and melt it over medium heat. Sprinkle the cinnamon over the butter and then drizzle the mixture over the dish.

6. Place the dish in the oven and bake until it is golden brown, about 40 minutes.

7. Remove the dish from the oven and let it rest for 10 minutes before serving.

INGREDIENTS:

6	CUPS BRODO DI CARNE (SEE PAGE 805)
4	LARGE SAVOY CABBAGE LEAVES, FINELY CHOPPED
5½	OZ. UNSALTED BUTTER, PLUS MORE AS NEEDED
1	LB. STALE CRUSTY BREAD, SLICED
14	OZ. FONTINA CHEESE, GRATED
⅓	TEASPOON CINNAMON

CASONSEI ALLA BERGAMASCA

YIELD: 4 SERVINGS / **ACTIVE TIME:** 30 MINUTES / **TOTAL TIME:** 30 MINUTES

Casonsei are a filled pasta typical of Lombardia, especially the cities of Bergamo and Brescia. Their filling is quite unique, combining sweet and savory ingredients like amaretti cookies, raisins, and meat.

1. Warm the oven to 200°F. Place the pancetta in a large skillet and cook it over medium heat until the fat renders, about 4 minutes. Remove the pancetta with a slotted spoon, place it in a crock, and place it in the oven to keep it warm.

2. Bring water to a boil in a large saucepan. Add salt and the Casonsei and cook until they float to the top and the meat is cooked through, about 4 minutes. Remove the Casonsei with a pasta fork and set them aside.

3. Place the butter in the skillet and melt it over medium heat. Add the sage and cook, stirring continually, for 2 minutes.

4. Add the Parmesan and some pasta water and stir until you have a creamy sauce.

5. Add the Casonsei and pancetta to the pan, toss to combine, and serve immediately.

INGREDIENTS:

3½ OZ. PANCETTA, CUT INTO STICKS (OPTIONAL)

SALT, TO TASTE

CASONSEI (SEE PAGE 69)

4 TABLESPOONS UNSALTED BUTTER

HANDFUL OF FRESH SAGE

3½ OZ. PARMESAN CHEESE, GRATED

CANEDERLI IN BRODO

YIELD: 4 SERVINGS / **ACTIVE TIME:** 40 MINUTES / **TOTAL TIME:** 1 HOUR

Canederli are the Italian version of German semmelknödel, bread dumplings, and come from the Alpine region Trentino-Alto Adige, which borders the German-speaking countries of Switzerland, Liechtenstein, and Austria.

1. Place the butter in a saucepan and melt it over medium heat. Add the onion and cook, stirring occasionally, until it is translucent, about 3 minutes.

2. Add the speck and cook, stirring occasionally, until it starts to brown, about 5 minutes.

3. Place the bread and speck mixture in a mixing bowl and stir to combine. Add the milk, parsley, half of the chives, and the eggs, season lightly with salt and pepper, and work the mixture until it is well combined. Cover the bowl and chill it in the refrigerator for 30 minutes.

4. Remove the mixture from the refrigerator and check the consistency. If it feels too loose to shape into balls, incorporate a little bit of flour until it has the desired consistency.

5. Form the mixture into 2-inch balls, trying not to make them too compact.

6. Place the broth in a medium saucepan and bring it to a boil. Add the canederli, reduce the heat, and simmer until the canederli are cooked through, about 15 minutes. Sprinkle the remaining chives over the top and serve immediately.

INGREDIENTS:

- 2 TABLESPOONS UNSALTED BUTTER
- ¼ ONION, FINELY DICED
- 5½ OZ. SPECK FROM TRENTINO-ALTO ADIGE, FAT REMOVED, FINELY DICED
- 9 OZ. STALE BREAD, CRUSTS REMOVED, CUBED
- 8.8 OZ. WHOLE MILK
- 2 TABLESPOONS FINELY CHOPPED FRESH PARSLEY
- 2 TABLESPOONS FINELY CHOPPED FRESH CHIVES
- 2 EGGS, LIGHTLY BEATEN
- SALT AND PEPPER, TO TASTE
- ALL-PURPOSE FLOUR, AS NEEDED
- 6 CUPS BRODO DI CARNE (SEE PAGE 805)

MINESTRONE DI VERDURE

YIELD: 4 SERVINGS / **ACTIVE TIME:** 40 MINUTES / **TOTAL TIME:** 24 HOURS

There are dishes that unite all of Italy, and minestrone di verdure is one of them. While it is found throughout the whole country, it is particularly popular in Central and Northern Italy, with local variations occurring everywhere, of course.

1. Place the olive oil in a large pot and warm it over medium heat. Add the onion, celery, and carrots and cook, stirring occasionally, until they have softened, about 5 minutes.

2. Add the potato, green beans, borlotti beans, Parmesan rinds, and water, season with salt, and cook for 1 hour.

3. Add the peas, zucchini, chard, and tomatoes and cook until the borlotti beans are tender, about 1 hour. If the dish starts to look too dry, add more water as necessary.

4. Season with salt, remove the Parmesan rinds, and discard them. Garnish the soup with the Parmesan and additional olive oil and serve.

INGREDIENTS:

- 3 TABLESPOONS EXTRA-VIRGIN OLIVE OIL, PLUS MORE FOR GARNISH
- ½ ONION, FINELY DICED
- ½ CELERY STALK, FINELY DICED
- 1½ CARROTS, PEELED AND FINELY DICED
- 1 POTATO, PEELED AND DICED
- 7 OZ. GREEN BEANS, TRIMMED AND CHOPPED
- 6 OZ. DRIED BORLOTTI BEANS, SOAKED OVERNIGHT AND DRAINED
- 2–3 PARMESAN RINDS
- 6 CUPS WATER, PLUS MORE AS NEEDED
- SALT, TO TASTE
- 6 OZ. PEAS
- ½ LARGE ZUCCHINI, FINELY DICED
- 3½ OZ. CHARD LEAVES, CHOPPED
- ½ CUP WHOLE PEELED TOMATOES, CRUSHED
- 2 TABLESPOONS GRATED PARMESAN CHEESE, FOR GARNISH

JOTA TRIESTINA

YIELD: 4 SERVINGS / **ACTIVE TIME:** 40 MINUTES / **TOTAL TIME:** 24 HOURS

This is a soup derived of probable ancient origin, which features as main ingredients beans, fermented cabbage in local dialect, and leftover pork. You can use any cut of pork you please here, but spareribs are traditional.

1. Place the peas, broth, and bay leaves in a large pot and bring to a boil. Reduce the heat and simmer until the peas are tender, about 1 hour.

2. Place the lard in a large saucepan and melt it over medium heat. Add the garlic and cook, stirring occasionally, until it is browned, 2 to 3 minutes.

3. Remove the garlic and discard it. Add the sauerkraut and cover it with warm water. Season with salt and pepper, reduce the heat to low, and cook for 30 minutes. Remove the pan from heat and set it aside.

4. Add the sausages to the peas and cook until the sausages are cooked through, about 15 minutes.

5. Add the potatoes to the peas and cook until they are tender, about 20 minutes.

6. Remove half of the peas and potatoes from the pot and mash them. Return them to the pot, add the sauerkraut, and stir to combine.

7. Place the olive oil in a skillet and warm it over medium heat. Add the flour, whisking continually, and cook until it turns golden brown.

8. Stir the flour mixture into the soup, season it with salt and pepper, and serve.

INGREDIENTS:

- 2   CUPS BLACK-EYED PEAS, SOAKED OVERNIGHT AND DRAINED
- 6   CUPS BRODO VEGETALE (SEE PAGE 806)
- 2   BAY LEAVES
- 2   OZ. LARD
- 4   GARLIC CLOVES, LIGHTLY CRUSHED
- 1½   LBS. SAUERKRAUT
      SALT AND PEPPER, TO TASTE
- 2   SMOKED CRAGNO SAUSAGES, CHOPPED
- 4   POTATOES, CUBED
- 3   TABLESPOONS EXTRA-VIRGIN OLIVE OIL
- 2   TABLESPOONS ALL-PURPOSE FLOUR

POLENTA TARAGNA

YIELD: 4 SERVINGS / **ACTIVE TIME:** 15 MINUTES / **TOTAL TIME:** 1 HOUR AND 15 MINUTES

Polenta taragna is a very special type of polenta made with about 2 parts buckwheat and 1 part cornmeal. It is very common in upper Lombardy, especially in the Bergamo valleys and in Valtellina. It is generally served smothered with a large amount of local Alpine cheese, which varies depending on the specific area where polenta taragna is being made.

1. Place the water and salt in a large saucepan and bring to a boil.

2. While whisking continually, slowly stream in the flour and polenta. Reduce the heat to low and cook, stirring continually, until the polenta is thick and creamy, about 1 hour. If the polenta thickens too quickly, add water as necessary.

3. Place the butter in a large skillet and melt it over medium heat. Add the sage and garlic and cook, stirring continually, for 1 minute.

4. Remove the garlic and discard it. Stir the sage and butter into the polenta.

5. Remove the polenta from heat, add the cheese, and stir until it has almost melted. Serve immediately.

INGREDIENTS:

8	CUPS WATER, PLUS MORE AS NEEDED
1	(SCANT) TABLESPOON COARSE SEA SALT
1¾	CUPS BUCKWHEAT FLOUR
1	(SCANT) CUP POLENTA
4	TABLESPOONS UNSALTED BUTTER
5	FRESH SAGE LEAVES
1	GARLIC CLOVE
11	OZ. SEMISOFT CHEESE SUCH AS ALPINE BRANZI OR EMMENTAL CHEESE, CUBED

POLENTA CONCIA ALLA VALDOSTANA

YIELD: 4 SERVINGS / **ACTIVE TIME:** 15 MINUTES / **TOTAL TIME:** 1 HOUR AND 15 MINUTES

In both Valle d'Aosta and Piedmont, the most popular way to cook polenta is smothered with local cheese. Here is a recipe for polenta concia from Valle d'Aosta, which features the fontina cheese that is popular locally.

1. Place the water and salt in a large saucepan and bring to a boil.

2. While whisking continually, slowly stream in the polenta. Reduce the heat to low and cook, stirring frequently, until the polenta is thick and creamy, about 1 hour. If the polenta thickens too quickly, add water as necessary.

3. Stir the butter into the polenta.

4. Remove the polenta from heat, add the cheese, and stir until it has almost melted. Serve immediately.

INGREDIENTS:

- 6 CUPS WATER, PLUS MORE AS NEEDED

- 1 (SCANT) TABLESPOON COARSE SEA SALT

- 2 CUPS POLENTA, PLUS MORE AS NEEDED

- 4 TABLESPOONS UNSALTED BUTTER

- 12 OZ. FONTINA CHEESE, CUBED

POLENTA AL SUGO DI SALSICCIA

YIELD: 6 SERVINGS / **ACTIVE TIME:** 30 MINUTES / **TOTAL TIME:** 2 HOURS

Although one generally associates polenta with Northern Italy, where the cultivation of corn has thrived, polenta is also very popular in Southern Italy, particularly in Basilicata and Apulia. There, just like in Veneto, one of the most treasured ways to eat polenta is with sausage and tomato sauce.

1. Place one-quarter of the olive oil in a large skillet and warm it over medium-high heat. Add the onion and cook, stirring occasionally, until it has softened, about 5 minutes.

2. Add the sausage and cook, stirring occasionally, until it is browned all over.

3. Add the wine and cook until it has evaporated.

4. Add the tomatoes and bay leaves, reduce the heat to medium, and cook, stirring occasionally, until the sauce has thickened, about 30 minutes.

5. Place the water and salt in a large saucepan and bring to a boil.

6. While whisking continually, slowly stream in the polenta. Reduce the heat to low and cook, stirring frequently, until the polenta is thick and creamy, about 1 hour. If the polenta thickens too quickly, add water as necessary.

7. Remove the polenta from heat, add the remaining olive oil and half of the Parmesan, and stir until the Parmesan has almost melted.

8. Ladle the polenta into the serving bowls and let it rest for 5 minutes. Top it with the sauce and remaining Parmesan and serve immediately.

INGREDIENTS:

7	OZ. EXTRA-VIRGIN OLIVE OIL
½	ONION, FINELY DICED
1½	LBS. LUGANEGA-STYLE ITALIAN SAUSAGE, CUT INTO LARGE CHUNKS
½	CUP DRY WHITE WINE
2.2	LBS. WHOLE PEELED TOMATOES, CRUSHED
3	BAY LEAVES
8	CUPS WATER, PLUS MORE AS NEEDED
1	(SCANT) TABLESPOON COARSE SEA SALT
3	CUPS POLENTA
2	CUPS GRATED PARMESAN CHEESE

NOT SIMPLY CORN:
A BRIEF HISTORY OF POLENTA

What we now call polenta is one of the oldest ways to consume cereals. In early agricultural settlements, cereals were ground into a coarse flour, mixed with water, and then cooked into a thick cream that must have had a consistency not that far from modern cornmeal polenta. This way of processing and eating grains was much simpler than making bread, and was certainly very common among the Italic populations that existed before the advent of the Roman Empire.

Romans, even if devoted to bread, also loved their puls, made of ground barley flour. Puls was the main staple food of Roman peasants, which often did not have the knowledge or means to make bread.

Over time, puls (polenta) started to be made from a variety of inexpensive cereals that were not ideal to make bread with, such as rye, millet, and sorghum, and even noncereals, like ground dried chestnuts, acorns, and legumes.

A polenta (then called "pulmentario") made of ground dried fava beans and panicum is mentioned in a document from Lucca dated 765 BCE, as food to feed the poor.

The role of polenta as a staple for the poor continued through the Middle Ages, based mostly on millet and legumes, until a new crop arrived from the Americas. Corn started to be cultivated in Northeast Italy, specifically in Veneto, and quickly became the staple of a whole region. The intensive cultivation of corn in Veneto was pushed by the landowners, who were focused on profits, and these landowners forced the population to only live on the corn they cultivated. This in turn caused a tragic epidemic of pellagra in the region, because Italians were not aware that corn contains toxins and needs to undergo special treatment before being consumed in large amounts. The local population was also unaware that corn has a much poorer nutritional profile compared to the cereals Italians traditionally relied upon.

Nowadays, people from Veneto and other regions, particularly on the eastern side of the peninsula, have learned how to eat corn polenta safely, and they have since turned it into a gourmet food with infinite iterations, both savory and sweet. Polenta is made from different varieties of corn, features grains of various grinds and consistencies, and, like the ancient puls, is also made with different cereals and nuts, like chestnut polenta and buckwheat polenta. So much for polenta being a food that was restricted to the poor!

RISOTTO ALLA PIEMONTESE

YIELD: 4 SERVINGS / *ACTIVE TIME*: 30 MINUTES / *TOTAL TIME*: 30 MINUTES

This is possibly the simplest risotto out there, and also the original one, first developed in Piedmont, at the Savoia court.

1. Place the broth in a saucepan and bring it to a simmer. Turn off the heat under the broth but leave it on the burner.

2. Place half of the butter in a large, deep skillet and melt it over medium heat. Add the onion and cook, stirring occasionally, until it has softened, about 5 minutes.

3. Add the rice and cook until it gives off a nutty aroma, about 2 minutes.

4. Add the wine and cook, stirring continually, until the rice absorbs it.

5. Add a few ladles of warm broth to cover the rice and cook, stirring frequently, until the rice absorbs it. Continue adding broth until the rice is al dente and the dish is creamy.

6. Season the risotto with salt and pepper and remove the pan from heat. Stir the Parmesan and remaining butter into the risotto and serve immediately.

INGREDIENTS:

- 4 CUPS BRODO VEGETALE (SEE PAGE 806)
- 4 TABLESPOONS UNSALTED BUTTER
- 1 SMALL ONION, FINELY DICED
- 11.3 OZ. CARNAROLI RICE
- ½ CUP DRY WHITE WINE

  SALT AND PEPPER, TO TASTE
- ½ CUP GRATED PARMESAN CHEESE

RISOTTO ALLA MILANESE

YIELD: 4 SERVINGS / **ACTIVE TIME:** 30 MINUTES / **TOTAL TIME:** 1 HOUR AND 30 MINUTES

Risotto alla Milanese is one of the most popular dishes from Lombardy and, specifically, its main city, Milan. It has a vivid color thanks to the saffron and a distinctive taste thanks to the bone marrow. In the absence of this latter ingredient one cannot talk of risotto alla Milanese, but keep in mind that the saffron-enriched risotto you'll end up with is still a lovely dish to make and eat.

1. Place the broth in a saucepan and bring it to a simmer. Turn off the heat under the broth but leave it on the burner. Remove 1 cup of broth, place it in a bowl, and add the saffron. Let the saffron steep for 1 hour.

2. Place two-thirds of the butter in a large, deep skillet and melt it over medium heat. Add the bone marrow and onion and cook, stirring occasionally, until it has softened, about 5 minutes.

3. Add the rice and cook until it gives off a nutty aroma, about 2 minutes.

4. Add the saffron and the broth it soaked in, season the risotto with salt, and stir to combine.

5. Continue adding broth until the rice is al dente and the dish is creamy.

6. Remove the pan from heat, stir the Parmesan and remaining butter into the risotto, season with salt, and serve immediately.

INGREDIENTS:

6   CUPS BRODO DI CARNE (SEE PAGE 805)

1   SACHET OF SAFFRON THREADS

4   TABLESPOONS UNSALTED BUTTER

2   TABLESPOONS ROASTED VEAL BONE MARROW

1   SMALL ONION, FINELY DICED

11.3 OZ. CARNAROLI RICE

     SALT, TO TASTE

½   CUP GRATED PARMESAN CHEESE

HOME OF RISOTTO:
A BRIEF HISTORY OF ITALIAN RICE

Rice cultivation in China started as early as 10,000 years ago, but this crop arrived in Europe much later, following Alexander the Great's expeditions to Asia, in the fourth century BCE.

Even if rice did reach the Greeks and the Romans, it did not immediately become a staple. Rice was considered merely a medicine for decoctions and potions against dysentery and intoxications, or as a beauty product.

Rice was reintroduced in Italy by the Arabs, probably through Sicily, where we find the popular rice-based arancini. At the same time, the Arabs also spread the use of rice to Spain, and from there rice started to be known also in Northern Italy, but not yet grown.

Until the fifteenth century, rice was largely considered an exotic item, but after the Black Death and several famines, there was a need for new cereals that the population could rely upon, which prompted the cultivation of rice in Lombardy. In this region, rice found ideal conditions to grow, as the swampy Pianura Padana plains were perfect for rice.

One of the first and most cited documents on rice cultivation in Lombardy is a letter from Gian Galeazzo Sforza, Duke of Milan, written in 1475, in which he donates 12 sacks of rice seeds to the d'Este dukes of Ferrara, assuring that each sack would yield up to 12 times as much rice.

By the beginning of the sixteenth century, rice fields in Lombardy covered over 5,500 hectares, and rice cultivation bloomed under the subsequent Spanish rule.

Rice cultivation arrived one century later in Piedmont, and then spread to Emilia-Romagna and later to Veneto.

Rice was mostly cultivated to be exported, and, to this day, Italy is still the biggest European producer of rice. However, initially rice was eaten mostly by the poor workers that were growing it, and it took a couple of centuries for rice to reach the elites' kitchens, with some exceptions.

In the nineteenth century, Italian rice started to undergo intensive genetic selection, starting with the contribution of Jesuit Father Calleri, who apparently smuggled the seeds of 43 varieties of Asian rice during his stay in the Philippines.

Further steps to refine Italian varieties were carried out by the agronomists Novello Novelli and Giovanni Sampietro, who were the first in Italy to successfully carry out the artificial hybridization of rice, which up till then had been considered impossible.

From these efforts derived the highly prized Vialone Nano, Carnaroli, and Arborio rice that today form the base of every well-made dish of risotto.

RISOTTO AL RADICCHIO ROSSO

YIELD: 4 SERVINGS / *ACTIVE TIME:* 50 MINUTES / *TOTAL TIME:* 50 MINUTES

Typical of the city of Verona, risotto al radicchio rosso has an appealing pink-purple color thanks to the inclusion of red wine. Any Italian red will do here, but Valpolicella is the best option.

1. Place the broth in a saucepan and bring it to a simmer. Turn off the heat under the stock but leave it on the burner.

2. Place two-thirds of the butter in a large, deep skillet and melt it over medium heat. Add the onion and cook, stirring occasionally, until it has softened, about 5 minutes.

3. Add the radicchio and a ladle of warm stock, season with salt and pepper, and cook until the radicchio has softened and the stock has evaporated, about 10 minutes.

4. Add the rice and cook until it gives off a nutty aroma, about 2 minutes.

5. Add the wine and cook, stirring continually, until the rice absorbs it.

6. Add a few ladles of warm broth to cover the rice and cook, stirring frequently, until the rice absorbs it. Continue adding broth until the rice is al dente and the dish is creamy.

7. Season the risotto with salt and pepper and remove the pan from heat. Stir the cheese and remaining butter into the risotto and serve immediately.

INGREDIENTS:

4	CUPS BRODO VEGETALE (SEE PAGE 806)
6	TABLESPOONS UNSALTED BUTTER
1	SMALL ONION, FINELY DICED
11	OZ. RADICCHIO ROSSO, FINELY DICED
	SALT AND PEPPER, TO TASTE
11.3	OZ. VIALONE NANO RICE
½	CUP RED WINE
2	OZ. MONTE VERONESE OR PARMESAN CHEESE, GRATED

RISOTTO ALLA PILOTA

YIELD: 4 SERVINGS / **ACTIVE TIME:** 30 MINUTES / **TOTAL TIME:** 50 MINUTES

This dish owes its name to the term used to refer to the workers involved in husking the rice, piloti. As these laborers did not have time to make a proper risotto, this dish, where the rice is first boiled, then left to steam, and finally smothered with butter and cheese and topped with stir-fried sausage, came to be.

1. Place the water in a medium saucepan and bring to a boil.

2. Add salt and the rice, ideally making the rice descend from a funnel-shaped sheet of paper. The tip of the funnel should be ½ inch above the water.

3. When the rice starts simmering, shake the saucepan and cook over high heat for about 12 minutes.

4. Remove the pan from heat, cover it, and let the rice rest for about 15 minutes.

5. While the rice is resting, place the butter in a large skillet and melt it over medium heat. Add the sausage and cook, stirring occasionally, until it is browned and cooked through, about 10 minutes.

6. Top the rice with the Grana Padano and sausage. Toss to combine and serve immediately.

INGREDIENTS:

4	CUPS WATER
	SALT, TO TASTE
14	OZ. VIALONE NANO RICE
3½	OZ. UNSALTED BUTTER
6	OZ. SALAMELLA MANTOVANA OR OTHER ITALIAN SAUSAGE, CASING REMOVED AND CRUMBLED
1	CUP GRATED GRANA PADANO CHEESE

RISOTTO AI FUNGHI E TALEGGIO

A classic mushroom risotto smothered in Taleggio, the delicious creamy cheese from Lombardy.

1. Place the broth in a saucepan and bring it to a simmer. Turn off the heat under the broth but leave it on the burner.

2. Place half of the butter in a large, deep skillet and melt it over medium heat. Add the onion and cook, stirring occasionally, until it starts to brown, about 8 minutes.

3. Add the mushrooms and parsley and cook until the mushrooms release their liquid, about 8 minutes.

4. Add the rice and cook until it gives off a nutty aroma, about 2 minutes.

5. Add the wine and cook, stirring continually, until the rice absorbs it.

6. Season with salt and pepper, add a few ladles of warm broth to cover the rice, and cook, stirring frequently, until the rice absorbs it. Continue adding broth until the rice is al dente and the dish is creamy.

7. Season the risotto with salt and pepper and remove the pan from heat. Add the taleggio and remaining butter to the risotto and stir until the cheese has melted. Serve immediately.

INGREDIENTS:

4	CUPS BRODO VEGETALE (SEE PAGE 806)
4	TABLESPOONS UNSALTED BUTTER
½	SMALL ONION, FINELY DICED
1	LB. MUSHROOMS, CLEANED AND CHOPPED
	HANDFUL OF FRESH PARSLEY, FINELY CHOPPED
11.3	OZ. VIALONE NANO RICE
½	CUP DRY WHITE WINE
	SALT AND PEPPER, TO TASTE
6	OZ. TALEGGIO CHEESE, CUBED

RISI E BISI

YIELD: 4 SERVINGS / **ACTIVE TIME:** 40 MINUTES / **TOTAL TIME:** 1 HOUR

Typical of Veneto, in particular the area of Vicenza, risi e bisi means "rice with peas." Pancetta is traditionally incorporated, but vegetarian versions also have a long history.

1. Place the broth in a saucepan and bring it to a simmer. Turn off the heat under the broth but leave it on the burner.

2. Place half of the butter in a large, deep skillet and melt it over medium heat. Add the onion and cook, stirring occasionally, until it starts to brown, about 8 minutes.

3. Add the peas and pancetta (if desired), season with salt and pepper, and add the wine, parsley, and ½ cup of warm broth. Cook, stirring continually, until the peas are tender and the pancetta is browned, 6 to 8 minutes. Remove the pan from heat.

4. Place the rice in a dry skillet and toast over medium heat until it gives off a nutty aroma, about 2 minutes.

5. Add half of the pea mixture, add a few ladles of warm broth to cover the rice, and cook, stirring frequently, until the rice absorbs the broth. Continue adding broth until the rice is al dente and the dish is creamy.

6. Season the dish with salt and pepper and stir in the remaining pea mixture, the remaining butter, and the Parmesan. Stir until the cheese has melted and add more stock if a soupy risi e bisi is desired. Serve immediately.

INGREDIENTS:

- 4 CUPS BRODO VEGETALE (SEE PAGE 806)
- 4 TABLESPOONS UNSALTED BUTTER
- ½ SMALL ONION, FINELY DICED
- 1.3 LBS. PEAS
- 3½ OZ. PANCETTA, DICED (OPTIONAL)
- SALT AND PEPPER, TO TASTE
- ½ CUP DRY WHITE WINE
- HANDFUL OF FRESH PARSLEY, FINELY CHOPPED
- 11.3 OZ. CARNAROLI OR VIALONE NANO RICE
- ½ CUP GRATED PARMESAN CHEESE

GNOCCHI DI PATATE AL GORGONZOLA E NOCI

YIELD: 4 SERVINGS / ACTIVE TIME: 15 MINUTES / TOTAL TIME: 25 MINUTES

Potato gnocchi are a popular Italian primo, with origins more modern than the average Italian specialty. Apparently, potato gnocchi appeared in Lombardy at the end of the nineteenth century. Here is a scrumptious and easy way to eat this delicacy, with Gorgonzola and walnuts.

1. Place the milk and Gorgonzola in a large saucepan and warm over low heat until the Gorgonzola has melted. Remove the pan from heat and set the sauce aside.

2. Bring water to a boil in a large saucepan. Add salt and the gnocchi, let the gnocchi rise to the surface, and cook for another minute once they do.

3. Drain the gnocchi and add them to the sauce along with the walnuts and parsley. Season with pepper, toss to combine, and serve immediately.

INGREDIENTS:

½   CUP MILK

6   OZ. GORGONZOLA CHEESE

    SALT AND PEPPER, TO TASTE

1.1   LBS. GNOCCHI DI PATATE (SEE PAGE 65)

½   CUP WALNUTS, TOASTED AND COARSELY CRUMBLED

1   TABLESPOON FINELY CHOPPED FRESH PARSLEY

GNOCCHI ALLA BAVA

YIELD: 4 SERVINGS / ACTIVE TIME: 20 MINUTES / TOTAL TIME: 30 MINUTES

Gnocchi alla bava are a type of gnocchi developed in Valle d'Aosta, and were likely the original Italian gnocchi.

1. Place the cream in a small saucepan and warm it over low heat.

2. Add the fontina and let it melt very slowly over low heat.

3. Season the sauce with salt and pepper, remove the pan from heat, and cover it.

4. Bring water to a boil in a large saucepan. Add salt and the gnocchi, let the gnocchi rise to the surface, and cook for another minute once they do.

5. Drain the gnocchi and add them to the sauce. Toss to combine and serve immediately.

INGREDIENTS:

1½   CUPS WHIPPING CREAM

9   OZ. FONTINA CHEESE,
      CUBED

      SALT AND PEPPER, TO
      TASTE

      GNOCCHI DI GRANO
      SARACENO (SEE PAGE 70)

TORTELLINI MODENESI AL SUGO

YIELD: 6 SERVINGS / **ACTIVE TIME:** 40 MINUTES / **TOTAL TIME:** 1 HOUR AND 30 MINUTES

Tortellini are originally from Modena, and they are typically served in broth, like cappelletti. The difference between tortellini and cappelletti lies in the details: tortellini are slightly smaller and have a visible hole in the middle, due to the slightly different shaping technique; tortellini feature mortadella in the filling, which should not be present in cappelletti, and, finally, tortellini are generally made with ground meat.

1. Place the butter in a Dutch oven and melt it over medium heat. Add the veal and pork and sear until they have browned, turning them as necessary. Remove the meats from the pot, season with salt and pepper, and set them aside.

2. Add the mortadella, ham, Parmesan, and nutmeg. Cook, stirring occasionally, until they have been incorporated. Remove the pan from heat and add the mixture to the pork and veal. Toss to combine and set the filling aside. If a smoother consistency is desired for the filling, place it in a food processor and blitz until it is a paste.

3. Run the pasta dough through a pasta maker until it is a ¹⁄₁₆-inch-thick sheet and place it on a flour-dusted work surface.

4. Using a ravioli wheel, cut the sheet into 2½-inch squares.

5. Form small amounts of the filling into balls. Place a ball in the center of each square and fold one corner of the square over the filling, creating a triangle. Press down on the edges to seal the tortellini. If the pasta dough feels a bit too dry, moisten the edges of the squares before sealing. Join the two ends of the base of the triangle together and gently press to seal.

6. Place the tortellini on flour-dusted baking sheets and let them dry for 30 minutes.

7. Place the sauce in a large saucepan and warm it over medium-low heat.

8. Bring water to a boil in a large saucepan. Add salt, let the water return to a full boil, and add the tortellini. Cook until they rise to the surface.

9. Remove the tortellini with a slotted spoon and add them to the sauce. Gently toss to combine and serve with additional Parmesan.

INGREDIENTS:

2	TABLESPOONS UNSALTED BUTTER
5½	OZ. VEAL, MINCED
5½	OZ. PORK TENDERLOIN, MINCED
	SALT AND PEPPER, TO TASTE
3½	OZ. MORTADELLA, FINELY DICED
3½	OZ. PARMA HAM, FINELY DICED
3	CUPS GRATED PARMESAN CHEESE, PLUS MORE FOR SERVING
2	PINCHES OF FRESHLY GRATED NUTMEG
1½	BATCHES OF PASTA ALL'UOVO (SEE PAGE 73)
	ALL-PURPOSE FLOUR, AS NEEDED
	SUGO AL BASILICO (SEE PAGE 806)

GNOCCHI ALLA ZUCCA

YIELD: 4 SERVINGS / **ACTIVE TIME:** 40 MINUTES / **TOTAL TIME:** 1 HOUR AND 30 MINUTES

These lovely orange gnocchi are common in Mantua, where, soon after the discovery of the Americas, pumpkin began to be successfully cultivated. If you can locate Mantua or Hokkaido pumpkins, those will serve you best here.

1. Preheat the oven to 390°F. Wrap the pumpkin in aluminum foil, place it in a baking dish, and place it in the oven. Bake until the flesh is tender, about 1 hour.

2. Remove the pumpkin from the oven and scrape the flesh into a mixing bowl. Mash the pumpkin until smooth.

3. Add the egg white, flour, and a couple of pinches of salt to the pumpkin and work the mixture until it comes together as a smooth dough. If the dough is a little too loose for your liking, incorporate a little more flour until it has the desired consistency.

4. Place the dough on a flour-dusted work surface and divide it into 6 pieces. Roll each piece into a 1-inch-thick log.

5. Cut each log into 1-inch gnocchi and gently press down on them with the tines of a fork to give the traditional gnocchi shape.

6. Bring water to a boil in a large saucepan. Place the butter in a small skillet and melt it over medium heat. Add the sage, reduce the heat to medium-low, and cook for 2 to 3 minutes. Remove the sage butter from heat.

7. Add salt and the gnocchi to the boiling water, let the gnocchi rise to the surface, and cook for another minute once they do.

8. Remove the gnocchi from the pan with a slotted spoon and add them to the sauce. Top with the Grana Padano, gently toss to combine, and serve immediately.

INGREDIENTS:

- 2.2 LBS. PUMPKIN, HALVED, SEEDED, AND CUT INTO WEDGES
- 1 EGG WHITE
- 7 OZ. ALL-PURPOSE FLOUR, PLUS MORE AS NEEDED
- SALT, TO TASTE
- 6 TABLESPOONS UNSALTED BUTTER
- HANDFUL OF FRESH SAGE
- ½ CUP GRATED GRANA PADANO CHEESE

ISABELLA D'ESTE:
MARCHIONESS OF MANTUA
AND RENAISSANCE FOODIE

In the past, famous dishes that end up entering the culinary tradition of an entire region were oftentimes developed for the tables of notable historical personalities. This was the case for the baba au rhum, for instance, which was created by the exiled King Stanislaus of Poland in tandem with his chef, and may be the case with tortelli di zucca, which were possibly created under the food-savvy influence of Isabella d'Este, Marchioness of Mantua.

Mantua is a beautiful city in Southern Lombardy, bordering with Emilia-Romagna and Tuscany, and it was an independent city-state during the Middle Ages. Isabella d'Este, even being a woman, became a driving force in Mantua's support of the arts and culture, as she was granted extreme freedom and power—to the point that she ruled Mantua on her own for several years, first during her husband's imprisonment, and then again after his death. Respected as very few leaders were, she became one of the most important engines of the Renaissance.

Among the many things Isabella d'Este became known for were her classy and delicious banquets which introduced new dishes that then became traditional. One of them could have been tortelli di zucca. Isabella was originally from Ferrara, in Emilia-Romagna, where pasta all'uovo was already blooming by the beginning of the sixteenth century. When she married the head of Mantua, Francesco Gonzaga, in 1490, she brought her know-how and the head chef in the Ferrara court, Cristoforo di Messisbugo. Soon after Isabella moved to Mantua, the pumpkin reached Italy and found a fertile soil in Mantua. The local variety that resulted, zucca mantovana (pumpkin from Mantua), is highly prized and still at the center of Mantua's rich culinary scene.

We now know that Isabella's favorite soup was pumpkin based, and from there we can speculate that tortelli di zucca was developed based on her wishes, since they featured her native pasta all'uovo and her beloved pumpkin. The first written report of the pumpkin-filled ravioli is from a master of ceremonies, Giovanni Battista Rossetti, at the service of Lucrezia d'Este, one of Isabella d'Este descendants, in Ferrara.

It is also believed that gnocchi di zucca was developed at Mantua's court, as they were pumpkin based and Mantua was an early adopter of this new crop. Since pumpkin never really became a staple in Italy, gnocchi spread to the rest of Italy only at the end of the nineteenth century, following the late but widespread diffusion of potatoes in the peninsula.

TORTELLI DI ZUCCA

YIELD: 8 SERVINGS / **ACTIVE TIME:** 2 HOURS / **TOTAL TIME:** 3 DAYS

Tortelli di zucca are born from the careful hands of the Mantua court's chefs. With this in mind, it does not surprise that they are a refined labor of love. One needs to make fresh pasta all'uovo, bake amaretti, hunt for the right type of pumpkin (one that is not too watery), and then spend a few days preparing one of the main ingredients, mostarda mantovana, which is an essential part of the filling, and pretty much impossible to swap out.

1. Preheat the oven to 390°F. Wrap the pumpkin in aluminum foil, place it in a baking dish, and place it in the oven. Bake until the flesh is tender, about 1 hour.

2. Remove the pumpkin from the oven and scrape the flesh into a mixing bowl. Mash the pumpkin until smooth.

3. Add the Grana Padano, Amaretti, and Mostarda Mantovana, season with salt and nutmeg, and stir until combined. Set the filling aside.

4. Run the pasta dough through a pasta maker until it is a 1⁄16-inch-thick sheet and place it on a flour-dusted work surface.

5. Using a ravioli wheel, cut the sheet into 2½-inch squares. Place a generous teaspoon of the filling in the center of every square and fold each square over the filling. Press down on the edges to seal the tortelli. If the pasta dough feels a bit too dry, moisten the edges of the squares before sealing.

6. Bring water to a boil in a large saucepan. Place the butter in a large skillet and melt it over medium heat. Add the sage and cook for 2 minutes. Remove the sage butter from heat.

7. Add salt, let the water return to a full boil, and add the pasta. Cook until the torelli rise to the surface.

8. Remove the tortelli with a pasta fork and add them to the sage butter. Top with a generous amount of Grana Padano, shake the pan to distribute the sauce, and serve immediately.

INGREDIENTS:

- 2.2 LBS. PUMPKIN, HALVED, SEEDED, AND CUT INTO WEDGES
- 5 CUPS GRATED GRANA PADANO, PLUS MORE FOR TOPPING
- 11 OZ. AMARETTI (SEE PAGE 741), CRUMBLED
- 7 OZ. MOSTARDA MANTOVANA (SEE RECIPE), MINCED
- SALT, TO TASTE
- FRESHLY GRATED NUTMEG, TO TASTE
- 2 BATCHES OF PASTA ALL'UOVO (SEE PAGE 73)
- ALL-PURPOSE FLOUR, AS NEEDED
- ½ CUP UNSALTED BUTTER
- 2 HANDFULS OF FRESH SAGE

MOSTARDA MANTOVANA

- 1.1 LBS. QUINCE, PEELED, CORED, AND SLICED THIN
- 1¼ CUPS SUGAR
- 6–8 DROPS MUSTARD ESSENCE

MOSTARDA MANTOVANA

1. Place the quince and sugar in a bowl, cover it with plastic wrap, and let the mixture macerate for 1 day.

2. Collect the juice from the quince and place it in a saucepan. Cook over low heat until it has thickened, about 10 minutes.

3. Add the juice back to the mixture, toss to combine, and cover the bowl. Let the mixture macerate for 1 day.

4. Repeat Steps 2 and 3.

5. Place the mixture in a saucepan and cook until it has caramelized, about 10 minutes.

6. Remove the pan from heat and let the mixture cool.

7. Add the mustard essence and transfer the mostarda to sterilized mason jars. Use immediately or store in the refrigerator.

CAPPELLACCI DI ZUCCA

YIELD: 4 SERVINGS / **ACTIVE TIME:** 1 HOUR / **TOTAL TIME:** 2 HOURS

Ferrara is home to cappellacci di zucca, a large, tortellini-type pasta. It is similar to Mantua's tortelli di zucca, and although shaping the pasta is slightly more difficult, the filling is simpler.

1. Preheat the oven to 390°F. Wrap the squash in aluminum foil, place it in a baking dish, and place it in the oven. Bake until the flesh is tender, about 40 minutes.

2. Remove the squash from the oven and scrape the flesh into a mixing bowl. Mash the squash until smooth.

3. Add the Parmesan and egg, season with salt, pepper, and nutmeg, and stir to combine. If the filling is too soft, incorporate some bread crumbs until it has the right consistency. Cover the bowl with plastic wrap and chill it in the refrigerator.

4. Run the pasta dough through a pasta maker until it is a ⅟₁₆-inch-thick and place it on a flour-dusted work surface.

5. Using a ravioli wheel, cut the sheet into 2½-inch squares. Place a generous teaspoon of the filling in the center of every square and fold one corner of the square over the filling, creating a triangle. Press down on the edges to seal the cappellacci. If the pasta dough feels a bit too dry, moisten the edges of the squares before sealing. Join the two ends of the base of the triangle together and gently press to seal.

6. Place the cappellacci on flour-dusted baking sheets and let them dry for 30 minutes.

7. Bring water to a boil in a large saucepan. Place the butter in a large skillet and melt it over medium heat. Add the sage and cook for 2 minutes. Remove the sage butter from heat.

8. Add salt to the boiling water and let the water return to a full boil. Add the cappellacci to the boiling water and cook until they rise to the surface.

9. Remove the cappellacci with a pasta fork and add them to the sage butter. Top with a generous amount of Parmesan, shake the pan to distribute the sauce, and serve immediately.

INGREDIENTS:

- 1.3 LBS. BUTTERNUT SQUASH, HALVED, SEEDED, AND CUT INTO WEDGES
- 1½ CUPS GRATED PARMESAN CHEESE, PLUS MORE FOR TOPPING
- 1 EGG
- SALT AND PEPPER, TO TASTE
- FRESHLY GRATED NUTMEG, TO TASTE
- BREAD CRUMBS, TO TASTE
- PASTA ALL'UOVO (SEE PAGE 73)
- ALL-PURPOSE FLOUR, AS NEEDED
- 4 TABLESPOONS UNSALTED BUTTER
- HANDFUL OF FRESH SAGE

AGNOLOTTI ALESSANDRINI

YIELD: 8 SERVINGS / **ACTIVE TIME:** 1 HOUR AND 20 MINUTES / **TOTAL TIME:** 27 HOURS

In Piedmont, filled pasta is known as agnolotti, and the most beloved filling for it is a meat-based ragù.

1. Place the beef, wine, onion, garlic, carrot, celery, cinnamon stick, juniper berries, and bay leaves in a large bowl and stir to combine. Cover the bowl with plastic wrap and let the beef marinate in the refrigerator for 24 hours.

2. Drain the mixture, reserving the liquid. Remove the beef from the mixture and set the vegetables and aromatics aside.

3. Place the butter in a Dutch oven and melt it over medium heat. Pat the beef dry and add it to the pot along with the spleen (if desired) and sausage. Cook until the meats have browned, turning them as necessary.

4. Add the vegetables, season with salt and pepper, and cook, stirring occasionally, for 5 minutes.

5. Strain the wine into a small saucepan and warm it over medium heat.

6. Add the wine to the Dutch oven, reduce the heat to low, and cover the pot. Cook until the meat starts to fall apart, about 2 hours.

7. While the beef is braising, bring water to a boil in a large saucepan. Add salt and the escarole and cook for 2 minutes. Drain the escarole, finely chop it, and set it aside.

8. Remove one-third of the meat from the Dutch oven and finely chop it. Remove the ragù from heat.

9. Place the finely chopped meat, salami, and escarole in a bowl and stir to combine. If necessary, add the egg to bind the filling together. Set the filling aside.

10. Run the pasta dough through a pasta maker until it is a 1/16-inch-thick sheet and place it on a flour-dusted work surface.

11. Using a ravioli wheel, cut the sheet into 2½-inch squares. Place a generous teaspoon of the filling in the center of every square and fold one side over the filling. Press down on the edges to seal the agnolotti. If the pasta dough feels a bit too dry, moisten the edges of the squares before sealing.

INGREDIENTS:

- 2.2 LBS. STEW BEEF, CUT INTO LARGE CUBES
- 26.4 OZ. BARBERA OR OTHER MEDIUM-STRONG RED WINE
- 1 SMALL ONION, CHOPPED
- 2 GARLIC CLOVES, HALVED
- 1 CARROT, PEELED AND CHOPPED
- 1 CELERY STALK, PEELED AND CHOPPED
- 1 CINNAMON STICK
- 4 JUNIPER BERRIES
- 2 BAY LEAVES
- 2 OZ. UNSALTED BUTTER
- 3½ OZ. SPLEEN, CHOPPED (OPTIONAL)
- 5 OZ. ITALIAN SAUSAGE, CASING REMOVED AND CRUMBLED
- SALT AND PEPPER, TO TASTE
- 1 HEAD OF ESCAROLE
- 3½ OZ. SALAMI, FINELY DICED
- 1 EGG (OPTIONAL)
- 2 BATCHES OF PASTA ALL'UOVO (SEE PAGE 73)
- ALL-PURPOSE FLOUR, AS NEEDED
- 1 CUP GRATED GRANA PADANO

12. Bring water to a boil in a large saucepan. Warm the ragù over medium-low heat.

13. Add salt to the boiling water and let the water return to a full boil. Add the agnolotti to the boiling water and cook until they rise to the surface.

14. Remove the agnolotti with a pasta fork and add them to the ragù. Top with the Grana Padano, gently toss to combine, and serve immediately.

CAPPELLETTI IN BRODO

YIELD: 6 SERVINGS / ACTIVE TIME: 1 HOUR / TOTAL TIME: 5 HOURS

Cappelletti in brodo are nowadays the typical Christmas primo for many Italians across the peninsula. Cappelletti are different from Modena's tortellini in that they are larger and have no hole in the center. Traditionally cappelletti are served in a stock made with a capon, which is generally fattier. If you cannot find a capon, regular chicken stock will be fine.

1. Place the butter in a Dutch oven and melt it over medium heat. Add the carrot, celery, and onion and cook, stirring occasionally, until they have browned, about 8 minutes.

2. Add the beef, veal, and pork and sear until they have browned, turning them as necessary.

3. Add the wine and cook until it has evaporated.

4. Add the beef broth, cinnamon, cloves, and nutmeg, season with salt and pepper, and reduce the heat to low. Braise until the meats start to fall apart, about 3 hours. Drain the meat and the vegetables, place them in a bowl, and let them cool.

5. Mince the meat, return it to the bowl, stir in the ham and Parmesan, and cover with plastic wrap. Chill the filling in the refrigerator for 30 minutes.

6. Run the pasta dough through a pasta maker until it is a 1/16-inch-thick sheet and place it on a flour-dusted work surface.

7. Using a ravioli wheel, cut the sheet into 1⅓-inch squares.

8. Remove the filling from the refrigerator and form small amounts of it into balls. Place a ball in the center of each square and fold one corner of the square over the filling, creating a triangle. Press down on the edges to seal the cappelletti. If the pasta dough feels a bit too dry, moisten the edges of the squares before sealing. Join the two ends of the base of the triangle together and gently press to seal.

9. Place the cappelletti on flour-dusted baking sheets and let them dry for 30 minutes.

10. Place the chicken broth in a large saucepan and warm it over medium heat.

11. Add salt and let the broth return to a full boil. Add the cappelletti to the broth and cook until they rise to the surface.

12. Remove the cappelletti with a pasta fork and divide them among the serving bowls. Ladle some broth into each bowl and serve with additional Parmesan.

INGREDIENTS:

½	CUP UNSALTED BUTTER
1	MEDIUM CARROT, PEELED AND FINELY DICED
1	CELERY STALK, FINELY DICED
1	SMALL YELLOW ONION, FINELY DICED
7	OZ. LEAN BEEF
5½	OZ. LEAN VEAL
5½	OZ. PORK TENDERLOIN
1	CUP RED WINE
2	CUPS BRODO DI CARNE (SEE PAGE 805)
	PINCH OF CINNAMON
2	PINCHES OF GROUND CLOVES
2	PINCHES OF FRESHLY GRATED NUTMEG
	SALT AND PEPPER, TO TASTE
3	OZ. PARMA HAM, FINELY DICED
2½	CUPS GRATED PARMESAN CHEESE, PLUS MORE FOR SERVING
1½	BATCHES OF PASTA ALL'UOVO (SEE PAGE 73)
	ALL-PURPOSE FLOUR, AS NEEDED
	BRODO DI POLLO (SEE PAGE 805), STRAINED TO REMOVE ALL IMPURITIES

PASTA ALL'UOVO:
THE GOLD OF THE NORTH

While in Southern and Central Italy we find mostly pasta made from durum wheat and water, in Northern Italy pasta all'uovo, egg pasta, rules.

There is surprisingly very little knowledge as to why we have this big division between North and South regarding pasta, so we can only speculate as to the reasons for this divergence.

We do know that pasta was first developed in the South, using flour and water, and that, around the turn of the first millennium, Sicily started to produce several types of dried pasta.

Regarding the North, we know that pies (torte) were commonly used to encase all sorts of fillings in an easy, transportable way. The pastry that encased the fillings in these torte was probably hard and not particularly tasty, so it is possible that egg pasta developed as an alternative way to encase a filling in a dough that was pleasing to the palate, for a change. Indeed, it is difficult to ignore the similarity between the word "torta" and the words "tortelli" and "tortellini," two popular types of filled egg pasta.

Egg pasta developed around the Po Valley, a marshy area that was far from ideal for growing wheat. During the Middle Ages, wheat in this area was scarcely available or weak at best. The substitution of eggs for water in the making of pasta dough was probably done to correct defects present in the wheat, which thanks to the eggs became extensible and elastic enough to be molded into pasta. The scarcity of wheat was probably the reason why pasta, around the Po Valley, developed more as a means of making miniature pies, or mini torte—tortellini—rather than to be eaten as it is. Unfilled egg pasta, like tagliatelle, was surely also popular but was overshadowed by a myriad of filled pastas, where the sfoglia, the pasta sheet, is so thin that only a small amount of flour is enough to feed many mouths. As is always the case in traditional cooking, di necessità virtù, something wholesome and delicious was indeed created out of necessity, and we probably have to thank the Po River and its marshy valley for the incredible gift of egg pasta.

RAVIOLI RICOTTA E SPINACI

YIELD: 4 SERVINGS / **ACTIVE TIME:** 40 MINUTES / **TOTAL TIME:** 2 HOURS

The most popular ravioli are filled with ricotta cheese and spinach, and while they probably originated in Emilia-Romagna, they are enjoyed all over Italy. The older versions of this filled pasta probably featured different vegetables than spinach, such as chard, as well as other types of cheese than ricotta, so feel free to alter the recipe as desired.

1. Place the 1 tablespoon of butter in a large skillet and melt it over medium heat. Add the spinach and cook until it has wilted, 2 to 3 minutes. Remove the spinach, place it in a colander, and let it drain and cool.

2. Squeeze the spinach to remove any excess liquid and chop it. Set the spinach aside.

3. Place the ricotta, half of the Parmesan, and the spinach in a bowl, season with nutmeg, salt, and pepper, and stir to combine. Set the filling aside.

4. Divide the pasta dough into two pieces. Cover 1 piece with plastic wrap and set it aside. Run the other piece of pasta dough through a pasta maker until it is a 1⁄16-inch-thick sheet and place it on a flour-dusted work surface.

5. Distribute dollops of the filling over the sheet, leaving 1.2 inches between each dollop. Moisten the pasta around the filling with water.

6. Run the remaining piece of pasta dough through the pasta maker until it is a 1⁄16-inch-thick sheet that is as long as the sheet with the filling on it.

7. Lay the second sheet of pasta over the first. Pinch the pasta around the filling so that the 2 sheets get sealed together. Using a ravioli wheel and possibly a ruler, cut the ravioli into squares.

8. Bring water to a boil in a large saucepan. Place the remaining butter in a large skillet and melt it over medium heat. Add the sage and cook for 2 minutes. Remove the sage butter from heat.

9. Add salt to the boiling water and let the water return to a full boil. Add the ravioli to the boiling water and cook until they rise to the surface.

10. Remove the ravioli with a pasta fork and add them to the sage butter. Top with the remaining Parmesan, shake the pan to distribute the sauce, and serve immediately.

INGREDIENTS:

- 1⁄2 CUP PLUS 1 TABLESPOON UNSALTED BUTTER
- 14 OZ. FRESH SPINACH
- 7 OZ. RICOTTA CHEESE, DRAINED IN THE REFRIGERATOR FOR 1 HOUR
- 7 OZ. PARMESAN CHEESE, GRATED
- FRESHLY GRATED NUTMEG, TO TASTE
- SALT AND PEPPER, TO TASTE
- PASTA ALL'UOVO (SEE PAGE 73)
- ALL-PURPOSE FLOUR, AS NEEDED
- 2 HANDFULS OF FRESH SAGE LEAVES

PASSATELLI IN BRODO

YIELD: 4 SERVINGS / **ACTIVE TIME:** 40 MINUTES / **TOTAL TIME:** 3 HOURS

Most popular in Romagna, but treasured throughout Northern Italy, passatelli are a lovely handmade pasta that are easy to make and delicious. If you're using bread crumbs made from homemade bread, make sure they come from a loaf containing no fat.

1. Place the bread crumbs and Parmesan in a bowl and stir to combine. Set the mixture aside.

2. Place the eggs, nutmeg, and lemon zest in a separate bowl, lightly season with salt, and whisk to combine.

3. Add the egg mixture to the bread crumb mixture and work it with a fork until well combined.

4. Knead the dough until it has the consistency of short-crust pastry. If the dough feels too soft, incorporate equal amounts of bread crumbs and Parmesan. If it is too hard, incorporate some stock.

5. Form the dough into a ball, cover it with plastic wrap, and chill it in the refrigerator for 2 hours.

6. Place the stock in a large saucepan and bring it to a boil. Place a piece of dough in a potato ricer with large holes and squeeze out passatelli that are about 3 inches long.

7. When all of the dough has passed through the potato ricer, add the passatelli to the stock and cook until they rise to the surface.

8. Divide the passatelli and broth among the serving bowls, top each portion with a generous sprinkle of Parmesan, and serve.

INGREDIENTS:

- 7 OZ. BREAD CRUMBS, PLUS MORE AS NEEDED
- 7 OZ. PARMESAN CHEESE, PLUS MORE AS NEEDED
- 4 LARGE EGGS
- 2 PINCHES OF FRESHLY GRATED NUTMEG

ZEST OF ½ LEMON

SALT, TO TASTE

- 6 CUPS BRODO DI CARNE (SEE PAGE 805), PLUS MORE AS NEEDED

TAGLIATELLE RAGÙ ALLA BOLOGNESE

YIELD: 4 SERVINGS / **ACTIVE TIME:** 40 MINUTES / **TOTAL TIME:** 3 HOURS AND 30 MINUTES

There is a book about it—*Gli spaghetti alla bolognese non esistono* by Filippo Venturi—but it is worth repeating it: spaghetti Bolognese do not belong to Italian cuisine, and definitely do not belong to Bologna. Spaghetti are a dry pasta format typical of Central and Southern Italy that are almost never eaten with a meat ragù. What we find in Bologna is instead tagliatelle ragù alla Bolognese, a local fresh egg pasta that is perfect to withstand such a rich condiment. When making Bolognese, make sure the carrot, onion, celery, and pancetta are very finely chopped—they should almost disappear in the sauce.

1. Place the butter in a Dutch oven and melt it over medium heat. Add the carrot, onion, celery, and bay leaf and cook, stirring occasionally, until the vegetables have softened, about 5 minutes.

2. Add the pancetta and cook, stirring occasionally, until it starts to brown, about 5 minutes.

3. Add the pork and beef and cook, breaking them up with a wooden spoon, until they have browned, about 6 minutes.

4. Add the wine and cook until it has evaporated.

5. Remove the bay leaf and discard it. Add the tomatoes and tomato paste, reduce the heat to low, and cover the pot. Cook until the sauce has thickened considerably, stirring occasionally and adding stock as necessary, about 3 hours.

6. Stir in the milk, season with salt and pepper, and raise the heat to medium-high. Let the sauce cook until it becomes creamy and then remove it from heat.

7. Bring water to a boil in a large saucepan. Add salt, let the water return to a full boil, and add the pasta. Cook until the pasta is al dente.

8. Drain the pasta and place it in a large serving bowl. Add the sauce and half of the Parmesan and toss to combine. Top each portion with the remaining Parmesan and serve.

INGREDIENTS:

2	TABLESPOONS UNSALTED BUTTER
1	CARROT, PEELED AND MINCED
1	SMALL ONION, MINCED
1	CELERY STALK, PEELED AND MINCED
1	BAY LEAF
6	OZ. PANCETTA, MINCED
11	OZ. GROUND PORK
1.1	LBS. GROUND BEEF
⅔	CUP DRY WHITE WINE
1.3	LBS. WHOLE PEELED TOMATOES, CRUSHED
2	TABLESPOONS TOMATO PASTE
	BEEF STOCK, TO TASTE
⅔	CUP WHOLE MILK
	SALT AND PEPPER, TO TASTE
	TAGLIATELLE (SEE PAGE 74)
3½	OZ. PARMESAN CHEESE, GRATED

LASAGNE ALLA BOLOGNESE

YIELD: 4 SERVINGS / **ACTIVE TIME:** 40 MINUTES / **TOTAL TIME:** 1 HOUR AND 20 MINUTES

While possibly the most famous Italian lasagna, lasagne alla Bolognese is not the oldest form, as it appears that Neapolitan lasagne came first. But it is the Bolognese version that conquered the world, thanks to its use of egg-based pasta and béchamel.

1. Preheat the oven to 320°F. Place the pasta dough on a flour-dusted work surface and roll it into a ⅕-inch-thick rectangle. Cut the dough into 7 sheets that will fit your baking dish (8 x 10–inch sheets should be good for four generous portions).

2. Bring water to a boil in a large saucepan. Add salt, let the water return to a full boil, and add the pasta. Cook until the pasta has just softened.

3. Drain the pasta and place it on a kitchen towel to dry.

4. Spread a thin layer of béchamel over the baking dish. Top with a sheet of pasta, cover the pasta with a layer of béchamel, spread a layer of the ragù over the béchamel, and finish with a generous sprinkle of the Parmesan. Repeat until all of the pasta sheets have been used up.

5. Top the last pasta sheet with bèchamel, ragù, the butter, and the remaining Parmesan.

6. Place the lasagna in the oven and bake until the cheese has melted and the top is golden brown, about 30 minutes.

7. Remove the lasagna from the oven and let it rest for 20 minutes before slicing and serving.

INGREDIENTS:

PASTA ALL'UOVO VERDE (SEE PAGE 77)

ALL-PURPOSE FLOUR, AS NEEDED

SALT, TO TASTE

BESCIMELLA (SEE PAGE 810)

RAGÙ ALLA BOLOGNESE (SEE OPPOSITE PAGE)

7 OZ. PARMESAN CHEESE, GRATED

2 TABLESPOONS UNSALTED BUTTER, CHOPPED

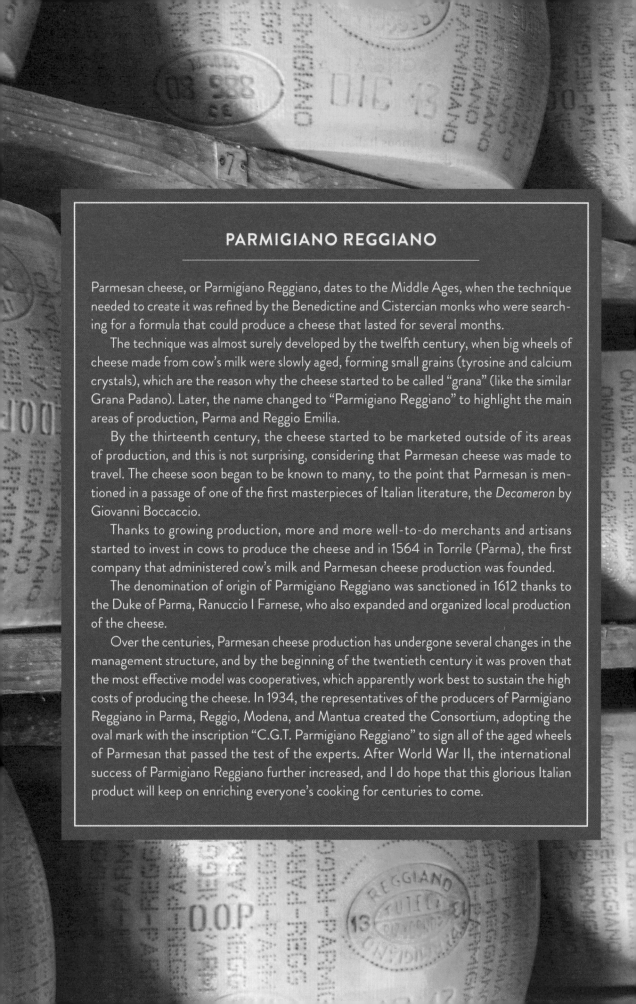

PARMIGIANO REGGIANO

Parmesan cheese, or Parmigiano Reggiano, dates to the Middle Ages, when the technique needed to create it was refined by the Benedictine and Cistercian monks who were searching for a formula that could produce a cheese that lasted for several months.

The technique was almost surely developed by the twelfth century, when big wheels of cheese made from cow's milk were slowly aged, forming small grains (tyrosine and calcium crystals), which are the reason why the cheese started to be called "grana" (like the similar Grana Padano). Later, the name changed to "Parmigiano Reggiano" to highlight the main areas of production, Parma and Reggio Emilia.

By the thirteenth century, the cheese started to be marketed outside of its areas of production, and this is not surprising, considering that Parmesan cheese was made to travel. The cheese soon began to be known to many, to the point that Parmesan is mentioned in a passage of one of the first masterpieces of Italian literature, the *Decameron* by Giovanni Boccaccio.

Thanks to growing production, more and more well-to-do merchants and artisans started to invest in cows to produce the cheese and in 1564 in Torrile (Parma), the first company that administered cow's milk and Parmesan cheese production was founded.

The denomination of origin of Parmigiano Reggiano was sanctioned in 1612 thanks to the Duke of Parma, Ranuccio I Farnese, who also expanded and organized local production of the cheese.

Over the centuries, Parmesan cheese production has undergone several changes in the management structure, and by the beginning of the twentieth century it was proven that the most effective model was cooperatives, which apparently work best to sustain the high costs of producing the cheese. In 1934, the representatives of the producers of Parmigiano Reggiano in Parma, Reggio, Modena, and Mantua created the Consortium, adopting the oval mark with the inscription "C.G.T. Parmigiano Reggiano" to sign all of the aged wheels of Parmesan that passed the test of the experts. After World War II, the international success of Parmigiano Reggiano further increased, and I do hope that this glorious Italian product will keep on enriching everyone's cooking for centuries to come.

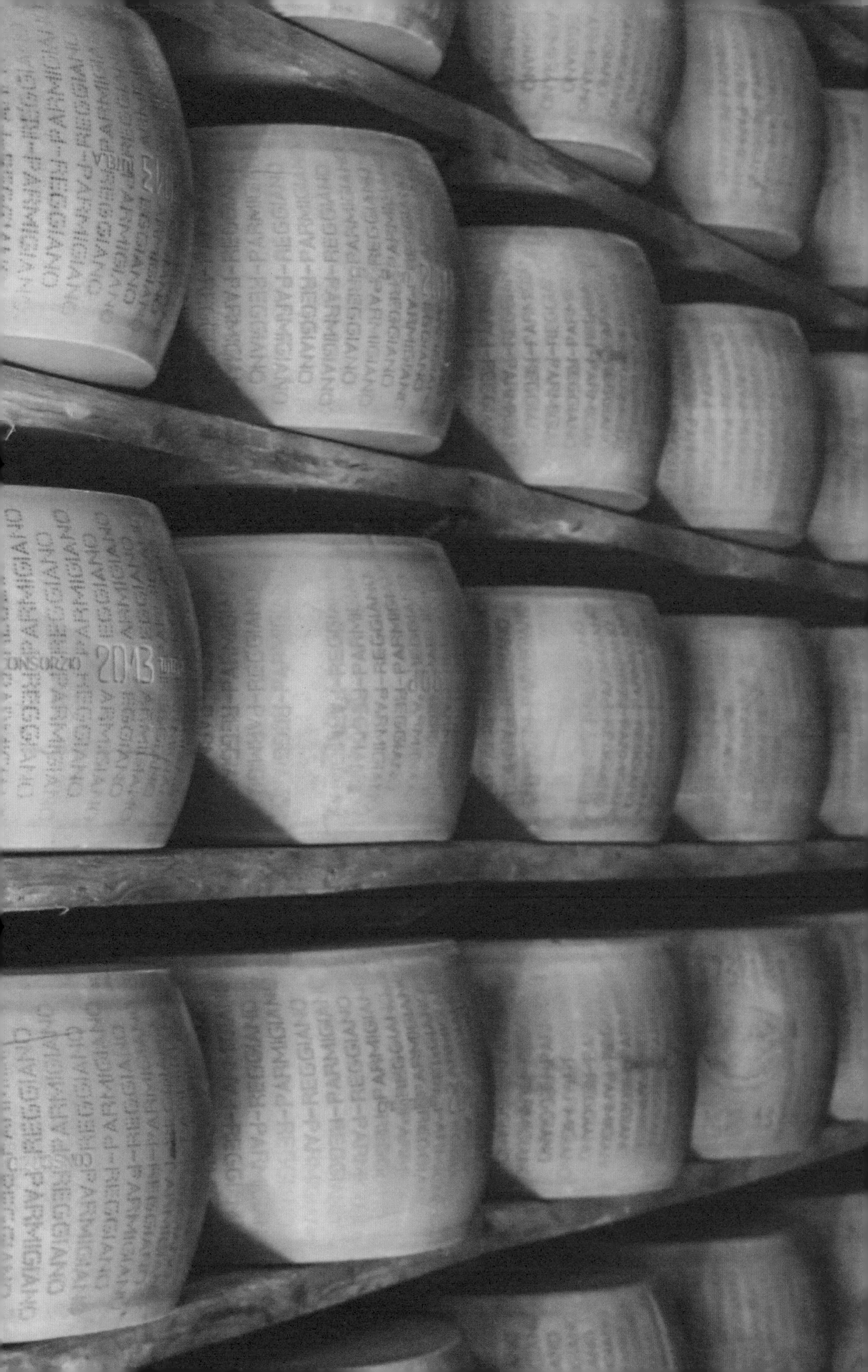
PARMIGIANO-REGGIANO
CONSORZIO
2013

TROFIE AL PESTO GENOVESE

YIELD: 4 SERVINGS / **ACTIVE TIME:** 20 MINUTES / **TOTAL TIME:** 40 MINUTES

Although abroad pasta with pesto Genovese is mostly consumed with just those two elements, in Liguria, the most popular pasta with pesto also includes potatoes and green beans. The addition of the vegetables does help to balance the rather strong taste of the basil pesto, and does not add too much work.

1. Bring water to a boil in a large saucepan. Add salt and the potatoes and boil for 7 minutes.

2. Add the green beans and boil for another 5 minutes.

3. Add the pasta and cook until it is al dente.

4. Drain the pasta and vegetables and place them in a large bowl. Add the pesto and toss to combine, trying not to break the potatoes.

5. Top the dish with the basil and serve.

INGREDIENTS:

SALT, TO TASTE

2 MEDIUM POTATOES, PEELED AND DICED

2 CUPS GREEN BEANS, TRIMMED

1 LB. TROFIE

1 CUP PESTO GENOVESE (SEE PAGE 811)

HANDFUL OF FRESH BASIL

PANSOTI ALLA GENOVESE

YIELD: 4 SERVINGS / **ACTIVE TIME:** 1 HOUR / **TOTAL TIME:** 1 HOUR AND 30 MINUTES

The typical Ligurian filled pasta is called pansoti, which look like Ferrara's pumpkin cappellacci but are made with a dough that contains not only eggs but also wine and water. If using ricotta in the filling, drain it for 1 hour in the refrigerator.

1. To begin preparations for the pasta, pile the flour on a clean work surface. Make a well in the center, place the eggs in the well, and beat the eggs with a fork until scrambled.

2. Add the wine, water, and salt and incorporate the flour, a little at a time, until the dough starts to come together.

3. Work the dough vigorously until it is smooth and elastic. If the dough feels too dry, incorporate a small amount of water.

4. Form the dough into a ball, cover it with plastic wrap, and place it in the refrigerator.

5. To prepare the filling, place all of the ingredients in a bowl and stir until well combined.

6. Run the pasta dough through a pasta maker until it is a 1/16-inch-thick sheet and place it on a flour-dusted work surface.

7. Using a ravioli wheel, cut the sheet into 3-inch squares.

8. Place a spoonful of the filling in the center of each square and moisten the edges of the square with water. Fold one corner of the square over the filling, creating a triangle. Press down on the edges to seal the pansoti. Join the two ends of the base of the triangle together and gently press to seal.

9. Place the pansoti on flour-dusted baking sheets and dust them with flour.

10. Bring water to a boil in a large saucepan. Place the sauce in a large saucepan and warm it over medium-low heat.

11. Add salt to the boiling water and let the water return to a full boil. Add the pansoti to the boiling water and cook for about 8 minutes.

12. Drain the pasta and place it in a large serving bowl. Add the sauce, toss to combine, and serve immediately.

INGREDIENTS:

FOR THE PASTA

1.1 LBS. ALL-PURPOSE FLOUR, PLUS MORE AS NEEDED

2 EGGS

¼ CUP DRY WHITE WINE

¼ CUP WATER, PLUS MORE AS NEEDED

PINCH OF FINE SEA SALT

FOR THE FILLING

2.2 LBS. PREBUGGIÙN (SEE PAGE 623)

1 EGG

3½ OZ. LIGURIAN PRESCINSÊUA OR RICOTTA CHEESE

3½ OZ. PARMESAN CHEESE, GRATED

1 TABLESPOON CHOPPED FRESH MARJORAM

PINCH OF FRESHLY GRATED NUTMEG

SALT AND PEPPER, TO TASTE

SALSA DI NOCI (SEE PAGE 812)

CIUPPIN

Ciuppin was originally a dish born to feed the fishermen, who used lower-quality fish to make a soup that was good enough to lift the stale bread they dipped into it. You can use any seafood you like here, but the ideal version of this dish would contain some mix of redfish, tub gurnard, hake, red mullet, weever, conger eel, octopus, and/or cuttlefish.

1. Place the olive oil in a Dutch oven and warm it over medium heat. Add the onion, carrot, celery, and garlic and cook, stirring frequently, until the onion is translucent, about 3 minutes.

2. Add the octopus or cuttlefish (if using) and wine and cook until the wine has evaporated.

3. Add the tomatoes, mash them with a wooden spoon, and cover the pot. Cook for 20 minutes.

4. Bring water to a boil in a large saucepan. Add salt and the biggest fish. After a few minutes, add the second biggest, and so on. Cook the fish until they are cooked through, about 10 minutes for the medium and small fish, and 15 to 20 minutes for the larger fish.

5. Drain the fish, reserve the broth, and remove the heads, skin, and all of the bones.

6. Add the fish to the Dutch oven and break it up with a wooden spoon.

7. Stir in 2 to 3 ladles of the reserved broth and parsley. Cook for 3 minutes.

8. Season the ciuppin with salt and pepper and serve with crusty bread.

INGREDIENTS:

5	TABLESPOONS EXTRA-VIRGIN OLIVE OIL
1	ONION, FINELY DICED
1	CARROT, PEELED AND FINELY DICED
1	CELERY STALK, PEELED AND FINELY DICED
2	GARLIC CLOVES, MINCED
3.3	LBS. MIXED SEAFOOD
½	CUP DRY WHITE WINE
1.1	LBS. WHOLE PEELED TOMATOES, CRUSHED
	SALT AND PEPPER, TO TASTE
	HANDFUL OF FRESH PARSLEY, FINELY CHOPPED
	CRUSTY BREAD, TOASTED, FOR SERVING

SECONDI

FRITTATA DI CARCIOFI

YIELD: 4 SERVINGS / **ACTIVE TIME:** 30 MINUTES / **TOTAL TIME:** 1 HOUR

This lovely artichoke frittata from Liguria also features porcini mushrooms and is flavored with marjoram, a favorite Ligurian herb.

1. Clean the artichokes, removing the tough leaves and thorns. Trim and peel the stems, place the artichokes in a bowl, and cover them with water. Stir in the lemon juice and set the artichokes aside.

2. Place half of the olive oil in a large skillet and warm it over medium heat. Drain the mushrooms and squeeze them to remove any excess liquid. Add them and the onion to the pan and cook, stirring occasionally, until they start to brown, about 8 minutes.

3. Cut the artichokes into thin wedges and add them to the pan. Cook, stirring occasionally, until they have softened, adding water if the pan starts to look dry. Remove the pan from heat and let the mixture cool.

4. Place the bread and milk in a bowl and let the mixture soak.

5. Place the eggs, Parmesan, marjoram, and garlic in a large bowl and whisk to combine.

6. Add the vegetable mixture. Squeeze the bread, add it to the egg mixture, season with salt and pepper, and whisk to combine.

7. Place the remaining olive oil in a large, shallow skillet and warm it over medium heat. Pour the egg mixture into the pan and shake the skillet to evenly distribute the mixture. Cook until the bottom of the frittata is set and starting to brown.

8. Place a large plate over the skillet and invert the frittata onto the plate. Place the frittata back in the pan and cook until it is completely cooked through.

9. Remove the frittata from the pan and let it cool to room temperature before serving.

INGREDIENTS:

4	SMALL ARTICHOKES
	JUICE OF 1 LEMON
6	TABLESPOONS EXTRA-VIRGIN OLIVE OIL
2–3	DRIED PORCINI MUSHROOMS, SOAKED IN WARM WATER
½	ONION, FINELY DICED
2	OZ. STALE BREAD, CRUSTS REMOVED
2	TABLESPOONS WHOLE MILK
5	EGGS
½	CUP GRATED PARMESAN CHEESE
¼	TEASPOON DRIED MARJORAM
½	GARLIC CLOVE, FINELY CHOPPED
	SALT AND PEPPER, TO TASTE

TORTA PASQUALINA

YIELD: 6 SERVINGS / **ACTIVE TIME:** 1 HOUR / **TOTAL TIME:** 3 HOURS

Torta pasqualina means "Easter pie," and it is indeed a Ligurian savory pie from Genoa, traditionally served on Easter. Besides eggs, the main symbol of Easter, the filling is usually made with chard, but nowadays a mix of chard and spinach is often used.

1. To begin preparations for the crust, place all of the ingredients in a large bowl and work the mixture until it starts to come together as a dough.

2. Transfer the dough to a flour-dusted work surface and knead it until it is smooth and elastic.

3. Divide the dough into 6 pieces, form them into rounds, and wrap each one with plastic wrap. Chill the dough in the refrigerator for 1 hour.

4. To begin preparations for the filling, place the olive oil in a large skillet and warm it over medium heat. Add the onion, chard, and spinach and cook, stirring occasionally, until the onion has softened and the greens have wilted, 5 to 7 minutes.

5. Remove the vegetables from the pan and let them cool. When they are cool enough to handle, squeeze them to remove any excess liquid and finely chop them.

6. Place the mixture in a large bowl, add 2 of the eggs, two-thirds of the Parmesan, the pecorino, the marjoram, and 1 pinch of nutmeg. Season with salt and pepper and stir until well combined. Set the mixture aside.

7. Place the ricotta, 2 of the eggs, the cornstarch, the remaining Parmesan, and the remaining nutmeg in a separate bowl, season with salt, and stir until the mixture is smooth and creamy.

8. Preheat the oven to 355°F. Place the pieces of dough on a flour-dusted work surface and roll them into very thin 12-inch rounds.

9. Coat a round 10-inch cake pan with olive oil and place a round over the bottom. Spread a tablespoon of olive oil over the dough and cover with another round, making sure that there are no air bubbles between the disks and that they adhere perfectly to each other. Repeat with 2 more rounds, reserving the last 2 for the top of the pie.

10. Top the fourth round with the vegetable mixture. Top with the ricotta mixture and level it with a spatula.

INGREDIENTS:

FOR THE CRUST

21.1 OZ. ALL-PURPOSE FLOUR, PLUS MORE AS NEEDED

12.3 OZ. WATER

2 TABLESPOONS EXTRA-VIRGIN OLIVE OIL

PINCH OF FINE SEA SALT

FOR THE FILLING

2 TABLESPOONS EXTRA-VIRGIN OLIVE OIL, PLUS MORE AS NEEDED

½ ONION, FINELY DICED

1.1 LBS. CHARD, HARD STEMS REMOVED, RINSED WELL AND CHOPPED

1.1 LBS. FRESH SPINACH, RINSED WELL AND CHOPPED

10 EGGS

1⅓ CUPS GRATED PARMESAN CHEESE

⅓ CUP GRATED PECORINO CHEESE

HANDFUL OF FRESH MARJORAM, FINELY CHOPPED

2 PINCHES OF FRESHLY GRATED NUTMEG

SALT AND PEPPER, TO TASTE

1.1 LBS. RICOTTA CHEESE, DRAINED IN THE REFRIGERATOR FOR 1 HOUR

1 TABLESPOON CORNSTARCH

11. Make six hollows in the ricotta filling, leaving equal space between each one, and crack the remaining eggs into them.

12. Top the filling with another round and spread 1 tablespoon of olive oil over it. Top with the last round and spread olive oil over it.

13. Place the pie in the oven and bake for about 50 minutes.

14. Remove the pie from the oven and let it cool slightly. Serve warm or at room temperature.

TORTA PASQUALINA:
THE QUEEN OF
LIGURIAN PIES

Torta pasqualina is a savory pie from Genoa in Liguria, prepared with a sort of olive oil–based pastry that is made by thin layers of dough separated by olive oil, resulting in a crust that is way different from puff pastry, and is more similar to phyllo dough. Traditionally, there were specifics regarding the number of dough sheets needed to make a proper pasqualina, an impressive 33 layers, a number symbolizing the years Jesus Christ lived according to Christian doctrine. Nowadays, many households use a simplified recipe with fewer layers, but one can surely increase the amount of dough required and make a pie with the traditional 33 layers.

Another potent symbol in the torta pasqualina is the eggs, which are not a merely Christian symbol but a universal one, representing and celebrating the rebirth that arrives with the spring solstice.

While outside of Genoa the pie is made with ricotta, the elective cheese for torta pasqualina is the local prescinsêua, a curdled, acidic Ligurian cheese that is hard to find elsewhere.

The pie was, and is, so popular that in older times, besides making it at home for Easter, the pie was sold by shops called sciamadde as a street food. Similarly, nowadays it is often found in gastronomy shops as a takeaway item.

Torta pasqualina is surely the queen of Ligurian savory pies, though it is not the only one, as the region has a real vocation for pies filled with any sort of vegetables and herbs mixed with cheese, as the climate and geography of Liguria are optimal for the cultivation of greens.

ERBAZZONE

YIELD: 6 SERVINGS / **ACTIVE TIME:** 40 MINUTES / **TOTAL TIME:** 1 HOUR AND 30 MINUTES

A farmer's pie from the area around Reggio-Emilia, erbazzone is also called scarpazzone because the impoverished people who depended on it for sustenance also used the tough stems of the chard, which are called scarpa, meaning "shoe."

1. To begin preparations for the crust, place all of the ingredients in a large bowl and work the mixture until it starts to come together as a firm dough. Add 1 to 2 tablespoons of water if the dough appears too dry.

2. Transfer the dough to a flour-dusted work surface and knead it until it is smooth and elastic.

3. Divide the dough into 2 pieces, form them into rounds, and wrap each one with plastic wrap. Let the dough rest for 30 minutes.

4. To begin preparations for the filling, place the lard in a large skillet and melt it over medium heat. Add the garlic and spring onions and cook, stirring frequently, until they have softened, about 5 minutes.

5. Add the chard and spinach and cook until they have wilted and all of the liquid they release has evaporated, about 15 minutes.

6. Remove the vegetables from the pan and let them cool. When they are cool enough to handle, squeeze them to remove excess liquid and finely chop them.

7. Place the mixture in a large bowl, add the Parmesan, season with salt and pepper, and stir until well combined. Set the mixture aside.

8. Preheat the oven to 390°F. Place the pieces of dough on a flour-dusted work surface and roll them into 14-inch rounds.

9. Coat a round 12-inch cake pan with lard and place a round over the bottom. Spread the vegetable mixture over the dough, making sure it is level.

10. Top with the remaining round, trying to make it wrinkly. Prick the top crust with a fork.

11. Place the pie in the oven and bake for 25 minutes.

12. Remove the pie from the oven, brush it with lard, and return it to the oven. Bake until the top is lightly browned, 5 to 10 minutes.

13. Remove the pie from the oven and let it cool slightly before slicing and serving.

INGREDIENTS:

FOR THE CRUST

10.6 OZ. ALL-PURPOSE FLOUR, PLUS MORE AS NEEDED

2 OZ. LARD

½ TEASPOON FINE SEA SALT

3½ OZ. LUKEWARM WATER (90°F), PLUS MORE AS NEEDED

FOR THE FILLING

¼ CUP LARD, PLUS MORE AS NEEDED

1 GARLIC CLOVE, FINELY DICED

2 SPRING ONIONS, TRIMMED AND FINELY DICED

2.2 LBS. CHARD LEAVES, HARD STEMS REMOVED, RINSED WELL AND CHOPPED

1.1 LBS. FRESH SPINACH, RINSED WELL AND CHOPPED

2 CUPS GRATED PARMESAN CHEESE

SALT AND PEPPER,, TO TASTE

VITELLO TONNATO

YIELD: 6 SERVINGS / **ACTIVE TIME:** 30 MINUTES / **TOTAL TIME:** 16 HOURS

Piedmont's elegant vitello tonnato, veal in a tuna-enriched sauce, is a delicacy served as an appetizer on festive occasions like Christmas, or as a secondo in the summertime.

1. Tie the veal with kitchen twine and place it in a Dutch oven with the wine, garlic, bay leaves, carrot, onion, and celery. Cover the Dutch oven and let the veal marinate in the refrigerator for 12 hours.

2. Drain the veal, reserving the liquid. Strain the liquid and return it to the Dutch oven with the veal.

3. Add the water, season with salt, and place the Dutch oven over medium heat. Bring to a simmer.

4. Reduce the heat to low, cover the Dutch oven, and cook until the veal is tender, about 1 hour, turning it occasionally.

5. Drain the veal, reserving 2 ladles of broth for the sauce. Let the veal cool to room temperature.

6. Place the veal in the refrigerator and chill it for 2 hours.

7. Cut the veal into thin slices and serve alongside the sauce.

SALSA TONNATA

1. Place the tuna, egg yolks, anchovies, capers, vinegar, and lemon juice in a blender and puree until smooth.

2. With the blender running, slowly stream in the olive oil until it has emulsified. Slowly stream in the reserved broth until the sauce is creamy.

INGREDIENTS:

2.1	LB. PIECE OF VEAL TOP ROUND
3	CUPS DRY WHITE WINE
5	GARLIC CLOVES, HALVED
2	BAY LEAVES
1	CARROT, PEELED AND CHOPPED
1	ONION, CHOPPED
1	CELERY STALK, CHOPPED
6	CUPS WATER
	SALT, TO TASTE
	SALSA TONNATA (SEE RECIPE), FOR SERVING

SALSA TONNATA

9	OZ. TUNA IN OLIVE OIL, DRAINED
3	HARD-BOILED EGG YOLKS
4	ANCHOVIES IN OLIVE OIL, DRAINED
3½	TABLESPOONS CAPERS PACKED IN BRINE, RINSED AND SQUEEZED DRY
1	TABLESPOON WHITE WINE VINEGAR
1	TABLESPOON FRESH LEMON JUICE
¼	CUP EXTRA-VIRGIN OLIVE OIL
2	LADLES OF RESERVED BROTH FROM COOKING THE VEAL

COTOLETTA ALLA MILANESE

YIELD: 4 SERVINGS / **ACTIVE TIME:** 15 MINUTES / **TOTAL TIME:** 30 MINUTES

The Italian answer to German schnitzel is cotoletta alla Milanese. The meat here is veal, rather than the pork that commonly features in Germany, but otherwise the recipes are quite similar.

1. Place the eggs and 2 pinches of salt in a shallow bowl and whisk to scramble the eggs.

2. Place bread crumbs in a separate shallow bowl. Dredge the veal chops in the eggs and then in the bread crumbs until they are completely coated.

3. Place the butter in a large skillet and melt it over medium heat. Add the veal and cook until it is browned on both sides and the interior temperature is 125°F.

4. Transfer the veal to a paper towel–lined plate and let it drain. Serve with lemon wedges.

INGREDIENTS:

2   EGGS

       SALT, TO TASTE

       BREAD CRUMBS, AS NEEDED

4   VEAL CHOPS (EACH ABOUT 1 INCH THICK)

7   OZ. UNSALTED BUTTER

       LEMON WEDGES, FOR SERVING

BRASATO AL BAROLO

YIELD: 6 SERVINGS / **ACTIVE TIME:** 40 MINUTES / **TOTAL TIME:** 16 HOURS

The king of Italian roasts is for sure brasato al Barolo, slow-cooked beef in the most celebrated Piedmont wine, Barolo. Barolo can also be substituted with the more affordable Langhe Nebbiolo.

1. Tie the beef with kitchen twine, place it in a roasting pan, and add the Barolo, onion, celery, carrots, bay leaves, and garlic. Cover the pan with plastic wrap and let the beef marinate in the refrigerator for 12 hours.

2. Drain the beef, reserving the marinade and vegetables. Pat the beef dry with paper towels.

3. Place the butter and olive oil in a Dutch oven and warm the mixture over medium heat. Add the beef and sear until it is browned all over, turning it as needed.

4. Remove the beef from the pot and set it aside.

5. Add the reserved vegetables and cook, stirring occasionally, until they start to brown, about 5 minutes.

6. Return the beef to the pot and cover the dish with the reserved marinade. Bring to a boil, reduce the heat to low, and cover the pot. Cook until the beef is very tender, 3 to 4 hours. Turn the beef occasionally as it cooks, and season it with salt and pepper halfway through cooking.

7. Remove the beef from the pot and let it cool completely before slicing.

8. Place the Dutch oven over high heat and stir in the flour. Cook until the cooking liquid has thickened slightly.

9. Serve the brasato with the cooking liquid and vegetables.

INGREDIENTS:

2.6	LB. BEEF SHOULDER
2	CUPS BAROLO
1	LARGE WHITE ONION, CHOPPED
1	CELERY STALK, CHOPPED
2	LARGE CARROTS, PEELED AND CHOPPED
2	BAY LEAVES
2	GARLIC CLOVES
2	TABLESPOONS UNSALTED BUTTER
2	TABLESPOONS EXTRA-VIRGIN OLIVE OIL
	SALT AND PEPPER, TO TASTE
1	TABLESPOON ALL-PURPOSE FLOUR

ARROSTO MORTO

YIELD: 8 SERVINGS / ACTIVE TIME: 30 MINUTES / TOTAL TIME: 3 HOURS

Arrosto morto translates to "dead roast"—a cheeky name that refers to the fact that the meat is slow cooked for so long that it definitely ends up well-done. As with most Italian roasts, this is not cooked in the oven but on the stove, an oddity that is likely due to the latter being far more common throughout the country in the past.

1. Tie the tenderloin with kitchen twine. Stick the herbs under the twine so that they are in contact with the tenderloin.

2. Place the butter and olive oil in a Dutch oven and warm the mixture over medium-high heat.

3. Add the tenderloin and sear until it is browned all over, turning it as needed and basting it. Use two spoons to turn the tenderloin, as you want to avoid piercing it.

4. Add the wine and cook until it has evaporated, turning the tenderloin frequently.

5. Reduce the heat to low, add the garlic, onion, carrot, and celery, season with salt and pepper, and cook for 10 minutes.

6. Add a few ladles of broth and cook until the tenderloin is cooked through, about 2 hours, turning it occasionally and adding more broth as needed. The broth should not cover the meat entirely, instead it should be added in small amounts, as the aim is making a roast and not a stew.

7. Remove the tenderloin from the pot and let it cool completely.

8. Taste the cooking liquid and strain it. Taste and adjust the seasoning as necessary.

9. Slice the tenderloin and serve it, reheated or cold, with its cooking liquid.

INGREDIENTS:

2.2 LB. VEAL OR PORK TENDERLOIN

2 SPRIGS OF FRESH ROSEMARY

2 SPRIGS OF FRESH SAGE

2 TABLESPOONS UNSALTED BUTTER

3 TABLESPOONS EXTRA-VIRGIN OLIVE OIL

1 CUP DRY WHITE WINE

2 GARLIC CLOVES

1 ONION, CHOPPED

1 LARGE CARROT, PEELED AND CHOPPED

1 CELERY STALK, CHOPPED

SALT AND PEPPER, TO TASTE

BRODO DI CARNE (SEE PAGE 805), AS NEEDED

BOLLITO MISTO ALLA PIEMONTESE

YIELD: 8 SERVINGS / **ACTIVE TIME:** 30 MINUTES / **TOTAL TIME:** 6 HOURS

Every region has its recipe for boiled meat, but in Piedmont this method has likely achieved its most elaborate form. In the traditional recipe for bollito, the mix of boiled meats included seven different cuts, accompanied by seven different sauces, and five side dishes. Nowadays, the recipe is much simplified and includes *only* five cuts of meat and three sauces.

1. Tie the beef with kitchen twine and set it aside.

2. Bring water to a boil in a stockpot. Add salt and half of the carrots, onions, and celery and cook for 15 minutes.

3. Add the beef and half of the parsley, garlic, and peppercorns. Boil for 15 minutes.

4. Reduce the heat to medium-low, cover the pot, and cook until the beef is very tender and falling apart, 2 to 3 hours, occasionally skimming any impurities that rise to the surface.

5. Place the pieces of beef that you remove in a serving dish and cover them with aluminum foil to keep warm.

6. While the beef is cooking, bring water to a boil in a large saucepan. Add salt, the chicken, and the remaining vegetables, peppercorns, and parsley and cook until the chicken is cooked through, about 1½ hours.

7. Bring water to a boil in another large saucepan. Add the cotechino and cook for 1 hour.

8. Slice the beef and cotechino. Place the chicken in the center of a very large serving platter and surround it with the beef and cotechino.

9. Serve with the sauces and enjoy.

INGREDIENTS:

3   (1 LB.) PIECES OF ASSORTED CUTS OF BEEF

    SALT, TO TASTE

4   CARROTS, PEELED AND CUT INTO BIG PIECES

3   ONIONS, CUT INTO BIG PIECES

4   CELERY STALKS, CUT INTO BIG PIECES

2   SPRIGS OF FRESH PARSLEY

4   GARLIC CLOVES

10 BLACK PEPPERCORNS

1   WHOLE CAPON, CLEANED

1   COTECHINO

    BAGNET VERT (SEE PAGE 811), FOR SERVING

    SALSA RUBRA, FOR SERVING

    SALSA AL CREN (SEE PAGE 812), FOR SERVING

RIFREDDO

YIELD: 4 SERVINGS / ACTIVE TIME: 30 MINUTES / TOTAL TIME: 1 HOUR AND 30 MINUTES

Rifreddo is the Italian version of meatloaf, and this is a typical one among the many variants, featuring a tuna-centered sauce similar to Piedmont's salsa tonnata.

1. Place the ground meats, mortadella, Parmesan, and eggs in a bowl, season with salt and pepper, and stir until well combined.

2. Spread the mixture over a clean kitchen towel. Roll it up and tie the ends closed with kitchen twine.

3. Bring water to a boil in a large saucepan. Add the rifreddo and boil until it is cooked through, about 1 hour.

4. While the rifreddo is boiling, place the tuna, olives, capers, olive oil, and lemon juice in a bowl and stir until well combined. Store the sauce in the refrigerator.

5. Remove the rifreddo from the boiling water. Unwrap it from the kitchen towel and let it cool completely.

6. Slice the rifreddo and drizzle the sauce over the top. Garnish with additional capers and olive oil and serve.

INGREDIENTS:

- 11 OZ. GROUND PORK
- 11 OZ. GROUND CHICKEN OR VEAL
- 6 OZ. MORTADELLA, FINELY DICED
- 1½ CUPS GRATED PARMESAN CHEESE
- 2 LARGE EGGS
- SALT AND PEPPER, TO TASTE
- 11 OZ. TUNA IN OLIVE OIL, DRAINED
- 1 (HEAPING) CUP PITTED GREEN OLIVES, FINELY DICED
- 2 TABLESPOONS CAPERS PACKED IN BRINE, DRAINED, SQUEEZED, AND MINCED, PLUS MORE FOR GARNISH
- 3 TABLESPOONS EXTRA-VIRGIN OLIVE OIL, PLUS MORE FOR GARNISH
- JUICE OF ½ LEMON

ÀNARA COL PIÉN

YIELD: 6 SERVINGS / **ACTIVE TIME:** 40 MINUTES / **TOTAL TIME:** 3 HOURS

A gem from the rural culinary tradition in the areas surrounding Verona, ànara col pién is a decadent secondo that should be reserved only for the most important occasions.

1. Place the rolls and milk in a bowl and let the rolls soak.

2. Remove the duck's innards, finely chop them, and place them in a bowl.

3. Add the softened rolls to the chopped innards and stir to combine. Add the sausage, garlic, parsley, egg, Grana Padano, and half of the olive oil, season with salt and pepper, and work the mixture with your hands until combined.

4. Preheat the oven to 390°F. Stuff the duck with the mixture and tie it closed with kitchen twine. Season the duck's skin with salt.

5. Place the remaining olive oil in a Dutch oven and warm it over medium heat. Add the duck, celery, onion, carrot, rosemary, and bay leaves and sear the duck until it is browned all over, turning it as needed.

6. Add the wine and cook until it has evaporated.

7. Cover the Dutch oven and place it in the oven. Braise the duck until it is cooked through, about 2 hours, basting the duck frequently.

8. Remove the duck from the oven, slice it, and serve.

INGREDIENTS:

2	STALE ROLLS
½	CUP WHOLE MILK
1	WHOLE DUCK
1	ITALIAN SAUSAGE, CASING REMOVED AND CRUMBLED
1	GARLIC CLOVE, MINCED
	HANDFUL OF FRESH PARSLEY, CHOPPED
1	EGG, BEATEN
⅔	CUP GRATED GRANA PADANO CHEESE
½	CUP EXTRA-VIRGIN OLIVE OIL
	SALT AND PEPPER, TO TASTE
1	CELERY STALK, CHOPPED
1	ONION, CHOPPED
1	CARROT, PEELED AND CHOPPED
1	SPRIG OF FRESH ROSEMARY
2	BAY LEAVES
½	CUP DRY WHITE WINE

CAPPONE RIPIENO

YIELD: 10 SERVINGS / **ACTIVE TIME:** 40 MINUTES / **TOTAL TIME:** 3 HOURS

Common in Central and Northern Italy but most popular in Piedmont, cappone ripieno is stuffed capon, a castrated cock that is known to be particularly tasty due to its fatty, tender flesh. In Morozzo, Piedmont, there is a yearly festival dedicated to their local capons, which are renowned for their quality. Even without access to Morozzo's famed capon or to any capon at all, this dish can be made with a regular chicken with pleasing results.

1. Preheat the oven to 355°F and coat a baking dish with olive oil. Remove the capon's innards and rinse out the cavity.

2. Place the veal, sausage, bread crumbs, Parmesan, eggs, onion, garlic, parsley, sage, rosemary, and olive oil in a large bowl, season with nutmeg, salt, and pepper, and work the mixture with your hands until well combined.

3. Stuff the capon with the mixture and tie it closed with kitchen twine. Season the capon with salt, place it in the baking dish, and place it in the oven.

4. Combine the wine and broth in a bowl. Roast the capon until it is cooked through, about 2 hours, basting it with the wine mixture frequently and turning it occasionally, making sure not to pierce the flesh when you do.

5. Remove the capon from the oven, slice, and serve.

INGREDIENTS:

¼   CUP EXTRA-VIRGIN OLIVE OIL, PLUS MORE AS NEEDED

4.4   LB. WHOLE CAPON

7   OZ. GROUND VEAL

7   OZ. ITALIAN SAUSAGE, CASING REMOVED AND CRUMBLED

1½   CUPS FRESH BREAD CRUMBS, SOAKED IN WATER AND SQUEEZED DRY

1   CUP GRATED PARMESAN CHEESE

2   EGGS

1   WHITE ONION, FINELY CHOPPED

1   GARLIC CLOVE, MINCED

  HANDFUL OF FRESH PARSLEY, FINELY CHOPPED

  HANDFUL OF FRESH SAGE, FINELY CHOPPED

1   TEASPOON FINELY CHOPPED FRESH ROSEMARY

  FRESH GRATED NUTMEG, TO TASTE

  SALT AND PEPPER, TO TASTE

1   CUP DRY WHITE WINE

1   CUP BRODO DI CARNE (SEE PAGE 805)

OSSOBUCO ALLA MILANESE

YIELD: 4 SERVINGS / ACTIVE TIME: 30 MINUTES / TOTAL TIME: 1 HOUR

This secondo is traditionally served with risotto alla Milanese, a classic primo, making this dish a rare example of an all-in-one recipe in Italian cuisine.

1. Clean any residual fragments of bones from the veal shanks. Cut away the connective tissue surrounding the meat with scissors.

2. Rinse the veal and pat it dry with paper towels. Place flour in a shallow bowl and dredge the veal in it until completely coated.

3. Place the olive oil and butter in a large, deep skillet and warm the mixture over medium heat. Add the onion and cook, stirring occasionally, until it has softened, about 5 minutes.

4. Add the shanks and sear until they are browned all over, turning them as necessary.

5. Add the wine and cook until it has evaporated.

6. Add the broth, cover the pan, and reduce the heat to low. Cook until the veal is very tender, about 40 minutes.

7. Place the parsley, lemon zest, and garlic in a bowl and stir to combine.

8. Stir the parsley mixture, which is known as gremolata, into the pan and serve the veal and liquid over the risotto.

INGREDIENTS:

4	VEAL SHANKS (EACH ABOUT 9 OZ.)
	ALL-PURPOSE FLOUR, AS NEEDED
¼	CUP EXTRA-VIRGIN OLIVE OIL
2	TABLESPOONS UNSALTED BUTTER
1	LARGE WHITE ONION
½	CUP DRY WHITE WINE
2	CUPS BRODO DI CARNE (SEE PAGE 805)
	HANDFUL OF FRESH PARSLEY, FINELY CHOPPED
	ZEST OF 1 LEMON
1	GARLIC CLOVE, MINCED
	RISOTTO ALLA MILANESE (SEE PAGE 674), FOR SERVING

TRIGLIE ALLA GENOVESE

YIELD: 4 SERVINGS / **ACTIVE TIME:** 30 MINUTES / **TOTAL TIME:** 1 HOUR

Mullet cooked in a tomato sauce flavored with mushrooms and fennel seeds is a classic dish in Genovese cuisine.

1. Clean the fish, removing the innards and most of the scales. Rinse the fish and pat it dry. Chill it in the refrigerator.

2. Place the olive oil in a large, deep skillet and warm it over medium heat. Add the onion, parsley, fennel seeds, anchovies, and mushrooms and cook, stirring occasionally, for 5 minutes.

3. Add the tomatoes, season with salt, and reduce the heat to low. Cook, stirring occasionally, for 20 minutes.

4. Add the fish and cook until it is flaky and opaque, 15 to 20 minutes.

5. Season with salt and serve immediately.

INGREDIENTS:

4	MULLET
¼	CUP EXTRA-VIRGIN OLIVE OIL
1	SMALL ONION, FINELY DICED
	HANDFUL OF FRESH PARSLEY, CHOPPED
1	TABLESPOON FENNEL SEEDS
2	ANCHOVIES IN OLIVE OIL, DRAINED AND CHOPPED
2	OZ. DRIED PORCINI MUSHROOMS, SOAKED, DRAINED, AND SQUEEZED DRY
1	LB. WHOLE PEELED TOMATOES, CRUSHED
	SALT, TO TASTE

TROTE ALLA PIEMONTESE

YIELD: 4 SERVINGS / **ACTIVE TIME:** 30 MINUTES / **TOTAL TIME:** 1 HOUR

Trout is the traditional choice for the fish here, but other whitefish such as sea bass, flounder, or tilapia are more than workable substitutions.

1. Clean the trout, removing the innards and most of the scales. Rinse the fish and pat it dry. Chill it in the refrigerator.

2. Place the olive oil in a large, deep skillet and warm it over medium heat. Add the onion, carrot, celery, garlic, rosemary, and sage and cook, stirring occasionally, for 5 minutes.

3. Add the raisins, 2 ladles of broth, the vinegar, and lemon zest, place the fish on top, and season with salt. Cover the pan and reduce the heat to low.

4. Cook until the fish is flaky and opaque, 15 to 20 minutes.

5. Remove the fish from the pan. Remove the skin and bones, taking care not to break the fillets. Serve the fish with the sauce.

INGREDIENTS:

4	TROUT
¼	CUP EXTRA-VIRGIN OLIVE OIL
1	ONION, FINELY DICED
½	CARROT, PEELED AND FINELY DICED
1	CELERY STALK, FINELY DICED
1	GARLIC CLOVE, MINCED
1	TEASPOON FINELY CHOPPED FRESH ROSEMARY
	HANDFUL OF FRESH SAGE, FINELY CHOPPED
3	OZ. RAISINS, SOAKED IN WARM WATER, DRAINED, AND SQUEEZED DRY
1½	CUPS BRODO VEGETALE (SEE PAGE 806)
¼	CUP WHITE WINE VINEGAR
	ZEST OF 1 LEMON
	SALT, TO TASTE

DOLCI E PANE

CANESTRELLI LIGURI

YIELD: 100 CANESTRELLI / **ACTIVE TIME:** 40 MINUTES / **TOTAL TIME:** 2 HOURS

These cookies from Liguria are famed for their crumbly nature, which is likely due to the presence of hard-boiled egg yolks in the mix.

1. Place the flour, potato starch, confectioners' sugar, lemon zest, and vanilla seeds in the work bowl of a stand mixer fitted with the paddle attachment and beat until combined.

2. Gradually add the butter and beat to incorporate. Add the egg yolks and beat until the dough just comes together.

3. Place the dough on a flour-dusted work surface and flatten it slightly. Cover the dough with plastic wrap and chill it in the refrigerator for 1 hour.

4. Preheat the oven to 350°F and line a baking sheet with parchment paper. Place the dough on a flour-dusted work surface and roll it out into a ⅓-inch-thick round. Cut the dough into cookies with a flower-shaped cookie cutter. Roll out any scraps of dough and cut into cookies.

5. Cut a ⅓-inch hole in the center of each cookie with a ring cutter.

6. Place some canestrelli on the baking sheet, place them in the oven, and bake until they are golden brown, about 15 minutes. Repeat with the remaining canestrelli.

7. Dust the canestrelli with confectioners' sugar before enjoying.

INGREDIENTS:

10.6 OZ. ALL-PURPOSE FLOUR, PLUS MORE AS NEEDED

7 OZ. POTATO STARCH

5.3 OZ. CONFECTIONERS' SUGAR, PLUS MORE FOR TOPPING

ZEST OF 1 LEMON

SEEDS OF 1 VANILLA BEAN

11 OZ. UNSALTED BUTTER, CHOPPED

6 HARD-BOILED EGG YOLKS, CRUSHED

ZALETTI

YIELD: 25 ZALETTI / *ACTIVE TIME:* 40 MINUTES / *TOTAL TIME:* 1 HOUR

Zaletti are popular in Venice, where they are generally dipped in a glass of wine after dinner. The name refers to their vibrant yellow color, which is conferred by the cornmeal.

1. Preheat the oven to 375°F and line two baking sheets with parchment paper. Place the raisins in a bowl, cover them with grappa, and let them soak for 30 minutes.

2. Drain the raisins and squeeze them dry.

3. Sift the flour, cornmeal, baking powder, brown sugar, and salt into the work bowl of a stand mixer fitted with the paddle attachment.

4. Add the butter, eggs, lemon zest, and raisins and beat until the mixture comes together as a smooth dough.

5. Divide the dough into 25 pieces and form them into rounds. Place the zaletti on the baking sheets and place them in the oven.

6. Bake the zaletti until they are golden brown, about 20 minutes. Remove the zaletti from the oven, transfer them to wire racks, and let them cool completely before enjoying.

INGREDIENTS:

1	CUP RAISINS
	GRAPPA, AS NEEDED
1¾	CUPS ALL-PURPOSE FLOUR, PLUS MORE AS NEEDED
1	CUP FINE CORNMEAL
1	TEASPOON BAKING POWDER
¾	CUP BROWN SUGAR
	PINCH OF FINE SEA SALT
3½	OZ. UNSALTED BUTTER, SOFTENED
2	EGGS
	ZEST OF ½ LEMON

AMARETTI

YIELD: 50 AMARETTI / *ACTIVE TIME:* 40 MINUTES / *TOTAL TIME:* 24 HOURS

Amaretti are popular throughout the North but are most closely associated with Piedmont, where we find them in many variations.

1. Preheat the oven to 390°F. Place the blanched almonds on a baking sheet, place them in the oven, and toast until golden brown, about 5 minutes.

2. Remove the toasted almonds from the oven and let them cool.

3. Place the toasted almonds in a food processor, add the confectioners' sugar and bitter almonds, and pulse until finely ground, taking care not to overwork the mixture and release the fat in the almonds.

4. Transfer the mixture to a bowl, add the egg whites and baker's ammonia, and work the mixture until well combined.

5. Cover the bowl with plastic wrap and chill it in the refrigerator overnight.

6. Preheat the oven to 300°F and line two baking sheets with parchment paper. Working with slightly wet hands, form the mixture into balls the size of a small walnut.

7. Place the amaretti on the baking sheets. Bake the amaretti until they are golden brown, about 20 minutes. Remove the amaretti from the oven, transfer them to wire racks, and let them cool completely before enjoying.

INGREDIENTS:

1¼	CUPS BLANCHED ALMONDS
5.3	OZ. CONFECTIONERS' SUGAR
2	TABLESPOONS CHOPPED BITTER ALMONDS
2	OZ. EGG WHITES
1	TEASPOON BAKER'S AMMONIA

BACI DI DAMA

YIELD: 22 BACI DI DAMA / **ACTIVE TIME:** 1 HOUR / **TOTAL TIME:** 3 HOURS

Having originated in the town of Tortona in Piedmont, baci di dama translates to "lady's kisses."

1. Place the butter and sugar in the work bowl of a stand mixer fitted with the whisk attachment and whip until the mixture is fluffy, about 10 minutes.

2. Add the egg and whip to incorporate.

3. Add the salt and whip for 2 minutes.

4. Sift the flours into the work bowl and whip until the mixture comes together as a smooth dough.

5. Transfer the dough to a flour-dusted work surface and form it into a log. Cover the dough with plastic wrap and chill it in the refrigerator for 1 hour.

6. Line two baking sheets with parchment paper. Cut the dough into 44 pieces, shape them into small rounds, and place them on the baking sheets. Chill the baci di dama in the refrigerator for 30 minutes.

7. Preheat the oven to 355°F. Place the cookies in the oven and bake until set, about 20 minutes.

8. Remove the cookies from the oven, transfer them to wire racks, and let them cool.

9. Bring a few inches of water to a simmer in a medium saucepan. Place the gianduja in a heatproof bowl, place it over the simmering water, and stir until the gianduja is melted and smooth.

10. Remove it from heat and let it thicken as it cools. Transfer the gianduja to a piping bag fitted with a plain tip and pipe some onto half of the cookies. Assemble the baci di dama with the remaining cookies and let the chocolate set before enjoying.

INGREDIENTS:

7   OZ. UNSALTED BUTTER, SOFTENED

⅔   CUP SUGAR

1   MEDIUM EGG

        PINCH OF FINE SEA SALT

8.8   OZ. ALL-PURPOSE FLOUR, PLUS MORE AS NEEDED

4   OZ. HAZELNUT FLOUR

2   OZ. GIANDUJA

SAVOIARDI

YIELD: 50 SAVOIARDI / **ACTIVE TIME:** 40 MINUTES / **TOTAL TIME:** 1 HOUR

Probably the most popular Italian cookies, along with Tuscan cantucci, savoiardi, known in America as ladyfingers, are thought to have originated in Piedmont.

1. Preheat the oven to 355°F and line two baking sheets with parchment paper. Place the egg whites, two-fifths of the sugar, and the vanilla in the work bowl of a stand mixer fitted with the whisk attachment and whip until the mixture holds stiff peaks.

2. Place the egg yolks and remaining sugar in a mixing bowl and beat with a handheld mixer until the mixture is frothy and has almost tripled in volume, about 10 minutes.

3. Add the egg white mixture and fold to incorporate. Gradually add the flour and potato starch and fold until they have been incorporated.

4. Transfer the batter to a piping bag fitted with a plain tip and pipe 4-inch-long strips of batter onto the baking sheets.

5. Dust the cookies with confectioners' sugar and additional sugar. Place them in the oven and bake until they are golden brown, 15 to 20 minutes.

6. Turn off the oven, crack the oven door, and let the cookies sit in the cooling oven for 5 minutes.

7. Remove the cookies from the oven, transfer to wire racks, and let them cool completely before enjoying.

INGREDIENTS:

6	EGGS, AT ROOM TEMPERATURE, SEPARATED
3½	OZ. SUGAR, PLUS MORE FOR TOPPING
½	TEASPOON PURE VANILLA EXTRACT
3½	OZ. ALL-PURPOSE FLOUR
1	OZ. POTATO STARCH
	CONFECTIONERS' SUGAR, FOR TOPPING

CASTAGNOLE

YIELD: 30 CASTAGNOLE / **ACTIVE TIME:** 40 MINUTES / **TOTAL TIME:** 1 HOUR AND 30 MINUTES

In Romagna it is common to drizzle the popular, red-colored liqueur known as Alchermes over hot castagnole, which is a delicious variation if one can get hold of this unique ingredient.

1. Place the flour, sugar, orange zest, salt, and baking powder in a mixing bowl and whisk to combine.

2. Add the eggs, butter, and rum and work the mixture until it just comes together. Place the dough on a flour-dusted work surface and knead until it is soft and smooth. Cover the dough with a kitchen towel and let it rest for 30 minutes.

3. Add olive oil to a narrow, deep, heavy-bottomed saucepan with high sides until it is about 2 inches deep and warm it to 350°F. Divide the dough into ¾-oz. pieces and shape them into rounds.

4. Working in batches to avoid crowding the pot, gently slip the castagnole into the hot oil and fry until golden brown.

5. Transfer the fried castagnole to a paper towel–lined plate to drain. Dust them with confectioners' sugar and serve them warm.

INGREDIENTS:

8.8 OZ. ALL-PURPOSE FLOUR, PLUS MORE AS NEEDED

2.8 OZ. SUGAR

ZEST OF ½ ORANGE

PINCH OF FINE SEA SALT

1½ TEASPOONS BAKING POWDER

2 EGGS, LIGHTLY BEATEN

2 OZ. UNSALTED BUTTER, SOFTENED

2 TABLESPOONS RUM

EXTRA-VIRGIN OLIVE OIL, AS NEEDED

CONFECTIONERS' SUGAR, FOR TOPPING

TORTA PARADISO

YIELD: 1 CAKE / **ACTIVE TIME:** 40 MINUTES / **TOTAL TIME:** 1 HOUR AND 30 MINUTES

Torta paradiso, "heaven's cake," is one of the symbols of Pavia in Lombardy, where this simple, delicious cake was created at the end of the nineteenth century. Vigoni's pastry shop, where the founder, Enrico Vigoni, invented it, is still open and worth a visit if one happens to be in Pavia.

1. Preheat the oven to 340°F. Coat a round 10-inch cake pan with butter and dust it with flour, knocking out any excess. Sift the flour, confectioners' sugar, sugar, potato starch, and baking powder into a mixing bowl and set the mixture aside.

2. In a separate bowl, combine the butter, vanilla seeds, lemon zest, and orange zest and beat the mixture with a handheld mixer until it is soft and airy.

3. Add the egg yolks and salt and beat until the mixture is creamy.

4. In a third bowl, whip the eggs and sugar until the mixture is frothy.

5. Add the whole egg mixture to the egg yolk mixture and fold to combine.

6. Gradually add the dry mixture and fold until the mixture is a smooth batter.

7. Pour the batter into the cake pan and knock it on the counter to evenly distribute the batter and remove any air bubbles.

8. Place the cake in the oven and bake until a toothpick inserted into the center comes out clean, about 45 minutes.

9. Remove the cake from the oven and let it cool for 20 minutes.

10. Remove the cake from the pan, dust it with confectioners' sugar, and enjoy.

INGREDIENTS:

- 6 OZ. UNSALTED BUTTER, SOFTENED
- 3½ OZ. ALL-PURPOSE FLOUR, PLUS MORE AS NEEDED
- 6 OZ. CONFECTIONERS' SUGAR, PLUS MORE AS NEEDED
- 2.4 OZ. POTATO STARCH
- 1 (SCANT) TEASPOON BAKING POWDER
-    SEEDS OF 1 VANILLA POD
-    ZEST OF ½ LEMON
-    ZEST OF ½ ORANGE
- 2.8 OZ. EGG YOLKS
-    PINCH OF FINE SEA SALT
- 3½ OZ. EGGS
- 1.4 OZ. SUGAR

STRUDEL

YIELD: 1 STRUDEL / **ACTIVE TIME:** 50 MINUTES / **TOTAL TIME:** 4 HOURS

The most popular dessert from South Tyrol, in Trentino-Alto Adige, Italian strudel is the local interpretation of baklava. The dough is often made with puff pastry, but the locals make it with a simple pie dough consisting of flour, water, and a little vegetable oil (which was originally lard). If the dough is not extensible enough, a small egg is added. For the filling, any variety of apple will work, but Granny Smith, golden delicious, and Fuji are all good options.

1. To begin preparations for the dough, pile the flour on a clean working surface.

2. Make a well in the center and put the salt and water in it. Gradually incorporate the flour into the water. Add the vegetable oil and work the mixture until it starts to come together as a dough. Check the dough to see if the consistency is right. Depending on several factors (strength of the flour and ambient humidity), you may need to incorporate an additional 1 or 2 tablespoons of water.

3. Work the dough until it is smooth and elastic, about 10 minutes. Form the dough into a ball, cover it with plastic wrap, and let it rest for 2 to 3 hours.

4. To begin preparations for the filling, place the apples, sugar, pine nuts, raisins, cinnamon, and lemon juice in a bowl and stir to combine. Set the mixture aside.

5. Place the butter in a large skillet and melt it over medium heat. Add the bread crumbs and toast, stirring frequently, until they are slightly browned. Remove the pan from heat and set the bread crumbs aside.

6. Preheat the oven to 355°F. Line a baking sheet with parchment paper and coat it with some melted butter. Dust a large kitchen towel with flour. Place the dough on the towel and roll the dough out into a very thin rectangle.

7. Brush the edges of the dough with melted butter and sprinkle half of the bread crumbs over the dough, leaving a 1-inch border around the edges. Top the bread crumbs with the apple mixture and then sprinkle the remaining bread crumbs.

8. Working from a long side, roll the dough up, finishing with the seam side down. Pinch the dough at both of the short sides to seal the strudel.

9. Transfer the strudel to the baking sheet and place it in the oven. Bake until the strudel is golden brown, about 40 minutes.

10. Remove the strudel from the oven and let it cool completely.

11. Dust the strudel with confectioners' sugar and enjoy.

INGREDIENTS:

FOR THE DOUGH

10.6 OZ. ALL-PURPOSE FLOUR, PLUS MORE AS NEEDED

PINCH OF FINE SEA SALT

3½ OZ. LUKEWARM WATER (90°F), PLUS MORE AS NEEDED

1½ OZ. VEGETABLE OIL OR LARD

FOR THE FILLING

2.2 LBS. APPLES, PEELED, CORED, AND FINELY DICED

⅓ CUP SUGAR

½ CUP PINE NUTS

½ CUP RAISINS, SOAKED IN WARM WATER, DRAINED, AND SQUEEZED DRY

1 TEASPOON CINNAMON

JUICE OF ½ LEMON

4 TABLESPOONS UNSALTED BUTTER, PLUS MORE, MELTED, AS NEEDED

1 CUP BREAD CRUMBS

CONFECTIONERS' SUGAR, FOR TOPPING

TORTA SBRISOLONA

YIELD: 1 CAKE / **ACTIVE TIME:** 20 MINUTES / **TOTAL TIME:** 1 HOUR

Born at the court of the Gonzaga, sbrisolona (or sbrisolina, sbrisulusa, or sbrisulada), means "crumbling," a reference to the extreme friability of this cake. Another name for torta sbrisolona is torta delle tre tazze, "3 cups cake," as it traditionally requires equal quantities of white flour, yellow flour, and sugar, although modern versions do not retain these proportions.

1. Preheat the oven to 355°F. Coat a round 10-inch cake pan with butter. Place the flour, cornmeal, and salt in a large mixing bowl and stir to combine.

2. Add the almonds, make a well in the center, place the egg yolks, lemon zest, and butter in the well, and work the mixture with your hands until it comes together as a crumbly dough.

3. Place the dough in the cake pan, leveling it without pressing down. Place the cake in the oven and bake until cooked through, about 30 minutes.

4. Remove the cake from the oven and let it cool completely before removing it from the pan.

5. Torta sbrisolona is generally broken by hand rather than cut. Drizzle grappa over it (if desired) and enjoy.

INGREDIENTS:

- 7 OZ. UNSALTED BUTTER, SOFTENED AND CHOPPED, PLUS MORE AS NEEDED
- 7 OZ. ALL-PURPOSE FLOUR
- 7 OZ. FINE CORNMEAL
- 6.3 OZ. SUGAR
- PINCH OF FINE SEA SALT
- 7 OZ. ALMONDS, CHOPPED
- 2 EGG YOLKS
- ZEST OF 1 LEMON
- GRAPPA, FOR TOPPING (OPTIONAL)

ZUPPA INGLESE

YIELD: 1 CAKE / **ACTIVE TIME:** 40 MINUTES / **TOTAL TIME:** 24 HOURS

Even if the name zuppa Inglese means "English soup," this dessert is unquestionably Italian. One of the main theories regarding its origins attributes the recipe to the royal kitchen of the Estense court in Emilia-Romagna. Thanks to some English visitor, the court's pastry chef learned about the trifle popular in Britain, and remade it his way.

1. Place the water, liqueur, and sugar in a bowl and stir to combine. Set the bagna aside.

2. Cut the Pan di Spagna, horizontally, into 3 equally thick pieces. Cut each layer into large strips and layer one-third of the strips in a 13 x 9–inch baking dish.

3. Drizzle the bagna over the cake. Cover the cake with half of the Crema Pasticcera evenly.

4. Cover the custard with the second layer of cake and drizzle half of the remaining bagna over the cake. Spread the chocolate custard over the cake evenly.

5. Top with the last layer of cake, drizzle the remaining bagna over it, and cover with the remaining custard.

6. Dust the cake with cocoa powder, cover it with plastic wrap, and refrigerate it for 24 hours before serving.

INGREDIENTS:

1¾ CUPS WATER

1¾ OZ. ALCHERMES LIQUEUR

2 TABLESPOONS SUGAR

PAN DI SPAGNA (SEE PAGE 819)

CREMA PASTICCERA (SEE PAGE 819)

½ BATCH OF CREMA PASTICCERA AL CIOCCOLATO (SEE PAGE 821)

COCOA POWDER, FOR TOPPING

TORTA DI NOCCIOLE

YIELD: 1 CAKE / **ACTIVE TIME:** 40 MINUTES / **TOTAL TIME:** 1 HOUR AND 30 MINUTES

A popular dessert throughout Piedmont, where hazelnut trees are ubiquitous, and hazelnut flour is widely available.

1. Preheat the oven to 340°F. Coat a round 10-inch cake pan with butter and dust it with flour, knocking out any excess. Place the hazelnuts, half of the sugar, and the flour in a food processor and pulse until the hazelnuts are chopped.

2. Place the mixture in a large bowl and add the baking powder. Stir to combine and set the mixture aside.

3. Place the egg yolks and remaining sugar in a separate bowl and beat with a handheld mixer until it is frothy.

4. Add the melted butter and beat to incorporate. Set the mixture aside.

5. Place the egg whites in the work bowl of a stand mixer fitted with the whisk attachment and whip until they hold stiff peaks.

6. Add the whipped egg whites to the egg yolk mixture and fold to combine. Add the dry mixture and fold until the mixture is a smooth batter.

7. Pour the batter into the cake pan and place it in the oven.

8. Bake until the cake is a dark golden brown, 30 to 40 minutes. Remove the cake from the oven and let it cool in the pan.

9. Dust the cake with confectioners' sugar and serve.

INGREDIENTS:

7	OZ. UNSALTED BUTTER, MELTED, PLUS MORE AS NEEDED
2.8	OZ. ALL-PURPOSE FLOUR, PLUS MORE AS NEEDED
7.8	OZ. BLANCHED HAZELNUTS, TOASTED
6	OZ. SUGAR
1	TEASPOON BAKING POWDER
3	EGGS, SEPARATED
	CONFECTIONERS' SUGAR, FOR TOPPING

A BRIEF HISTORY OF PIEDMONT'S
FAMED HAZELNUTS

Hazelnuts are indigenous to Italy since ancient times and were celebrated by the Romans for their nutritional value, so much so that
Cato recommended planting them in the city gardens of Rome.

Piedmont's weather and soil are particularly favorable to the
cultivation of this delicious nut, but it is uncertain when hazelnuts
started to be grown in the region. We do know that by the end of the
nineteenth century, high-quality hazelnuts grew in the Alta Langa
hills, a Unesco heritage site that is also home to other Piedmont
extravagances such as the Alba white truffle and Barolo wine.

From the Alta Langa comes the tonda gentile trilobata variety of
hazelnut, which is the base of the protected geographical denomination Nocciola del Piemonte IGP, and it is the type of hazelnut
that Turin's pastry chefs found to be the best suited for use in their
confections.

Piedmont's hazelnut came to prominence after 1806, following
the Napoleonic Wars. Due to the conflict, cocoa had become difficult to get hold of, and thus, Turin's pastry chefs started to grind
hazelnuts and mix them with the little available cocoa, creating a
new, delicious product known as gianduja. This paste, so called in
honor of the homonymous Turin carnival mask, was born out of
necessity, and ended up revolutionizing confectionery production
in Piedmont and in the rest of the world. Again, di necessità virtù,
great food often arises out of need.

Stemming from the gianduja lucky creation, so many other
hazelnut-related products quickly originated, especially at the end
of the nineteenth century, when the industrialization of both agri-
culture and confectionery production was booming. Soon Piedmont
became the center of a flourishing confectionary industry, among
which Ferrero from Alba stood out with its world-renowned Nutella
spread, among other successful products.

TIRAMISÙ

YIELD: 1 CAKE / **ACTIVE TIME:** 20 MINUTES / **TOTAL TIME:** 4 HOURS

Likely the most popular Italian dessert worldwide, tiramisù is a rather recent creation, entirely absent from Italian cookbooks before the 1970s. Many are the stories behind its origins, but there is evidence that the dessert was born in Veneto, in the area around Treviso, as a late-night pick-me-up.

1. Place the egg yolks and sugar in a mixing bowl and beat until frothy.

2. Place the mascarpone in a separate bowl and beat until fluffy.

3. Add the mascarpone to the egg yolk mixture and fold to combine.

4. Soak the sugary sides of the Savoiardi in espresso for a few seconds and layer them in a small rectangular baking dish.

5. Cover the Savoiardi with some of the mascarpone cream. Repeat with the remaining Savoiardi and mascarpone cream.

6. Chill the tiramisù in the refrigerator for 2 to 3 hours.

7. Dust the tiramisù with cocoa powder and serve.

INGREDIENTS:

3   EGG YOLKS

⅓   CUP SUGAR

11   OZ. MASCARPONE CHEESE

7   OZ. SAVOIARDI (SEE PAGE 745)

FRESHLY BREWED ESPRESSO, SLIGHTLY SWEETENED, AS NEEDED

COCOA POWDER, FOR TOPPING

PANDOLCE GENOVESE

YIELD: 1 CAKE / **ACTIVE TIME:** 30 MINUTES / **TOTAL TIME:** 1 HOUR AND 30 MINUTES

Traditionally baked for Christmas, pandolce Genovese is a rather simple sweet bread enriched with raisins and citrus. Also known as panettone Genovese, this simple cake is possibly how panettone used to look before evolving into its current, masterful form.

1. Preheat the oven to 320°F and line a round 10-inch cake pan with parchment paper. Sift the flour into a large bowl, add the salt, sugar, and baking powder, and stir to combine.

2. Add the melted butter, egg, lemon zest, and Marsala and work the mixture until it comes together as a smooth dough.

3. Add the raisins, pine nuts, and candied citrus peels and work the dough until they have been evenly distributed.

4. Form the dough into a round and flatten it slightly. Place it in the pan, slash a cross on the top of the dough, and place it in the oven.

5. Bake until a toothpick inserted into the center of the cake comes out clean, about 1 hour.

6. Remove the cake from the oven and let it cool completely before slicing and serving.

INGREDIENTS:

17.6 OZ. ALL-PURPOSE FLOUR

2 PINCHES OF FINE SEA SALT

7 OZ. SUGAR

1 TABLESPOON BAKING POWDER

5½ OZ. UNSALTED BUTTER, MELTED

1 EGG

ZEST OF 1 LEMON

3½ OZ. MARSALA

⅔ CUP RAISINS, SOAKED IN WARM WATER, DRAINED, AND SQUEEZED DRY

1 OZ. PINE NUTS

1 OZ. CANDIED CITRUS PEELS, CHOPPED

I GRANDI LIEVITATI: A BRIEF HISTORY OF
PANETTONE, PANDORO & COLOMBA

Northern Italy has the merit of having developed possibly the most ambitious sweet breads in Italian cuisine. The term grandi lievitati, "big leavened breads," is used mainly to describe Milan's panettone and Verona's pandoro, with the addition of Milan's somewhat less popular colomba pasquale. All of these breads are modern evolutions of much simpler traditional celebrative breads, with panettone and pandoro belonging to the Christmas festivities, and colomba to the Easter ones.

The original panettone has a centuries-old tradition and probably looked more like the flat pandolce Genovese, a simple bread enriched with honey, eggs, raisins, and spices, than anything like the astounding cake we are now familiar with. With time and progress in baking techniques, panettone achieved a lighter texture, and, at the beginning of the twentieth century, it finally reached the shape we know today, thanks to pastry chef Angelo Motta. Motta pastry shops soon became factories, which enabled panettone to be distributed to the whole of Italy and become the nation's traditional Christmas cake.

Pandoro's origins are less obscure than those of panettone. While the name is likely a reference to a bread that in Renaissance-era Venice was covered with golden leaves, called pane d'oro, "golden bread," the real antecedent of pandoro is instead a sweet bread called nadalin that was created in Verona in the thirteenth century to celebrate the first Christmas of the city under the lead of the Scala dynasty. Nadalin has the shape of an eight-pointed star, is leavened with sourdough, and is simply flavored with lemon and vanilla, without any nuts or dried fruit (which are characteristic of pandoro).

Modern pandoro was created at the end of the nineteenth century by pastry chef Domenico Melegatti, who later started to produce it industrially. It is possible that Motta was inspired by the success of Melegatti's pandoro in pursuing the same type of transformation for the panettone.

It should be pointed out that Veneto has a much richer tradition of light festive breads compared to Lombardy. In fact, many households in Veneto used to make another type of sweet bread, called fugassa. This Easter bread is shaped like a shorter panettone, has a light crumb, and is fermented traditionally with sourdough. Nowadays it is mostly produced by local pastry shops rather than made at home.

And what about colomba, the dove-shaped Easter panettone from Milan? Surprisingly, colomba has no antecendent in Milan's tradition. It was created for Angelo Motta's factories in the 1930s, relying on the same method and machines used to make panettone around Christmas.

In recent times, both artisan pastry shops and home bakers have interpreted the industrial panettone, pandoro, and colomba recipes with quite convincing results, and in the surrounding pages we offer you a chance to join them.

PANETTONE MILANESE

YIELD: 3 PANETTONE / **ACTIVE TIME:** 3 HOURS / **TOTAL TIME:** 2 TO 3 DAYS

Considered the king of Italian sweet breads, and maybe the king of sweet breads in general, panettone milanese is a brioche that defies gravity.

1. Begin preparations for the pasta madre 2 to 3 days before you are going to start baking. Combine the starter with 1¾ oz. water and 3½ oz. flour in a large bowl. Cover the bowl with plastic wrap and let it rest for 12 hours.

2. Combine 1¾ oz. of the pasta madre with 1¾ oz. water and 3½ oz. flour.

3. Perform three feedings of the pasta madre, one every 3 to 4 hours. The fed starter should be kept in a naturally warm spot, ideally about 79°F. The schedule should look like this: first feeding (morning): 1¾ oz. of the stiff starter with 1¾ oz. water and 3½ oz. flour; second feeding (lunchtime): 3½ oz. stiff starter, 1¾ oz. water and 3½ oz. flour; final feeding (late afternoon): 3½ oz. stiff starter, 1¾ oz. water and 3½ oz. flour.

4. To begin preparations for the first dough, place the egg yolks and water in the work bowl of a stand mixer fitted with the paddle attachment and beat to combine. Fit the mixer with the dough hook, add the flour and sugar, and work the mixture on low until combined. Gradually add the pasta madre and knead to incorporate. Add the butter in three increments and knead the dough for about 6 minutes on low if using a stand mixer. The first dough should be mixed for no more than 10 minutes after the flour has been added.

5. Place the dough in a deep bowl and let the the dough rise at room temperature until it is 3 to 4 times its original size, 10 to 12 hours.

6. To begin preparations for the second dough, place the first dough and two-thirds of the flour in the work bowl of a stand mixer fitted with the dough hook and mix on low speed for 2 minutes. Add the egg yolks and the remaining flour and knead on medium speed for about 2 minutes.

7. Add the powdered milk and malt and mix for 1 minute. Add the honey, orange extract, vanilla seeds, and salt and mix for 1 minute. Add the sugar and mix at medium-high speed until the sugar is fully dissolved and the dough attaches to the hook, 2 to 5 minutes.

Continued . . .

INGREDIENTS:

FOR THE PASTA MADRE

½	OZ. SOURDOUGH STARTER (SEE PAGE 822)
	WATER, AS NEEDED
	ALL-PURPOSE FLOUR, AS NEEDED

FOR THE FIRST DOUGH (END OF DAY 1)

3½	OZ. EGG YOLKS
1	CUP WATER
16.9	OZ. STRONG BREAD FLOUR OR PANETTONE FLOUR
3½	OZ. SUGAR
6.3	OZ. PASTA MADRE
4.3	OZ. UNSALTED BUTTER, CHOPPED, PLUS MORE AS NEEDED

FOR THE SECOND DOUGH (START OF DAY 2)

8½	OZ. STRONG BREAD FLOUR OR PANETTONE FLOUR
6.7	OZ. EGG YOLKS
⅓	OZ. POWDERED MILK
1	(SCANT) TEASPOON BARLEY MALT
1.2	OZ. HONEY
1	TEASPOON ORANGE EXTRACT
	SEEDS OF 2 VANILLA BEANS
2	(SCANT) TEASPOONS FINE SEA SALT
4.9	OZ. SUGAR
4	OZ. UNSALTED BUTTER, CHOPPED, PLUS MORE AS NEEDED
5	OZ. DICED CANDIED ORANGE PEELS
5	OZ. CHOPPED CANDIED CITRUS PEELS
10	OZ. RAISINS

Gradually add the butter and work the dough at medium speed until it wraps tightly around the hook and is elastic when pulled, about 10 minutes. Add the candied peels and raisins and work the dough until they are evenly distributed.

8. Let the dough rest in the mixing bowl for 30 minutes. Coat a work surface with butter and place the dough on it. Shape the dough into 3 tight balls that are each 30 oz and place them in three 26 oz. panettone molds.

9. Place the panettone molds on baking sheets. Let the rounds rise in a naturally warm spot until the dough reaches the edges of the molds, 5 to 10 hours.

10. Preheat the oven to 350°F. Gently score a cross on top of each panettone and slightly pull up on the edges of each cross. Ideally you want to perform a scarpatura, detaching the edges from the dough with a razor, but if you are making your first tries, just place a small piece of butter in the center of each cross, on top of the panettone.

11. Place the panettone in the oven and bake until the internal temperature is around 200°F, 35 to 45 minutes. Do not open the oven until at least 35 minutes have passed.

12. Remove the panettone from the oven, put 2 skewers in the bottom part of the panettone, and flip them upside down. Hang the panettone by the skewers and let them remain upside down until cool, 2 to 3 hours.

13. Spray fitted cellophane sheets with grain alcohol and wrap the panettone with them. Stored this way, the panettone will keep for several weeks.

GALLETTE DEL MARINAIO

YIELD: 8 TO 9 GALLETTE / **ACTIVE TIME:** 30 MINUTES / **TOTAL TIME:** 2 HOURS AND 30 MINUTES

This flatbread was born in Liguria around the fifteenth century to sustain fishermen during their lengthy trips. Gallette del marinaio are not eaten as they are but need to be softened, often in water and vinegar, and are a popular ingredient in many Ligurian recipes.

1. Line three baking sheets with parchment paper. Place the yeast and water in the work bowl of a stand mixer fitted with the dough hook, gently stir, and let the mixture proof until it starts to foam, about 10 minutes.

2. Add the flour and work the mixture on low until it comes together as a firm dough.

3. Raise the speed to high and work the dough until it is smooth and elastic, about 10 minutes.

4. Divide the dough into 3 oz. pieces and shape them into tight rounds.

5. Place the dough balls on one of the baking sheets, cover them with a kitchen towel, and let them rise for 1 hour.

6. Roll each ball into a ¼-inch-thick disk, place them on the baking sheets, and cover with a kitchen towel. Let them rise for 45 minutes.

7. Preheat the oven to 430°F. Poke holes in the tops of the gallette with a fork and place them in the oven. Bake for about 10 minutes.

8. Remove the gallette from the baking sheets and place them directly on the oven's racks. Bake until golden brown, about 5 minutes.

9. Turn the oven off, crack open the oven door, and let the gallette cool in the oven.

INGREDIENTS:

- ½ TEASPOON ACTIVE DRY YEAST
- 8.8 OZ. LUKEWARM WATER (90°F)
- 17.6 OZ. BREAD FLOUR, PLUS MORE AS NEEDED

GUBANA

YIELD: 1 GUBANA / **ACTIVE TIME:** 30 MINUTES / **TOTAL TIME:** 24 HOURS

Gubana is a delicious, sweet bread that is enjoyed year round in Friuli-Venezia Giulia, and particularly around Christmas.

1. The day before you are going to prepare the dough, begin preparations for the filling. Coat a clean, heat-resistant work surface with olive oil. Place the raisins and the rum in a bowl and let the raisins soak.

2. Place half of the sugar, the water, and vinegar in a medium saucepan and cook over medium heat, swirling the pan occasionally, until the mixture starts to caramelize. Add half of the walnuts and cook, stirring continually, until they are coated. Pour the mixture onto the work surface and let it cool.

3. Place the butter in a large skillet and melt it over low heat. Add the pine nuts and toast, stirring occasionally, until they are browned, about 5 minutes. Remove the pan from heat and let the pine nuts cool.

4. Crush the Amaretti and the biscuits and place them in a bowl. Chop the caramelized walnuts and the remaining walnuts and add them to the bowl.

5. Drain the raisins and squeeze them dry. Add them, the toasted pine nuts, butter, lemon zest, salt, vanilla, cinnamon, remaining sugar, and enough rum for the mixture to be spreadable to the bowl. Stir to combine, cover the mixture with plastic wrap, and chill the filling in the refrigerator overnight.

6. To begin preparations for the dough, warm the milk to 90°F. Add the yeast, gently stir, and let the mixture proof until it starts to foam, about 10 minutes.

7. Place two-thirds of the flour, the egg, egg yolks, and yeast mixture in the work bowl of a stand mixer fitted with the dough hook and work the mixture until it comes together as a soft, smooth dough. Cover the work bowl with a kitchen towel, place it in a naturally warm spot, and let the dough rise for 1 hour.

8. Add the remaining flour, the salt, honey, butter, and sugar to the work bowl and work the dough vigorously until it is elastic. Cover the bowl with a kitchen towel, place it in a naturally warm spot, and let it rise for 30 minutes. Remove the filling from the refrigerator and let sit at room temperature.

Continued . . .

INGREDIENTS:

FOR THE FILLING

	EXTRA-VIRGIN OLIVE OIL, AS NEEDED
⅔	CUP RAISINS
1	CUP RUM OR MARSALA, PLUS MORE AS NEEDED
½	CUP SUGAR, PLUS MORE FOR TOPPING
3	TABLESPOONS WATER
½	TEASPOON WHITE VINEGAR
2	CUPS WALNUTS
2	TABLESPOONS UNSALTED BUTTER, PLUS MORE, CHOPPED, AS NEEDED
⅔	CUP PINE NUTS
7	AMARETTI (SEE PAGE 741)
1½	OZ. DRY, BISCUIT-STYLE COOKIES (PETIT BEURRE OR SIMILAR)
	ZEST OF ½ LEMON
1	TEASPOON PURE VANILLA EXTRACT
2	TEASPOONS CINNAMON

9. Place the dough on a flour-dusted work surface and roll it into an 8 x 12–inch rectangle. Spread the filling over the dough and dot it with pieces of butter. Working from a long side, roll the dough up, finishing with the seam side down. Pinch the dough at both of the short sides to seal the gubana.

10. Stretch the gubana until it is about 30 inches long. Coat a round, 10-inch cake pan with high edges with butter. Place the guabna in the pan in a tight spiral, making sure one end is underneath to seal it. Cover the pan with a kitchen towel and let the gubana rise until it has doubled in size, about 1½ hours.

11. Preheat the oven to 320ºF. Brush the gubana with the egg white, sprinkle some sugar over the top, and place it in the oven.

12. Bake until the gubana is golden brown and a toothpick inserted into the center comes out clean, about 1 hour. Remove it from the oven and let it cool before slicing and serving.

INGREDIENTS:

FOR THE DOUGH

2.1	OZ. WHOLE MILK
⅔	PACKET OF ACTIVE DRY YEAST
11.6	OZ. STRONG BREAD FLOUR, PLUS MORE AS NEEDED
1	EGG
2	EGG YOLKS
⅓	TEASPOON FINE SEA SALT
⅔	OZ. HONEY
2	OZ. UNSALTED BUTTER, SOFTENED
1¾	OZ. SUGAR

1 EGG WHITE, LIGHTLY BEATEN

GRISSINI

YIELD: 50 GRISSINI / **ACTIVE TIME:** 30 MINUTES / **TOTAL TIME:** 2 HOURS

Grissini, the popular Italian breadsticks, originated in Turin and were created by Antonio Brunero, baker at the Savoia court, for the considerable needs of the child heir to the throne, Vittorio Amedeo II, who was not able to digest the crumb of regular bread due to his poor health. The original method to produce grissini is quite complex—here is a relatively simple adaptation that approaches the real thing.

1. Line a baking sheet with parchment paper. Place the yeast and water in the work bowl of a stand mixer fitted with the dough hook, gently stir, and let the mixture proof until it starts to foam, about 10 minutes.

2. Add the flour and work the mixture on low until incorporated. Add the malt, salt, and olive oil and work the mixture until it comes together as a firm dough.

3. Raise the speed to high and work the dough until it is smooth and elastic, about 10 minutes.

4. Place the dough on the baking sheet, flatten it into a ⅓-inch-thick rectangle, and brush the top with olive oil. Cover with plastic wrap and let the dough rise for 1 hour.

5. Preheat the oven to 375°F and line two more baking sheets with parchment paper. Cut the dough into ⅓-inch-thick strips and place them on the baking sheets.

6. Sprinkle semolina flour over the grissini and place them in the oven.

7. Bake until the grissini are golden brown, 15 to 20 minutes. Remove the grissini from the oven and let them cool slightly before serving.

INGREDIENTS:

1   PACKET OF ACTIVE DRY YEAST

9.9   OZ. LUKEWARM WATER (90°F)

17.6   OZ. BREAD FLOUR

1   TEASPOON BARLEY MALT

2   TEASPOONS FINE SEA SALT

2.1   OZ. EXTRA-VIRGIN OLIVE OIL, PLUS MORE AS NEEDED

SEMOLINA FLOUR, AS NEEDED

PANE BIOVE

YIELD: 2 LOAVES / **ACTIVE TIME:** 40 MINUTES / **TOTAL TIME:** 2 HOURS AND 30 MINUTES

While the most popular bread in Lombardy is michette, a roll with a hollow inside that is almost impossible to get right at home, in Piedmont the daily bread is la biova, or pane biove, which is a rather simple bread that can easily be produced by home bakers.

1. Line a baking sheet with parchment paper. Place the yeast and water in the work bowl of a stand mixer fitted with the dough hook, gently stir, and let the mixture proof until it starts to foam, about 10 minutes.

2. Add the flour and work the mixture on low until incorporated. Add the malt, salt, and lard and work the mixture until it comes together as a firm dough.

3. Raise the speed to high and work the dough until it is smooth and elastic, about 10 minutes. Form the dough into a ball and place it on the baking sheet. Cover it with a kitchen towel and let it rise for 30 minutes.

4. Place the dough on a semolina-dusted work surface, divide it in half, and shape each piece into a round. Stretch each round into a log.

5. Using a rolling pin, flatten each log into 2⅓-inch-thick rectangles. Starting from a long side, roll each rectangle up tightly.

6. Roll each piece of dough into a long, 2-inch-wide strip. Roll each strip up and place the dough, seam side down, on the work surface. Cover it with kitchen towels and use some object to prevent the dough from expanding horizontally.

7. Preheat the oven to 390°F and line a baking sheet with parchment paper. Place the loaves on the baking sheet and make a deep incision in each one.

8. Place the loaves in the oven and bake until they are golden brown, about 30 minutes. Remove the bread from the oven and let it cool completely before slicing and serving.

INGREDIENTS:

1 PACKET OF ACTIVE DRY YEAST

9.9 OZ. LUKEWARM WATER (90°F)

17.6 OZ. BREAD FLOUR

1 TABLESPOON BARLEY MALT

1½ TEASPOONS FINE SEA SALT

1 OZ. LARD, PLUS MORE AS NEEDED

SEMOLINA FLOUR, AS NEEDED

COPPIA FERRARESE

YIELD: 3 LOAVES / **ACTIVE TIME:** 50 MINUTES / **TOTAL TIME:** 6 HOURS

I n Northern Italy, bread doughs are drier compared to those from Central and Southern Italy. Coppia Ferrarese, from the city of Ferrara, is a classic example of this tendency. Its special shape and the addition of olive oil make the bread crunchy on the outside and at the ends, and soft at the junction of the two arms.

1. Place the yeast and water in the work bowl of a stand mixer fitted with the dough hook, gently stir, and let the mixture proof until it starts to foam, about 10 minutes.

2. Add the flour and work the mixture on low until incorporated. Add the olive oil and work the mixture, gradually increasing the speed with the intent to reach medium after 10 to 15 minutes.

3. Add the salt and work the dough until it is smooth and elastic, about 5 minutes. Form the dough into a ball and place it in a mixing bowl. Cover it with plastic wrap and let the dough rise until it has doubled in size, 2 to 2½ hours.

4. Preheat the oven to 430°F and line a baking sheet with parchment paper.

5. Remove a small piece from the dough (smaller than a golf ball), cover it, and set it aside. Form the remaining dough into a ball, place it on a flour-dusted work surface, and roll it out into a large, ⅛-inch-thick disk. Using a pizza cutter or another sharp implement, cut the disk into 6 triangles.

6. Roll each triangle up into a log, starting from the base. Take 2 rolled-up logs and place them next to each other, lengthwise, on the baking sheet. Use a small piece of the dough you put aside to join the rolled-up logs at their centers, leaving most of each log uncovered. Turn the free ends of each log so that they form an arch facing away from the center. Repeat with the remaining rolled-up logs.

7. Cover the coppia with a kitchen towel and let them rest for 20 minutes.

8. Place the coppia in the oven and bake until they are golden brown, about 20 minutes.

9. Remove the coppia from the oven, transfer them to wire racks, and let them cool completely before enjoying.

INGREDIENTS:

⅔ PACKET OF ACTIVE DRY YEAST

6.2 OZ. WATER

17½ OZ. ALL-PURPOSE FLOUR, PLUS MORE AS NEEDED

1¾ OZ. EXTRA-VIRGIN OLIVE OIL

2 TEASPOONS FINE SEA SALT

FOCACCIA DI GIAVENO

YIELD: 1 LARGE FOCACCIA / **ACTIVE TIME:** 30 MINUTES / **TOTAL TIME:** 4 HOURS

The north of Italy is characterized by several versions of sweet focaccia. The one from Giaveno, a beautiful town in Piedmont, is very soft and utterly delicious, due in large part to the citrus zests.

1. Place the yeast and water in a bowl and gently stir. Let the mixture sit until it starts to foam, about 10 minutes.

2. In a large bowl, combine the two flours. Add the milk and yeast mixture and work the mixture until it just comes together. Transfer it to a flour-dusted work surface and knead the dough until it is compact, smooth, and elastic.

3. Incorporate all of the remaining ingredients, except for the butter, into the dough one at a time. When incorporated, knead until the dough is developed, elastic, and extensible, about 5 minutes.

4. Gradually incorporate the butter and work the dough until it does not feel sticky. Let the dough rest in a warm spot until it has doubled in size, about 2 hours.

5. Coat an 18 x 13–inch baking sheet with butter. Place the dough on the baking sheet and gently flatten it into an approximately ¾-inch-thick disk. There is no need to cover the whole pan with the dough. Cover the dough with a kitchen towel and let it rest at room temperature for 1 hour.

6. Preheat the oven to 430°F.

7. Dip your fingers in butter and press down on the dough to make deep indentations in it. Sprinkle sugar generously over the focaccia, place it in the oven, and bake until the focaccia is a light golden brown, 15 to 20 minutes.

8. Remove the focaccia from the oven, sprinkle more sugar over it, and let it cool briefly before slicing and serving.

INGREDIENTS:

2½ TEASPOONS ACTIVE DRY YEAST

3½ TABLESPOONS LUKEWARM WATER (90°F)

7 OZ. ALL-PURPOSE FLOUR, PLUS MORE AS NEEDED

17.6 OZ. BREAD FLOUR

15½ OZ. WHOLE MILK

2.6 OZ. SUGAR, PLUS MORE FOR TOPPING

3 EGG YOLKS

ZEST OF ½ LEMON

ZEST OF ½ ORANGE

1 TEASPOON FINE SEA SALT

½ TEASPOON PURE VANILLA EXTRACT

3½ OZ. UNSALTED BUTTER, CHOPPED, PLUS MORE AS NEEDED

SMACAFAM

YIELD: 1 MEDIUM FOCACCIA / **ACTIVE TIME:** 10 MINUTES / **TOTAL TIME:** 1 HOUR

The name of this dish from Trentino-Alto Adige means "keep away the hunger," scaccia fame in Italian. Something between a focaccia and a quiche, smacafam is typically served in bite-size pieces.

1. Preheat the oven to 360°F and grease a 13 x 9–inch baking pan with butter. Add all of the ingredients, except for about 3 oz. of the sausage, to a mixing bowl and stir until the batter looks smooth. Pour the batter into the pan and sprinkle the remaining sausage over the top.

2. Place the focaccia in the oven and bake for 30 to 40 minutes, until the edges are golden brown. Remove and let it cool briefly before serving.

INGREDIENTS:

	BUTTER, AS NEEDED
14	OZ. ALL-PURPOSE FLOUR, PLUS MORE AS NEEDED
2½	CUPS WHOLE MILK
2	EGGS
½	LB. SWEET ITALIAN SAUSAGE, CHOPPED
2	TEASPOONS TABLE SALT
2	PINCHES OF BLACK PEPPER

PINZA ONTA POLESANA

YIELD: 1 LARGE FOCACCIA / **ACTIVE TIME:** 40 MINUTES / **TOTAL TIME:** 4 HOURS

Most versions of this recipe include ciccioli, a type of processed pork that pancetta or bacon can be substituted for; the meat can also be removed altogether. This focaccia is traditionally made with lard, but feel free to use butter or margarine if you prefer.

1. Place half of the pancetta in a skillet and cook over medium heat until the fat has rendered, about 4 minutes. Transfer the pancetta to a paper towel–lined plate to cool.

2. Place the water and yeast in a bowl and gently stir. Let the mixture sit until it starts to foam, about 10 minutes.

3. In a large bowl, combine the flour, milk, half of the lard, and the yeast mixture and work the mixture until it just holds together. If kneading by hand, transfer the dough to a flour-dusted work surface. Work the dough until it is compact, smooth, and elastic.

4. Add the fine sea salt, pepper, and cooled pancetta and work the dough until it is developed, elastic, and extensible, about 5 minutes. Let the dough rest in a naturally warm spot until it has doubled in size, about 2 hours.

5. Coat an 18 × 13–inch baking pan with lard and sprinkle a light coating of bread crumbs over the pan. Place the dough in the pan and stretch it into a thick rectangle, making sure not to stretch it all the way to the edges of the pan. Cover the pan with plastic wrap and let the dough rest at room temperature for 1 hour.

6. Gently stretch the dough until it covers the entire pan. Let it rest for another 30 minutes. Preheat the oven to 410°F.

7. Sprinkle coarse sea salt over the focaccia and top with the remaining lard. Place the focaccia in the oven and bake until it is crispy and golden brown, 30 to 35 minutes.

8. Remove the focaccia from the oven and let it cool briefly before slicing and serving.

INGREDIENTS:

- 7 OZ. PANCETTA, DICED
- 4.6 OZ. LUKEWARM WATER (90°F)
- 2 TEASPOONS ACTIVE DRY YEAST
- 21.1 OZ. ALL-PURPOSE FLOUR, PLUS MORE AS NEEDED
- 7 OZ. WHOLE MILK
- 4.2 OZ. LARD, AT ROOM TEMPERATURE AND CHOPPED, PLUS MORE AS NEEDED
- 2 TEASPOONS FINE SEA SALT
- 2 PINCHES OF BLACK PEPPER
- BREAD CRUMBS, AS NEEDED
- COARSE SEA SALT, AS NEEDED

TIROT

YIELD: 1 LARGE FOCACCIA / **ACTIVE TIME:** 40 MINUTES / **TOTAL TIME:** 4 HOURS AND 45 MINUTES

Typical of Lombardy, the region surrounding Milan, this focaccia is enriched with yellow onions that confer a sweet note and provide a contrast to the crunchy crust.

1. Place the water and yeast in a bowl and gently stir. Let the mixture sit until it starts to foam, about 10 minutes.

2. In a large bowl, combine the flour, two-thirds of the lard, and the yeast mixture and work the mixture until it just holds together. If kneading by hand, transfer the dough to a flour-dusted work surface. Work the dough until it is compact, smooth, and elastic.

3. Add the onions and salt and work the dough until the onions are well incorporated. Shape the dough into a ball and let it rest in a naturally warm spot until it has doubled in size, about 2 hours.

4. Coat an 18 × 13–inch baking pan with lard and sprinkle a light coating of bread crumbs on top to prevent the focaccia from sticking to the pan. Place the dough on a flour-dusted work surface and press it out into a thick rectangle that is smaller than the pan. Place the dough in the pan, brush the surface with olive oil, and cover the dough with a kitchen towel. Let it rest for 30 minutes.

5. Gently stretch the dough until it covers the whole pan. Let it rest for another hour.

6. Preheat the oven to 390°F.

7. Season the focaccia with salt and top with the remaining lard. Place it in the oven and bake until the focaccia is golden brown and crispy, 30 to 35 minutes.

8. Remove the focaccia from the oven and let it cool briefly before serving.

INGREDIENTS:

- 13 OZ. LUKEWARM WATER (90°F)
- 2 TEASPOONS ACTIVE DRY YEAST
- 21.1 OZ. ALL-PURPOSE FLOUR, PLUS MORE AS NEEDED
- 5.3 OZ. LARD, CHOPPED AND AT ROOM TEMPERATURE, PLUS MORE AS NEEDED
- 1 LB. YELLOW ONIONS, SLICED THIN
- 2 TEASPOONS FINE SEA SALT, PLUS MORE AS NEEDED
- BREAD CRUMBS, AS NEEDED
- EXTRA-VIRGIN OLIVE OIL, AS NEEDED

SCHIZOTO

YIELD: 1 LARGE FOCACCIA / **ACTIVE TIME:** 15 MINUTES / **TOTAL TIME:** 1 HOUR AND 30 MINUTES

A very simple, unleavened focaccia, which means it can be prepared relatively quickly. The use of lard produces a crispy and light focaccia, even in the absence of yeast.

1. Preheat the oven to 375°F and line an 18 × 13–inch baking pan with parchment paper. In a large bowl, combine all of the ingredients and work the mixture until it is smooth and elastic. Cover the bowl with plastic wrap and let the dough rest at room temperature for 30 minutes.

2. Place the dough on a flour-dusted work surface and flatten it into a 1-inch-thick disk. Place the disk in the pan and score the surface in a crosshatch pattern.

3. Place the focaccia in the oven and bake until it is a light golden brown, 30 to 40 minutes.

4. Remove the focaccia from the oven, brush it with water, and let it cool briefly before slicing and serving.

INGREDIENTS:

21.1 OZ. ALL-PURPOSE FLOUR, PLUS MORE AS NEEDED

8.8 OZ. WATER, PLUS MORE AS NEEDED

5.3 OZ. UNSALTED BUTTER

2 TEASPOONS FINE SEA SALT

FUGASCINA DI MERGOZZO

YIELD: 1 LARGE FOCACCIA / **ACTIVE TIME:** 10 MINUTES / **TOTAL TIME:** 1 HOUR AND 30 MINUTES

This sweet and crispy focaccia is typical of the dreamy lakeside town of Mergozzo. It pairs really well with grappa or a sweet wine, but it is also great with coffee or tea.

1. Preheat the oven to 340°F and coat an 18 × 13–inch baking pan with butter. Combine all of the ingredients in a large bowl and work the mixture until it comes together as a smooth dough. Form the dough into a ball, cover it with plastic wrap, and chill in the refrigerator for 1 hour.

2. Place the dough on a flour-dusted work surface and roll it out so that it fits in the baking pan and is approximately ¼ inch thick. Place the dough in the pan and make deep cuts in it, as though you were dividing it into squares, making sure not to cut all the way through.

3. Place the focaccia in the oven and bake until it is golden brown, about 20 minutes. Remove the focaccia from the oven, cut it into squares, and let it cool completely before serving.

INGREDIENTS:

7	OZ. UNSALTED BUTTER, MELTED, PLUS MORE AS NEEDED
21.1	OZ. ALL-PURPOSE FLOUR, PLUS MORE AS NEEDED
10½	OZ. SUGAR
3½	OZ. GRAPPA OR BRANDY
5	EGG YOLKS
2	PINCHES OF FINE SEA SALT
	ZEST OF 1 LEMON

PIZZA AL PADELLINO

YIELD: 1 SMALL FOCACCIA / **ACTIVE TIME:** 15 MINUTES / **TOTAL TIME:** 4 HOURS AND 30 MINUTES

This delicious focaccia is also called pizza al tegamino, and it is a popular street food in Turin. Although nowadays it is considered a local delicacy, pizza al padellino does not have a centuries-old tradition like most local focaccia. Instead, it is a relative newcomer on the scene, brought by immigrants from Southern Italy.

1. Place the ball of dough on a piece of parchment paper, cover it with a kitchen towel, and let it rest at room temperature until it looks soft and fully risen, 2 to 3 hours.

2. Place the dough in a 10-inch cast-iron skillet and gently spread it to the edge of the pan, being careful not to deflate the dough. Brush the dough with olive oil, cover the skillet with plastic wrap, and let the dough rest at room temperature for 30 minutes.

3. Preheat the oven to 480°F.

4. Place the tomatoes, salt, dried oregano, and olive oil in a mixing bowl and stir to combine. Spread the sauce over the focaccia, season it with salt, and generously drizzle olive oil over the top.

5. Place the focaccia in the oven and bake for about 10 minutes, until it is a light golden brown. Remove the focaccia, top it with the mozzarella, and return it to the oven. Bake until the mozzarella has melted and the edges of the focaccia are golden brown, about 10 minutes.

6. Remove the focaccia from the oven and let it cool briefly before serving.

INGREDIENTS:

1   BALL OF NEAPOLITAN PIZZA DOUGH (SEE PAGE 397)

1   TABLESPOON EXTRA-VIRGIN OLIVE OIL, PLUS MORE TO TASTE

1   CUP CRUSHED TOMATOES

½   TEASPOON (SCANT) FINE SEA SALT, PLUS MORE TO TASTE

2   PINCHES OF DRIED OREGANO

7   OZ. FRESH MOZZARELLA CHEESE, SLICED

FOCACCIA GENOVESE

YIELD: 1 LARGE FOCACCIA / **ACTIVE TIME:** 30 MINUTES / **TOTAL TIME:** 2 HOURS

The quintessential focaccia hails, without a doubt, from Genoa. This focaccia is generally of medium height, salty, and soft. Producing a high-quality version of this at home can be challenging, but it is achievable after a few attempts.

1. Place the dough on a flour-dusted work surface and form it into a loose ball, making sure not to compress the core of the dough and deflate it. Grease an 18 ×13–inch baking pan with olive oil, place the dough on the pan, and gently flatten the dough into an oval. Cover with a kitchen towel and let it rest at room temperature for 30 minutes to 1 hour.

2. Stretch the dough toward the edges of the baking pan. If the dough does not want to extend to the edges of the pan right away, let it rest for 15 to 20 minutes before trying again. Cover with the kitchen towel and let it rest for another 30 minutes to 1 hour.

3. Place the olive oil, water, and fine sea salt in a mixing bowl and stir to combine. Set the mixture aside. Lightly dust the focaccia with flour and press down on the dough with two fingers to make deep indentations. Cover the focaccia with half of the olive oil mixture and let it rest for another 30 minutes.

4. Preheat the oven to 445°F. Cover the focaccia with the remaining olive oil mixture and sprinkle the coarse sea salt over the top. Place in the oven and bake for 15 to 20 minutes, until the focaccia is a light golden brown. As this focaccia is supposed to be soft, it's far better to remove it too early as opposed to too late. Remove and let it cool briefly before serving.

INGREDIENTS:

FOCACCIA CLASSICA (SEE PAGE 420)

ALL-PURPOSE FLOUR, AS NEEDED

3 TABLESPOONS EXTRA-VIRGIN OLIVE OIL, PLUS MORE AS NEEDED

⅔ CUP WATER

1 TEASPOON FINE SEA SALT

COARSE SEA SALT, FOR TOPPING

FUGÀSSA CO A CIÒULA

YIELD: 1 LARGE FOCACCIA / **ACTIVE TIME:** 20 MINUTES / **TOTAL TIME:** 4 HOURS AND 45 MINUTES

Don't be turned off by the amount of onions, as they will caramelize in the oven and add a sweetness that contrasts wonderfully with the savory dough.

1. Remove the dough from the refrigerator and let it rest at room temperature for 30 minutes.

2. Place the dough on a flour-dusted work surface and form it into a loose ball, making sure not to compress the core of the dough. Coat an 18 x 13–inch baking sheet with olive oil, place the dough on the pan, and gently flatten it into an oval. Cover the dough with plastic wrap and let it rest at room temperature for 1 hour.

3. Stretch the dough toward the edges of the baking sheet. If the dough does not want to extend to the edges of the pan right away, let it rest for 15 to 20 minutes before trying again.

4. Add the olive oil, water, and salt to a mixing bowl and stir to combine. Cover the focaccia with half of the mixture, cover it with plastic wrap, and let it rest for another hour.

5. Preheat the oven to 445°F.

6. Distribute the onions over the focaccia and drizzle the rest of the olive oil mixture over the top. Place the focaccia in the oven and bake until the onions look slightly charred and the focaccia is a deep golden brown, 20 to 25 minutes.

7. Remove the focaccia from the oven and let it cool slightly before serving.

INGREDIENTS:

FOCACCIA CLASSICA (SEE PAGE 420)

ALL-PURPOSE FLOUR, AS NEEDED

3 TABLESPOONS EXTRA-VIRGIN OLIVE OIL, PLUS MORE AS NEEDED

½ CUP WATER

1 TEASPOON FINE SEA SALT

2 LARGE WHITE ONIONS, SLICED THIN

FOCACCIA CON LE OLIVE

YIELD: 1 LARGE FOCACCIA / **ACTIVE TIME:** 20 MINUTES / **TOTAL TIME:** 3 HOURS AND 30 MINUTES

This is a typical Ligurian focaccia, but similar versions exist in other regions. You can use any type of olives, but Ligurian Taggiasca olives are a great choice.

1. Place the dough on a flour-dusted work surface and form it into a loose ball, making sure not to press down too hard on the core of the dough and deflate it. Coat an 18 x 13–inch baking sheet with olive oil, place the dough on the pan, and gently flatten the dough into an oval. Cover the dough with a linen towel and let it rest at room temperature for 1 hour.

2. Stretch the dough toward the edges of the baking sheet. If the dough does not want to extend to the edges of the pan right away, let it rest for 15 to 20 minutes before trying again. Cover the dough with the linen towel and let it rest for another 30 minutes.

3. Add the olive oil, water, and salt to a mixing bowl and stir to combine. Cover the focaccia with half of the mixture and let it rest for another hour.

4. Preheat the oven to 445°F. Distribute the olives over the focaccia, pressing each of them into the dough until they don't bounce back. Brush the focaccia with the remaining olive oil mixture.

5. Place the focaccia in the oven and bake until it is golden brown, about 15 minutes. Remove the focaccia from the oven and let it cool briefly before serving.

INGREDIENTS:

FOCACCIA CLASSICA (SEE PAGE 420)

ALL-PURPOSE FLOUR, AS NEEDED

3½ TABLESPOONS OLIVE OIL, PLUS MORE AS NEEDED

5⅓ OZ. WATER

1 TEASPOON TABLE SALT

10 OZ. GREEN OLIVES, PITTED

PISSALANDREA

YIELD: 1 SMALL FOCACCIA / **ACTIVE TIME:** 45 MINUTES / **TOTAL TIME:** 3 HOURS AND 30 MINUTES

Often referred to as the Ligurian take on Neapolitan pizza, this actually dates back to long before the famous pie became popular in Naples. While it does have tomato sauce, a spongy crust, olives, and anchovies put pissalandrea in a world all its own.

1. Coat a round, 10-inch cake pan with olive oil, place the dough in the pan, and flatten it slightly. Cover the dough with a kitchen towel and let it rest at room temperature for 1 hour.

2. Place the onion and olive oil in a saucepan and cook, stirring occasionally, over medium-high heat until the onion starts to soften, about 5 minutes. Add the tomatoes, salt, and oregano and simmer until the flavor is to your liking, about 30 minutes. Remove the pan from heat and let the sauce cool completely.

3. Gently stretch the dough toward the edge of the pan. If the dough does not want to extend to the edges of the pan right away, let it rest for 15 to 20 minutes before trying again. When the dough is covering the pan, brush it with olive oil, cover it with the kitchen towel, and let it rest until it looks completely risen, about 45 minutes.

4. Preheat the oven to 430°F.

5. Spread the sauce over the focaccia, taking care not to press down too hard on the dough and deflate it. Top the focaccia with the anchovies, olives, and, if desired, the garlic and capers. Season with salt and drizzle olive oil over the focaccia.

6. Place the focaccia in the oven and bake until it is golden brown, 20 to 30 minutes.

7. Remove the focaccia from the oven and let it cool briefly before serving.

INGREDIENTS:

3 OZ. EXTRA-VIRGIN OLIVE OIL, PLUS MORE AS NEEDED

½ FOCACCIA CLASSICA (SEE PAGE 420)

1 ONION, SLICED THIN

21.1 OZ. WHOLE PEELED TOMATOES, CRUSHED BY HAND

¾ TEASPOON FINE SEA SALT, PLUS MORE TO TASTE

2 PINCHES OF DRIED OREGANO

2.1 OZ. CANNED ANCHOVIES, DRAINED AND CHOPPED

8.8 OZ. BLACK OLIVES (IDEALLY TAGGIASCA), PITTED

9 GARLIC CLOVES, UNPEELED (OPTIONAL)

1 TABLESPOON CAPERS PACKED IN BRINE, DRAINED, RINSED, AND SQUEEZED DRY (OPTIONAL)

FARINATA

YIELD: 1 LARGE FOCACCIA / *ACTIVE TIME:* 20 MINUTES / *TOTAL TIME:* 3 TO 24 HOURS

Born during a time when wheat was scarce, farinata is a true poor man's focaccia. Though, believe me, it does not lack for flavor.

1. In a large bowl, combine the chickpea flour and salt. While whisking constantly, gradually add the water. If possible, use a handheld mixer, as you do not want lumps to form in the dough. When all of the water has been incorporated, cover the batter with a kitchen towel and let it rest at room temperature for 2 to 3 hours. If time allows, let the batter rest overnight.

2. Preheat the oven to 480°F.

3. Remove the foam that has gathered on the surface of the batter and discard the foam. Stir the olive oil and, if desired, the rosemary into the batter.

4. Coat an 18 x 13–inch baking sheet with olive oil, pour the batter into the pan, and use a rubber spatula to even the surface. Drizzle olive oil generously over the focaccia.

5. Place the focaccia on the upper rack of the oven and bake until it is set and lightly brown, 10 to 15 minutes.

6. Remove the focaccia from the oven and let it cool briefly before seasoning it with pepper and cutting it into squares.

INGREDIENTS:

14 OZ. CHICKPEA FLOUR

2 TEASPOONS FINE SEA SALT

5 CUPS WATER

3½ OZ. EXTRA-VIRGIN OLIVE OIL, PLUS MORE AS NEEDED

1 TABLESPOON FRESH ROSEMARY (OPTIONAL)

BLACK PEPPER, TO TASTE

FOCACCIA DI RECCO

YIELD: 1 MEDIUM FOCACCIA / **ACTIVE TIME:** 45 MINUTES / **TOTAL TIME:** 1 HOUR AND 20 MINUTES

A beloved focaccia from the town of Recco in Liguria. It is stuffed with fresh, local cheeses, and the surprising contrast created by the thin, mildly flavored, crispy outside and the slightly sour, melted cheese on the inside can raise goose bumps. The cheeses used in Recco, stracchino and crescenza, may be difficult to find outside of Italy, so feel free to use taleggio cheese in their place.

1. In a large bowl, combine the flour and salt. Add the water and work the mixture until it just comes together. If kneading by hand, transfer the dough to a flour-dusted work surface and work it for at least 10 minutes. You want it to be very smooth and elastic. Form the dough into 2 balls, place them in an airtight container, and let them rest at room temperature for 30 minutes.

2. Coat a 13 × 9–inch baking dish with olive oil. Transfer one of the balls to a flour-dusted work surface and roll it into a rectangle that will fit in the pan. Stretch the dough with your hands until it is about 1/25 inch thick, taking great care not to tear the dough.

3. Preheat the oven to the maximum temperature. With the help of a flat flour-dusted baking sheet or peel, transfer the rolled and stretched dough onto the baking sheet and cover it with the cheese. Roll and stretch the other piece of dough to the same thickness and place it over the cheese. Remove any excess dough with a sharp knife and crimp the edges to seal the focaccia. Make a few holes in different parts of the focaccia by pinching the surface with your fingers until it breaks.

4. Drizzle olive oil over the focaccia and season it with salt. Place the focaccia on the top rack of the oven and bake until dark spots begin to appear on its surface, about 10 minutes.

5. Remove the focaccia from the oven and let it cool briefly before serving.

INGREDIENTS:

14 OZ. BREAD FLOUR, PLUS MORE AS NEEDED

1/2 TEASPOON (SCANT) FINE SEA SALT, PLUS MORE TO TASTE

7.8 OZ. WATER

EXTRA-VIRGIN OLIVE OIL, AS NEEDED

28.2 OZ. STRACCHINO, CRESCENZA, OR TALEGGIO CHEESE, TORN

TIGELLE

YIELD: 20 TO 30 SMALL FOCACCIA / **ACTIVE TIME:** 30 MINUTES / **TOTAL TIME:** 3 HOURS AND 30 MINUTES

A yeasted version of piadina, these small, round focaccia are traditionally cooked in a specific double cast-iron pan with built-in molds, but a standard skillet with a lid will work just fine.

1. Place the yeast and water in a bowl and gently stir. Let the mixture sit until it starts to foam, about 10 minutes.

2. In a large bowl, combine the flour, milk, lard, and yeast mixture and work the mixture until it just comes together. If kneading by hand, transfer the dough to a flour-dusted work surface. Work it until it is compact, smooth, and elastic.

3. Add the salt and work the dough until it is developed, elastic, and extensible, about 5 minutes. Coat an airtight container with lard, shape the dough into a ball, place it in the container, and let it rest at room temperature until it has doubled in size, about 2 hours.

4. Place the dough on a flour-dusted work surface and roll it out until it is approximately ¼ inch thick. Using a water glass or round cookie cutter, cut 20 to 30 rounds out of the dough. Place the rounds on a parchment-lined baking sheet, dust them with flour, cover with a kitchen towel, and let them rest at room temperature for 1 hour.

5. Lightly coat a 10-inch cast-iron skillet with lard and warm it over medium heat. Working in batches, cook the focaccia for 5 to 6 minutes per side in a covered skillet. You want the tigelle to remain flat; if necessary, place a weight on them during the last minute of cooking. Cut the warm tigelle open and eat as is or fill with whatever your heart desires.

INGREDIENTS:

1¾ TEASPOONS ACTIVE DRY YEAST

4.6 OZ. LUKEWARM WATER (90°F)

17.6 OZ. ALL-PURPOSE FLOUR, PLUS MORE AS NEEDED

4.6 OZ. WHOLE MILK

1.4 OZ. LARD, PLUS MORE AS NEEDED

1½ TEASPOONS FINE SEA SALT

CHISOLA PIACENTINA

YIELD: 1 SMALL FOCACCIA / **ACTIVE TIME:** 40 MINUTES / **TOTAL TIME:** 4 HOURS

In Piacenza, like in other parts of the Emilia-Romagna region, focaccia is enriched with different types of cured pork and lard. This is a tremendous treat every once in a while—any more frequent than that and it becomes dangerously decadent.

1. Place the pancetta and lard in a skillet and cook over medium heat, stirring occasionally, until the pancetta is browned, about 6 to 8 minutes. Transfer the pancetta to a bowl, making sure to reserve the rendered fat as well.

2. Place the yeast and water in a bowl and gently stir. Let the mixture sit until it starts to foam, about 10 minutes.

3. In a large bowl, combine the flours, wine, and yeast mixture and work the mixture until it just comes together. If kneading by hand, transfer the dough to a flour-dusted work surface. Work it until it is compact, smooth, and elastic.

4. Add the salt, pancetta, and rendered fat and work the dough until they have been incorporated and the dough is developed, elastic, and extensible, about 5 minutes. Coat an airtight container with lard, shape the dough into a ball, place it in the container, and let it rest at room temperature until it has doubled in size, about 2 hours.

5. Place the dough on a flour-dusted work surface and roll it out until it is an approximately ⅓-inch-thick disk. Coat a round 10-inch cake pan with lard and place the focaccia in the pan. Brush the focaccia with lard, cover it with a kitchen towel, and let it rest for 1 hour.

6. Preheat the oven to 390°F.

7. Top the focaccia with more lard, place it in the oven, and bake until it is golden brown, about 30 minutes.

8. Remove the focaccia from the oven and let it cool briefly before serving.

INGREDIENTS:

7 OZ. PANCETTA

1¾ OZ. LARD, PLUS MORE AS NEEDED

1¾ TEASPOONS ACTIVE DRY YEAST

5.3 OZ. LUKEWARM WATER (90°F)

10.6 OZ. BREAD FLOUR

10.6 OZ. ALL-PURPOSE FLOUR, PLUS MORE AS NEEDED

3½ OZ. WHITE WINE

1½ TEASPOONS FINE SEA SALT

CRESCENTA BOLOGNESE

YIELD: 1 LARGE FOCACCIA / **ACTIVE TIME**: 45 MINUTES / **TOTAL TIME**: 5 HOURS

Hailing from the city of Bologna, crescenta is a tall and fluffy focaccia enriched with prosciutto and pancetta. It was once the breakfast of the city's bakers, who made this focaccia using leftover dough from their morning preparations and scraps of cured meat from nearby butchers.

1. Place the yeast and water in a bowl and gently stir. Let the mixture sit until it starts to foam, about 10 minutes.

2. Place the prosciutto and pancetta in a food processor and blitz until very finely chopped. Set the mixture aside.

3. In a large bowl, combine the flour, lard, Biga, sugar, and yeast mixture and work the mixture until it just comes together. Transfer the dough to a flour-dusted work surface and knead the dough until it is compact, smooth, and elastic.

4. Add the salt and the cured meat mixture and knead the dough until it is developed, elastic, and extensible, about 5 minutes. Cover the dough with a kitchen towel and let it rest in a warm spot until it has doubled in size, about 2 hours.

5. Place the dough on a flour-dusted work surface and form it into a ball. Coat an 18 x 13–inch baking sheet with lard and place the dough in the center. Brush the surface of the dough with lard and gently press it into an oval. Cover the dough and let it rest for 1 hour.

6. Stretch the dough toward the edges of the baking sheet. If the dough does not want to extend to the edges of the pan right away, let it rest for 15 to 20 minutes before trying again. Once it has been stretched to the edges of the pan, cover it with a kitchen towel and let it rest until fully risen, about 1 hour. You may need to stretch the dough again halfway through this final rise to get the desired result.

7. Preheat the oven to 430°F and position a rack in the center. Brush the focaccia with lard, place it in the oven, and bake until it is golden brown, 25 to 30 minutes.

8. Remove the focaccia from the oven and let it cool slightly before serving.

INGREDIENTS:

⅔	TEASPOON ACTIVE DRY YEAST
11	OZ. LUKEWARM WATER (90°F)
½	LB. PROSCIUTTO
½	LB. PANCETTA
24¾	OZ. BREAD FLOUR, PLUS MORE AS NEEDED
2½	OZ. LARD, PLUS MORE AS NEEDED
½	LB. BIGA (SEE PAGE 596)
1	TABLESPOON SUGAR
2⅔	TEASPOONS FINE SEA SALT

PIADINA

YIELD: 4 PIADINA / **ACTIVE TIME:** 30 MINUTES / **TOTAL TIME:** 1 HOUR AND 30 MINUTES

This small, round, and flat focaccia from the Romagna side of the Emilia-Romagna region is more reminiscent of pita bread than its Italian relatives. Unleavened and cooked on the stove, piadina used to be made with cereals that were not optimal for bread baking. It is delicious filled with creamy cheese and ham, but innumerable other fillings can be used.

1. Combine the salt and water and stir until the salt has dissolved. In a large mixing bowl, combine the flour and baking soda. Add the lard and the salted water and work the mixture until it just comes together. Transfer the dough to a flour-dusted work surface and knead the dough until it is compact, smooth, and elastic. Coat an airtight container with lard, form the dough into a ball, place it in the container, and let the dough rest at room temperature for 30 minutes.

2. Place the dough on a flour-dusted work surface and divide it into 4 pieces. Form the pieces into balls and roll each one until it is an approximately ⅛-inch-thick disk.

3. Warm a dry skillet over medium-high heat. When the skillet is hot, cook 1 piadina at a time. Cook until dark brown spots appear on both sides, about 5 minutes per side. Pop any big bubbles with a fork as the piadina cooks.

4. Serve once all of the piadina have been cooked.

INGREDIENTS:

2	TEASPOONS FINE SEA SALT
4.8	OZ. LUKEWARM WATER (90°F)
18	OZ. ALL-PURPOSE FLOUR, PLUS MORE AS NEEDED
1½	TEASPOONS BAKING SODA
3½	OZ. LARD, PLUS MORE AS NEEDED

SCHÜTTELBROT

YIELDS: 8 SCHÜTTELBROT / **ACTIVE TIME:** 40 MINUTES / **TOTAL TIME:** 2 HOURS AND 30 MINUTES

This crunchy flatbread is common in Trentino-Alto Adige, where it is enjoyed with earthy cheeses and/or speck. An everyday staple during the Middle Ages, it was made to sustain the common people during the long winters when food was scarce.

1. Place the yeast and water in a bowl, gently stir, and let the mixture proof until it starts to foam, about 10 minutes.

2. Place the remaining ingredients in the work bowl of a stand mixer fitted with the dough hook, add the yeast mixture, and work the mixture until it is a smooth, well-developed dough, about 15 minutes.

3. Form the dough into a round, transfer it to a clean bowl, and cover the bowl with a kitchen towel. Let the dough rest for 40 minutes.

4. Line a baking sheet with parchment paper. Place the dough on a flour-dusted work surface and roll it into a long log. Divide the dough into 8 pieces, form them into rounds, and place them on the baking sheet. Cover the rounds with a kitchen towel and let them rest for 1 hour.

5. Working with 1 round at a time, place it on a flour-dusted work surface and flatten it with your hands or a rolling pin until it is a ⅓ inch thick disk. Cover the disks with a kitchen towel and let them rest for 20 minutes.

6. Preheat the oven to 410°F and place a baking stone in it as it warms.

7. Use a peel to slide the schüttlebrot onto the baking stone. Bake until they are lightly browned, about 20 minutes.

8. Remove the schüttlebrot from the oven and let them cool before serving.

INGREDIENTS:

2½ TEASPOONS ACTIVE DRY YEAST

12 OZ. WARM WATER (105°F)

12.8 OZ. MEDIUM RYE FLOUR

5.3 OZ. ALL-PURPOSE FLOUR, PLUS MORE AS NEEDED

2 TEASPOONS MIXED SEEDS (FENNEL, CARAWAY, CORIANDER, AND ANISE RECOMMENDED)

1½ TEASPOONS FINE SEA SALT

1 TEASPOON SUGAR

1¾ OZ. BUTTERMILK

APPENDIX

BRODI, SUGHI E PESTI

BRODO DI CARNE

YIELD: 6 CUPS BEEF BROTH / **TOTAL TIME:** 2 TO 3 HOURS

1. Rinse the beef and place it in a stockpot. Add the water and bring to a boil.

2. Add the remaining ingredients, reduce the heat, and simmer the broth until the flavor has developed to your liking, 2 to 3 hours, skimming to remove any impurities that rise to the surface. Halfway through cooking, crush the tomato so that its juices infuse the broth.

3. Strain the broth and use as desired. The meat can be used for other preparations, such as the Bollito Misto alla Piemontese on page 727.

INGREDIENTS:

1.1	LB. PIECE OF BONE-IN STEW BEEF
10	CUPS WATER
1	CARROT, PEELED AND CHOPPED
½	ONION, CHOPPED
1	MEDIUM TOMATO
1	CELERY STALK, CHOPPED
1	TEASPOON FINE SEA SALT

BRODO DI POLLO

YIELD: 6 CUPS CHICKEN BROTH / **TOTAL TIME:** 2 HOURS

1. Rinse the chicken and place it in a stockpot. Add the remaining ingredients and bring to a boil.

2. Reduce the heat and let the broth simmer until the flavor has developed to your liking, about 2 hours, skimming to remove any impurities that rise to the surface.

3. Strain the broth and use as desired. The chicken can be used for another preparation.

INGREDIENTS:

1	WHOLE CHICKEN
1	CARROT, PEELED AND CHOPPED
1	ONION, CHOPPED
1	CELERY STALK, CHOPPED
10	CUPS WATER
1	SPRIG OF FRESH PARSLEY
1	TABLESPOON WHOLE PEPPERCORNS
1	TEASPOON FINE SEA SALT

BRODO VEGETALE

YIELD: 6 CUPS VEGETABLE BROTH / **TOTAL TIME:** 1 HOUR AND 30 MINUTES

1. Place all of the ingredients in a stockpot and bring to a boil.

2. Reduce the heat and let the broth simmer until the flavor has developed to your liking, about 1½ hours, skimming to remove any impurities that rise to the surface. Halfway through cooking, crush the tomatoes and let their juices infuse the broth.

3. Strain the broth and use as desired.

INGREDIENTS:

2	POTATOES, PEELED AND CHOPPED
1	ZUCCHINI, CHOPPED
1	CARROT, PEELED AND CHOPPED
1	ONION, CHOPPED
1	CELERY STALK WITH LEAVES LEFT ON, CHOPPED
2	MEDIUM TOMATOES
10	CUPS WATER
1	SPRIG OF FRESH PARSLEY
	SALT, TO TASTE

SUGO AL BASILICO

YIELD: 8 CUPS BASIC TOMATO SAUCE / **TOTAL TIME:** 40 MINUTES

1. Place the olive oil in a medium saucepan and warm it over medium heat. Add the garlic and cook until it starts to brown.

2. Add the tomatoes, partially cover the pan, and cook the sauce for 20 minutes, stirring occasionally.

3. Remove the garlic, season the sauce with salt and red pepper flakes (the latter is optional), and add the basil leaves.

4. Cook until the taste has developed to your liking and the consistency is correct, 5 to 10 minutes. During this last phase, leave the pan uncovered if the sauce is too liquid, or reduce the heat and add a splash of water if it is too thick.

INGREDIENTS:

¼	CUP EXTRA-VIRGIN OLIVE OIL
2	GARLIC CLOVES
1.8	LBS. WHOLE PEELED TOMATOES, CRUSHED
	SALT, TO TASTE
	RED PEPPER FLAKES, TO TASTE
	HANDFUL OF FRESH BASIL, TORN

SUGO CON SOFFRITTO

YIELD: 8 CUPS RICH TOMATO SAUCE / **TOTAL TIME:** 40 MINUTES

1. Place the olive oil in a medium saucepan and warm it over low heat. Add the carrot, onion, celery, and garlic and cook, stirring frequently, until the vegetables have softened, about 5 minutes, taking care to make sure that they do not brown.

2. Add the tomatoes, season the sauce with salt and red pepper flakes (the latter is optional, but will benefit the sauce), and partially cover the pan. Raise the heat to medium and cook the sauce for 20 minutes, stirring occasionally.

3. Cook until the taste has developed to your liking and the consistency is correct, 5 to 10 minutes. During this last phase, leave the pan uncovered if the sauce is too liquid, or reduce the heat and add a splash of water if it is too thick.

INGREDIENTS:

- ¼ CUP EXTRA-VIRGIN OLIVE OIL
- ½ CARROT, PEELED AND CHOPPED
- ½ ONION, CHOPPED
- ½ CELERY STALK WITH ITS LEAVES, CHOPPED
- ½ GARLIC CLOVE, MINCED
- 1.8 LBS. WHOLE PEELED TOMATOES, CRUSHED
- SALT, TO TASTE
- RED PEPPER FLAKES, TO TASTE

SUGO AI PEPERONI

YIELD: 8 CUPS RED PEPPER TOMATO SAUCE / **TOTAL TIME:** 50 MINUTES

1. Place the olive oil in a medium saucepan and warm it over medium heat. Add the garlic and onion and cook until the onion is translucent, about 3 minutes.

2. Add the peppers, season with salt, and cook, stirring frequently, until they have softened, about 10 minutes.

3. Add the tomatoes, partially cover the pan, and cook the sauce for 20 minutes, stirring occasionally.

4. Remove the garlic and season the sauce with salt, oregano, and red pepper flakes (the latter two are optional, but will benefit the sauce).

5. Cook until the taste has developed to your liking and the consistency is correct, 5 to 10 minutes. During this last phase, leave the pan uncovered if the sauce is too liquid, or reduce the heat and add a splash of water if it is too thick.

INGREDIENTS:

- ¼ CUP EXTRA-VIRGIN OLIVE OIL
- 1 GARLIC CLOVE
- ½ ONION, MINCED
- 2 MEDIUM RED BELL PEPPERS, STEMS AND SEEDS REMOVED, SLICED THIN
- 1.8 LBS. WHOLE PEELED TOMATOES, CRUSHED
- SALT, TO TASTE
- DRIED OREGANO, TO TASTE
- RED PEPPER FLAKES, TO TASTE

RAGÙ CLASSICO

YIELD: 8 CUPS CLASSIC RAGOUT / **TOTAL TIME:** 1 HOUR AND 30 MINUTES

1. Place the olive oil in a large, deep skillet and warm it over medium heat. Add the carrot, onion, and celery and cook, stirring occasionally, until they have softened, about 5 minutes.

2. Add the pork and beef and cook, breaking them up with a wooden spoon, until they are browned, about 8 minutes.

3. Add the wine and cook until it has evaporated.

4. Add the tomatoes and season with salt and pepper. Reduce the heat to low, partially cover the pan, and cook for 1 hour, stirring occasionally.

5. When the taste has developed to your liking and the ragù has the right consistency, use it as desired.

INGREDIENTS:

- ¼ CUP EXTRA-VIRGIN OLIVE OIL
- 1 CARROT, PEELED AND FINELY DICED
- 1 SMALL ONION, FINELY DICED
- 1 CELERY STALK, PEELED AND FINELY DICED
- 9 OZ. GROUND PORK
- 9 OZ. GROUND BEEF
- ⅔ CUP DRY WHITE WINE
- 1.8 LBS. WHOLE PEELED TOMATOES, CRUSHED
- SALT AND PEPPER, TO TASTE

RAGÙ RICCO

YIELD: 8 CUPS RICH RAGOUT / **TOTAL TIME:** 2 HOURS AND 30 MINUTES

1. Place the olive oil in a large, deep skillet and warm it over medium heat. Add the carrot, onion, and celery and cook, stirring occasionally, until they have softened, about 5 minutes.

2. Add the beef, chicken liver, rosemary, and bay leaf, and cook, stirring occasionally, until the meat is browned, about 8 minutes.

3. Add the wine and cook until it has evaporated.

4. Remove the bay leaf and discard it. Add the tomatoes, reduce the heat to low, partially cover the pan, and cook for about 2 hours, stirring occasionally and seasoning the ragù with salt and pepper halfway through. If the ragù becomes too thick, add the broth as needed.

5. When the taste has developed to your liking and the ragù has the right consistency, use it as desired.

INGREDIENTS:

- 1 ONION, FINELY DICED
- 1 CARROT, FINELY DICED
- ½ CELERY STALK, FINELY DICED
- 3 TABLESPOONS EXTRA-VIRGIN OLIVE OIL
- 11 OZ. STEW BEEF, FINELY DICED
- 11 OZ. CHICKEN OR VEAL LIVER, FINELY DICED
- 1 TEASPOON FINELY CHOPPED FRESH ROSEMARY
- 1 BAY LEAF
- ½ CUP RED WINE
- 10.6 OZ. WHOLE PEELED TOMATOES, CRUSHED
- ½ CUP BRODO DI CARNE (SEE PAGE 805), HOT
- SALT AND PEPPER, TO TASTE

RAGÙ BIANCO

1. Place the olive oil in a large, deep skillet and warm it over medium heat. Add the carrot, onion, celery, and garlic and cook, stirring occasionally, until they have softened, about 5 minutes.

2. Add the pancetta and cook, stirring occasionally, until it has browned, about 4 minutes.

3. Add the beef, pork, bay leaves, rosemary, and marjoram, and cook, stirring occasionally, until the meat starts to brown, about 5 minutes.

4. Add the wine and cook until it has evaporated.

5. Reduce the heat to low and add 2 ladles of the broth. Partially cover the pan and cook for about 2 hours, stirring occasionally and seasoning the ragù with the cloves, cinnamon, salt, and pepper halfway through. If the ragù becomes too thick, add the remaining broth as needed.

6. Stir in the milk, uncover the pan, and cook until the ragù has the right consistency. Use as desired.

INGREDIENTS:

3	TABLESPOONS EXTRA-VIRGIN OLIVE OIL
1	LARGE CARROT, PEELED AND FINELY DICED
½	WHITE ONION, FINELY DICED
1	CELERY STALK, FINELY DICED
1	GARLIC CLOVE, MINCED
2	OZ. PANCETTA, FINELY DICED
14	OZ. GROUND BEEF
14	OZ. GROUND PORK
2	BAY LEAVES
1	TEASPOON FINELY CHOPPED FRESH ROSEMARY
	HANDFUL OF FRESH MARJORAM, FINELY CHOPPED
½	CUP DRY WHITE WINE
2	CUPS BRODO DI CARNE (SEE PAGE 805), HOT
	PINCH OF GROUND CLOVES
	PINCH OF CINNAMON
	SALT AND PEPPER, TO TASTE
½	CUP WHOLE MILK

RAGÙ DI CINGHIALE

YIELD: 8 CUPS WILD BOAR RAGOUT / **TOTAL TIME:** 2 HOURS AND 30 MINUTES

1. Place the olive oil in a large, deep skillet and warm it over medium heat. Add the carrot, onion, celery, and garlic and cook, stirring occasionally, until they have softened, about 5 minutes.

2. Add the pancetta and cook, stirring occasionally, until it has browned, about 4 minutes.

3. Add the boar, thyme, and juniper berries and cook, stirring occasionally, until the meat starts to brown, about 5 minutes.

4. Add the wine and cook until it has evaporated.

5. Add the tomatoes and water, season with salt and pepper, and reduce the heat to low. Partially cover the pan and cook for about 2 hours, stirring occasionally.

6. When the taste has developed to your liking and the ragù has the right consistency, use as desired.

INGREDIENTS:

3	TABLESPOONS EXTRA-VIRGIN OLIVE OIL
1	CARROT, PEELED AND FINELY DICED
½	WHITE ONION, FINELY DICED
1	CELERY STALK, FINELY DICED
1	GARLIC CLOVE, MINCED
3½	OZ. PANCETTA, FINELY DICED
14	OZ. WILD BOAR, FINELY DICED
1	TEASPOON FRESH THYME
5	JUNIPER BERRIES
½	CUP RED WINE
1.8	LBS. WHOLE PEELED TOMATOES, CRUSHED
1	CUP WATER
	SALT AND PEPPER, TO TASTE

BESCIAMELLA

YIELD: 2½ CUPS BÉCHAMEL SAUCE / **TOTAL TIME:** 30 MINUTES

1. Place the milk in a small saucepan and warm it over low heat, taking care not to let it come to a boil.

2. While the milk is warming, place the butter in a separate pan and melt it over medium heat.

3. Season the milk with nutmeg and salt and remove the pan from heat.

4. Add the flour to the butter and stir continually until the mixture gives off a nutty aroma and turns golden brown, 2 to 3 minutes.

5. While whisking continually, add the milk in 3 increments. Reduce the heat to low and cook, stirring frequently, until the sauce thickens to the desired consistency. Use as desired.

INGREDIENTS:

2	CUPS PLUS 2 TABLESPOONS WHOLE MILK
	PINCH OF FRESHLY GRATED NUTMEG
	SALT, TO TASTE
1¾	OZ. UNSALTED BUTTER
1¾	OZ. ALL-PURPOSE FLOUR

BAGNET VERT (SALSA VERDE LIGURE)

YIELD: 4 CUPS SALSA VERDE / **TOTAL TIME:** 25 MINUTES

1. Place the bread in a bowl, add the water or vinegar, and toss it to combine. Let the bread soak for 10 minutes.

2. Place the remaining ingredients in a food processor and blitz until the mixture is pureed.

3. Add the bread and blitz to incorporate. Incorporate more water if the sauce seems too thick.

INGREDIENTS:

2	CUPS DAY-OLD BREAD PIECES
½	CUP WATER, PLUS MORE AS NEEDED
1	TABLESPOON RED WINE VINEGAR
2	CUPS FRESH FLAT-LEAF PARSLEY
1	CUP EXTRA-VIRGIN OLIVE OIL
1	TABLESPOON CAPERS IN BRINE, DRAINED AND RINSED
4	ANCHOVIES IN OLIVE OIL, DRAINED
½	TEASPOON FINE SEA SALT

PESTO ALLA GENOVESE

YIELD: 3½ CUPS PESTO / **TOTAL TIME:** 15 MINUTES

1. Using a mortar and pestle, grind the garlic and salt into a paste.

2. Add the basil and grind until it is pulpy.

3. Add the pine nuts and grind until they are fine.

4. Place the Parmesan and pecorino in a separate bowl and stir to combine.

5. Add one-quarter of the cheese mixture and grind until it has been incorporated. Add one-quarter of the olive oil and grind until it has been incorporated. Continue alternating the cheese mixture and olive oil until the pesto has the desired, creamy yet grainy, consistency. Use as desired.

INGREDIENTS:

2	(HEAPING) CUPS FRESH BASIL
2	SMALL GARLIC CLOVES
½	CUP EXTRA-VIRGIN OLIVE OIL (LIGURIAN OLIVE OIL PREFERRED)
⅔	CUP GRATED PARMESAN CHEESE
⅓	CUP GRATED PECORINO CHEESE (SARDINIAN PREFERRED)
2	TABLESPOONS PINE NUTS
	PINCH OF FINE SEA SALT

SALSA DI NOCI

YIELD: 3 CUPS WALNUT CREAM SAUCE / **TOTAL TIME:** 20 MINUTES

1. Place the bread and milk in a bowl and soak for 10 minutes. Drain the bread and squeeze it to remove any excess liquid.

2. Place the bread in a blender, add the walnuts, garlic, marjoram, Parmesan, and salt and puree until the mixture is a paste.

3. With the blender running, add the olive oil and water and blend until the sauce is thick and creamy. When using this sauce for pasta, dilute it with pasta water until it reaches the desired level of creaminess.

INGREDIENTS:

1	SLICE OF WHITE BREAD, CRUST REMOVED
7	OZ. WHOLE MILK
1⅔	CUPS WALNUTS
½	GARLIC CLOVE
	HANDFUL OF FRESH MARJORAM LEAVES
1	TABLESPOON GRATED PARMESAN CHEESE
2	PINCHES OF FINE SEA SALT
5	TABLESPOONS EXTRA-VIRGIN OLIVE OIL
2	TABLESPOONS LUKEWARM WATER

SALSA AL CREN (SALSA DI RAFANO)

YIELD: 8 CUPS HORSERADISH SAUCE / **TOTAL TIME:** 10 MINUTES

1. Place all of the ingredients in a food processor and blitz until the sauce is creamy and spreadable. Use as desired.

INGREDIENTS:

11	OZ. HORSERADISH, FINELY GRATED
1	CUP FRESH BREAD CRUMBS
⅓	CUP WHITE WINE VINEGAR
3	TABLESPOONS EXTRA-VIRGIN OLIVE OIL
2	PINCHES OF FINE SEA SALT
2½	TEASPOONS SUGAR

BAGNET ROSS

YIELD: 10 CUPS PIEDMONTESE PESTO / **TOTAL TIME:** 3 HOURS AND 30 MINUTES

1. Bring water to a boil in a large saucepan. Add salt and the tomatoes and cook for 30 minutes.

2. Drain the tomatoes and let them cool.

3. Peel the tomatoes and puree them in a blender or with a food mill. If using a blender, strain the puree to remove the seeds.

4. Place the tomato puree in a saucepan, add the celery, carrots, onion, garlic, chile, bell pepper, parsley, and sage, and cover the pan. Cook the sauce over low heat until the flavor has developed to your liking, about 2 hours.

5. Pass the sauce through a sieve or a food mill. If it is too thin for your liking, return it to the pan and cook it over medium heat until it has thickened.

6. Let the sauce cool and add the olive oil and vinegar. Season the sauce with salt, pepper, cinnamon, and mustard powder and use as desired.

INGREDIENTS:

	SALT AND PEPPER, TO TASTE
2.2	LBS. RIPE TOMATOES
2	CELERY STALKS, FINELY DICED
2	CARROTS, PEELED AND FINELY DICED
1	LARGE ONION, FINELY DICED
2	GARLIC CLOVES, MINCED
½	SMALL FRESH CHILE PEPPER, MINCED
1	LARGE RED BELL PEPPER, STEM AND SEEDS REMOVED, FINELY DICED
1	TABLESPOON FINELY CHOPPED FRESH PARSLEY
1	TABLESPOON FINELY CHOPPED FRESH SAGE
1	CUP EXTRA-VIRGIN OLIVE OIL
1	TABLESPOON RED WINE VINEGAR
	CINNAMON, TO TASTE
	MUSTARD POWDER, TO TASTE

BASI DOLCI E PANE

PASTA SFOGLIA

YIELD: 1 SHEET OF PUFF PASTRY / **TOTAL TIME:** 4 HOURS

1. To begin preparations for the dough, place the flours, salt, and the butter in the work bowl of a stand mixer fitted with the paddle attachment.

2. Combine the ice water and lemon juice and then add the mixture to the work bowl. Beat the mixture until it is combined.

3. Fit the mixer with the dough hook and work the mixture until it comes together as a smooth dough.

4. Form the dough into a ball, cover it with plastic wrap, and chill it in the refrigerator for 1 hour.

5. While the dough is in the refrigerator, begin preparations for the butter block. Place the butter on a clean work surface and sprinkle half of the flour over it.

6. Begin pounding the butter with a rolling pin until it is in 1 smooth, flat piece. Incorporate the remaining flour as needed to keep the butter from sticking to the rolling pin and work surface.

7. Fold the butter over itself into a rectangle. Pound it until it is pliable. Shape the butter block into a 5-inch square and chill it in the refrigerator.

8. Remove the dough from the refrigerator, place it on a flour-dusted work surface, and use a sharp knife to slash a 1-inch-deep crosswise cut into the top of the dough ball.

9. Gently pull one corner of the dough at a time until it is a square. Place the butter block in the center of the dough.

10. Take each corner of the dough and pull it up and over the butter block until the butter block is completely covered by the dough.

11. Roll the dough into a rectangle that is approximately 10 inches long and 5 inches wide.

12. Working from the short sides, fold 1 end of the dough to the center. Fold the other end so that it meets the opposite end in the center. Fold the dough in half so that it resembles a book. Chill the dough in the refrigerator for 20 minutes.

13. Repeat Step 12 three times. After the final fold, let the puff pastry chill in the refrigerator for 1 hour before using or storing in the refrigerator.

INGREDIENTS:

FOR THE DOUGH

11.6 OZ. BREAD FLOUR

2.1 OZ. CAKE FLOUR, PLUS MORE AS NEEDED

1½ TEASPOONS FINE SEA SALT

2 TABLESPOONS UNSALTED BUTTER, SOFTENED

¾ CUP PLUS 2 TABLESPOONS ICE WATER

1 TABLESPOON FRESH LEMON JUICE

FOR THE BUTTER BLOCK

4 STICKS OF UNSALTED BUTTER, CHILLED AND CUT INTO 1-INCH CUBES

5 TABLESPOONS BREAD OR ALL-PURPOSE FLOUR

PASTA FROLLA

YIELD: 1 SHORT-CRUST PASTRY / **TOTAL TIME:** 1 HOUR AND 15 MINUTES

1. Place the sugar and butter in the work bowl of a stand mixer fitted with the paddle attachment and cream until the mixture is light and fluffy.

2. Add the egg, egg yolks, and lemon zest and beat until incorporated.

3. Sift the flour, baking powder, and salt into the work bowl and beat until the dough just comes together.

4. Form the dough into a ball, cover it with plastic wrap, and chill it in the refrigerator for 1 hour before using.

INGREDIENTS:

4.2   OZ. SUGAR

5.4   OZ. UNSALTED BUTTER,
      SOFTENED

1   EGG

2   EGG YOLKS

      ZEST OF 1 LEMON

10.6 OZ. ALL-PURPOSE FLOUR

      PINCH OF BAKING
      POWDER

      PINCH OF FINE SEA SALT

PASTA FROLLA PER CROSTATE

YIELD: 1 SWEET PIECRUST / **TOTAL TIME:** 1 HOUR AND 15 MINUTES

1. Place the sugar and butter in the work bowl of a stand mixer fitted with the paddle attachment and cream until the mixture is light and fluffy.

2. Add the eggs and lemon zest and beat until incorporated.

3. Sift the flour, baking powder, and salt into the work bowl and beat until the dough just comes together.

4. Form the dough into a ball, cover it with plastic wrap, and chill it in the refrigerator for 1 hour before using.

INGREDIENTS:

7   OZ. SUGAR

4½   OZ. UNSALTED BUTTER OR
      LARD

4   SMALL EGGS

      ZEST OF 1 LEMON

4   CUPS ALL-PURPOSE FLOUR

1   TEASPOON BAKING
      POWDER

      PINCH OF FINE SEA SALT

PASTA FROLLA AL LARDO

YIELD: 1 SHORT-CRUST PASTRY WITH LARD / **TOTAL TIME:** 1 HOUR AND 15 MINUTES

1. Place the sugar and lard in the work bowl of a stand mixer fitted with the paddle attachment and cream until the mixture is light and fluffy.

2. Add the eggs and lemon zest and beat until incorporated.

3. Sift the flour, baking powder, and salt into the work bowl and beat until the dough just comes together.

4. Form the dough into a ball, cover it with plastic wrap, and chill it in the refrigerator for 1 hour before using.

INGREDIENTS:

8.8	OZ. SUGAR
8.8	OZ. LARD
3	SMALL EGGS
	ZEST OF 1 LEMON
17.6	OZ. ALL-PURPOSE FLOUR
½	TEASPOON BAKING POWDER OR ¼ TEASPOON BAKER'S AMMONIA
	PINCH OF FINE SEA SALT

PASTA FROLLA NAPOLETANA

YIELD: 1 NEAPOLITAN SHORT-CRUST PASTRY / **TOTAL TIME:** 1 HOUR AND 15 MINUTES

1. Place the sugar, lard, and butter in the work bowl of a stand mixer fitted with the paddle attachment and cream until the mixture is light and fluffy.

2. Add the water, vanilla, and lemon zest and beat until incorporated.

3. Sift the flour, baker's ammonia, and salt into the work bowl and beat until the dough just comes together.

4. Form the dough into a ball, cover it with plastic wrap, and chill it in the refrigerator for 1 hour before using.

INGREDIENTS:

3½	OZ. SUGAR
1¾	OZ. LARD
1¾	OZ. UNSALTED BUTTER
1¾	OZ. WATER
1	TEASPOON PURE VANILLA EXTRACT
	ZEST OF ½ LEMON
8.8	OZ. ALL-PURPOSE FLOUR
	PINCH OF BAKER'S AMMONIA
	PINCH OF FINE SEA SALT

PASTA FROLLA AL MARSALA

YIELD: 1 SHORT-CRUST PASTRY WITH MARSALA / **TOTAL TIME:** 1 HOUR AND 15 MINUTES

1. Place all of the ingredients in the work bowl of a stand mixer fitted with the paddle attachment and beat until the mixture just comes together as a smooth dough.

2. Form the dough into a ball, cover it with plastic wrap, and chill it in the refrigerator for 1 hour before using.

INGREDIENTS:

10.6 OZ. ALL-PURPOSE FLOUR

3½ OZ. UNSALTED BUTTER

2½ TABLESPOONS SUGAR

1 EGG YOLK

3 OZ. MARSALA

3 OZ. WHOLE MILK

PINCH OF FINE SEA SALT

PASTA FROLLA DI SEMOLA

YIELD: 1 SEMOLINA SHORT-CRUST PASTRY / **TOTAL TIME:** 1 HOUR AND 15 MINUTES

1. Place the sugar and butter in the work bowl of a stand mixer fitted with the paddle attachment and cream until the mixture is light and fluffy.

2. Add the egg yolks and water and beat until incorporated.

3. Sift the flours, baking powder, and salt into the work bowl and beat until the dough just comes together.

4. Form the dough into a ball, cover it with plastic wrap, and chill it in the refrigerator for 1 hour before using.

INGREDIENTS:

7 OZ. SUGAR

7 OZ. UNSALTED BUTTER

4 EGG YOLKS

3.2 OZ. COLD WATER

8.8 OZ. ALL-PURPOSE FLOUR

8.8 OZ. FINELY GROUND DURUM WHEAT FLOUR (SEMOLA RIMACINATA)

PINCH OF BAKING POWDER

PINCH OF FINE SEA SALT

PAN DI SPAGNA

YIELD: 1 SPONGE CAKE / **TOTAL TIME:** 1 HOUR AND 30 MINUTES

1. Preheat the oven to 355°F. Place the egg yolks, confectioners' sugar, and lemon zest in a mixing bowl and beat the mixture until it is foamy.

2. Place the egg whites in a separate bowl and whisk until they hold stiff peaks.

3. Add the egg whites to the egg yolk mixture and fold to incorporate them.

4. Sift the flour over the mixture and fold to incorporate.

5. Coat a round 10-inch cake pan with butter, dust it with flour, and knock out any excess. Pour the batter into the pan, place it in the oven, and bake until a toothpick inserted into the center of the cake comes out clean, about 40 minutes.

6. Remove the cake from the oven and let it cool in the pan before slicing, serving, or using in another preparation.

INGREDIENTS:

5	EGGS, SEPARATED
5.3	OZ. CONFECTIONERS' SUGAR
	ZEST OF 1 LEMON
4.4	OZ. CAKE FLOUR, PLUS MORE AS NEEDED
	BUTTER, AS NEEDED

CREMA PASTICCERA

YIELD: 3 CUPS PASTRY CREAM / **TOTAL TIME:** 1 HOUR

1. Place the milk and lemon peel in a small saucepan and warm over low heat.

2. Place the egg yolks and confectioners' sugar in a mixing bowl and whisk to combine.

3. Sift the flour over the egg yolk mixture and stir until the mixture is combined.

4. When the milk is just about to simmer, remove the lemon peel and, while whisking continually, gradually add the milk to the egg yolk mixture until all of the milk has been incorporated.

5. Add the tempered egg yolk mixture to the saucepan and cook it over low heat, stirring frequently, until the custard has thickened.

6. Add the butter, stir vigorously until it has been incorporated, and remove the pan from heat.

7. Pour the custard into a bowl, place plastic wrap directly on the surface, and chill it in the refrigerator until it has cooled completely.

INGREDIENTS:

17.6	OZ. WHOLE MILK
	PEEL OF ½ LEMON
3	EGG YOLKS
3.2	OZ. CONFECTIONERS' SUGAR
2.6	OZ. ALL-PURPOSE FLOUR
1	TEASPOON UNSALTED BUTTER

CREMA PASTICCERA NAPOLETANA

YIELD: 3 CUPS NEAPOLITAN PASTRY CREAM / TOTAL TIME: 1 HOUR

1. Place the milk, whipping cream, and lemon peel in a small saucepan and warm over low heat.

2. Place the egg yolks and sugar in a mixing bowl and whisk to combine.

3. Sift the flour over the egg yolk mixture and stir until the mixture is combined.

4. When the milk mixture is just about to simmer, remove the lemon peel and, while whisking continually, gradually add the milk mixture to the egg yolk mixture until all of the milk mixture has been incorporated.

5. Add the tempered egg yolk mixture to the saucepan, stir in the potato starch, and cook the custard over low heat, stirring frequently, until it has thickened.

6. Pour the custard into a bowl, place plastic wrap directly on the surface, and chill it in the refrigerator until it has cooled completely.

INGREDIENTS:

14	OZ. WHOLE MILK
3½	OZ. WHIPPING CREAM
	PEEL OF 1 LEMON
6	EGG YOLKS
5.3	OZ. SUGAR
1	OZ. ALL-PURPOSE FLOUR
⅔	OZ. POTATO STARCH

CREMA PASTICCERA SICILIANA

YIELD: 3 CUPS SICILIAN PASTRY CREAM / TOTAL TIME: 1 HOUR

1. Place the milk and lemon peel in a small saucepan and warm over low heat.

2. Place the egg yolks and sugar in a mixing bowl and whisk to combine.

3. Sift the potato starch over the egg yolk mixture and stir until the mixture is combined.

4. When the milk mixture is just about to simmer, remove the lemon peel and, while whisking continually, gradually add the milk mixture to the egg yolk mixture until all of the milk mixture has been incorporated.

5. Add the tempered egg yolk mixture to the saucepan and cook the custard over low heat, stirring frequently, until it has thickened.

6. Pour the custard into a bowl, place plastic wrap directly on the surface, and chill it in the refrigerator until it has cooled completely.

INGREDIENTS:

17.6	OZ. WHOLE MILK
	PEEL OF 1 LEMON
2	EGG YOLKS
5.3	OZ. SUGAR
1.6	OZ. POTATO STARCH

CREMA PASTICCERA AL CIOCCOLATO

YIELD: 3 CUPS CHOCOLATE PASTRY CREAM / **TOTAL TIME:** 1 HOUR

1. Place the milk and lemon peel in a small saucepan and warm over low heat.

2. Place the egg yolks and confectioners' sugar in a mixing bowl and whisk to combine.

3. Sift the flour starch over the egg yolk mixture and stir until the mixture is combined.

4. When the milk mixture is just about to simmer, remove the lemon peel and, while whisking continually, gradually add the milk mixture to the egg yolk mixture until all of the milk mixture has been incorporated.

5. Add the tempered egg yolk mixture to the saucepan and cook the custard over low heat, stirring frequently, until it has thickened.

6. Pour the custard into a bowl, place plastic wrap directly on the surface, and set it aside.

7. Bring a few inches of water to a boil in a medium saucepan. Place the chocolate in a heatproof bowl, place it over the simmering water, and stir until it is smooth. Remove the chocolate from heat.

8. Stir the vanilla into the melted chocolate. Stir the chocolate into the custard, place a fresh piece of plastic wrap directly on the surface, and chill it in the refrigerator until it has cooled completely.

INGREDIENTS:

17.6 OZ. WHOLE MILK

PEEL OF ½ LEMON

3 EGG YOLKS

3.2 OZ. CONFECTIONERS' SUGAR

2.6 OZ. ALL-PURPOSE FLOUR

3 OZ. BITTERSWEET CHOCOLATE, BROKEN INTO SMALL PIECES

1 TEASPOON PURE VANILLA EXTRACT

HOW TO MAKE A SOURDOUGH STARTER

It is possible to get a starter from a friend or to buy it online from trusted sellers. However, making your own starter is a highly rewarding endeavor that you do not want to miss out on. Once a stable starter has been created, it can be maintained indefinitely, assuming it receives proper care. There are several ways to create a starter. The most straightforward method is to make use of the many wild yeasts and good bacteria naturally occurring in flour and in the air, and allow time to do the rest.

DAY 1, MORNING

1   OZ. LUKEWARM WATER (AROUND 80°F)

0.2 OZ. WHOLE-GRAIN RYE FLOUR

0.8 OZ. ALL-PURPOSE FLOUR

Mix the ingredients together and put the mixture in a washed and rinsed container, making sure that the mixture takes up no more than one-third of the container. Put the lid on (if you are using a glass jar, do not screw the lid on tightly). Place the container in a naturally warm (but not hot) spot. Ideally, the temperature should be around 80°F, so if you do not have a place in your home that gets this warm, consider investing in an incubator.

You may also want to use bottled water to create a starter, because chemicals in tap water could inhibit the starter's development in the early stages.

DAY 2, MORNING

1   OZ. OF YOUR STARTER FROM THE DAY BEFORE

1   OZ. LUKEWARM WATER (80°F)

0.2 OZ. WHOLE-GRAIN RYE FLOUR

0.8 OZ. ALL-PURPOSE FLOUR

Discard the rest of your starter. Add the water and mix. Then add the flours, mix, and scrape the walls of the container well to keep it clean. Place the container back in the warm spot.

DAY 2, EVENING

1   OZ. OF YOUR STARTER FROM THE MORNING

1   OZ. LUKEWARM WATER (80°F)

0.2 OZ. WHOLE-GRAIN RYE FLOUR

0.8 OZ. ALL-PURPOSE FLOUR

Discard the rest of your starter. Add the water and mix. Then add the flours, mix, and scrape the walls of the container well to keep it clean. Place the container back in the warm spot.

At this point, you should be seeing some signs of life, some activity, which will manifest itself as bubbles.

DAY 3, 4, 5, AND SO ON

Continue to do what was described for Day 2, until your starter can double itself within 12 hours, is all bubbly, and smells good (not too acidic, the aroma of a healthy starter is similar to a freshly cut green apple). Make sure that the color stays within the yellow-brown shades, and does not take an orange or blueish tone.

By Day 6 or 7, you may have successfully created a starter. Does it double in 12 hours? Does it smell sweet and is it full of bubbles? If the answer to any of these is no, then continue as in the previous days. Hopefully, your sourdough culture will soon come to life, but if it does not, discard and start over.

If instead you have given birth to a stable sourdough culture, the task now is keeping it healthy.

HOW TO MAINTAIN A SOURDOUGH STARTER

If you just started a sourdough culture, it is not recommended to shift to refrigerated maintenance for a few weeks. During those first few weeks at room temperature, strains of yeast and bacteria that are optimal for bread baking will be selected. Once the culture is stable, periods of refrigeration will not disrupt its main composition. Of course, this all depends on how good you are at feeding your starter at the right time.

When keeping the starter at room temperature, it is ideal to feed it once every 12 hours. In the beginning, use the same amount of starter, water, and flour, in a 1:1:1 ratio for each feeding. This means that every 12 hours you will take some of your starter and combine it with equal amounts of water and flour (in terms of weight, not volume).

The remaining starter can be discarded or used for other preparations.

After several days at room temperature, your starter should become very active and you will need to change the ratio. The relative amounts for your feedings could then become, for instance, 1:2:2.

This means that you will use half the amount of starter, keeping the same amounts of water and flour. What matters is that the hydration (the proportion of water to flour) remains constant. The amount of starter from the previous feeding can instead change depending on how active the starter is from day to day, how warm the place where you are storing the starter is, and how capable you are of doing two feedings a day. If you want to feed your starter only once a day, you can inoculate a small amount of starter in your mixture of water and flour.

When your sourdough culture has stabilized, you can make life easier by alternating between leaving the starter unfed in the fridge, and bringing it to room temperature, feeding as described previously. Ideally, you want to leave the starter unfed in the fridge for no more than 5 days, and then feed it at room temperature at least three times before putting the starter, just fed, back into the fridge.

Always choose the least cold spot of your fridge to keep your starter, and make sure the overall temperature of the fridge does not go below 36°F.

Although not optimal, if it does happen that you leave your starter unfed in the refrigerator for a prolonged amount of time, do not worry.

It takes a very long time to kill a stable sourdough culture. If this occurs, let your sourdough starter stay at room temperature longer, with repeated feedings, to regenerate all of the yeast cells and the good bacteria.

MAKING PASTA MADRE (STIFF SOURDOUGH STARTER)

To convert your 100 percent hydration sourdough starter (equal amounts of water and flour) into a pasta madre that has 50 percent hydration, take ⅚ oz. of sourdough starter straight from the refrigerator and combine it with 1¾ oz. water and 3½ oz. all-purpose flour.

After 12 hours, perform another feeding using 1¾ oz. of the new stiff starter, 1¾ oz. water, and 3½ oz. all-purpose flour.

CONVERSION TABLE

WEIGHTS

1 oz. = 28 grams

2 oz. = 57 grams

4 oz. (¼ lb.) = 113 grams

8 oz. (½ lb.) = 227 grams

16 oz. (1 lb.) = 454 grams

VOLUME MEASURES

⅛ teaspoon = 0.6 ml

¼ teaspoon = 1.23 ml

½ teaspoon = 2.5 ml

1 teaspoon = 5 ml

1 tablespoon (3 teaspoons) = ½ fluid oz. = 15 ml

2 tablespoons = 1 fluid oz. = 29.5 ml

¼ cup (4 tablespoons) = 2 fluid oz. = 59 ml

⅓ cup (5 ⅓ tablespoons) = 2.7 fluid oz. = 80 ml

½ cup (8 tablespoons) = 4 fluid oz. = 120 ml

⅔ cup (10 ⅔ tablespoons) = 5.4 fluid oz. = 160 ml

¾ cup (12 tablespoons) = 6 fluid oz. = 180 ml

1 cup (16 tablespoons) = 8 fluid oz. = 240 ml

TEMPERATURE EQUIVALENTS

°F	°C	Gas Mark
225	110	¼
250	130	½
275	140	1
300	150	2
325	170	3
350	180	4
375	190	5
400	200	6
425	220	7
450	230	8
475	240	9
500	250	10

LENGTH MEASURES

1/16 inch = 1.6 mm

⅛ inch = 3 mm

¼ inch = 1.35 mm

½ inch = 1.25 cm

¾ inch = 2 cm

1 inch = 2.5 cm

ABOUT THE AUTHOR

Dr. Barbara Caracciolo has a background in both psychology and epidemiology, and published relevant articles on the epidemiology of cognitive aging before deciding to pursue her life-long interest in cooking and baking.

Born in Rome, she relocated to Stockholm, where she founded Spigamadre, a bakery-café that offers baked goods and traditional dishes from her homeland. Through the years, Barbara studied the history of Italian regional cooking and baking (once a researcher, always a researcher), and this passion is deeply intertwined with her creations at Spigamadre, as well as her writing.

Her works include two food and baking blogs, contributions to international baking publications, and, more recently, a series of books for Cider Mill Press. If you have any questions or comments for Barbara, feel free to reach out to her at breadandcompanatico@gmail.com

INDEX

ABOUT CIDER MILL PRESS BOOK PUBLISHERS

Good ideas ripen with time. From seed to harvest, Cider Mill Press
brings fine reading, information, and entertainment together between
the covers of its creatively crafted books. Our Cider Mill bears fruit
twice a year, publishing a new crop of titles each spring and fall.

"Where Good Books Are Ready for Press"

501 Nelson Place
Nashville, TN 37214

cidermillpress.com